LEARNER-CENTERED THEORY AND PRACTICE IN DISTANCE EDUCATION

Cases From Higher Education

LEARNER-CENTERED THEORY AND PRACTICE IN DISTANCE EDUCATION

Cases From Higher Education

Edited by

Thomas M. Duffy
Jamie R. Kirkley
Indiana University

LEA
LAWRENCE ERLBAUM ASSOCIATES, PUBLISHERS
2004 Mahwah, New Jersey   London

Senior Acquisitions Editor:	Naomi Silverman
Editorial Assistant:	Erica Kica
Cover Design:	Kathryn Houghtaling Lacey
Textbook Production Manager:	Paul Smolenski
Full-Service Compositor:	TechBooks
Text and Cover Printer:	Hamilton Printing Company

This book was typeset in 10/12 pt. New Baskerville Roman, Bold, and Italic.
The heads were typeset in New Baskerville, Bold, and Bold Italic.

Lawrence Erlbaum Associates, Inc., Publishers
10 Industrial Avenue
Mahwah, New Jersey 07430
www.erlbaum.com

Library of Congress Cataloging-in-Publication Data

Duffy, Thomas M.
    Learner-centered theory and practice in distance education : cases
from higher education / Thomas M. Duffy and Jamie R. Kirkley.
        p.   cm.
    ISBN 0-8058-4576-3 (casebound : alk. paper) — ISBN 0-8058-4577-1
(pbk. : alk. paper)
    1. Distance education—United States—Case studies.   2. Internet in
higher education—United States—Case studies.   3. Instructional
systems—United States—Design—Case studies. I. Kirkley, Jamie R. II. Title.
    LC5803.C65D86   2003
    378.1′75—dc21
                                                        2003014682

Books published by Lawrence Erlbaum Associates are printed on
acid-free paper, and their bindings are chosen for strength and durability.

Printed in the United States of America
10 9 8 7 6 5 4 3 2 1

This book is dedicated to William E. Montague, mentor, friend and the inspiration for the interactive nature of this book. We only hope we can keep the conversation going as well as he has done.

Contents

Preface

In this volume, we have focused on two objectives. First, we want to bring the voice of the learning sciences to the study and design of distance education. Over the past 2 decades, we have learned a tremendous amount about how people learn and how to engage them in the learning process (see, e.g., National Academy of Science, 2000). However, we find little of that work applied to the design of distance learning environments. It is not that the principles of teaching and learning change when we look at distance education—it is that the context for learning results in markedly different constraints and affordances when compared to face-to-face teaching. How do we promote engaged learning when students are distributed around the world? What should it mean pedagogically to put a course on the web?

In seeking to meet this goal, we invited individuals who were a part of distance education programs that reflected the principles for engaged learning and asked them to describe their programs from the perspective of the pedagogical design but also focus on issues of assessment, retention, and workload. These programs are from business, education, library science, and bioengineering, as well as campus- and system-wide efforts.

Our second goal was to assure that the programs are presented in enough detail so that readers with different interests will have the detail they need to understand the pedagogical approaches and the implications of implementing those approaches. Of course, fully achieving this goal was quite impossible without supporting an ongoing dialogue. So we tried to approach the goal by bringing together a diverse group of specialists working in distance education to comment on and discuss the chapters. We invited those from the learning sciences, professionals in educational evaluation and policy, administrators, and professionals from the corporate sector, all with expertise in issues of distance learning, to review, discuss, and write reactant chapters on each of the programs. The group met at a symposium held at the Asilomar Conference Center in Pacific Grove, California, to discuss these chapters, as well as larger issues in the design of distance learning environments. In fact, key elements of the discussion at Asilomar were captured and are included in this book. The result of this effort is an edited volume that describes eight distinct distance education programs. For each program, there is a chapter describing the program with a focus on the pedagogy, a formal reactant to the chapter, and an edited transcript of the group discussion of the chapter. This is our attempt to provide the level of detail and the perspective taking that is too often missed in many program and course descriptions.

This book is intended for a wide audience of those engaged in delivering, support-ing, or administrating distance education programs at the postsecondary level. The descriptions, strategies, and principles will inform the design of continuing education, as well as degree-based education and corporate education and training. This book also has relevance to the broad audience engaged in distance education for adults.

Finally, let us acknowledge the support that made this book possible. First, and certainly the critical factor, is the support from the U.S. Department of Education's Fund for the Improvement of Postsecondary Education's (FIPSE) Learning Anytime Anywhere Program (U.S. Department of Education Grant No. P339B990108-01). Brian Lekander, coordinator of the Learning Anytime Anywhere Partnerships Program, and Joan Krejci Griggs, program officer and coordinator, were immensely helpful in identifying participants and planning the Asilomar meeting.

We also appreciate the support of the Naval Postgraduate School in Monterey, California, and Provost Dick Elster for providing equipment and technical support at the Asilomar symposium. We also thank Martha Zuppann at the Center for Research on Learning and Technology at Indiana University for her administrative support and Trena Paulus, Rohany Nayan, and Nellie Beatty for their Web-site development, editing, and transcribing services. Finally, Naomi Silverman and Lori Hawver, our editorial crew, have been a joy to work with. We appreciate Naomi's enthusiastic embracing of this book, her thoughtful editing, and her support in moving it through the system.

—Thomas M. Duffy
—Jamie R. Kirkley

About the Authors

Authors at the Asilomar Conference Center, California

Kneeling (L to R) Matt Champagne, Karen Ruhleder, Linda Polin, Tom Duffy, Prasad Kaipa

Second Row (L to R) Bob Wisher, José Rafael López Islas, Jim Botkin, Scott Grabinger, Brian Lekander, Jamie Kirkley, Carson Eoyang

Third Row: John Bransford, Terry Anderson, Peter Shea, John Stinson, Lani Gunawardena, Sally Johnstone, Dick Lesh, Mark Schalger

Photo courtesy of Sonny Kirkley

Terry Anderson, Professor and Canada Research Chair in Distance Education at Athabasca University, Canada's Open University. Terry has published widely in the area of distance education and educational technology and has recently co-authored two new books: *eResearch: Methods, Issues and Strategies* and *E-Learning in the 21st Century: A framework for research and practice.* Terry is a lead investigator on a number of research and development projects and has been instrumental in the development of the CAN-CORE metadata specification for identifying and retrieving educational objects. He teaches in the Masters of Distance education program at Athabasca University.

Helen Bateman, Research Fellow, Vanderbilt University. Helen has a Ph.D. in cognitive studies and is the recent recipient of a two-year fellowship award in the area of cognitive studies for educational practice from the J.S. McDonnell Foundation. Her research involves program design and evaluation. She is presently developing an evaluation rubric for assessing community in different types of learning environments and its relationship to social, motivational, and learning outcomes. Her present work examines which learning environment characteristics promote sense of community and how to facilitate community in educational settings. Her past work focused on anchored instruction, mathematical efficacy, and the effectiveness of early academic and social interventions on high-risk children.

Jim Botkin, Executive Coach, Entrepreneur, and Author. Jim has spent his career on the leading edge of contemporary thinking about business issues such as knowledge creation, executive development, and creative innovation in large corporations and entrepreneurial start-ups. In 1990, Jim founded InterClass, a unique learning consortium of premier global companies such as AT&T, Dupont, BP, Volvo, Shell, GM, Xerox, KPMG, Sun Microsystems, Deloitte & Touche, Pfizer, and the World Bank. In 2002, Jim started his executive coaching practice in leadership and life coaching. He holds a Ph.D. and M.B.A. from the Harvard Graduate School of Business Administration. He has written seven books on business, learning, and technology including *No Limits to Learning* and *Smart Business*.

John Bransford, Centennial Professor of Psychology, Vanderbilt University. Since 1984, John has co-directed the Learning Technology Center where he and his colleagues have conducted extensive research on learning, thinking, and problem solving, and they have also developed several technology applications such as the Jasper Woodbury Problem Solving Series and the Little Planet Literacy Series. More recently, ideas from this work have led to research on development projects on "challenge-based design." Bransford won the Thorndike Award from the American Psychology Association and the Southerland Award from Vanderbilt University. He and his colleagues have received five "article of the year" awards. Bransford has co-chaired several reports for the National Academy of Science and is a member of the National Academy of Education.

Sean P. Brophy, Assistant Research Professor in the Department of Biomedical Engineering, Vanderbilt University. Sean is currently co-leader of the learning sciences thrust of the VaNTH Engineering Research Center (ERC). He collaborates with various domain experts to explore instructional and technological methods for enhancing students' learning. His research interests focus on optimizing the cognitive benefits of using simulations and models to facilitate students' understanding of difficult engineering concepts. He also works with the Learning Technology Center at Vanderbilt. Sean received his B.S. degree in mechanical engineering from the University of Michigan, an M.S. in computer science from DePaul University, and a Ph.D. in education and human development from Vanderbilt University.

Susan K. Byrne, Research Assistant, Purdue University. Susan is a graduate research assistant in the School of Education, Department of Curriculum and Instruction. She received her Master of Science degree in education with a mathematics education emphasis in 2002. Her research interests include pre-service teacher education, and reflections in teaching and learning in mathematics education.

Matthew V. Champagne, Co-Founder and CEO, IOTA Solutions, Inc. Matt has led the development of feedback and embedded evaluation tools that are considered the standard practice for distance education. He has served as a researcher, faculty member, practitioner, consultant, and Senior Research Fellow in the areas of learning and evaluation for more than 10 years, and he is program evaluator for the U.S. Department of Education, the National Science Foundation, and numerous training organizations. He was founder of the *IDEA Lab,* the first university laboratory dedicated to the assessment of e-learning. Matt received his doctorate from Purdue University.

Thomas M. Duffy, Barbara Jacobs Chair of Education and Technology at Indiana University Indiana University Bloomington. Tom is the founding director of the Center for Research on Learning and Technology. He received his doctorate from University of Illinois, Urbana-Champaign and has been a faculty member in the School of Education and Cognitive Science at Indiana for 16 years. His research interests are in the design of learning environments and the study of learning processes and technology tools to support inquiry in those environments. Previous books include *New Learning* (with R.J. Simons and J. van der Linden) and *Constructivism and the Technology of Instruction* (with D. Jonassen).

Carson K. Eoyang, Naval Postgraduate School, Monterey, CA. Carson is the Associate Provost for Academic Affairs at NPS. Besides his Ph.D. in business from Stanford, he holds an M.B.A. from Harvard, and a B.S. in physics from MIT. In addition to his academic career at NPS, his public service experience includes being the Director of Training at NASA, the Director of Training at FAA, and two short tours in the White House, the second involved coordinating distance learning initiatives across the Federal government. His publications include a book on citizen espionage, journal articles on organization development, and book chapters on program design.

Eric E. Fredericksen, Director of Distributed Learning Services, Cornell University. As a senior manager in Cornell Information Technologies, he is responsible for supporting faculty in their use of technologies to support teaching and learning in and out of the classroom. Prior to joining Cornell, he was Assistant Provost for Advanced Learning Technology in the State University of New York System Administration where he was responsible for the nationally recognized SUNY Learning Network. He was also co-Principal Investigator and Administrative Officer for three multi-year, multimillion dollar grants from the Alfred P. Sloan Foundation. Under his leadership, the program grew from just two campuses offering eight courses with 119 enrollments to 53 campuses offering 2,500 courses to more than 40,000 enrollments in just seven years. He is currently completing his Ph.D. in at the University at Albany.

Scott Grabinger, Director, Center for Innovations in Teaching and Technology, University of Colorado at Denver. Scott directs the Center for Innovations in Teaching and Technology, a team that works with faculty to integrate technology in their on-site classes and to design online courses. Scott holds an appointment as Associate Professor in the information and learning technologies program. He teaches classes in message design, student-centered learning environments, problem-based learning, and the application of computers in instruction. He and Joanna Dunlap collaborated to formulate the rich environments for active learning (REALs) model of instruction. His previous books are *Building Expert Systems for Education and Training* (with Brent Wilson and David Jonassen), and *Hypermedia Learning Environments* (with Piet Kommers and Joanna Dunlap).

Charlotte N. (Lani) Gunawardena, Professor of Distance Education and Instructional Technology, University of New Mexico. As a principal investigator, Lani is currently researching and evaluating a federally funded web-based math and science teacher professional development project. Her recent research examines knowledge construction in online communities, social presence theory, and the sociocultural context of online learning, and the design and evaluation of distance education systems. Lani enjoys her work as an international consultant. She has worked as a World Bank Consultant in Sri Lanka and has consulted in Brazil, Mexico, Norway, and Turkey.

Sally M. Johnstone is Founding Director of WCET. Sally leads WCET, which is the Cooperative advancing effective use of technology in higher education. Her areas of expertise include the effects of the integration of technology on higher education institutions and system organizations, collaborations, quality assurance issues, project development and evaluation, international projects, and supporting WCET members in the implementation of e-learning. She writes a regular column for *Syllabus* magazine on distance learning and a semi-annual column for *Change*. She has authored dozens of articles, book chapters, and reports on distance and distributed learning. She earned her Ph.D. in experimental psychology from the University of North Carolina at Chapel Hill.

Prasad Kaipa, CEO, SelfCorporation. Along with heading an executive development company, Prasad also teaches leadership, innovation, and organizational learning part-time at Saybrook Graduate School. Prasad has a Ph.D. in physics from IIT Madras, and he has worked as a technology advisor as well as fellow and marketing manager in Apple. He has written a book *Discontinuous Learning: Aligning Work and Life* that was published in 2003. Along with being on the board of five start-up companies, including a public company, he is also a trustee of Society for Organizational Learning and Foundation for Human and Economic Development. He is a founding director of the TiE Institute for Entrepreneurship in the Silicon Valley.

Jamie R. Kirkley, Research Scientist, Information in Place, Inc. Jamie conducts research and development on projects focusing on the use of wireless and mixed reality technologies to support contextualized learning. She has also managed development of a range of technology-based learning projects, including the Learning to Teach with Technology Studio at Indiana University. Jamie is completing a dual Ph.D. in instructional systems technology and language education at Indiana University. Her research focuses on developing a framework for examining asynchronous collaborative and problem-based learning environments. She has taught courses at Indiana University in adult and adolescent reading as well as K-12 use of the Internet.

Brian Lekander, Learning Anyplace Anytime Partnerships (LAAP). Brian is Coordinator of LAAP, a program through the U.S. Department of Education's Office of Postsecondary Education. LAAP is the only Department of Education grant program devoted to programmatic improvements in postsecondary distance learning.

Richard Lesh, R.B. Kane Distinguished Professor of Education, Purdue University. Dick also serves as the Associate Dean for Research and is the Director for Purdue's Center for Twenty-first Century Conceptual Tools and School Mathematics & Science Center. He has been a professor and has held administrative positions at Northwestern University and UMass-Dartmouth, and he was a principal scientist at the Educational Testing Service in Princeton. His recent publications include *The Handbook of Research Design in Mathematics & Science Education* (Kelly & Lesh, 2001) and *Beyond Constructivism: Models & Modeling Perspectives on Mathematics Problem Solving, Learning & Teaching* (Lesh & Doerr, 2003). His Ph.D. was granted jointly by Indiana University's Mathematics Department and School of Education.

José Rafael López-Islas, Director for Curricular Innovation, Instituto Tecnologico de Monterrey University System (Mexico). Rafael did graduate studies at Oklahoma State University and The University of Texas at Austin. His career at the Tecnologico de Monterrey includes several years as a faculty member, Director of the undergraduate and graduate programs in communication, and researcher and administrator. Until 2002, he was a faculty and administrator at the Tecnologico de Monterrey's Virtual University. He has conducted research mostly on the violent content of television, as well as on the relationship between interaction and learning in online environments. His current interest is on the design of a higher education student-centered curriculum and use of technology to support it.

William E. Pelz, Chancellor's Awarded Professor of Psychology, Herkimer County Community College. Bill coordinates the HCCC Internet Academy, provides instructional design support to HCCC faculty, and trains new online professors for the SUNY Learning Network. He represents SUNY in the discipline of Psychology on the national Merlot Project Editorial Board. Bill has published an odd assortment of articles, most recently focused on student and faculty satisfaction with asynchronous teaching and learning. His current research interest is in isolating the pedagogical factors influencing student achievement in virtual learning environments. He has developed and taught twelve asynchronous courses since 1997.

Alexandra M. Pickett, Assistant Director of the SUNY Learning Network (SLN), State University of New York. Since 1994, Alexandra has led the development of the instructional design methods, support services, and resources used by SLN to support the development and delivery of full web online courses by SUNY campuses and faculty. One of the original SLN design team members, she co-designed the course management software and authored the 4-stage faculty development process and 7-step course design process used by the network. She has co-authored a number of studies on these topics and has published and presented the results both nationally and internationally.

Linda Polin, Professor of Education and Technology, Pepperdine University. Linda received her doctorate from UCLA in learning and instruction where she worked in writing assessment in the UCLA Center for the Study of Evaluation (now CRESST). She has been involved in online computing communities since 1985, including sysop'ing a 4-line dial-up BBS on her desktop computer back in 1987. Linda teaches learning and design and action research courses in the master's and doctoral programs in educational technology. She was instrumental in the development of both of these blended programs and directed the online M.A. in Educational Technology for its first four years. Her research interests are in online communities of practice, networked knowledge sharing and distributed collaborative work, and measurement issues in the analysis of online interaction.

Robert J. Roselli, Professor of Biomedical Engineering and Chemical Engineering, Vanderbilt University. Bob serves as Director of Graduate Studies for the Department of Biomedical Engineering at Vanderbilt, Biotransport Domain Leader for the VaNTH Engineering Research Center in Bioengineering Learning Technologies, and he is an active contributor to the VaNTH Biomechanics Domain. He has also served as Education Director for VaNTH. His research concentrates on fluid and solute exchange in the lung microcirculation. Bob has developed graduate and undergraduate courses in biomechanics and biotransport at Vanderbilt University and is a strong advocate of the challenge-based approach to instruction. He received his B.S. (1969) and M.S. (1972) degrees in mechanical engineering and a Ph.D. (1975) in bioengineering from the University of California, Berkeley.

Karen Ruhleder, Assistant Research Professor, University of Illinois, Urbana-Champaign (UIUC). As a member of the faculty of the Graduate School of Library and Information Science at UIUC, Karen is part of a research concentration that examines social informatics and computer supported cooperative work in particular settings or types of work. She is also interested in the development of complex sociotechnical infrastructure to support distributed work and learning. She has been at Illinois since 1995 and has also taught at Worcester Polytechnic University in Worcester, MA, and at the University of Houston. She received her Ph.D. in information and computer science from the University of California, Irvine, in 1991.

Mark Schlager, Associate Director of Learning Communities, Center for Technology in Learning, SRI International. Mark, who earned his doctorate in cognitive psychology from the University of Colorado, Boulder, specializes in the application of cognitive and social learning theory to the development of educational technology. As Director of the Tapped In project (www.tappedin.org), his recent work has focused on online infrastructure and strategies for cultivating and supporting communities of education professionals and how online community concepts and design principles can play a more integral role in local and state teacher professional development. Mark serves as an advisor for two U.S. Department of Education Regional Education Laboratories: AEL's Institute for the Advancement of Emerging Technologies in Education and NCREL's Blue Ribbon Panel on Emerging Technologies and Education.

Peter J. Shea, Interim Director of the SUNY Learning Network. Peter is also Director of the SUNY Teaching, Learning, and Technology Program and serves as coordinator for SUNY's participation in the MERLOT Project (Multimedia Educational Resource for Learning and Online Teaching), a national consortium for the collection and peer review of online teaching and learning materials. Peter is also a visiting assisting professor in the Department of Educational Theory and Practice at the University at Albany, where he has taught at the graduate level both online and in the classroom. He is the author of many articles and several book chapters on the topic of online learning and co-author of a new book, *The Successful Distance Learning Student.*

John Stinson, Professor Emeritus at the College of Business, Ohio University. John is former Dean of the College of Business at Ohio University and has served as Director of Management Development for two divisions of Litton Industries. He is an active consultant, focusing on strategic transformation and design of technologically mediated action learning systems. John is the author of six books and more than 100 journal articles, professional papers, and grants. He was selected by the Society of Alumni and

Friends at Ohio University to receive the Faculty Contribution Award in 1991, and he was twice nominated by students to serve as a University Professor and was given the Excellence Award for Graduate Teaching.

Pamela A. White, Graduate Student, Purdue University. Pam is the Technology Professional Development Coordinator at North West Hendricks School Corporation and a Graduate Student at Purdue University. She received both her master's in education in 2002 and her bachelor's in technology in 1998 from Purdue. Pam served as a graduate assistant for Richard Lesh, the Associate Dean for the School of Education, and has studied the effects of using collaborative software in his classroom. Her research interests are in the use of technology as a tool for learning and the effect of design on learning and retention. She has written and presented papers at national conferences including AECT, AERA, SITE, and ED-MEDIA.

Robert A. Wisher, Senior Research Psychologist, Department of Defense. Bob is a Senior Research Psychologist with the Office of the Secretary of Defense, and he specializes in issues related to the instructional effectiveness of technologies for training and education. Bob previously worked in the research laboratories in the Army and Navy for 20 years. His research interests are on long-term retention of learning, collaborative learning environments, and the development of repositories of sharable learning content. Bob received his doctorate in cognitive psychology from the University of California, San Diego.

Nancy Vye, Director of Education, American Healthways, Inc. Nancy is a learning scientist and received her Ph.D. from Vanderbilt University in 1983. From 1983 to 1987, she was on the faculty in the Department of Psychology at the University of Western Ontario, Canada. In 1987, she joined the Learning Technology Center at Peabody College of Vanderbilt University where she was Senior Research Associate and Co-Director until 2003. Nancy has been associated with various initiatives, including the development of *The Adventures of Jasper Woodbury*, a CD-based, middle school mathematics curriculum, and research and development on e-learning, computer agent software, and problem-based training.

LEARNER-CENTERED THEORY AND PRACTICE IN DISTANCE EDUCATION

Cases From Higher Education

I

Introduction

1

Introduction: Theory and Practice in Distance Education

Thomas M. Duffy and Jamie R. Kirkley
Indiana University

Controversies over the impact and role of distance education abound. On one hand, we hear that distance education will never survive. The estimates of and interest in the market for distance education have been overblown (NEA Higher Education, 2002). Just look at the struggles of Western Governors University (Carnevale, 2000), the demise of the for-profit NYU Online (Carlson & Carnevale, 2001), Open University United States (Arnone, 2002), California Virtual University[1], Cognitive Arts, and Fathom and the near demise of Unext.com's Cardean University. And it is not just the for-profit companies. Arizona Learning Systems (Carnevale, 2001), funded by the state, closed its doors for lack of students. Every week, it seems *The Chronicle of Higher Education* has new articles on "distance education ventures" in trouble. And, as Stein (2001) notes, venture capital for distance education has dried up: "After pouring billions of dollars into e-learning startups over the past two years, venture capitalists are now pulling back. Many of the companies they funded face excessive competition, layoffs, and bankruptcy. Even the relatively successful startups in the sector have very little hope of going public, at least for the time being."

On the other hand, distance education has grown at an explosive rate. At the University of Maryland, University College, distance education enrollments have grown from 4% of total enrollments in 1997 to 64% in 2002 and now stand at over 26,000 (Allen, 2002). In the State University of New York system, distance education has grown from eight courses and 119 students in 1995–1996 to more than 1,500 courses and 38,000 students in 2000–2001 (Fredericksen, Pickett, Shea, & Pelz, 2000; Shea, Fredericksen, Pickett, & Pelz, Chap. 16, this volume). The rate of growth of online courses at University of Phoenix online appears to be exceeding the record growth of its face-based programs, with the distance courses expanding to 49,000 online students in just 3 years. The University of Central Florida enrolls approximately 4,000 students each

---

[1]Although the for-profit California Virtual University closed, the California Virtual Campus site, which catalogs and coordinates all of the California online courses, is thriving.

semester in their courses taught fully through the Web. (Dziuban & Moskal, 2001). Finally, more than 3,000 courses are offered online through the Illinois Virtual Campus (www.ivc.illinois.edu), and the California Virtual Campus catalog contains 4,400 courses (http://www.cvc.edu).

These contrasting perspectives characterize the polarized discussions that have arisen around distance education. On the one hand, it is viewed as the next revolution in education, extending the reach of education to those who cannot come to campus, making education more affordable, providing new models for lifelong learning (e.g., through communities of practice), and reforming teaching practices through the emphasis on student discussion and activity, and the elimination of the lecture as the central teaching activity. On the other hand, distance education is seen as lowering the quality of instruction, a moneymaking rather than educational enterprise, an environment where cheating cannot be controlled, and an environment that threatens the teaching role both through the lack of any physical constraints on class size and through the objectification of the "course," thus threatening course ownership and potentially leading to the disaggregation of the roles of faculty.

Of course, both sides of these arguments take a very narrow view of distance education, failing to recognize the diversity of practices and goals. One cannot say that, in general, distance education is of high or low quality any more than we can commend or condemn lectures or seminars. The quality depends on the design of and the student's engagement in the learning environment. There are poorly designed lecture courses and seminars, just as there are poorly designed distance education courses. In an American Federation of Teachers (AFT, 2001) survey of 200 members who teach online, 84% said they would teach online again. Fifty-four percent felt that their online students learned as much as students in their campus-based classes, whereas 18% felt the distance students performed more poorly and 28% felt they outperformed students in the campus-based courses. In essence, distance education courses were right in the mix with all other courses on the dimension of quality.

The one thing we think distance education has done is to force a closer examination of and attention to teaching practices in higher education regardless of whether the teaching is at a distance or in the classroom. Perhaps one of the most interesting issues that has arisen in these debates is the quality of learning that occurs online. Although the AFT survey indicated that the learning in online and face-to-face classes was basically equal, the AFT nonetheless expressed a concern over the quality of online classes when it questioned whether "deep understanding of difficult material—beyond amassing facts—can occur in the absence of same-time same-place interaction" (AFT, 2001).

This concern is particularly interesting given the lack of research on learning in the undergraduate classroom. Most higher education research relies on survey data; for example, class ratings and specialized survey's like the National Survey of Student Engagement (Koljatic & Kuh, 2001; Kuh, in press), infer, based on student report, that learning has occurred. Very little research has actually looked at student learning in the classroom. The work that has been done leads us to question the efficacy of our current classroom-based model.

Hayes and his colleagues (Chenoweth, Hayes, Gripp, Littleton, Steinberg, & Van Every, 1999) examined learning in four different undergraduate classrooms. They worked with the faculty to clearly define the objectives for the course and to collaboratively build an objective test to assess the degree to which the students achieved those objectives. The test had to be approved by the faculty member as a fair test of the absolute core of the learning expected of every student. Learning was then assessed using both pretest postpost design and a no-treatment control. There were five objectives defined for the first year English class—and remember that these were the objectives reflecting core expectations, not the lofty hopes of the faculty member. The tests on these five objectives indicated that the students showed significant gains on only one of the five goals relative to the control group. Work with a faculty member teaching a history survey course identified two core goals, and testing showed only one of those goals showed significant gains. As we noted, there is seldom an opportunity to experimentally evaluate learning. Thus, these faculty, like most of us, had been certain that their students were learning, and they were shocked by the results.

A similar critique can be made of the quality of discussion in the college classroom. The AFT worries that a face-to-face class experience is needed to develop a deep understanding of difficult topics. One must assume that the benefit of face-to-face is the lively interaction that can occur in the classroom. But Mikulecky (1998) presents evidence that questions that conclusion. He compared the classroom discussions of an online class, a classroom-based whole class discussion, and classroom-based small group discussion (when the instructor asked the students to get in groups to discuss an issue). This was not a controlled study: Students in each condition were at different levels in their studies and enrolled in different courses. However, the focus was on the discussion of a single topic common to all three courses. The contrasts were quite striking. The whole class "discussions" amounted to repeated sequences of a student asking the instructor a question and the instructor answering—or vice versa. The small group discussion was mostly off topic, for example, social issues from the night before or the next evening, or organizational, for example, what is required, who will report out, and so forth. In contrast, the online students pursued the issues deeply in a problem-centered discussion and integrated their relevant personal and professional experiences into the discussion.

Nunn (1996) and others (e.g., Smith, 1983) further suggest that quality of discussion in a college classroom is not a forgone conclusion. Nunn examined the level of discussion in medium-sized classes (15 to 44 students) and found on average that only 2.3% of class time (1 minute out of 40) involved student talk. Further, only 25% of the students in a class were involved in that talk.

Once again, this is not to suggest that there is not rich discussion in campus-based courses. But it does suggest that rich discussion will not occur simply as a function of bringing students together. In the same vein, we note that distance education also does not necessarily lead to rich discussion. Web-based courses typically consist of resource materials, assignments, and discussion environments. The success of the course often depends on how that discussion space is used. It is a common experience for faculty teaching online to struggle to get students to participate. As in the classroom, there is a lot of wasted discussion time—time when students are simply talking or doing a project rather than thinking deeply about issues and using the learning resources to ground their thinking. And there is a lot of time when students simply do not participate. As Riel and Harasim (1994) found, discussion must be an integral and required part of the course. Then, as Mikulecky's (1998) and many others (Collison, Elbaum, Haavined, & Tinker, 2000) have found, rich discussion is possible.

But how do we design courses to be taught at a distance? What are the best practice models that will inform our own design efforts? What are effective models? As we looked through the literature, we found little to inform our thinking. There is a lot of advice on the components of design, for example, on how to facilitate groups effectively and on the support faculty require. But the actual course designs tended to be in the vein of "transferring a course to the Web." Although we are sure that there were many excellent courses out there, we found two problems.

First, there were few instances of principle-based design. The learning sciences have made tremendous gains in understanding how people learn (e.g., Bransford, Brown, & Cocking, 2000). However, it is primarily K–12 education that has been the database for our new understandings, and the bulk of the application of our new understandings has been to the design of K–12 educational programs. We see little attention to higher education generally and a definite absence in distance education. There is little discussion of constructivist learning theory guiding the design and practice of distance education beyond stating the need for active discussion among students. It is important to clarify that we do not think that a different theory of learning applies just because we have moved to a distance environment. We certainly see learning as a constructive process (Barab & Duffy, 2000; Duffy & Cunningham, 1996; Duffy & Jonassen, 1992). That is, in our view, learners are goal directed, and they use learning environments to construct an understanding to aid them in achieving their goal. Unfortunately, that goal is typically to pass a test, and the learning needed to "pass a test" often has little to do with being able to use the resources to function outside of the classroom (Bransford & Schwartz, 2001; Honebein, Duffy, & Fishman, 1993).

This book is an attempt to meet that need. That is, we sought authors who had principle-based distance learning efforts and who could talk about the design of their distance learning program from a conceptual perspective. Of course, we were looking for program designs consistent with a learner-centered perspective. (Note that we were looking for programs rather than individual courses.) It is interesting that we were able to identify very few programs in North America that were consistent with a learner-centered perspective. The programs that we, found are represented in this book. There are likely many other programs that are pedagogically and theoretically interesting; we are sure we missed some and perhaps many. However, that just reinforces our belief that little attention is being paid to the rich and growing number of well-designed and theory-based distance learning environments. The programs are not well-known.

The second problem we encountered in looking at the literature was that the distance education courses were simply not described in very much detail, especially the detail that would help us interpret the theory–practice linkages. There were many questions we wanted to ask as we read each article, but that simply was not feasible. So in designing this book, we sought to establish a context in which the questions people have might be answered. Thanks to the support of the Fund for the Improvement of Postsecondary Education (FIPSE), we were able to bring all of the participants in the book, and a few others, to Asilomar, California, where papers were presented and then discussed. That discussion led to revisions and clarification of the chapters, and much of the discussion was captured and is included in this book.

For each of the eight programs presented, a formal discussant critiques the chapter and places the key issues in a larger context. After the discussant presentation, we present the open discussion among the participants that followed the formal presentations. We are very pleased with the diversity of discussants who contributed to the success of this book and to the interaction at Asilomar. We sought learning science researchers and practitioners in distance education, but we also wanted to make sure that the array of issues relating to distance education were addressed, so the participants included specialists in evaluation, policy, and organizational management and communication. Reflecting this goal of obtaining multiple perspectives, we asked Sally Johnstone (of WICHE), with her focus on policy, and Jim Botkin (of Natural Voice Coaching), with his organizational management perspective, to offer the final reflections on the papers and the discussions.

Most of the program designs are problem-centered designs, but the variation between them is considerable. A comparison of these contrasting strategies alone is extremely informative. José Rafael Lopez-Islas (of the Monterrey Technological Institute) has tried to institutionalize a team-based and instructor-driven online problem-based learning approach modeled after the University of Maastricht, the Netherlands. Thomas Duffy and Jamie Kirkley (of Indiana University) and John Bransford, Nancy Vye, Helen Bateman, Sean Brophy, and Bob Roselli (of Vanderbilt University) describe design problems presented in an engaging multimedia format and a rich set of resources. John Stinson (at Ohio University), on the other hand, presents real, whole-business problems with students beginning their work initially in a face-to-face environment and then continuing to work at a distance over a period of 2 months, using only a rich discussion forum. Finally, the work of Richard Lesh, Susan Byrne, and Pamela White (of Purdue University), although not formally in a problem-centered learning environment, explores a rich array of environments that support students in exploring teaching practices in education, mathematics, and engineering.

The designs of these environments have significant scaling implications. The programs at Monterrey Tech Virtual University and the State University of New York (Shea) are clearly the most scalable. However, as Karen Ruhleder (at the University of Illinois, Champaign-Urbana) noted in reflecting on the papers, the programs that were guided by the most detailed models were also those that appeared to be least scalable.

The different models also have cost implications for both the university and the student. Face-to-face meetings are the greatest cost factor for delivery of instruction, whereas development costs are heavily impacted by the use of multimedia and the amount of material that is written specifically for the course, as, for example, in the work of Duffy and Kirkley, and Bransford and his colleagues. Although our focus was on the learning design, it is clear that additional discussion is needed to consider the cost-effectiveness trade-offs of these different approaches. This is certainly an area where learning sciences research and cost model approaches advocated by Erhmann (2002) would aid the discussion.

Perhaps the issue that stood out most clearly was the complexity of the concepts of collaboration, community, and interaction. There was a clear bias among the authors toward a rich collaborative community environment. However, the relationship between community and collaboration is complex. For example, the face-to-face meetings that were central to the work of John Stinson and Linda Polin seemed to produce a rich community environment in which graduates choose to remain affiliated with the program and even volunteered to help teach the next group of cohorts. The students did not necessarily collaborate on team projects, but rather seemed more involved in learning about and helping one another with their action research project and discussing issues in a seminar type of format. It seemed clear, though there is no data to support the conclusion, that the synchronous component and the face-to-face meeting in particular are critical to this community building. In contrast, while Ruhleder provides students with a preliminary face-to-face meeting and meetings include synchronous chat, there did not seem to be the same sort of community building as reported by Polin and Stinson. Perhaps Ruhleder was less community and team focused—with the chats being open channels for student-initiated discussion during lectures. Thus, it is not just that face-to-face and chat that are important, but rather that there are principles of community development that are critical. However, once again, we return to the question as to whether the community "spirit" impacts learning or simply leads to more socializing.

In contrast to the synchronous efforts, López-Islas and Shea both emphasize asynchronous learning and the reflective process associated with problem solving and discussion. It is clear from the descriptions that although these environments may lead to knowledge construction as López-Islas describes, there is not the sense of community and commitment among students. Clearly, collaboration and dialogue do not necessarily lead to community—but perhaps it leads to better understanding of the concepts and processes being taught. It is often through discussion as well as collaboration that concepts and relationships are visited, revisited, and enhanced. In addition, with asynchronous discussion, students can be challenged to communicate and negotiate perspectives on various issues in a reflective environment, address issues within context, and manage group production as well as their own learning.

Finally, Duffy and Kirkley argued that the instructor may well be able to fulfill the role of challenging the student's assumptions and engaging in the dialogue if not the dialectic that seems to be important to learning. That is, they argue that students can function in a self-paced environment with the student having access to an online mentor. Although the mentor or teacher is one of the most important factors impacting learning (Bloom, 1984), they argue that we have tended to ignore the mentor role and indeed emphasize its subservience to the group process (Collison, Elbaum, Haavind, & Tinker, 2000).

Individual mentoring permits the design of self-paced learning environments, and this, in turn, led to a discussion of the goals and needs of the learners. Many students, especially working professionals, come to distance learning because of the opportunity it offers to manage learning along with job, family, and community responsibilities. It is not just any place, but also anytime (and hence not synchronous) and any pace (hence not cohort based) that is important to their success. Indeed, the recent work by Duffy and Kirkley (Duffy & Grabinger, 1999; Malopinsky, Kirkley, & Duffy, 2002) focuses on the design of self-paced, mentored professional development for teachers because teachers told us that flexibility in pacing is more important than having a peer group. As one of our teachers told us, "I always have access to the mentor if I need help or want to try out an idea." The teachers in professional development are certainly frustrated by time-based requirements and perhaps even the requirement to spend time interacting with others. On the other hand, other students entering distance education may find it a lonely space and look for the camaraderie of the classroom. The students are likely to find the synchronous environment and the opportunity for face-to-face meetings as central to their motivation to learn.

All of this is to say that the online learning environment provides a rich research context in which to probe more deeply into the issues that are so central in the learning sciences. As Anderson and Lekander both noted in their reflections on the chapters, the theories of learning may be too tied to the classroom model of learning. Certainly, Resnick (1989) has made this point very strongly in distinguishing in-school and out-of-school learning. Perhaps we should be considering the contrasts in the classroom and distributed learning environments in a similar way as we seek to evaluate and extend theory. As Andersen noted, we would do well to heed Glaser's and Strauss' (1967) grounded theory approach, with the emphasis that theory is a process grounded in the data, and hence the theory grows and evolves as new sources of rich data, like the distance learning environment, enter the discussion.

SECTION 1: INTRODUCTION

The program descriptions and discussions in this book provide a rich array of approaches to distance education, all within the learner-centered framework. The issues raised in this chapter are all explicitly discussed or implicit in the work. There are four sections following this introduction, each focused on a critical issue in distance education today: "Community Building," "Problem-Centered Learning," "Innovative Uses of Technology," and "Scaling Up." In each of these sections, there are two primary chapters and a response chapter for each of the primaries. In addition, there is a transcribed and edited representation of the whole group discussion of each primary chapter. The final section of the book, "Alternate Views," provides chapters focusing on policy issues in corporate America and higher education.

SECTION 2: COMMUNITY BUILDING

Community is a theme that emerges throughout the book and seems to be associated with the use of face-to-face meetings and chat. Both of the programs described in this section use both of these strategies to encourage students to get to know one another and to support open dialogue on issues. Although both are very successful programs as gauged by student enrollment growth and interest in the program, one led to very strong community among students whereas the other did not.

In the first primary chapter, Linda Polin (of Pepperdine University) uses a community of practice lens to examine a master's degree program in teacher education. The program utilizes an asynchronous learning environment supplemented with chat sessions using Tapped In, which is a virtual moo (see http://www.tappedin.org). Face-to-face meetings and an extended action research project serve as cohesive organizers for community building and learning activities across courses. Scott Grabinger (of the University of Colorado at Denver) responds to Polin's chapter by examining her theory-into-practice approach, as well as by contrasting traditional instructional design processes with those using a sociocultural approach. He also addresses how theoretical components and the use of learning tools affects the design of online courses. The open discussion focuses on developing online communities of practice, the importance of tool design to support learning, and issues related to assessing quality in learning.

In the second primary chapter, Karen Ruhleder (of the University of Illinois, Urbona-Champaign [UIUC]) describes an online masters' degree program in library science that uses live audio-streamed lectures accompanied by student chat. An asynchronous learning environment is also an integral part of the learning environment. She addresses issues of managing chat and lecture, as well as the rationale for using this unusual approach. Research outcomes on virtual interaction with this approach are also presented. Mark Schlager (of SRI International) responds to Ruhleder with an assessment of the UIUC strategy, as well as a discussion of the challenges of designing distance learning environments to support a community of learners engaged in multiple collective and individual activities. The open discussion focuses mainly on using synchronous technology to support learning and issues related to the role of adjunct faculty in online learning programs.

SECTION 3: PROBLEM-CENTERED LEARNING

Most of the programs in this book used some form of problem-centered learning. However, the two programs in this section had problem-centered learning at the core of their approach. In addition, as with the chapters in the previous section, the two programs provide a study in contrasts: one focused on meeting individual needs through individual study; the other a very collaborative problem-solving approach with an emphasis on community building.

In the first primary chapter, Thomas Duffy and Jamie Kirkley (Indiana University) begin with a discussion of the principles for the design of a learner-centered or constructivist distance learning environment. These principles are then used to examine an MBA curriculum offered by a for-profit virtual university, Unext.com's Cardean University. The courses are entirely asynchronous and have a self-paced, problem-centered learning format. In addition to the linkage of design and conceptual goals to practice, they discuss the competition between pedagogical goals and business rules in this for-profit effort. Finally, they question the role and necessity for student interaction in online courses. In her response, Lani Gunawadena (of the University of New Mexico) examines issues related to designing online inquiry-based learning environments using constructivist and socioconstructivist theories of learning, including challenges with balancing structure and dialogue in distance education design and issues related to collaboration, assessment, and transfer of learning. The open discussion focuses on how the business rules of Unext shaped the design of its courses. This also contains interesting commentary on the role and relationship of community and collaboration within online learning environments.

In the second primary chapter, John Stinson (of Ohio University) describes an MBA program that is a mixture of face-to-face and Web-based asynchronous learning. The program uses a problem-based learning format that contrasts significantly in strategy from the program described by Duffy and Kirkley. This is a cohort-based program with student's working in teams. All work, other than start-up and reporting out at the end of a problem, occurs in the asynchronous discussion environment. Robert Wisher (of the Army Research Institute) responds with commentary on the design of the Ohio University program with regard to pedagogy and community. He also focuses on how it might better be evaluated by using specific guidance from the training literature. The open discussion focuses on issues of measuring intellectual capital, the scalability of a program like MBA Without Boundaries, and the roles of faculty teaching in the program.

SECTION 4: INNOVATIVE USES OF TECHNOLOGY

Of course, all of distance education makes use of technology, and all of the programs described are innovative. However, in this section, we focus on two programs where the technology is central to engaging the learners.

In the first primary chapter, John Bransford, Nancy Vye, Helen Batemen, Sean Brophy, and Bos Roselli (of Vanderbilt University) describe the AMIGO project, a problem centered approach to distance education that emphasizes strategies for engaging students in professional issues. Several examples of the use of the AMIGO design in teaching educational psychology and biotechnology are discussed. Terry Andersen (of Athabasca University) responds to Bransford and his colleagues by focusing on the issue of quality in online learning and the variety of techniques that can be used to assess the quality of online learning. The open discussion includes an elaboration of the How People Learn framework (Bransford, Brown, & Cocking, 2000) and how to design challenges that are engaging and truly useful for learning rather than exercises that are neither relevant nor useful.

In the second primary chapter, Richard Lesh, Susan Byrne, and Pamela White (of Purdue University) focus on using a specialized version of constructivism called a models perspective, which is being used within a variety of distance learning settings in teacher education to help improve pedagogical and technology integration skills. They examine how technology is used to support strategies and goals for real world, complex learning. Matthew Champagne (of the Iota Corporation) responds with a discussion of challenges of and solutions for evaluating technology-based, and specifically Web-based, learning environments. He offers embedded assessment as one key strategy. The open discussion focuses on the systems approach to thinking and how that informs the design of learning environments. Other issues include the function of roles in learning, as well as the scalability of the types of approaches discussed by Lesh, Byrne, and White.

SECTION 5: SCALING UP

Most of the chapters in this book can be considered describing "boutique" programs, programs that are focused first on creating a rich learning experience, and second on scaling the process. Here we focus on two programs where scaling is central—with the emphasis on supporting an entire university system in the movement to distance education. The concern is the development of scalable models.

In the first primary chapter, José Rafael López-Islas (of Instituto Tecnológico de Monterrey (known in English as Monterrey Tech or MT–VU)) examines the efforts of the Virtual University to mount a wide-scale implementation of a problem-based learning (PBL) model. He takes us through the experiences of moving faculty along the path to an increasingly interactive environment and the problems that ensue. MT eventually adopts the University of Massstricht's problem-based learning approach (where PBL has been a required approach in all classes for the last 25 years), with the goal of applying it to all of the classes taught at Monterrey Tech Virtual University. Data on student interaction in the classes is described in some detail as Monterrey Tech Virtual University moved toward the PBL approach. In her response to López-Islas, Jamie Kirkley discusses the challenges of using theory to guide the design and assessment of distance learning environments. She examines the challenges with using theory as a design tool. She also addresses specific analytical research methods for examining constructivist learning environments. Open discussion focuses on the role of tools to support the PBL learning process, as well as how students are assessing the online learning environment.

In the second primary chapter, Peter Shea, Eric Fredericksen, Alexandra Pickett, and William Pelz report (of the State University of New York [SUNY]) survey data from students and faculty in the distance education programs in the SUNY system (20,000 students last year). It contrasts from the other chapters in that the design of the courses in a program is not the focus because there are a variety of strategies used across the system. Rather, the emphasis is on students' perception of depth of learning, interaction, and quality of the experience, as well as the faculty members reports of their teaching strategies and their satisfaction. Carson Eoyang (of the Naval Postgraduate School) examines the SUNY research and offers insights into SUNY's role as a large, nationally recognized program and discusses the conceptual and methodological challenges in conducting large-scale research. Open discussion addresses issues of research design for surveys, specifically with regard to sample bias. Other interesting issues include the role of synchronous and asynchronous technologies to support learning and the political and research issues that surround this issue.

SECTION 6: ALTERNATIVE VIEWS

In these final two chapters, we bring fresh eyes to bear on the issues of distance learning in higher education. Rather than provide a traditional reflection on the book, we asked leaders outside the instructional design, evaluation, and learning science perspectives to offer their views on the approaches and the thinking reflected in the rest of the book.

First, Sally Johnstone (of WICHE) addresses the plethora of challenging policy issues for distance education at the national, regional, state, and local levels. She states that for distance education to continue to advance and grow, we must address many difficult policy issues along the way. The open discussion addresses the possible complexities of the policy issues, as well as some ideas for addressing these. Other issues include the impact of using knowledge objects, as well as the role of the cost of technology in forcing many to deal with policy.

In the second chapter, Jim Botkin (of Natural Voice Executive Coaching) and Prasad Kaipa (of SelfCorporation) discuss the interesting intersection of learning in business and education. They address future trends in learning and the need for businesses to find creative solutions for meeting the educational needs of the workforce. The open discussion of the Botkin–Kaipa chapter addresses issues related to the potential use of learning objects. It also contains an excellent discussion of the role of theory in designing learning environments, which is an appropriate ending point given the focus of this entire work.

With this book, we aim to advance the discussion of how the learning sciences can inform the theory, research, and practice of distance learning, as well as face-to-face learning. There is much to learn about the design of learning environments and tools as well as the pedagogy and support needed to provide a high quality educational experience. We hope that others continue the conversation as we strive to better understand the role and impact of distance learning on the learning process and outcomes.

REFERENCES

Allen, N. (2002, November). *Climbing a mountain (and finding a range!)*. Paper presented at the annual meeting of the Western Cooperative of Educational Telecommunications, Denver, CO.

American Federation of Teachers. (2001, January). *Distance education guidelines for good practice*. Washington, DC: Author.

Arnone, M. (2002, February 15). United States Open U. to close after spending $20 million. *The Chronicle of Higher Education*, p. 35.

Barab, S., & Duffy, T. (2000). From practice fields to communities of practice. In D. Jonassen & S. M. Land (Eds.), *Theoretical foundations of learning environments* (pp. 25–56). Mahwah, NJ: Lawrence Erlbaum Associates.

Bloom, B. S. (1984). The two sigma problem: The search for methods of group instruction as effective as one-to-one tutoring. *Educational Researcher, 13*, 4–16.

Bransford, J. D., Brown, A., & Cocking, R. (Eds.). (2000). *How people learn: Mind, brain, experience and school*. Washington, DC: National Academy Press.

Bransford, J. D., & Schwartz, D. L. (2001). Rethinking transfer: A simple proposal with multiple implications. *Review of Research in Education, 24*, 61–100.

Carlson, S., & Carnevale, D. (2001, December 14). Debating the demise of NYUonline. *The Chronicle of Higher Education*, p. A31.

Carnevale, D. (2000, July 14). Legislative audit criticizes Western Governors University [Online]. *The Chronicle of Higher Education*. Available: http://chronicle.com/weekly/v47/i06/06a04802.htm

Chenoweth, N., Hayes, J. R., Gripp, P., Littleton, E., Steinberg, E., & Van Every, D. (1999). Are our courses working? Measuring student learning. *Written Communication*, 16:29–50.

Collison, G., Elbaum, B., Haavind, S., & Tinker, R. (2000). *Facilitating online learning: Effective strategies for moderators*. Madison, WI: Atwood.

Duffy, T. M., & Cunningham, D. J. (1996). Constructivism: Implications for the design and delivery of instruction. In D. H. Jonassen (Ed.), *Handbook of research for educational communications and technology*. (pp. 170–198). New York: Simon & Schuster.

Duffy, T., & Grabinger, S. (1999). *The learning to teach with technology studio*. Unpublished paper, Center for Research on Learning and Technology, Bloomington, IN.

Duffy, T. M., & Jonassen, D. H. (1992). (Eds.). *Constructivism and the technology of instruction: A conversation*. Hillsdale, NJ: Lawrence Erlbaum Associates.

Dziuban, C., & Moskal, P. (2001). Evaluating distributed learning in metropolitan universities. Educause Quaterly, *24*(4), 60–61.

Ehrmann, S. (2002). *Flashlight cost-analysis handbook: Modeling resource use in teaching and learning with technology, Version 2.0*. Washington, DC. TLT Group.

Fredericksen, E., Pickett, A., Shea, P., & Pelz, W. (2000) Factors influencing faculty satisfaction with asynchronous teaching and learning in the SUNY learning network. *Journal of Asynchronous Learning Networks, 4*(3). pp. 245–278.

Glaser, B., & Strauss, A. (1967). *The discovery of grounded theory: Strategies for qualitative research*. Chicago: Aldine.

Honebein, P., Duffy, T., & Fishman, B. (1993). Constructivism and the design of learning environments: Context and authentic activities for learning. In T. Duffy, J. Lowyck, & D. Jonassen (Eds.). *The design of constructivist learning environments: Implications for instructional design and the use of technology*. (pp. 87–108) Heidelberg, Germany: Springer-Verlag.

Koljatic, M., & Kuh, G. (2001). A longitudinal assessment of college student engagement in good practices in undergraduate education. *Higher Education, 42*, 351–371.

Kuh, G. D. (in press). Student engagement in the first year of college. In L. M. Upcraft, J. N. Gardner, & B. O. Barefoot (Eds.), *Meeting challenges and building support: Creating a climate for first-year student success*. San Francisco: Jossey-Bass.

Malopinsky, L., Kirkley, J. R., Duffy, T. (April, 2002). *Building performance support systems to assist preK–12 teachers in designing online, inquiry-based professional development instruction*. Paper presented at the annual meeting of the American Educational Research Association, New Orleans, LA.

Mikulecky, L. (1998) Diversity, discussion, and participation: Comparing Web-based and campus-based adolescent literature classes. *Journal of Adolescent and Adult Literacy, 42*(2), 84–97.

NEA Higher Education. (2002). The promise and the reality of distance education. *Update, 8*(13), pp. 1–4.

Nunn, C. E. (1996). Discussion in the college classroom. *Journal of Higher Education, 67*, 243–266.

Resnick, L. B. (1987, December). Learning in school and out. *Educational Researcher, 16*(9), 13–20.

Riel, M., & Harasim, L. (1994). Research perspectives on network learning. *Journal of Machine-Mediated Learning. 4*(23), 91–114.

Smith, D. G. (1983). Instruction and outcomes in an undergraduate setting. In C. L. Ellner & C. P. Barnes (Eds.), *Studies in college teaching* (pp. 83–116). Lexington, MA: Heath.

Stein, T. (2001, February 25). VCs go back to the drawing board. *Red Herring Magazine*. Available: http://www.redherring.com/mag/issue92/680015468.html

II

Community Building

2

Learning in Dialogue With a Practicing Community

Linda Polin
Pepperdine University

This chapter is not about how to port a successful graduate program online, although that describes the initial intent behind the "substantive change" proposal sent to the Western Accreditation of Schools and Colleges, to allow the graduate school to move the 15-year-old master of arts in educational technology to an online format and have it remain accredited. This chapter is not about how to adapt instruction or curriculum to take advantage of the affordances of network software applications, although that is exactly what the graduate school hoped to do. This chapter is about how a particular theory of learning underlying the redesign of the program as a specifically online program led to changes in curriculum and pedagogy. More important, it is about how those changes were possible largely because the program was online. In other words, the features of the tools and the elements of the pedagogical model created a synergy that transformed the program for the better.

In this online program,[1] the goal of graduate education is to increase the extent of students' participation in their field of practice. The program attempts to do this by bringing together the academic scholars (faculty and guests) and the active practitioners (students themselves) on equal footing. This has become possible by leaving the university classroom behind and moving the learning conversation online. Key synchronous and asynchronous communication tools support the construction of a

---

[1]Though there are two online programs at the Graduate School of Education at Pepperdine University, this chapter focuses on the online master of arts program in educational technology (hereafter OMAET), which began its fifth year in the fall of 2002. The program is conducted almost entirely through the Internet. Students and faculty have only three face-to-face meetings over the 13 months of the program. The first is a mandatory, 5-day, preprogram, VirtCamp, held in July on campus. The second 5-day, face-to-face meeting takes place at midprogram in conjunction with a national educational computing conference. The third is a 4-day meeting, which encompasses the end-of-program juried exhibition of student projects, conducted at Pepperdine. The remainder of program interaction takes place online. Students and faculty use asynchronous and synchronous tools such as newsgroups, web pages, groupware, chat shells, and e-mail to greatly expand the variation in participation, observation, and interaction structures available to them (Polin, 2000).

new discourse community of scholars and practitioners working together to improve practice.

A SOCIAL–CULTURAL MODEL OF LEARNING IN HIGHER EDUCATION

Over the past decade, mainstream learning theory has evolved yet again, producing models that view learning as a function of social, historical, and cultural activity (Cole, 1996; Cole & Engestrom, 1993). Sociocultural theories describe the learning process, and the knowledge that is "learned," as distributed among participants and located within a context of activity. From this perspective, children don't acquire reading skills, but rather they join the "literacy club" (Smith, 1992). Educated consumers don't rely on school math to calculate per unit prices in the grocery store; they rely on the "tools" in the grocery store environment to reason their way toward "best" purchases (Lave, Murtaugh, & de la Rocha, 1984).

Sociocultural learning theory describes a family of models of learning that share a common ground but foreground different aspects of the developmental process. For some, the development of the individual *in situ* is the focus (Bruner, 1992, 1998; Vygotsky, 1978). For others, the larger organizational system of activity within which the individual operates is the focus (Engestrom, 1999; Lave & Wenger, 1991). Building on seminal work by the Russian psychologist Vygotsky (1978), current activity theory is one model that describes learning as the consequence of interaction with people, objects, and culture, in goal-oriented, organized, collective effort (Engestrom, 1999). The "community of practice" concept is a closely related model that describes learning as a consequence of organized, goal-directed, social activity (Lave & Wenger, 1991). For both models, in a healthy system, the individual learns through a process of enculturation into a slowly but constantly evolving practice.

From this perspective, learning is often described as identity transformation within a community (Wenger, 1998). That is, the learner does not merely acquire knowledge or add to his or her repertoire of abilities. She or he becomes a different member of the practice community, taking on different roles, responsibilities, or status in the practice (e.g., Polman, 2000). Among the K–12 teachers who are students in our program, this transformation can be quite profound. For instance, students cease perceiving and being perceived of as isolated classroom practitioners and are viewed as highly valued, sought-after leaders on the school site, even as active members of regional and national organizations in their field. For these students, job titles or responsibilities often change; opportunities open up for them that lead to deeper involvement in the practice. Students from settings other than K–12 education also find themselves acquiring a different status within their setting, leading change, and participating in the planning and development of new workplace learning strategies.

Graduate School as a Practice Community

Part of what defines a "good" graduate school is its ability to offer its full-time students easy access to apprenticeship relationships with junior and senior faculty, the opportunity to be immersed in an intellectual and professional community, to work alongside more advanced students and faculty experts, to hear faculty conversations, to attend guest lectures, to connect with the professional culture, and to practice it in animated, collegial, intense conversations with peers over coffee before or after class.

In graduate education students on campus have additional opportunities to work on funded research under the mentorship of faculty sponsors and to gain experience in college teaching as teaching assistants. Indeed, many of the factors in the ranking of graduate schools are derived from variations on the theme of external funding and faculty research production. In this model, junior research opportunities are located on campus and cannot translate into an online environment.

However, the majority of graduate students in the field of education in the United States are not full-time students. They do not spend their days on campus in coffee-houses, faculty offices, or research enclaves in the departments in which they study. At the master's level, nationwide, two thirds of education students are employed full-time while enrolled in school, compared to less than half of those enrolled in M.A. and M.S. programs other than education (National Center for Educational Statistics [NCES], 1996). At the doctoral level, 82.6% of students in Ed.D. programs are engaged in full-time work, compared to barely one third of those enrolled in Ph.D. programs (NCES, 1996). Ph.D. students who work are self-described as "students working to meet expenses" rather than as full-time "employees enrolled in school" (NCES, 1996). Most likely, these students are employed on campus and most likely as junior research staff on externally funded research projects. They are able to experience the apprenticeship relationship described above. However, Ed.D. and master of arts students are overwhelming fully employed within their careers. These students are not working on campus with program faculty; their access is severely limited.

These data suggest that the needs of M.A.- and Ed.D.-seeking students in education are different from those of other graduate students, and even from Ph.D. students in education. The university that serves commuter and part-time students with very little alteration of its traditional means of doing business cannot support a community of practice in education for students; it leaves them isolated and without access to the practice or to experts, peers, and near-peers engaged in practice.

Although the Pepperdine University program specializes in educational technology, the students and program faculty view technology not only as subject matter, but also as a resource for organizational learning and change in the educational systems in which they both work. This broader view enables the program to assume the lofty goal of mediating students' engagement with a larger professional community in technology and education. It redefines the collective activity as joint knowledge building in the service of constructive action, as opposed to individual acquisition and storage of abstract knowledge from academic authority.

OMAET students come from a variety of specific workplace contexts. Though most are in K–12 education, increasingly the program draws people from higher education and corporate training. This variation in workplace setting is perceived of as a powerful feature of the program, and there is an intentional effort to balance and distribute variation rather than track it into homogeneous groupings.

The K–12 practitioners in the program are primarily classrooms teachers, but also include site- and district-level technology specialists, from network administrators to staff development coordinators. The K–12 group, though it may not share a common job title, generally shares a common vision: the desire to make pedagogical change by leveraging classroom and district technology use. The students from higher education settings are generally not full-time, tenure-track faculty, but represent media and technical support departments on campus. They describe themselves as caught between administrators pressuring faculty to move online and faculty rebuffing that pressure. The students from the corporate world report their organizations increasing interest in providing networked support for "just-in-time" learning, moving away from traditional models of self-contained, face-to-face training classes (Berge, 2001). These students are further enmeshed in the growing corporate interest in knowledge management and knowledge sharing.(Davenport & Prusak, 1998; Nonanka & Takeuchi, 1995) For many students, these workplace ideas are becoming human resource department directives affecting their jobs.

Supporting the Community by Relocating the Activity

Locating students in a community of practice for their graduate schooling means locating the program in that community setting as well. It has been difficult to imagine how to accomplish this for graduate programs in education, which tend to enroll full-time working adults who cannot spend their day on campus. In building the structure of the online master of arts program, the faculty intended to address this problem by re-vision of the central activities of graduate school. The program, its faculty, and curricula would explicitly function to mediate connections between students' local, personal experience of practice and the larger field of professional activity and the theoretical knowledge in which that practice is embedded.

The program accomplished this in five ways. First, the program is explicitly anchored in real world practice. Students are required to contribute from their experiences at work. This begins in the application process. The program explicitly requires applicants to have at least 3 years of full-time work experience in their careers. In the application interview, students are told that their local work setting will be the context for course work. In their application essay, they are asked to describe a problem, project, idea, issue, or plan in their workplace that they think they would like to focus on in the program.

Second, the program makes extensive use of the notion of generations. Selected alumni of the program work as paid teaching assistants to organize and conduct the summer VirtCamp for the incoming generation. This task is not merely a matter of implementing an existing faculty design. Camp staff plan the agenda, content, and activities, taking into account the history and experiences of prior generations of students. This group uses documents and materials from prior years, as well as members' own experiences from VirtCamp. Selection to the VirtCamp staff is a highly sought-after privilege, reinforced by the distribution of black, program polo shirts with the program logo, which distinguish staff from new student campers, who wear blue.

Third, the midprogram, face-to-face meeting is always held in conjunction with a national educational technology conference on the East Coast. As Pepperdine University is on the West Coast, this was initially done to facilitate students' departure from their workplace for an extended period of time and to offer East Coast students a chance to meet on their side of the continent. Over time, this notion has developed as an effort to connect students to the larger professional community in educational technology. In the first 3 years, the program relied on large K–12 educational computing conferences, but in the fourth year the opportunity arose to build the face-to-face meeting around a more scholarly venue, the Computer-Supported Collaborative Learning (CSCL) conference (CSCL, 2002). In this setting, students were able to interact with academics and developers on issues and ideas in the program curriculum. Program faculty members were able to hold debriefing and reflection seminars, and help students realize the different opportunities and roles in the educational technology practice.

Fourth, the program faculty continually invites guest experts into the virtual classroom, either asynchronously through threaded discussions or synchronously in the virtual chat environment, called Tapped In. (These media are described later in this chapter.) Over the past 4 years, students have interacted with text authors, researchers, software developers, and principals of exemplary schools.

Fifth, the masters program connects with near peers in the doctoral program in educational technology leadership, and even with students in comparable programs at other institutions. The program involves second-year doctoral students in a couple of ways. They assist with VirtCamp, often in the role of OMAET graduates who are heading into the doctoral program, and, in their second year of doctoral work, a select number are offered the opportunity to teach a course section in the OMAET program. Graduate students in comparable programs at other institutions regularly interact with Pepperdine students about their online program experience itself, as well as about course work and practical experiences.

IMPLICATIONS FOR CURRICULUM: FROM PRESCRIPTION TO CO-CONSTRUCTION

For newcomers then the purpose is not to learn from talk as a substitute for legitimate peripheral participation; it is to learn to talk as a key to legitimate peripheral participation. (Lave & Wenger, 1991, p. 109)

Learning by doing and learning by enculturation into a practice are at once desirable for their power and frustrating for their implementation difficulty. Short of placing students in the field of practice, how can formal education support an authentically situated approach to learning? Some have argued that simulations, problem-based learning scenarios, and time-limited opportunities for collaboration with "real" practitioners accomplish this (Riel, 1998; Schank, 1997; Scardamalia & Bereiter, 1994). However, these opportunities are constrained by time, curriculum, and access. They are, at best, tourist opportunities for students. Barab and Duffy (2000) have referred to these opportunities as "practice fields," that is, near-practice settings that share many of the critical characteristics of the real practice but are bounded and controlled experiences.

However, when students come together as a group in the online program, they each come with a personal reality—a local version of the practice of technology in education. The program was designed to take advantage of this, to connect the academic world of the university with the various local work settings for technology and learning. The chief structural support for this is the year-long action research project (ARP), described in the next section, which engages students in cycles of local intervention, data collection, reflection, revision, and repair (Coghlan & Brannick, 2001; McNiff, Lomax, & Whitehead, 1996). Involving students in mentored action research overcomes the limitations of the practice field.

The Action Research Project

When building the curriculum for the online master of arts, the faculty took a long hard look at necessary conditions for learning that are troublesome enough in a traditional academic setting and potentially exacerbated in an online environment: the ever troublesome course in the traditional masters' curriculum: the obligatory "introduction to research." Historically, here, and in most master of arts programs in the social sciences, this course is problematic for two reasons. First, it is very much outside most students' personal world experience. Second, even when students are asked to do "real" research in the course, it rarely succeeds either as an elegant and appropriate research design or as a reliable and valid data analysis activity. It is simply too hard for students to plan and carry out meaningful research inside the space of a semester at the same time they are learning about research design, instrumentation, and data analysis.

The decision was made to unfold the research course and stretch it out over the duration of the program. In addition, the yearlong course was redesigned as an action research project, thus enabling the nexus of theory and practice. The action research project begins with the student's essay in the application process, in which she or he is asked to describe a problem, idea, issue, project, or concern in the workplace that she or he will focus on during the program. The ARP ends with the formal, juried, public exhibition of ARP project work at the end of the year. It is the most powerful learning tool in the program, providing the integrative structure for course work.

Each group, or "cadre," of 20 to 24 students is assigned a faculty member who serves as the ARP mentor and remains with the group during the 13 months of the program. The faculty member establishes a rapport with the students, comes to know them intimately, and is able to experience a genuine apprenticeship relationship with each. This faculty mentor mediates peer-to-peer relationships while developing a sense of "cadre" among the group, and is instrumental in developing a climate to support risk taking in the yearlong project.

Students with a year to spend on project work and a sense of peer and faculty support are able to carve out truly powerful projects that engage them deeply and very often lead them through the dramatic personal transformation that the program faculty believe is the hallmark of deep learning.

The Action Research Project as Curricular Backbone

In the third year of the program, during the final face-to-face session, Cadre Three students participated in a "future search" about the program (Weisbord & Janoff, 1995) as a culminating activity in their leadership class, and also as a feedback mechanism for the program. Students remarked on the value of connections they made between classes and their ARP work. In exhibition displays, we found over and over again that students had references to specific courses activities and readings anchoring the "big ideas" in their local project work. But, of course, different courses were more and less important in different projects.

By virtue of its duration over all three and a half semesters of the program, the ARP grounds the work in other courses. The courses acquires the potential to serve as frames of reference, or points of viewing, for ARP content, to operate as lenses, or perspectives, on the year-long project. This a powerful role for courses to play, that is, supporting real world action and reflection as a frame for change efforts.

Once we realized what we had, we could intentionally exploit the connections between course work and the ARP. Faculty members could shape course work and activities to support the relationship and were rewarded by deep engagement by students. Course instructors could harvest fertile examples and activities from students' "real world" contexts for the material they were focusing on in their course readings, activities, and discussions. Students could function as peer-to-peer mentors in their courses in very powerful ways, as one student's exciting view of the connection of the course to his or her ARP subject matter enabled another student to find a way into the otherwise "abstract" theory and concepts in the course.

It would be dishonest to claim that we were that clever in our first construction of the program curriculum. We weren't. Much of what we initially built was the result of a combination of luck and experience. However, the close relationship between students and their ARP faculty mentor through the year, and the deliberate efforts to understand how students were making sense of the program, allowed us to see these relationships and then to intentionally exploit them as we revised and refined program content and structure. In short, as the program has progressed, we have found, through intentional self-study and serendipity, that the more closely the program connects students' workplace experience with course work, and the more fully it can provide stability, security, and presence, the more powerful the program can be for the students in it. Our experience of program revision is much like the way buildings learn and grow (Brand, 1994), that is, by accommodating the lives of the inhabitants.

In their seminal work on situated learning, Lave and Wenger (1991) distinguish between "talking about" and "talking within" a practice. The danger of talking about a practice, from outside of its enactment, arises as "didactic instruction" and "creates unintended practices" (Lave & Wenger, 1991, p. 108). That is, the language of instruction becomes what is learned. Students acquire a vocabulary of concepts, but it is an inert collection. Talk that arises from within ongoing practice can carry the same information, but it is anchored to practical activity: "Apprenticeship learning is supported by conversations and stories about problematic and especially difficult cases" (Lave & Wenger, 1991). The central action research project is a mother lode of problems as students try to make changes in their workplaces.

In the online program, students are doing both kinds of talking. They are speaking from within practice to others, and they are learning how to speak about their practice the way experienced, knowledgeable, grounded, practitioners do. The curriculum intentionally supports this, but the pedagogy makes it possible.

IMPLICATIONS FOR PEDAGOGY: FROM TRANSFER TO DIALOGUE

> . . . knowledge construction and theory development most frequently occur in the context of a problem of some significance and take the form of a dialogue in which solutions are proposed and responded to with additions and extensions or objections and counter-proposals from others. (Wells, 1999, p. 51)

Theories of learning as a social activity describe cultural mechanisms that help learning along. The chief mechanism is discourse, specifically, dialogues between more and less experienced people, engaged in joint activity toward a shared goal (Brown, Collins, & Duguid, 1989; Lave & Wenger, 1991; Vygotsky, 1978; Wells, 1999). In the traditional university classroom, social interaction is constrained by a transmission culture that discounts dialogue in favor of faculty presentation, and in favor of "talk about" a field of practice from outside of it.

For teachers and other professional educators, such as corporate trainers, coming to the university for an education degree is a mixed experience: "Within education, most discourse that stands for theory about educational practice has been produced within a division of labor between those who construct theory and those for whom it might have some pragmatic value" (Simon, 1992, p. 85). This perceived disconnect between university as the source of theory and the field as the location of practice becomes problematic when we ask students to embrace theory that requires them to reject their own experience and identity as faulty, obsolete, unfounded, or inadequate. Theory in the graduate classroom "authorizes a particular discourse" while disrupting and marginalizing another. Part of what makes this so is the context, history, and constraints of the university classroom.

Yet this is also the potential power of graduate education, at its best a transformative experience for the student. The university classroom might offer the student "access to a discourse and, through this discourse, the possibility of engaging the social world differently ... " (Simon, 1992, p. 91). But first, students and teachers must engage in genuine dialogue that divulges, honors, and explores their own situated perspectives. Unfortunately, shared time is severely limited when constrained by traditional, face-to-face class meeting times. However, when dialogue is relocated from a course classroom to a collegial working community, a social learning model can thrive.

Getting to Dialogue

Formal education relies on written and oral language almost entirely. Relatively little communication arises in other semiotic channels. But amidst all that language there is very little dialogue. What looks like discussion is often recitation or patterns referred to as I–R–E or I–R–F (Lemke, 1990; Mehan, 1979). This sequence begins with the teacher posing a question (*I* for initiation), a selected student offering an answer (*R* for response), and the teacher then commenting on the quality on the student's response (*E* for evaluation or *F* for feedback). These conversational sequences are also found in the higher education classroom under the guise of discussion, as faculty check on student comprehension of required reading for the week. This kind of interaction is the consequence of a theory that teaching–learning is the transmission and acquisition of information from an authoritative source.

Another way to interpret the construction of this traditional classroom talk is from the point of view of the identities of the people involved. If teachers carry with them a notion of the teacher as an authority and near expert on the topics in the curriculum, and if students carry a complementary view of themselves as receptors of given knowledge, then this I-R-E conversational experience makes perfect sense for all involved in it. It doesn't take much of a stretch to consider how this is possible. Certainly, the role of the teacher as content matter expert and disseminator of knowledge is reinforced by credentialing systems, by teachers' right and duty to grade or certify student knowledge, and by their formal relationship to a specific curriculum.

If, however, the people involved in the interaction share a different relationship to one another, their conversation might look different. In the OMAET program, the inclusion of students' workplace experiences and identity as a focus for curriculum and course work acknowledges and supports students as people with relevant expertise, and it creates an arena in which peers are viewed as having legitimate authority as well. Research in the K–12 classroom has identified how this can be achieved, by incorporating students' commonsense knowledge and experience into the instructional discourse (Lemke, 1990), by allowing that students "make sense," (Schon, 1987), and honoring their "funds of knowledge" as legitimate curricular material (Moll & Greenberg, 1990). Graduate professional education can be infused with these same cultural values and reap similar benefits. With this very different set of identities and relationships, verbal interaction can become joint inquiry. This verbal interaction has been labeled dialogue (Bohm & Nichol, 1996; Dixon, 1996; Isaacs, 1999; Senge, 1990), and in this chapter, dialogue refers to linguistic interaction in which participants act together in pursuit of understanding on a topic of mutual interest.

THE TOOLS OF ONLINE DIALOGUE

Finally, for many people, the transforming potential of collaborative knowledge building is most fully realized when the progressive discourse is conducted in writing, since in this mode the writer enhances his or her understanding by dialoguing with his or her emerging text as well as with the community for whom the text is intended. (Wells, 1999, p. 87)

Ironically, for a distance education program, the main pedagogical method in the OMAET program is group dialogue, though almost all this dialogue is written rather than spoken. Written language and public conversation, in particular, make student and faculty thinking accessible for others to view, consider, expand, or modify. Communities engaged in online dialogue offer a hybrid of both: public conversation that is written.

There are two main dialogue tools in the online program: (1) Tapped In, a multi-user, real-time, virtual chat environment and (2) newsgroups, an asynchronous, public, threaded discussion forum. Both of these tools are fairly "old," even predating the World Wide Web, though each has been greatly enhanced by virtue of Web access, Java applets, and html. Both chat and newsgroups are tools shaped by their use to support community. They arose in networked environments to support interaction among members of cohesive social groups. Both rely heavily on "written talk" as the medium for communication.

Threaded, Public, Asynchronous Discussion Groups

Server-hosted threaded discussions, or newsgroups, were not developed for teaching, but for supporting groups of people with common interests who wished to discuss and share experience and expertise, that is, "news" on a topic. Newsgroups have a long and colorful history on the Internet as Usenet forums for geographically dispersed members of communities with a common interest, such as owners of diabetic cats, wine connoisseurs, recreational pilots, cancer survivors, and parents of children with attention deficit hyperactivity disorder. These forums allow experts and novices to interact on issues, pose questions, offer advice, share experiences, barter merchandise, and argue opinions. In other words, newsgroups come from a tradition that supports the kind of communication and interaction that a social, situated model of learning holds as a central mechanism of learning.

Newsgroup discussions do not contain formal academic writing, such as a student might produce in a term paper or project report. The writing in newsgroups is a hybrid of speech and prose (Davis & Brewer, 1997). The register is often informal, misspellings show interference from oral language (they're and their), sentence fragments are common, and vernacular expressions abound. Despite this informality, or perhaps because of this, newsgroups are an ideal place for reflecting on course ideas. In contrast to ephemeral chat, they provide an enduring reflective space for thinking aloud, for using writing to share thinking. They put students' remarks in close proximity with each other, and they structure the response format to encourage building directly on prior remarks of others.

In the online program, students are exhorted to consider their course newsgroup as a main venue for class participation, and because of the way in which the program faculty make use of newsgroups, participation means discussion and dialogue. In addition to course-based newsgroups, the program maintains non-course-specific newsgroups for the discussion of social, logistical, or personal topics. This supports the continued social interaction among students but keeps most of the chitchat out of course discussions areas. Occasionally, a student group will request the creation of a newsgroup for use by a work group that wishes to "talk more" about a particular subject that has come up online. Recent examples of student-requested newsgroups include: ARP-talk, to discuss the action research project; kids2kids, to allow the elementary students of the various teachers to interact online; highered, to support a discussion of issues involved in supporting technology use among faculty; and exhibitions, to discuss the logistics and do some problem solving around the final exhibitions in July.

Course newsgroups are where most of the intellectual work of the online course takes place, in large part because of the special features of newsgroups that make them a powerful tool for using writing as a tool for thinking and sharing thinking. In newsgroups, students have the time and space to reference their workplace, in anecdotes or as examples to illustrate course ideas. This sharing is probably most useful to the student as he or she ports pieces of his or her reality onto the countertop to mix with academia. This opportunity is heightened by the responses of peers and the opportunity to see peer versions of the workplace as an application or illustration of theory. It all goes a long way toward helping students broaden their vision from the narrow confines of the specifics of their school or organization, to a more expansive view of many schools and organizations.

Writing allows access to thinking (Langer & Applebee, 1987). Rarely are there opportunities in traditional courses for instructors and students to view each other's thinking other than in formal, lengthy papers or presentations that run uninterrupted by classmates or the teacher. Like classroom talk, writing done for a traditional class is usually a formal display for evaluation purposes, rather than an opportunity for genuine interaction (Applebee, 1981; Britton, 1975). Rarely do students have the chance to craft written rejoinders to teachers' remarks on their papers or revisit their contributions to class discussion. Again, this is often the result of time constraints, as well as the constraints of tradition in a culture of learning as knowledge transfer. The further away teaching is from the context in which that knowledge is used, the more important assessment becomes for the teacher.

Further, students in traditional classes very rarely get to see the instructor thinking or interacting with his or in her colleagues in the department or in the specialization. However, in the online program, instructors frequently interact with each other in the public asynchronous spaces of the newsgroup around issues, such as standards, assessment, and the politics of education.

There are many features of threaded newsgroups, some of which are dictated by the browser or "newsgroup viewing client" used to read news. Four key features are common to all, however, and are critical to the power of newsgroups to support a successful online intellectual community. These are threading, quoting, embedding, and open access.

Threading

The defining characteristic of the newsgroup is its ability to hold together, or thread, responses on the same topic, in the order in which they were generated, regardless of the amount of intervening time or activity on other topics (see Fig. 2.1).

Some topic threads will run over a 1- or 2-day period, others as long as several months. Anyone can post at any time to respond to any thread or to initiate a topic of his or her own choosing. It is possible for a writer to alter the subject heading on the posting and still have his or her post show up within the original thread of subject matter. Students

Subject	To/From	Total	Date	Lengt
▽ Brain Drain (Interesting Article)	Cathy ...	43	10/22/00 12:13 PM	64
Re: Brain Drain (Interesting Arti...	Kris Te...		10/22/00 2:44 PM	98
Re: Brain Drain (Interesting A...	Jessic...		10/22/00 7:00 PM	126
Re: Brain Drain (Interesting...	Kris Te...		10/23/00 3:33 PM	35
Re: Brain Drain (Interesti...	Jennife...		10/23/00 5:12 PM	81
Re: Brain Drain (Interesting Arti...	kyle ▼...		10/22/00 5:03 PM	81
Re: Brain Drain (Interesting Arti...	Marty ...		10/22/00 6:48 PM	93
Re: Brain Drain (Interesting A...	Jennife...		10/22/00 7:48 PM	52
Re: Brain Drain (Interesting...	Tom S		10/23/00 7:43 PM	16
Re: Brain Drain (Interesting Arti...	Jessic...		10/22/00 6:54 PM	87
Re: Brain Drain (Interesting Arti...	Linda P...		10/23/00 9:08 PM	77
Re: Brain Drain (Interesting Arti...	Patrici...		10/23/00 9:33 PM	40
Re: Brain Drain (Interesting Arti...	Cathy ...		10/25/00 5:16 PM	93
Re: Brain Drain (Interesting A...	Jennife...		10/25/00 6:15 PM	138
Re: Brain Drain (Interesting A...	Jessic...		10/25/00 8:13 PM	105
Re: Brain Drain (Interesting...	Cathy ...		10/30/00 7:50 PM	113
Re: Brain Drain (Interesting A...	Kris Te...		11/12/00 1:21 PM	132
Re: Brain Drain (Interesting A...	kyle ▼...		10/28/00 3:30 PM	22
Re: Brain Drain (Interesting...	Kris Te...		11/12/00 1:26 PM	33
Re: Brain Drain (Interesti...	kyle ▼...		11/12/00 4:57 PM	39
Re: Brain Drain (Intere...	Jennife...		11/13/00 5:47 PM	61
Re: Brain Drain (Intere...	Cathy ...		11/13/00 8:25 PM	43
Re: Brain Drain (Intere...	Stuart ...		11/19/00 1:56 PM	47
Re: Brain Drain (Int...	kyle ▼...		11/19/00 3:39 PM	51
Re: Brain Drain (Interesti...	Jessic...		11/17/00 9:53 PM	39
Re: Brain Drain (Intere...	Kris Te...		11/25/00 2:55 PM	45
Re: Brain Drain (Interesting A...	Adrien...		10/25/00 8:20 PM	44
Re: Brain Drain (Interesting...	Jendy ...		10/28/00 9:50 AM	51
Re: Brain Drain (Interesting...	Suzann...		10/31/00 5:39 PM	61
Re: Brain Drain (Interesti...	Jennife...		10/31/00 6:57 PM	75
Re: Brain Drain (Interesti...	Adrien...		11/3/00 11:09 PM	70
Re: Brain Drain (Interesting...	Kris Te...		11/12/00 1:32 PM	84
Re: Brain Drain (Interesting...	Cathy ...		11/13/00 8:24 PM	14
Re: Brain Drain (Interesting A...	Stuart ...		10/24/00 9:41 PM	105
Re: Brain Drain (Interesting A...	Cathy ...		10/25/00 5:12 PM	102
Re: Brain Drain (Interesting...	Jessic...		10/25/00 8:16 PM	116

FIG. 2.1. A discussion thread.

are encouraged to do this when they are taking a thread off on a tangent, for instance, when a thread on national curriculum standards heads off into a discussion of large-scale testing. Figure 2.1 shows how students' responses vary in date and time, how they are physically connected, and how the horizontal listing with indentations offers a visual indication of where in the chain of conversation the response arises. Most newsreader clients allow the reader to reorganize the threads according to several dimensions. Sorting messages by date, subject, or sender is a useful way to find a specific posting. It is also possible to flag a message and later search for flagged messages.

Quoting

When a writer responds to a posted message, he or she can make use of a newsgroup function to include a copy of the message to which he or she is responding. This shows up as quoted text, set off from the text being created in response. The respondent can pare down the quoted original to reveal just the section of prose being responded to in the new message. Unless a student is initiating a new topic thread, a post is always in response to some prior message and linked to it.

Even though the newsgroup is public, students will often write a response that addresses, by name, the person whose message they are responding to. This tendency to name and quote a specific student-speaker-writer in one's own responses leads to students to build on prior commentary rather than simply assert their own prose without connecting it to ongoing discourse. This is an interesting phenomenon: directing one's prose to an individual and realizing that the entire group will read it. While building on prior prose, a student's own response introduces new ideas or builds selectively on prior remarks, and so the threaded dialogue can migrate slowly toward a different aspect of the topic. This can lead to a long thread with an interesting duality: messages are tightly woven together around a topic and yet are also expansive in regard to particular elements of that topic. However, because of the mechanics of threading, it is possible for a sidebar conversation to emerge in a thread, run its course, and end without interrupting the ongoing flow of discussion on the main theme.

Embedded Objects

A third critical feature of newsgroups is the ability to embed images, links, and html commands in the body of the message. Or, these objects may also be sent along as file attachments to the message. This feature makes it easy for students to share articles, Web sites, digital images, or any other relevant objects with the class. Further, these objects can be embedded in an introductory or explanatory context, penned by their contributor.

The objects students choose to embed are offerings they make to the newsgroup, most often as the result of one or two kinds of personal experiences. First, and most often, students find something of use to them in their course work, and it occurs to them that others might benefit from it. Or, they find something that they know will be of interest to so-and-so, who is working on that topic. They have a desire to share that resource rather than hoard it. Second, and almost as common, students run across something that is relevant to any topic in the program and want to talk about it; it is controversial, or exciting, or startling, and they want to engage with others about it. Their sharing is actually a bid for discussion, and sometimes they will solicit peer reactions.

Open Access

Though newsgroups look like written talk, they are very different from face-to-face conversations. For one thing, the turn-taking norms of conversation are irrelevant, and the linearity of chronological order is as well. Students can read and respond to any posting anytime, and indeed, sometimes students respond several days or even a week or two after a message has been placed in play or after other responses have been made to it by other writers. In the latter instance, it is possible to make a response to a message without reading what others have already said in reply to that message. There is much we don't know about how students interact with the structure of newsgroups.

Students do not need to get permission from the teacher to post, and only the person whose IP address matches the author's can cancel or delete a posted message. This open access also means students and faculty from other classes can participate actively or by simply lurking (reading without posting). Faculty will often intentionally cross-post messages to more than one newsgroup to facilitate interaction across cadres in the same course, or between doctoral and masters students on a subject of interest to both groups. Students tend not to cross-post, and when faculty members do so without mentioning it to their class first, students tend to react to the "intrusion" of "outsiders" in their newsgroup. This happens so consistently that faculty members have learned the hard way that they must take a more active brokering role and not simply drop in cross-posted messages. This behavior also reveals how the students view their cadre newsgroup as a private space, despite knowing that it is not truly private.

In addition to cross-posting, faculty will also "drop in" on a newsgroup and interact for a few turns on a topic, often responding to messages posted by the faculty member teaching the class. This kind of limited guest participation has also been used for guest speakers who choose not to interact with a class in chat mode. A book author can interact with the class from anywhere at times convenient to him or her by agreeing to respond for a few days in a course newsgroup.

Asynchronous Dialogue

The voice and presence of the faculty member, even novice faculty members, is much less dominant in the newsgroup than in the face-to-face classroom. Among OMAET faculty, the more experience an instructor has teaching in the program, the lower the proportion of messages she or he posts, and the fewer the postings she or he initiates in the newsgroup (Sheingold & Polin, 2002). Novice online instructors tend to overrespond, as if obliged to enact the I–R–E sequence mentioned earlier in this chapter. Often, by their second online teaching experience, faculty members have learned to ease up on their responses to student posting, to adopt a virtual version of "wait time" sufficient to entice peer-to-peer interaction. This, in turn, reinforces students' tendency to read and respond to each other, not just to the instructor. Faculty still initiate topics to accomplish their course intentions, but the conversation in the newsgroup ranges far and wide around those topics. Students truly have control of the floor and exert that control.

Although there is more room for the student voice, the functional role of threaded discussions is still dictated by instructors' use of them, and that also appears to be related to the extent of their experience teaching in the online program (Sheingold & Polin, 2002). Novice online instructors may tend to occupy a greater proportion of initial postings and ask for displays of knowledge, for example, posing questions about the readings or requesting responses to a prompt of some sort. More experienced faculty members are more often able to initiate discussion topics than their inexperienced peers, and their own responses to postings make up a smaller proportion of the total message count. Newsgroups of experienced teachers contain a lot of peer-to-peer conversation and often considerably more total postings than same-sized classes of novice instructors. In other words, there is a lot more turn taking on the same topic as students work out their ideas.

When they first encounter newsgroups, some students will craft postings as if they were penning a series of academic essays. It is not unusual to have edited, spell-checked, multiparagraph postings at the beginning of the first semester. It may be that the medium of the written word is largely, historically, encountered as a formal academic display of knowing, rather than as a means of communication. Instructors' responses in a more casual register begin to penetrate the misunderstanding that is the main obstacle to dialogue. Only initially must students be reminded that postings should be addressed to each other, as well as to the faculty members. Students quickly learn to compose on the fly in newsgroups, rather than offline in a word processor. Faculty members do urge them to do some minimal spell checking and to use pseudonyms when talking about real people and organizations with whom they work.

One of the remarkable things about the function of newsgroups is how well suited they are for the nuances of conversation, albeit written conversation. The quoting and linking in particular seem to support the use of assumptions, inferences, and referents. The language in the examples below, drawn from one class newsgroup, shows some of the dimensions of the language of relationships that helps hold the group together over distance and time.[2] Most messages manage to combine academic talk with social connection.

In Fig. 2.2, Kyle shares resources with his cadre and experiences appreciation for his help (from Adrienne), as well as ratification of its utility (from Suzanne). This thread, coming as it does early in the first semester, helps establish norms of sharing: that it is good, that it is directed to specific individuals, that folks should acknowledge its utility.

In Fig. 2.3, Jendy does weave a complex message to Veronica. She sees common ground in their ARP plans and makes a bid to buddy up for mutual support and help; she even goes so far as to implicate a third person in this idea. She offers an explanation of how she sees the topic for herself; she shares her thinking under the presumption that it is compatible with Veronica's interests, and thus presumes to understand Veronica. Finally, she tempers her remarks about buddying up by embedding them in the real-life concern she has as a working mother of four. She alludes to Veronica's imminent motherhood and, by calling her brave, implies that Veronica is also about to find herself in a time crunch as a working mother. So Jendy's brief note to Veronica attempts (successfully, as it turns out) to connect with Veronica on two levels—academic and personal.

Figures 2.4 and 2.5 offer a typical interaction that arises in a fairly long thread occasioned by an issue of interest in the reading on dialogue at work. Again, as with the students in the other examples, this student addresses the previous writer by name and makes overt efforts to forge connections between people. Marty tells Judy, "You are far from being alone" and then proceeds to bear witness to her point by offering a personal confession. But he doesn't stop there. Marty offers an insight, his "plan" to deal with the problem of "quoters and educspeak." As it turns out, Marty's plan, "to speak from the heart," connects with Judy, and they have another conversation later in the thread.

Figure 2.6 illustrates another kind of experience of sharing and relationships of trust and support. Sue has posted her first cycle reflections on her ARP, and in those reflections, she discusses her insight that she needs to move on from where she is working. Several students read her document (a web page) and comment on her "difficult decision" and her "bravery." But Pat asks, "I'm wondering what you think of how you were able to come to your decision." Sue's reply captures the whole point of the program and offers the best example of how learning in an online community works. She acknowledges that the academic program made her look at her work through particular lenses: mentoring, learning, leadership, and management. Most of this analysis has been done online in newsgroup discussions and in reflective journaling. Sue adds, "It has been a

---

[2]Though these examples are drawn from one course newsgroup, specifically the ARP seminar, these characteristics describe the look, function, and feel of all newsgroups in the OMAET program.

Subject: Re: Relevant Literature

From: kyle

 For those of you who's ARP has anything to do with mentoring, I
ran across a great website that lists the top 7 ways to mentor. You can
find it at www.ivillage.com/workingdiva/mentoring/mentor/articles/0,6894,54856,00.html

 Also, I ran across this book for you science types: Mentoring for
Science Teachers by Terry Allsop. B and N has it for $27.00.

Kyle

Adrienne wrote:

>Hello Kyle,

>Thanks for sharing these resources. We have talked about a mentoring

>program in our diversity office but thus far have not made any strides

>towards putting one together. I will review this site and see if they

>can offer some good advice on things to do/avoid.

 >Suzanne wrote:

 >

 >Kyle--

 >Thanks for sharing these points. I recognized that I've

 >personally been guilty of the traps. I really like the SAGE

 >recipe for mentoring. The surrendering part especially makes

 >sense, but is so hard to do.

FIG. 2.2.   Kyle shares information.

huge help to have the support of this group as I've contemplated this difficult decision,"
indicating the depth and utility of her relationship within the group.
 Students do a lot of talk-writing in this online social group called the OMAET program. They "listen to" each other and are very responsive and attentive to their colleagues' remarks. They offer and receive emotional support, often as empathy and
validation. They find in each other, and their faculty, comparable and distinct experience and expertise that are accessible to them through interaction online. They are
able to take advantage of it, to admit confusions and past "mistakes," to speculate about
different possible futures for themselves and the people they work with, and to practice
new academic ideas and vocabulary in a community that offers help and support.

```
Subject: Re: Veronicas ARP

From: Jendy

Veronica,

        I think that this may be my ARP as well. I'm doing the Lego thing

for my semester project, but I am more interested in improving my

teaching practices and getting my philosophy clearly defined for myself

and others.

        Since I was the founder of our school I have been very concerned

about my practices and what I'm modeling for others. We have had so many

changes in our Faculty and our school has grown so fast that I am very

concerned that we have gotten off our original path. It has actually been

a very difficult September for me and I'm still concerned about sharing

too much on NGs.

        I would love to buddy up with you and Jessica to work out some of

our ideas. I'm teaching Kdg. and it is quite a challenge with 4 kids. The

last time I taught Kdg. I only had 3 kids. It is amazing the dimension

kids add to our profession! How are you doing? Isn't that baby coming

soon? You are very brave to do this and teach and have a baby! ;-)

Jendy
```

FIG. 2.3. Jendy connects with Veronica on several levels.

Virtual Environments for Synchronous Interaction

The real-time, synchronous chat environment is generally eschewed as a learning environment. Chat is considered a resource-poor environment for conversation, especially for "intellectual" conversation (Palloff & Pratt, 1999). After all, it cannot support critical prosodic elements: intonation, volume, stress, variations in vowel length, phrasing, and other acoustic features that support meaning (Gumperz, 1981). It deprives participants of access to each other's facial expressions, gestures, and body language, all of which are considered critical devices for assisting in meaning making in conversation. An additional objection to chat rooms as learning spaces must be attributed to still dominant cognitive theories of how people learn, none of which place "conversation" at the top of the list of strategies for knowledge acquisition.

Chat predates the World Wide Web, but this "old" network application still enjoys a tremendous popularity. Chat environments were little more than rapidly scrolling screens of badly typed, jargon-laced lines of text, with no scenic embellishment other than what the participants generated as narration in their own typed text: "Hagrid waves at Dumbledore. Dumbledore pours Hagrid a steinful of ale." Chat was barren.

Subject: Re: Larson and Dialogue

From: Marty

Judy,

   Your discussion of the barriers and resistance to "evangelism" and your own concerns of how people will perceive your actions.... well just know that you are far from being alone. As I reflect upon, consider, plan, and act within my decision to promote a CoP [community of practice] and my mentoring project at the school I too am frightened of the possible responses that I will elicit. My own reactions to people, in the past, who pepper their conversations with quotes and references to others, of whom I was not familiar, have, quite frankly, been quite judgmental. Unconsciously allowing myself to go on the defensive, I always questioned why they could not talk to me plainly, as I would speak to them to insure that they understood; because in challenging my intellect, I felt that they placed themselves above me. Yet, as I look back to others who have presented ideas & knowledge to me I remember that the ones who spoke with fervor, excitement, with commitment to new ideas were, for the most part, ones with whom I was far more accepting of what knowledge that they had to offer. So, acknowledging my own prejudice against "quoters" & "educspeak" my plan is to speak from my heart of what has effected me and why. To speak of new plans, new directions, and of my new experiences, asking what their reactions are to my actions, will be more likely to elicit interest. Of course, once I have that interest, their questions will permit the quotes, references, and the "whole magilla".

Judy wrote:

>*As I was getting towards the end of this very enjoyable book and*
>*read one of the letters Larson wrote the faculty in which he quoted*
>*from a book -- my thoughts were that I bet the faculty started seeing*
>*him as a know-it-all sort of guy. ...... Still, even people who want*
>*things to change are often suspect of outside authority, of people*
>*that have not really lived what they have lived.*

FIG. 2.4. Marty expands Judy's point.

Subject: Re: Larson and Dialogue

From: Judy

Marty,

This year I have felt so behind at work -- so much to do, so much
catching up to do, so many new ideas, want to develop some vision, be
proactive, blah, blah, blah. I realized by being so busy, I was not just
hanging out with my coworkers. I now try to remember to go to the coffee
room in the mornings and just talk about the weekends football games or
what people are doing for the holidays., etc. It really makes for many
casual opportunities to also talk about tech things and sometimes new
books I have read (for Pepperdine.)

Marty wrote:

> *As the guy in charge of the technology at the school.... I have become*
>*isolated. There are those that come to me to solve a problem, those*
>*that avoid me because of their fear of being deemed less than expert,*
>*and those that avoid me because engaging me in conversation would*
>*acknowledge their lack of mastery in tech. I'm the tech teacher. I*
>*wish that I was a math teacher that coincidently knew a lot about*
>*tech.... I believe that I would be accepted more as a peer who can help*
>*mentor.*

>*In discussions with people if I acted out the typical characterization*
>*of a tech guy.... I would use "tech-talk" that would be beyond many.*
>*Instead my habit is to take the logical route and talk simply, building*
>*upon concepts to the same end goal, and then I run the risk of*
>*resentment because people may (mistakenly) perceive that I am talking*
>*down to them when, in fact, I am making sure that I don't assume what*
>*their knowledge is.*

FIG. 2.5. Judy engages Marty.

Nothing existed before the participants created it in prose, on the fly, and when they left, there was no enduring residue of their presence.

However, in the early 1980s, the role-playing game community, for example, of games like Dungeons and Dragons, was constructing and disseminating networked, multiuser, real-time, virtual worlds that moved beyond chat into group collaboration and

>IMHO the first thing you must recognize is "what pack do you want to

>belong to?" Is it the one that sits back, reveling in the status quo?

>Is it the one that sits back, complaining that nothing changes? Or is

>it the one that acts to change and, in doing so, risk success &

>failure?

> IMHO the second thing you must recognize is that not everyone is

>created equal! But everyone, for the most part, wants to believe that

>we are equal.... and so our social interaction, the rules of our

>memberships are that we must perceive each other as equals because we

>all want equal power. Call me silly, but I believe that you must offer

>others equal authority to avoid resentment, minimize resistance, and,

>possibly, overt criticism. This has been true, for me, in all

>relationships, no matter how my abilities compared to others; and I

>remember those times when I was, undeservedly, offered equality and

>the strength of the trust that developed. You may be ahead of the pack

> (you might be behind), just don't challenge others as the "alpha male"

>but, rather, as "fellow betas" that can benefit from each other's

>experiences and judgment.

FIG. 2.5.   (Continued)

interaction in imaginary landscapes (Rheingold, 1993). Rather than rely on sustaining group play over slow asynchronous homegrown bulletin board systems, gamers on the Internet could engage with each other in real-time, text-based fantasy scenarios, limited only by their own descriptive and programming capabilities. Referred to variously as MOOs, MUDs, MUSHes, MUSEs, and MUVEs, these program shells supported enduring databases that comprised "landscaped" worlds with objects that could be handled, shared, and employed instrumentally. These worlds existed independent of the typed talk of the participants.

A number of postsecondary educators and researchers found their way to these programs, downloaded the free program shell, and managed to find support at their university to install and maintain it on a server. This is no small task. Clearly, they recognized in these environments the potential for supporting learning in a variety of subjects, including composition and rhetoric (LinguaMOO), foreign language learning (MundoHispano MOO), biological sciences research (BioMOO), among others (e.g., Haynes, 1998).

In 1994, the Pepperdine graduate school of education downloaded one of the early freeware shells, LambdaMOO, from Xerox PARC (Curtis, 1998) and initiated its own virtual world for student and faculty use in educational technology courses. In 1998, with the increased 24/7 demands of the online master of arts and Ed.D. programs,

Subject: Re: Sue's First Cycle

From: "PatP"

Sue,

I've just had time to read your Cycle1 document. What a tough decision you are having to make! I am sorry that this is happening to you - you have given so much to <Name> School - it is sad your new administrator doesn't see it. You will be in my thoughts as you move forward with this decision.

I do think you are right on in your assessment of this person's leadership style, etc. I agree that placing you in the other teacher's position is a poor solution. It's clear that she has little understanding of the support needs for technology. Or that even infrequent users of tehcnology (sic) claim that poor support keeps them from using their computers. I'm wondering what you think of how you were able to come to your decision. Is it one you would have made just as easily (not that it's an easy decision) pre-Pepperdine? Have the Pepperdine readings, topics, and class discussions helped support you as you made the decision? Maybe you'll go on to the Doctoral Program. :)

Pat

Subject: Re: Sue's First Cycle

From: Sue B

Pat,

>Thanks for your comments. I do think that the Pepperdine program

>influenced me to make this decision. For one thing, I have been so

>busy running so fast and working so hard on the computer program at my

>school during the past 10 years, that I really had not taken time for

>personal reflection until I started this program. When we were asked

>to determine an ARP, I did a lot of soul searching and thought that if

>I just worked harder, I could influence more teachers to integrate

>technology. After studying communities of practice, looking at the

>administrative and scheduling roadblocks, and the limited help I was

FIG. 2.6.   Practicing a new identity.

>getting from my new employee, I realized that I am simply one person

>and I cannot do it all. Our mentoring class helped me to reflect on my

>relationships with the members of my Tech Department and accept their

>strengths and weaknesses.

>I also came to respect my interest and talent with Mac hardware, and

>realized that I don't want to totally neglect that part of my self. I

>could not be satisfied with only doing training and administrative

>paper pushing. When my new Head of School's leadership style and

>ethics clashed with mine, and she proposed this new job description for

>me next year, I knew that I'd have to think about leaving the school

>that I've been so invested in. Actually, I've been a wreck -- due to

>the demands of the program and the stress at school. It has been a

>huge help to have the support of this group as I've contemplated this

>difficult decision.

>I need to turn in my letter to the Head of School this week so that

>she'll know I'm not renewing my contract and they can look for another

>person. My mentor told me today that she wants me to offer to be a

>hardware consultant next year. She doesn't want to lose me completely,

>but I can't imagine the rigid Head of School considering another

>paradigm. I'm going to have to pray and sleep on this, and confer with

>my friends and family again. I'll let you know how it all turns out.

>Sue

FIG. 2.6.   (Continued)

the graduate school subcontracted with SRI for expanded access to its enhanced version of the same MOO program, called Tapped In (Schlager, Chap. 5, this volume). Pepperdine maintains its own virtual campus building in Tapped In. It is twelve stories high, housing classrooms, student and faculty offices, and the interstitial spaces of those virtual locations (hallways, elevators, and entryways). Figure 2.7 shows the terrain in Tapped In, in which the Pepperdine building is a prominent feature.

In Tapped In, graduate students obtain their own offices and decorate them through description and object construction. As a group, teachers in the Pepperdine online programs tend to revel in the possibilities a virtual reality affords them and relish the possession and development of their office spaces. Most of the objects they create reference worlds other than the classroom: saunas, massage tables, pets, rocking chairs, entertainment devices, pitchers of margaritas, aquariums, and pictures. Figure 2.8 shows the interior of a student office as the student has remodeled it.

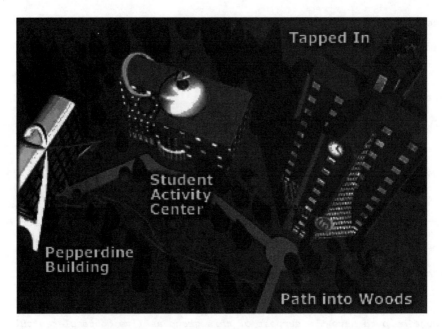

FIG. 2.7.   The Pepperdine building in Tapped In.

Organizing for Online Chat

In online programs that draw students from across the globe, there is always a big spread in time zones, making it difficult to schedule synchronous ('real-time') meetings. One solution is to group students by time zone, to facilitate easier scheduling of online sessions. However, time zone groupings leave students in regional clusters, and a critical value in the pedagogical model that guides this program is heterogeneity. Students in Texas must be able to share experiences with students in Alaska or Kuwait. Thus, students admitted into the program are placed in groups somewhat randomly. However, this means that all students cannot be online together at the same time; Japan is going to bed when California is eating breakfast. The time zone gap isn't the only obstacle to online classroom chat. A second implementation problem is subtler. It arises from the tension between the freedom of online chat and the constraints of human processing.

The Tapped In chat environment is not a classroom, It doesn't look like a classroom, and it doesn't function like a classroom. There are fewer traditional signs, tools, and symbols demarcating authority and control. There is no "front of the room," and there are no lecterns. The instructor's name takes the same form as the students' names: first name and last initial. As a function of the way in which one "speaks" in the chat environment, there is no need to go through the teacher to get the floor. As a result, students do not behave as if they are in a classroom (Polin, 2000). When there are 20 to 24 people claiming the floor to express themselves, the result is a tangle of topics and a rapidly scrolling screen of text that is almost impossible to keep up with. Yet, a critical value central to the OMAET program is the free flow of discussion.

To manage both these problems of synchronous contact, the program has adopted several conventions. First, each instructor partitions his or her synchronous meeting time into two sessions scheduled at different times in the day, depending on the time

```
Murph's Place
-----------------------------------------------------------------------
A gorgeous mutli-level corner suite. There's much to explore... have fun!
          _____
     **   /(*)  _____     (*)\
    *{*}*/(*)  /  ~~       ~~~        ~~    \  (*)\
    *\\/      /  ~           _____    ~~~  \    _____
_____\\   /  ~~~ / (*)_(*)_(*) \ ~~      \     ==]       \
|[====]  {} /_____/  /_____\ \____\      ==]        \
|[ HT ]     _____              _____    ==]         |
|[====]   | W I N D O W \[ PT ]/ W I N D O W \___[ South ]|
|      o|                          |Library      |
|:(*)   -S  \/ |/                  [ LI ]  (*) |
|:(*)   |L  \|/                    |       (*) |
|:(*)   |D   |         (*) (*) (*)  |(*)(*)(*) |
|:(*)   |N   ----      -------------|_____[ ]_|
|       |G  \_/   (*)|           |(*)  |Lounge     |
|~      |D        ------------       [ LO ]   (*)|
| ~     -R         (*) (*) (*)        (*) (*)|
|  ~   [ PT ]                         |_____[ ]_|
|_____   /(~)\  ~###############~  |Kitchen    |
|          | ()===()  ~###############~  [ KI ]    |
|          |___|   ~###############~  |           |
|          |\        ._____.  |_[WndwBar]|
|          | \       |-------------|              |
|          |FirePlace  ()============() (~)        [ OUT ]
|          |  \       \(**)(**)(**)/  (~)          |
|_____[ WHITEBOARD ]__|

Who is here? LindaX.

What is here? Whiteboard, Supplies, Clock. Fly on the Wall, The

Fireplace, Josie, Raja, Dog_53364, and Ella. Plant, Table, Chair, and

overstuffed couch.

Greetings!  Make yourself at home.  If you need anything, just ask!
-----------------------------------------------------------------------
```

FIG. 2.8. Amy's Tapped In office.

zone spread in the cadre. Students are free to choose which schedule suits them as long as the resulting subgroups are fairly evenly distributed. For instance, in a cadre of 24 people, 10 may decide to avail themselves of Dr. Smith's 6:00 a.m. class session, and the other 14 to may decide to appear in Dr. Smith's 6:00 p.m. section of same course. By the middle of the first semester, this becomes routine. Some folks are morning people; some prefer evening. The most common dual-session schedules are 6:00 a.m. and 4:30 p.m., or 5:00 p.m. and 9:00 p.m., Pacific Time.

Another characteristic that shapes scheduling is the nature of online sessions. They are intense; everyone is very focused. Talk in the chat room is, after all, written speech and is unconstrained by hand raising or "passing the microphone" (as in some integrated online courseware packages). This means several students can speak at once, and they do, posting comments simultaneously. Though this hour of time is shared by an instructor and only half the class, or 10 to 12 students, the pace of online talk can be quite fast, and because this equates to rapidly scrolling text, students must pay close attention. It is not surprising then that over the years of using chat environments with students in the doctoral program, faculty members have determined that an hour is the best duration for an online chat session. At the end of an hour or so, students and their instructor are worn out. After an hour, the conversation tends to wander. Less than an hour doesn't not allow sufficient time to discuss in depth. These are experience-based conclusions from the Pepperdine doctoral program that have been validated in the OMAET program.

Critical Features of Synchronous Virtual Environments

Interaction in Tapped In is possible in a several modes. People may "speak" to every-one in the room, or "whisper" or "page" one another: "Professor Polin says, 'I don't understand your question.'" People may also emote, or describe emotions or actions for themselves, for instance: "Bob waves to Tony" or "Professor Polin sighs." Finally, people may interact with objects in the environment, objects that they have made or that others have made and left in the area. Actions taken with objects show up as nar-rative description in the scene: "Brad sits down in the hot tub" or "Tomas writes on the whiteboard."

Turns

Unlike the face-to-face classroom, the Tapped In classroom makes it possible for anyone to speak up at any time. In a real world environment, this would result in an indistinguishable babble of voices, but online, everyone's words come through clearly as written text. Generally, in face-to-face classroom conversation, one person speaks at a time and the conversation is constrained by having one topic in play at a time. In the chat session, parallel processing abounds. Sometimes two or three lines of discussion are moving forward at once. In class, this feature provides students and their instructor a continuing opportunity to choose from an interesting array of related ideas and points of view at any given moment. The conversation bobs and weaves with the attention of the group, as discussants choose, moment to moment, which line of conversation to pursue. In this way, a class and instructor can jointly construct the focus of the discussion, though instructors can assert their authority quite easily should they choose to do so.

In the chat space, everyone can get the floor, and one-to-one side conversations, as whispers, can be carried on without being seen by the group. Sometimes instructors use whispers to encourage students privately, whispering, "say that again Ted, that's an interesting idea" or "hey Rosella, are you awake? We're missing your voice in this discussion."

Another feature of the chat environment is the social constraint on turn-taking length. In the face-to-face classroom, one student can monopolize the discussion by taking a long turn in the conversation. In Tapped In and other chat environments, there is a long-standing tradition of reperteé or banter: very brief and very rapid con-versational turns. This tradition is passed along to students in VirtCamp, but every now and then, early in the first semester, a student will attempt to talk too long in one turn, writing a long remark or dropping a prewritten paragraph into the flow. After some teasing by classmates, and after the unmistakable visual cues in the length of other people's turns, that behavior disappears.

Objects and Landscapes

People rely on shared understanding of cultural metaphors from the real world to make sense in the virtual one. In the setting for an online class, familiar objects like blackboards and more novel objects like hot tubs can function as conversational props, signaling and supporting meaning in an otherwise unreal setting. Students and teachers make sense of who they are and what is happening at the moment, based in part on the cues in the setting.

In the Tapped In environment, school objects and landscapes don't function the way they do in the university classroom. They invite different sorts of relationships and interactions among students and instructors and even guest speakers. Everyone still knows he or she is "in class," but "class" now has a different look and feel that supports a more collegial, less hierarchical relationship among participants. For instance, in Tapped In, rooms have whiteboards. It is possible for anyone in the room to write on the whiteboard with minimal disruption of the ongoing scene. The student doesn't have to make a physical move to occupy what is traditionally the teacher's domain. To write on the board, a student merely types, unseen by others, for instance: "writeb motivation." The room reports that the student has written, telling the class: "TeriN writes on the whiteboard." Anyone present can choose immediately to read the board without generating text intrusions into the public conversation.

Because the whiteboard is available to everyone, the Tapped In environment has effectively removed it from the teacher's exclusive control. This virtual classroom setting has altered the power structure in the classroom, and in our class sessions, students do take advantage of the new arrangements (Polin, 2000), often using it as a shared tool for co-constructing group memory. This interpretation is further supported by the additional functionality of the virtual whiteboard as a shared text tool. In class transcripts, we see students make use of the whiteboard options to print and e-mail themselves a copy of its contents at any time, simply by issuing line commands to do so. Access to and functionality of the board places it in a different role in the virtual classroom than it typically fills in the real world. These features of easy access to posting on the board and obtaining copies of the whiteboard contents suggest use of the whiteboard as a tool for collaboration and a cue that shared use is not merely possible, but expected.

Text

The nature of talk in the synchronous chat environment is less a hybrid of prose and speech than is its asynchronous newsgroup counterpart. People are clearly engaged in speaking to one another in Tapped In. However, experienced instructors also make use of nonverbal behavior and "thought bubbles" to share emotions and ideas. Students quickly pick up this additional channel for making meaning. All these communication ploys appear on the screen as words—text—and they stay on the screen for a while. People engaged in online conversation can literally see themselves speak and think.

Tapped In has made it quite simple for members to receive a literal text transcript of the entire public conversation and interaction that takes place online. The system generates a text file of every session from the moment of log-on to log-off, and then delivers the transcript via e-mail. Traditionally, OMAET instructors post an official transcript of class sessions; this allows students from one session, for example, the morning group, to read what transpired in the session of the evening group, or for students and faculty to revisit the session. Students do read these transcripts, as evidenced by their reference to things they read "in the tranny from last night," for example.

Figure 2.9 offers a 1-minute excerpt from a transcript of an online session. In this excerpt, many things are going on at once. Stacy is thinking about taking notes from interviews and observations. She mentions how this is going to test her listening skills.

[5:17:01 pm]MaureenE says, "Frequent journal entries would be important too"

[5:17:01 pm]

[5:17:09 pm]LindaX says, "now, you are going to have to get through two complete

        cycles of your ARP data collection process next semester."

[5:17:09 pm]

[5:17:14 pm]LindaX nods at Maureen

[5:17:14 pm]

[5:17:28 pm]LindaX says, "you might start thinking about the calendar on that."

[5:17:28 pm]

[5:17:30 pm]RafaelM says, "nice"

[5:17:30 pm]

[5:17:31 pm]BrendaL says, "VERY important, Maureen. How quickly we forget important

        thoughts."

[5:17:31 pm]

[5:17:32 pm]StacyRV says, "Oh my goodness. This is going to strength my listening

        skills."

[5:17:32 pm]

[5:17:41 pm]TammyAF exclaims, "Our plan, right Linda!"

[5:17:41 pm]

[5:17:42 pm]AmyMur feels like she's already been through two cycles.. oh maybe that

        was just me through the ringer....

[5:17:42 pm]

[5:17:42 pm]DanaCo says, "/look"

[5:17:42 pm]

[5:17:42 pm]DonSe asks, "How long is a typical cycle?"

[5:17:42 pm]

[5:17:43 pm]LindaX says, "you need to try, gather, analyze, reflect, try again"

[5:17:43 pm]

[5:17:45 pm]StacyRV says, "Or ability to recite 'as is'"

[5:17:45 pm]

FIG. 2.9.   One-minute excerpt of a Tapped In session.

After a short pause, she modifies her remarks to: "or the ability to recite 'as is.'" She sees a difference to be made between "listening" and taking notes, and recording talk "as is," without adding to or interpreting what the speaker has said. This distinction has been the focus of the instructor's class session. However, it is a very difficult distinction for students to make. Here, without explicit intervention or apparent ratification, Stacy works it through, but she does it with the support of the text tool that is the central mechanism of Tapped In.

Stacy has made a conversational response, and she sees it on the screen. For whatever reason, without explicit responses from other speakers, she decides that it requires further clarification; it is not adequate. Her addition can only be described as a "repair" in that it revisits the earlier remark, barely 13 seconds later. By explicitly using quotation marks to encompass "as is," she indicates her mindful incorporation of talk from earlier in-class conversation. Here is a moment of learning for Stacy, as she first expresses an idea she has "heard" and then repairs her own expression of it. In face-to-face conversation, this usually happens with the support of others who respond to the remark in ways that may help the speaker reshape it. However, no one here is obviously interacting with Stacy. She is thinking aloud, probably intending to share her nervousness about doing the impending interviewing task the right way. But in doing this, she has to put her thoughts into words; she has to choose a way to say it. She generates a concrete representation of her understanding of the idea: she speaks. This is the sort of externalization Vygotsky describes in his analysis of learning (Vygotsky, 1978). However, where another might be involved in working through the idea with Stacy, in Tapped In the visual text serves as the mediational device that supports her reconsideration of her own utterance as she finds the words to make the critical distinction in the idea.

In this snippet, everyone, including the instructor, is focused on the logistics of the task. Maureen suggests journaling as a useful device for the project; Brenda notices that idea and ratifies it. Tammy, Amy, and Don are thinking about earlier remarks by the instructor about completing two action research cycles in the next semester. If the instructor were mediating this conversation through serial turn taking in a face-to-face class, Stacy would not have gotten the floor, or might have decided not to make a claim for the floor, as her thoughts are off the topic of logistics. She might have still had these thoughts, but they would have been ephemeral, and she would not have had a way to look at, tinker with, and clarify her own words as a representation of her understanding, if, indeed, that is what transpired.

ONLINE CULTURE

Curricula and pedagogy are traditionally the main considerations in discussing quality and structure of a degree program. The physical setting, and the academic culture that comes with it, are tacit dimensions of the university. The power and function of these elements becomes obvious when the campus is removed and the program goes virtual. This has been a liberating realization, encouraging risk taking and experimentation in program construction and implementation.

The setting in this online program is a strange hybrid. It is composed of one part fantasy and one part reality. The fantasy of the virtual classroom is liberating, furnished as it is with objects foreign to higher education, such as hot tubs and sofas, and with familiar objects that just don't work in the usual way, such as the whiteboard, with its equitable, unimpeded access for all. The setting is also partly real, but the reality is an amalgamation of workplace and home realities that students are asked to foreground in their discussions and projects.

There is no prior history or tradition for this strange half-real, half-fantasy learning space. There are no routines governing virtual interaction that students have absorbed as they've made their way through years of schooling. There are no norms for their behavior in these classrooms. However, because this program was constructed from a specific point of view about learning, there are intentional structures in place to temper student and faculty behavior, and that are in turn tempered by each generation of student cadre in the program. We are building, shaping, evolving an online culture. In this regard, we have moved our view of online learning out of the realm of instructional technology, that is, of online learning as another delivery system. We are instead operating in a new world in which learning is situated in real world practice outside the walls of the university, and in which the role of the university is not to deliver knowledge but to mediate interaction among more and less knowledgeable practitioners, including faculty as practitioners in their own right. Moving graduate programs online has freed us from the cultural history of traditional, campus-based course delivery, and the tools available for our use online have further pushed and shaped our instructional interactions to more resemble the free flowing give-and-take of online communities of practice. In this new realm, we are cultural workers, crafting interactional space, tools, and objects of meaning; roles and identities for participants; and norms for behaving.

An Example of Critical Cultural Ceremony: VirtCamp

One of the ways in which cultures pass knowledge along to participating members is through rituals. The OMAET online community does this as well, in many different ways. Two cultural rituals in particular are key. One marks the legitimate entry of "newbies" into the community: through VirtCamp. The other marks their achievement of a central task, the action research project: through Exhibitions.

Since its inception, the OMAET program has included a mandatory 5-day, intensive, preprogram experience, held on campus, and called VirtCamp. VirtCamp has three functional goals: learn the online tools, meet the faculty, and begin bonding with cadre classmates. As they work through these goals, students are also reexamined by VirtCamp staff in terms of their likelihood of success in this program. This is a subjective call based in part on how well students handle the online tools, but more critically, on their ability to actively participate in a group. Every now and then, a student applies for admission to OMAET, looking at online education as a way to work alone along the lines of the traditional correspondence course. VirtCamp staffers—recall that these are all graduating students from the prior cadre—identify those who seem unable to engage with cadre mates, contribute to their group, or embrace the variation in personalities with which they must deal. This is actually a fairly rare occasion. Over the past 4 years, only one person has been counseled out of the program based on VirtCamp experiences.

VirtCamp sets the culture of the program, and it is deliberately organized in ways to emphasize features of culture. Clues and manifestations of "who we are" and "how we do things around here" are all around from the moment the new students set foot on the campus for VirtCamp. The VirtCamp rooms are set up in modular seating arrangements to support group work. Digital cameras, digital camcorders, powerful desktop computers, and computer peripherals abound, as part of the VirtCamp process includes a group effort to document the VirtCamp experience. Snack food and beverages are omnipresent and abundant. Dress is casual. During camp, students work on a wireless laptop network, encouraging their free and easy movement around in the room.

From its inception, camp has always been run by former online students. In the first year, those students came from the online doctoral program. Each year since, camp has been organized and staffed by former OMAET students. The two coleaders of VirtCamp are always more than 1 year out from their master's experience, but the camp staff comes from the most recent graduating cadre. Though students are paid for their time, the opportunity to work on VirtCamp stuff is seen as a privilege. Staff members are upgraded from the blue T-shirt to the blue polo shirt, camp coleaders to the black polo shirt. This shirt hierarchy is one cultural sign supporting the notion of experience as expertise, and demonstrating a route to full participation in the online community of OMAET.

Like the content of the program itself, the content of VirtCamp is embedded in project activity. As in the program, in VirtCamp students also approach their task with partial knowledge, access to materials and support, and peers with whom to collaborate. On the morning of the second day, students form small groups complete a challenge, the solution to which they must demonstrate on the last day of camp. The challenges involve building and programming a Lego device to solve a problem and then documenting the process (Papert, 1996). These are hard tasks, and groups quickly learn to share information and materials across teams. Recent tasks have included: building an automatic luggage sorter, an audible record player, a functional fax machine, and a Coke machine that changes the price of the drink based on temperature. At the same time they are working on their Lego challenges, students in different small groups are working on a digital movie that documents their VirtCamp experience. These movies are shown on the last day as well, and are usually funny and endearing montages of high and low moments during camp.

During camp, all learning about the program tools—web page development, digital media-making, Tapped In, newsgroups—arises in the context of the group projects and camp life. There are no training sessions about Dreamweaver; there are sessions in which groups work together on their documentation page using Dreamweaver and with the support of VirtCamp staff. There are no training sessions about how to post to newsgroups; there are end-of-day personal journals that must be posted in the cadre newsgroup, with the support of VirtCamp staff. Indeed, camp staff is alert to requests from students for workshops on the fly, for example, in Flash or sound editing. Often, staff turn to students in the cadre who know these tools and can step up to lead a small group on the subject. To operate in this fashion requires a deep faith in the underlying principle that the knowledge resides in the community and can be most effectively learned by supporting access to expertise at work rather than by organizing transmission of information. For the new students, the enculturation process into OMAET culture has begun.

By the end of VirtCamp, we see the beginning of a cohesive, socially interdependent group of eager and nervous students that has begun to value peer, near peer, and expert knowledge through collaboration. On the last day of camp, after the Lego projects have been demonstrated, after the movies have been shown, the last official bit of business is the distribution of cadre T-shirts. The T-shirts are designed by and paid for by the graduate school, emblazoned with the OMAET logo, and represent an official welcome into the program and an endorsement of the student's right to be there. It is interesting that it is not unusual for cadres to have managed to design, purchase, and distribute their own logo T-shirts before the end of VirtCamp.

VirtCamp is just one of several key structures that are used to manifest ideas and values in the program, for example, to create moderated opportunities for students to learn how to learn from and with each other.

LESSONS LEARNED

This chapter has described how a particular theoretical framework has guided one online graduate program to design curricula and select tools to support a particular kind of interaction between students and faculty working at a distance. This chapter has described two common online software tools, and the features of those tools that support a learning experience that is community based. These are very low-cost, low-maintenance, low-tech tools, but they derive great power from their reliance on written talk and the ability to link commentary, synchronously or asynchronously. Whether it is the slow pace of asynchronous conversation in threaded newsgroups or the fast-paced repartee of a virtual classroom, the centerpiece is language, specifically, dialogue. Also, that dialogue is situated in the intersection of academe and real world practice. That virtual intersection is possible, because the graduate program is outside the university box. It is able to develop within a new cultural tradition.

These online community tools were historically constructed to support human interaction, and it is no surprise that a program that values human interaction finds them powerful. However, the same tools could be used other ways. The software tools are themselves neutral devices, and they derive their power from the cultural surround in which they are used. Thus, for the model of learning that underlies this OMAET program, the single most important tool is the program culture, a self-sustaining system that supports the entire enterprise over time and through troubles. In this regard, it is easier to bring an entire program online than a course or two, for a program provides a broader canvass on which to paint a "big picture" for students and faculty. In contrast to single courses, the program contains more elements and processes that can be marshaled to support a vision of online learning, and in this case, of learning by dialogue within a community of practice.

REFERENCES

Applebee, A. (1981). *Writing in the secondary school: English and the content areas.* Urbana, IL: National Council of Teachers of English (NCTE).

Barab, S., & Duffy, T. (2000). From practice fields to communities of practice. In D. Jonassen & S. Land (Eds.), *Theoretical foundations of learning environments* (pp. 25–55). Mahwah, NJ: Lawrence Erlbaum Associates.

Berge, Z. (2001). The context of distance training: Predicting change. In Z. Berge (Ed.), *Sustaining distance training* (pp. 3–12). San Francisco: Jossey-Bass.

Bohm, D., & Nichol, L. (1996). *On dialogue.* New York: Routledge.

Brand, S. (1994). *How buildings learn: What happens after they're built.* New York: Penguin.

Britton, J., Burgess, T., Martin, N., McLeod, A., & Rosen, H. (1975). *The development of writing abilities* (11–18). Urbana, IL: National Council of Teachers of English.

Brown, J. S., Collins, A., & Duguid, P. (1989). Situated cognition and the culture of learning. *Educational Researcher, 18*(1), 32–42.

Bruckman, A. (1992). *Identity workshops: Emergent social and psychological phenomena in text-based virtual reality.* Unpublished master's thesis, MIT Media Laboratory Cambridge, MA.

Bruner, J. (1992). *Acts of meaning.* Cambridge, MA: Harvard University Press.

Bruner, J. (1998). Infancy and culture: A story. In S. Chaiklin, M. Hedegaard, & U. Jensen (Eds.), *Activity theory and social practice* (pp. 225–234). Oxford, UK: Aarhus University Press.

Coghlan, D., & Brannick, T. (2001). *Doing action research in your own organization.* London: Sage.

Cole, M. (1996). *Cultural psychology: A once and future discipline.* Cambridge, MA: Belknap.

Cole, M., & Engestrom, Y. (1993). A cultural-historical approach to distributed cognition. In G. Salomon (Ed.), *Distributed cognitions: Psychological and educational considerations* (pp. 1–46). New York: Cambridge University Press.

Computer Supported Collaborative Learning (Jan. 2002) Boulder, CO. A special interest group of the Association of Computer Machinery. Now combined with ICLS as ISLS, the International Society of the Learning Sciences (home page www.isls.org)

Curtis, P. (1998). Not just a game: How LambdaMOO came to exist and what it did to get back at me. In C. Haynes & J. Holmevik (Eds.), *High wired: On the design, use, and theory of educational MOOs* (pp. 25–42). Ann Arbor, MI: University of Michigan Press.

Davenport, T., & Prusak, L. (1998). *Working knowledge: How organizations manage what they know.* Cambridge, MA: Harvard Business School Press.

Davis, B., & Brewer, J. (1997). *Electronic discourse: Linguistic individuals in virtual space.* Albany: State University of New York Press.

Dixon, N. M. (1996). *Perspectives on dialogue: Making talk developmental for individuals and organizations.* Greensboro, NC: Center for Creative Leadership.

Engestrom, Y. (1999). Activity theory and individual and social transformation. In Y. Engestrom, R. Miettinen, & R. Punamaki (Eds.), *Perspectives on activity theory* (pp. 19–38). New York: Cambridge University Press.

Gee, P. (1999). *An introduction to discourse analysis: Theory and method.* New York: Routledge.

Gumperz, J. (1981). The linguistic bases of communicative competence. In D. Tannen (Ed.), *Analyzing discourse: Text and talk* (pp. 323–334). *Georgetown University roundtable on language and linguistics.* Washington, DC: Georgetown University Press.

Harlow, H. F. (1958). The nature of love. *American Psychologist, 13,* 573–685.

Haynes, C. (1998). There's a MOO in this class. In C. Haynes & J. Holmevik (Eds.), *High wired: On the design, use, and theory of educational MOOs* (pp. 161–176). Ann Arbor, MI: University of Michigan Press.

Hymes, D. (1974). *Foundations in sociolinguistics: An ethnographic approach.* Philadelphia, PA: University of Pennsylvania Press.

Isaacs, W. (1999). *Dialogue and the art of thinking together.* New York: Currency Doubleday.

Langer, J., & Applebee, A. (1987). *How writing shapes thinking: A study of teaching and learning* (NCTE Rep. No. 22). Urbana, Il: National Council of Teachers of English.

Lave, J., Murtaugh, M., & de la Rocha, O. (1984). The dialectic of arithmetic in grocery shopping. In B. Rogoff & J. Lave (Eds.), *Everyday cognition: Its development in social context* (pp. 67–94). Cambridge, MA: Harvard University Press.

Lave, J., & Wenger, E. (1991). *Situated learning: Legitimate peripheral participation.* New York: Cambridge University Press.

Lemke, J. L. (1990). *Talking science: Language, learning, and values.* Norwood, NJ: Ablex.

McNiff, J., Lomax, P., & Whitehead, J. (1996). *You and your action research project.* New York: Routledge.

Mehan, H. (1979). *Learning lessons: Social organization in the classroom.* Cambridge, MA: Harvard University Press.

Moll, L. C., & Greenberg, J. B. (1990). Creating zones of possibilities: Combining social contexts for instruction. In L. Moll (Ed.), *Vygotsky and education: Instructional implications and applications of sociohistorical psychology* (pp. 319–348). New York: Cambridge University Press.

National Center for Educational Statistics. (1996). Graduate and first-professional students. In *National Postsecondary Student Aid Study* (pp. 989–139). Washington DC: U.S. Department of Education, Office of Educational Research and Improvement.

Newman, D., Griffin, P., & Cole, M. (1989). *The construction zone: Working for cognitive change in school.* New York: Cambridge University Press.

Nonaka, I., & Takeuchi, H. (1995). *The knowledge-creating company.* New York: Oxford University Press.

Oldenburg, R. (1989). *The great good place: Cafes, coffee shops, community centers, beauty parlors, general stores, bars, hangouts, and how they get you through the day.* New York: Marlowe.

Palloff, R., & Pratt, K. (1999). *Building learning communities in cyberspace: Effective strategies for the online classroom.* San Francisco: Jossey-Bass.

Papert, S. (1996). Learning. In S. Papert, *The connected family: Bridging the digital generation gap* (pp. 35–62). Atlanta, GA: Longstreet.

Polin, L. (2000, April). *Affordances of a VR world as a place for learning: Discourse patterns and contextualization cues framing learning experiences for adults in a real-time, text-based, virtual reality setting.* Paper presented at the annual meeting of the American Educational Research Association, New Orleans, LA.

Polin, L. (2001, April). *Access is everything: The technology of access in online community.* Paper presented at the annual meeting of the American Educational Research Association, Seattle, WA.

Polin, L. (2002, April). *Creating norms for thinking publicly together: Becoming part of an online graduate community.* Paper presented at the annual meeting of the American Educational Research Association, New Orleans, LA.

Polman, J. L. (2000). Identity development through participation in an informal setting. In B. Fishman & S. O'Connor-Divelbiss (Eds.), *Proceedings of the Fourth International Conference of the Learning Sciences* (pp. 340–341). Mahwah, NJ: Lawrence Erlbaum Associates.

Rheingold, H. (1993). *The virtual community: Homesteading on the electronic frontier.* New York: Addison-Wesley.

Riel, M. (1998). Learning communities through computer networking. In J. Greeno & S. Goldman (Eds.), *Thinking practices in mathematics and science learning* (pp. 369–398). Mahwah, NJ: Lawrence Erlbaum Associates.

Rogoff, B. (1984). Introduction: Thinking and learning in social context. In B. Rogoff & J. Lave (Eds.), *Everyday cognition: Its development in social context.* (pp. 1–8). Cambridge, MA: Harvard University Press.

Scardamalia, M., & Bereiter, C. (1994). Computer support for knowledge-building communities. *The Journal of the Learning Sciences, 3,* 265–283.

Schank, R. (1997). *Virtual learning: A revolutionary approach to building a highly skilled workforce.* New York: McGraw-Hill.

Schon, D. (1987, April). *Educating the reflective practitioner.* Paper presented at the annual meeting of the American Educational Research Association, Washington, DC. Available: http://hci.stanford.edu/other/schon87.htm.

Senge, P. M. (1990). *The fifth discipline: The art and practice of the learning organization.* New York: Currency Doubleday.

Sheingold, K., & Polin, L. (2002, January). *Letting go of the reins: The evolution of pedagogy in an online graduate program.* Paper presented at Computer Supported Collaborative Learning Conference, Boulder, CO.

Simon, R. (1992). *Teaching against the grain.* Westport, CT: Bergin & Garvey.

Smith, F. (1992). *Joining the literacy club: Further essays into education.* Portsmouth, NH: Heinemann.

Turkle, S. (1997). *Life on the screen: Identity in the age of the Internet.* New York: Touchstone.

Vygotsky, L. S. (1978). Mind in society: The development of higher psychological processes (pp. 56–57). Cambridge, MA: Harvard University Press.

Weisbord, M. R., & Janoff, S. (1995). *Future search: An action guide to finding common ground in organizations and communities.* San Francisco: Berrett-Koehler.

Wells, G. (1999). *Dialogic inquiry: Toward a sociocultural practice and theory of education.* New York: Cambridge University Press.

Wenger, E. (1998). *Communities of practice: Learning, meaning, and identify.* New York: Cambridge University Press.

3

Design Lessons for Social Education

Scott Grabinger
University of Colorado at Denver

GENERALIZABLE LESSONS

This chapter is not about how to port a successful graduate program online, although that describes the initial intent behind the "substantive change."... This paper is not about the way to adapt instruction or curriculum to take advantage of the affordances of network software applications.... This chapter is about how a *particular theory of learning* underlying the redesign of the program as a specifically 'online' program led to changes in curriculum and pedagogy [my italics]. More importantly, it is about how those changes were possible largely *because* the program was online. (Polin, Chap. 2, this volume)

Polin's Chapter

Polin's chapter describes a program to move the 15-year-old master of arts in educational technology to an online format—the online master's of art in educational technology (OMAET). The program is conducted almost entirely through the Internet, with only three face-to-face meetings during a 13-month program. The vast majority of interactions take place online using asynchronous and synchronous tools such as newsgroups, web pages, groupware, chat shells, and e-mail. Her chapter describes the application of sociocultural learning theory to design changes in curriculum and pedagogy, and more important, how those changes were possible largely because the program was online.

Polin's action research project (ARP) provides the central unifying concept in her overall program; therefore, my comments on her chapter focus on two ARP features. First, the ARP teaches us important lessons for designing instruction, not just "online" instruction. For several years, those advocating a sociocultural approach to instruction have claimed that it also requires a new approach to instructional design, yet there have been no new models of instructional design that reflect the sociocultural approach. Some make the mistake of thinking that since both approaches to learning deal with goals, learners, strategies, and assessment, that there really isn't much of a difference in design models. However, Polin's approach to the design of the OMAET program illustrates that there are significant differences between traditional and sociocultural instructional designs. Yes, her design process deals with the common elements within the learning environment; yet the entire process is different. The manner in which she and her team designed the ARP reflects her goal "to increase the extent of students' participation in their field of practice ... by bringing together the academic scholars [faculty and guests] and the active practitioners [students themselves], on equal footing" (Polin, Chap. 2, this volume). It provides a clear look at how the design process reflects theory.

Second, we learn from her deliberative use of theory to shape and drive the use of tools. Despite her denials (see the previous quotation from her chapter), the ARP *is* about the successful adaptation of instruction and curriculum to utilize the affordances of network software applications. It *is* about the elegant use of theory to create effective practice. It *is* easy, while reading her chapter, to imagine her team working around a table and constantly asking the question: "How can we create and foster dialogue and learning within a community of practice with _____ [insert any of the following: chat rooms, e-mail, web sites, discussion forums, and so on]?" They weren't sitting around the table saying, "Let's make the learners use a chat room, because it's fun." The ARP is successful because it uses tools in a reflective manner to implement a sociocultural theory of learning to solve a learning problem. Studying her approach helps us in our own theory-based online designs.

THEORY-BASED INSTRUCTIONAL DESIGN: TWO DISTINCT APPROACHES

Traditional and sociocultural approaches to instruction and its design have distinctly different views of learning, the roles of learners and teachers, instruction, and the use of tools (see Table 3.1 for a summary of the following discussion).

Traditional instructional design (ID) breaks instruction down to small units of knowledge classes (e.g., verbal information, concepts, rules, or problem solving) and recommends prescriptions for each classification. These units are then taught "out of context," that is, outside the community in which the knowledge and skills would be put to practice. A sociocultural approach, in contrast, questions traditional ID models, because their molecular approach focuses on controlling the learner and environment, and fails to emphasize the integration of all the small units of knowledge to enable learners to create flexible knowledge structures that facilitate problem solving in new situations. Where traditional ID views learning as a result of controlled responses to exercises and information, the sociocultural approach views learning as a consequence of authentic interactions with people, objects, and culture in a collective effort. Traditional ID takes a linear approach to instruction, whereas a sociocultural approach takes a more integrated and global perspective (see Fig. 3.1 for a depiction of both approaches).

TABLE 3.1
Beliefs and Characteristics Affecting Instructional Design Models

ID Components	Traditional Instructional Design	Sociocultural Instructional Design
Learning	• Information processing and behaviorist learning theories form the basis of traditional ID models. The fundamental idea is that errors in performance can be corrected or that new behaviors can be created through the acquisition of information and practice. • The primary goal of learning is to teach knowledge or skills that may be applied at a later date in a variety of circumstances. • It takes a molecular view of knowledge elements. • The instructional designer determines the goals and objectives of units of instruction from the observation of inappropriate behaviors and errors (e.g., arithmetic errors, failure to identify a geologic formation, rude treatment of a customer, etc.) that they believe can be fixed through the delivery of correct information and practice. • Learners must become novices before they become experts. They must learn "the basics" before they can participate in an authentic community of practice. • Learning and teaching is a process that can be controlled. Successful teaching and learning comes about through the precise arrangement of information, practice, and testing. • Each learner learns the same things in basically the same way.	• Sociocultural models of instructional design are based on cognitive learning theories that emphasize collaborative and generative learning strategies in authentic environments. • The primary goal of learning is to enculturate the learner into an authentic community of practice, providing learners the opportunities to learn authentic cognitive, affective, and psychomotor skills and knowledge. Learners practice higher order thinking and problem-solving skills that can be applied immediately in an authentic context. • It takes a broad view of learning, focusing on valuable participation in a community. • The instructional designer sets the overall goals of the unit. Goals are based on real problems, cases, or projects within the community of practice. Goals are complex and often require collaboration. • Learners are considered members of a community of practice and work within the community from the beginning of the learning experience. • Learning and teaching is a continuous process that is mediated by the learner's prior knowledge, experience, and personal goals; the learning environment; strategy selection; and interpersonal interactions. • Each student constructs his or her own meaning.
Roles of learners and teachers	• Designers view learners as responders to the instructional design. Designers prepare information that learners will process and activitis in which the learners will practice the ideal behaviors needed to demonstrate learning. In other words, they believe that learners can be controlled and led to specific performances.	• Designers view learners as collaborators in the learning process. The teacher helps each learner work in a personal way toward the goal. In other words, they believe that learners can be responsible for their own learning and need to guided rather than controlled. The learner's dignity is a critical feature of the learning process.

(Continued)

TABLE 3.1
(Continued)

ID Components	Traditional Instructional Design	Sociocultural Instructional Design
	• Though designers generally treat all learners alike, they do attend to general (e.g., intelligence, socioeconomic status and age) and specific characteristics (e.g., attitude, prior knowledge, and experience). • Learners assume the traditional role of students—listening and reacting to the teacher. They make few decisions about what to learn, how to study, and which resources to use. The have no responsibility for the learning process. • Teachers pass on information to the learner. The clearer the information, the more the learner will acquire.	• Designers recognize the individuality of learning. Each learner has knowledge, experience, and strengths on which to capitalize. Each learner have weaknesses that can be strengthened. One learner's strengths and weaknesses are different from another's. • Learners assume a critical role in their own learning and in the learning of their peers. They make most of the decisions related to what to learn, how to study, and which resources to use. Their decisions are valued, and they are given responsibility for designing the learning process. • Teachers help learners solve problems, determine goals, gather resources and participate in the community.
Instruction and the environment	• Learning often takes place in a decontextualized environment. The learners are not considered worthy of participation until they have learned the basics. • All learners perform the same activities. • Learning is an individual responsibility and activity. • Teaching strategies transmit information in small chunks, leading to the practice of desired behaviors. • Teachers focus on assigning the correct strategies. If the correct strategies are used, then all learners will learn. Learners make few, if any, decisions about how and what they study. • Evaluation takes place at the end of instruction. • Evaluation takes place in the classroom rather than in an authentic situation • Evaluation often focuses on giving a grade based on memory as reflected in the ability to pass a test. • Insufficient learning or failure indicates that there is a problem in the learning environment, because the instructional strategies failed to pass on the necessary information. Failure is undesirable, because it may lead to a habit of inappropriate behaviors.	• Learning occurs through learner interaction with the environment and others. The learning of each individual is different and based on evolving and valued participation in a community of practice. • Learners participate in activities according to their needs, strengths, and weaknesses. • Collaboration and discourse with other members of the community—the social construction of knowledge—play a major role in learning. • Teaching strategies focus on creating discourse among teachers, learners, and other members of the community. • Teachers focus on interacting at a metacognitive level with learners. Teachers guide the students in solving their own problems. Learners make most of their own decisions about how to achieve the learning goal. • Assessment and evaluation is an ongoing process taking place throughout instruction. • Assessment of learning takes place by observing actual practice within the community. • Assessment is paired with detailed, constructive feedback aimed at improving performance.

(Continued)

TABLE 3.1
(Continued)

ID Components	Traditional Instructional Design	Sociocultural Instructional Design
	Corrective feedback is usually not a part of the evaluation. • Instruction is successful if learners have mastered the objectives.	• Insufficient learning or failure is regarded as an opportunity—even desirable—because it leads to the refinement of learning through discourse and practice. Corrective feedback is standard. • Instruction is successful if learners have reached the general goals established at the beginning and have become more enculturated with the community.
Use of tools	• Tools support the teaching and learning process. • Teachers use tools to transmit information and demonstrate concepts. Clearly transmitted information leads to successful learning. • Students use tools to solve classroom-based problems. • Teachers view the student use of tools as artificial aids to be phased out over time. • If a tool is the object of instruction, then using the tool is taught as a separate piece of instruction rather than in its practice-based context.	• Tools support the learning process. • Tools are enablers of theory-based instructional strategies within the unique community of practice. • Learners use tools to participate within the community, to learn, and, ultimately, to improve the community. • Teachers view learner use of tools as a means to an end. Tools enable learners to contribute to the community. • Tools are not objects of instruction. Rather, tools help learners participate as equals with the community of practice.

LEARNING

Traditional Designs

Behaviorist and information processing learning theories provide the basis for traditional ID models. Generally, these models begin with a learning problem or goal and proceed to break down the learning–teaching process into a series of small objectives. The behaviorist approach (Dick & Carey, 1990; Gagné & Briggs, 1979; Merrill, 1983) emphasizes the learning of a series of observable behaviors that lead to the overall goal—the ideal or desired behavior. The theory posits that once a behavior is learned, it may be applied and practiced anywhere.

Similarly, information-processing theorists (Anderson, 1995; Chi & Cesi, 1987; Glazer, 1990) emphasize the organization of information through phased processes, making a distinction between novice and expert thinkers. Again, the focus is on smaller, more discrete pieces of knowledge that will be organized into a larger, more complex knowledge structure. A novice's knowledge tends to be declarative—information about facts and rules. An expert's knowledge is procedural—the ability to link facts and rules to perform and solve problems. Both of these approaches lead to instruction that

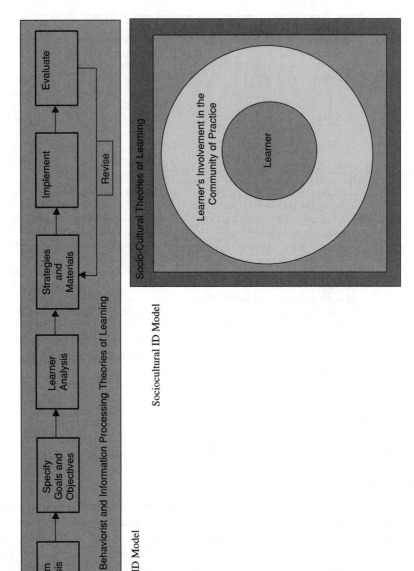

Traditional ID Model

Behaviorist and Information Processing Theories of Learning

Problem Analysis → Specify Goals and Objectives → Learner Analysis → Strategies and Materials → Implement → Evaluate

Revise

Sociocultural ID Model

Socio-Cultural Theories of Learning

Learner's Involvement in the Community of Practice

Learner

FIG. 3.1. ID Models.

attempts to control the learner and environment, that isolates the learner from real communities of practice, and that emphasizes the learning of knowledge and skills before one can begin to practice and solve real-world problems. Learner analyses provide information only to the point of shaping the environment to better control the learner. Fundamentally, learning is an exercise in acquisition.

Traditional ID has designed millions of successful instructional interventions over the years; however, we have also found that knowledge learned but not explicitly related to relevant problem solving remains inert and is not readily available for problem solving, application, or transfer to novel situations (Butterfield & Nelson, 1989; Clark & Voogel, 1985; Perfetto, Bransford, & Franks, 1983; Whitehead, 1929). Thus, over the last decade and a half, constructivist, social, historical, and cultural models of learning (Bull, Kimball, & Stansberry, 1998; Cunningham & Duffy, 1993; Dijkstra, 1997; Duffy & Jonassen, 1992; Staupe & Hernes, 2000; Willis, 2000) have increasingly provided guidance to the teaching and learning process.

Sociocultural Designs

Sociocultural instructional designers (Dijkstra, 1997; Willis & Wright, 2000; Winn, 1993) question the applicability of traditional ID models, because their molecular approach focuses on controlling the learner and environment, and leads to inert knowledge. In a sociocultural view of knowledge and learning, the learning goal is enculturation as legitimate members of a community of practice. This authentic world of practice is a community to which learners aspire—or aspire to so that they may take on greater responsibility. Polin views learning as a consequence of interactions among people, objects, and culture in a collective effort to solve problems, create products, or perform service. Learning, then, is transformative rather than acquisitive. This emphasis creates flexible knowledge structures that facilitate problem solving in new situations (Bednar, Cunningham, Duffy, & Perry, 1991; Cunningham & Duffy, 1993; Grabinger, 1993).

LEARNER, DESIGNER, AND TEACHER ROLES

Traditional ID

Students in a traditional environment are part of the process in that they respond to stimuli. They listen and take in knowledge. Teachers and designers analyze their students for general and specific traits will affect the design of instruction. General traits include those that cannot be changed, for example, age, IQ, gender, travel time, and so on. For instance, if the students are young, then instruction may be simplified. Specific traits include those that can be affected as part of the instructional plan, for example, prior knowledge and skills, attitude toward the class, comfort, and so on. For instance, the extent of prior knowledge will affect where a lesson may begin. The idea is to control student responses and thinking, because it is assumed that there is single, best way of organizing and presenting information. If that single best way is found, then the instruction will work. If the instruction works, it can be repeated with the same results with different students.

The relationship between student and teacher is generally hierarchical. Teachers are the masters, and students are the novices. The master presents information, and the students acquire it. When a student asks a question, the teacher provides the answer. Teachers must always know more than their learners. Students make few decisions about what and how to learn, instead waiting to be told by the teacher what to do. Students work independently, but together. In that, I mean that each student is responsible for his/or her learning and demonstrates that learning through individual assignments. By "together," I mean that all students work on the same content, tasks, and exercises.

Sociocultural ID

The learner's ability, responsibility, and dignity are central components in sociocultural designs and in Polin's design of the ARP. Rather than looking at the learner as something manipulated by the learning environment, Polin believes that learning comes from learner participation within the learning environment by the learner. She views her job as one to empower the learners and help them transform themselves into participating members of the community. Polin designed the ARP to take advantage of each students abilities and environment by making it possible for students to work on projects meaningful to them within their own environments. In that way, the learners are working to provide contributions to improving their communities.

The relationship between teachers and learners is on a more equal footing than hierarchical. Teachers are facilitators who lead the students in meaningful discourse (see "Instruction and the Environment," the next section). Teachers are members of the same community and are working with the student toward the same goals. Polin's learners and teachers worked together to conduct action research, with the goal of improving education within the community. Both the faculty and learners made changes in their own environments: the learners in the schools that provided the context for their work and the faculty at the university in integrating the ARP in their classes to create more authentic learning environments.

Teachers in Polin's program were to interact with students at a metacognitive level rather than an informational level. For example, if a teacher education student asks a question such as "I had an angry parent at parent–teacher conferences last night. How do I handle a confrontational situation with a parent whose child is failing my class and won't be able to play sports?" In a traditional environment, the teacher would answer, "The best way to diffuse a crisis is by reflecting the emotions of the angry parent in a calm and detached manner" or "Well, if you are threatened, call security."

However, in a dialogue between teacher and learner, the sociocultural teacher may ask a series of questions that would help lead the learner to find the solution, such as "How did you handle it last night?" "What were the parent's reactions?" "What do you think you might have done to calm the parent down?" "Have you encountered anything like this before in your life?" "Have you seen other people deal with this? What did they do?" "What resources might you use?" "You know, Rachel had the same problem. Have you talked to her about how she handled it?" and so on. The object is to encourage the learner to think through the problem and carry on a conversation, rather than to expect to receive "the answer." Carrying on a dialogue like this tells students that they are equal members of the community and that what they think is just as important as what the teacher thinks.

INSTRUCTION AND THE ENVIRONMENT

Traditional Designs

In traditional course designs, instruction is a matter of creating the proper environment and materials that can be passed on to the learners to help them respond appropriately (learn). Teachers and the designer select instructional strategies and materials based on goals, objectives, and the learners. By responding to the strategies and materials, the students acquire information and skills. Again, recall that the objectives are based on learning pieces of knowledge (e.g., verbal information, concepts, rules, or principles) so small that it wouldn't make sense to try to learn them in an authentic environment. For example, an aerospace engineer learns the rule for determining the amount of lift a specific airfoil (wing) will provide based on its shape. The teacher prescribes a mnemonic as a memorization strategy and provides practice by using the formula with word problems. The engineer learns the formula out of a real context and, thus, does not learn when or how to apply it. However, the instruction is successful if the engineer can repeat and use the formula on a test.

Evaluation is a critical strategy within traditional learning environments and points out whether students have learned what they were supposed to learn, but because the learning occurred out of context, so does the evaluation. The evaluation focuses on the smaller objectives rather than the whole performance (as seen with the engineer in the preceding paragraph).

It is also important to note that most instructional strategies, although not individualized, are based on the individual as a sole learner. Each learner is assumed to learn in the same way and follows the same strategies as every other learner—strategies prescribed by the teacher. Therefore, there is practically no dialogue among the students or between the students and teacher. Interactions between students and teachers are usually confined to questions and answers that pass on more information to the student.

Sociocultural Designs

Conversation, discourse, talking, chat, dialogue, exchange, banter, discussion, communication, dissertation, critique, and *exposition* are all synonyms for the primary learning strategy in a sociocultural environment. For Polin, the activation of discourse is everything—the chief mechanism for learning. Discourse governed most of her thinking about instructional strategies and decisions about which tools to use, especially because she based her program within an online environment. As previously described (in the "Learner, Designer, and Teacher Roles" section), conversation between learner and teacher is more than passing on and acquiring information—it is thinking through the aspects of a problem.

In addition, discourse among other learners and other members of the community is equally important as discourse between learner and teacher. Polin created the ARP distance education project to keep meaningful, situated, community-based discourse going through chat rooms, e-mail, web pages, and listservs. Students worked together to help each other learn and grow as members of the community. They shared their findings, problems, and data via the tools that encouraged discourse.

A sociocultural approach does not eliminate the need for other types of learning strategies, including mnemonics for memorization, practice for rules, or outlining for organization. However, the learners choose which strategies are applicable to their needs, rather than having the strategies foisted on them. In that way, each of Polin's learners can contribute something individually meaningful to the conversation by learning what they decide they need rather than what someone else has decided they need.

Performance-based assessment is another important strategy and a way to respect the learner and develop lifelong learning skills. Assessment is both ongoing and summative. It provides specific, constructive information about improving learner performance. Learners are not penalized for making mistakes; rather, a mistake is an opportunity to learn. Performance-based assessment does not ask learners if they have memorized terms or procedures. Rather, it asks whether or not they contribute in a positive way to the community of practice. Positive, constructive participation will indicate whether the terms, rules, or principles were learned. Performance-based assessment prepares the learner for a continuing, evolutionary, and growing role in the community, because in a community of practice, constant change is desirable and a sign of learning and growth. Who within a school or business never changes?

USE OF TOOLS

Traditional Designs

In traditional ID, tools and materials support the teaching and learning processes. Teachers use tools primarily to pass information on to the learners with the assumption that if they pass it on clearly then it will be learned. The military and industry designed overhead projection, film, filmstrips, slides, and opaque projectors to help military and industrial trainers deliver information. Schools adopted them for the same purpose.

Students use tools to solve decontextualized problems. For example, calculators support learning in math, physics, science, and chemistry. Word processors support learning in languages and social sciences. Video cameras support learning in the arts. However, the use of tools by students is also viewed suspiciously, as though they were crutches holding up a person with a broken leg until he or she can stand on two feet. Students use tools to help them learn, though a "real expert" doesn't need a tool. When it is important for students to learn to use tools for job performance, then the tool becomes a focus of instruction rather than a means to an end—another form of decontextualization.

Sociocultural Designs

Tools take on a major role in supporting learning and enculturation into a real community of practice. Experts in a community use tools to perform their jobs every day. We are all grateful that surgeons have microscopic video cameras, aerospace engineers have calculators and wind tunnels, and firemen have ladders and hazardous materials suits.

Polin considered tools in terms of how they may enable learning—more specifically, how they enable discourse. Because the tools in the ARP are enablers of a theoretical approach to instruction, they are, in one sense, the least important part of her project. Students participating in the ARP use tools to facilitate learning within a community of practice, but not for the sake of using newsgroups, e-mail, chat, or web pages—they are a means to an end, a way to talk about learning and improving the community.

Yet, in another sense, the tools are the most important part of the project. Polin was able to meet the unique distant learning needs of her students because tools for building an online community existed. This convergence of tools and theory has enabled Polin to discuss, plan, create, and implement unique strategies for providing instruction within a unique environment.

CONCLUSION AND QUESTIONS

Polin works with an extremely challenging audience.[1] Many of us who work with mature, part-time students often complain about their lack of "dedication" to learning. We describe them as too busy to be good students, more interested in parking than actually attending class, not wanting to read or do homework, prone to whining instead of discussing, and failing to go "above-and-beyond" the class requirements. We plead with them, try rewards, try punishment, and bring in food. We are still caught up in the environmental approach and thinking, "If I just find the right combination of rewards, punishments, materials, and assignments, it will be better. If I can just create a better environment, learning will burst forth." But, in reality, nothing changes.

On the other hand, Polin's action research provides meaningful ways to make instructional changes with a high degree of generalizability for a couple of reasons. First, theories of learning as social experience are relatively elegant in their simplicity. Learners feel valued as participants within a community. They rely on learning materials and resources that exist. They learn to contribute as individuals and to work collaboratively.

Polin views the learner as more important than the environment. Rather than complaining about them, she chooses to respect them. Rather than creating a learning environment that manipulates and controls behaviors, she creates an environment that the learners control. Traditional ID looks linear because it takes a step-by-step approach to the design of instruction. Sociocultural design is far from procedural in its appearance (see Fig. 3.1). The sociocultural part of Fig. 3.1 reflects layers of context that become the focal point of interactions, and the learner is immersed within those contexts.

Second, discourse and participation in a community of practice do not need complex technologies. Newsgroups, web pages, e-mail, and chat are available to everyone. There will be technological improvements in communication technology in the future, so when something comes along that will help make discourse more efficient and effective, it will be easy to adopt because the learning theory is not tied to a specific technology.

Polin's program points up the differences between traditional and sociocultural ID in clear ways. The importance of respect for her students should not be underestimated in clarifying these differences. She respected their maturity, independence, and learning needs. Rather than force her square pegs into a round hole, she made a square hole. It isn't that adult learners don't want to read, come to class, or write papers. It is that their time is valuable and they are extremely goal driven. They'll read, write papers, and discuss issues as long as they believe that these activities will help them achieve their goals. They want to manage their own behaviors and make decisions about what and how they should learn. They also want to be part of a rich community of practice that will support them in reaching their goals. This does have a profound implication

---

[1]When I read the description of the working graduate students in her school of education, I thought that she was describing the students in my school.

for education. Learners will not continue to adopt the teacher's goals as their own. The teacher must find a way to use the learners' goals to meet the her teaching goals.

REFERENCES

Anderson, J. R. (1995). *Learning and memory: An integrated approach.* New York: Wiley.

Bednar, A. K., Cunningham, D., Duffy, T. M., & Perry, J. D. (1991). Theory into practice: How do we link? In G. J. Anglin (Ed.), *Instructional technology: Past, present, and future* (pp. 88–101). Englewood, CO: Libraries Unlimited.

Bonk, C. J., & Reynolds, T. H. (1997). Learner-centered web instruction for higher-order thinking, teamwork, and apprenticeship. In B. H. Kahn (Ed.), *Web-based instruction* (pp. 167–175). Englewood Cliffs, NJ: Educational Technology.

Bull, K. S., Kimball, S. L., & Stansberry, S. (1998). Instructional design in computer mediated learning. In *Coming together: Preparing for rural special education in the 21st century* (pp. 34–41). Charleston, SC: Conference Proceedings of the American Council on Rural Special Education.

Butterfield, E., & Nelson, G. (1989). Theory and practice of teaching for transfer. *Educational Technology Research and Development, 37*(3), 5–38.

Chi, M. T. H., & Cesi, S. J. (1987). Content knowledge: Its role, representation, and restructuring in memory development. *Advances in Child Development and Behavior, 20,* 90–91.

Clark, R. E., & Voogel, A. (1985). Transfer of training principles for instructional design. *Educational Communication and Technology Journal, 33*(2), 113–125.

Cunningham, D., & Duffy, T. M. (1993). In D. H. Jonassen (Ed.), *Handbook of research for educational communications and technology* (pp. 665–692). New York: Macmillan.

Dick, W., & Carey, L. (1990). *The systematic design of instruction* (3rd ed.). Glenview, IL: Scott, Foresman.

Dijkstra, S. (1997). The integration of instructional systems design models and constructivistic design principles. *Instructional Science 25,* 1–13.

Duffy, T. M., & Jonassen, D. H. (1992). *Constructivism and the technology of instruction: A conversation.* Hillsdale, NJ: Lawrence Erlbaum Associates.

Gagné, R. M., & Briggs, L. J. (1979). *Principles of Instructional Design* (2nd ed.). New York: Hold, Rinehart & Winston.

Glazer, R. (1990). The reemergence of learning theory within instructional research. *American Psychologist, 45,* 29–39.

Grabinger, R. S. (1993). Rich environments for active learning. In D. H. Jonassen (Ed.), *Handbook of research for educational communications and technology* (pp. 665–692). New York: Macmillan.

Grabinger, R. S., & Dunlap, J. (1995). Rich environments for active learning: A definition. *Association for Learning Technology Journal, 3*(2), 5–34.

Graziadei, W. D., & McCombs, G. M. (1995). The 21st century classroom–scholarship environment: What will it be like? *Journal of Educational Technology Systems, 24*(2), 97–112.

Lave, J., & Wenger, E. (1991). *Situated learning: Legitimate peripheral participation.* New York: Cambridge University Press.

Merrill, M. D. (1983). Component display theory. In C. M. Reigeluth (Ed.), *Instructional design theories and models* (pp. 279–333). Hillsdale, NJ: Lawrence Erlbaum Associates.

Perfetto, B. A., Bransford, J. D., & Franks, J. J. (1983). Constraints on access in a problem solving context. *Memory and Cognition, 11,* 24–31.

Staupe, A., & Hernes, M. S. (2000). How to create a learning environment on the Internet, based on constructivism and sociocultural approaches? [sic] In G. H. Marks (Ed.), *Society for information technology & teacher education international conference: Proceedings of SITE 2000* (pp. 819–825).

Wells, G. (1999). *Dialogic inquiry: Toward a sociocultural practice and theory of education.* New York: Cambridge University Press.

Whitehead, A. N. (1929). *The aims of education and other essays.* New York: Macmillan.

Willis, J. (2000). The maturing of constructivist instructional design: Some basic principles that can guide practice. *Educational Technology 40*(1), 5–16.

Willis, J., & Wright, K. E. (2000). A general set of procedures for constructivist instructional design: The new R2D2 model. *Educational Technology 40*(2), 5–16.

Winn, W. (1993). A constructivist critique of the assumptions of instructional design. In T. M. Duffy, J. Lowyck, & D. H. Jonassen (Eds.), *Designing environments for constructive learning* (pp. 189–21). New York: Springer-Verlag.

Open Discussion of Chapter 2

Scott Grabinger: To follow up on my comments in my discussion, the action research project seems to be central to the program and perhaps sets you off as something different. But how do you expect new students to pick a worthwhile research project almost before they start the program? That's like, "Bring me a crisis." But what if the crisis is gone in 2 or 6 months?

Linda Polin: Really good question. I think you are on to something about the ARP being a different beast. We [at Pepperdine] actually have a thread going on about this right now. Most, not most, probably about a third of our students change job titles before the end of the project. I think the action research project is an important factor, because what happens with the action research project is they start rattling cages and showing up at meetings, and people start noticing them and going "Oh, you're pretty interesting," and they start getting offers. Things move for them, and that amazes them and they are energized. It's a great big ball of snow rolling down the hill. So in that sense, it is pretty easy to tell who is moving along and who is not.

The action research project then becomes the backbone of all the rest of the curriculum. Each class is a lens on the problem. Let's look at this problem, or let's look at this—it's not really a problem—let's look at this project as a curriculum project or a leadership project or a technology project. People look at it in different ways. It's like a giant mentoring experience, which I think is good, but it's also a huge time sink. I mean massive quantities of time. Students are constantly interacting with you, and you have to learn to not answer them all the time. If you teach in the program, it helps if you have kids (*laughs*).

Scott Grabinger: One more question. In your paper, you mention heavy lifting. What do you mean by heavy lifting? And if you are not getting this heavy lifting, what are you doing in the course? How do you get it? In one class, I was really unhappy with the level of discourse I was getting from people in discussions. They had readings from all these sources they could fall back on, so I sent out a memo in frustration, which I am sure was not tactfully presented . I said, "People stop this bloody whining and use your readings, think about the questions, and get this information and use it." This immediately cut down on our messages by 90%. (*Group laughs.*) That lasted for quite a while. So how do you improve, or how do you step in to improve the discourse?

Linda Polin: Because so much of it is online, we say right out from the beginning that participation is absolutely critical in this program. And we encourage our faculty to send out midpoint reports individually to students, saying, "You're doing ok" or "We need to hear more from you in the newsgroup." The big lesson that everyone has to learn is to get the kids to talk to each other. There is an earlier paper that Karen Sheingold and

I just worked on—we looked at a new instructor, a veteran faculty member who is new to online. What we saw over time in this instructor's use of the newsgroup is a gradual change in the way she handles newsgroups. In the beginning, she handled it very much like a face-to-face-class: "Here are some questions about the readings, answer them." So the thread you get is the teacher posts, and then—bing, bing, bing—you get 24 little answers, and the kids don't talk to each other because they are answering the instructor. The instructor occupies a lot of the space and initiates a lot of the discussion in the newsgroup. Over time, she starts to back out more, and the students start to take over more. The big hard lesson in our program and the way it is designed is for the instructor to back the heck out of it. Give control over to the students. It is about herding cats— you want to keep them roughly in the same direction and keep them out of trees. But you have to give them their head. At first, this is new to them. The students have been through schooling; they know what it is about—what you are supposed to do and what they are supposed to do, what a syllabus should look like. At the beginning, there will be pauses in the newsgroups while they are waiting for you to post your response. And when that is not forthcoming, eventually some students step in and at the halfway point through the first semester, they usually figure out that they are going to have to talk to each other. That is something they definitely have to learn.

Jim Botkin: I thought this was a terrific presentation, so I hope that I've captured all the wisdom. I'd like to go a bit deeper into this communities of practice thing. I have worked with executives primarily over the years and, one of the things has been the question of trust. It's central, especially when we are dealing with the executive level.

Linda Polin: I agree. Every year, something happens; they'll say something personal, and that opens the floodgates. Once someone goes on the record... I mean, there's something every year. Once that happens, it's public and everybody responds, because everybody is very careful with each other and because everybody is stressed, it's like "Oh, if there is anything can I do for you?" or "Oh, that's awful" or "that happened to my mother, and here's what we did." People are very forthcoming, and they are doing this in newsgroups, and it's public—they're not doing this in e-mail. I don't know— they could just e-mail each other, but they put it in newsgroups. And that is interesting ... that lays the trust right there. If you're telling me your kid is in drug rehab—that is revealing.

Carson Eoyang: Question/clarification: you are talking about a whole program, a degree program. So you are talking about a closed community for 13 months. They are taking all the classes, and they are taking one class at a time?

Linda Polin: No, they are taking multiple classes at a time.

Carson Eoyang: But they are taking classes with each other, which is different from most other programs, where you have stranger groups at different times, and their affinity and cohesion is very weak from class to class. So you really have a year-long cohort that you totally control and shape and engineer?

Linda Polin: Yes.

Scott Grabinger: I almost hate to ask this one: What are they learning? How is their performance? The reason I hate to ask this is because I am not sure that what they are learning is all that important. Because if they are legitimate members of this community of practice and they are growing and evolving in this community of practice, can we assume they are learning?

Linda Polin: Quality—we are still wrestling with that. I hope we discuss this—how we should assess online. I mean, there is no reason why it could not be identical to how you do it face-to-face. A lot of the elements are still in the papers, and you can worry about whether they are authentic to the same extent that you worry about if they are authentic in your face-to-face class. You can have interactions with them online and see whether they can respond to questions. Twice I've called groups on the carpet and said, "You guys haven't done the reading, have you?" And I wish to God I could tell you how I knew, because I don't. I looked at the transcript, and I can't figure it out. In both cases, I was right and they 'fessed up. I sent them off packing. I said, "Go read, go away." So there is something there I don't know what. These are good questions for me to ponder.

Bob Wisher: The chats over time: Did you look at any trends in terms of the types of chats? Do some seem to be more social in nature, and do some seem to be more task-oriented, and did that hold constant? Any ideas on how to manage it or how it fluctuated and why it did?

Linda Polin: In my experience, you can't go too deep in chat, because you are so constrained by turn taking. You only get a line or two out before someone else's turn—it's a social norm. Or, if you write a paragraph, people will look at you and say, "Stop dropping slides in the middle of the discussion." So that constrains things. As you saw, there are multiple threads. The chats tend to be of two sorts—the social stuff, and then they tend to be logistical—we have this project coming up, let's talk about how we're going to do it. If you are good, you can peel that back and say, "Let's talk about logistics, but let's talk about logistics in terms of some ideas. Let's not just talk bout how long it has to be—let's talk about what it's supposed to be about."

We have seen the doctoral students (we had one group which was largely Type A) decide that didn't like all of the chitchat at the beginning of Tapped In, as it wasted too much time. So they passed a rule among themselves that if you were going to do chat, you would log in early and talk to each other. So when it was time to start class, you started class. The very next time they were in Tapped In, they did what they always do: They showed up for class, had about 5 or 6 minutes of "How's the cat, how's the husband?" They went right into chitchat, and they couldn't even police themselves. That got me to thinking that that serves a function, especially when you are out of body. It sort of locates everybody. So one of the things I have taken to doing with my classes is that I'll let it go a while, and then I'll start the clock and do a roll call and have everyone say we're here—here, here, here. It sort of puts people in the frame of mind that we have started. They can't even do away with it when they want to do away with it. It serves a function.

Peter Shea: I'm not very well versed in synchronous distance learning, but I imagine there are some affordances and constraints that a synchronous environment carries with it. Do you think, relative to an asynchronous environment, that a synchronous environment has certain advantages for engaging a safer and more thoughtful discussion? When I think about a moment-to-moment negotiation that happens in the face-to-face classroom, a lot of people have the disadvantage that they are not good at thinking on their feet. So the same thing seems to happen in a synchronous online environment

Linda Polin: You know, there's that fantasy that we all hear about that the shy person will be online and will blossom. Well, shy people are shy online too. At least they are in ours. I mean, there are people who will whisper, "We need to hear your voice in the discussion." They'll say, "Well I'm happy here, I'm getting a lot out of it, and I'll speak when I have something to say." We have this fallacy that shy people will suddenly blossom.

Peter Shea: Are shy people shy in synchronous environments?

Linda Polin: Yes.

Peter Shea: And not in asynchronous environments?

Linda Polin: Asynchronous is different, because there is a lot more control. In the beginning, you have students who word process and edit, and write fine essays— you have to work really hard to get them to write off the top of their head. Most of them make it there by getting a lot more control in an asynchronous environment, where you can pull your own message off the system. You can cancel it after you post it.

Jenny Franklin: Anecdotally, I've had a lot of people tell me that shy students come out in anonymous environments like group decision labs, and people that have not spoken all semester will be there frantically typing away. And it seems to me that the security of anonymous environment will allow them to come out, and not in an asynchronous environment, where they know each other.

Linda Polin: These guys know each other pretty well, though.

Terry Anderson: I think we've got a huge confound between synch and asynch text and voice. Sometimes we're talking about synch when we really mean text, and sometimes we're talking about asynch when we really are talking about voice, or vice versa. So I think we have a helluva lot of work before we can flesh out what the difference is between synchronous and text and asynchronous and voice, because it's a possibility that both are happening.

Linda Polin: We have toyed with voice, because after a while the students usually say, "This isn't very sophisticated stuff we're doing here. So we'll do CUSeeMe, and we'll do NetMeeting" and some things like that as well. It usually doesn't work as well. Now we don't have as much practice with it, and we've been doing this other thing quite a while. To be fair, people who are slow typists use Dragon Speak to do text-to-talk and talk-to-text, and that's okay. But the guy gave it up because he had to spend too much time teaching it words.

   I believe that it matters that they write it—I think that really matters. That's my interest currently. I think talk is cheap, and it disappears. I like that there is a transcript that comes out of Tapped In, even though if I'm not sure if anybody goes back and looks at it. We set up classes so that they don't overlap. What happens in the morning class is not the same thing that happens in the afternoon class. So you have to read each other's transcripts.

Tom Duffy: Stinson had things related to that in terms of your students meeting by phone as opposed to using the asynchronous discussion. You might want to relate to that.

John Stinson: Yeah, I think that the way that our students tended to come at it was that they are primarily executives and are not used to typing. Typing and chat was not particularly comfortable for them. Yet there are times when you need to be in a synch-type of communication environment. So you get an awful lot of conference calling to make decisions and brainstorm.

Linda Polin: I know that students used the phone to do the project, and I know that they are in Tapped In—in the instant messaging area. And then there is a whole back channel communication that I don't even know about, So . . . .

Jenny Franklin: I have a question for you about the faculty and the degree to which they work in a collaborative model: How many faculty are there, and how do you bring newcomers into the community? How do you meet their learning needs in terms of pedagogy and issues like that?

Linda Polin: We've had some interesting issues around that in a master's course—it's not something the faculty happily wanted to do. So in the beginning, it was mostly adjuncts. This gave me a lot of control, because I could pick and choose who I wanted and could talk to them about the history of the place. For the first couple of years, I had an in-house newsletter—I asked faculty who had taught in the program to contribute. For example, I'd ask John to "write a tip for this month . . . something you want to write about and share with people. Write something about a book you are using in class and why you picked that book." This was a semiregular newsletter that went around to all people who were teaching, and who were about to teach in that program.

Suddenly, with the circulation of the newsletter, the full-time faculty wanted to teach in the program. I haven't figured out how to make it work with the full-time faculty who are my colleagues. It's much more difficult than with adjuncts. We've had students come in and say "Some people need to go to culture camp, some of the faculty need to go to Virt Camp." So it's become a problem with the full-time faculty. With the adjuncts, it's not a problem. It's very political.

Tom Duffy: I'd like to dive in and ask a couple of different questions about switching the topic from community to the outcome sort of thing. And they are short questions. Dropout rate?

Linda Polin: Out of 65 or 70 kids coming in (give or take), we'll usually lose 3, 4, 5. They'll usually leave for one of two reasons. Some of them have a crisis they can't overcome financial or personal, and we've had one case of plagiarism where we threw the person out.

Peter Shea: How does that compare to the face-to-face dropout rate?

Linda Polin: I don't know—I'll have to look and see what our rate is—our rate might be different. We are expensive—if you are coming here, you are committed—you've got loans, ya know?

Tom Duffy: In terms of following through on the outcome question, you talked about the sense of trust leading them to feel more comfortable in honestly critiquing each other and being tougher on each other. Do you see that? Do you see higher quality resulting from that?

Linda Polin: Not in critiquing. I see higher quality from people more publicly working through things, saying, "I don't quite get this idea, here's what I think it means, it confuses me," and someone else responding to it. I think that's where the payoff is.

Tom Duffy: Part of that is talking to each other— but how deeply do they push on the issues when they are going back and forth? One of your opening issues was that their trust would lead to that kind of behavior.

Linda Polin: I don't see it as much in critiquing, and I don't see it as much in evaluating each other. I see it more in problem sharing and being more forthright about confusion and seeking.

Tom Duffy: It's an honesty of interaction. I wanted to push on the quality. So the third question is: What are the kinds of primary strategies used to promote quality thinking in the students?

Linda Polin: We have some little tricks that we use (*laughs*), and one little trick that we found on reading. For instance, we'll start a thread that says, "Pick a quote out of the book, write it there, and put the page number. It has to be something you like, or that you think is absolutely correct, and tell us why." Real simple—so pick a quote and write a paragraph about it. What happens in doing that is that someone will say something that sets off a discussion, or someone will have the same quote but a different response. Or you ask them to pick something they didn't like. So these are like conversation starters. What we do with a conversation starter is make it clear that the texts in the class are the anchor points for discussion. It's not just what do you in your work place, and isn't that interesting. It's about going back to the text material. As you saw from that person who started off that thread I presented—had internalized that model and was doing the same sort of thing. Other ways we do it are to just tell them, "Hey, you guys aren't discussing, so let's revisit that." And we have participation count as a huge part on the syllabus—may be 40% of the grade—so that's clearly defined. The pressure is on.

Jamie Kirkley: How is it defined? Is it numbers of messages, or . . . ?

Linda Polin: No, that's a mistake (*laughs*). At first, I tried that and it didn't work at all because some people are gung ho. We have this one woman right now who is in the hundreds already. They are mostly good, but she clearly has no job and just sits at her computer. We tell them they have to make comments of the following kind: One, they have to connect to what they are doing at work (we are looking for that explicitly). Two, they have to provide help to peers—they are explicitly tasked with responding to peers and doing it in a way that is helpful. We define help as helping people find and shape ideas, helping people find resources, so they have to do that. There are about five things off the list, but I can't remember the other two. There is sort of a bulleted list—do these things. It comes from students concerned about grades: "How come I got a B and she got an A?"

Carson Eoyang: The real aha for me, and the thing that I'm so excited about, is the unit of analysis is not the teacher. And it's not the individual student—it's the social group. You have talked about this for about an hour now, and I still have no clue about what the content is. (*Group laughs.*) But I don't care.

Linda Polin: It's educational technology.

Carson Eoyang: But the point is that we do not know what the course is about. But we are so fascinated because what you are focusing on is basically social dynamics and evolution of this community. You said that the focus is on the cohort. Well, now what you are focusing on is a social engineer of their learning. You were concerned that senior colleagues who are beginning to take part in the program did not have the skills in social engineering and group dynamics? I'm thinking that in my own school, I could have this discussion with my math faculty, and they would think I was talking Chinese. They are thinking about second order differential equations, and what I need to do is to make sure that each and every one of them needs to know how to structure— and social dynamics form a lot of courses and disciplines. The group social dynamic is something that faculty ignore or think it gets in the way of what they want to accomplish: "Stop talking in the back there! This is what my lecture is about ... " So it's a whole new dimension of what it is to be an instructor or professor—to think about the social dynamic of the people in the class.

Linda Polin: That gives me an idea of how to approach the faculty now, thank you (*laughs*). What is interesting is that I'm really awful at face-to-face instruction now. I'm just ruined. I've had to do a couple of them recently, and I go in there and everyone is just ready, and I'm not going to stand up there and talk anymore. They are just not happy with that at all.

Terry Anderson: I guess I'm a little suspicious if the goal is to create a community of inquiry or learning. we've had them from the Well to the MOOs to the palaces. We can create virtual communities—we've been doing it for 10 years. They have spawned businesses and love and life. So I think we have to get beyond just sort of creating communities. I guess that goes back to the discussion of what did they learn. One of the things I remember someone saying is that nobody agrees as to what an undergraduate education should look like—how much science, how much humanities, how much service—the only thing that everyone agrees on is that it should take 4 years. (*Group laughs.*) And it's a little bit based on some research on time on task with kids—the more time you spend on things, the more time you learn. So when I see that you have created a community, and we give an Ed.D. ....

Linda Polin: No, it's a master's program. There is a doctoral program, but it's not 15 months. It's 2 years of course work plus a dissertation.

Terry Anderson: Just pushing the point ...

Linda Polin: Yeah, they are there to get a degree. But what we want to do is connect them—we want to get them to look up a bit. I mean, they are leading tiny lives. I hate to sound kind of cold here, but they are leading very tiny lives when they come to graduate school. They know their world, so in my opinion the whole point of graduate school is to connect them with the universe and their field. So yeah, what we are looking at is that community and not the cohort. We've had this discussion with the kids after they read Lave and Wenger—they all decided they are a community of practice. I said, "What's the practice? Where are the experts? You're not a community of practice—you have access to the community of practice." That is what we them to do—look up and connect. In fact, they'll be at the CSCL conference if any of you are going to be there. It's a midpoint meeting, and they are there. They have to go to the conferences and listen to academic presentations on computer-supported collaborative learning. The idea is to connect them with the real field—let them read the journals and talk to people who work in the field. You think about how you got your doctorate, and I think that's a great way to learn. So it can look very social because there is a lot of talk involved, a lot of interaction. But there is content. I gave a bunch of Cs last semester. There clearly is content, and some people did not get it or didn't show they got it. That was a wake up call for a number of folks, that you can't just schmooze through this.

Terry Anderson: I guess it does depend a bit on the community and what the discipline is in. Your mathematicians—those are not the kinds of things they are trying to do. It's more important in an educational realm for practicing teachers to want to become communicators within their community.

Linda Polin: Let me put it this way—I think there is a lot more to debate about in education. We've had a huge discussion about standards and testing, and that serves a really useful purpose, because teachers have to make decisions about that and have to be able to articulate it to administrators. So in that regard, there might be a different role for this course. I don't know—I'm not a mathematician. I've always imagined that mathematicians stood at the board together and sort of argued about stuff.

John Stinson: One of the things I hear us needing to discuss is what learning outcomes are and how the methodologies and architectures related to those outcomes are. I think that could help clarify some of the outcomes.

Jim Botkin: Building on what Carson said and Terry's response, I think what Carson is saying is that the unit of analysis has become a community or group of people. I think that is a fundamental shift in the educational world no matter what the subject is. I hope we can find ways to debate these issues over the couple of days that we are here. No one really knows how to measure communities. I have spent the last 10 years encouraging, nurturing, and building executive communities, so I know how difficult it is. Sometimes you get the feeling that this is really terrific and our whole goal is that we are going to build this community. The community gets built, and then guess what—the community has these really tough barriers, and it won't let anybody else in. The members all think alike—talk alike—they've got the same answers. I think even Wenger would quickly point out that there are some negatives . . .

Linda Polin: I don't think we're trying to get everybody to the same place, because they are not the same people. Like I said, some are corporate trainers at Boeing, and some people are fifth-grade teachers.

Jim Botkin: The other way to say that is that some communities are really good and effective, and some are just plain lousy.

Linda Polin: Yeah, that too.

Lani Gunawardena: I am interested in learning how you facilitate this community of practice. Are you looking at how people learn from each other? Have you done any evaluation or research on how people teach, teach others ideas, and learn from that?

Linda Polin: I've just started looking at that stuff now. I do know there is one person I hired 2 years after they graduated, because in the public exhibition, every single person cited that that person helped them make decisions about their research project, and I thought "Wow, he's really impressive." And he is—I'll probably use him again. The analysis turns out to be very hard. I don't go deep enough linguistically—I'm doing a lot of back reading trying to figure out how to capture the learning—and because it's all there. I've got literal transcriptions, threaded newsgroups, so I'm hoping that if anyone has ideas . . .

Mark Schlager: I've tried to listen here for what is social engineering and what is pedagogy. We kept flowing back and forth so easily between pedagogical strategies and things that are social strategies that I don't even know if anybody recognized it. I just wanted to point that out.

(End of session)

4

Interaction and Engagement in LEEP: Undistancing "Distance" Education at the Graduate Level

Karen Ruhleder
University of Illinois, Urbana–Champaign

Distributed, online technologies are dramatically changing opportunities for education by supporting new forms of engagement between students and instructors. As computing technologies become increasingly integrated into other aspects of people lives, the ease with which they can be extended into the realm of education increases, supporting trend toward distance education and lifelong learning (Beller & Or, 1998). The Internet enables instructors to craft extensive resources that freely combine text, images, video, and audio. Instructors and students can communicate asynchronously through computer conferences. They can communicate synchronously using video teleconferencing and text-based chat. They can provide forms of interaction and collaborative activity that were once solely the province of face-to-face, same-time-and-place classroom, internship, or apprenticeship experiences (Twidale & Ruhleder, 2000).

Collectively, we are committing an enormous amount of resources to these new virtual forms of education. We ask instructors to wholeheartedly embrace the concept of online education and to invest time and effort in developing new course materials and modes of delivery (Visser, 2000). We assure students in virtual degree programs that our technologies will help fulfill their needs for continued education, training, and professional advancement. We ask institutions to invest monies that might go to other pursuits. Finally, we ask the professional community to consider the products of a "virtual" education as equivalent to one acquired through more traditional means.

What kind of detailed understanding do we have about the nature of these interactions? Our current understanding of how people interact comes primarily from research in face-to-face settings. This body of research tells us how participants use verbal and nonverbal signals to take or grant a turn, how they communicate interest or attention, and how they interpret interruptions. New media challenge this understanding by removing or altering the cues available to participants in an interaction. They offer participants new ways in which to shape and exercise control over interactions and affect the ease with which participants can communicate with others and maintain their visibility in a virtual community.

This chapter outlines the ways in which one set of technologies supports interaction within a particular virtual classroom that combines instructor audio with student chat. Multiple dialogues can take place at once, and students can direct the dialogue in ways not possible in a face to-face classroom. Instructors, in turn, must take on roles that involve not only imparting information but also monitoring ongoing student chat. They must find new ways to assert their own authority across the different media. The resulting changes have broad implications for the many kinds of virtual spaces, not only those established for educational purposes. The following sections describe the online venue, the data, and method in more detail. They then present and analyze a set of excerpts from several online classes. The chapter concludes with a discussion of the implications not only for students and instructors, but for those who design, implement, and study venues for virtual learning.

THE LEEP DISTANCE EDUCATION PROGRAM

> We aren't ordinary commuting students. We're a little shaky here and don't have the kind of informal access to students and staff that produces a feeling that we are not alone. (Martin, LEEP student)

This chapter draws on experiences with LEEP, an internet-based master's program in library and information science (LIS) offered through the Graduate School of library and information science (GSLIS) at the University of Illinois at Urbana–Champaign (Estabrook, 1999; Haythornthwaite, Kazmar, & Robins, 2000).[1] The on-campus program goes back over 100 years and has undergone many revisions of its mission and curriculum. The master's program as a whole is based on a commitment to guiding students in entering a profession through their interactions not only with faculty, but with their peers. The school offers a wide variety of courses to help students prepare for jobs in public, academic, and corporate libraries; in museums and archives; as web masters and content providers; and more.

GSLIS already supports a kind of reverse-distance program designed for students who live some distance away[2] and come to campus only on Fridays, taking up to three classes at a time. Many students enrolled in the "Fridays-only" option already hold jobs in libraries, but need additional skills and the formal degree in order to advance professionally. Others are making a career change to LIS after working within another profession. The courses are organized so that the program can be completed in 2 years and, strictly speaking, it is not a separate program but a scheduling option.[3] The limitations of this arrangement are clear. The goal of LEEP is to offer an LIS education to students regardless of geographic location. Like their Fridays only counterparts, these students are often looking for advancement in the library profession or making a career change. As with the Fridays-only option, it extends the already successful master's

---

[1] School URL: http://alexia.lis.uiuc.edu. LEEP program URL: http://leep.lis.uiuc.edu/.

[2] Students enrolled in this options come from all over the state, including Carbondale (4-hrs. drive), Peoria (2 hrs.), and the northern suburbs of Chicago (3½ hrs.).

[3] The courses are the same, the faculty are the same, and on-campus students may also register, but Friday students get first pick. For instance, the library administration course is generally offered every semester, including the summer term, but it is periodically offered on a Friday to offer it to Friday students first.

program to a broader population and is considered a scheduling option, not a separate program from what is offered on campus. Students admitted to the master's program through any option may enroll in any course, no matter what the mode of delivery (though students within a particular option get first choice). Faculty and on-campus adjuncts also teach across all options. In addition, a number of remote adjuncts teach in LEEP.[4]

LEEP was launched in the fall of 1996 and, although there have been some technology changes and adaptations, there has been no fundamental change in its organization. Starting with a cohort of 30, the program now enrolls 50 to 60 new students each year and maintains a high retention rate.[5] At any given time, about 140 are actively taking classes. Full-time students generally finish in a calendar year. In the distance program, however, the pace varies more widely because of the high number of participants with part- or full-time jobs. More than half of these students are out-of-state (actual numbers fluctuate), and there are a few foreign students as well, though students living outside of the United States tend to be U.S. citizens working at English language schools or connected with the military. Students must have access to a certain level of computer hardware, software, and support, and are expected to enter the program with basic technical skills.[6] They and their instructors "meet" in a virtual space, described in more detail later. The average LEEP class size is 25, with the exception of one introductory course in which all members of each incoming cohort enroll. This class is the only one with teaching assistant support to help monitor online activity.

The LEEP Experience: Face-to-Face and Online

What is it like to be a LEEP student? LEEP is an online program that starts with a face-to-face experience. The first aspect of the program is a 10-day orientation in late summer, during which students take an initial class together, participate in a set of technology workshops, learn about available resources such as interlibrary loan or online reserves, and are introduced to faculty and staff. In addition, each semester one extended weekend is set aside for on-campus class meetings, with each class offered that semester convening for part of that weekend. This is a chance for meeting with the instructor, working on group projects, carrying out library research,[7] and socializing:

"The face-to-face meetings are definitely important so you can create real people. Then when you talk to them over the net, they're your friends, you know who they are" (Melissa, LEEP student).

---

[4]One criticism raised against the LIS program as a whole is in the high use of adjuncts. Many of the adjuncts who teach in the program work in academic libraries at the UIUC and other universities. They come with special skills or experience that the full-time faculty may not have and are essential to maintaining a year-round program, as most full-time faculty do not teach in summer.

[5]Actual retention rates for the master's program are not tracked for any of our options. Most students do finish. Those who drop out tend to do so for personal reasons, not out of dissatisfaction with the program.

[6]Skills include elementary knowledge of a microcomputer operating system, information retrieval skills using online databases and CD-ROMs, e-mail and bulletin board skills, and some basic HTML coding ability. Details can be found at http://alexia.lis.uiuc.edu/gslis/degrees/leep.html#technology, which includes a link to the hardware and software requirements: http://leep.lis.uiuc.edu/info/techreq.html.

[7]All students have access to online reference and class materials provided through LEEP. However, these resources may not suffice for research papers or special projects. The on-campus weekend offers them access to the UIUC library.

Most class contact is online, however. Classes "meet" online weekly for 2 hours. Students listen to an instructor's presentation via RealAudio and view Web-based overheads. The students and the instructor all connect to a class chat room, to which students can post comments or questions at any time.[8] The term *chat* is a misnomer, because little casual chat takes place once class has begun, and participants are generally very much focused on the topic at hand. Instructors could also use this time for group discussion by sending different groups of students into a chat room of their own to discuss a preset topic.

In addition to these synchronous interactions, each class uses computer conferences, called WebBoards, through which students can post and comment on assignments, ask questions, discuss readings, and share useful resources. Individual instructors decide how they will set up and use the WebBoards for a given class. For instance, students used the WebBoards to discuss the weekly readings and share related experiences. Students in a young adult literature course may share stories about their own early reading experiences students taking an administration course talk about problems they have had in the workplace and how they resolved them. These posts lay the foundation for the next "live" session. In other classes, students post draft proposals (the grant writing course) or interface prototypes (the interface design course), to which other students respond asynchronously prior to the synchronous class discussion.

An extensive "tour" of a LEEP class is available online and includes screen shots of the LEEP interface (developed in-house).[9] Although it is presented through one instructor's experience with one particular class on young adult literature, it is representative of the ways in which many instructors use LEEP technologies. It also illustrates use of the chat room for small group work during a live session.

The use of Web-based technologies isn't limited to the classroom. All students have access to the same school-wide WebBoards. These are used for broadcasting information about course offerings, technical problems, new publications, and other matters. A new WebBoard was recently created for sharing "LEEP lore": stories about students' experiences in LEEP. Students also have access to archives of on-campus presentations. When special presentations are given at the school, they are frequently recorded and added to a "guest speakers" web page as RealAudio clips with accompanying PowerPoint slides or text materials. For instance, a recent presentation by a candidate for the deanship was made available via this archive.

Students come with reservations and apprehensions, because they have no idea what to expect from an online a program. Many have fairly traditional academic backgrounds and are used to lecture and small seminar formats. They look to the professor to map out a new territory for them and are not always comfortable with the free form of the chat room or the WebBoards:

> There's no professor to say, "You're wrong," or "Yes, I see your point."... It was nothing like sitting in a class and getting lectured at by this wealth of knowledge," (Katherine, on-campus student taking a LEEP class).[10]

---

[8]Students can also send private messages, called whispers, to others in the chat room. These are only seen by the person (instructor or other students) to whom they send the whisper.

[9]A tour of LIS 406, Youth Services Librarianship is available at: http://leep.lis.uiuc.edu/demos/jenkins/.

[10]Anecdotal evidence suggests that on-campus students tend to be younger and less experienced in the field, which may lead to a preference for a more "traditional" classroom experience.

Others, however, value a venue in which they can learn from their peers:

> One thing I really like about LEEP is that a lot of people who are professionals in the field are taking the classes. By working with them on group projects you get insight into their job and what their work experience is, (Madeline, LEEP student).

Despite the challenges of LEEP, hundreds of students have found it a viable and welcome option in their lives. What makes LEEP a tractable environment for students whose interests, work experience, and technological competence varies greatly? LEEP students start out as cohorts and have a sense of belonging to that cohort even when individuals move along at different paces. LEEP offers a fairly standard form of course organization and an established "look and feel" for its online class spaces and public forums. It builds on the established rhythms of semesters, midterms, finals, academic years, and, of course, matriculation and graduation, thus including all of the key rhythms and markers of academic life.[11] Overall, the LEEP program offers students great flexibility and rich potential for interaction while grounding these interactions in recognizable metaphors and organizational structures.

Evaluating LEEP

LEEP is evaluated and regulated on a number of levels. Students fill out course evaluations at the end of each semester, and there has been no striking difference between on-campus and LEEP instructor or course rankings. Proposals for new courses must be approved by the faculty and at the campus level. Most recently, the Graduate College Committee on Extended Education and External Degrees conducted a 5-year review of LEEP. It was rated as a very strong program and was recommended for renewal for another 5 years. The master's program as a whole is accredited by the American Library Association. These forms of evaluation are an extension of standard academic and professional procedures to include online environments.

This makes LEEP very different from programs such as the one Polin describes (Chap. 2, this volume). She and others are using new technologies as a way of implementing pedagogical models that they believe will enhance or improve on traditional models. LEEP was not implemented to explore ideas about pedagogy. More like the views of Duffy and Kirkley (Chap. 6, this volume), LEEP was a response to a need within a professional community—library schools were closing while the demand for information professionals was growing—that could now be offered through a new set of technologies.

Studying the "Live" Online Classroom

How do we collect and analyze data in virtual settings? In observing on-campus classes, we have many cues available to us that don't easily translate into an online environment. Seating patterns, body language, and the rate of note taking inform us about students' engagement with the instructor and each other. Working in a virtual setting

---

[11] Anyone applying to LEEP has at least one bachelor's degree. Some number of those admitted in any given year have some form of advanced degree, with a few students holding J.D.s or doctorates (no statistics are kept on this). LEEP students thus come with a set of experiences and skills that faculty can build on from the very first day of orientation.

challenges us to think about the adaptation of methods and frameworks from sociology, anthropology, and other disciplines (Bruckman, 1998; Haythornthwaite, 1998, 2000; O'Day, Bobrow, Bobrow, Shirley, Hughes, & Walters, 1998; Koschmann, 1996; Lombard & Ditton, 1997; Mynatt, O'Day, Adler, & Ito, 1998; Ruhleder, 2000). We lose many cues available to us in face-to-face settings. In addition, when the "site" of an interaction is distributed over multiple physical locations, each participant's class experience is shaped both by virtual activity and local activity. Virtual participants may interact with local nonparticipants, such as coworkers or family members, during the course of the interaction (Ruhleder, 1999b). Part of the challenge, then, is to capture these interactional data and to analyze them in ways that help us understand what the new technologies afford and require of students and instructors.

This particular paper is focused on the audio-chat "live" classes that are central to the LEEP model. It draws specifically on transcriptions of audio-chat classes in the summer semesters of 2000 and 2001, and considers only interactions in the shared virtual space.[12] The LEEP Web archive provided access to audio recordings and chat logs of past classes. This work is part of a stream of research being carried out at GSLIS that considers a variety of face-to-face, audio, and online interactions, aimed at helping us better understand how to design for the online experience of a distributed student body (Kazmer, 2000; Haythornthwaite, 1998, 2000; Ruhleder, 1999a). The data extend an earlier project in which several graduate students and I interviewed faculty, students, and staff involved in the LEEP program, some of whom have been quoted above (Ruhleder, 2002).

Data Presentation: Using the Chat–Audio Data

This chapter focuses specifically on two components of the online classroom interaction, the chat dialogue and the audio lecture, to outline the ways in which these LEEP technologies change the avenues for participation available to student and instructor during a "live" class. The set of data was drawn from six classes offered in the summer of 2000 and the summer of 2001. In collecting and analyzing it, I built on established methods for recording, transcribing, and analyzing talk between participants. The preparation of these transcripts is outlined later.[13] In the summer of 2000, classes included Business Reference and Indexing and Abstracting. In the summer of 2001 classes included these topics again (with the same instructors) and two additional classes, Library Administration and Grant Writing.

Adjunct instructors living in other states taught all but one of these courses. They called in to the LEEP office on a telephone, where they were connected to a line that would broadcast them online to the LEEP class members. As described above, students listened to an audio broadcast of the lecture via their computers, simultaneously reading

---

[12]I tried to capture nonverbal cues and local interactions by videotaping both the instructor and selected students during class. This turned out to be ineffective. A student in a virtual class looks much like any person anywhere staring at a screen and occasionally typing something, even when the chat room contained a lively discussion. Instructors, too, focused on the screen and their notes as they carried out the audio broadcast. How representative is this? We did not have permission to videotape children, so we could not include the students who were most likely to have to respond to other demands during class. The few students we did videotape cleaned up their work areas, sent their spouses away, and were clearly on their best behavior. Videotaping was more effective in capturing the interactions between and among two multiperson groups (c.f. Ruhleder & Jordan 1997, 1999; drawing on Jordan & Henderson, 1996).

[13]The analysis of these transcripts is particularly informed by conversation analysis (Goodwin, 1981; Sacks, Schegloff, & Jefferson, 1974).

Time	Content of AUDIO BROADCAST (What students hear through their computer speakers)	Postings in the CHAT ROOM (What students see in the chat window on their monitors)
19:52:08	Instructor lectures on web sites for novice investors.	
19:52:15	Instructor says sites for novices lack resources for sophisticated investors.	**Student A:** Are any of these sites regulated in any way? They are giving advice to people.
19:52:21	Instructor says he is posting a list of resources Silence for 9 seconds [posting doesn't work]	
19:52:35	Instructor says: "That should be coming through to you now."	**Student B:** Nope, it's defnitely caveat emptor.
19:52:56	Instructor comments on list he has posted	
19:53:01	Instructor continues: "They are designed to help a prospective investor make decisions..."	**Student C:** Isn't a commission being established to set some guidelines?
19:53:22	Instructor comments on chat room activity: "**Let me go back to Student A's question.** As Student B says, no, they are not regulated, and it does make it dificult for novices. Hmm, Student C. I haven't heard anything..."	

FIG. 4.1.   Sample audio–chat dialogue.

and posting comments to the chat room. Some instructors also use PowerPoint slides or text files that students can view during the instructor's presentation. Asynchronous postings to class Web conferences are not directly considered in this analysis.

In a face-to-face classroom, generally only one person will speak at a time. The speaker may be either the instructor or a student, but the instructor holds the floor most frequently and is in charge of deciding to whom to grant the floor, at what point, and for how long. The instructor thus remains the focal point of interaction. The organization of LEEP classes, however, enables students to take the floor in the chat room without having to wait for permission from the instructor. Further, it allows students to exchange information and engage in dialogue with other students even while the instructor is speaking.[14]

For each class studied, I transcribed some or all of each audio broadcast and then matched up the instructor's spoken comments with a transcript of the chat room posts. Figure 4.1 shows how these two transcripts would be combined for analysis.[15] The far-left column notes the time of a post or utterance. The middle column shows what the instructor said during the audio broadcast and the right-hand column is a transcription of postings to the chat room.[16]

Student A's question opens up a new topic not addressed in the lecture. The instructor doesn't respond, being first engaged in the lecture and then engaged with some technical problems. However, two students respond, one flippantly and one with

[14]This analysis does not include "whispers," private messages only viewable by selected individuals.

[15]The hypothetical example used here is drawn from real data, but it is streamlined for presentation.

[16]Text in the chat room appears exactly as in the log. In the real data, that often means the inclusion of misspellings, nonstandard abbreviations, all lowercase typing—the chat equivalent of colloquial speech.

a serious question. Not until both Students B and C have responded does the instructor break off to comment on this set of posts. Students are able to post responses while the instructor is lecturing or engaged in some other way. This represents a significant change from how a face-to-face classroom setting operates. Examples from audio–chat classes later illustrate this in more detail.

REDISTRIBUTING PARTICIPATION AND AUTHORITY: CLASS EXCERPTS

Before discussing particular excerpts, let us consider the ways in which the technologies of the online classroom break down at least some of the factors that structure interactions between students and instructor. One traditional function of the professor has been to serve as a guide and be the person who knows the trail: "When it's a very large area or a new area, you've got somebody who's already walked through the woods pointing to the blazes on the tree" (Ed, on-campus student). In the open forum of the chat room and computer conference, many potential guides are available, and some students may know parts of the trail better than the instructor. Authority may need to be renegotiated at different points in time as the ease with which students may introduce new information and answer questions increases.

In the excerpts below, student contributions become an increasingly focal point of overall class activity. This series of excerpts is taken from the two online classes previously described. They illustrate a range of ways in which the chat and audio threads can be interrelated. Student names have been replaced with a letter and number: S1, S2, etc. The chat dialogue is presented as it appeared in the chat room, complete with misspellings, grammatical errors, and abbreviations.

Excerpt 1: Providing New Information

The chat room is a forum for information sharing. Small comments that might seem too unimportant to make in a classroom can be posted concurrently with the lecture. In this example, the instructor mentions the 1997 economic census as a potential information source, and a student says that it will be online by the end of the year. The instructor thanks him. One students posts information about a conference he recently attended, another posts a pointer to CD-ROM versions of the economic census, and several students begin to talk about a class article. This all takes place while the instructor continues to talk about online resources.

The online classroom retains the traditional lecture framework in which the instructor is the primary presenter of new information. The chat room, however, provides a channel for students to share their own bits of information without stopping the lecture. In Fig. 4.2, S1 contributes information that is new to the instructor. The source to which S1 refers isn't one that the instructor wants to talk about. The chat room, however, lets another student add to S1's post. The ability to make such contributions does not mean that there will be uptake of the topic on the part of other students. In fact, no discussion develops either about the availability and use of the economic census or about S2's conference experience.

The chat room also lets students engage in discussion while the instructor encounters a technical problem. S3's comment kicks off a series of posts on students' reactions to a class article. This highlights the new role the instructor must take on. Instead of managing student discussion, the instructor must now monitor and respond (or

Time	Content of Audio Broadcast	Postings in the Chat Room
19:17:58	Instructor uses the 1997 economic census as an example of a government database organized around NIAC numbers.	
19:18:21	Instructor talks about search strategies for commercial on-line databases and refers to a class article by Jan Tudor.	
19:19:30	Instructor continues to talk about strategies for getting information on specific industries.	S1: I spoke to someone at the census bureau a few weeks ago and they are still working on getting the complete 1997 Economic census online. End of the year they hope.
19:20:05	Instructor responds to S1's post: "I did not know that, S1. Thank you for letting us know."	
19:20:25	Instructor acknowledges the future utility of on-line economic census: "it definitely will be easier."	S2: As an aside, I was amazed at how many us govt agencies had booths at the ALA conference.. with some great information on searching
19:20:29	Instructor starts talking about useful web sites.	S3: I enjoyed Tudor most. She offers additional tips for gathering information like job announcements.
19:20:51	Instructor has some problems sending a URL (17 sec. of indistinct talk sotto voce in background).	S4: The econ census is available via cd-rom at government depository libraries. (ideally)
19:21:12	Instructor continues to have technical problems: "Sorry, I'm having dificulties, it is completely my fault. . ."	S5: Jan Tudor's article was really helpful. I like the specific hints and examples she gave. Having a starting place always helps.
19:21:34	Instructor starts lecturing about the URL: "I want to call your attention to. . ."	
19:21:42	Instructor continues lecturing. "What's really absolutely terrific about this site. . ."	S5: Not to mention that the reading is not dense.
19:22:28	Instructor comments on posts: "I'm just looking at some of your reactions that people have to Jan Tudor's article. . ."	

FIG. 4.2.   Economic census online.

choose not to respond) to student posts even while lecturing or dealing with technical problems. In the example above, the instructor acknowledges S1's post, ignores S4's post, but does comment on the posts sparked by S3. This new role and responsibility on the part of the instructor is discussed in more detail in a later section.

Excerpt 2: Peer Response to Questions

In Fig. 4.3, student posts affect the flow of the lecture as they ask questions and respond to each other. The instructor begins to reply not only to questions, but also to students'

Time	Content of Audio Broadcast	Postings in the Chat Room
19:32:53	Instructor lectures on abstract construction: "For an indicative abstract, that includes..."	S6: Is the last sentence about the conclusion or is it evaluative? The word "superior" seems critical ratherthan informative."
19:33:04	Instructor reads S6's question and responds: "I'm assuming here that the abstractor took this from the conclusion of the paper..."	
19:34:18	Instructor explains about formative abstracts.	S6: OK.
19:34:35	Instructor continues lecturing.	S7: How would the abstractor have stated it if this were "critical"?
19:34:40	Silence for 4 seconds. Instructor says: "Right. Thank you for that clarification, S8." Instructor begins gives an example of an indicative abstract.	S8: "Superior" refering to accuracy, not quality?
19:35:12	Instructor continues lecturing.	S6: Probably a poor word choice?
19:35:47	Instructor stops to read messages in the chat room: "Let's see, let me just check here..." [doesn't respond to posts] Instructor continues lecturing.	S9: maybe that was the word used in the paper, S6, by the authors.
19:35:59	Silence for 5 seconds. Instructor responds to S9: "As far as the wording of the original article, I don't know..."	S6: Perhaps
19:37:17	Silence for 6 seconds. Instructor responds to S9: "They did sort of tell us the outcome in the title..." Instructor talks about decisions in the abstracting process.	S9: The conclusive statement corresponds with the title somewhat–and the title is the author's we assume.
19:46:47	Instructor continues lecturing.	S6: Good point S9

FIG. 4.3.   How is the word *superior* used?

responses to each other, taking on a role as monitor rather than initiator. In this class, students are analyzing abstracts constructed by a professional abstracting service. The abstractor has used the word *superior* in an abstract provided with the citation for a research paper. A student, S6, questions the appropriateness of its use. Discussion between S6, the instructor, and other students (who respond to each other, as well as to the instructor) centers on why that particular word was used and whether or not it was a good choice.

The instructor must monitor and respond to what is happening in the chat room, even as he continues his lecture. He tries to clarify a student's interpretation of class material. In this case, however, the process of clarification is more complex and drawn out, and involves both the instructor and several students. During the course of this excerpt, one student, S6, moves from the role of student-novice asking a question of the instructor-expert to taking on a guiding role and having the final word in a discussion. He posts an answer to S8's question and an evaluative comment in response to S9. The segment concludes with S6 making another evaluative comment directed at the previous student poster.

The instructor, meanwhile, must balance his own responses to students' posts with the need to cover a certain set of material for the day. The instructor's response is first triggered by a direct question from S6's, then by S6's comments to other people in the chat room. S6 offers a lukewarm reaction to S9's suggestion that the word *superior* came directly from the authors' writing. The instructor thus needs to set the record straight or at least to give support to posts he believes offer the most appropriate analyses. This management of the chat room is done at the expense of maintaining a coherent lecture narrative.

Excerpt 3: Students Help Clarify a Question

In Fig. 4.4, one of the students, S8, asks a question about how to include particular terms in an index. The instructor answers her but misunderstands her question. Over the course of the excerpt, S8 tries to reframe her question, and the instructor tries again to answer her, after which other students help S8 clarify what she wants to ask. These posts provide a jumping-off point for the instructor to readdress the indexing problems to which S8's question refers.

Instructors in both face-to-face and online classrooms must deal with questions from many different students. Sometimes they fail to correctly understand or fully answer a question, frustrating a student who must then decide whether to repeat the question or to push for a more detailed answer. In the chat room, other students can help reinterpret or reframe an answer. Their efforts, however, may still require instructor comment or intervention.

In this example, the instructor does not give a satisfactory answer to S8's question before resuming the lecture. Other students begin to probe, suggest interpretations, and offer answers. The work of probing takes place concurrently with the lecture and is interspersed with questions on other, unrelated topics from students in the chat room. The instructor responds to both the suggested interpretations and, finally, to S8's response to S11. The instructor does this while answering other student questions and continuing his planned lecture.

Both students and instructor may benefit from involving a wide range of people in interpreting and answering a question—students in particular may be better able than the instructor to recognize what other students have trouble understanding. However, the instructor cannot control the quality of the chat dialogue that arises around that question and needs to monitor that dialogue to make sure that the question is being interpreted and answered in a useful way. Student participation in this kind of interpretive work implicitly challenges the instructor's authority by asserting itself as a source of interpretation and knowledge.[17]

---

[17]During this time, I also saw one example of a student offering to post a web page explaining something that other students found confusing in the "live" class. This puts that student in the position of creating and making available resources in direct response to what happens in the class. The instructor must decide how to respond to such initiatives. Student postings may be a good way to deal with questions that the instructor cannot take on at that point in the class (or specialty topics about which a particular student is the expert). However, it also places on the instructor the burden of monitoring not only the chat, but posted resources.

Time	Content of Audio Broadcast	Postings in the Chat Room
20:00:53	Instructor is lecturing about index construction, using an example that cross-references the terms "lawyer" and "attorney."	S8: In regard to omnibus references— would it be taboo to include those Native American groups right under that heading, even though the heading has no locator?
20:01:07	Instructor answers: "It would be if you put a page number. . ." Instructor continues lecture, giving several examples.	
20:02:28	Instructor continues an example using coal and acid rain.	S9: So if lawyer had several subheadings, it would be better to use Attorney—see lawyer instead of using the double entry?
20:03:08	Instructor answers S9: "Right, thank you, Linda, for putting it in much clearer than I did. . ."	
20:04:18	Instructor finishes his answer to S9.	S8: I guess what I really mean is, Can you make up a heading for a list of common entries even through it does not have its own locator in order to minimize cross referencing and achieve better co-location?
20:04:25	Instructor answers: "I'm not sure if I get the gist of that, S8. . ."	
20:05:43	Instructor continues coal/acid rain example. Instructor sees S7's question and reads it aloud.	S7: Going back to Coal—would you include the acid rain alphabetically under coal with the pages acid rain, 152–153
20:05:59	Instructor continues to read S7's question aloud.	S6: So acid rain under Heading "environment" with other page numbers than found under coal?
20:06:00	Instructor continues to read S7's question aloud.	S10: S8, are you suggesting indexing several specifics under a broader term for better collocation, the point from the specifics to the BT? For example, you'd put the locators under Native Americans with see references from Hopi, Iroquis, and Seminole?
20:06:02	Instructor addresses S7 and S6: "OK, what I'm going to do, I'm sending acid rain to its own heading. . ."	S11: S8, do you mean can you have a heading without a locator but with subheading that DO have locators?

FIG. 4.4.   Students helping a student reframe a question.

Time	Content of Audio Broadcast	Postings in the Chat Room
20:06:54	Instructor reads S10's question aloud. Instructor starts to read S11's question aloud.	
20:07:29	Instructor finishes reading S11's question.	S6: Sorry! [no apparent reason for the apology]
20:07:40	Instructor addresses S10 and S8's questions: "I think an answer is, it's better to have them underneath a heading..."	
20:08:26	Instructor finishes addressing S10 and S8's questions.	S7: With malocclusion, there are no pages listed. Why not?
20:08:28	Instructor starts to read S7's question aloud.	S12: malocclusion is a heading without a locator, but the subheadings have locators... ??? that's OK?
	Instructor answers: "Thank you, S7 and S12, let me get back to that malocclusion...."	
20:09:33	Instructor continues to answer the questions on malocclusion.	S8: Right, S11—I'm sort of begging the question of why you would want to employ an omnibus heading—that is, if you can gather Hopi, Sioux, etc. under Native American (even though there are no references in the text to Native Americans in general), why not? Why make the reader go look up each tribe individually? But you may have already answered by question by saying that you do always need a locator.
20:09:48	Silence for 5 seconds.	S12: Thank you
20:09:53	Instructor responds to S8: "OK, ominbus heading is not something to use..."	

FIG. 4.4.   (Continued)

Excerpt 4: Shift in Authority

Finally, sometimes the instructor's voice even gets lost in student explanations and discussions. In Fig. 4.5, the instructor discusses guidelines for effective abstracting. He refers to a Web-based "overhead" to which all students have access. The instructor has been speaking to point 5, "eliminating excess words," and responds to a student question about the submission of abstracts with a manuscript. When a student misinterprets a particular concept, it isn't ever clear that the instructor manages to correct the thinking of that person or of other students who jump into the discussion.

In the face-to-face classroom, the instructor controls the pace of the dialogue. In the chat-audio setting, a student can continue to pursue a line of questioning even after the instructor has moved on. If interest persists, other students can turn to that person with their own questions, continuing the thread. Students benefit from being able to have their say without overtly stopping or impeding the lecture. However, they can also

Time	Instructor Audio Lecture	Chat Room Dialogue
20:18:17	Instructor is lecturing on abstract construction. Instructor reads S9's question aloud. Instructor answers S9: "That's going to be completely dependent on the database it goes to..."	S9: [Instructor], I'm curious. Authors in cell/molecular biology are required to submit an abstract with the manuscript and when it's published, the author's abstract appears with the article. Do abstracting services use that abstract, or do they write a second one for the databases?
	Instructor lectures on the use of abbreviations. Instructor lectures on judging the intended audience.	
20:21:33	Instructor introduces the term, "findings-oriented abstracts." Silence for 4 seconds. Instructor clarifies that "slanted abstracts" is not pejorative, but means slanted to a specific audience. Instructor lectures on selection of verb tense.	S9: Thanks [Instructor]—of course us author sare not skilled abstractors and we write them for different reasons and with different slants than a professional abstractor would.
20:21:33	Instructor encourages people to look at some sample abstracts and see if they find a pattern. Instructor laughs and says he'll take it that way.	S9: I probably should have used "prejudices" than slants — thank you,
20:23:57	Instructor starts moving on to the next point on his overhead. Instructor responds to S13: "I'm looking at it a little bit differently than that...."	S13: Are you saying an abstractor would slant it to make it more understandable to a particular audience while the author would slant it to make it appear to be a more scholarly article than it is
20:24:52	Instructor talks about writing at different levels for different user populations.	S9: I think [Instructor] hit it on the head S13—authors often talk of what they would have liked to have done or obtained in results.
20:25:00	Instructor continues.	S7: Aren't some abstracts submitted prior to the article—so, if all research has not been finished, the abstract might not completely reflect the paper, or might say what is expected to be discovered, but, at the end of the research, the conclusion isn't quite the same as the abstract says.. (Hope this makes sense)
20:25:12	Silence for 1 second, says "um." Silence for 3 seconds.	
20:25:16	Instructor responds to S9: "And S9 is mentioning this information, too, ..." Instructor responds to S7: "I think that would be true if we're talking about meeting abstracts..."	S11: Slanting=emphasizing?

FIG. 4.5. Defining the "slanted" abstracts.

20:26:19	Instructor explains that those abstracts aren't going into an abstracting and indexing service directly.	S9: In the natural sciences S7, you have to submit the abstract with the completed manuscript and the research has to be complete prior to submitting the paper for peer review.
20:27:41	Instructor responds to S11 saying that slanting is emphasizing, but in a non-pejorative way.	
20:28:01	Instructor says: "Thank you, S9, for putting in the real story. . . . That put it in a much clearer way than I did."	
20:28:38	Instructor continues: "If we move along here. . ."	S13: Is the author's slanting of an abstract considered bad or just par for the course?
	Instructor repeats S13 question, laughs and says, "I'll let S9 handle that one."	
20:29:21	Instructor continues lecture	S14: Passing the buck [Instructor]
	Silence for 2 seconds. Instructor laughs. Instructor says, "I am passing the buck because, you know, I open up my MedLine and I take the abstracts as they are. . ." Instructor returns to lecture: "But since I'm talking about the writing of them . . . as opposed to the reading of them . . ." Instructor continues lecture	
20:31:11	Instructor returns to earlier topic: "Now, I go back to the possibility of a modular or slanted abstract. . ."	
20:32:20	Instructor refers to a page in an article the class read on indexing vs. abstracting skills.	S9: Yes–it's bad S13 if it's done deliberately, which it is. Those of us in the field know who does this–others out of the field may not know. But it happens unconsciously, no matter how hard all of us try to be critical of our own studies–we often (includingme) would send the manuscript with the abstract to our peers and competitors asking for a critical evaluation and how the manuscript was written. Many do not do this though–i
20:32:25	Silence for 6 seconds. Instructor says he'll wait while people read S9's post. Silence for 5 seconds. Instructor starts to continue the lecture.	
20:32:54	Instructor stops mid-sentence. Silence for 5 seconds. Instructor reads aloud S9's post at 20:32:20, thanks S9. Instructor continues lecture, referring to another class article.	S9: That's why I asked the question of [Instructor] in the first place

FIG. 4.5. (Continued)

disrupt an instructor's presentation of ideas or techniques through their questions or comments.

In this example, S9 disrupts the flow of the lecture by framing responses to the instructor and other students in such a way that the instructor stops lecturing to comment on what S9 is saying. S9 takes the word *slanted* (as applied to abstracts) in a negative way, attributing some form of deception to the abstracting and indexing service. The instructor tries to correct this view, but at some point stops pursuing the matter—thus letting "bad" information go unchallenged to keep on track with the presentation of material. Although it is not impossible for this kind of exchange to take place in a face-to-face classroom, its likelihood is increased by the openness of a forum in which S9 can continue to press the point even as the instructor moves on.

Changes in the Role of the Instructor

The excerpts above highlight changes for the student—each one now has a voice online and can contribute comments, questions, and ideas at any point in the audio-chat class. This arrangement makes it possible to deal with questions more quickly and within the context of a broader interaction:

> The live broadcast session allows a bit more spontaneity—it allows students to type in questions on the fly (Mark, LEEP instructor).

The examples also illustrate some of the ways in which instructors must alter their own behavior in response to the new affordances of the medium. The instructor must monitor the chat while lecturing to respond in an appropriate and timely manner.[18] Some instructors try to monitor constantly while speaking from their own notes and materials. Others deliberately do not look at the screen except at specific break points in their presentation, assuring students that they will periodically stop to scan the chat or call for questions (this will not stop chat, but it changes the expectation of instructor response).

No matter which approach the instructor chooses, the activity in the chat room must be dealt with. Some student comments can be handled quickly and within the context of the broader topic at hand. For instance, in Excerpt 1, the student posts a specific fact that is tied to a comment the instructor has just made. In other cases, student posts become not only disruptive but also counterproductive to the instructor's goal. In Excerpt 4, for example, students began interpreting an idea from the lecture—the use of *slanted* abstracts—in ways that are not in keeping with the way the terminology is actually used within the field of indexing and abstracting. The instructor here is fighting a losing battle in terms of reclaiming the definition.

How different is this from a face-to-face lecture or even a discussion-based class, in which the instructor periodically takes the floor to influence the discussion? In a lecture, students can raise their hands at any time. In a discussion, some voices often predominate. Student questions or comments may not be central to the instructor's goals. Face-to-face, however, the instructor has some control over their participation by not calling on them, asking them to defer questions, declining to address a part of their comment or refocusing the direction of a remark. In LEEP, the instructor can certainly do some of that in the chat room, but has no real control over what is posted or how other students will respond.

---

[18]This project has no formal data on instructor strategies. These comments reflect informal discussions with instructors and inferences made from working with the audio–chat data.

CONCLUSION

The weekly audio–chat sessions from which the previous excerpts are drawn serve as both intellectual and social touchstones for students participating in the LEEP program. For 2 hours a week per class, they know that they are not working alone toward a degree, no matter how physically distanced they may be from other students or from the University of Illinois itself. What they find online, however, is more than an extension of the traditional face-to-face classroom. The virtual classroom also enables significantly different forms of interaction. Viewed through the lens of who may hold the floor, who may comment to whom, and what kinds of contributions may be made, the above excerpts illustrate changes that affect roles and relationships among participants.

Aspects of the LEEP experience parallel observations made in the 1980s and early 1990s, when e-mail was introduced into business organizations on a wide scale. Employee communications began to cross traditional hierarchical boundaries once they gained access to this new medium. Someone might include their boss's boss on a "cc" list, or directly request information from someone in a different department instead of "going through channels" (Markus, 1994; Sproull & Kiesler, 1991). Similarly, students no longer need to go through the proper channel of raising their hand and hoping to be recognized; class is never strictly divided into a lecture and a discussion component, but might have elements of both at any point in time. Other media choices will expand or constrain these impacts, but the previous example illustrates how even relatively "low-tech" media can dramatically begin to alter key features of an interaction.

While it does not build on any particular pedagogical framework, LEEP is an extension of a successful on-campus program that is already committed to small classes with lots of student involvement. The technologies used have grown out of a desire to maintain as much spontaneous interaction as possible while also staying as low-tech as possible (video, for instance, requires more bandwidth than most students and adjuncts have available to them). Technical decisions have also been influenced by the desire to give instructors as much flexibility as possible in organizing their courses. The audio–chat combination is one technical expression of a broader set of values that shape classes offered via any of the three scheduling options. The new interactional possibilities require both students and instructors to reassess who holds expertise and authority within a class.

For designers, the experiences of students and faculty in the virtual classroom point to particular features of online interactions that could be better supported by distributed technologies. In the chat room, technology design could support the tracking of multiple threads and make it easier to incorporate multiple forms of material into real-time venues such as the chat room. Data about chat room and WebBoard participation could help instructors (and students) get a better view of who is participating and who is talking to whom, not just in a particular session but over time. A "good" post might be defined in terms of content, but might also be defined in terms of how many responses it generated.

This chapter described one feature of LEEP, an internet-based approach to delivering instruction that combines on-line and face-to-face, asynchronous and synchronous communication. In particular, this chapter focused on the use of the weekly "live" class sessions in which an instructor broadcasts a lecture via RealAudio while students participate through a chat room in which they can post questions or comments at the same time. This simple combination of media adds a powerful synchronous component to the on-line learning experience. Students connect with each other not just in terms of the shared formal learning, but by being able to offer their own expertise within the same forum. Participants must reconsider old classroom expectations of whose voice may be heard and whose knowledge is privileged. The LEEP audio+chat "live" sessions represent one exploration into these new possibilities.

ACKNOWLEDGMENTS

I wish to thank the students, faculty, and staff of the LEEP program for giving me access to their classes. I also wish to thank Brigitte Jordan of Xerox Palo Alto Research Center for her helpful comments on an earlier draft of this chapter. This research was supported by NSF Grant No. 9712421 and by the Graduate School of Library and Information Science.

REFERENCES

Beller, M., & Or, E. (1998). The crossroads between lifelong learning and information technology: A challenge facing leading universities. *Journal of Computer-Mediated Communication 4*(2). Available: http://www.ascusc.org/jcmc/vol4/issue2/beller.html

Bruckman, A. (1998). Community support for constructionist learning. *Computer Supported Cooperative Work: The Journal of Collaborative Computing, 7*(1–2), 47–86.

Estabrook, L. (1999, April). *New forms of distance education: Opportunities for students, threats to institutions* [Online]. Paper presented at the Association of Colleges and Research Libraries (ACRL) National Conference, Detroit, MI. Available: http://www.ala.org/acrl/estabrook.html

Goodwin, C. (1981). *Conversational organization: Interaction between speakers and hearers*. New York: Academic Press.

Haythornthwaite, C. (1998). A social network study of the growth of community among distance learners [Online]. *Information Research, 4*(1). Available: http://www.shef.ac.uk/~is/publications/infres/paper49.html

Haythornthwaite, C. (2000). Online personal networks: Size, composition and media use among distance learners. *New Media and Society, 2*(2), 195–226.

Haythornthwaite, C., Kazmer, M. M., & Robins, J. (2000). Community development among distance learners: Temporal and technological dimensions. *Journal of Computer Mediated Communication, 6*(1). Available: http://www.ascusc.org/jcmc/vol6/issue1/haythornthwaite.html

Jordan, B., & Henderson, A. (1995). Interaction analysis: Foundations and practice. *The Journal of the Learning Sciences, 4*(1), 39–103.

Kazmer, M. (2000). Coping in a distance environment: Sitcoms, chocolate cake, and dinner with a friend [Online]. *First Monday, 5*(9). Available: http://www.firstmonday.dk/issues/issue5_9/index.html

Koschmann, T. (1996). *CSCL: Theory and practice of an emerging paradigm*. Mahwah, NJ: Lawrence Erlbaum Associates.

Levin, J., & Waugh, M. (1998). Teaching teleapprenticeships: Frameworks for integrating technology into teacher education. *Interactive Learning Environments, 6*(1–2), 39–58.

Lombard, M., & Ditton, T. (1997). At the heart of it all: The concept of presence [Online]. *Journal of Computer Mediated Communication, 3*(2). Available: http://www.ascusc.org/jcmc/vol3/issue2

Markus, M. L. (1994). Electronic mail as the medium of managerial choice. *Organizational Science, 5*(4), pp. 119–149.

Mynatt, E., O'Day, V., Adler, A., & Ito, M. (1988). Network communities: Something old, something new, something borrowed . . . *Computer Supported Cooperative Work: The Journal of Collaborative Computing, 7*(1–2), 123–156.

O'Day, V., Bobrow, D., Bobrow, K., Shirley, M., Hughes, B., & Walters, J. (1988). Moving practice: From classrooms to MOO rooms. *Computer Supported Cooperative Work: The Journal of Collaborative Computing, 7*(1–2), 9–45.

Rowling, L. (1997). Creating supportive environments. In D. Colqhoun, M. Sheehan, & K. Golz., *The Health Promoting School*. Sydney: Harcourt Brace.

Ruhleder, K. (1999a). Creating network community: Workable space in a virtual landscape. In C. Hoadley & J. Rochelle (Eds.), *Proceedings of the Third Conference on Computer Support for Collaborative Learning, December 12–15* (pp. 503–519).

Ruhleder, K. (1999b). On the edge: Learning through sidework and peripheral participation. In M. Easterby-Smith, L. Araujo, & J. Burgoyne (Eds.), *Proceedings of the Third International Conference on Organizational Learning* (pp. 862–876). Lancaster, England: Lancaster University Press.

Ruhleder, K. (2000). The virtual ethnographer: Fieldwork in distributed electronic environments. *Field Methods, 12*(1), 3–17.

Ruhleder, K., & Jordan, B. (1997). Capturing complex, distributed activities: Video-based interaction analysis as a component of workplace ethnography. In A. S. Lee, J. Liebenau, & J. I. De Gross (Eds.), *Information systems and qualitative research* (246–275). London: Chapman & Hall.

Ruhleder, K., & Jordan, B. (1999). Meaning-making across remote sites: How delays in transmission affect interaction. In S. Bodker, M. Kyng, & K. Schmidt (Eds.), *Proceedings of the Sixth European Conference on Computer-Supported Cooperative Work* (pp. 411–427). Cophenhagen, Denmark: Kluwer Academic Dordrecht.

Ruhleder, K., & Twidale, M. (2000). Reflective collaborative learning on the Web: Drawing on the master class [Online]. *First Monday, 5*(5). Available: http://www.firstmonday.org/issues/issue5_5/ruhleder/index.html

Sacks, H., Schegloff, E, & Jefferson, G. (1974). A simplest semantics for the organization of turn-taking for conversation. *Language, 50,* 696–735.

Sproull, L., & Kiesler, S. (1991). *Connections: New ways of working in the networked organization.* Cambridge, MA: MIT Press.

Visser, J. A. (2000). Faculty work in developing and teaching Web-based distance courses: A case study of time and effort. *American Journal of Distance Education, 14*(3), 21–32.

5

Enabling New Forms of Online Engagement: Challenges for E-learning Design and Research

Mark Schlager

SRI International

OVERCOMING CONSTRAINTS AND ACHIEVING PEDAGOGICAL GOALS

Web-based distance learning researchers, technology designers, and practitioners (i.e., course developers and instructors) have been on a quest to construct online environments that satisfy a wide range of cognitive, pedagogical, motivational, and social goals while overcoming a range of practical constraints (e.g., temporal, geographical, technological, financial, and organizational). The U.S. Department of Education program that sponsored the symposium leading up to this volume—Learning Anytime, Anywhere—conveys one category of goals: overcoming practical constraints of temporal or geographical copresence, or both. The focus is to design environments that (a) increase the availability of learning experiences to learners who cannot or (for many reasons) choose not to attend traditional face-to-face offerings, (b) assemble and disseminate instructional content more cost-efficiently, or (c) enable instructors to handle a larger number of students. These goals are justifiable in their own right, and technology designers, as reflected in this volume, have done an excellent job building delivery platforms to meet those goals. At one end of the continuum are technologies that support asynchronous communication only, such as threaded discussion boards and newsgroups, which enable users to contribute at their own convenience (e.g., Duffy & Kirkley, Chap. 6, this volume; Shea, Fredrickson, & Pickett, Chap. 14, this volume). At the other end are technologies designed to recreate copresent teaching strategies, such as delivering lectures and holding discussions with both large and small groups of students (e.g., Webcasting, whiteboards, chat rooms, and desktop video technology, which are used to deliver lectures and hold discussions with large and small groups of students; e.g., Ruhleder, Chap. 4, this volume; Polin, Chap. 2, this volume).

A second category of goals is aimed at developing sociotechnical structures and pedagogical strategies that use the unique affordances of online environments to enhance the quality of learning experiences and outcomes. The primary goal is to apply

Web-based distance learning technology in ways that maximize cognitive, social, and motivational benefits.[1] Some of this work is theoretically grounded, and much more is based on the experience and intuitions of creative practitioners. A common theme is that effective learning of a complex body of knowledge involves a community of learners engaged in multiple collective and individual activities, such as formal composition and informal conversation, lecturing and coaching, reflecting and critiquing (Bransford, Brown, & Cocking, 1999). Designing distance learning environments that support this set of goals has been much more difficult than overcoming temporal and geographical constraints, because of differences in student populations, subject domains, and pedagogical preferences as much as technological challenges. The diversity of papers in this volume alone attests to the number and complexity of issues that must be addressed, the gaps that still exist among the researcher, designer, and practitioner communities, and the sometimes conflicting goals that work in this area tries to satisfy.

The "Holy Grail" of this quest is, of course, a system that satisfies both sets of goals (and others, such as easy authoring and reuse of content). But does the grail actually exist? Distance education is rife with attempts to justify severely constraining pedagogical approaches, such as courses that are conducted entirely via asynchronous postings or streaming video lectures, in terms of metacognitive (more reflective than . . .), social (more participative than . . .), and motivational benefits (more feeling of presence than . . .) when the systems they use were designed primarily to overcome practical constraints, not to satisfy theoretically grounded pedagogical goals.

Efforts by researchers and creative practitioners to design and implement innovative pedagogical and social strategies have been hampered by distance learning systems that are not flexible enough to adapt to the subtleties of diverse learning styles and innovative pedagogies. Programs that are able to show significant learning outcomes are often criticized as one-time solutions that cannot be replicated (e.g., it works with you running the program, but our faculty would never do that); as heavy on social affordances but light on content (e.g., sure, the students learn to form strong bonds and support one another, but are they learning the content?); or as not "anywhere-anytime-any-number" enough (e.g., sure, it works for a small program, but we have thousands of students!). Thus, it is encouraging to see distance learning approaches that blend synchronous and asynchronous, high- and low-bandwidth discourse, and formal and informal group and individual activities to achieve pedagogical goals rather than approaches that strictly adhere to technologically driven pedagogical conventions. Such was the feeling I got when I read Karen Ruhleder's and Linda Polin's chapters, in this volume.

The LEEP master's degree program is the result of empirical implementation and refinement over several years (and Ruhleder acknowledges that continued refinement is necessary). The overarching objective of the LEEP online program is to extend a successful face-to-face program to students whose schedule or location makes it difficult to participate in the face-to-face program (because of practical constraints) while enhancing the quality of the learning experience. The designers of the LEEP program (if not the LEEP technology) were clearly interested in the quality of the learning experience at least as much as the constraints of time and distance. I encourage the reader to note the innovative blend of strategies and modes of interaction, for example, the role of face-to-face events and the flow of synchronous and asynchronous communication

---

[1]The field has not yet reached consensus on what combinations of activity structures make up "high-quality" learning processes or how to assess "high-quality" learning outcomes, regardless of whether the learning takes place online or in conventional classrooms.

over time. Contrary to conventional wisdom, that online courses requiring synchronous interaction are overly burdensome for faculty and students, LEEP has been very successful in attracting, retaining, and graduating students, with its blend of online and face-to-face strategies.

Yet, I struggled with the section of Ruhleder's chapter that described the primary pedagogical strategy—weekly lecture and discussion meetings using audio Webcasting and chat technology—and the quality of dialogue that it fostered. More than once, I found myself asking, "Why did Ruhleder and her colleagues design the system to do that?" only to recall that Ruhleder and her colleagues had little control over the technologies they were using. Here was a classic case of a distance learning program attempting to hold to deeply felt social and pedagogical principles while struggling to make the best use of a technological platform that was clearly not designed for the task. The result was an online experience that had both positive and clearly negative aspects from the perspectives of the instructor and students.

UNDERSTANDING THE LEEP LECTURE–CHAT STRATEGY

Ruhleder does an excellent job of documenting the combined effects of technology-mediated communication and the unique pedagogical strategy of concurrent lecture (via audio) and group discussion (via chat). The analysis is careful to document both the desirable and not so desirable effects of the strategy. One question that came to mind was: Does this combination of pedagogy and technology lead to effective learning outcomes? If so, must we take the desired effects with the undesired? Can we keep what is good and prune away what is not? For example, Ruhleder argues that one affordance of the technology is that students can engage in conversation without interrupting the instructor; yet most of the transcripts appear to show repeated disruptions.

To understand the implications of Ruhleder's paper, I needed to understand how the LEEP instructors arrived at the concurrent lecture (audio) and group discussion (chat) strategy. It couldn't be that the technology enforced this strategy only. I was able to come up with several other pedagogical variations that would use the same technology (described later). Nor was it clear to me that this was an optimal strategy. There were too many problems that came out in the transcripts, so, I constructed the following story (which, I hope isn't too far off the mark).

One key factor in understanding the success of the LEEP program is its understanding of, and sensitivity to, its students. LEEP recognizes that its student population is different in important ways from other student populations. The program is a graduate program involving practitioners of a specific profession—library science. Because many of the students are practicing LIS professionals, the students are viewed as having a great deal of practical knowledge, professional interpersonal skills, and expertise that they can share with one another. As professionals, we can also expect that they have developed effective social norms for engaging in meaningful dialogue.

We might contrast the LEEP student population with high school advanced placement (AP) students or undergraduate English literature majors. Would the same strategies work for all three populations? Would the same social norms of engagement apply? My answer to both questions was no. Although we might give professionals taking a course free rein to raise and discuss the topics of their choosing, we might want to have more instructor control over the AP or literature class. Of course, all good instructors want their students to engage in "reflective" dialogue. The design issue here is the degree of structure required and how best to achieve it.

Most online courses for undergraduate and high school populations use well-structured asynchronous tools as the communication backbone (e.g., WebCT, Blackboard, and other course management systems). The LEEP program went in a different direction. Based on the backgrounds of the students, LEEP established the goal of enabling students to freely interact with one another through frequent unstructured dialogue, primarily in real time (synchronous). Thus, it is uncertain whether the design implications would apply to graduate-level programs that currently rely primarily on asynchronous communication and whether the lessons generalize beyond graduate-level programs.

Another key driver of the LEEP pedagogical approach appears to be sensitivity toward the teaching styles of the faculty. It was difficult for me to discern the backgrounds of the faculty from the paper. Were they technologically sophisticated radical constructivists (like the Pepperdine faculty described in Polin's chapter) or more traditional stand-and-deliver instructors? My guess was that they were, at least at first, more the latter. The LEEP faculty clearly felt a need for regularly scheduled lectures. Thus, it appeared that a second pedagogical goal of the LEEP program was to enable instructors to deliver lectures.

So, my thought experiment derived two design goals—support lectures and support free dialogue—that on the surface appear, if not conflicting, at least different enough so that a designer would not attempt to achieve both with the same concurrent pedagogical strategy. In most traditional courses, lectures are followed by a recitation or study group discussion. Instead, LEEP chose a pedagogical strategy in which two teaching strategies—lectures and discussions—go on concurrently (with the added degree of difficulty that the dialogue occurs in two modalities competing for the same cognitive resources).

I had seen this format used effectively in Webcasts, in which a speaker or panel talk via an audio channel and audience members engage in text-based chat. In those sessions, the speaker may take questions (usually funneled through a moderator, but I had never seen a situation in which the speaker was expected to pay close attention to the chat while speaking). As Ruhleder points out, this is a significant change from how face-to-face classes operate. Moreover, it is a significant change from how most online courses operate, flying in the face of conventional distance learning wisdom in (at least) two ways:

- Conventional wisdom says that in online courses, asynchronous communication should be the dominant mode of interaction because of its purported "reflective" and time-flexibility benefits. Ruhleder's data and interviews with instructors and students indicate the opposite. They prefer more synchronous interaction.
- Conventional wisdom says that during disembodied online lectures, people tune out, read e-mail, or get a sandwich. One thing is certain from the LEEP transcripts: The LEEP program has found a very interesting way to promote online dialogue during lectures.

Were the designers of LEEP crazy to go against convention or "crazy like a fox"? What we have in LEEP is a solution to a unique combination of participant needs, pedagogical goals, and available technology that leads to certain type of experience. LEEP has, in fact, accomplished its design goal. It has a program that encourages a great deal of interaction among students. The students (at least some—we are not told what percentage of them engage in chat discussions) appear to enjoy and derive benefit from the ability to hold side conversations as a lecture is being given (haven't we all had that experience in the back of a conference hall?). And the instructors do not seem to mind their extra cognitive load—or do they?

ASSESSING THE AUDIO LECTURE–CHAT DISCUSSION STRATEGY

As I read the transcripts, I began to "feel the pain" of the lecturer trying to deliver a lecture, diagnose errors in the students' comments, respond to the students' questions, and add depth to side conversations (all the while having technical problems). The instructor must lecture aloud and read at the same time; she or he must gauge when to stop talking and shift gears to engage in an ongoing conversation that may not be going where she or he would like it to go. From the interview clips and transcripts, I also felt the confusion and frustration of some of the students struggling with whether to listen, read, or talk; of discerning when it is reasonable to spin off their own conversation while not risking missing a point made by the instructor.

From my own substantial online experience, I have no doubt that participants improve at this hybrid form of engagement over time, but aren't there other ways to achieve the same goals without all the problems? For example, Ruhleder indicates that the LEEP lectures are recorded. One solution, then, could have been to record the lectures in advance, require students to listen to it offline at their convenience, and then discuss it in groups facilitated by the instructor. Another variation would have been to record the lectures in advance and then listen to and discuss it in real time with the instructor turning on and off the recording at key points (e.g., Sipusic, Pannoni, Smith, Dutra, Gibbons, & Sutherland, 1999). Both of these approaches may have enabled the instructor to participate more effectively in the discussions than the concurrent lecture–discussion strategy. An even simpler solution would be if the instructor insisted that the chat may be used only for questions to the instructor or only to respond to a question asked by the instructor—same technology, different pedagogical norms. Would the learning experience and the learning outcomes be significantly different—better or worse?

In some respects, Ruhleder's paper is warning online technology and instructional designers: Be careful what you wish for, you may get it! Designers can engineer situations that break down traditional rules of social engagement (i.e., the instructor lectures and the students listen) and encourage new ones (i.e., the instructor lectures while the students discuss), but are the new rules any better than the old? When LEEP students are having their own conversation, are they missing important points that the instructor is trying to get across? Do students actually go back and review the recording to get what they missed? Do certain students tend to dominate conversation? Do the conversations distract other students from the lecture? What proportion of assertions that are factually or conceptually inaccurate are taken as truth by others? How much lecture material is never covered at all by the instructor?

Analyzing transcripts alone is not sufficient to answer these questions. We need to know not only what is going on during the sessions; clearly there is a lot of dialogue in the LEEP sessions (which is generally considered a good thing). We need to know what is retained by the participants (e.g., lecture facts, and comments and assertions by other students); what meaning is given to the information (e.g., do students distinguish supposition from fact, or comments made by the instructor versus other students); how knowledge is used later in the course (e.g., in subsequent discourse and work samples); and how the particular session fits in the larger context of the community of participants.

These questions are important in any learning context, but they take on special significance when we set out to design new forms of online engagement, especially when they require participants to use multiple, concurrent sensory and cognitive channels. As in medicine, an e-learning designer's code of ethics must start with: First, do no harm. But how can we know if certain forms of online engagement cause harm to the learning experience? Chances are, we would not be able to detect the adverse effects using traditional measures, such as grades or student work artifacts. For example, it would be difficult to trace a student's mistaking an inaccurate supposition by another student as fact back to the instructor's inability to detect and correct the erroneous supposition because she was busy lecturing and could not concurrently keep track of the chat dialogue. In such a case, I would argue, the fault is not with the student or the instructor, but with the form of online engagement. I would argue that the same inability to detect adverse effects holds true for pedagogically constraining form of online engagement, such as those enforced by strictly asynchronous e-learning systems. Students do get good grades in asynchronous online courses (so they must be learning the content, right?), but what are they not getting by being deprived of other (synchronous online or face-to-face) forms of social discourse with other students and instructors? We simply do not know.

How, then, can we research the relative effects of different forms of online engagement on students (and instructors)? A view shared by several of the participants at the Learning Anytime Anywhere Program symposium was that the field simply does not have analytical frameworks and tools to answer the questions previously raised in both an effective and efficient manner. I offer no ready solutions. My colleagues and I (as well as other researchers represented in this volume; see also Barab, Kling, & Gray, in press; Dede, Whitehouse, & Brown-L'Bahy, 2002) are attempting to develop convergent analytical methods that we hope will help address these issues. In closing, I give a brief introduction to our work in an effort to spur further dialogue on methods for researching online learning processes and outcomes. I encourage the reader who is interested in more details to see Gray and Tatar (in press) and Tatar, Gray, and Fusco (2002), from which much of the discussion below is drawn.

TOWARD A FRAMEWORK FOR RESEARCHING AND IMPROVING ONLINE LEARNING

Traditionally, online communication has been studied either through the mechanisms provided by the system—transcripts of interactions (Baym, 1997; Bruckman, 1998; Cherny, 1999; Herring, 1999)—through ethnography (Gray, 1999; O'Day, Ito, Linde, Adler, & Mynatt, 1999), or by using both approaches. Ethnographic description gives us the big picture but may overlook influential but unmemorable background factors. In our own studies (Schlager, Fusco, & Schank, 2002), we have used transcript data to understand how groups of teachers and professional development staff became progressively more adept at engaging in online meetings in the Tapped In online community environment (Schlager, Fusco, & Schank, 1998; Schlager & Schank, 1997). As the participants' facility with the technology and modes of online engagement increased, so did the productivity and efficiency of the meetings. We were able to show that after participants acclimated to the online environment, meetings exhibited the same proportions of business-oriented, social, and group management dialogue as commonly found in face-to-face business meetings.

The study also documented the important ways that face-to-face and online meetings differ. Whereas in conversation and interaction analysis there is a core assumption that the participants are experts in the communicative system and that we may therefore treat their behaviors as finely tuned performances, we cannot assume such accomplished expertise in online interaction. For example, in face-to-face meetings, there are visual and auditory cues and social taboos that prevent people from talking over one another, ignoring a question, or holding unrelated conversations. New ways to accomplish these meeting management and facilitation norms online had to be learned over time before the group could work at peak efficiency. The implications for online courses that subject students and instructors to new technology and rules of engagement are clear: Participants may never reach a level of facility that is needed to focus on learning rather than the mode of interaction.

However, we have come to recognize that transcripts alone do not give us enough information about the meaning of online events for the participants. To understand and appreciate the activity that constitutes learning, we must understand the meaning of communication as situated in its context. For example, Tatar, Gray, and Fusco (2002) suggest that many background factors could contribute to the ability to engage in effective discourse in synchronous, text-based online seminars. These factors include the codification of the seminar structure, the presence of a facilitator who fields technological and procedural problems, the technological and pedagogical experience of the leader, the experience of the participants with the system, and whether participation is voluntary or required.

Consequently, we have expanded our analytical framework to include personal, interpersonal, and community aspects of the sociotechnical systems within which learning experiences occur (Rogoff, Baker-Sennett, Lacasa, & Goldsmith, 1995). The personal plane of analysis focuses on how individuals change through involvement in sociocultural activity. This perspective leads us to ask questions about the relationship between the long-term aims of the individuals, how participants' identity shapes their online participation, and how that participation in turn shapes their identity. The interpersonal plane focuses on how people communicate and coordinate their activities. This perspective leads to questions about the processes that are involved in engagement, understanding, and meaning making. Who is able to participate in different aspects of discussions and to what effect? Do people have a sense of what behaviors are appropriate and useful at different points in time? When someone makes a comment, do others understand the point or force of the comment in an appropriately contextualized way? The community plane of analysis (Wenger, 1998) focuses on people participating with others in a culturally organized activity, leading us to ask questions about what the participants know about one another coming into the learning encounter, their relative status in the group, and the social norms and conceptual tools they share.

To address issues particular to online communication, learning, and community, we add the technology plane of analysis, which focuses on how technology mediates activities at each of the other planes. Although the design of a technology may afford various kinds of interactions, it does not guarantee them. Rather, interactions are determined by factors in all four planes—the personal goals of the individuals involved, their interpersonal history and relationships, the prevailing cultural models of communication shared by participants, and the communicative affordances of the technology.

Over the past year, we have developed a method for looking at both behaviors and the meaning that the behaviors have for the participants in synchronous online interactions. Our method focuses on the investigation of specific focal events, which are used as the central organizing occasion for data gathering. We select events because they represent situations that are either known to be problematic in the face-to-face world or because they have particular importance for learning. By picking a focal event, we are able to gather data from several sources about how a particular group of people came to be assembled, what those people think about the activity that they caused to happen, and their more general experiences in the learning environment.

Our major methodological innovation is to combine the internal analysis of the events (transcripts and artifacts) with participant accounts of the interaction (phone interviews conducted as soon after the event as possible) and patterns of interaction outside the chosen event (log-in, chat, and asynchronous posting records). The interviews constitute a "focused ethnography" in which we ask not only about the participants' general views and identity, but also about their memory and understanding of particular events and bits of dialogue. In this way, we combine behavior, reflection on that behavior, and more general attitudinal and affective information. We are as interested in what people dismiss as in what they value. Sometimes, participants mention these events themselves in the course of answering general questions, such as "What happened in the session?" Sometimes, we prompt them by describing the situation and reading from the transcript. Participants' memory for events and attitudes toward events is not always veridical. However, our interest is in the subjective ways in which each participant constructs meaning. Whenever possible, we also collect data regarding previous interactions among participants and with others outside the core group. Social network analysis (Wellman, 1997) enables us to position specific interactions in the broader context of relationships and activities that take place within a community over time. Knowledge of previous social interaction among the participants is important not only in illuminating individual relationships, interactions, expertise, and attitudes, but also in delineating the kind of sociality we are talking about when we describe the focal event.

We do not assume a one-to-one correspondence between the types of data we gather and the conclusions we draw. For example, information about the social network of the participants comes in part from activity records in the system and in part from self-reports during the interview. Evidence about the meaning of discourse is drawn partly from actual discourse and partly from interview-based recollections. Tatar, Gray, and Fusco (2002) and Gray and Tatar (in press) examine the same online event, illustrating our methodologically interwoven approach to understanding processes of learning and development in relation to multiple contexts. Tatar, Gray, and Fusco (2002) introduce our approach and the particular event from which we gathered our data. They offer an analysis of a particular interaction between the event leader and a participant in the session, and the meaning of the interaction for the two actors and the other participants. Gray and Tatar (in press) draw on sociocultural theory and use ethnographically oriented case study methods to highlight the interconnections between online and offline contexts in the professional trajectory of another participant in the event. The study addresses how learning and development occur in computer-mediated environments, and how these processes may compare and contrast with similar processes in traditional offline cultural settings.

Our work is proof that convergent methods based on different planes of analysis can lead to a deeper understanding of online learning than we can expect from the same methods alone, but we acknowledge that we are still in the early stages of developing and testing this set of techniques. We would welcome a Learning Anytime Anywhere Program symposium that focuses on frameworks and analytical methods, so that our field can continue to build consensus on the methods and metrics used to understand and assess forms of engagement and environments that are intended to support learning at a distance.

ACKNOWLEDGMENTS

This research was supported by the National Science Foundation through grants to SRI International (REC-9720384 and REC-9725528). I am grateful to Tom Duffy and Jamie Kirkley for inviting me to participate in the symposium and for their insightful comments on drafts of this chapter. I am indebted to my colleagues Deb Tatar, Judi Fusco, and Jim Gray for demonstrating that clarity, depth, and focus can emerge from three different views of the (online) world.

REFERENCES

Barab, S., Kling, R., & Gray, J. (in press). *Designing for virtual communities in the service of learning.* New York: Cambridge University Press.

Baym, N. K. (1997). Interpreting soap operas and creating community: Inside an electronic fan culture. In S. Keisler (Ed.), *Culture of the Internet* (pp. 103–120). Mahwah, NJ: Lawrence Earlbaum Associates.

Bransford, J., Brown, A., & Cocking, R. (Eds.). (1999). *How people learn: Brain, mind, experience, and school.* Washington, DC: National Academy Press.

Bruckman, A. (1998). *Community support for constructionist learning. CSCW, 7:47–86.*

Cherny, L. (1999). *Conversation and community: Chat in a virtual world.* Stanford, CA: CSLI.

Dede, C., Whitehouse, P., & Brown-L'Bahy, T. b (2002). Designing and studying learning experiences that use multiple interactive media to bridge distance and time. In C. Vrasidas & G. V. Glass (Eds.), *Current perspectives on applied information technologies: Vol. 1. Distance education* (pp. 1–30). Greenwich, CN: Information Age Press.

Gray, J. (1999). *Understanding online peers: Sociocultural and media processes among young adolescent students in the United States.* Unpublished doctoral dissertation, Harvard University, Cambridge, MA.

Gray, J., & Tatar, D. (in press). Sociocultural analysis of online professional development: A case study of personal, interpersonal, community, and technical aspects. In S. A. Barab, R. Kling, & J. Gray (Eds.), *Designing for virtual communities in the service of learning.* Cambridge, UK: Cambridge University Press.

Herring, S. (1999). Interactional coherence in CMC. Journal of computer-mediated communication 4(4). http://www.ascusc.org/jcmc/vol4/issue4

O'Day, V. L., Ito, M., Linde, C., Adler, A., & Mynatt, E. D. (1999). Cemeteries, oak trees, and black-and-white cows: Learning to participate on the Internet. In C. Hoadley (Ed.), *Computer support for collaborative learning* (pp. 360–367). Hillsdale, NJ: Lawrence Erlbaum Associates.

Rogoff, B., Baker-Sennett, Lacasa, P., & Goldsmith, D. (1995, Spring). Development through participation in sociocultual activity. In J. J. Goodnow, P. J. Miller, & F. Kessel (Eds.), *Cultural practices as contexts for development, 67.* (pp. 45–65). San Francisco: Jossey-Bass.

Schlager, M. S., Fusco, J., & Schank, P. (1998). Cornerstones for an online community of education professionals. *IEEE Technology and Society, 17*(40), 15–21.

Schlager, M., Fusco, J., & Schank, P. (2002). Evolution of an online education community of practice. In K. A. Renninger & W. Shumar (Eds.), *Building virtual communities: Learning and change in cyberspace* (pp. 129–158). New York: Cambridge University Press.

Schlager, M. S., & Schank, P. K. (1997). Tapped In: A new online teacher community concept for the next generation of Internet technology. In R. Hall, N. Miyake, & N. Enyedy (Eds.). *Proceedings of CSCL '97, the Second International Conference on Computer Support for Collaborative Learning* (pp. 230–241). Hillsdale, NJ: Lawrence Erlbaum Associates.

Sipusic, M. J., Pannoni, R. L., Smith, R. B., Dutra, J., Gibbons, J. F., & Sutherland, W. R. (1999). *Virtual collaborative learning: A comparison of face-to-face tutored video instruction (TVI) and distributed tutored video instruction (DTVI)* (Report No. SMLI TR-99-72). Palo Alto, CA: Sun Microsystems.

Tatar, D., Gray, J., & Fusco, J. (2002). Rich social interaction in an online community for learning. In G. Stahl (Ed.), *Proceedings of the Computer Support for Collaborative Learning Conference* (pp. 633–634). Mahwah NJ: Lawrence Erlbaum Associates.

Wellman, B. (1997). An electronic group is virtually a social network. In S. Keisler (Ed.), *Culture of the Internet* (pp. 179–205). Mahwah, NJ: Lawrence Erlbaum Associates.

Wenger, E. (1998). *Communities of practice: Learning, meaning, and identity.* New York: Cambridge University Press.

Open Discussion of Chapter 4

Bob Wisher: Let me start off with a question about the chat environment. In the chapter, you say one affordance of the technology is that students can engage in conversations without interrupting the instructor, but most of the transcripts appear to show disruptions. Are these representative? And, of course, there is the whispering factor—students can whisper, and we don't hear anything about that.

Karen Ruhleder: No one monitors whispers, and no one would give us permission to. We have no idea as to the amount of back channel discussion between students. The chat can be disruptive, but at the same time it provides an indication to the instructor of how well the students understand. In particular, the students' answers to each other's questions provide that "understanding" feedback for the instructor and permit midcourse corrections. But, of course, you are right—this is a difficult environment for both students and faculty.

Peter Shea: When you talk about the complexity of the technologies and the difficulty that instructors could have in sustaining interaction and participating in what is a simultaneous audio–text–chat environment, I was wondering who the heck could do this? What students are able to do this? Can you talk a little bit about the background of the students?

Karen Ruhleder: They are all highly educated, and about 50% are from out of state. We have network administrators from Alaska; we have children's librarians. We have the best set of students you could possibly want for a distance education program in that most already have higher education experience—they all have a bachelor's degree, most have a masters', and some have a doctorate. They are almost all working in libraries where salaries are low, so they come with all this intelligence and motivation.

Peter Shea: And you guys almost have a corner on the market—you are the crème de la crème of the online libraries.

Karen Ruhleder: That's what I was pointing out. I'm not sure if anybody here really buys those *U.S. News and World Report* rankings, but we have been number one for a long time. It really means something to people. It's something they can cite as a reason to attend.

Peter Shea: So you get the best students in the best program. No wonder they can use this technology.

Mark Schlager: Karen, could you talk a bit about the technology choices. You started the program with a MOO environment but then switched to the current technology. What motivated you to change the format. Was somebody complaining?

Karen Ruhleder: We didn't choose the technology that we used—it was someone else's technology. After the first year, our technical staff wanted something in house, so the tech staff chose what we are using now. I would be willing to say that while all of the faculty care about teaching, nobody cares about taking on another committee that sets guidelines on technology. We do not live in a world where the faculty sit around and discuss and describe strategies they want implemented. We know the technology is not ideal in some ways, and we care, but not enough to do something about it in the face of other things that we care about. This ended up as kind of a compromise between wanting to have free interaction and wanting to hear a voice. It's not a very good pedagogical answer, but it's a practical answer. And from that perspective, I might note that all of our online classes are duplicated in the face-to-face program, and that's a pretty good program. And students in the online program end up doing work that's no worse than that.

Terry Anderson: Karen, did I hear that most of the faculty in your program are adjuncts?

Karen Ruhleder: Well, not most overall. In summer, we have almost 100%. During the year, it is mostly regular faculty, but we also use adjuncts because we cannot cover classes in some traditional library areas. So we do tend to have the adjuncts, and they tend to be practitioners in those areas. The problem this presents is what Linda said earlier: Our adjuncts are very limited in what they can do in these classes because many have a limited technology infrastructure. We don't always know what kind of computer they have locally, so it's a whole pot of issues with quality monitoring. We have been pretty successful in building a group of adjuncts who are reliable, who do research in the field, and who have taught at least one class. So they are strong adjuncts but not necessarily in terms of technology.

Sally Johnstone: If you do not address some policy issues, you could be seeing some problems with the way you are using adjuncts in this capacity. It makes tremendous sense to do so—it's a more flexible workforce for what you are doing because your program is not a campus system. But it does mean that the issues you have raised with regard to having adjuncts as a teaching population, particularly within a very traditional setting that you're using, need to be addressed. What are the quality control systems that are in place to review their performance? Have you developed an equitable compensation system? There are models out there. There are a lot of institutions that have been doing this for a long time and have policies in place for how they gauge the quality of adjunct populations. You may want to look at the open universities around the world or some of the institutions that have developed in an exclusively online environment.

Karen Ruhleder: We also have a lot of adjuncts speaking on campus. I taught library administration for a number of years despite the fact that I've never administered a library. So is it better to have the adjunct? I would rather have the adjunct! So I could actually have someone that knows something about it.

Sally Johnstone: What is the tuition policy for out-of-state students.

Karen Ruhleder: It's out-of-state.

Sally Johnstone: So the cost to them is the out-of-state tuition, which is usually substantial, as well as the cost of coming to the campus at least once a semester.

Karen Ruhleder: Yes, but some are in organizations that will often pick up part of these costs.

Jim Botkin: Is this seen as a net revenue generator for you? Increasing the out-of-state enrollments should help the model. And why not? What should be wrong with that? A business would expand.

Karen Ruhleder: We get the money for it, but it's also very expensive. It's self sustaining—we have stopped losing money.

Tom Duffy: There should also be pressure to not recruit out-of-state students. At IU at least, there is pressure to serve the students of the state.

Jenny Franklin: I have two questions—the first is a very quick one. These are two programs that rely heavily on adjuncts, and adjunct faculty are really doing sort of piece work. Coming from a unionized campus, I am concerned and wondering if adjuncts have noticed they are doing more piecework than their colleagues doing face-to-face classes.

Second, in thinking about the curriculum, I'd like to know more about how the faculty collaborate and if there is some process for looking at outcome data, student outcomes specifically, and at the choices you're making in the design of the course. When I observe course curriculum planning sessions, I typically see them as driven by convention, that is, the curriculum is based on the conceived wisdom of "this is how we teach this subject." But this is likely very different from how people are integrating this knowledge and where a planning session focused on integration might go. It would seem that there must be some anchor in strategies to understand what you're students will be able to do. So I wonder if your faculty have some sort of active inquiry cycle where they are learning and making choices that interact with the curriculum design at the content and course level, as well as the delivery strategy.

Karen Ruhleder: The first question is an easy one. We also have the best population you could want for adjuncts, because we tend to get people who have full-time jobs in libraries and feel it is a privilege to teach in our program. They may like the extra money. They are generally not doing it for the money, because they tend to be full-time salaried personnel somewhere. We have had a few people teaching who are doctoral students somewhere, but they are the exception. I think that is one of the reasons that we do not have the same adjunct problem, because they want to do it again, and they are highly qualified to be teachers.

I don't know how to answer the second question, because we have a much more pragmatic approach to curriculum. We have a curriculum committee that oversees it. We have had a faculty retreat about who are we as a school. The big issue to us is not how to design specific courses. It is all part of a bigger question of who are we now as an LIS field. The curriculum is part of that bigger question. We talked a few years ago about getting rid of the traditional boundaries between public libraries and academic libraries and this and that, and talking more broadly about what we want people to learn about managing information, understanding information, and so on, and how to structure the program where we have courses that address these different conceptual approaches. But I don't think that we do the kind of work that you mean, where, for instance, we would structure a set of courses to interlock.

Jenny Franklin: Does the curriculum committee actually review student learning outcomes data in making those curriculum decisions?

Karen Ruhleder: I have no idea. I don't think so.

Linda Polin: This is related to the comments you and Sally made. One of the things that strikes me is that there seems to be a cultural difference in how you approach online teaching in that you seem to feel more responsible to care for the students online than face-to-face. In a face-to-face, if a student is not participating, then screw him, that's his problem. But online, it's my problem: "Where's Bob—he hasn't been on for two weeks," and where is his paper and all that. The tradition of face-to-face is, "I'm there, I do my thing, you take notes, and we'll see what happens. "I'm not sure if it's our anxieties about whether distance education is good enough or are we just helping—and God forbid if too many kids drop out. It strikes me that I hear a lot of deep concern about how kids are doing.

Tom Duffy: I think it rests in the fact that when you go online, you've got a lot of material online, and now what's my role as an instructor? In fact, what is an online class if students aren't talking?

Linda Polin: That's kind of the reconceptualization of the role of faculty.

Tom Duffy: Yes, it forces that reconceptualization.

Carson Eoyang: I would like to say thank you to both Karen and Mark for puncturing the academic conceit that our students' sole motivation is to hang on to every word and that our words are so eloquent as to elicit their attention. I think we now recognize that multitasking is the norm rather than the exception. After all, how many windows do you have open on that computer? Don't we all multitask most of the time—we're writing while we're listening, reading while we're eating, showering while we're reflecting. I think if we now focus more on the learning design as the engineering of the tension, it raises some interesting design questions, such as designing lectures as experiences—sequence, tempo, emphasis, volume.

John Bransford: I thank both of you. I really appreciate your thoughts here. One thing—your use of the Excel spreadsheets to find outliers—one use of it is that one of my colleagues in engineering is doing this. He has created what he calls knowbots. So if the student is an outlier and has not responded, for example, he sends an e-mail on behalf of the professor, "Hey are you feeling ok? I noticed you haven't talked," and this kind of thing has a huge effect. It absolutely changes all kinds of things. So you could add that to your database.

Second, this whole idea of tending toward a community online more than face-to-face. One of the things I have discovered is how easy it is to fake ourselves out face-to-face that things are going okay. I cotaught a course on cognition and culture with Xiadong Lin. It's a very diverse course. So I am just pleased as punch that by the third week everything is just going great. Then we instituted an e-mail task where each student has to say on each Friday what is going on. Unbelievable! Below the surface we found people felt cut off, really angry. They said that if they had even come to talk to us face-to-face, they would have cried. So this social distance thing then led us to totally restructure this course. I would have absolutely missed it in the face-to-face. I think we are getting cues in this environment that we may get not otherwise.

Third, one of the issues we know from cognitive sciences whether you can multitask or not depends on what your knowledge base is about what you are doing. So, when you are first learning to drive a car, you cannot carry on a conversation at the same time. If these people are really knowledgeable about the content in a lecture they can multitask, or if they are really good at typing they can multitask, but whether people can do it or not really depends the level of expertise.

Fourth, I hear a lot about "let's get away from the sage on the stage" and that constructivism is not lecture. Actually, I think that is absolutely wrong. I think constructivism is a theory of how we know. We construct new knowledge based on what we already know. It is not a theory of pedagogy. There are some times when the most powerful way to learn is to have a sage on the stage come in. It's only if you are prepared in certain ways, but all communities, or most communities of practice, in fact, revere the sage on the stage if they choose when the sage come, in to solve a problem that they already want to solve. So I think it is important.

Tom Duffy: I agree.

Bob Wisher: I was caught by your comment that your on-campus students perceive that they work much harder than the remote students. I wonder if there are any obvious explanations.

Karen Ruhleder: I think it is the other way around.

Bob Wisher: The other way around?

Karen Ruhleder: The big difference here is that LEEP students have more experience but often have more constraints. A lot of them have full-time jobs, families—other responsibilities. They want to be able to really structure what they do and when they do it, but they work really intensely and have a lot of practical experience to draw on. Maybe they have another graduate degree already, maybe they've already done report writing and grant writing. On-campus, you have a lot of students who got a bachelor's degree pretty recently. They're full-time students, they're getting their first real library experience as a graduate assistant. Grad school is what they are doing on their way to something else, but a lot of LEEPers have already gotten somewhere and are improving on it. That's a bit of an overgeneralization, but these differences really do affect how students work together in a group or a class.

(End of session)

III

Problem-Centered Learning

6

Learning Theory and Pedagogy Applied in Distance Learning: The Case of Cardean University[1]

Thomas M. Duffy and Jamie R. Kirkley
Indiana University

In the past decade, education and training has seen incredible growth in Web-based learning. From corporate training to higher education, many institutions are now providing online courses and modules so learners can gain access to education anytime and anywhere there is an Internet connection. Currently, more than 50,000 university courses are taught online, and more than 1,000 universities are developing and offering these courses (Carnavale, 2000; National Center for Education Statistics, 1999). Corporations are also embracing the Web for instructional delivery. From 1996 to 1998, the proportion of companies using their intranet for training increased from 3.5% to 33.2% (ASTD career center, 2001), and nearly all of the Fortune 100 companies already offer some form of online computer-based training (Herther, 1997).

The surge in Web-based education reflects the institutional goals of meeting the needs of those who cannot come to campus, capturing a larger share of the education market, seeking to survive in the education market, or reducing education and training costs. However, in these distance learning initiatives the focus, for the most part, has been limited to selecting the "right" technology and transferring courses to the Web. An examination of the literature most often yields personal descriptions of the transfer process and the technology used. The one exception to this has been a focus on how to facilitate discussion on the Web (Collison, Elbaum, Haavind, & Tinker, 2000; Salmon, 2000).

The online environment dramatically impacts teaching methods, so simply importing traditional models of instruction and tacking on discussion is not likely to work. Although we do not share the calls of alarm of those who question the quality of Web-based distance education (e.g., AAUP, 2001), we do agree that the distance environment, just like the campus classroom, must be informed by our best understanding of how people learn (see Bransford, Brown, & Cocking, 2000).

[1] Preparation of this chapter was funded in part by the U.S. Department of Education's Fund for Improvement in Postsecondary Education, Learning Anytime Anywhere Program, grant number P339B990108–01.

The goal of this chapter is to address issues in the real world design and implementation of an online university offering MBA courses. Cardean University is an interesting case study, because it was well financed, was released from many of the constraints of traditional universities, and was committed to educational excellence through the design of courses based on an implementation of constructivist learning theory. But, of course, the world is never so easy. There are real business goals, real world constraints, and the medium of delivery that drive the design and implementation of online learning. In this chapter, we discuss how people learn and our commitment to a constructivist pedagogical stance, how theory is applied through design, and how design and delivery are impacted by real world issues through a case study of Cardean University. The first author served as a vice president and the chief learning officer at Cardean and led the development of the basic course architecture that will be discussed in the chapter. Thus this is a firsthand perspective on the meeting of theory, educational practice, and the business world. Although this provides an up-close and personal view, it is also subject to the biases of the first author's perspective.

We begin with a discussion of a constructivist perspective on how we learn and, in the examination of five pedagogical implications of that stance on learning, how that theory is applied through design. The theory and pedagogical strategies apply to both distance and classroom-based settings; what differs between these contexts are the tactics for achieving the pedagogical goals. Thus, we examine the specific tactics related to taking the pedagogy to the distance learning environment. We then turn to an examination of Cardean University, first examining the design process and then examining how the theory and pedagogical goals were approached in the design. Throughout this discussion, we will identify nine tensions among the pedagogical, practical, and business demands in the design process that led to struggles in making key design decisions.

HOW WE LEARN

Our understanding of how people learn has grown dramatically over the last 20 years. There was a long tradition of understanding learning as knowledge transmission, a process whereby the student processes information provided to him or her and stores it in a network of information (Gardner, 1985). This perspective leads to a focus on the design of content so that it is easy to process, and hence "learn" (Sweller, 2000). It is reflected in the widespread notion that "moving a course to the Web" is a matter of designing the content for the Web. In many of these cases, there is not even a mention of the learners and what they will do (Janicki & Liegle, 2001).

In a seminal article in the field of education, Resnick (1987) offered an alternative perspective, one focused on the goals and activities of the learner rather than on the presentation of content. She pointed to both the active construction of understanding and to the situated nature of understanding as she contrasted learning out of school to what we do with children in school. School learning tends to be individual work, focused on mastery of the text. The student's goal is to pass a test that typically involves the ability to recall or recognize information in the text. In contrast, the out-of-school learning—the learning that individuals do as part of their everyday life—reflects a focus on the use of information outside of the learning context, where collaboration is the norm and where information is a resource to be used rather than mastered.

Resnick's argument that the out-of-school learning reflects the process by which we learn reflects the basic tenets of the two dominant theoretical positions in education today, constructivism and situated cognition.[2] From these perspectives, there is recognition of the active construction of understanding by the learner and of the situated nature of learning. At the most fundamental level, constructivism and situated cognition offer a view of learning as "sense making": Learning is a process of making sense of the world and of seeking useful understanding—an understanding that aids in resolving uncertainty. Constructivism is an action-oriented perspective in that understanding is in the doing. As Barab and Duffy (2000) noted:

a) Knowing refers to an activity, not a thing;
b) Knowing is always contextualized, not abstract;
c) Knowing is reciprocally constructed in the Individual–environment interaction, not objectively defined or subjectively created; and
d) Knowing is a functional stance on interaction—not a truth. (p. 32)

The view of learning as "sense making" is not a pedagogical stance on the way we teach people. Nor is it a proposal that this is the way learning occurs sometimes or in some situations. It is a proposal that this is what learning is all about. Regardless of age, whether we are in school or out, whether we are working adults or traditional college students, or whether learning is online or in the classroom, the process of learning is driven by the learner's goal of making sense of the world and of resolving uncertainty (Brookfield, 1986; Cross, 1992; Knowles, 1984; Piaget, 1932; von Glasersfeld, 1995).

From this perspective, learning resources are just that—resources. Knowledge is not contained in those resources, but rather the knowledge is in the goal-oriented use of those resources in a specific context and for a specific purpose. What is learned is a function of the learner's goals and is impacted by the constraints and affordances of the particular situation. Certainly, we have all had the experience of going back to a book for a different purpose or in a different context (e.g., as an administrator rather than a researcher) and coming away with new understandings of familiar text. As Brown and Duguid (2000) have noted, nurses and physicians read the same documents as do accountants and financial planners, but because of their goals, they come away with different understandings. (Bransford and Johnson, 1972) have amply demonstrated this impact in an experimental setting where students having memorized the punch lines for jokes for one purpose (not knowing they were punch lines) and did not recognize the relevance of these punch lines when presented with the jokes. Similarly, the same paragraph of text can be understood very differently, depending on the perspective with which one approaches the text (Bransford and Schwartz, 2001; Gick and Holyoak, 1983).

Entwistle, Entwistle, and Tait (1991) have demonstrated the same impact of goals in student learning in university courses. In surveys and interviews with students, they found that regardless of the students' goals for taking a class, the testing process determined their study strategy and what they learned. In summarizing their data, they noted, "It might be said that students were, to varying degrees, developing understanding which was situated in the perceived requirements of the examination questions rather than in the discipline or profession, thus restricting the likelihood of ready knowledge transfer to the outside world." (Entwistle, Entwistle, & Tait, 1991, p. 350). Or, as is the common saying to new entrants to the workforce, "You have had your schooling, now it is time to really learn."

---

[2]In this chapter, we will not distinguish between these views. We will simply speak of constructivism to represent these views of learning.

As adults come back to university and as companies send their employees back to school, many adults are seeking understanding that they can apply to their jobs. Indeed, vocational application is one of the three major learner goals expressed by students even 20 years ago (Taylor, 1983). Unfortunately, as Entwistle, Entwistle, and Tait (1991) note, these students will typically encounter a conflict between the demands of the course (e.g., to pass a test) and their goal of being able to use the information outside of school (e.g., use what they have learned at work). But it is not just the vocational linkage that makes this an issue. Certainly, most individuals entering college anticipate that their learning will be usable outside of the classroom context. So what does this mean for the design and implementation of online learning environments?

KEY PEDAGOGICAL GOALS OF A CONSTRUCTIVIST LEARNING ENVIRONMENT

The goal in this section is to discuss five design objectives that we feel are central to the constructivist framework and hence are central in creating inquiry environments. The goals, as outlined in Table 6.1, are to engage and support the student in an inquiry process, which will result in the development of usable knowledge, that is, knowledge that will serve the student outside of the classroom. By inquiry, we mean that the individual is engaged in a domain-relevant issue and is seeking to resolve or gain a richer understanding of that issue. Any assessment process must be in the service of that inquiry. Finally, collaboration can both support the student as learner and provide a mechanism for testing ideas.

These objectives apply whether the learning is at a distance or in the face-to-face classroom. It is when we instantiate these objectives that the learning context becomes critical. Thus, in the discussion that follows, we will discuss each of these goals as they apply in any learning environment, and then we examine how each may be impacted in a distance learning environment.

Engage in Inquiry

Colleges are increasingly attempting to meet the lifelong learning needs of older adults. These students come to a course because the topic and issues have meaning for them, meeting their professional development or general interest needs. They are already engaged in the inquiry and anticipate the course helping their efforts. If the course does not serve their needs, they will leave. Here the task is straightforward: the

TABLE 6.1
Pedagogical Goals for a Constructivist Learning Environment

1. Engage the student in inquiry that will lead to the student's useful understanding of the concepts and skills identified in the course objectives.
2. Provide structure and support to the learners as they engage in goal-oriented inquiry and problem solving.
3. Facilitate interaction, collaboration, and a community-based learning environment.
4. Design an assessment system that is performance oriented, calling for a demonstration of useful understanding.
5. Promote transfer of knowledge to other contexts through reflective activities and diverse experiences.

objectives of the course and the course design are driven by these learner needs. However, in most of our educational environments, there are specified curricular goals, which are typically established by the instructor or the department. There is a professional preparation that is necessary, and thus the courses cannot simply be tailored to the user but must meet these professional or intellectual preparation objectives. However, even with curricular requirements, we can still engage the student in authentic inquiry either by finding the link between the course goals and the student interests or by developing the students' interests in an inquiry that is consistent with the prespecified goals of the course.

Linking to Student Interests

There are several strategies for linking course goals to student interests. Scardamalia and Bereiter (1991) and Bransford and Schwartz (2001) have demonstrated that students often have questions about a subject that are fully consistent with the goals for the course. Simply asking students, before they study, what questions they have about a curriculum topic often yields a list of issues that will meet curricular goals. Capitalizing on those student-generated issues is one strategy for giving ownership while still maintaining the prespecified learning objectives for the course.

Action learning (Revans, 1997) is another strategy for meeting both institutional and individual goals. In the action learning format, institutional goals are sought that are relevant to the individual, and these goals become the drivers of the learning experience. In the corporate environment, this typically involves defining a broad-based problem or issue of future direction that is relevant to a team of employees. Developing strategies for addressing the problem or future then becomes the focus of the course. Service learning and adult functional literacy similarly situate learning in a real world context meaningful to the learner while meeting curricular goals.

Creating Student Interest

It is not always possible to adapt goals to the interests of the learners. In these circumstances, the strategy is to create environments that will create a puzzlement that engages the learner in inquiry activities consistent with the goals of the course. In contrast to the adaptive approach in the previous paragraphs, here the course is designed, but there is a direct effort to engage the learner in an issue that they may not have considered previously. There are many strategies for this: problem-based learning (Barrows, 1992), learning by design (Kolodner, Crismond, Gray, Holbrook, & Puntambekar, 1998), project-based learning (Bloomenfeld, Soloway, Marx, Krajcik, Guzdial, & Palinczor, 1991), case-based learning (Christensen, Hansen, & Moore, 1989), and experiential simulation (Gredler, 1996) environments are some examples. It should be clear that the problem or project is not just a functional one, but may involve creating an intellectual curiosity in some issue, for example, in using the principle of force from physics to understand how roller coasters work or in understanding how drama is created in a film.

Simply confronting the student with an issue is very different from engaging the student in that issue. As Barrows (1992) has argued, it is critical that we "bring the problem home" for the student and help the student establish personal relevance to the problem, issue, or goal. Further, the inquiry will only be sustained if the student has primary responsibility for the process, taking ownership in examining and investigating the issues, as well as proposing a solution. Teachers' interactions and responses should not focus on content, as this takes away student ownership. Rather, the focus is at the metacognitive level, where they model, scaffold, and support student thinking (Savery & Duffy, 1996; Stepien & Gallagher, 1993).

Application to Distance Learning

A distance learning or computer-mediated environment does not change the issues in creating an inquiry environment; there is always the challenge of engaging and sustaining engagement in an issue. The online environment presents different challenges. For example, the fact that the course is taken from home or the office is likely to make it difficult to sustain engagement in the issue. Also, the current internet technologies limits strategies for engaging the Learner—in particular, the extemporaneous discussions about issues and discussions embedded in the viewing or presentation of a real world context that are often so important in stirring excitement in an issue. Nonetheless, the goals are the same.

Whether in a classroom or at a distance, the designer must identify the problem or issue that, with student engagement, will lead to learning consistent with the course objectives. Given the problem, the instructor or the instructional designer must develop a well designed method for:

- Engaging the learner (e.g., presentation of problem and issues from the real world or linking student interests to curriculum goals)
- Establishing ownership of the problem (e.g., sharing the impact of the problem on the learner and others; bringing the problem home; working on a student-generated problem)
- Developing a commitment to solve the problem (e.g., learners believe they can address the problem with some degree of success).

Facilitating student engagement and ownership can be done through:

- Resources (including multimedia, such as Flash animation, demonstrating the issues)
- Discussion among learners (e.g., debate on pros and cons of the issue)
- Group projects (e.g., collaborative report proposing solutions to the problem presented)

These choices should be guided based on the characteristics of the specific learning environment. For example, in a learning anytime anywhere environment, where there may limited learner interactions, providing some compelling resources may be more appropriate than a group project. However, it must be remembered that the strategy is not the end in itself—the goal is to engage learners in the issue, and this is most likely to occur when the issue is relevant and authentic to their context.

Provide Structure

Once students are engaged in the problem, it is critical that we effectively support their learning process. There are three issues in providing that support:

1. The student must continue to feel ownership of the problem. The presentation of the problem served to engage the student in the problem, and now the goal is to sustain that engagement in the inquiry process for the duration of the course (Savery & Duffy, 1992).

2. There must be enough structure so that the student does not become overly frustrated. Although we agree that frustration can be one of the stimuli for learning (Schank, 1996), the frustration cannot be such that the student feels helpless (Bandura, 1997) or that the level of effort expended in sorting through issues exceeds the payoff expected. These frustrations can lead to students leaving the course or the inquiry.

3. The student's inquiry into the concepts and skills as defined in the performance objectives must be maintained. The support and structure cannot replace the problem-solving activities that are central to the learning outcomes. Instead, the instructor's role is to help learners maintain focus on the performance objectives and not wander too far off track while examining these issues.

In sum, providing structure requires a very difficult balancing act. We must give the students ownership and keep them engaged in an inquiry into the critical concepts but not leave the environment so unspecified that there is a sense of helplessness or wasted effort. The goal is to provide structure within which the student is engaged in critical thinking and problem solving relevant to the performance objectives.

One issue that frequently arises in the inquiry environments is that instructors err on the side of giving the student total ownership and providing little structure for the learning process or the learner. As noted by Wherry (2001), "learner-centered" too often means that materials are simply made available and that it is the student's job to figure it out. However, the instructor is critical to providing structure within which the student can be engaged in problem solving. Fosnot (1989) put it very nicely in noting that one of the instructor's roles is to ask questions at the "cutting edge of the learner's understanding," thus supporting the structure of the students thinking while still pushing it ahead. Finkle and Torp (1995) described the facilitator's role as "cognitive coaching," something quite different from the more typical "content coaching."

Application to Distance Education

Distance education environments are noted for the impoverished cue environment they provide. There are few social cues, because there is no ability to look around and see if everyone else is looking puzzled. There is also much less informal discussion, the sort of before and after class chatter (as well as outside of the classroom environment) in which students can clarify expectations, perceptions, and requirements. These informal cues are central to helping students get a "sense" of the class and to define the structure where it is unclear, yet they are minimally available to distance students. Thus, students can go pretty far off track before they receive the feedback that gets them consistent with the class activities and thinking again.

A second factor impacting the need for structure in online classes is the work style of the students and the frequency of class meetings. In a face-to-face class, it is not unusual for the instructor to evolve a syllabus as the class progresses or to make significant modifications in the syllabus during the semester. However, because distance students are "at home" taking a course rather than being traditional students, they typically are more "planful" of their work efforts and are taking a course because they can plan work schedules. Thus, changes in schedule can have an even more significant impact on these students.

Finally, the written communication in an asynchronous environment does not allow for the easy exchange that is essential to clarifying meaning. Indeed, students face challenges online with regard to interpreting one another's ideas and solving problems

(McLoughlin & Luca, 2000). It is for these reasons that structure is, after collaboration, the most important contrast between classroom and online courses. There are at least four strategies to use in providing structure in the online environment:

- Provide times and formats for discussing the progress of the course and the expectations. This needs to be a facilitated discussion, as it is unlikely students will contribute without facilitation.
- Provide a structure within which the students can work. This includes having consistent and fixed events, such as short-term goals (Bandura, 1997), deadlines, meeting times, and office hours. This all provides markers students can use to plan and complete their work.
- Set out the requirements and expectations at the beginning of the course and try to avoid making changes. With asynchronous communication, students receive change information at different times (e.g., many students are in vastly different time zones) and perhaps after considerable offline work. It is frustrating to feel one is the last to know of a change and that work was done unnecessarily.
- Provide clear instructions for procedures that are time-consuming and unfamiliar to students. Online learning is still new, and there are many variations in the technologies used that will impact the student. For example, a simple assignment of exchanging papers and providing feedback to one another can involve very time-consuming processes of uploading, downloading, and commenting—and be extremely frustrating to the individual who does not understand the procedure or who did not plan for the time necessary to complete the string of actions.

Although there is an increased need for clear structure in the course, this should not negate the opportunities for critical thinking and problem solving. Indeed, the structure is meant to permit the students to expend their energy focused on problem solving related to the core concepts—not problem solving the course structure. If a course is well designed and well facilitated, the learner can focus on the inquiry and learning.

Support Collaborative Inquiry

Student collaboration has been the focus of considerable research and theory development in recent years and is a central component of constructivist theory (Barab & Duffy, 2000; von Glasersfeld, 1995). Here we use the term *collaborative inquiry* broadly to include teamwork, whole class discussions, and even the mutual support students in a class can provide as each is involved in an inquiry. It is, quite simply, the lively interaction that we all cherish in teaching.

There are many practical reasons for forming collaborative groups, including dividing up a large workload and teaching students to be effective group members. However, from a constructivist perspective, the benefits include the following:

- Scaffolding of the critical thinking and inquiry process. Students have an opportunity to test their ideas publicly. Through verbalizing their ideas to others and engaging in debate, they can begin to internalize their understanding. Further, colleagues can provide assistance in enriching and expanding the thinking as they assist students to reach just beyond their zone of development (Vygotsky, 1978).

- Challenging perspectives. In some sense, this is the flip side of the previous point. Although the collaborative environment supports the individuals' development of their perspective, the group is also there to challenge the ideas. Thus, the dialectic serves to present the learner with alternative perspectives and conflicting data that must be assimilated or accommodated in the current thinking (von Glasersfeld, 1995).
- Providing a support environment. Students become a part of a learning community, sharing common goals and motives. There is value in being "in it" together that provides motivation and encourages persistence in the effort (Barab & Duffy, 2000).

That is the theory, and practice in K—12 and out-of-school environments seems to support the theory. There is a wide variety of evidence of the value of collaborative inquiry in K—12, including the benefits of collaborative teams (Johnson & Johnson, 1990) and mutually supportive learning communities (Hewitt, in press; Scardamalia & Bereiter, 1991).

Of course, collaboration is invaluable in our daily lives, outside of the classroom. We cherish the meetings with peers where we have an opportunity to discuss conceptual or research issues of common interest. The general effectiveness of work teams, properly established, has also been well documented. And we are gaining increasing evidence of the value of workplace communities of practice (Botkin, 1999; Brown & Duguid, 2000; Wenger, McDermott, & Snyder, 2002), though the underlying mechanisms are not well understood (Kling and Courtright, in press; Schwen, in press).

On college campuses, students actively seek to form study groups to study for exams. More generally, Kuh (1995), reports that the collaborative learning experiences outside of the classroom may be a greater source of learning during the college years than any in-class experiences. In qualitative data reporting, a Stanford University senior noted, "It is funny that we are talking about things outside the classroom because I feel like that is the place that I have done my most growing" (p. 123), and a Grinnell College senior reported, "I remember my mother telling me... not to let my studies interfere with my education... She was right" (p. 149). Light's (2001) interviews with Harvard University students affirm the findings of Kuh in indicating the centrality to the college learning experience of out of class collaborative and community activities.

The results of the National Survey of Student Engagement (at Indiana University, 2001) would lead us to believe that the students are also highly engaged in collaborative activities in the classroom. Fifty-seven percent of freshman reported that they asked questions in class or contributed to class discussion often or very often, whereas 71% of seniors report a similar level of participation. However, classroom observation data would suggest that much of this participation simply involves asking questions that the instructor answers. For example, Nunn (1996) examined 20 classes taught by faculty who were highly rated for their teaching and where the students were primarily majors and class size ranged from 15 to 44. In what might be thought to be an ideal setting, there was an average of only 2.3% (1 minute out of 40 minutes) of class time that involved student talk. Further, only 25% of the students in the class were involved in that talk. It would seem to us that Nunn's 25% participation rate in a single class session would be reasonably comparable to the 57% and 70% participating often or very often of reported in NSSE. But, of course, the nature of that frequent participation leaves much to be desired from the perspective of collaborative inquiry.

Nunn's classes were in a large university. An earlier study by Smith (1983) suggests that participation rates might be higher at small liberal arts colleges—but not much higher. Smith found only 14% of class time involved student talk, and this seemed consistent for classes regardless of time of semester or level of the class. One might hope that much has changed since 1983, when this study was conducted. However, Koljatic (2000), using data from large national samples, found no difference from 1983 to 1997 in the student report of level of class participation.

So, why is there not more collaborative inquiry in the college classrooms? Of course, large class sizes are one factor, but the studies described above were not large classes. One important factor is the inquiry in which the students are engaged. If it is to understand the text and to identify what is on the test, then the discussion is going to center around the instructor, and there will be little inquiry. If, however, the students are engaged in the issues of the domain being studied, then there is a greater likelihood for successful collaboration.

However, the classroom collaborative groups differ from our out-of-class collaborations in one important way: We typically cannot choose our in-class collaborators. The work of Light (2001) pointed to the importance of this factor, suggesting that a shared commitment is critical to successful collaboration. In his interviews, students reported that they placed a high value on collaborative inquiry with their peers. However, they noted that shared values were critical to the success of any peer collaboration. In particular, they noted a commitment to learning, inquiry, and hard work. For the most part, their collaborative activities in secondary school were not seen as useful, because this common commitment was too often absent. We have informally asked college students at all levels and from a range of institutions about working in groups, and the vast majority respond by indicating that group work is seldom effective. Like the students in Light's study, they note that the failure is because of a lack of a shared commitment.

In sum, an effective collaborative environment would seem to require an inquiry task that is meaningful to the students and that they own, and team members who are committed to learning, inquiry, and hard work. These factors suggest two strategies for the effective design of collaborative environments.

One strategy is to focus on collaborative teams but to assure that everyone brings a level of expertise and commitment to the meetings. Ochoa (2002) for example, asked students to first conduct their individual analyses of a problem situation and provide rationale for their analysis. In Phase 2, the students worked in teams, taking different perspectives on the problem but also evaluating the perspectives each brought to the situations. Of course, the well-established jigsaw strategy (Aronson & Patnoe, 1997) is similar to this. Different student groups develop different areas of expertise, and then the groups are reformed to capture the diversity of expertise in each new group. Both of these strategies serve to scaffold the expertise of the learners prior to collaborative inquiry, but it is still essential that all of the students be engaged in the problem if the approach is to be successful.

A consultancy model is an alternative to the team effort. In the consultancy model, the individual seeks out those he feels may be of help. The consultant selected focuses on aiding the individual in developing his or her understanding, testing ideas, and assisting in other ways. This does not preclude teams forming, but it does not mandate them. In essence, the discussion will be focused on the learner's issues—the value is clearly established. Further, the student can seek out consultants he or she feels will provide the necessary expertise and quickly move on if they do not meet the needs.

These consultants could be classmates, and grading could be based in part on the rated helping value of the consultant. The consultants could also be graduate students as part of their mentoring experience, or even faculty. This strategy differs from the traditional collaborative inquiry in that the focus of the exchange is on an individual's particular issues and needs as they are engaged in the inquiry and allows the students to seek the help judged of most potential benefit.[3]

Application to Distance Education

The distance and classroom environments are most diverse on the dimension of collaboration. Student interaction, much less student collaboration, as noted above, is simply not common in the college classroom. In the traditional college classroom, the instructor's lecture tends to serve as the central event of a learning session. But in the asynchronous environment, there are no lectures, or they are available in a resource area just like any other readings or resources. Being part of a class comes not from sitting in a room together but in talking together. It is the communication with peers that has been seen as central to the distance learning environment. A second difference is that the distance student does not have the community membership associated with being on campus. It is not only the class "community" but the campus community and culture that the individual becomes a part of and that is central to growth during the college years (Kuh, 1999).

Barab and Duffy (2000) have talked about community as being an important contributor to the development of an identity as a potential member of a profession. Collaborative inquiry is more critical in the distance environment, because it is a mechanism to provide a community for students through which they can develop their identity as a student and receive motivation for persisting. Distance learning environments are new to people. Without the interaction, there is uncertainty as to how to proceed, of how well the concepts are understood, of what is required, and how much work is expected—of all of those things that students get informally when they are together. Also, because the academic environment is embedded in the everyday context of the distant student, the community is important to help the student prioritize the academic requirements. There is a pull of the community in addition to the pull of the requirements. This is just as it is with students on a campus who are encouraged in their persistence by seeing other students expending effort and meeting requirements. Data suggests that specific strategies for interacting will increase the sense to which students feel they know other students and feel a part of a group (Abdullah, 1999). These include using names, referring directly to other students comments, and including personal reference, for example, following up with inquiries as to health when a student reports having been ill or having a sick child.

In addition to collaboration as a tool for community, it is also critical in the on-line environment to support learning by both having ones ideas challenged and engaging alternative perspectives. Although this is also important in the campus-based classroom, because discussion is so central to the distance environment, it is likely to be more readily achieved. However, the cautions about teamwork also apply even more strongly in the online environment. People taking online courses are generally even more focused on the efficient use of their time and will be more rebellious of

---

[3]This strategy also counteracts the competitiveness associated with many students. That is, if a significant component of the grading is the degree of help you provide others, then it is no longer beneficial to keep information from fellow students.

teamwork or class interaction that does not help them enrich and challenge their understanding

We suspect that the logistics of the jigsaw method and even the prestudy methods described by Ochoa (2002) are too complex to manage in the asynchronous environment. However, the distributed problem based learning approach is being implemented in several areas of education including nursing (Naidu & Oliver, 1996) and business (Stinson, Chap. 8, this volume; Stinson & Milter, 1996). The second author of this chapter has found successful collaborations in her PBL-based distance course in instructional technology. However, as in the discussion of Cardean that follows, it is also clear that a problem-centered approach does not always lead to collaboration.

We also think that the consultancy model has much to offer in the distance learning environment, because it allows students to work at their own pace—one of the benefits of distance learning—yet provides a collaborative process for testing ideas. The work of Polin (Chap. 2, this volume) with individual projects that span the length of a master's program reflects what appears to be a very successful application of this consultancy model.

A third alternative is the use of practice problems—not "end of the chapter" problems, but problems that present real situations of application that will challenge the students preconceptions and serve as a basis for discussion with the instructor or other students. The problems can run parallel to the course work and require contribution from students. Stinson (personal communication, May 16, 2002) has used this strategy effectively in an online executive education program and, as we will discuss in the next section, it was also a strategy used in the Cardean courses.

The instructor plays a critical role in all of these collaborative strategies. In contrast to the typical central role of the instructor in the campus classroom, the instructors can end conversations very easily through the type or amount of contribution they make. In contrast to the classroom, it is very difficult to reinvigorate a conversation once it is stopped, because it involves even more input and direction from the instructor. Fortunately, there are several excellent resources on effective strategies for promoting quality discourse in the asynchronous discussion (Collison, Elbaum, Haavind, & Tinker, 2000; Salmon, 2000).

Conduct Performance-Based Assessment

Assessment drives learning. Thus, if there is a conflict between the critical thinking and problem solving demanded by the problem and what and how we test, then the test is almost certainly to win out. It is for these reasons that the assessment strategy must be performance based (Wiggins, 1998). Performance assessment requires students to demonstrate their knowledge, skills, and strategies by creating a response or a product (Rudner & Boston, 1994), including the "application of knowledge, skills, and work habits through the performance of tasks that are meaningful and engaging to students' learning and outcomes" (Hibbard, Van Wagenen, Lewbit, & Waterbury, 1996, p. 5).

There are a variety of assessment strategies, the important point being that they must extend or validate the student's work rather than sit separate from it. It may be that the assessment is on the ability of the student to explain and defend the results of his or her inquiry in terms of use of the concepts and methods employed. Alternatively, the student may be asked to apply the concepts and methods in a new or related manner.

Rubrics or checklists can be used to evaluate both product and process. A rubric is a rating system by which a judge determines at what level of proficiency a student is able to perform a task or display knowledge of a topic. Instructors or students can use rubrics to evaluate everything from the final product to the process.

Application to Distance Learning

The distance learning environment does not impact the assessment strategy from a pedagogical perspective. However, because text-based discussion is the norm, the collaborative component of the performance can more easily be assessed, and feedback on collaboration and analysis of issues can be better grounded. This is a strong advantage over the face-to-face environment. Also, because distance courses tend to be "designed" and there is the potential for multiple teachers of the course over time, rubrics may play a more central role in assuring the consistency in applying performance standards.

Promote Reflection and Transfer

The goal of education is not to master information for use in the classroom, but rather to be able to apply the concepts in real world settings, for example, developing useful understandings. The inquiry-based approach is ideal for supporting real world transfer, because the problem, project, design task, or puzzlement simply needs to be a real world context (Honebein, Duffy & Fishman, 1993). However, transfer should not be assumed. As the literature amply demonstrates, transfer of learning to new situations is difficult to achieve.[4] In problem- or project-centered environments, it is easy to focus on "doing the problem." Learning occurs only to the extent necessary to move forward on the problem; understanding is, at best, very narrow (Spiro, Feltovich, Jacobson, & Coulson, 1992).

There are four strategies for promoting the development of useful understanding that transfers to other environments:

1. Emphasize to the students that the problem is simply a vehicle for thinking about the use of the concepts and methods identified as the learning outcomes or goals for the course. Stinson (Chap. 8, this volume) carries this further by assigning students to learning issues that they explore in parallel with their work on the problem. There is an interplay between the broader examination of the concept and its application in the problem.
2. Work (and the checks along the way) should never be focused on simply developing a position on a problem. Rather, and most critically, the focus should be on being able to explain the underlying concepts and defend their use. It is the critical evaluation of alternative strategies and alternative understandings that is important.
3. Asking "what if" questions and bringing in related situations for discussion can be very effective. Reflective activities during the course can help extend the student's thinking. Even asking students to summarize the current understanding can help in focusing attention on the concepts to be learned and the learning issues related to them (Barrows, 1992).

---

[4]Bransford and his associates, in recent work, have argued for a richer notion of transfer. Rather than thinking of it as "stored knowledge" that can be applied in new situations, they propose that we should think of transfer in terms of "preparing for future learning." That is, in a new situation, the individual can use the resources (as in original learning) to solve problems, that is, they can critically think and use resources to solve new problems. This is consistent with the work of Farr & Greene (1994) in problem-based assessments.

4. Reflection or debriefing at the end of the course is important to help students step back from the "work" and focus on the learning. Industry refers to this as debriefing, whereas the military calls it after-action-review. The goal is to focus on what was learned, what still needs to be learned, and to consider other contexts in which the concepts apply.

Application to Distance Learning

Distance learning has little impact on the goals or strategy for supporting reflection and transfer. All of the strategies outlined above can be used in the online environment. The critical issue will be the skills of the facilitator in promoting the "what if" and reflective discussions. For the learners, the goal is to produce models of thinking and not focus solely on solving the problem. These models should be sharable and useful for thinking in other contexts.

IMPLEMENTING THE MODEL IN AN ONLINE LEARNING ENVIRONMENT

We now turn to the case of Cardean University's Web-based master's in business administration to examine the issues of implementing these pedagogical principles in an online format. Cardean is a valuable case study, because it was well financed, released from many of the constraints of traditional universities, and committed to educational excellence through the design of courses based on an implementation of constructivist learning theory. Thus, Cardean had the financing, the freedom, and the intent of doing things "right." However, there are always constraints and affordances of the particular context that impact how the design of the distance courses can be approached. In the case of Cardean, this is reflected in the business model and rules. After reviewing the business model and the development process, we will discuss the course design, highlighting nine tensions that arose in making design decisions.

Goals and Business Model

Cardean University[5] is a for-profit institution that is approximately 4 years old at this writing. The core of the business model (see Table 6.2) for Cardean is providing high-quality business education to large numbers of students worldwide. The first initiative in seeking quality was to partner with the leading universities in the world: The University of Chicago, Columbia University, Stanford University, Carnegie Mellon University, and the London School of Economics. Through these partnerships, courses are codeveloped and cobranded in delivery. Cardean also sought to define quality in terms of the pedagogical approach. Nearly from the inception there was a goal of supporting learning by doing, and leading cognitive scientists were brought in to help give greater substance to that concept. Both the university affiliations and the problem-centered pedagogy have been key in the marketing of the Cardean courses.

The second component of the business model argued that students must be able to begin a course at anytime and move at their own rate. The courses were marketed

---

[5] Cardean University is owned by Unext. Although courses are actually developed in Unext under Cardean guidance, for ease of communication we will not distinguish which entity does what, but rather simply refer to Cardean University for all of the activity.

TABLE 6.2
Business Rules That Governed the Design and Delivery of Cardean Courses

---

- Cardean courses will all have the highest quality content.
- The pedagogical design of Cardean courses will reflect the best understanding from the learning sciences.
- Cardean courses' delivery will accommodate the busy schedule of working professionals.
- Cardean courses will capitalize on the power of the Web (in comparison, e.g., to CD-ROMs).

---

through business alliances, so all the students were working full time. The assumption was that these were busy people who needed flexibility. Hence, the "anytime, anywhere" mantra of distance education was taken seriously. Finally, the business model called for assuring that the Web was integral to the courses. What distinguishes the Web from CD-ROM-based training, and hence the focus of this business rule, is the ability to support interaction and personalized feedback with a distributed student body.

COURSE DEVELOPMENT PROCESS

We begin with a brief discussion of the Cardean course development process for two reasons. First, we have argued that Cardean has made significant efforts to create high-quality courses. A review of the development process provides substance for that argument. Second, Cardean's disaggregation of the faculty role as part of the strategy to achieve quality presents an interesting case for the debate about such disaggregation (Dolence & Norris, 1995).

A core team of three types of people are involved in developing a course: editors, subject matter experts, and instructional designers. The core team is small, three to six people, but it is supported by a large cadre of specialists. The faculty member from the partner university (e.g., the University of Chicago) and a course architect are central early in the process, as they are involved in developing the course definition. Media specialists, Web developers, and information technology specialists provide support in creating media resources and placing materials on the Web. Cardean University faculty and administration, as well as the partner university faculty, are available to consult and review the content and the course design. As the course is completed, user experience personnel test the course with representative students.

Faculty Roles

Table 6.3 summarizes the faculty roles in the course development and delivery process. There are two types of Cardean faculty involved in development: senior faculty and development faculty. The senior faculty are close to the traditional role of faculty in a university: They work with the dean in defining courses that need to be developed and in setting student policies on prerequisites and grading. They also oversee the entire course development process, assuring that the course content is of high quality and the design is consistent with the pedagogical standards that we will discuss in the next section.

The faculty member from the partner university provides the foundation for specifying the course content requirements and the course goals. It is that person's course

TABLE 6.3
Disaggregation of Faculty Roles at Cardean University

Role	Qualifications	Responsibilities
Partner school faculty*	Faculty member at one of the partner schools	Lead in defining course content and in review and final approval of a course. It is this faculty member's course that is the basis for the development of the Cardean course.
Senior faculty	Ph.D. in the relevant field	Leadership in defining curriculum and in assuring that courses meet content and pedagogy goals
Development faculty	Significant work experience and advanced degree work, or faculty position at another university	Subject-matter expert working day-to-day in developing course material
Teaching faculty	Minimum of master's degree in the area of the course and work experience	Course facilitators who serve as adjunct faculty to Cardean
Advisory faculty	Minimum of a master's degree and significant work experience	Serve to advise teaching faculty on the teaching of the Cardean courses

*Partner school faculty are not employed by Cardean University or Unext.

objectives and basic content that is being adapted by the Cardean faculty and who works with the Cardean senior faculty to define the course requirements. He or she is also generally responsible for representing the partner university in signing off on the course as meeting content and design requirements.

Development faculty are generally faculty from other universities or senior people in the business world who write and design the course following the specifications. These development faculty work closely with an editor and an instructional designer to realize the design goals for the course.

Teaching faculty are adjunct faculty, hired to teach a specific section of a course. Although the minimum requirement is a master's degree and work experience in the topic of the course, almost all have teaching experience, and many are faculty at another university. These faculty are in training for 6 weeks, including 2 days on-site at Cardean, before they are permitted to teach. Training includes becoming familiar with the course content and requirements, learning the problem-centered pedagogical framework, learning how to use the course rubrics to grade student work, and practice in being an effective facilitator in the discussion forum. They must also teach under supervision and submit a portfolio of their teaching that demonstrates their understanding of the goals of the course and their role as a facilitator.

Advisory faculty are full-time faculty at Cardean who serve to support and coordinate the teaching faculty. The advisory faculty develop and support the use of a course guide, which provides the teaching faculty with an overview and orientation to the particular course, detailed grading rubrics, and examples for all of the student work.

Course Development

The development of a course can be divided into five phases:

1. Course definition
2. Development of course materials
3. User testing
4. Technical testing
5. Course maintenance.

In the course definition phase, a course architect and senior faculty from Cardean meet with a partner university faculty member to develop a plan for the course suite. For example, working with the faculty member who teachers Data Mining at Carnegie Mellon, the team would lay out the specifications for a suite of four Cardean courses that meet the goals of that Data Mining course.

This definition phase is not a matter of transferring the course from one institution to another. Typically, the partner university faculty have never taught a problem-centered course before, so the entire process is new (and sometimes uncomfortable) for them. In principle, the process should begin with the Cardean team asking the faculty member what the students should be able to do outside of the course once they complete it. These performance goals are then used to ask the faculty for examples in which this would occur. The examples, in turn, serve as grist for developing problem scenarios. Finally, the faculty member's on-campus course materials are collected and places where students have difficulties are identified. If the faculty has resources for helping the student through the difficult point, they are also collected. I noted that this is how the planning process proceeds in principle. In fact, in many cases the process is very gradual, and the focus is simply on understanding the faculty member's goals and requirements, and on collecting the resources.

Given a course plan, the development team—development faculty, course designer, and editor—go to work in developing the course. There are informal and fixed review points along the way for Cardean faculty, the course architect who oversees the group, and the partner school faculty member. And, as noted, there is also close interaction with the technology teams to build the multimedia tools and address any Web-based requirements. The team can, and frequently does, call for consultation on content, pedagogy, or technology.

When the course is developed, it is submitted to a user-testing group to test all facets of the course. Although the process varies, this group runs students through the course both on-site (for close observation and interview) and at a distance to identify points requiring revision. The development team is debriefed daily during user testing so they can immediately begin revising the course based on the test data. Once revised, the course is submitted for a technology quality testing, with the course release following. Following the course release, students are monitored to identify any persisting problems, and student course evaluations are used to identify strengths and weaknesses in the course.

Clearly, the intended process was to provide very careful development of Courses—and the news reports on Cardean noted just how expensive this development process was. (*Newsweek* [McCormick, 2000] reported that courses cost $1 million to develop.) For the most part the development process was also rigorous. However, as the pressure for turning out courses more rapidly increased, the process of testing courses was modified and at times minimized, relegating quality assurance to expert judgment. Also, the pressure short-circuited the review and sign-off process, with the core course development team making final decisions.

COURSE DESIGN

Courses were designed to require approximately 30 hours of work and were offered for one graduate credit hour. They were grouped into suites of three to five courses; thus, the suite stood as an approximate equivalent to the traditional semester course at a university. Consistent with the business rules, students could begin the courses anytime and complete them at their own pace. However, this self-paced mode was combined with a cohort model. Students were grouped with up to 20 other students enrolling in the same course over an approximate 2-week window. Class sizes varied, depending on the number of enrollees during that window. The students were in a cohort in that they shared the same instructor and the same discussion board. The design of the courses was an adaptation of the problem-based learning model. The courses have five basic components:

1. Problem–based scenarios provide the framework for the course work.
2. Tasks provide the framework and guidance for working on the problem outlined in the scenario and define the work to be submitted.
3. Project resources provide data about the company and the situation that is needed to work on the problem.
4. Learning resources provide the conceptual or textbook content.
5. Asynchronous discussion is used for all collaboration except for personal communications, which is done using e-mail. There is no synchronous environment.

We now examine these components in the context of the key pedagogical features discussed in the previous section.

Inquiry

The inquiry environment is initiated by beginning every course with a problem scenario. The scenario places the student in a business context, provides some background on the context, presents a current tension or problem and some of the issues or points of view underlying that problem, and ends with a statement of the student's assignment in helping to resolve the problem. The problems are designed to serve two roles. First, the problem is the vehicle for engaging students in learning the concepts relevant to the course and is designed so that those concepts are central to the work. Second, the problems are meant to present realistic situations in which the students applied their understanding. The problems are presented as flash animations and as a text transcript. See Fig. 6.1 for an example of a problem.

As we noted in the discussion of pedagogy, one of the keys to effective design of inquiry environments is to bring the problem home to the student, so the student adopts the problem as her or his own. Because of the individualized starting times for the course, there is little that could be done to bring the problem home. The instructors can talk about the generality of the problem and ask about relations to the students work, but these are not particularly engaging strategies in an asynchronous

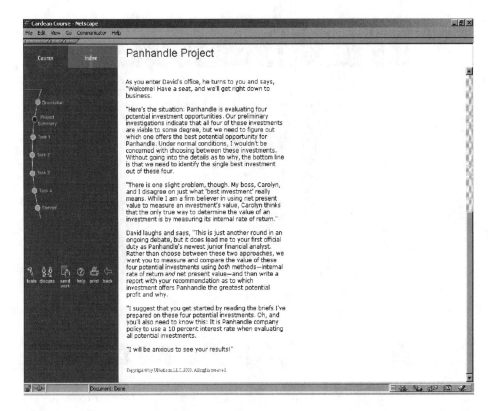

FIG. 6.1.   Transcript of the problem presented to students in the first finance course using the new interface. The problem is presented as an animation with this transcript also available to students. (Reprinted with permission of Unext.com LLC. Copyright 2000 Unext.com LLS. All rights reserved.)

environment. Thus, to the extent that the student is engaged in a problem-centered inquiry, the engagement comes through the problem design and the associated tasks.

Tension 1: Doing the Problem Versus Understanding the Concepts

In the early design of our courses, we found that many students would read all of the learning resources before even looking at the scenario. They took a traditional learning approach of studying the material and then testing themselves by seeing if they could apply it. Once they turned to the problem and tasks, these students would often report that they did not understand the concepts in a way that would allow them to work on the problem. They had to return to the learning resources, this time with a learning goal related to the use of the concepts.

Although this was satisfactory confirmation of the theory and pedagogy, it presented a significant design problem. Part of the solution was a new interface design. In the original interface, all learning resources were listed along the left margin of a single screen, which was the main work area (see Fig. 6.2), and this lent itself to a linear reading strategy. In the new design (see Fig. 6.3), the resources related to each student task are listed separately. Hence, the design promotes a linking of resources to tasks. The course guidance was also modified to provide a more detailed explanation of problem-centered learning, how learners should approach the course, and the benefits of that approach. Finally, instructor training focused on helping instructors in understanding

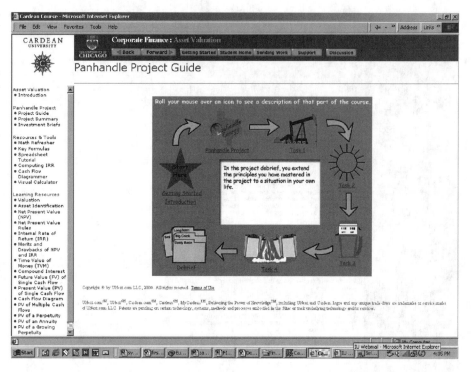

FIG. 6.2. Original course interface when a student enters a course. Note the list of all resources down the left side. (Reprinted with permission of Unext.com LLC. Copyright 2000 Unext.com LLS. All rights reserved.)

the pedagogy and in developing strategies for focusing students on the problem in their welcoming message.

These redesign strategies seemed to work. There were few if any students reporting that they read everything first. In the student evaluations, the value of the problem for organizing their work and thinking is one of the highest rated components of the course. However, focusing the students on the problem raised a new issue. Many students saw their task as doing the problem rather than understanding the concepts. Although the goal was to involve the students in the problem-centered inquiry, the intent was not for the students to simply "do the problem." Consistent with our goal of promoting transfer, the problem is intended as a vehicle for developing a usable understanding of the concepts and methods that can be applied to a variety problems.

Several strategies were used in the course to focus on a broader conceptual understanding. First, "guided problems" were provided within the learning resources. The guided problems presented a mini problem to the students or a real life situation in which the relevant concept is central and the students are asked to think about how they would approach the problem. After self-initiated work on the problem, they can then look at the course designer's (the expert's) approach (see Fig. 6.4 for an example).

Thus, these were transfer problems that focused on key concepts. Second, the learning outcomes presented at the beginning of the course emphasized the concepts to be learned and noted that the problem is a vehicle for understanding the concepts. Third, the final task was designed to promote reflection in which the student is asked to apply what was learned to a familiar situation, for example, to identify a workplace

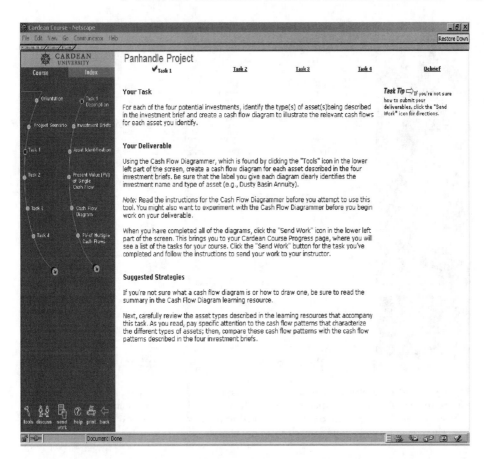

FIG. 6.3. The new interface lists the problem and tasks on the left. When a task is selected, the task description and relevant resources are listed. The text presents the first task in the first finance course, including task description and suggested strategies for working on the task. (Reprinted with permission of Unext.com LLC. Copyright 2000 Unext.com LLS. All rights reserved.)

issue where this applies. However, although reflection is great in theory, it is not clear that it is very effective in this implementation, as we shall discuss later.

Those were all course content-based strategies. However, we think the solution to focusing the students on useful understanding of concepts must come through the work of the instructors. The instructors must engage, motivate, and challenge the students to extend their thinking. To this end, the instructors are encouraged to engage the concepts (rather than the problem) in a variety of ways:

- They are provided with "what if" questions that they can ask students after they turned in work. The "what if" questions are near transfer questions that ask the students how their answer would change, if something specific about the scenario changed, or how they would respond in a different situation.
- Instructors are encouraged to introduce current events or work experience relevant to the problem and concepts, asking students their views of how the concepts would apply.
- Instructors are encouraged to develop strategies to engage students in discussions about the concepts and strategies. For example, it was suggested that instructors

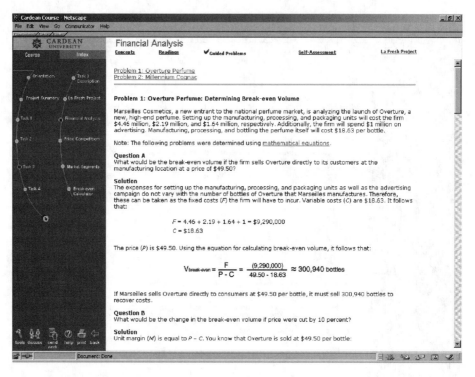

FIG. 6.4. Guided problems are presented with most learning resources to provide mini-problems for the student, focused on particular concepts. This is one guided problem related to "financial analysis" in the first marketing course. (Reprinted with permission of Unext.com LLC. Copyright 2000 Unext.com LLS. All rights reserved.)

use e-mail to contact a few students and ask them to post their analysis of the critical information in a learning resource or what they saw as the most difficult concepts to work with in this particular phase of the course. However, because of the self-paced format, there was little motivation for students to engage in discussion beyond that dealing with the practicalities of the course (e.g., due dates and technology questions).

Structuring and Sustaining the Inquiry

Much of the course development work focused on creating the structure to maintain and support the inquiry and minimize the engagement in activities not central to it. The tasks, project resources, and learning resources provided this structure.

Tasks

The underlying assumption in the design of the courses was that students in an online environment require more structure than those in a face-to-face environment. The uncertainty of how to get started on a problem was seen as presenting particular difficulties that could lead to frustrations and retention problems. Therefore, a series of tasks that as a whole represented the strategy for working on the problem were provided to help structure the learning activities. The tasks were meant to represent the intermediate tasks and guidance a good manager might give a new employee. Much as on the job, it was within the task structure that the student engaged in critical thinking and problem solving.

The task presentation included a statement of the product the student was to submit, the rationale for that product, and the critical criteria for an acceptable product. In addition to the description of the deliverable, the students were provided guidance on the strategy for how they might approach the task and what resources might be key. Again, this is much like a good manager giving the employee a heads up on how she is thinking about the task and what resources she thinks are relevant.

Tension 2: An Academic Versus a Situated Learning Perspective

Because the tasks were the "manager'" assignments to the students, the goal was to present them in the context of the scenario, thus reinforcing the scenario and hopefully helping to sustain the learner's engagement in the problem (the inquiry). In some cases, additional Flash animations were used to continue the story, with the appropriate people in the scenario presenting the task and relating it to the prior tasks and the overall goal.

The details of the assignment that the student had to complete were presented in a business context, specifying the audience and what was considered important. For example, a product might be

> A memo report to the board with recommendations on a pricing strategy. The board is very focused on competitive analysis, and so it will really focus on how your recommendations were based on an analysis of the competition. The board members will certainly want details and the methods of your competitive analysis so they can feel comfortable that your recommendations are based on a sound analysis.

Initial testing of the courses indicated that students often did not perceive the task as a clearly defined assignment. They are use to a traditional course structure and so ask, "What do you want? How long should it be? How are you going to grade it?" Somehow, because it was presented in a scenario context, it was not seen as a real assignment. In some sense, that is good news: The problem-centered focus was working. However, it is clear that students are also focused on grades and want a clear definition of assignments and grading. This issue of integrating the grading and course context and the problem context is critical to the inquiry approach and likely could have been managed simply through the instructor's guidance to students. However, many of the course developers decided that the tasks needed to be presented as academic tasks, in keeping with student expectations. Although the scenario may be referenced, the student assignment is presented as a course assignment, and the criteria for grading and issues about format and length are presented as grading criteria.

In our own analysis, presenting the tasks as academic assignments has serious consequences for the integrity of the courses. Most important, there is a loss of the interrelationship of the tasks and the sense of the whole problem. The student will begin seeing individual assignments as tasks to be completed rather than understanding them as steps in the problem-solving process for problems like this. The structure, rather than orienting the student to the problem, replaces the problem as the focus.

The effect also impacts developers. If the goal is to maintain the scenario, then there needs to be a clear logic linking the tasks so they build toward the student developing a final position on the problem. In essence, the problem-solving strategy is built in. However, as the tasks are increasingly seen as "homework," there is less focus in developing cohesion between tasks and the logic of the tasks. Other factors, like coverage of content, could and did begin to drive the specifications of the tasks.

Task and Learning Resources

The task resources are related to the situation represented in the scenario and basically provide the data needed to work on the problem, for example, financial data on companies, minutes from meetings, organizational charts, and notes from interviews. The learning resources are the primary learning materials. There is a separate learning resource for every major concept or procedure, generally resulting in 15 to 25 learning resources in a one-credit course. The intent is for the learning resources to stand independent of the scenario. There are two reasons for this. First, at a pedagogical level, the goal is for the student to learn to use resources, gathering, interpreting, and synthesizing the information to apply it to a problem. To the extent the learning resource is written for the scenario, there would be an increasing tendency to design it as a guide (or procedure) for action, thus defeating the pedagogical goal. Second, from a practical perspective, the goal is to be able to reuse the learning resources for other courses or as part of a larger library.

Tension 3: Authored Versus Adopted Learning Resources

To what degree is learning to use resources a part of the learning process? In a university, a key learning objective of any course should be to learn to find and evaluate resources relevant to an issue. However, in the corporate environment, the resources are typically available in the corporate library, and it is only those resources that are generally expected to be used. Hence, the "search" task is not essential. If the focus of a course is on understanding and being able to apply the concepts, then the use of resources can be even more narrowly defined. Cardean developers argued that textbooks and articles will always contain considerable material that is irrelevant to the concepts in the course. Hence, they argued, they could prepare learning materials that were more targeted to the concepts being studied and reduce learner frustration in reading material that was "irrelevant" to the task at hand. As a consequence, all Cardean learning resources were written in-house. Although there were articles and book chapters from other sources, these were always supplementary to the course.

This is an interesting issue, not easily resolved. The Cardean approach reflects a "learning objects" view currently popular in industry and even in some university contexts. Here, the idea is to provide "just-in-time" learning targeted to the specific learning requirements at hand. The view is that learning needs are very specific to the problem at hand, and hence materials should be designed to support work on that particular problem. In a practical sense, we have all experienced the frustration of sorting through a text trying to find the bit of discussion or explanation we need. Why make the learner do that?

This approach leaves us with two concerns. First, context is important. The ability to see the linkages of concepts provides a richer understanding and also provides for serendipity. Second, learning is not just the acquisition of the concepts as objects stored in the head, but rather it is the development of the ability to problem solve in the domain using the resources of the domain (Bransford & Schwartz, 2001; Savery & Duffy, 1996).

Tension 4: Online Versus Hard-copy Resources

A second resource issue is the decision as to what materials should be put online. Cardean University put all learning and project resources online and did not provide hard copy. There were two arguments for this strategy, both of which are very important from a business perspective:

- The materials could be easily updated.
- Consistent with the business model, a student can begin the course at anytime. There is no requirement to wait for course materials to be mailed.

Of course, there are also negatives associated with providing materials online:

- Students print the materials anyway, so they can read while traveling and at other times when they do not have an Internet connection. In response to a question-naire sent to students in two Cardean courses, all but 3 of 43 students reported printing out at least 70% of the material. The Masie Institute (Masie, 2001) report that 35% print out the material, but their survey is for all kinds of courses (including procedure training) and all types of e-learning (including computer based training).
- It is very expensive to put the materials online.

These are practical issues and in some sense pit student versus university convenience. However, we do think there is an underlying pedagogical issue here that relates to one's conception of a "course." In writing all of the course material and in putting all of it online, there is a focus on content as the definition of a course. Indeed, when looking at a Cardean course, it is the content that stands out. We do think that part of this focus of putting content on the Web rests with an anxiety, or at least a lack of understanding, as to what a course online can be if not a repository of materials. This reflects a content acquisition perspective and the CD-ROM course development environment from which many of the developers came. The role of the instructor was seldom considered by the developers. Rather, the goal was to make stand-alone courses. The developers often had to be reminded that there were things the instructor could do to elaborate on tasks and create inquiry activities. This contrasts to a view of courses as places for collaborative inquiry, where the tools for collaboration and sharing of resources stand out. As we shall discuss in a moment, this perspective was a major factor impacting the ability to establish a collaborative environment.

So what should be online or at least be on a computer? We would argue that there are three types of resources. First, there are resources that structure the course. For Cardean courses, this includes the scenario and the task. In a traditional course, it is the syllabus. Second, multimedia resources, including simulations, animations, graphics, and video that aid students in visualizing or gaining a greater understanding of a complex concept, are one of the real educational values of computer technology (Barab, Hay, & Duffy, 1999). Cardean makes considerable use of multimedia technology throughout the courses. Finally, tools designed to support collaborative inquiry obviously should be online.

Collaborative Inquiry and Community

Collaborative inquiry among students was considered a necessary component of the courses for two reasons. First, it was consistent with the business rule (see Table 6.2) of capitalizing on the "power" of the Internet. That is, distributed students could talk to one another, something not possible in a CD-ROM environment. Second, collaboration was seen as pedagogically important. It was the vehicle to build a learning community that would help students feel less isolated and have more affinity to the course, and it was a vehicle for students to test their understanding without overburdening the instructor. However, it became clear that the instructor, rather than students, could fulfill the business rule or provide real time interaction, and the instructor could and should also fulfill the pedagogical role through feedback and grading, as well as through answering questions online.

Student collaboration also took a back seat, because of two other business rules: accommodating the schedules of students (i.e., a self-paced environment) and providing quality content. Thus, although important, student collaboration was never a strong focus, and there was minimal interaction in the courses.

Tension 5: Collaboration as a Service Versus Content as a Product?

The core of the Cardean financial and developmental investment is in content. There was a very significant financial investment in the partnerships with the seven major universities and business schools to provide content and to sign off on the content of the Cardean courses, thus publicly endorsing the quality of that content. Although the content was obtained from the major universities at great expense, Cardean rewrote most of the materials and placed them online at considerable additional expense. Thus, content represented a very significant component of the overall course production labor. In addition, content was something that could be readily shown and evaluated for quality, both by its heritage (coming from premier business schools) and from a simple review. In contrast, the collaborative environment is a service. It is hard to show a customer the collaboration or even to demonstrate the importance of collaboration beyond the simple mantra that collaboration is important. Thus, from both a sale perspective and the perspective of developers, the product of content was clearly visible and essential, whereas collaboration was neither sellable, nor was it something the course developers could "design." Thus, the focus of the company was increasingly on manufacturing more courses for delivery with little attention paid to the instructional service.

This manufacturing model of Cardean contrasts sharply to the service model of more traditional universities. Universities seek to create a campus life, promote student discussion, and bring both social and intellectual richness to the university environment. Although the universities may not do as good a job as we would hope (Nunn, 1996), student collaboration in the learning process is a central goal of the educational process, as reflected in the ongoing efforts to create learning communities on campus (Tinto, 1993). Indeed, collaboration is central to most graduate educational programs.

This tension between manufacturing and service is one we suspect is encountered in many online efforts. In the classroom, it is the instructor holding court and orchestrating activities that is the focus. When moving to an online environment, there is by necessity greater emphasis on organizing and defining content. Even that dramatic lecture becomes content. This planning of content—and of seeing the course as finished once the content and structure is in place—lends itself easily to a manufacturing perspective.

Although a manufacturing model may define the development process, once the course is delivered the importance of student interaction becomes the focus of the instructor. In a traditional university environment, with a single faculty member involved in both development and delivery, there is a useful blending of the manufacturing and service models. Thus, we may speculate that one of the negative consequences of the disaggregation of the faculty roles is that there is a loss of a wholistic view of the educational process. Instruction is seen as two reasonable independent activities, manufacturing a course and delivering a course, rather than as creating a learning experience. Then, with a focus on income streams that dominates a business view of education, it is natural to focus on manufacturing, that part that is most visible and most costly. Although a hypothesis, this is not an unreasonable analysis of the Cardean environment.

Tension 6: What Kind of Community Can There Be in an Individualized Environment?

Perhaps the most critical factor impacting the building of a collaborative course environment was the business rule that students could start a course (literally) anytime and move at their own rate. This self-study environment is obviously at odds with any collaborative efforts.

Within the constraints of this business rule, Cardean attempted to create classes of students in which interaction could occur. Those students enrolling during a 2-week window, with a limit of 20, were grouped into a section that shared the same discussion space and the same instructor. Of course, these students not only started at somewhat different times, they also moved at their own pace. Thus, this was a class only in the sense that it shared a discussion board and an instructor. However, within this constraint, an attempt was made to conceptualize a community by analogy, comparing it to a neighborhood. Everyone is working on their own efforts, but neighbors help one another out. For example, all may be planting gardens, but at different times and with different plants. This diversity does not stop neighbors from helping one another in planning a garden. In addition, in a neighborhood, issues arise that everyone attends to and collaborates on, and for which there will be large variation in expertise on that issue.

This framework was used in training instructors. Instructors worked on strategies to take themselves out of the question–answer loop and encourage students to help one another. They were trained on techniques to get students to post notes on their strategies and learning issues in a way that could be used to prompt discussion, for example, by using e-mail messages to students, asking them to post on the discussion board what they feel are the most important issues in a particular learning resource or how they are approaching a particular problem. Several such postings would provide differing perspectives and, it was hoped, lead to discussion. Instructors were also encouraged to bring a current topic into the "class" and encourage students to discuss it.

There were three problems with this approach. First, there were simply not enough enrollments to yield a sizable cohort. It was not uncommon to have three or four students in a section—having started at different times and moving at their own rate. But even when there were larger classes, student collaboration was minimal, because of the second problem: The discussion was extraneous rather than integral to the requirements of the class. As research has shown, students will generally not engage in discussion unless it is integral to their class performance (Collison, et al., 2000; Riel & Harasim, 1994). Third, participation was not integral to the grading system. If students contributed significantly to the discussion, their grades were simply augmented with the phrase "with distinction"—the discussion could not increase the grade.

Although discussion remains minimal even though it is encouraged, the need for more interaction in the courses is the number one comment made by students in course evaluations when asked how courses can be improved.

Let us briefly mention two alternative strategies for engaging the student in a collaborative environment that were considered but could not be implemented. First, the new peer collaboration tools (e.g., Groove Networks, 2002), with online awareness, allow students to form study groups on issues or problems as they choose. All enrollees are visible, along with an indication of their progress in the course and whether or not they are online. With a large enough number of students enrolled in a course (and there is no upper limit) students can use the online awareness tool to form immediate study groups or to plan a meeting—working with students at the same point or soliciting help from students who are further along. All work sessions that a student participated in can be logged for later review.

Finally, given the constraints of the business rules, we wonder whether a stronger faculty mentoring focus might not be the most effective strategy. With support tools for faculty, they could provide rich resources and engage in one-on-one interactions. The testing and discussion associated with the feedback provides the challenges to the students and more informal instructional and social interactions and help form the student's identity as a learner.

Assessment

The student's expectations about assessment are a primary determinant of the learning focus and strategy. If our goal is usable knowledge, then we must assure that the focus of learning is on applying the concepts. Consistent with this goal, assessment in the Cardean courses is integral to the inquiry process. That is, the assessment is simply the evaluation of the student's performance on the tasks that are part of the problem-solving process. These are generally brief papers (less than a page) that provide the document required (e.g., a memo on the strategy to use in addressing some issue) and the rationale for the approach taken in the memo. The instructor provides feedback within 48 hours after submission, with a grade reflecting a mastery approach: exemplary, mastery, incomplete, or unacceptable. Cardean provides grading rubrics to the faculty to assure consistency in grading. The rubric gives the criteria and a sample answer to define each grade for each task. Although instructors vary considerably in the amount of feedback they give students, it is a source of reinforcement for them (it is their contact with the students) and students rate the feedback as one of the most valuable aspects of the course.

Tension 7: Efficient Assessment

Once courses are developed, the variable expense in delivering the courses has to do with the cost of teaching. Indeed, the limit to scaling the online educational environment has to do with extending the limits of the number of students an instructor can manage. And along with the scaling constraints is a constraint on the earnings per student enrollment that can be realized.

Of course, this business model applies to all universities. Our university has set minimum limits on graduate and undergraduate class sizes based on an economic analysis. The minimum class size could prevent classes being taught that are central to a given program—economics can override academics.

Cardean focused on strategies to make teaching most efficient. Instructors received considerable training, as described previously, with at least part of the rationale being that they could function more efficiently. There was also a focus on developing tools to monitor student performance and automate feedback given to students. The idea was that technology could help increase the efficiency of instructor performance and hence increase the scalability of the course delivery. The bottom line, however, was that instructors were expected to spend no more than 10 minutes grading a student's work. This impacted the design of assessments, as well as the strategy and attention the instructor could give to grading.

It is in this management of scaling that for-profit and traditional universities will show the greatest difference. Faculty at a traditional university have a course load and are expected to put in whatever time is required to create a quality academic experience. Increasingly, student ratings of teaching are a central part of the tenure process. In contrast, the for-profit business model emphasizes the time (cost) involved. Faculty hired to teach a course are told how many hours they are expected to work, and they are paid based on that hourly rate. Even if the faculty were willing to spend extra time, the business model creates a climate of pay per time spent.

Tension 8: Maintaining Test Security

Security is a complex issue in the online environment. Although we know cheating occurs on campuses, it is an issue of concern in the online environment as well. A variety of identity techniques have been developed that can be used to assure that the student is the person at the computer, for example, pupil and fingerprint identity and randomly generated personal questions that must be answered during testing (reference). However, these strategies only assure that the student is in the room; it does not inform us who else may be present to help.

The problem-centered approach of the Cardean courses provide an interesting tension in the assessment process. Testing is an integral part of the learning activities. Indeed, the tasks in the course that drive learning are also the assessment. Thus testing is not a one- or two-time event where someone could sit in, but rather is integral to the learning process. If someone were helping on a test, they would have to take the course. Although it is still possible to cheat, it is considerably more labor intensive. However, because the assessments are integral to the course, they cannot be easily changed. The answers can get out.

There were several checks planned to verify students' work if there were concerns about the individual's answer. First, "what if" questions (Bransford & Schwartz, 2001) were developed for each task to be used as an individualized assessment (or mentoring tool) if the instructor had any questions about the student's work or understanding. These were near transfer questions[6] that could be sent to the student after the task deliverable (homework or test, depending on your framework) was graded.

Second, if further security were needed, test centers could be used for administering the "what if" tests.[7] There are commercial test centers with worldwide affiliations and, within the United States, there is an affiliation of universities that share resources for proctoring tests for distance education (DE) students. The inconvenience of going to a center, however, would be a major factor.

---

[6]The questions asked about the problem the students were working on but changed the context somewhat, for example: What if the interest rate were higher? What if this were a recession? What if this were the electronics industry rather than retail clothing? How would your answer change, and why?

[7]The test centers could not be used with the task deliverables themselves. The deliverables are an integral part of the learning process and hence cannot be pulled out as a traditional test. The questions are known, because they are the organizer for the students' study.

Third, the use of click-stream data reports on student activity within the program could be used to see what resources the student used, including practice problems and self-tests, and how long the student used a resource or if it was printed out. Although imperfect, this data gives some evidence of the student's efforts in the course, which can help interpret performance on deliverables.

Of course, the best assessment of students is through their participation in the discussion throughout the course. For example, Stinson (personal communication, May 16, 2002) grades executive education students based on their ability to integrate ideas presented in discussion or to build off of someone else's comments with a link to the course concepts. But, with minimal student discussion, this was not an option at Cardean.

Finally, for students enrolled in the degree program, there were plans to develop a comprehensive test that a student would take at a proctored test center after completing the core courses in the MBA curriculum. This would be in a traditional test format but would be problem centered in content.

Transfer

Of course, the whole purpose of learning is the ability to use what is learned outside of the classroom. As we discussed at the outset of the chapter, although this goal is obvious, it is surprising how little transfer we typically find in school-based learning. In the Cardean courses, the problem itself served as a vehicle for transfer—it represented a real world context in which the concepts were applied. Transfer was also facilitated through the use of guided problems within each learning resource that gave the student the opportunity to think about the application of the concept in different contexts (Spiro et al., 1992). The "what if" questions served a similar transfer function (Bransford & Schwartz, 2001). Unfortunately, there is no data to indicate the degree to which the "what if" and guided problems were used.

Tension 9: General Problems Versus Individual Contexts

Although the problems provided as curriculum items provide real world contexts, for many students, the context is far removed from their workplace. Through the work on these problems, the students are developing an understanding of the concepts as they are applied in workplace settings, and they are learning how to use the resources to problem solve in the domain. Indeed, one of the primary goals of problem-centered learning is to develop domain-specific problem-solving skills (Honebein, Duffy, & Fishman, 1993; Savery & Duffy, 1996).

However, there is still the leap between the formal problems and the student's work environment and issues. An important instructional goal is to assure that the students are able to apply these concepts to their environment. The difference between the individual's business and that represented in the problem could impact ease of transfer. For example, the way in which some concepts apply may differ for the manufacturing and retail industries or as a function of the size of the company and its bureaucratic structure. A particularly difficult transfer variable is the cultural context (Hofstede, 1997). Cardean has students enrolled from around the world. For example, in one test of the system, a major technology corporation enrolled students from Australia, Europe, Asia, South America, and North America. In designing problems, Cardean did attempt to internationalize the contexts, and thus there were, for example, Swiss and Indonesian companies. Nonetheless, it is still a problem in the curriculum, and the generality to the individual's context may be difficult.

Cardean attempted to bridge the contexts in two ways. First, instructors were trained to use the discussion area to get students talking about how the concepts apply in their particular context, beginning by talking about their own business experiences. Second, the final task in most courses is a reflection task in which the students are asked to write a paper as to how the concepts apply to their context. Unfortunately, neither of these strategies was particularly effective. As we have already noted, the use of discussion was minimal in the course. Students were focused on their "tasks." There are two problems with the end-of-course reflection. First, it is at the end of the course, and hence there is the desire to finish the course. Because the problem presented in the course is completed, this feeling is likely enhanced—the course is over, and this reflection is simply something extra. The second problem is that it is very difficult for instructors to give meaningful feedback on the student's reflection. The instructor is simply not in that context and may not have experience with that culture, that size of a company, or that industry. Thus, to provide a meaningful dialogue for each student in a class and with a short turn around is unrealistic.

If the transfer to the personal context is to be supported, then the individual's context must become an integral part of the course activity and not an add-on to the end of the course or a voluntary discussion. One option is to have a "what if this were your company" as a part of each of the tasks. Thus, the student's submission would include the task solution, the rationale, and a reflection on the application to her or his company. If the last component of the answer became part of the course discussion space, the personalized views might well provide the spark needed for real collaborative discussion.

CONCLUSION

The goal of this chapter was to address theoretical and learning issues in regard to real world design and implementation of an online university offering MBA courses. This chapter provided a view of the application of theory through design, and of how design and delivery are impacted by real world issues.

Using a constructivist theory as a lens for understanding how we learn, we examined five pedagogical instantiations of the theory. Specifically, these were

- Engage the student in inquiry that will lead to the student's useful understanding of the concepts and skills identified in the course objectives.
- Provide structure and support to the learners as they engage in goal-oriented inquiry and problem solving.
- Facilitate interaction, collaboration, and a community-based learning environment.
- Design an assessment system that is performance oriented, calling for a demonstration of useful understanding.
- Promote transfer of knowledge to other contexts through reflective activities and diverse experiences.

In light of examining these strategies, we discussed how they apply to both distance and classroom-based settings. Thus, we examined the specific issues related to implementing the pedagogy to the distance learning environment.

Finally, we examined the case of Cardean University: the design of the courses, the pedagogical rationale, the process of developing courses, and the business rules that impacted design. The business rules were

- Cardean courses will all have the highest quality content.
- The pedagogical design of Cardean courses will reflect the best understanding from the learning sciences.
- Cardean courses delivery will accommodate the busy schedule of working professionals.
- Cardean courses will capitalize on the power of the Web (in comparison, for example, to CD-ROMs).

Critical discussions centered on the tensions that arose between realizing the pedagogical goals and the constraints of these business rules and the practicalities of the context. Designers of online courses often face issues similar to those experienced by Cardean. Depending on the context for which the course is developed, real world demands shape the learning design and process. Yet, where we as educational designers draw those lines is critical, as it may mean the difference between success and failure.

REFERENCES

Airasian, P. W. (1991). *Classroom assessment*. New York: McGraw-Hill.

Abdullah, M. H. (1999). *An examination of social presence cues in online conferences*. Unpublished doctoral dissertation, Indiana University, Bloomington.

American Association of University Professors. (2001). *Guidelines on distance education*. Washington, DC: American Association of University Professors. Also available: http://www.aaup.org/govrel/distlern/deguide.htm

Aronson, E., & Patnoe, S. (1997). *The jigsaw classroom: Building cooperation in the classroom* (2nd ed.). New York: Addison Wesley Longman.

ASTD Career Center. (2000). Human Resource Development Careers. Available: http://www.astd.org/virtual_community/comm_careers/t&d_career/HRD_intro.html

Bandura, A. (1997). *Self-efficacy: The exercise of control*. New York: Freeman.

Barab, S., & Duffy, T. (2000). From practice fields to communities of practice. In D. Jonassen & S. M. Land (Eds.), *Theoretical foundations of learning environments* (pp. 25–56). Mahwah, NJ: Lawrence Erlbaum Associates.

Barab, S., Hay, K., & Duffy, T. (1998). Rounded constructions and how technology can help. *Technology Trends, 43*(2) 15–23.

Barab, S., Makinster, J., & Scheckler, R. (in press). Designing system dualities: Building online community. In S. Barab, R. Kling, & J. Gray (Eds.), *Designing virtual communities in the service of learning*. Cambridge, UK: Cambridge University Press.

Barrows, H. S. (1992). *The tutorial process*. Springfield: Southern Illinois School of Medicine.

Bloomenfeld, P., Soloway, E., Marx, R., Krajcik, J., Guzdial, M., & Palinczar, A. (1991). Motivating project-based learning: Sustaining the doing, supporting the learning. *Educational Psychologist, 26*, 369–398.

Botkin, J. (1999). *Smart business: How knowledge communities can revolutionize your business*. New York: Free Press.

Bransford, J. D., Brown, A., & Cocking, R. (Eds.). (2000). *How people learn: Mind, brain, experience and school*. Washington, DC: National Academy Press.

Bransford, J. D., & Johnson, M. (1972). Contextual prerequisites for understanding. Some investigations of comprehension and recall. *Journal of Verbal Learning and Verbal Behavior, 61*, 717–726.

Bransford, J. D., & Schwartz, D. L. (2001). Rethinking transfer: A simple proposal with multiple implications. *Review of Research in Education, 24*, 61–100.

Brookfield, S. (1986). *Understanding and facilitating adult learning*. San Francisco: Jossey-Bass.

Brown J., & Duguid, P. (2000). *The social life of information.* Cambridge, MA: Harvard Business School Press.

Carnavale, D. (2000, March 31). Crowded Cal State U. campuses are asked to add distance education programs. *Chronicle of Higher Education,* p. A30.

Christensen, R. C., Hansen, A., & Moore, J. (1989). *Teaching and the case method: Instructor's guide.* Cambridge, MA: Harvard Business School.

Collison, G., Elbaum, B., Haavind, S., & Tinker, R. (2000). *Facilitating online learning: Effective strategies for moderators.* Madison, WI: Atwood.

Crook, C. (1994). *Computers and the collaborative experience of learning.* London: Routledge.

Cross, P. (1992). *Adults as learners: Increasing participation and facilitating learning.* San Francisco: Jossey-Bass.

Dolence, M. G., & Norris, D. M. (1995). *Transforming higher education: A vision for learning in the 21st century.* Ann Arbor, MI: Society for College and University Planning.

Dweck, C. S. (1986). Motivational processes affecting learning. *American Psychologist, 41,* 1040–1048.

Entwistle, N., Entwistle, A., & Tait, H. (1991). Academic understanding and contexts to enhance it: A perspective from research on student learning. In T. M. Duffy, J. Lowyk, & D. H. Jonassen (Eds.), *Designing environments for constructive learning* (Vol. 105, pp. 331–358). Berlin: Springer-Verlag.

Farr, R., & Greene, B. (1994, July.) College assessment project: Final report. Technical Report from the Center for Reading and Language Studies, Indiana University, Bloomington, IN.

Finkle, S. L., & Torp, L. L. (1995). *Introductory documents.* Aurora, IL: Illinois Math and Science Academy, Center for Problem-Based Learning.

Fosnot, C. (1989). *Enquiring teachers, enquiring learners: A constructivist approach for teaching.* New York: Teachers College Press.

Gardner, H. (1985). *The mind's new science: A history of the cognitive revolution.* New York: Basic Books.

Gick, S., & Holyoak, G. (1983). Schema induction and analogical transfer. *Cognitive Psychology, 15,* 1–38.

Gijselaers, W. H. (1996). Connecting problem-based practices with educational theory. *New Directions for Teaching and Learning, 68,* 13–21.

Gredler, M. E. (1996). Educational games and simulations: A technology in search of a (research) paradigm. In D. J. Jonassen (Ed.), *Handbook of research for educational communications and technology* (pp. 957–983). New York: Macmillan Library Reference USA.

Groove Networks. (2002) *Product Backgrounder white paper.* Beverley, MA: Groove Networks. Also available: http://www.intel.com/ebusiness/pdf/prod/desktop/p4p/wp021302.pdf

Harasim, L., Hiltz, S. R., Teles, L., & Turoff, M. (1995). *Learning networks.* Cambridge, MA: MIT Press.

Herther, N. K. (1997, September/October). Distance learning and the information professional. *Online,* 63–71.

Hewitt, J. (in press). An exploration of community in a knowledge forum classroom: An activity system analysis. In S. Barab, R. Kling, & J. Gray (Eds.) *Designing virtual communities in the service of learning.* Cambridge, UK: Cambridge University Press.

Hibbard, K. M., Van Wagenen, L., Lewbit, S., Waterbury, W. (1996), *A teacher's guide to performance-based learning and assessment.* Alexandria, VA: Association for Supervision and Curriculum Development.

Hofstede, G. (1997). *Culture and organizations: Software of the mind.* New York: McGraw-Hill.

Honebein, P. C., Duffy, T. M., & Fishman, B. J. (1993). Constructivism and the design of learning environments: Context and authentic activities for learning. In T. M. Duffy, J. Lowyck, & D. H. Jonassen (Eds.), *Designing environments for constructive learning* (pp. 87–108). New York: Springer-Verlag.

Janicki, T., & Liegle, J. (2001). Development and evaluation of a framework for creating web-based learning modules: A pedagogical and systems perspective. *Journal of Asynchronous Learning Networks, 5*(1), pp 58–84.

Johnson, D. W., & Johnson, R. T. (1990). Social skills for successful group work. *Educational Leadership, 47*(4), 29–33.

Keegan, D. (1990). *Foundations of distance learning.* London: Routledge.

Kling, R., & Courtright, C. (in press). Characterizing collective behavior online: The social organization of hangouts, clubs, associations, teams and communities. In S. Barab, R. Kling, & J. Gray (Eds.) *Designing virtual communities in the service of learning.* Cambridge, UK: Cambridge University Press.

Knowles, M. (1984). *Andragogy in action: Applying modern principles of adult learning.* San Francisco: Jossey-Bass.

Koljatic, M. (2000). *A longitudinal assessment of college student perceptions of good practices in undergraduate education.* Unpublished doctoral dissertation, Indiana University.

Kolodner, J., Crismond, D., Gray, J., Holbrook, J., & Puntambekar, S. (1998). Learning by design from theory to practice. In A. O. Bruckman, M. Guzdial, J. Kolodner, & A. Ram (Eds.), *Proceedings of the International Conference of the Learning Sciences 1998* (pp. 16–22). Charlottesville, VA: Association for the Advancement of Computing in Education.

Kuh, G. D. (1995). The other curriculum: Out of class experiences associated with student learning and personal development. *Journal of Higher Education, 66,* 123–155.

Kuh, G. D. (1999) *The college student report. National survey of student engagement.* Bloomington: Indiana University, Center for Postsecondary Research and Planning.

Kuh, G. (2001). *The National Survey of Student Engagement: The College Student Report.* Bloomington: School of Education, Indiana University. Available: http://www.iub.edu/%7Ensse

Light, R. (2001.) *Making the most of college: Students speak their mind.* Cambridge, MA: Harvard University Press.

Masie, E. (2001, July). To print or not to print? That is a question! *Learning Decisions Interactive Newsletter.* Sarasota, NY: Masie Center.

McCormick, J. (2000, April 24). New school. *Newsweek, 135*(17), 60.

McLoughlin, C., & Luca, J. (2000, December). *Lonely outpourings or reasoned dialogue? An analysis of text-based conferencing as a tool to support learning.* Paper presented at the annual conference of the Australasian Society for Computers in Learning in Tertiary Education, Brisbane, Australia. Available: http://www.ascilite.org.au/conferences/brisbane99/papers/mcloughlinluca.pdf

Mikulecky, L. (1998). Diversity, discussion, and participation: Comparing Web-based and campus-based adolescent literature classes. *Journal of Adolescent and Adult Literacy, 42*(2), 84–97.

Naidu, S., & Oliver, M. (1996). Computer-supported collaborative problem-based learning: An instructional design architecture for virtual learning in nursing education. *Journal of Distance Education.* Available: http://cade.athabascau.ca/vol11.2/naiduoliver.html

National Center for Education Statistics. (1999). *Internet access in public schools and classrooms: 1994–1998* (NCES 1999-017). Washington, DC: U.S. Department of Education, Office of Educational Research and Improvement.

Nunn, C. E. (1996). Discussion in the college classroom. *Journal of Higher Education, 67,* 243–266.

Ochoa, T. A. (2002). An interactive multimedia problem-based learning CD-ROM for teacher preparation: IDEA-97 guidelines for disciplining students with disabilities. *Journal of Special Education Technology, 17*(2), 39–45.

Phillips, R. (1998). What research says about learning on the Internet. In C. McBeath, C. McLoughlin, & R. Atkinson, (Eds.), *Planning for progress, partnership and profit.* Proceedings of EdTech '98. Perth, Australian Society for Educational Technology. Available: http://cleo.murdoch.edu.au/gen/aset/confs/edtech98/pubs/articles/p/phillips.html

Piaget, J. (1932). *The moral judgement of the child.* New York: Harcourt, Brace Jovanovich.

Resnick, L. B. (1987, December). Learning in school and out. *Educational Researcher, 16*(9), 13–20.

Revans, R. (1997). Action learning: Its origins and nature. In M. Pedler (Ed.), *Action learning in practice* (3rd ed., pp. 3–14) Brookfield, VT: Gower.

Riel, M., & Harasim, L. (1994). Research perspectives on network learning. *Journal of Machine-Mediated Learning, 4*(23), 91–114.

Rudner, L. M., & Boston, C. (1994, Winter). Performance assessment. *The ERIC Review, 3*(1), 2–12.

Salmon, G. (2000). *E-Moderating: The key to teaching and learning online.* London: Kogan Page.

Savery, J. R., & Duffy, T. M. (1996). Problem-based learning: An instructional model and its constructivist framework. In B. G. Wilson (Ed.), *Constructivist learning environments: Case studies in instructional design.* (pp. 135–148). Englewood Cliffs, NJ: Educational Technology.

Scardamalia, M., & Bereiter, C. (1991). Higher levels of agency for children in knowledge building: A challenge for the design of new knowledge media. *Journal of the Learning Sciences, 1*(1), 37–68.

Schank, R. C. (1996). Goal-based scenarios: Case-based reasoning meets learning by doing. In D. Leake (Ed.), *Case-based reasoning: Experiences, lessons & future directions* (pp. 295–347). Cambridge, MA: AAAI Press/MIT Press.

Schwen, T. (in press). Community of practice a metaphor for online design? In S. Barab, R. Kling, & J. Gray (Eds.) *Designing virtual communities in the service of learning.* Cambridge, UK: Cambridge University Press.

Simonson, M. (1995). Does anyone really want to learn? *Techtrends. 40*(5), p. 12.

Sloffer, S., Dueber, B., & Duffy, T. (1999). Using asynchronous conferencing to promote critical thinking: Two implementations in higher education. In R. H. Sprague (Ed.), *Proceedings of the 32nd Hawaii International Conference on the System Sciences* (Wailea, Maui, Hawaii). Institute of Electrical and Electronics Engineers (IEEE). Available: http://lilt.ics.hawaii.edu/resources/papers/Sloffer99.pdf

Soller, A., Linton, F., Goodman, B., & Lesgold, A. (1999). Toward intelligent analysis and support of collaborative learning interaction. In S. P. La Jole & M. Vivet (Eds.), *Proceedings of the Ninth International Conference on Artificial Intelligence in Education,* LeMans, France (pp. 75–82).

Smith, D. G. (1983). Instruction and outcomes in an undergraduate setting. In C. L. Ellner & C. P. Barnes (Eds.), *Studies in college teaching* (pp. 83–116). Lexington, MA: Heath.

Spiro, R. J., Feltovich, P. J., Jacobson, M. J., & Coulson, R. L. (1992). Cognitive flexibility, constructivism and hypertext: Random access instruction for advanced knowledge acquisition in ill-structured domains.

In T. Duffy & D. Jonassen (Eds.), *Constructivism and the technology of instruction* (pp. 57–75). Hillsdale, NJ: Lawrence Erlbaum Associates.

Stepien, W., & Gallagher, S. (1993). Problem-based learning: As authentic as it gets. *Educational Leadership, 50,* 25–28.

Sticht, T. G. (1975) *Reading for working: A Functional literacy anthology.* Alexandria, VA: Human Resources Research Organization.

Stinson, J. E., & Milter, R. G. (1996). Problem-based learning in business education: Curriculum design and implementation issues. In L. A. Wilkerson & W. H. Gijselaers (Eds.), *Bringing problem-based learning to higher education: Theory and practice* (pp. 33–42). San Francisco: Jossey-Bass.

Sweller, J. (2000). *Cognitive processes and instructional design in technical.* Herndon, VA: Stylus.

Taylor, P. C. (1983, September). The adult education act: Issues and perspectives on reauthorization. *Lifelong Learning, 7*(1), 10–11, 26–27.

Tinto, V. (1993). *Leaving college: Rethinking the causes and cures of student attrition* (2nd ed.). Chicago: University of Chicago Press.

Von Glasersfeld, E. (1995). *Radical constructivism: A way of knowing and learning.* London: Falmer.

Vygotsky, L. (1978). *Mind in society: The development of higher psychological processes.* Cambridge, MA: Harvard University Press.

Wenger, E., McDermott, R., & Snyder, W. (2002). *Cultivating communities of practice: A guide to managing knowledge.* Cambridge, MA: Harvard Business School Press.

Wherry, C. (2001) The work of education in the age of e-college. *First Monday, 6*(5). Available: http://www.firstmonday.dk/issues/issue6_5

Wiggins, G. P. (1998.) *Educative assessment: Designing assessments to inform and improve student performance.* San Francisco: Jossey-Bass.

Wilkerson, L. A., & Gijselaers, W. H. (Eds.). (1996). Bringing problem-based learning to higher education: Theory and practice. *New Directions for Teaching and Learning* (p. 68). San Francisco: Jossey-Bass.

7

The Challenge of Designing Inquiry-Based Online Learning Environments: Theory Into Practice

Charlotte N. (Lani) Gunawardena
University of New Mexico

When learning is defined as knowledge transmission, the focus becomes the design of content rather than the design of the process of learning, which is reflected in the widespread practice of putting content on the Web. However, as Bransford, Brown, and Cocking (2000) have observed, "New developments in the science of learning raise important questions about the design of learning environments—questions that suggest the value of rethinking what is taught, how it is taught, and how it is assessed" (p. 131). These new developments in understanding learning are the foundations of constructivist and social constructivist learning principles.

The purpose of this chapter is to address issues and challenges related to designing online learning environments based on constructivist and social constructivist learning principles. The chapter will review constructivist and social constructivist assumptions about learning, issues related to the design of inquiry-based learning environments, the balance between structure and dialogue in distance education design, and factors related to collaboration, assessment, and transfer of learning. This chapter builds off issues raised by Duffy and Kirkley (Chap. 6, this volume) when designing inquiry-based learning environments for Cardean University online courses. It also draws on distance education research and my own research on these issues to extend the discussion.

Teaching at a distance impacts how faculty teach and how students learn (Duffy & Kirkey, Chap. 6, this volume; Eastmond, 1994; Gunawardena, 1992); therefore, importing traditional models of pedagogy to the online context will not work. This is a premise that must be kept at the forefront of any effort to develop online distance education programs. It is a premise that has influenced the discussion on designing inquiry-based online learning environments in this chapter.

ASSUMPTIONS ABOUT LEARNING

If we define learning as knowledge construction rather than knowledge transmission, then learning becomes a "sense-making activity in which the learner seeks to build a coherent mental representation from the presented material. Unlike information, which is an objective commodity that can be moved from one mind to another, knowledge is personally constructed by the learner and cannot be delivered in exact form from one mind to another" (Mayer 2001, p. 13). Bransford, Brown, and Cocking (2000) have shown that students construct scientific understanding through an interactive process of theory building, criticism, and refinement based on their own questions, hypotheses, and data analysis activities. This process or structure helps students explore the implications of the theories they hold, examine underlying assumptions, formulate and test hypotheses, develop evidence, provide warrants for conclusions, and so forth. The process as a whole provides a richer, more scientifically grounded experience than the conventional focus on textbooks or laboratory demonstrations. These views provide the foundation for constructivist learning theory, which emphasizes the construction of meaning from personal values, beliefs, and experiences. The development of personal schemata and the ability to reflect on one's experiences are key principles in constructivist theory.

In developing their pedagogical model for inquiry-based learning, Duffy and Kirkley (Chap. 6, this volume) draw on constructivism and situated cognition, as exemplified in Resnick's 1987 work, as the learning theory foundation. Although I concur with Duffy and Kirkley's perspectives on constructivism and situated cognition as the foundations necessary for designing learning environments, I feel that in the context of distance education, where emphasis must be placed on reducing the loneliness of the distance learner by building learning networks, their perspectives on constructivist learning can be strengthened by an equally important emphasis on socially shared cognition (Resnick, 1991; Resnick, Levine, Teasley, 1991), and socioconstructivist and sociocultural views on learning (Vygotsky, 1978; Wertsch, 1985, 1991).

Resnick (1991) observes that in "most psychological theory, the social and the cognitive have engaged only peripherally, standing in a kind of figure-ground relationship to one another rather than truly interacting" (p. 1) and advocates that we undo this figure–ground relationship between cognitive and social processes. She points out that much of human cognition is so varied and so sensitive to cultural context that we must also seek mechanisms by which people actively shape each other's knowledge and reasoning processes. According to the strong constructivist assumption, everything an individual knows is personally constructed, but directly experienced events are only part of the basis for that construction. She argues that people also build their knowledge structures on the basis of what they are told by others, orally, in writing, in pictures, and in gestures.

Our daily lives are filled with instances in which we influence each other's constructive processes by providing information, pointing things out to one another, asking questions, and arguing with and elaborating on each other's ideas. She elaborates that recent theories of situated cognition are challenging the view that the social and the cognitive can be studied independently, arguing that the social context in which cognitive activity takes place is an integral part of that activity, not just the surrounding connect for it.

Recent theories of learning, therefore, have made an attempt to blend the social and the cognitive in the design of learning environments. These are exemplified in discussions on socially shared cognition (Resnick, Levine, & Teasley, 1991), socioconstructivism, which emphasizes the importance of social processes in individual knowledge building (Teasley & Roschelle, 1993; Vygotsky, 1978), and sociocultural perspectives that describe learning from a cultural point of view. By stressing the interdependence of social and individual processes in the coconstruction of knowledge, sociocultural approaches view semiotic tools or cultural amplifiers as personal and social resources, and, hence, mediating the link between the social and the individual construction of meaning (Vygotsky, 1978).

In an experimental study, Wegerif and Mercer (2000) sought to test the hypothesis that 8- and 9-year-old children learn to reason individually, in situations such as that of individual nonverbal reasoning tests, through prior participation in social reasoning. The statistical analysis of the results of individual reasoning tests provided support for the hypothesis that children learn to reason individually through prior participation in joint reasoning activity. In the distance education context, it has been a challenge to facilitate joint reasoning activities or collaborative learning that is so important for individual sense making till the advent of Internet-based asynchronous computer conferencing, which can link participants to engage in dialogue for a certain period of time. This is perhaps one of the greatest assets of the online medium. Although a few designers have utilized this feature to create online communities of inquiry, in many online designs, this feature remains an underutilized option.

Lave (1991) further extends the interdependence of social and individual processes in the coconstruction of knowledge by stating that we need to rethink the notion of learning, treating it as an emerging property of whole persons' legitimate peripheral participation in communities of practice. Such a view sees mind, culture, history, and the social world as interrelated processes that constitute each other, and intentionally blurs social scientists' divisions among component parts of persons, their activities, and the world. She recommends a decentralized view of the locus and meaning of learning, in which

> learning is recognized as a social phenomenon constituted in the experienced, lived-in world, through legitimate peripheral participation in ongoing social practice; the process of changing knowledgeable skill is subsumed in processes of changing identity in and through membership in a community of practitioners; and mastery is an organizational, relational characteristic of communities of practice. (p. 64)

Lave (1991) considers learning not as a process of socially shared cognition that results in the end in the internalization of knowledge by individuals, but as a process of becoming a member of a sustained community of practice. She notes that developing an identity as a member of a community and becoming knowledgeably skillful are part of the same process, with the former motivating, shaping, and giving meaning to the latter, which it subsumes. My own work in researching learning in the online environment has been greatly influenced by these socioconstructivist (Gunawardena, Lowe, & Anderson, 1997) and sociocultural (Gunawardena, Nolla, Wilson, López-Islas, Ramírez-Angel, & Megchun-Alpízar, 2001) views on learning. Therefore, my reaction to the Duffy and Kirkley chapter in this volume is through this lens. Computer-mediated communication (CMC) has led to the emergence of networked learning communities, or "cybercommunities," bound by areas of interest and transcending time and space (Jones, 1995, 1997). It is the ability to facilitate critical communities of inquiry that I think is the single most important contribution of this medium to distance learning. Perhaps it is the peripheral design of individual–peer interaction in Cardean University courses that led to problems associated with lack of interaction and peer learning.

A CONSTRUCTIVIST LEARNING DESIGN MODEL

One of the major contributions of Duffy and Kirkley's chapter is the discussion of the development and application of a constructivist learning design model for creating inquiry-based online learning environments. The model described has five components, which include (1) creating an inquiry environment, (2) providing structure, (3) supporting collaboration and a community-based learning environment, (4) designing an assessment system that is performance oriented, and (5) promoting transfer. Each of these components has significant implications for designing online courses, and I would like to engage in an extended discussion of the issues raised by these five components in the design model.

The Inquiry Learning Environment

Inquiry-based learning is founded on constructivist learning theory. The central theme is that learning is the process of constructing meaning. It is a student-centered active learning approach focusing on questioning, critical thinking, and problem solving. Students are engaged in finding solutions to authentic, socially valid problems through investigations and collaboration with others. Inquiry-based instruction should help students to communicate with those who have different perspectives, articulate problems out of complex and messy situations, and collaborate with others in finding solutions to problems. In an inquiry-based learning environment, the teacher becomes a partner in the inquiry, a guide and facilitator who presents challenging, interesting, curiosity-provoking problems that entice students to learn. The teacher also takes an active role in inquiring about the processes of teaching and learning.

In this section, I discuss the challenges of designing inquiry-based learning environments for the online context in relation to matching the pedagogical model to the business model, problem solving in a community of inquiry, presenting the problem to be solved, prespecifying objectives, faculty approaches to directing the inquiry, and designing the Web interface to support the inquiry. The Duffy and Kirkey chapter provides excellent examples that address these issues in a real world context.

Matching the Pedagogical Model to the Business Model

One of the critical challenges to implementing an inquiry-based learning environment in the online context is the conflict that often arises with the policies and administrative structures that govern the institutions that offer distance education. Many dual-mode higher education institutions (those that teach face-to-face and at a distance) have had to adjust their policies and administrative structures to accommodate distance education and new formats of instruction. Duffy and Kirkey note that a major problem in designing an inquiry-based learning environment for Cardean courses was the individualized starting times for the courses, as specified in the Cardean business model. According to this model, students must be able to begin a course at anytime and move at their own rate. They observe that there was little that could be done to "bring the problem home." The issue here is the mismatch of the business model with the inquiry-based learning format.

Problem Solving in a Community of Inquiry

I think, however, that there is a larger issue inherent in this mismatch—the inability of students to work together to solve the problem in a community of inquiry, as is necessary in an inquiry learning environment. As stated earlier, inquiry-based instruction should help students to communicate with those who have different perspectives, articulate problems out of complex and messy situations, and collaborate with others in finding solutions to problems. Another inquiry learning format, the problem-based learning (PBL) model, as it is used in medical education, may be a good alternative to providing the opportunity to dialogue and solve problems with a community of peers and a tutor or preceptor. Mayo, Donnelly, Nash, and Schwartz (1993) describe PBL as a pedagogical strategy for posing significant, contextualized, real world problems, and providing resources, guidance, and instruction to learners as they develop content knowledge and problem-solving skills. In problem-based learning, students collaborate to study the issues of a problem as they try to come up with viable solutions. Unlike traditional face-to-face instruction, which is conducted in a lecture format, with the instructor being in control, problem-based learning occurs in a small group facilitated by a faculty tutor (Aspy, Aspy, & Quimby, 1993). In this learning process, learners encounter a problem and attempt to solve it with information that they already possess, allowing them to appreciate what they already know. They also identify what they need to learn to better understand the problem and how to come up with a solution for it. These are called learning issues. Once they have identified what they need to learn to understand the problem better, learners engage in self-directed study and research searching for information in books, journals, on the Web, and by talking to a variety of people with appropriate expertise. The learners, then, return to the problem and try to apply what they have learned to resolve it. After they have finished their assessment of the problem, learners assess themselves and each other to develop skills in self-assessment and the constructive assessment of peers. Self-assessment is an important skill that leads to effective self-directed, independent learning.

The principle role of the teacher in problem-based learning is one of a facilitator (often referred to as tutor or preceptor) that guides learners through the learning process. The facilitator's role includes subject-matter expert, resource guide, and task group consultant. This arrangement promotes group processing of information rather than an imparting of information by faculty (Vernon & Blake, 1993). The facilitator's role is to encourage student participation, keep students on track, avoid negative feedback and assume the role of fellow learner (Aspy, Aspy, & Quimby, 1993). As learners learn to take more control of the learning process, the facilitator becomes less active. For example, in the PBL curriculum at the University of New Mexico's medical school, small groups of students (5–6, maximum of 8) work together with a preceptor (usually a faculty member) to solve a medical problem over an extended period of time following the PBL steps discussed above. We discuss the use of the Web for facilitating PBL and case-based reasoning in the training of preclinical medical students at Wake Forest University School of Medicine (Crandall & Gunawardena, 1999). In the Cardean example, the innovation is inherent in centering the design on solving problems, but, unfortunately, the format and structure of the design did not adequately support the problem-solving process in a community of inquiry. If it had been possible to create small groups to work on the problem for an extended period of time, students may have negotiated meaning and developed a solution using each other's experience.

Presenting the Problem to Be Solved

Another issue related to the difficulty of bringing the problem home to the student may be associated with how the problem was presented. The problem was presented from the instructor's or designer's point of view and not the students'. The students were not engaged in generating the problem, but solving one that was presented to them. Again, if it had been possible to establish a community of inquiry and engage the students in discussion, the students themselves could have come up with the problem to be resolved and thus assumed ownership of it. This may have taken more time, but it would have "brought the problem home."

Prespecifying Objectives

I believe that a related issue is the prespecification of objectives for an inquiry environment. Once objectives are presented to students at the beginning of the course, then the focus turns to achieving the objectives specified and not to the inquiry process. Therefore, designers need to seriously consider the role of instructional objectives in inquiry-based environments. In the traditional instructional design approach as exemplified in the ADDIE (Analysis, Design, Development, Implementation, Evaluation) model, the end goal of the analysis phase is the specification of intended learning outcomes or instructional objectives. Bednar, Cunningham, Duffy and Perry (1992) point out that "constructivists do not have learning and performance objectives that are internal to the content domain (e.g., apply the principle), but rather we search for authentic tasks and let the more specific objectives emerge and be realized as they are appropriate to the individual learner in solving the real-world task" (p. 25). They note that from the constructivist perspective, every field has its unique ways of knowing, and the function of analysis is to try to characterize this. If the field is history, for example, constructivists try to discover ways that historians think about their world and provide means to promote such thinking in the learner: "The goal is to teach how to think like a historian, not to teach any particular version of history" (pp. 24–25). Therefore, some of the questions designers need to ask as they design inquiry environments are: How can objectives emerge from real world problem-solving tasks? Can these objectives change and develop characters of their own as the inquiry progresses? Can objectives emerge from the online community of learners that has enrolled in a specific course?

I am currently evaluating the design of a Star Schools Web-based project, developed by Oklahoma State University, which is aimed at teaching middle school science and math teachers how to use hypothesis-based teaching methodology. The designers are grappling with the challenge of focusing on the inquiry rather than on meeting the objectives. The design begins by engaging the learner in the inquiry process, by asking students to make an observation of an event or phenomena, generate a hypothesis, test the hypothesis and engage in the scientific method to encourage students to think like a scientist, rather than prespecifying content objectives to be covered. Content is learned through the inquiry process (Gunawardena et al., 2001).

Faculty Approaches to Directing the Inquiry

As Duffy and Kirkley have pointed out (Chap. 6, this volume), another problem in designing inquiry-based environments is when faculty view the problem as a motivator rather than as integral to the learning process. Even if learning is driven by the inquiry, we still may not create an inquiry environment if the faculty member directs the student in detail on how to proceed. If the inquiry is controlled or directed, it is no longer an inquiry, but rather a series of tasks to be done for the instructor. Faculty perceptions of the problem, as well as the need to write prespecified learning objectives for the inquiry, may prove detrimental to the inquiry process.

Duffy and Kirkley (Chap. 6, this volume) describe a setback that occurred when focusing the students on the problem. Many students saw their task as doing the problem rather than understanding the concepts. To address this problem, Duffy and Kirkley developed several strategies to bring a focus on conceptual understanding, but these were all content-based strategies. They emphasize that the solution to focusing the students on usable understanding of concepts must come through the work of the instructors. The instructors must engage, motivate, and challenge the students to extend their thinking. This issue also stresses the importance of focusing the design on problem-solving activities that are carried out within a community of inquiry comprised of peers and the instructor. Unfortunately, the business model associated with the format of Cardean courses did not support the inquiry environment in many ways.

Designing the Web Interface to Support the Inquiry

One of my learning highlights is the example that Duffy and Kirkley (Chap. 6, this volume) provided to show how the interface design influences the learning process. In the early design of Cardean courses, many students would read all of the learning resources before even looking at the scenario. They took the traditional learning approach of studying the material and then testing themselves by seeing if they could apply it. Listing the learning resources on the left margin of a single screen led to a linear reading strategy. When the designers developed a new interface where the resources were linked to the tasks, the students found it to be more beneficial, and there were few if any students reporting that they read everything first. Duffy and Kirkley report that in student evaluations, the value of the problem for organizing their work and thinking is one of the highest rated components of the course. This is evidence of a good constructivist learning design. More systematic data collection, however, is necessary to support this finding. I believe that this is an excellent area for future research and evaluation—the development of studies to examine how the interface design supports the inquiry learning process.

Structure

The underlying assumption in the design of Cardean courses was that students in an online environment require more structure than those in a face-to-face environment. Therefore, the designers focused on structuring the work within which the student would be engaged in problem solving and critical thinking. They developed a series of tasks that as a whole represented the strategy for working on the problem. The tasks were meant to represent the intermediate tasks and guidance a good manager might give a new employee.

I think that structuring the tasks in this way may have led to directed inquiry rather than open inquiry, which seems to have been the goal of this program. In open inquiry, the learning process is more open-ended and open to change, whereas in directed inquiry, there are specific guidelines on how to conduct the inquiry. The former method provides more opportunity for creativity and unexpected answers, and is more suitable for students familiar with the inquiry process, whereas the latter method is more structured and a more suitable format for novice students to learn the inquiry process. Therefore, when designing distance education courses, it is important to examine means to balance structure and dialogue (or communication), which would help the instructor and students negotiate the structure designed into the course. The structure of a course is evident in the prespecified objectives, and teaching, learning, and assessment methods. When there is opportunity for students to negotiate these items with an instructor, the learning environment can be adapted to meet the needs of the learner. The negotiation process can happen when the entire class feels that a change in direction is necessary, or it can be done individually to meet an individual's unique learning needs. In disciplines that often deal with ill-structured and messy problems, this opportunity to negotiate structure with the instructor is an important aspect of the course design.

The distance education literature addresses this issue in the work done by Moore (1973), Moore and Kearsley (1996), Saba (1988), and Saba and Shearer (1994), who have shown the importance of balancing structure and dialogue, and the varying degrees of autonomy in designing distance education courses. Moore (1973) developed the theory of transactional distance where distance is conceived of as a pedagogical phenomenon rather than a geographical phenomenon consisting of three variables that interplay in an educational transaction: structure, dialogue, and autonomy. Dialogue is the opportunity for communication between instructor and students; structure refers to the elements in the course design, such as how objectives, learning methods, and evaluation are specified; autonomy refers to the degree of freedom learners have to select learning goals, methods, and evaluation. Moore and Kearsley (1996) note that what determines the success of distance teaching is the extent to which the institution and the individual instructor are able to provide the appropriate structure of learning materials, and the appropriate quantity and quality of dialogue between teacher and learner, taking into account the extent of the learner's autonomy. They argue that the more highly autonomous the learners, the greater is the distance they can be comfortable with—that is, less dialogue and less structure. For others, the goal must be to reduce distance by increasing dialogue perhaps through the use of computer conferencing or personal telephone contact. Moore and Kearsley (1996) observe further that at other times it may be appropriate to design highly structured courses or programs and to limit dialogue, given the type of learner and the discipline. For practitioners, the theory of transactional distance helps them understand the particular instructional problems they are faced with.

In the case of Cardean courses, where the learning was targeted toward middle managers who were new to distance education, starting the course in a structured format would have given learners a sense of direction. However, as the course progressed, if the opportunity for dialogue were available, the learners could have negotiated course structure with the instructor to see that the course fit with their learning needs. Saba (1988) and Saba and Shearer (1994) researched the relationship between structure and dialogue in instructional contexts using systems modeling techniques and observed that as dialogue increases, structure decreases to keep the system stable. In Saba's (1988) study, this relationship was displayed as a negative feedback loop in a system-dynamics causal loop diagram:

> The negative flow diagram represents an inverse relationship between levels of dialogue and structure. As dialogue increases, structure decreases, and as structure decreases dialogue increases to keep the system stable. In negative feedback loops, the stability of the system depends on interventions from outside the loop. The levels depend on the actions of teacher and learner. In a plausible scenario, the need for decreasing structure is communicated to the teacher. Consultation automatically increases dialogue; then adjustments in goals, instructional materials, and evaluation procedures occur and the learner achieves the desired level of autonomy. (Saba, 1988, p. 22)

Saba expanded the systems model in a subsequent study (Saba & Shearer, 1994), when he ran simulations of distance students' exchanges with instructors to measure relationships of transactional distance and autonomy using discourse analysis techniques. The theory of transactional distance provides guidance to designers on the necessity to balance structure, dialogue, and autonomy for a given group of learners. Garrison and Baynton (1987) have argued that it is pointless to give learners control or autonomy unless they have the necessary support (e.g., instructor and resources) and proficiency (capability) to use that control or autonomy. They note that Control is the dynamic balance between learner proficiency, learner support, and autonomy.

The initial testing of Cardean courses had shown that students often did not perceive the task or the problem to be solved as a real assignment. This may have been due to the way that the course structure was presented. This observation stresses the importance of dialogue between the instructor and students in negotiating the structure related to course assignments. The ability to dialogue with the instructor about the task or problem would have enabled learners to clarify the questions they had about the task or problem so that they understood its relevance and importance within the course structure.

Duffy and Kirkley (Chap. 6, this volume) have noted that a related issue is the presentation of tasks as academic assignments that can result in a loss of the interrelationship of the tasks. That is, the student will begin seeing individual assignments to be completed rather than understanding the problem-solving process. The structure, rather than orienting the student to the problem, replaces the problem as the focus. These are excellent observations on the challenge of designing inquiry learning environments for the online context. Even though the underlying philosophy supports an open inquiry approach, many online courses are designed with content as the focus or course structure as the focus rather than the development of ideas in a community of inquiry, which can overcome some of these pitfalls. As in problem-based learning formats, inquiry-based learning designs should encourage problem solving in small groups with the instructor as a resource and a guide, a format that can be supported by many online course development tools. Small group interaction can lead to the exchange of multiple perspectives necessary to solve ill-structured problems, and can also lead to the negotiation of structure designed into the course if the predesigned structure is not suitable for the learning task or the group of learners.

Another issue that designers must address is the need to provide a clear orientation for students and teachers on the learning and instructional philosophy embedded in the design of open-inquiry environments. As we move students to new paradigms of learning, this orientation is critical so that they do not resort to the traditional ways of progressing through a course.

Collaboration

Duffy and Kirkley (Chap. 6, this volume) quite rightly note that it is in terms of collaboration and community that the Web-based distance learning environment presents the greatest contrast to the classroom environment: "Discussion becomes the cornerstone of an online class. Without it, the class is little more than a correspondence course." While fully supporting this view, I would add that in many online course designs, collaboration remains an add-on feature rather than an integral part of course design. Although building community was considered critical to the Cardean learning environment, there was very little interaction. Duffy and Kirkley point to several factors for this lack of interaction: (1) the focus on course content at the expense of student interaction; (2) the Cardean business model, which allowed students to start and end at their own time; and (3) the focus on courses that ignored the importance of building a university community. This created a context where students saw themselves as individually focused and any discussion was considered extraneous to their goal of working on the course. Duffy and Kirkley observe that although discussion remained minimal even though it was encouraged, the need for more discussion is mentioned by students and faculty as the place where the courses need to be improved.

The major issue I see here is that the concept of a community of inquiry was not central to the course design; it was peripheral. The focus was on individual inquiry-based learning through problem solving and not problem solving in a collaborative group. Interaction was an add-on feature, and students did not see its relevance to meeting the course objectives. The focus on the individual rather than the learning community in the course design led to the problems observed in relation to interaction. If interaction and collaboration are going to be the cornerstone of online learning, then course designers must focus on community building as the central concept in course design.

When training faculty to emphasize student interaction, Cardean conceptualized community by analogy to a neighborhood where everyone works at their own efforts, but neighbors help one another out, as in planning a garden. Although this analogy has value in encouraging students to support one another, I would suggest an alternative analogy if a community of inquiry is to become central to the learning process. In this analogy, all the neighbors collaborate to plant one garden from which everyone benefits, planting a diversity of plants whose products would be shared among the community. When each neighbor knows that he or she can benefit from the products of this collaborative enterprise, individual effort will be put into maintaining the overall well-being of the garden. We have much to learn from collectivist societies such as our own Native American communities, and those in Asia such as Japan, on how to foster a community spirit among individuals that puts a premium on working for the common good. In Keresan Pueblo communities in New Mexico, giftedness (or the Western concept of intelligence) is defined as the individual's ability to contribute to the well-being of the entire community (Romero, 1994). However, building community also means that assessment must reward collaboration, and products developed within the community, rather than individual achievement. This is a difficult concept for many of the individualistic Western academic institutions to comprehend and integrate into course design.

In the online environment, we are currently beta testing an instructional design model that my students and I developed in an advanced instructional design course in the fall of 2001. Referred to as the FOCAL (Final Outcome Centered Around Learner) model, it aims at developing a wise community through the process of transformational learning in individuals and in the community as a whole. Assuming that wisdom is considered by many to be the pinnacle of adult learning, we arrived at the consensus that wisdom would anchor our model. We framed our work around the idea that the new age of bioengineering will require wisdom communities—a collective of people who build knowledge together to create wise products, take wise actions, and nurture relationships with wisdom. FOCAL is founded on constructivist and social constructivist assumptions of learning and is comprised of three elements: wisdom community, mentoring and learner support, and knowledge innovation. The desired outcome of the model is a wisdom community characterized by a collection of accessible knowledge contributed by each individual. The outcome of the FOCAL model is transformational learning within a wisdom community. The process of transformative learning is firmly anchored in life experience, and critical reflection, processes supported by the wisdom community. In this model transformational learning occurs through knowledge innovation, mentoring, support, and dialogue and reflection within the community.

Duffy and Kirkley (Chap. 6, this volume) raise other important issues related to discussion and interaction in online courses. Is discussion essential or not essential?

The role of interaction in an online course needs to be carefully considered by course designers. Discussion should not be an add-on; it should be designed and facilitated only if it is central to achieving the learning goals for the course. For example, if students can move through the course in a self-directed, self-paced manner and solve their own problems, then discussion is not essential. The course should be designed as an individualized learning course. As in Moore's theory of transactional distance, highly autonomous learners who have learned the skills of "learning how to learn" can be comfortable with less dialogue and less structure. However, if the course is designed with a focus on a community of inquiry that engages in inquiry-based learning or problem-based learning, where small groups engage in examining and resolving a problem, then discussion becomes essential.

A related issue that Duffy and Kirkley bring up is whether participation in discussion should be assigned a grade. If the objective to be achieved by the discussion is not central to the course goals, then grading participation does not make sense. Providing opportunity for discussion is not sufficient; it must be meaningful to the learners and facilitated by the instructors or students as moderators. The issue related to quality of discussion can be taken care of when students see its relevance to course goals.

Another important issue is the need to develop a sense of a community of practice or a learning community, an environment in which there are shared goals and in which there is a sense of being part of something larger. Duffy and Kirkey point out that too many online programs have ignored bringing students into the university community and have, instead, focused on courses. This lack of community may be a major contributor to the large dropout rate! I agree wholeheartedly with this point of view and see it as the major contributor to dissatisfaction and dropout in online courses. Students feel lonely, disconnected from the instructor, peers, and the institution, and eventually drop out or do not return. In a study that examined factors that could predict student satisfaction with online conferencing, we found that social presence (or the degree to which a person is perceived as a "real person" in mediated communication and the feeling of connection to others) was a very high predictor of satisfaction, compared to other variables such as equal opportunity to participate in the conference, prior technical skills, and attitude toward the medium (Gunawardena & Zittle, 1997). Duffy and Kirkley note several strategies for creating a learning community, such as blended programs, social activities, and synchronous conferencing. However, these strategies also may create communities as add-ons, and students may not perceive the value of community to achieving course objectives. Community must be central to the design of an online course. Polin (Chap. 2, this volume) and Stinson (Chap. 8, this volume) offer excellent models for centering community in course design and for creating communities of practice. Other examples are found in Wenger and Snyder (2000).

Liedtka (1999) compares the characteristics of communities of practice with contemporary management theories such as learning organization, total quality management, corporate reengineering, strategic thinking, collaboration, participative leadership, and servant leadership. She discovered qualities that are common to all these theories, which mirror the characteristics of communities of practice. If the Cardean business model can be changed, the problem-centered course design would benefit from the incorporation of communities of practice that reflect contemporary management practices, as well as accommodate the learners' request for more interaction.

With the increasing use of the Internet and the Web to offer courses in cross-cultural and cross-national environments, we need to make an attempt to understand how cultural differences influence the way groups interact and develop online. We conducted an exploratory study using survey and focus group data to determine if there are differences in the perception of online group development between participants from Mexico and the United States (Gunawardena et al., 2001). Survey data indicated significant differences in perception for the Norming and Performing stages of group development identified in the Tuckman (1965) model, with the Mexican group showing greater preference for collectivist group values. Mexican and American groups differed in their perception of collectivism, power distance, femininity, and high context communication. Country differences, rather than age and gender differences, accounted for the differences observed between the two groups. For the Mexican participants, the medium of CMC equalized status differences, whereas American participants were concerned that the lack of nonverbal cues led to misunderstanding. Both groups felt that the amount of time it takes to make group decisions in asynchronous CMC, and the lack of commitment to a fair share of the group work, were problems. Focus group participants in Mexico and the United States identified several cultural factors that influence online group process and development: (1) language, or forms of language used, (2) power distance in communication between teachers and students, (3) gender differences, (4) collectivist vs. individualist tendencies, (5) perception of "conflict" and how to manage it, (6) social presence, and (7) the time frame in which the group functions. A subsequent qualitative study (Gunawardena, Walsh, Reddinger, Gregory, Lake, & Davies, 2002) conducted with six different cultural groups investigated how individuals of different cultures negotiate "face" in a non-face-to-face learning environment. Results indicated that cultural differences do exist in online presentation and negotiation of "face." These exploratory studies have indicated the need for future research in this area if we are to design more inclusive computer conferences.

Assessment

Duffy and Kirkley observed (Chap. 6, this volume) that, in general, assessment drives learning. Therefore, the challenge in designing inquiry-based learning environments is to develop appropriate assessment of learning. My questions relate to whether Cardean University evaluated the problem-solving process or only the tasks associated with the process. Is the grade based on the process or the product, or both?

I believe that in inquiry-based learning, it is critical that we evaluate the process of learning, as the product may not turn out to be what the instructor or the student expected. For example, I observed how medical students work with a sophisticated technology-driven simulated patient at the University of New Mexico School of Medicine and learned from the instructor that often the process anesthesiology students go through to revive the patient is accurate, even though the patient may die. The instructor found it difficult to convince the students that the process was accurate, as they could only focus on the product—their responsibility in letting the patient die. The challenge-based design model developed for the AMIGO project, described by Bransford, Vye, Bateman, Brophy, and Roselli (Chap. 10, this volume), offers insight on how to evaluate process in a Web-based inquiry environment. Comparing students' later thoughts to their initial thoughts as described in this model will indicate how much their thinking has changed. This is only possible because their thinking process can be captured in the Web-based learning environment.

Assessment of learning in communities of inquiry or communities of practice presents a significant challenge to instructors and designers alike. The computer transcript provides an excellent data source for analysis of learning. My colleagues and

I took up this challenge in a study to assess the process and type of learning that occurred in an online professional development conference conducted as a debate across international time lines. The questions we were interested in examining were:

1. Was knowledge constructed within the group by means of the exchanges among participants?
2. Did individual participants change their understanding or create new personal constructions of knowledge as a result of interactions within the group?

Our efforts ended up in the development of an interaction analysis model (Gunawardena, Lowe, & Anderson, 1997) based on social constructivist theory to examine the negotiation of meaning that occurred in the online conference by analyzing the computer transcripts. We described the model in phases, as we saw the group move from sharing and comparing of information, through cognitive dissonance, to negotiation of meaning, the testing and modification of the proposed coconstruction, and to the application of the newly constructed meaning. This model was applied to a study in Mexico discussed by López-Islas (Chap. 16, this volume). An interesting observation is that the phases of cognitive dissonance, and the testing and modification of the proposed coconstruction, were almost absent in the conferences, as the Latin culture does not favor the open expression of disagreements, and therefore there is no need to extensively test and modify group proposals. Jeong (2001) applied the Gunawardena, Lowe, and Anderson (1997) model and developed a model of 12 critical thinking event categories, whereas Reschke (2001) applied the model and developed the Degree of Synthesis Model. Other interaction analysis models have been developed for understanding learning in constructivist and social constructivist learning environments (Garrison, Anderson, & Archer 2001; Kumpulainen & Mutanen, 2000; Rojas-Drummond, 2000). These interaction analysis models, an emerging area of research in distance education, present a means to evaluate the process of learning through the analysis of computer discussions. Although detailed analyses of computer transcripts fall within the realm of research and are very time-consuming, a practitioner with relevant skills should be able to analyze small segments of computer discussions (for example, a 2-week discussion) to determine the process of learning.

Transfer

Duffy and Kirkley (Chap. 6, this volume) observed that the inquiry-based approach is ideal for supporting real world transfer, because the problem, project, design task, or puzzlement simply needs to be a real world context. However, simply rooting the problem in a real world context may not lead to transfer of learning, and as Duffy and Kirkley have observed, transfer to new situations is difficult to achieve. Bransford, Vye, Bateman, Brophy, and Roselli (Chap. 10, this volume) provide a thought-provoking discussion of transfer of learning in terms of "preparing for future learning," rather than applying stored knowledge to new situations.

The discussion on transfer could have been enriched with data to support transfer of learning from Cardean courses. Duffy and Kirkley (Chap. 6, this volume) made a very important point about two strategies that were designed to promote transfer and that were largely ineffective. These strategies were the instructor's attempt to promote discussion about related applications and the use of a final "reflection" task in which students were asked to apply the learning to their workplace. The reflection task was largely ineffective because it came at the end of the course and it was an individual reflection on which no one could comment and about which there was no discussion except for comments the instructor might offer. If reflection was designed as a process that took place throughout the course, with instructors and peers commenting on the reflections, this may not have occurred.

CONCLUSION

This chapter addressed issues related to designing online learning environments based on constructivist and social constructivist learning principles. Some of these issues included the challenge of designing inquiry-based learning environments, balancing structure and dialogue in distance education course design, designing online collaboration, and assessment and transfer of learning. This chapter built off issues raised by Duffy and Kirkley (Chap. 6, this volume) when designing inquiry-based learning environments for Cardean University online courses and extended the discussion by citing my own research and research in distance education.

The significance of Duffy and Kirkley's chapter lies in its presentation of a pedagogical model for the design of inquiry-based learning environments for the online context, and the frank and open discussion of problems encountered when applying the pedagogical model to Cardean courses. The chapter shows us the challenge of matching a pedagogical model to a business model and the inability to generate sustained interaction and a community of inquiry because of this mismatch. I believe the pedagogical model can be enhanced by focusing the design on a community of inquiry where students collaborate on solving problems. Insights on centering the design on a community of inquiry are discussed by Linda Polin (Chap. 6) and John Stinson (Chap. 8) in this volume. To further develop the pedagogical model and provide guidelines for designers, future research should focus on gathering more systematic evaluation and research data.

REFERENCES

Aspy, D. N., Aspy, C. B., & Quimby, P. M. (1993). What doctors can teach teachers about problem-based learning. *Educational Leadership, 50*(7), 22–24.

Bednar, A. K., Cunningham, D., Duffy, T. M., & Perry, J. D. (1992). Theory into practice: How do we link? In T. M. Duffy & D. H. Jonassen (Eds.), *Constructivism and the technology of instruction: A conversation* (pp. 17–34). Hillsdale. NJ: Lawrence Erlbaum Associates.

Bransford, J. D., Brown, A. L., & Cocking, R. R. (Eds.). (2000). *How people learn: Brain, mind, experience, and school* (National Research Council). Washington DC: National Academy Press.

Crandall, S., & Gunawardena, C. N. (1999). Using the Web for facilitating problem-based learning and case-based reasoning in the training of pre-clinical medical students. In *Proceedings of the WebNet World Conference on the WWW and Internet* (pp. 1232–1233). Charlottesville, VA: Association for the Advancement of Computing in Education.

Eastmond, D. V. (1994). Adult distance study through computer conferencing. *Distance Education, 15*(1), 128–152.

Garrison, D. R., Anderson, T., & Archer, W. (2001). Critical thinking, cognitive presence, and computer conferencing in distance education. *The American Journal of Distance Education, 15*(1), 7–15.

Garrison, R., & Baynton, M. (1987). Beyond independence in distance education: The concept of control. *American Journal of Distance Education, 3*(1), 3–15.

Gunawardena, C. N. (1992). Changing faculty roles for audiographics and online teaching. *The American Journal of Distance Education, 6*(3), 58–71.

Gunawardena, C. N., Boverie, P., Wilson, P. L., Lowe, C. A., Ortegano-Layne, L., Lindemann, K., Mummert, J., & Rodriguez, F. (2001, December). *First-year evaluation report of the Star Schools Web-based math and science teacher education program developed by Oklahoma State University* (Study funded by the U.S. Department of Education, Office of Educational Research and Improvement, Grant No. R203f000039). Albuquerque, NM: University of New Mexico, Organizational Learning and Instructional Technologies, Program College of Education.

Gunawardena, C. N., Lowe, C. A., & Anderson, T. (1997). Analysis of a global online debate and the development of an interaction analysis model for examining social construction of knowledge in computer conferencing. *Journal of Educational Computing Research, 17,* 395–429.

Gunawardena, C. N., Nolla, A. C., Wilson, P. L., López-Islas, J. R., Ramírez-Angel, N., Megchun-Alpízar, R. M. (2001). A cross-cultural study of group process and development in online conferences. *Distance Education 22*(1), 85–121.

Gunawardena, C. N., Walsh, S., Reddinger, L., Gregory, E., Lake, Y., & Davies, A. (2002). Negotiating "face" in a non-face-to-face learning environment (pp. 89–106). In F. Sudweeks & C. Ess (Eds.), *Proceedings of Cultural Attitudes Towards Communication and Technology, 2002.* Quebec, Canada: University of Montreal.

Gunawardena, C. N., & Zittle, F. (1997). Social presence as a predictor of satisfaction within a computer mediated conferencing environment. *The American Journal of Distance Education, 11*(3), 8–25.

Jeong, A. (2001). *Supporting critical thinking with group discussion on threaded bulletin boards: An analysis of group interaction.* Unpublished doctoral dissertation, University of Wisconsin, Madison.

Jones, S. G. (1995). *Cybersociety: Computer-mediated communication and community.* Thousand Oaks, CA: Sage.

Jones, S. G. (Ed.). (1997). *Virtual culture: Identity and communication in cybersociety.* London: Sage.

Kumpulainen, K., & Mutanen, M. (2000). Mapping the dynamics of peer group interaction: A method of analysis of socially shared learning processes. In H. Cowie & van der Aalsvoort (Eds.), *Social interaction in learning and instruction: The meaning of discourse for the construction of knowledge* (pp. 144–160). Amsterdam: Pergamon, Advances in Learning and Instruction Series.

Lave, J. (1991). Situating learning in communities of practice. In L. B. Resnick, J. M. Levine, & S. D. Teasley (Eds.), *Perspectives on socially shared cognition* (pp. 63–82). Washington, DC: American Psychological Association.

Liedtka, J. (1999). Linking competitive advantage with communities of practice. *Journal of Management Inquiry, 8*(1), 5–17.

Mayer, R. E. (2001). *Multimedia learning.* Cambridge, UK: Cambridge University Press.

Mayo, P., Donnelly, M. B., Nash, P. P., & Schwartz, R. W. (1993). Student perceptions of tutor effectiveness in problem based surgery clerkship. *Teaching and Learning in Medicine, 5,* 227–233.

Moore, M. G. (1973). Towards a theory of independent learning and teaching. *Journal of Higher Education, 44,* 661–679.

Moore, M. G., & Kearsley, G. (1996). *Distance education: A systems view.* Belmont, CA: Wadsworth.

Reschke, K. (2001). *The family child care forum: An innovative model for effective online training for family child care providers.* Unpublished doctoral dissertation, Indiana State University, Terre Haute, Indiana.

Resnick, L. B. (1991). Shared cognition: Thinking as social practice. In L. B. Resnick, J. M. Levine, & S. D. Teasley (Eds.), *Perspectives on socially shared cognition* (pp. 1–20). Washington, DC: American Psychological Association.

Resnick, L. B., Levine, J. M. & Teasley, S. D. (1991). *Perspectives on socially shared cognition.* Washington, DC: American Psychological Association.

Rojas-Drummond, S. (2000). Guided participation, discourse and the construction of knowledge in Mexican classrooms. In H. Cowie & van der Aalsvoort (Eds.), *Social interaction in learning and instruction: The meaning of discourse for the construction of knowledge* (pp. 191–213). Amsterdam: Pergamon.

Romero, M. E. (1994, Fall). Identifying giftedness among Keresan Pueblo Indians: The Keres study. *Journal of American Indian Education, 34*(1), 35–58.

Saba, F. (1988). Integrated telecommunications systems and instructional transaction. *American Journal of Distance Education, 2*(3), 17–24.

Saba, F., & Shearer, R. (1994). Verifying theoretical concepts in a dynamic model of distance education. *American Journal of Distance Education, 8*(1), 36–59.

Teasley, S., & Roschelle, J. (1993). Constructing a joint problem space: The computer as a tool for sharing knowledge. In S. P. Lajoie & S. J. Derry (Eds.), *Computers as cognitive tools* (pp. 229–257). Hillsdale, NJ: Lawrence Erlbaum Associates.

Tuckman, B. W. (1965). Developmental sequence in small groups. *Psychological Bulletin, 63,* 384–399.

Vernon, D. T., & Blake, R. L. (1993). Does problem-based learning work? A meta-analysis of evaluative research. *Academic Medicine, 68,* 550–563.

Vygotsky, L. S. (1978). *Mind in society: The development of higher psychological processes* (M. Cole, V. John-Steiner, S. Scribner, & E. Souberman, Eds). Cambridge, MA: Harvard University Press.

Wegerif, R., & Mercer, N. (2000). Language for thinking: A study of children solving reasoning test problems together. In H. Cowie & G. van der Aalsvoort (Eds.), *Social interaction in learning and instruction: The meaning of discourse for the construction of knowledge* (pp. 179–192). Oxford, UK: Pergamon.

Wenger, E. C., & Snyder, W. M. (2000). Communities of practice: The organizational frontier. *Harvard Business Review, 78*(1), 139–146.

Wertsch, J. V. (1985). *Vygotsky and the social formation of mind.* Cambridge, MA: Harvard University Press.

Wertsch, J. V. (1991). A sociocultural approach to socially shared cognition. In L. B. Resnick, J. M. Levine, & S. D. Teasley (Eds.), *Perspectives on socially shared cognition* (pp. 85–100). Washington, DC: American Psychological Association.

)

Open Discussion of Chapter 6

Tom Duffy: Lani has emphasized the importance of collaboration and the sense of affiliation that arises from it. Let me clarify, or perhaps reemphasize. Absolutely, and without a doubt, this is a case of the business model conflicting with the pedagogical goals that we have. There is no doubt about it. Lani suggested that the garden metaphor should be one of everyone working on the same garden. Although it is nice to propose, the business model simply did not allow a model that reflected that metaphor. In any environment, we need to live within the business rules. (As an aside, Indiana University in recent years has begun to enforce a minimum class-size requirement—again, a business rule potentially impacting pedagogy—or more likely in this case, impacting curricular needs.)

Let me also note that my garden metaphor of consultants does in fact parallel at least at the metaphorical level, the learning circle approach that Margaret Reil has been developing for the last decade. So there is a reasonably well-worked-out conceptual framework for the consultancy strategy. However, this in no way implies that the business rules would not also hinder our ability to realize the conceptual richness of learning circles—it is just to note that there are different models.

I want to take a contrarian notion. We all acknowledge the fact that all we do happens in a social and community context. That is not the issue. However, I want to challenge people to defend the importance of formally building and supporting the social context or community in learning—what does one get out of the process—when you're talking about people who are already working in a community? Our students already have their community of practice. They're already learning together in the workplace. They are using these courses as resources; these are professional courses, right? They are not humanities or social science courses. They are, in fact, professional courses to develop intellectual skills that can then be applied to the workplace. (Of course, social sciences should do the same thing, but we don't think about them in that way.)

So our students already have their community. They have people to talk to. Do they need it in the course? We have to think of the cost benefits. What if we, in fact, force the collaboration, force a cohort. We would lose a lot of people. By the way, we already have high dropout rates. They already tell us they would not be able to complete the course with a fixed schedule imposed. One has to wonder, can we think of different models?

Let me offer a different model from a community one, and that's a mentoring model. Could we not just establish it by having a better tutoring system available, one where you have the central instructor but you have junior people who do a lot of interacting with the students, prodding them? Perhaps we have a lot of dropout because they don't have sense of community, but also perhaps because they don't have deadlines for turning anything in and are not getting adequate challenge from an instructor. If we

159

start instituting deadlines, would that, in fact, get the completion rate up? My suspicion is that it would—and the mentoring would also like build that sense of affiliation and identity.

Mark Schlager: You're discussing your own paper! (*group laughs.*)

John Stinson: I think we have to recognize the breadth of complexity of the content attempting to be addressed here. Each one of the courses is very, very focused, with not very much breadth of content. Given that, if you look at the learning outcome, I'm not certain that collaboration is very important in terms of learning from one another. Also, you're talking about being situated in a community, but I would focus more on them being situated more in the context of their work environment. Although there is a community in the workplace too, I think the context is perhaps more important than the community. Students might not discuss it with anyone else in their community, but if they have already been through that type of thing, there reaction will be, "oh, hell, I can use that for this." That is a powerful situating element. So I'm not certain for almost all of those learning objects that we need a hell of a lot of collaboration.

Bob Wisher: Tom, I understand that Cardean sold in blocks to General Motors and other corporations. So if you had a cohort from one corporate culture, would you then expect to get more of the interactivity that you are not getting because you are mixing across corporations?

Tom Duffy: The corporations are really mixed about that. Some want it to be internal and others—really both the corporate and student level—want to go intercorporate. It is a freedom of discussion versus a generation of new ideas. GM has really emphasized wanting a community environment. It will be interesting to see if it can be pulled off. But the community environment is stepping out of the course level and up to the university level. They want to think of the community in a university sense rather than a course sense.

Mark Schlager: That is the point I was actually going to address. We seem to get a little sloppy in equating collaboration and community here. Collaboration within a course is a pedagogical choice. Community, going back to Linda's students, exists or it doesn't exist, and we don't create community through the amalgamation of courses. The whole issue of the university is where the community needs to be, and then people can choose to become part of that community in addition to their own. But they have got to see what benefits in it. So it's almost a chicken or egg thing: You don't have community here, but then you want people to be part of a community. They don't know what they are going to be a part of, so what value is it? I would like try to keep separate the issue of collaboration within a course as a pedagogical issue and a community as a larger social entity issue.

Tom Duffy: I agree.

Jim Botkin: I think there are great advantages for communities, particularly when they do cross over company lines. There is no way to build these things magically.

Mark Schlager: They are emergent.

Jim Botkin: They *are* emergent. It is much easier to have them emerge when you are going across company lines or, dare I say, university lines, because you won't have the power and authority to control issues that you have in any single institutional hierarchy.

Tom Duffy: That is really an excellent point—one I have not heard raised in the community discussions except in terms of the concept of the value of boundary crossing. I would ask a question back to Mark regarding the relationship of community and collaboration. The paper that Sasha Barab and I did really talks about it directly in that fashion. But, in fact, it is really common in the learning sciences to talk about communities in the classroom. In online classes, we talk about social presence, this sense of affiliation with one another, which is really the beginning of the sense of community. It is important to create the persistence even within a class. I think at the community level . . .

Jim Botkin: You look to alternatives to the community level, the community of practice. At the individual level, you mention mentoring or coaching. The other famous one of course is apprenticeship. I never understood why that has not caught on bigger in other countries except Germany. It seems to me that is another viable alternative along the same lines.

Peter Shea: You mention that these folks are already members of a community, so they don't need community here. It immediately struck me to say that you really don't mean that, because if we buy into the notion that affect matters, that trust matters, that all things that go into building a community matter in supporting learning, then you would say, "Sure, I belong to lots of communities." But if I want to benefit from the role community plays in learning, there has to be sense of community in this classroom to benefit from that. Maybe there are other ways that individuals can learn. But if we think that having community is more efficient and effective method for supporting all kinds of learning outcomes, we need to find the best way to support it.

Tom Duffy: I would push back from a variable point of view. To talk about it that way—the community in a class—what is the benefit from the learning perspective of the community in the class?

Peter Shea: I think a lot is done with talking about all the variables that go into building a sense of belonging, a sense of trust, a sense of closeness. That makes it supportive of learning.

Dick Lesh: First, Tom, I want to say thanks for inviting me. I now have a sense of why I may have a contribution here. (*group laughs.*) This is such an interesting group of folks, it brings an interesting perspective. In this session, I was trying to figure out what is the problem for which we are the solution. I am getting a better sense of that now. I have heard two perspectives on whatever we think it is we're doing: the sociocultural perspective and the instructional design perspective. I think there is at least a third perspective, a content perspective—maybe I am a singleton as a math guy, but there is at least a physics guy here too. The instructional design perspective focuses on how to design the learning environment. The sociocultural perspective is more about how you learn it. The content view is simply what must be learned, not just what should the person be able to do at the end of the learning experience, but also what content encounters are required to get to that end.

I think maybe the shocker for people is that the content to be learned has changed, and really radically. Just to give you an idea, I spent years studying kids learning about fractions—just fractions. What people need to know about fractions today is radically different from what it was even 15 years ago, because math is now multimedia. It is now about complex systems, where there is integration, where you are quantifying qualitative information. It's really changed in a radical way. You can really get a sense of that if you think about the difference in what a teacher needs to know about fractions than what a kid needs to understand about fractions. Yet you say, so what is it they need to know? Sure, it involves something of how an idea develops logically, but also psychologically, historically, and in the curriculum and a variety of other things. Well, I think what "it" is, is smaller than people have led you to believe and that it does not need intense interaction. You suggested that. But let me mention a context in which this has occurred.

—I am at Purdue University, and it's a very applied kind of place with engineers and management people—I've gone to folks that teach courses like the one Tom was talking about. We have tried to get them to articulate for us what it is that kids need to know to prepare them to do what they want them to be able do. The truth is, they don't know. They have not thought about it very much. We call these instructors/faculty "evolving teaching experts", because we treat them as experts, but they are experts that have a lot to learn.

Basically, we get them to learn by getting them to express what they think in a form that needs to be tested and revised multiple times. One of the vehicles for doing that is to have them develop case studies for kids that get at what they think the kernel of the idea is. We have yet to find a case study in engineering or management that we cannot make accessible to a middle school kid in a project that would not take more than a couple of hours. But that is because we weed out all the crap and get down to the kernel of the idea. They often call it a model if they call it anything. It is a model for thinking about a class of things, and they are trying to get their students to develop a model, and the message is that the model doesn't take that long to develop—like 2 hours for middle schoolers.

I worked with a guy in the management school who was astounded that we got middle school kids who were not supposed to be terribly good—they were in the dropout class—to outperform his graduate students on the kid version of the task he helped us develop. One of the things that makes this doable is when we start to get clear of what the "it" is, models are constructs. That is what needs to be constructed—everything doesn't need to be constructed. Constructs need to be constructed.

In math, we have a long history of focusing on discovery learning, problem-based learning. What has been wrong with it is that we take a process and turn it into the product, and it goes awry. People start treating discovery as though it is great for it's own sake, don't care what was discovered. The thing that is nice about these case studies is that the product people produce isn't an answer to a question. It is a model for thinking about a class of things. There is an enormous difference.

A couple of other spinoffs, and then I'll shut up. I was quiet for too long. Sorry. (*Group laughs*). The other thing is if you produce the model you can look at it and see how someone was thinking. So the other bugaboo we are dealing with is, How in the hell do you get instructors to improve? The best way to change instructors, we found, is to see how their students teach. The most effective way we have found with these guys in management school is if we can get clearer with having them produce models for thinking. They are thought revealing . . . they do see their students think, and they start to teach better. So those are a bunch of leverage points that don't come unless you take a content perspective.

John Bransford: Quickly, as a learning scientist, I agree that the content issues are huge, and we haven't talked about those. I was just going to mention lessons I learned from working with Ann Brown and Joe Campione about how intricately related social context and content are. So, for example, if you really want social collaboration, you have to have a problem and a set of audiences that can actually make it more efficient to learn things from one another. You can actually engineer that. If you use the task structure, you have a really complex problem you start out with in your scenario, but now you have broken it down for people. Use the jigsaw approach to build specific expertise in specific subgroups of the class. Collaboration in a jigsaw mode, when the problem is complex, can result in more efficient learning, because everyone can take a different segment. But to integrate the work, they have to go back and teach the group what they learned in their segment . . .

Tom Duffy: I agree. Obviously, if we could run cohorts through the teaming process, I think it would be rich. Given we can't do that, I'd like some reflection on what we lose and what are the alternatives.

Rafael López: We face similar tensions and issues at Monterrey Tech. But what I want to say is that in this issue of collaboration, of whether it is important or not to do it collaboratively, what we decided was that collaboration is not only a pedagogy for learning something else, it's an objective by itself, and that is why we pay a lot of attention to it. I don't think we have found the answers to these questions, but collaboration is declared at the beginning in every course as a learning objective by itself, besides the other content-related issues.

Tom Duffy: I absolutely agree with you. A lot of corporations talk about wanting their people to be working in teams, because they wanted to develop the team skills. You know, it is really an interesting conflict. I find it fascinating. I am not sure that we don't create the social environment that invites the kind of the responses that we get from students and corporations. However, while they tell us teamwork and collaboration are important, when I tried to do that in two instances—where we truly wanted to create cohorts—I got back the responses, "Nope, I would love to do it, but no." When it comes down to the practicalities, they—both the corporation and the students—don't want the restrictions that arise in collaborative environments.

Rafael López: There are three things that I picked up from your context. First, the learning goals seems to be individually definable. So if you were to present the problem from the perspective of "apply it to your own scenario, apply it to your own company", and then as a second phase, within your team come up with what of this is relevant to your team, then maybe collaboration would become.

Second is the question of competence and transferability. Competence is not just whether you are competent to find the answers to the questions somebody else have given. The real competence is if you can you generate the questions yourself. Can you identify the kind of problems you are having in the company that you work for or the institution that you work for? Then it becomes provocative to collaborate naturally within that community to identify the right kinds of questions for which there could be answers.

Tom Duffy: There are three business roles I defined, but there is a fourth one that I guess I need to add. It is the notion that we are going to deal with millions of students, that we are going to scale very large, right? If you are scaling very large, you can't deal with the individual and their corporation and how it will apply to them. We cannot deal with Linda's kind of environment; it is too craft oriented. It really is a craft versus a technology orientation, I think. In scaling, you have to push more to the technology solution. I hate saying that.

Let me add one thing about one of the notions I had of how one could actually start building the community environment in here: How it could work well even in our current environment? If it's scaled large, if we started to have hundreds of students in the class, then if students had online awareness and were using a tool like Groove's peer-to-peer collaboration, people could spontaneously jump into groove discussions. Given this context—and it does require a lot of students in our environment—ad hoc groups could form. Students could get together in work groups to work on particular parts of the problem. That could become a really powerful kind of strategy for building those kinships, even in a fully self-paced environment. It's not a community in a larger sense like everybody else has been talking about: everyone getting to know everyone else. But it is kind of building a bunch of cohorts talking to each other over time and with the students mixing across different ad hoc groups. As their learning needs change, there would be the growing "class" or "community" environment. Students would begin to develop identities in the environment, recognized by other students.

Peter Shea: Okay, it seems to me that there were two things that were not working. One is that there was never a critical mass of students in any one class or in the whole system to have a sense of community or to benefit from collaboration and cooperation. Second, collaboration and community building was incompatibile with an idea that says that we are going to cater to these busy students, with our assumption that work takes precedence.

Tom Duffy: I think that is true. Absolutely. I think that is true, Peter.

Peter Shea: This is a learning network. All online students are busy. Everybody in the world is busy. Online students are no more busy than anybody else. The idea to say that we have to cater to these people so much to make this work sort of undermines the whole thing from the beginning.

Tom Duffy: I agree with that. Do let me note that there were enough students enrolling to support collaboration if we ran cohorts.

Linda Polin: I have two thoughts. As you were talking about the very thing you were bemoaning, I was thinking, That is interesting, how can I do that? Because I actually think it is very artificial if you try to get everyone in at one time and make them a cohort. I think we do it for reasons of structured university.

Bob Wisher: The corporations seem to be concerned about return on investment, and rightly so. Perhaps they need to move beyond the traditional view of how it affects earnings or new sales revenues and things like that to more judgments of the contributions of this to some new strategy. For example, the contributions of this might be toward envisioning a new product or some new manufacturing process that might not be realized for some years. But the fact that you made that contribution from these learning projects and we're able to come up with some kind of thinking capital, that is, some kind of transformation or change, that is an important return on investment.

Carson Eoyang: There is already some tracking of that. I know *Technology Review* evaluates universities on the basis of patents, copyrights, and royalties generated from patents over the last year. They rank universities over the last 10 years in terms of the amounts of revenues that comes from patents and royalties. They measure the number of patents and royalties themselves.

Linda Polin: That might be the analog in the program. It just appealed to me conceptually as the way to go. When you are working with project-based stuff and team-based stuff, then what is the metric?

John Stinson: Going there is a really difficult thing to do. The closest thing we get to in our assessment activity requires the individuals to do something that is very similar. New product development, for example, would be part of the individual assessment. The student has to demonstrate the capability of creating a new product and developing a model for bringing that product to market.

Tom Duffy: I know we would love to continue the discussion, but it is time to move on.
    (End of session)

8

A Continuing Learning Community for Graduates of an MBA Program: The Experiment at Ohio University

John Stinson
Ohio University Without Boundaries

As we enter what Peter Drucker (1994) has called the knowledge age, work and the environment of work is changing dramatically. Increasingly knowledge—intellectual capital—is becoming the most critical resource that a firm possesses. Increasingly, employees are being called on to continually expand their capabilities, not to do more work, but to do more complex work, to make more decisions and make them more independently. This implies that people need to be continually developing competencies—not just job skills, but also intellectual skills. It implies that learning opportunities need to be available to them anytime and anywhere, and that learning needs to be available just-in-time as needed for their use. As Tapscott (1997) noted in The Digital Economy

- Increasingly, work and learning are becoming the same thing.
- Learning is becoming a lifelong challenge.
- Learning is shifting away from formal schools and universities.

Changing learning needs present a threat to today's higher education institutions. Although many, if not most, have units focusing on continuing education, those units are typically outside the main mission of the institutions. They are generally not integrated with the major academic programs. They frequently focus on providing short courses for public consumption and seldom provided a framework for a continual relationship designed to meet the learning needs of an individual throughout his or her career and life.

Does this have to be the case? Can a higher education institution become a source for continual learning for its "students"? Can a learning community be established in formal degree programs and sustained so that it provides a source for continual learning?

This chapter reports on an attempt to develop such a continual learning community at Ohio University. Although it focuses on a single program—the MBA Without

Boundaries (MBAWB)—the effort is seen by the university as an experiment that, if shown to be feasible and desirable, could lead to the integration of such learning communities into a variety of programs.

Why use the MBAWB for the experiment? The MBAWB is an award-wining program that is widely recognized as being on the forefront of innovation. It is a blended program including both residential experiences and online learning. Based on a constructivist learning philosophy, it strongly emphasizes development and use of community. The program, now 6 years old, targets fast-tracking midlevel executives who continue to work during their participation. Thus, it provides many conditions that could lead to continued community; the existence of community, technology mediated collaboration, online learning, and a learning model that emphasizes the integration of work and learning.

Further, graduates of the program have expressed an interest in continuing the community. They understand their need for continual learning. They read about and to some extent experienced "Free Agent Nation" (Pink, 1997). They are familiar with Tapscott's view of work and learning (Tapscott, 1997). Because of their past relationship with Ohio University, their fellow students, and their faculty, they have expressed an interest in Ohio University providing that continual source of learning.

In the sections that follow, we describe the MBAWB and actions taken to develop community within the program. We then describe the effort to develop a primarily online continuing community for graduates of the program. Finally, we provide some preliminary results of the attempt to continue community and some comments on the educational policy issues raised.

THE MBAWB

MBA Without Boundaries utilizes a learning architecture that combines the learning power of project-centered action learning with the ease of access and learning enhancement of a virtual learning community. It is designed for individuals with the potential to lead global corporations in the information age. Participants are expected to have a record of increasingly responsible professional experience and participate fully without having to stop work. The design is partially based on that of a full-time MBA program delivered in a face-to-face setting that was initially implemented in 1987. The MBAWB took the pedagogical approach used in the full-time program and redesigned it for distance delivery using information technology (Stinson, 1997).

Initially, few changes were made in program structure. Lotus Domino was used to facilitate online team-based collaboration and faculty tutoring of participants. Over time, more interactive learning modules were added to enable more effective content acquisition.

The program, a lock-step, cohort program, is organized around nine learning projects, in contrast to being organized around the typical discipline-based courses, and requires 2 years of commitment. There are three 1-week residencies, one each at the beginning, middle, and end of the program, and three extended weekends meetings each of the 2 years. The residencies are designed to enable the development of interpersonal skills, allow accelerated project start-up, evaluate project deliverables, and assess student learning. Participants meet face-to-face every 3 months.

Rather than being vessels that are simply filled by faculty, participants learn by working their way through projects, usually in a team. As they need to know, they engage in research, work with faculty, and construct their learning in an active and contextualized way. The virtual community that permeates the program is built on Lotus Domino and enables online collaboration among learners and faculty, access of learning materials, and tutoring by faculty.

The MBAWB Structure

The MBAWB is based firmly on a constructivist approach to learning. The learning methodology has evolved experientially as we have used it during the last 14 years. As we evolved our approach, we have been significantly influenced by discussions with Barrows (1985) and Duffy (1991).

There are no discrete, discipline-based courses in the program. Rather, all learning is organized into nine separate learning units that in total form an integrated whole. Each unit is situated with an authentic and engaging project that provides the goal that engages the learners. Short descriptions of the nine units are provided in Fig. 8.1.

As they perform research to produce the project deliverable, participants are expected to make full use of sources available on the Internet. Although faculty package some learning exercises on the program intranet, the main effort is to help the participants develop an effective inquiry process; faculty help them learn how to develop a conceptual road map of the information they need and how they might obtain the needed information.

The curriculum is designed so that participants develop a broad conceptual framework first and then learn the specific detailed content that fits within it. (See Collins, 1990, for theoretical rationale.) For example, Project 1 is designed to focus on the business as a whole and develop an understanding of the business concept in action. The next three projects take a much more micro perspective and focuses in detail on making and selling (operations and marketing) and the financial activities of the firm. Later projects return to a more macro perspective, integrating the more micro perspectives into the larger environment of which business is a part.

Thus, the curricular structure is design to develop breadth of perspective and depth of understanding of the business as a whole, its component parts, and the environment in which it functions. This is accomplished through the sequencing of the learning units and the design of the projects. Recognizing the importance of iteration on the same content areas, discipline areas are addressed multiple times, each time with greater depth.

The project is central to each learning unit. Although the topic of each learning unit remains the same, a new project is developed for each iteration of the program. This is done to maintain currency of focus and to ensure that the content is being learned in the most timely context. Nothing turns off an adult student faster than studying a problem that a company had 10 years ago.

The project drives the learning and creates the "need to know." As Schank and Cleary (1995) have noted, too frequently inadequate attention is given to the design of problems. Those inexperienced with project-based action learning problems often make the mistake of selecting a project because it is convenient or interesting. They then "fudge" the development of learning outcomes to fit the selected project.

We have been very rigorous in the area of project design to protect against poor project selection. We first clearly identify the target learning outcomes for the unit. We then attempt to design a project that directly targets those learning outcomes and is at the same time authentic and engaging. Over the years, we have developed a set of guidelines for the design of projects. (See Fig. 8.2 for a summary of the guidelines.) More detail on the design of projects can be found in Stinson (1994) and Stinson and Milter (1996).

Project 1: Orientation—The Business Concept
The primary purpose of this project is to introduce students to the learning methodology that is used in the MBAWB program. They also become acquainted with each other and learn to use the information technology to both do research and collaborate.

This is a macro-level project that looks at the business as a business. In the past, the project has been based on questions such as, Should HP buy Compaq? and Can Enron survive? There is an attempt to ensure that the project utilizes a situation that is current in the news.

Project 2: Basic Business Concepts—Making and Selling and Financing Activities
This project is intended to allow participants to review and consolidate their understanding of basic business activities. We should remember that these topics are not new to the participants; they have some educational and experiential background. Thus, basic understanding of marketing, operations, accounting, and finance concepts and the interrelationships of the functions is the focus. The form typically is to require participants to make a business case for a new business effort.

Project 3: Developing Strategy
This project focuses on the future. The basic project requirement is to help a company determine what actions to take to maximize the probability of long-term success. Thus, it involves futures analysis, in-depth industry analysis, competitive intelligence, analysis of strategic and financial strength, identification of distinctive competencies, scenario development, and other activities. Participants are required to develop and articulate a vision for a company and develop a strategy to implement that vision.

Project 4: Global Competition and International Trade
In this project, participants develop an understanding of international trade and global business. They learn how to perform country analysis, how to understand and incorporate consideration of cultural differences, how to deal with international monetary issues, and other things. This is often an excellent project to do with a live company.

Project 5: Individual Project
This project focuses on an area of emphasis that is important to the individual participant. Participants are encouraged to engage in a project that is in some way related to current or anticipated work responsibilities. It often involves an operations improvement.

Project 6: Financing the Firm
This project is designed to develop in-depth understanding and abilities in financial analysis. It includes developing understanding of financial institutions, capital formation, financing activities, and financial analysis techniques. Participants will consider financial analysis from both a micro and a macro level. It often takes the form of developing a mutual fund and selecting an initial portfolio of stocks.

Project 7: Entrepreneurial Activity—Commercializing an Invention
This project helps participants understand the product (service) development and introduction process. They are confronted with the problem of determining the market for a product that does not exist and finding financing for an idea. As part of the project, they develop a business plan to present to venture capitalists.

FIG. 8.1.   The nine learning projects of the MBAWB.

Project 8: Business and Public Policy
This project focuses on the interrelationships between business and government. The consideration can range from government regulations to business lobbying efforts. Obviously, the issue of corporate social responsibility is also a part of the participant's consideration.

Project 9: Individual Project
This project focuses on an area of emphasis that is important to the individual student. Students are encouraged to do a transitional project that will help them establish a base for long development.

FIG. 8.1.   (Continued)

The Learning Process

The learning process that permeates the program is shared with the participants in model form at the first residency (see Fig. 3). The model is frequently referred to by faculty and participants in subsequent residencies and in online discussions.

With the exception of the first project, which is done during the first 1-week residency, each project starts and ends during a residency. All necessary collaboration to develop the deliverable for each project is accomplished through the MBAWB intranet.

At the start-up residency, participants identify learning outcomes that they will target, personally and as a class. They also identity issues that must be addressed to develop the deliverable and meet the requirements of the project charge. Finally, they develop an action plan and a team contract that governs how they will function as they collaborate in a distributed manner to complete the deliverable.

The ability to identify learning issues must be developed by the participants. They do not naturally look at a project and identify what they can use that project to learn. Over time, however, with modeling by the faculty and repeated efforts with feedback on the part of the faculty, they become proficient. Note that this is important not just in learning during the program; it gives the base for participants to learn from experience throughout their careers.

There is somewhat of a parallel track through the learning units. The project (generally a team effort) provides the context and is the driver for learning. It provides the need to know and the context in which to learn how to apply knowledge. The focus on identified learning issues—individual research, tutorial discussion with faculty regarding individual research, working through online exercises or learning objects—is primarily individual work. This is designed to help individuals develop conceptual knowledge that is applicable in the current project, but it is also generalizable. Together, the two tracks help individuals develop an active usable knowledge that is the basis for professional practice (Stinson & Milter, 1996).

Likewise, the faculty have multiple roles. In their facilitation, they have to focus on the project, the team functioning, and participant learning, all while working at a distance utilizing information technology. Although this introduces a considerable amount of complexity that does not exist in the normal faculty role, with appropriate training, most faculty can adjust to the role. As with project design, we have developed guidelines for faculty tutorial activity. (See a summary of these guidelines in Fig. 8.4.) For more detail, see Stinson (1994) and Stinson and Milter (1996).

Learning outcomes should be holistic rather than divided by narrow disciplinary boundaries. Focusing on content only within narrow discipline boundaries limits potential excursionary learning. Further, discipline boundaries are largely a construct of academic convenience.

Projects should mirror professional practice. They should be similar to situations found in professional practice and call forth the same types of skills and activities. Thus, content is learned in the context of practice so that, when needed for practice, the content can be more readily recalled and used. Over time, as the learner confronts and manages authentic situations, the process of learning and doing becomes intertwined and indivisible.

Projects should be ill structured. In practice, managers are seldom confronted with neat, well-structured situations. Rather, they are confronted with ill-defined situations that may or may not call for action, situations that the manager must examine and define into a reality on which he or she can act. Learners need to develop the ability to confront an ambiguous, ill-defined situation and make sense of it, and they need to be able to recall concepts and techniques and apply them in this sense-making process.

Projects should require the learner to engage in and develop an effective inquiry process. During the process of confronting and managing an ill-structured situation, the learner is required to gather and interpret information. The information required is not packaged, preanalyzed, and provided to the leaner. Once again, this is consistent with professional practice. Managers must be able to determine what information is needed and have the ability to obtain and interpret it.

Projects should be contemporary. Although authenticity is emphasized in the above principles, engagement is implied. In our experience, authentic projects are engaging. Learners see such problems as real and find them stimulating to attack. But these projects should also be based on current events. Learners are not engaged by a challenge to determine what a company should have done 10 years ago.

The educational process should be modeled as a pull process rather than a push process. Learners should be able to obtain knowledge units in a form that is best suited to learning styles at just the time it is needed for use (just-in-time learning), rather than knowledge units being provided within the boundaries of a physical location at a time that is convenient for the teacher (just-in-case learning).

FIG. 8.2.   Guidelines for project design.

THE MBAWB AND DEVELOPMENT OF COMMUNITY

When the MBAWB was designed, we were aware of the persistence problems with most online learning programs and wanted to maximize persistence and thus the effectiveness of the program.

When we did the initial design, the faculty was not thinking in terms of community. Rather, we wanted a design that was pedagogically sound and that would maximize persistence, engagement, and motivation. As we look back, however, there were several elements that did contribute to the development of community.

Sergiovanni (1994) noted that "communities are social units built around interpersonal relationships and the dependence among people that enhance those relationships." He further described them as "a collection of individuals who are bonded together by natural will and who are together bound to a set of shared ideas and ideals. This bonding and binding is tight enough to transform them from a collection of 'I' into a collective 'we'" (p. 4).

1. *The Challenge.* Participants are confronted with an unstructured situation, without prior preparation. It can be a problem, a question, or a project. It can be presented informally initially, but is always formalized into a charge.
2. *Issue Identification.* Participants identify the issues they must confront and manage to produce the deliverable required by the charge. Two types of issues are identified:
   - Project issues: information and data needs that are unique to the project situation, but must be collected and analyzed to develop the deliverable.
   - Learning issues: knowledge of concept and techniques and abilities that need to be present or developed to develop the deliverable. These are areas that are not unique to the project but are generalizable and applicable in many similar situations.
3. *Inquiry.* Based on the identified issues, participants engage in inquiry. They conduct research to collect information and data necessary for the project. They also engage in learning activities independently, in a tutorial relationship with faculty, and/or interactive learning modules developed and provided for their use.
4. *Action.* Participants then analyze the data collected, using the learning developed, and make decisions regarding the deliverable. Note that this frequently involves iteration with point 2 and 3 as more information or knowledge leads to the identification of additional issues and the need for more inquiry. At some point, however, the iteration must stop (usually caused by a time deadline), and the deliverable must be prepared and delivered.
5. *Reflection.* After the deliverable is presented and feedback is received, participants engage in reflection. We believe that practice unexamined does not lead to learning. Rather, the process of reflection is central to making learning explicit and being able to recall and use the content learned and skills developed in other situations. Many approaches are used to facilitate reflection, ranging from simple discussion to written diaries, written responses to questions, and confronting and managing a similar situation.

FIG. 8.3.   The MBAWB learning model.

In our effort to maximize persistence, engagement, and motivation, the faculty decided to emphasize mutual dependence among participants, relationships among participants, and interaction and collaboration, both required and emergent. Finally, we recognized that identity was important; the participants had to think of themselves as a part of a whole that was important to them. Thus, we did introduce many elements that, based on a post hoc analysis, did contribute to the development of what is today more popularly called community. Structural elements that encourage community are the following:

- The program is a cohort-based program. The same group of 20 to 30 students and 6 faculty work together in all projects throughout the 2 years.
- There are three 1-week and six long weekend residencies during the program. This face-to-face experience enables the establishment of relationships during an intense period of face-to-face exposure, a more familiar way for establishing relationships for most people.
- The residencies are held on the Ohio University campus. Although we knew we couldn't build community around place, we did have an asset in the beauty of

1. Focus on the project: Facilitate the team approaching the problem. Make certain that they are using a rational reasoning process, addressing the issues that are important to a quality deliverable.
2. Focus on the team: Facilitate team functioning. Make certain that the team is approaching the project efficiently and effectively, dividing labor, organizing itself, and managing its time.
3. Focus on learning: Facilitate individual learning. Make certain that individuals are learning concepts and techniques that they can generalize to situations in other contexts. Early on, make certain that learning objectives are established and that individuals are focusing on their learning, not just the deliverable. Toward the end, help them explicitly define what they have learned and verbalize how their learning can be applied in other contexts.

In accomplishing these activities, tutors should use their own personal style; be yourself. Do not, however, be directive. Don't tell the learners what they should be doing or learning. Likewise, don't push them off the dock. Rather, lead them by asking questions. Model the managerial reasoning process through your questions. Help them work through the process.

When learners ask questions (and they will) you will have to determine if it is appropriate for you to answer directly. If it is a question of fact, if you have the information, and if it is not a significant learning opportunity, you may answer the question directly. If, however, it is a significant learning opportunity, you may want to work through their question with them, helping them come to an answer.

Finally, learners will have a tendency to become fixated on the deliverable and forget that the real objective is learning. Thus, you must continually bring learners back to reflect on what they are learning and how that learning can be applied to other problems in other contexts.

FIG. 8.4. Guidelines for faculty tutorial activity.

the residential campus. (In research on why undergraduate students select Ohio University, "nature of the campus" is generally ranked second and sometimes has been first.) We have had a few residences in remote locations to be near live clients and theoretically could hold the residencies anywhere we had access to the Web. But, when given a choice, participants always vote to have the residencies in Athens, even though the nearest airport is 90 miles away and travel to Athens is always an issue.

- The first project is completed in 3 days during the first 1-week residency. The participants inevitably call this boot camp. The participants have a very short period of time to complete a complex project, and, at the end, they present the results of their effort to a group of visiting executives. This requires a tremendous amount of effort from all individuals, and it requires that a group of strangers form and start to function in a mutual dependent fashion in a very short period of time. Finally, because of the presentation to outsiders, the stakes are seen as very high.

- Seven of the nine projects in the program are team projects. These projects are large, complex, holistic projects that cannot be completed by a single individual during the 3-month time period. In addition, deliverables are evaluated and grades are given on a team, rather than individual, basis. Thus, team members are mutually dependent and must collaborate effectively online during the 3 months they are working on the project.

- New teams are established for each project. Thus, individuals must learn to form and function with a new group every 3 months. The objective is to maximize the possibility that each member of the class will work with every other member of the class in a team setting. Thus, the total community, not just the team, becomes the focus over time.
- During the two individual projects, there is required participation in a "Question of the Week" discussion. This is an activity where a provocative current event question is posted by a different faculty member each week. Participants then participate in an asynchronous discussion of the question. Four levels of participation are identified. Level 1 is comments based on prior experience. Level 2 is reporting the results of some type of research. Level 3 is advancing the discussion by building on others' contributions. Level 4 is synthesizing the discussion and providing an overall response to the question. Participants are expected to make multiple contributions to the discussion and to make contributions at Level 3 and/or 4. This discussion is designed to support continued community-level interaction and collaboration during the 3-month time period when the primary effort and the deliverable is individually based.
- At the end of each project, there is a community-level debriefing and reflection. The reflection reviews both performance and process, but focuses on learning. During the reflection, community members are encouraged to explicitly describe what they have learned and comment on the performance and learning of others. The reflection is accomplished through an individual assessment activity, a peer review that is shared with the peers, and a general community oral discussion. As mentioned earlier, this is considered to be a very important part of the learning process. Thus, we spend about half a day on the different activities involved in the reflection process. Some, such as the individual assessment, are graded. Others, such as the general community oral discussion, are not. It is important that individuals be very open in their discussions, and over time as trust develops they become very open. During the reflection process, the community support for individual learning is continually reiterated.

Nonstructural factors also encouraging community:

- We talk of the community as a community. This is modeled by faculty. We start calling the class a community during the first 1-week residency, identifying a community as a place where people care and share. Over time, participants also start to use the term and start talking about themselves as being a part of a community.
- Participants are encouraged to collaborate and share research results during individual work on learning issues. Although these activities often require individual deliverables that should represent individual syntheses and conclusions, faculty state and reinforce the value that sharing research results and information sources, even sharing ideas and reviewing and commenting on each other's work, is not cheating. Rather, it is a part of the sharing process and the mutual support of a learning community.
- Participants are encouraged to view one another as resources. The classes are, by selection, heterogeneous in nature. Participants have different educational backgrounds, bring different work experiences, and come from different industries and different parts if the United States and Canada. Thus, it is possible for them to learn a great deal form one another. This is strongly encouraged. They can

share their expertise to help another member of the community develop a weak competency. They can, and often do, call on other members of the community for advice and collaboration on nonprogram, generally work-related issues. The program encourages cooperation and discourages competition. Teams are not placed in competition during the projects; our goal is to provide a win–win environment, and it normally develops as community becomes established.

IS COMMUNITY DEVELOPED DURING THE PROGRAM?

Unfortunately, there has been no systematic empirical research performed on the effort to build community. The anecdotal evidence, however, answers with a resounding yes.

Four classes have graduated and in exit program reviews by an outside member of the executive review team (a group of outside businesspeople and learning experts who advise the program), participants frequently talk of the learning community. Participants further emphasize how much they have learned from one another. In fact, they frequently talk of the "cohesiveness" of the community.

Most faculty who have participated voice a similar feeling. Most note that they have never developed as close a relationship with a group of students. Note that this is not true of all faculty. A small minority of faculty have difficulty allowing "students" to have equal status in the learning community. In fact, two faculty have withdrawn from the learning community midway during a program. However, this doesn't question the development of community. In fact, it may do just the opposite. These faculty had a value structure that was not consistent with the design and values of community.

Is this really community, or is it some faux community? Without systematic research it is difficult to confirm.

The literature on communities of practice does provide some insight. Wenger (1998) notes three dimensions of practice as the property of community: mutual engagement, joint enterprise, and shared repertoire. These conditions clearly exist while individuals are participating in the MBAWB program.

While representing a diverse population in terms of background, occupation, geographic location, and other factors, they come together with the purpose of learning and ultimately obtaining a degree. This is what Wenger calls their enabling engagement. Further, they develop the mutual relationships and maintenance activities typical of community.

Participation in the learning projects becomes a joint enterprise for the participants. Defining and developing approaches to learning projects and then cooperatively working through them is indeed a negotiated enterprise. Further, because deliverables on learning projects are team responsibilities, individuals are mutually dependent and mutually accountable.

A shared repertoire develops during the life of the program. Practices evolve and are accepted. Norms develop. Stories are told and retold. Values are exemplified and expressed. Some of these continue from class to class, primarily communicated by the continuing faculty. Others come out of the interaction and development of community within the particular class.

Although Wenger's (1998) conceptualization is useful, there are some differences from his typical community of practice. For example, in his vignettes, the participants are colocated and interact and collaborate primarily face-to-face. In the MBAWB, individuals are geographically dispersed, and most of their collaboration is technologically mediated. In his vignettes, the practice involves work that requires rather low levels of cognitive demand. In the MBAWB, projects involve a rather high level of cognitive complexity. Finally, and perhaps most notable, In his vignettes the learning that occurs is developed to be applied to the practice, the joint enterprise. In the MBAWB, although learning is applied to the joint enterprise—the learning project—the community exists to develop learning that individuals will take away and apply in their individual enterprises and their personal growth.

Thus, there is at least some anecdotal evidence that a learning community is established during the 2 years of the MBAWB program. And, using Wenger's conceptualization, there is at least some support that the dimensions of a community are present. For our purposes here, we will use the old adage, "If it looks like a duck and walks like a duck and quacks like a duck, it probably is a duck."

CONTINUING COMMUNITY

The question facing us now is, Can the community be continued? There might be some expectation that because the members were part of a community when they were in the MBA program, the community would automatically continue. That seems not to be the case. We have graduated four classes from the MBAWB. In all cases, they have had continued access to their MBAWB intranet. This means they had the ability to continue to interact and collaborate on a voluntary basis. In actuality, there was very limited interaction after the first 3 to 4 months following graduation. This suggests that the opportunity to interact and collaborate in and of itself isn't sufficient to continue community. Participants must perceive that they are receiving some value if they are to put forth the effort to continue collaboration.

Further, just because the members are part of a learning community that is defined by a particular MBAWB class does not mean that the feeling of and involvement with community will automatically transfer to a larger online community that is composed of alumni of all MBAWB programs.

After graduation from the program, participation is voluntary on the part of the participants; they no longer have required participation to obtain a degree. They no longer have required collaboration and interaction. Nor do they not have required residential experiences. Thus, although there continues to be shared repertoire, some of the dimensions of mutual engagement and joint enterprise that did exist no longer exist in the same form.

There is significant question whether or not we can continue a learning community without the formality of a program, a course, or a grade. Does the community exist only because individuals are required to participate as a part of an academic course or program? Can we incorporate new ways to achieve joint enterprise and mutual engagement? These are questions that we face as we attempt to develop and engage alumni into a new online community.

THE ONLINE COMMUNITY EXPERIMENT

As indicated earlier, Ohio University has decided to use the MBAWB as a pilot of an effort to continue to add value to those who have had an association with the university. At this point in time, this is not done as a revenue-producing project. Nor is it intended to provide an entirely new focus for the university. Rather, the pilot focuses on the feasibility of providing a continuing learning community. Is it something that can be done, and if so, what resources will be required? Is it something that is valued by alumni, and if so, what are the elements they most value? If it is determined that it is feasible and desirable, then a number of educational policy issues will be raised.

This section and those that follow will describe an initial attempt to introduce the online learning community, very preliminary results of the effort, and note some of the educational policy issues that such an effort will raise if it is more broadly implemented.

REENGAGING THE COMMUNITY

All the target population for the pilot community had graduated between March 1999 and December 2001. Thus, technically, we were not attempting to simply continue community; we had to reengage alumni with the community. Thus, the decision was made to start with a live, face-to-face event. This was billed as a reunion that would have an educational component and would introduce the participants to the site that would support the online community experience. Eighteen of a possible 63 alumni (29%) returned to Athens for the activity. (Note that the alumni are spread throughout the United States and eastern Canada. Although there was only a banquet charge related to the reunion, they traveled back at their own expense; none of their companies provided funding.)

At the reunion, the purpose of the online community was discussed. (See Fig. 8.5 for the written description that was provided.) The online site was introduced as a prototype, and the alumni were asked to interact with it and use it for the next few

During the 2 years of the MBAWB program, we become members of a tight-knit community. We care and share. We learn from one another and provide support for one another. The association with a diverse but sharing group of people gives us a breadth of perspective on the world and enriches us.

This community is an effort to continue that experience. As we enter what Peter Drucker has called the knowledge age, work and the environment in which we work is changing dramatically. Increasingly, knowledge or intellectual capital is the most critical resource that a firm possesses. People are being called on to continually expand their capabilities, not to do more work, but to do more complex work, to make more decisions and make them more independently. This implies that people need to be continually developing competencies, not just job skills, but also intellectual skills. It implies that learning needs to be available anytime and anyplace, and that it needs to be available just-in-time as needed for use. As Tapscott (1997) said in *The Digital Economy*, "Work and learning are becoming the same thing and learning is becoming a lifelong challenge."

The MBAWB community provides an opportunity for us to cooperatively continue our learning. It is a place where we can initiate collaboration on issues that are important to us and share stories and wisdom relative to those issues. It is a place where we can go to review business concepts and further develop our abilities to apply those concepts in our environment. It is a place that we can go to broaden our perspectives, and review and discuss ideas and issues that are outside of our day-to-day experience. It is a place that provides stimulation and encourages creativity.

This is our dream. Working together, we can continue a community that adds learning value and integrate that community into our life on a continual basis.

FIG. 8.5. The description of the purpose of community.

months. They were also asked to provide critiques and make suggestions regarding changes to the site.

The discussion evolved into more than a simple discussion of the online community; it also addressed the general question of how we could best continue as a community. In the discussion that followed, two factors came from the group. It wanted regularly scheduled face-to-face events to supplement the online experience, and it wanted those events to be educational experiences that used the learning architecture used in the MBAWB. In essence, the alumni were going back to their shared repertoire, the blend of online and residential experience and the use of project-based action learning. Thus, the community as it goes forward will be a blended community; it will contain both online and face-to-face activities and events. As it now stands, the online community site contains the following elements (also see Fig. 8.6):

- A statement of purpose for the community
- An address book with contact information and biographical sketches of all members of the community
- An "Idea Factory," in which "What's Hot" provides links to some recent articles or news reports that have caught our attention. Community members can go to the Collaboration Center to share their ideas about any of the articles. What's Hot is refreshed every week to 10 days. Old entries are archived.

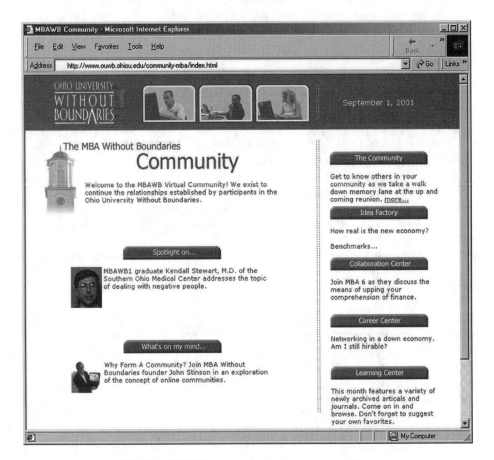

FIG. 8.6.   MBAWB community site homepage prototype

- The benchmark section of the Idea Factory provides stories of best practices. Also included are video interviews and presentations by executives.
- The Collaboration Center provides an area for community members to collaborate, either around practice issues or social issues.
- The Career Center is an area where individuals can obtain information regarding career planning and career development. Two additional elements are being considered. One is an area where they can get advice on career searching, and resume and portfolio development. The other is a job listing service.
- The Learning Center contains a set of e-learning experiences that can be utilized by community members on an anytime-anyplace basis. For example, the Valerie Perotti series (prepared by a revered former faculty member) provides workshop information on a series of communication skills. The Learning Center also contains some more involved e-learning workshops (such as an interactive workshop on e-business) that may involve some cohort activity. Finally, there are links to relevant external resources.
- "What's on My Mind" is a provocative statement, set up as a monthly event, by a prominent faculty member or outside resource. The first in the pilot is simply a written statement. It is likely that future entries will be video.

Thus, the online community site provides an integrated learning and community environment. The site is updated at least every 2 weeks. Note, however, that by itself the online site does not provide the same type of mutual engagement and joint enterprise that was central to the development of community within the program.

PRELIMINARY PARTICIPATION RESULTS

How has the community site been received? Initial results after 4 months of existence are not encouraging. Although 93% of the participants have visited the community site at least two times, regular visitation is significantly less. A usage analysis indicates that 35 of the 63 participants visit the site on the average of once per month. Fifteen participants visit on the average of at least weekly, but many of the visits are primarily in response to e-mail, indicating that we have placed a new item on the site (updated "What's Hot," etc.). There has been little use of the community site for collaboration. Two articles have been received from participants and placed as a part of the Learning Center.

An e-mail request for nonstructured feedback resulted in a response by 20 of 63 potential participants. Comments indicated a favorable response to the community. No direct criticism of any part of the community was offered. Likewise, no direct suggestions for change were offered.

Although all but one of the respondents noted that they visit the site on a more or less regular basis and reviewed the updates and "What's Hot," many mentioned reasons for their lack of active participation and collaboration discussion. Many mentioned time pressures and a feeling of being already overloaded at work. Given those pressures, they noted that they simply didn't get around to the site. One noted, "It seems strange, but making a 2-year commitment is/was almost easier than signing up for a short-term engagement of collaboration on the site."

What explains the level of participation? Perhaps it is simply time and job pressures, but people tend to make time when an activity has some type of priority. Perhaps the components of the online community do not provide a value that is important for many of the participants. Perhaps, as one individual indicated, they are "overloaded" with formal education from the MBA and not yet ready for continual self-development. Perhaps the group is too small to support an active, collaborating community. As noted earlier, without requirements, required interaction, and grades, it may be that proportion of the total group that is interested in active participation purely for self-development may be too small to make up a critical mass.

At this time we can only speculate. There will be, however, a formal user study done at the end of 6 months. This will provide better data and will lead to some alterations in the community. Based on informal results, however, and based on discussions with participants, some additions to the community experience will be added even before the user survey.

A series of blended learning projects will be provided for the community on a regular basis. These may be taken as credit or certificate "courses." These learning units will utilize the learning architecture used in the MBAWB. They will center on a significant learning project and will combine face-to-face residency experience with online collaboration and e-learning experiences. (Note that as the community matures and as technology becomes more accessible, these face-to-face experiences may actually utilize videoconferencing.)

In addition, a series of structured completely online learning experiences involving active discussion by participants will also be introduced. These may involve Webcasting with subsequent asynchronous participation in the discussion.

It is hoped that participation in these learning experiences will reengage community members through the mutual engagement and joint enterprise that they had in the program. Although participation in these projects will, of course, be voluntary, once members are involved, the elements of the old community will be present, and it is expected that this will also encourage more participation and more use of the online community site. These elements will increase the "instructional" element of the community. They will also put additional demands on resources to support the community. Up to now, little time and effort has been required for community support. An estimate is that two 4-hour periods of "faculty" time and 1 hour of technical time per week has been invested. Building in the stronger instructional components, while providing significant value-added potential, will also require additional funding. It is expected that, after initial pilots, participants will be required to pay for participation in the instructional portions of the community.

This experiment is just that: an experiment. During the next year, we will be continually assessing and evaluating the impact and the value. We will also be making changes, additions, and subtractions as they are called for. Hopefully, at the end of a year, we will be able to draw some conclusions and determine whether or not the experiment should be institutionalized as a part of Ohio University.

THE EDUCATIONAL POLICY ISSUE

Although this paper has concentrated on the attempt to develop a continuing community for a single program, we should keep in mind that it is also a pilot test of a larger concept. Is it possible for a traditional university to refocus and add to its traditional "product mix" an educational structure and infrastructure to provide a continual learning community for its members?

At this level, it becomes more than a simple question of can community be developed and continued; it becomes a question of educational policy. If, indeed, the experiment is positive and Ohio University decides to increase its efforts in this direction, a myriad of other institutional issues come into play. In particular, the issues involving faculty governance may become particularly difficult.

For example, when a department moves a program into an online format, it frequently has to obtain curricular approval through all levels of the curricular approval process. This can be very time-consuming, requiring 1 to 3 years. In the rapidly evolving world of e-learning, this is an eternity. In addition, faculty governance structures are not known to be particularly supportive of innovation.

Likewise, when new pedagogical approaches are utilized, there tends to be significant resistance on the part of more traditionally oriented faculty. The full-time MBA program at Ohio University was an award-winning program developed in conjunction with the professional business community, based on clearly defined externally validated learning outcomes, and utilized a project-based action learning approach (Milter & Stinson, 1995; Stinson, 1997). As the champions that developed the program retired, younger, more traditionally oriented faculty migrated the program back to one controlled exclusively by faculty, based on coverage-oriented learning objectives and incorporating a course-based structure.

These are examples of constraints already experienced by numerous innovators. Imagine the resistance if an institution tries to extend the learning relationship with the student throughout the student's life. How will such things as credit, faculty role, and faculty load be redefined? Can that redefinition be implemented? Can the concept of education really be transformed, given the self-interests and the strengths of the internal constituencies of educational intuitions? That is very much an open question.

REFERENCES

Barrows, H. S. (1985). *How to design a problem-based curriculum for the preclinical years.* New York: Springer.

Collins, A. (1990, April). *Generalizing from situated knowledge to robust understanding.* Paper presented at the annual meeting of the American Educational Research Association, Boston.

Drucker, P. F. (1994). The age of social transformation. *Atlantic Monthly, 271*(5), 53–80.

Duffy, T., & Jonassen, D. (1991). Constructivism: New implications for instructional technology. *Educational Technology, 21*(5), 7–12.

Milter, R., & Stinson, J. (1995). Educating leaders for the new competitive environment. In Gijselaers, Tempelaar, Keizer, Blommaert, Bernard, & Kasper (Eds.), *Educational innovation in economics and business administration: The case of problem-based learning* (pp. 30–38). Dordrecht, the Netherlands: Kluwer.

Pink, D. H. (1997). Free agent nation. *Fast Company,* (12), 131–150.

Schank, R., & Cleary, C. (1995). *Engines for education* [Tech. Rep. No. 58, Online]. Available: http://www.ils.nwu.edu/~ e_for_e/index.html

Seely Brown, J., & Duguid, P. (1991). Organizational learning and communities-of-practice: Toward a unified view of working, learning, and innovation. *Organizational Science 2,* 40–57.

Sergiovanni, T. (1994). *Building community in schools.* San Francisco: Jossey-Bass.

Stinson, J. (1994, July). *Can digital equipment corporation survive? An introductory learning problem.* Paper presented at the Sixth International Conference on Thinking, "Improving the Quality of Thinking in a Changing World," Massachusetts Institute of Technology, Cambridge, MA.

Stinson, J. (1997, May). *The Ohio University MBA Without Boundaries.* Paper presented at the International University Consortium and Institute for Distance Education Conference, "The Potential of the Web," University of Maryland, College Park.

Stinson, J., & Milter, R. (1996). Problem-based learning in business education: Curriculum design and implementation issues. *New Directions for Teaching and Learning, 68,* 33–42. San Francisco: Jossey-Bass.

Tapscott, D. (1997). *The digital economy,* New York: McGraw-Hill.

Wenger, E. (1998). *Communities of practice.* Cambridge, England: Cambridge University Press.

9

Learning in the Knowledge Age: Up-Front or at a Distance

Robert A. Wisher*

U.S. Army Research Institute

Advances in technology have historically led to changes in the workplace and in the practice of work. With the infusion of information technology at the office, such as e-mail, videoconferencing, and sophisticated groupware applications, there are time demands on information analysis and problem solving. Decision cycles are becoming compressed. Priorities and deadlines must be carefully balanced. Further, the knowledge age is unmistakably changing the manner of collaboration among workers. Employees need to become engaged in different ways, and work must be reorganized to construct a high-performance workplace (McCain, 2002).

Although the preparation of workers for the knowledge-age economy has been under way for years, the knowledge and skills of this workforce demand continual advancement. Technical skills, communication skills, and the capacity to adapt quickly and fit into high-performance teams are placing new demands on preparing knowledge-age workers. It is also forcing change on those responsible for educating and training this workforce. Didactic models of instruction are becoming outdated, whereas problem solving, inquiry, and critical thinking are becoming crucial features of learning environments for the contemporary workplace. One illustration of such change is the reorientation experiment at Ohio University described by Stinson (Chap. 8. this volume).

THE OHIO PROGRAM

John Stinson provides a description of one university's effort to go beyond its physical boundary to reach learners preparing for the knowledge age. The place is a blend of virtual engagement over computer networks and periodic returns to the academic

---

*The views expressed are those of the author and do not necessarily reflect the views of the U.S. Army Research Institute for the Behavioral and Social Sciences or the Department of the Army.

splendor of Athens, Ohio. The Masters of Business Administration (MBA) Without Boundaries (hereafter, the Ohio program) is a learner-centered environment that connects innovations from the distance-education toolbox with learning projects oriented to the workplace. In phase with most other chapters in this volume, the constructivist perspective underpins the design of instruction. In contrast to self-contained online programs, there is a concerted effort to develop a sense of community within a cohort as it progresses through the program. This is accomplished through recurring interpersonal contact, and virtual and live collaboration during seven of the nine learning projects. Two projects involve independent work guided by faculty.

There is recognition up front that persistence must be addressed and steps taken to ensure that diligence, engagement, and motivation are maintained at high levels. Students recognize that team members are depending on each other's regular participation and input as part of the learning process. The instructional design encourages this dependence and the interchanging of students across project teams stimulate fresh engagements. Of the several innovations of the Ohio program described by Stinson (Chap. 8, this volume), the notion to extend learning beyond the MBA degree as part of a voluntary, continuing learning community of alumni was groundbreaking. Comments on the design of this feature and thoughts on how to evaluate it are provided in my discussion.

Education and Training

The distance education approach exemplified in the Ohio program, like all problem-based learning programs, has both a training and educational bearing. Training and education clearly share the psychological constructs of learning and memory, but for different purposes. The Ohio program reflects traditional training in that it seeks to improve an individual's capacity to perform a work-related activity (i.e., developing a competency). Apart from traditional training, however, it is not geared to a specific skill certificate or job requirement, as with certification programs, nor is it directed to problems unique to a particular employer, as can be the case with corporate universities. The program requires that a student understand the underlying principles of business activities, the educational component, and demonstrate the application of those principles while solving realistic problems under the guidance of faculty. For example, learning the principles underpinning financial analysis and capital formation (education) are applied to a project on financing the firm (training).

There is a complementary relationship between the design of the educational and training components in the Ohio program. Generally speaking, training that does not include a broader, educational understanding of "knowing why" may inadequately prepare workers, who must generalize and transfer what is learned to the circumstances of their own jobs. Without knowing the reasons why certain analyses must be conducted, or how task constraints can sway the interpretation of the analytic results, the knowledge gained is inert (Barab & Duffy, 2000). On the other hand, without putting in to practice the concepts and principles learned, there is no anchoring of the knowledge in a work context. As described by the nine learning projects of the Ohio program, the balance between education and training appears to have been nicely achieved. Participants review and consolidate their conceptual understanding of models and theories related to a project area, and then apply the understanding to circumscribed activities identified in the project. The result appears to be the creation of practice field in which activities are contextualized and anchored in authentic tasks (Senge, 1994).

The successful completion of these project leads to an MBA degree, which is likely to satisfy a participant's goal of obtaining the credentials needed for career advancement. One should also expect that what is learned in the program will transfer positively to a host of job titles, a variety of corporate cultures, and an assortment of leadership responsibilities. As one measure of effectiveness, the graduates should become "better employees," because of what they learned and how they learned it. Did the design of the learning environment lead to a positive transfer to the workplace environment?

Framework for Discussion

The issues I have chosen as a framework to discuss the Ohio program cluster into three categories—pedagogical design, evaluation, and implementation. These were among the set of nine issues of Web-based learning environments raised by the conference participants months prior to the symposium at Asilomar. My choice of these categories was based on what I perceived as a linking of the program from a start point (design), to an in-process point (evaluation), to a final state (implementation). This framework allows for thoughts and suggestions on how feedback from one point can influence another, such as how the evaluation can recommend changes to the design. My professional background is in training research and educational technology. This, too, influenced my selection of the three discussion categories. As a research psychologist, I have conducted field research on training design and effectiveness, long-term retention of knowledge and skills, the impact of "new" technologies on learner reactions, immediate learning outcomes, and eventual job performance. I could, thus, draw from my experience in critiquing other standards, conditions, and designs of learning environments in preparation for real jobs.

The Ohio program is based on a constructivist approach. There are no traditional disciplined-based courses, lectures imparting commodities of knowledge, or endless readings of case studies. Students are situated in nine appealing learning projects. With the exception of the first, each project begins in one residency period and ends in another. During the 3-month interlude between the start and finish of a project, learners engage in research, collaboration, online exercises, tutorials with faculty, and so forth while working with their group toward project completion. This is all accomplished over the Internet using Lotus Domino as the groupware facility handling the interactions. The program is, thus, a blended approach between online activities and face-to-face participation.

Pedagogical Design

Too often, learning content is a static commodity, outlined in a syllabus as an inflexible list of topics. A distinguishing feature of the Ohio program is that students themselves have a voice in determining the learning issues for a particular learning project. Faculty offer a core set of issues related to a project. During the participation process, students define their individual learning issues within the context of a larger group project. By doing so, other students are brought into a dialogue that reflects their prior knowledge, experiences, and personal learning goals. The result is a negotiation of interests supervised by faculty, who themselves establish an initial set of issues related to the desired learning outcome.

The expectation is that an individual's influence in defining learning objectives will direct learning toward a specific current or future workplace need. The opportunities to explore a specific learning issue more deeply, through research and dialogue with faculty during the individual projects, allows students with different strategies, approaches, and prior knowledge to personalize the learning experience. This adds to their ownership of the learning environment. Personal choice is clearly an innovation that sets the Ohio program apart from most other approaches to online education. A student's specific objectives become a theme in which others can contribute and participate, broadening the sense of learning as a social experience. Such a social learning model can prosper when genuine dialogue is driven by situated perspectives (Polin, Chap. 2, this volume).

Learner-Centered Paradigm

Another dimension of the pedagogical design concerns its learner-centered approach. Learner-centered pedagogy addresses what students need to learn, what their learning preferences are, and what is meaningful to them. Principles from learner-centered instruction, such as those from the American Psychological Association set of 14 learner-centered psychological principles (American Psychological Association, 1993), can be encountered throughout the Ohio program. The principles address areas such as curiosity and intrinsic motivation, linking new information to old in meaningful ways, providing choice and personal control, promoting social interaction and interpersonal relations, encouraging thinking and reasoning strategies, and constructing meaning from information and experience. These principles have significant promise for Web-based instruction. Bonk and Cummings (1998), for example, documented a dozen recommendations for designing online instruction from a learner-centered perspective.

One example from the program is the principle of the influence of intrinsic motivation on learning. Intrinsic motivation suggests that students are compelled to learn by a motive to understand. That is, they have a driving interest to be self-determining and competent (Deci & Ryan, 1985). Designing problems of optimal novelty and difficulty stimulates intrinsic motivation. These problems should be relevant to personal interests and provide for personal choice and control. In the Ohio program, the students' participation in the definition of the learning issues is a way to personalize the content of the learning environment. Their desire to learn is thus driven by objectives that are, in part, self-determined.

Social interactions, interpersonal relations, and communication with others also influence learning. The Ohio program builds conditions to support these social influences in two ways: in the design of the residency periods and in the design of online participation by small groups in the learning projects. The influence is probably evident during the residency periods, when face-to-face interaction and customary social exchanges are prevalent. Indeed, one motivation for the design of the residency period was to develop interpersonal skills. Participation in the online group projects, through the electronic collaboration software, augment the social influence stemming from the residency periods.

Researchers argue that when coupled with text-based communication, online instruction can create a "social presence," in which students project their personalities as well as their ideas (Garrison, Anderson, & Archer, 2000). When properly structured, students perceive the process of interaction and the nature of group communications as being fundamental to the learning experience (Henri, 1992). However, lacking any specific content analysis or student reactions to the online experience of the Ohio program, it is not possible to indicate just how much this contributes to the overall success. Based on the success of prior practices (e.g., Gunawardena, Lowe, & Anderson,

1997), the components for a positive influence of social interactions on learning were evidently in place.

Learning environments such as the Ohio program provide a more authentic learning than typically found in conventional educational environments. Here, students are not subject to lectures, memorization routines, detached textbook readings, or other devices of the didactic classroom. The Ohio program provides opportunities to construct knowledge, actively share and seek information, and generate and engage in social interaction and dialogue, all ingredients of a learner-centered approach (Oliver & McLoughlin, 1999).

Question Asking

The learning projects and the goal for an MBA degree provide a common ground for dialogue and questions. The Ohio program uses a "Question of the Week" discussion while students are engaged in their individual projects, but it seems designed more to foster group cohesion rather than satisfy a specific learning objective. The role of question asking in the design of distance education programs, how it can influence learning, and how it may play a more prominent role in the future are also important factors of a learner-centered approach.

Researchers in cognitive science and education have often advocated learning environments that encourage students to generate questions (Dillon, 1988). There are several reasons why question generation may play a central role in learning. The most encompassing reason is that it promotes active learning and construction of knowledge rather than passive reception of information (Brown, 1988). Other reasons relate to: (1) metacognitive factors, in which learners become more sensitive to their own knowledge deficits and comprehension failures; (2) self-regulated learning factors, in which learners take charge of both identifying and correcting comprehension problems; and (3) common ground factors, in which learners build shared knowledge with those authoring or responding to questions. It is well documented that improvements in the comprehension, learning, and memory of material can be achieved by training students to ask questions during learning (Ciardiello, 1998; Rosenshine, Meister, & Chapman, 1996).

Future Directions for Question Reply

Establishing methods to increase question asking is desirable in any learning environment, particularly those that are asynchronous (Graesser & Wisher, 2001). An inherent drawback, however, is that replies to questions are usually not prompt. The problem arises when a student is working online and poses a question, but no faculty member is available to offer an answer, at least not soon enough. It is technically possible to accumulate previous question–answer sets, those that occurred from previous cohorts, for example, and then index the question–answer sets by learning project, which are further indexed by content. The opportunity to refer to a previous question–answer set, or sets, on similar questions provides the student with a reply that is prompt and germane. Doing so also poses a responsibility for the student to judge whether the answer was informative, and, if not, post it to the faculty for further clarification.

The evolution and maintenance of such a facility could be a self-organizing system if there was some principled way of automating judgments on similarity of meaning. Is one question semantically similar to another? What sets of questions should be clustered by virtue of having similar meaning? The field of computational linguistics is progressing toward such automated solutions. For example, metadata tagging schemes, lexical semantic analysis, and data structure languages, such as XML, are making headway on the problem of determining similarity of meaning. Future versions of the Ohio program may someday have such a capability.

Sense of Community

Throughout his discussion of the Ohio program, Stinson (Chap. 8, this volume) refers to the sense of community that is nurtured throughout the 2-year program. During the learning projects, features of a community of practice (Wenger, 1998) are in evidence, with mutually defined practices and understandings among the students while pursuing shared goals—completing a project and completing an MBA degree. One reason for the interest in a community is to maximize persistence, the sense being that interpersonal relations and social interactions will lead to a "Let's get through this together" attitude. Another reason is to cultivate a learning benefit. This is particularly apparent during the debriefs and reflection at the conclusion of the project, which include peer reviews that are shared with the peers. All through the Ohio program, the community support for individual learning is underscored.

The interest in developing a continuing learning community after completion of the MBA degree is a striking feature of the program. This is initially conceived as a campus-wide opportunity, to include all alumni of Ohio University. The pilot test limits participation to those who had completed the online MBA program. The implications of such a lifelong learning capability are really far-reaching. Clearly, the prominence of the Internet in the home and workplace supports the technical feasibility of the concept. How such a community, however, will become central to a lifelong learner in business is difficult to judge. Persistence could become a problem, particularly if a few prominent members of the community become inactive or change professions. The lifelong learner has many choices, from self-development to local and online alternatives to social and trade organizations. Also, communities of practice naturally arise at the workplace and within one's profession, both sources of lifelong learning. How the Ohio program can find a niche for continuing learning against these competing sources will be a challenge. The very early indications reported by Stinson (Chap. 8, this volume) are that student's want face-to-face events to blend with the online experience, which to me indicates the importance of the social ties. I hope we hear more about the success of the Ohio program as it progresses.

Program Evaluation

Evaluations are a means toward improving an educational program. They should identify what types of activities were of greatest value to students and compare performance with purpose and expectations. In this section, I briefly review the generally regrettable state of affairs in evaluating distance education programs. I also discuss the inherent difficulties in judging the value of programs such as the Ohio program, where the benefits are realized well after the completion of the program rather than at the end of any learning project. Finally, I step through a framework of evaluation common in training settings and suggest how parts of it may be adapted in the Ohio program.

Evaluations of online and other distance learning environments on learning outcomes have become a shortcoming of the field. In a study that examined practices in educational environments, Phipps and Merisotis (1999), for example, point out that most research on distance learning does not control for extraneous variables, and the validity and reliability of the instruments used to measure outcomes are often questionable. In a parallel report on the literature as it pertains to training, Wisher and Champagne (2000) conclude: Most research is anecdotal; when examining effectiveness, it is usually based on an ambiguous experimental design; when measuring effectiveness, comparative results are reported only approximately one third of the time; and when reporting data, there are analytic problems and errors in reporting that are often overlooked by researchers. The lack of, or problems with, assessments seems to be par for the course for distance learning programs.

Lack of Empirical Evidence

For the Ohio program, it is indeed unfortunate that no empirical evidence was obtained to measure the impact of the design of the environment on learning. What students benefited the most from which learning projects? How much did prior knowledge matter? What role did the three face-to-face weekend meetings play versus the online exercises? The relative contributions of the many innovations cannot be explicitly determined, so any benefits are left to subjective judgments. For example, was a learning community really formed? I'm not sure how this could be validated externally, but anecdotal evidence indicated it was resoundingly positive. The indication of success was based on participants mentioning a "learning community" and their use of the term *cohesiveness* to describe the experience. This is a positive development, but examples of behaviors or attitudes that illustrate the formation, development, and progression of the learning community are of greater value to the field. The faculty's perception of the development of community, also anecdotal, was interesting to note but not particularly informative.

Evaluating Community

The broader issue is how to go about evaluating a community that is supposed to form in an online or blended learning environment. Based on an analysis of the contemporary usage of the term *community* in an educational context, Barab and Duffy (2000) point to three key components: a common cultural and historical heritage, inclusion in an interdependent system, and the ability to reproduce. In the Ohio program, the common heritage and inclusion relate to active participation in the MBA program. An indicator may be the peer reviews offered at the end of each learning project, which could, if properly structured, indicate the degree of participation per individual and how this increased or decreased over the 2-year period. An increase in participation would point toward an increase in the value of community membership. Another indicator is the frequency of online interactions during the program, as well as during the continuation of the community of learners. If there is a sharp drop in participation, the inclusion component suffers and the longevity of the community is at risk. The nature of the participation would also be a factor, such as the elimination of spiteful comments or an increase in goal-oriented dialogue.

In terms of the reproduction component, the extent to which veteran members of the continuing community interact with new members reflects acceptance into the community. The extent to which new members advise veteran members on their work practices and are accordingly accepted as peers would be a convincing indicator that a true community is in place and is sustainable. Overall, the evaluation of community is not straightforward. Qualitative judgments by experienced observers of community formation will remain an assessment practice.

Program Evaluation Framework

Evaluations of programs such as the Ohio program can take several forms, and success can be measured in several ways. A rationale for conducting a more formal, empirical evaluation is both to judge the program's overall value and to inform the provider of strengths that should be replicated and weaknesses that should be avoided. I will attempt to outline some general evaluation strategies and procedures that may be applied to online learning environments. These may be useful to include in future iterations of the Ohio program. Phillips (1991) described 11 myths of evaluation, three of which bear repeating here: The results of my training effort can not be measured; evaluation will lead to criticism; evaluation will probably cost too much. These are, indeed, myths.

Early evaluations of distance learning were mostly descriptive case studies that focused on learner satisfaction. They were often anecdotal. But the new genre of Web-based, collaborative instructional methods emerging in higher education and corporate training call for an examination of new evaluation dimensions, such as content analysis of threaded discussions (Bonk & Wisher, 2000). The development of these measures and the value of their feedback are still at an early stage. A still useful framework to approach an evaluation is the four-level model proposed by Kirkpatrick (1994): student reactions, learning outcomes, behavioral effects, and organizational results. Although the Kirkpatrick model is oriented more toward training in business and industry, it is a widely recognized framework that is relevant to educational programs such as an MBA. A brief description of the four levels follows:

> Level 1, Reactions: A measure of how students react to aspects of a program. Examples include ratings of instructor effectiveness, adequacy of facilities, and quality of audio and video signals. Course satisfaction is another example.
> Level 2, Learning outcomes: A measure of how much a student increased knowledge, improved a skill, or changed an attitude. Examples include measures of performance on a written test, quality of a project, or a hands-on assessment of a skill.
> Level 3, Job Performance (Behavior): A measure of the extent to which there has been a change in behavior due to participation in a program. Examples include supervisory assessments, ratings by subordinate personnel, job samples, and on-the-job observations.
> Level 4, Organizational results: A measure of the final bottom-line results that occurred due to participation in a program. Examples include increased sales, decreased costs, and a reduction in turnover.

In the context of the Ohio program, student reactions were apparently positive, and learning outcomes were presumably manifested in the successful completion of the learning projects. Stinson (Chap. 8, this volume) did note that one purpose of the three residences was to "assess student learning," but additional details were not offered. Although it may seem evident that learning occurred, even a modicum of evaluation data can provide feedback for adjustments in the design of future programs. I now examine each of the four levels of the Kirkpatrick model vis-à-vis the Ohio program.

Suggested Evaluation Approach

As a first step in evaluating the Ohio program, I suggest a determination of which demographic variables are relevant. Several that come to mind for the Ohio program are: (1) years since undergraduate degree, (2) who is paying (student or employer), (3) importance for career advancement, (4) importance of learning projects for immediate job duties, (5) convenience to return to the Ohio University campus for residences (e.g., travel time and cost), (6) some indication of preference for working in group versus working independently, (7) prior distance learning experiences, (8) point in career (early, middle, late), (9) job duties (e.g., manager, account executive, marketing), and (10) career goals. These data should be gathered at the beginning of the program, and several of the suggested variables (such as numbers 3 and 4) could be resampled at the midpoint and end of the 2-year program.

Reaction Measures

The next step is to measure satisfaction (Level 1) with each learning project. To any organization exploring distance learning, it is of practical value that participants have a positive attitude from the learning experience. For universities anticipating that students, or their employers, will pay for these courses, stakeholders need to understand how well the consumer is satisfied with the learning process and its product. Obviously, word-of-mouth advertising, low attrition rates during the program, and increased enrollment are signs that things are working, but there are more direct ways to quantify student reactions and interpret the implications.

The satisfaction scale represents numerous items—overall satisfaction, the degree to which the learning project was relevant to one's current work, the quality of the learning project, perceptions of overall effort, and other factors. The items can take many forms, such as a 7-point Likert scale, but a simple 5-point, low–high scale would suffice, particularly for obtaining reasonable statistical power for a relatively small sample size (Zickar, 2002).

The satisfaction ratings can then be related to specific demographic variables to uncover what needs adjustment. For example, if satisfaction ratings on a certain learning project results in wide variability, then this variability may be accounted for by the demographic variable on importance for immediate job duties. An adjustment to the program may have this learning project become an individual one rather than one performed as a group. As a general rule, faculty may want to reexamine the learning issues involved with projects that exhibit high variability in satisfaction ratings.

Learning Outcomes and Utility Judgments

In some distance learning programs, objective learning measures are often not available or simply not feasible to collect, such as in a satellite broadcast for a 1-hour learning event. In such cases, affective reaction measures are often used in lieu of objective learning measures. However, the literature clearly demonstrates that there is no consistent relationship between satisfaction (Level 1) and learning (Level 2) in at least one common form of distance learning, namely, video teletraining (Payne, 1999). In a study reported by Wisher, Curnow, Borman and Chase (2001), a further lack of agreement was noted between satisfaction (Level 1) and job performance (Level 3), as measured by supervisor ratings in a military course for staff officers. This underscores the importance of measuring beyond the level of affective student reaction when one is seeking feedback on how to improve the effectiveness of a program. Although the research cited was conducted in distance learning environments, it probably applies equally to conventional classroom-based instruction.

An alternative evaluation approach to affective reactions is the use of utility judgments. These are student ratings concerning the usefulness of the course, the relevance of the course to job requirements, or a metacognitive assessment of the amount learned compared to what was previously known. In a meta-analysis of training outcomes, Alliger, Tannenbaum, Bennet, Traver, and Shotland (1997) found significant positive correlations between utility judgments and learning outcome measures, whereas there was essentially no statistical relationship between affective reactions and learning measures. Alliger and colleagues (1997) made a distinction between affective reaction measures, which measure such things as how much students enjoyed the training and utility judgments that ask students to judge the amount that they have learned or the perceived usefulness of the training for eventual job performance. The Alliger et al. (1997) meta-analysis of 34 studies reported that affective reactions correlated "about zero" with objective measures of immediate learning. Utility judgments, on the other hand, did correlate with immediate learning.

Example of Utility Judgments

I will illustrate how a utility judgment can be employed in the Ohio program. This is based on research that I conducted for a military training program involving innovative instruction on threats to computer security. The course used a whiteboard over the Internet, coupled with separate audio and video links (Wisher & Curnow, 1999). Students observed the information presented on the whiteboard while listening to, and being able to view, the instructor—much like the classroom. The point of the study was to examine the effect of disabling the instructor video while maintaining the audio and whiteboard links. In a counterbalanced design, the students had a negative affective reaction to not seeing the instructor for certain modules, rating that it negatively affected their ability to learn. However, an analysis of both the utility judgments for individual modules and corresponding items on an objective written test confirmed that it had no impact on learning.

In the analysis, utility judgments of prior knowledge on each of 11 modules were cross-tabulated with utility judgments of the amount learned for each module. Figure 9.1 depicts the result of the tabulation. Both prior knowledge and amount learned were measured on 5-point scales. For each module, ratings were segmented in to "low prior knowledge" (a rating of 1 or 2) and "high prior knowledge" (a rating of 4 or 5). The midpoint responses for this scale (22% of all cases) were dropped from the analysis, resulting in a clearer comparison between low– and high–prior knowledge categories. The results are displayed in Fig. 9.1.

Effect of Prior Knowledge

Learners bring various degrees of prior knowledge to the learning environment. Tobias (1994) determined that prior knowledge accounts for between 30% and 60% of explained variance in post test scores. This knowledge is not always assessed prior to an instructional treatment, leading to a potential confounding in the interpretation of learning outcome data. As is evident in Fig. 9.1, there is a trend for students with low prior knowledge to report learning more than students with high prior knowledge. The left panel of Fig. 9.1 depicts students with low previous knowledge: 70% of these reported learning "a lot." On the right panel, there is an opposite trend: About half of the students with high prior knowledge reported learning little, whereas only 21% reported learning "a lot." This is what should be expected, and it supports the construct validity of the utility judgment measure. In this particular research, the finding was also confirmed with an objective written test.

The point is quite simple: Ask two questions regarding each learning project, and then look for trends such as those reported above. The surrogate learning measures can

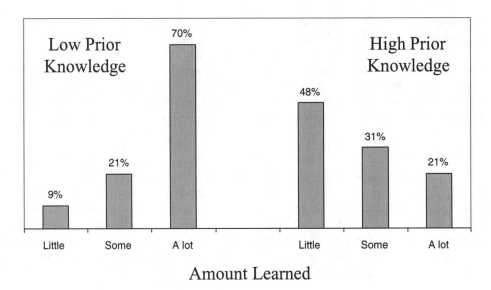

FIG. 9.1.   Self-Assessment of prior knowledge by amount learned for all modules.

further be tabulated against demographic variables, such as the 10 suggested earlier, producing a basis for adjustments at the outset of subsequent programs. For example, a certain learning project may result in low satisfaction and low judgments of learning for students who identify themselves with marketing duties on their regular jobs. Situating that learning project with optional activities of greater relevance to marketing could lead to an improvement in learning. In this way, the evaluation can influence the redesign of the course.

Behavioral Results

This measurement would indeed be difficult to conduct, for both theoretical and practical reasons. The ideal variable would be job performance. The reliable measurement of job performance, of course, has been subject to debate (Conway & Huffcutt, 1997). The three sources most often used to rate job performance are self, peers, and supervisors. Self-ratings tend to be more lenient than supervisor or peer ratings. Peer raters can be a viable alternative to self-ratings, because peers should have a great deal of information about a coworker's typical performance. However, peers often lack experience in judging performance, whereas supervisors usually have better calibrated performance norms because of their experience in evaluating subordinates. Perhaps the most compelling argument for using supervisory ratings is that they are more reliable. Viswesvaren, Ones, and Schmidt (1996) found in their meta-analysis that supervisor ratings had higher interrater reliability than did peer ratings. Similarly, Conway and Huffcutt (1997) found supervisory ratings to be more reliable than both peer and subordinate ratings.

Reliability is critical to performance ratings, because it puts an upper limit on validity. Consequently, supervisors would be the most appropriate source to make job performance ratings for such an analysis. But how could this be done for the Ohio program? With the multitude of employers, the absence of common job dimensions, the manifold career paths the students are following, and the varying degree of relevance to job duties, the prospect of measuring the direct impact of learning on one's job performance appears impractical. Factors influencing individual performance have been studied in the laboratory, in educational settings, and in the workplace. There have been problems in generalizing findings from one environment to another (Fleishman & Quaintance, 1984). Still, some feedback, even in the form of testimonials from employers, would provide evidence of behavioral results. Doing so in a scientific manner would be quite difficult. If the educational provider is interested in expanding to a potentially large corporate customer, such evidence can be persuasive.

Organizational Results

For reasons similar to those discussed above, documenting organizational results from the Ohio program would be a challenge. Evaluations of the impact of training in workplace settings would be expected to link outcome variables to measures of productivity. But what are the common job dimensions of the students in the program, and how do they affect an output? The job responsibilities of the students in the program must vary tremendously. There are too many uncontrolled variables that would threaten the internal validity of any measure.

Evaluation Summary

Evaluations can provide a basis for making rationale adjustments to a program. As I have suggested for the Ohio program, relating a set of demographic variables to a learning outcome, even if limited to a utility judgment, offers practical comparisons. A basis forms for understanding which students benefit from which learning projects or for knowing how much prior knowledge affects certain learning projects. These can be linked back to students' interests or professional backgrounds, setting the stage for tailoring and tuning future iterations of the program. Some of the steps outlined here can be applied quite easily. The evaluations can be further used to demonstrate to those paying the tuition and fees—the employers—that the program is sensitive to their employee's needs.

Implementation

I generally view implementation as a matter of scaling up to a larger student population and to other domains. Scaling up to a larger student population is a matter of resources, primarily faculty, to maintain the high degree of interactivity and personalization. Scaling up to other domains may be more restrictive. The Ohio program is oriented to a popular professional area, where the concepts and principles of business are apparent to the learning projects. A difficulty in scaling up can come from domains with a low demand, where there may be only dozens rather than hundreds of potential students. Will sufficient resources be available to design such a well-reasoned learning enterprise, with a challenging set of well-conceived learning projects? Will students in these low-demand domains have an option similar to the Ohio program, or will their alternatives be the conventional classroom or its online version? Broader implementation of the approach taken in the Ohio program may be restricted to the high-density professional areas.

Higher education has had a difficulty in not always tuning to a specific set of needs, in contrast to corporate universities who have a firsthand awareness of their needs. However, what may be central to the knowledge-age worker is the ability to solve problems. The acceptance of new learning paradigms is predicated on the changing nature of work. Stinson (Chap. 8, this volume) equates work with learning, in accordance with Tapscott's observation, and he further equates knowledge with intellectual capital, in accordance with Druker's view. By imposing a premise that learning implies the construction of knowledge, an argument follows that in the knowledge age, work equates to intellectual capital. The ability to create intellectual capital is the new measure of productivity (Stewart, 1997). Solving problems is a pathway to intellectual capital. There is a perceived need, then, to implement programs that equip the worker with the ability to solve problems.

These problems are situated in a workplace context. They may be ill structured, rarely algorithmic, and usually require some relevant strategic knowledge. Implementing the approach advocated in the Ohio program has remedies for such constraints. Learning projects can be made to appear ill structured, so the early phase of a project involves adding structure to a problem. Algorithmic solutions are the mainstay of a training approach. The Ohio program, as described earlier, moves between education and training components within the projects. Learning concepts and principles underpins their application in the projects. Students are prepared beyond the algorithmic method. Strategic knowledge can be gained during the interactions with other learners, who possess views based on their work experiences, which can enlighten a new approach to the problem. For workers in the knowledge age, the primary purpose for continuing education may be to improve problem-solving abilities.

Problem Solving

From the description of the learning projects, several problem-solving activities that are likely to be prevalent concern the acts of defining a problem, allocating resources, tracking progress (Sternberg, 1997), and tests or assessments to see whether the team is progressing toward a solution (Glaser, 1989). It would be elucidating to relate qualitative characteristics of the messages to specific projects, demographic variables, and any measures of the quality of a solution. Such an analysis could clearly illustrate the how, why, and when of problem-solving behaviors. This provides a baseline for the design and implementation of future learning projects for the growing demands on the knowledge-age worker.

For the knowledge-age worker, it is learning the strategies and tactics needed to achieve a goal—to understand why certain information must be manipulated in certain ways—that is a desired learning outcome. The knowledge-age worker will increasingly belong to team-based work structures, continually learning to solve problems while critiquing the strategies and methods of others (National Research Council, 1999). Although the knowledge-age workplace is shifting toward team structures, an ability to work both dependently and independently will be needed. In the Ohio program, learners have two independent projects to foster their individual problem-solving ability.

CONCLUSIONS

Who will be responsible for the change to the new paradigm of learning—higher education or the corporate trainers? Joining the ranks of educational providers are corporate universities, for-profit universities and learning centers, government agencies, and, of course, the traditional university. Each is exploring online alternatives to the conventional classroom. Not all online providers, however, are breaking from pedagogical traditions. For example, Jonassen (2002) argued that consensus practices in online learning suffer from a focus on memorizing preset material. Even in the dynamic era of online learning, conventional classroom practices are often merely replications of classroom traditions. Jonassen advocates taking advantage of online technology by shifting away from the traditional patterns of interaction common in the classroom.

The call for a redirection of pedagogical practice from the mastery of text and subsequent testing of recognition is echoed by Duffy and Kirkley (Chap. 6, this volume) and others in this volume. Learning should be viewed as a process of making sense of a domain. This "sense making" relies on an environment of inquiry in which learners are absorbed in solving a problem by interacting with resources, instructors, and peers throughout the process. In concert with the pace of change in the workplace, researchers contend that there is an opportunity for online environments to emphasize learning through social interactions that parallel the workplace.

The Ohio program is one example of this fresh look at learning environments that blend online instruction with a residency. In my review of the Ohio program, I discussed its design and how this reflects inquiry and sense making, how it could better be evaluated with specific suggestions from the training literature, and issues related to a broader implementation to other domains. The lack of specific evidence of learning outcomes for the separate learning projects, even if obtained through a surrogate measure of learning, limit the extent to which the design could be adjusted based on empirical results. Another innovation, the life-long learning community, is in a very early stage of development.

The Ohio program is obviously a well-planned undertaking, one that looks to a learner-centered paradigm and applies the constructivist approach so well. It also focuses on the development of a community, within the 2-year program and beyond. One indicator of its immediate success is the persistence of students in completing the program, as described by John Stinson (Chap. 8, this volume). How well this community sustains itself during the next few years should be of great interest to those interested in models of lifelong learning. It is hoped that the overall approach of the Ohio program can be replicated in other domains, as it offers much to the serious student.

REFERENCES

Alliger, G. M., Tannenbaum, S. I., Bennett, W., Traver, H., & Shotland, A. (1997). A meta-analysis of the relations among training criteria. *Personnel Psychology, 50*, 341–358.

American Psychological Association. (1993). *Learner-centered psychological principles: Guidelines for school reform and restructuring.* Washington, DC: Author and Mid-continent Regional Educational Laboratory.

Barab, S. A., & Duffy, T. M. (2000). From practice fields to communities of practice. In D. H. Jonassen & S. M. Land (Eds.), *Theoretical foundations of learning environments* (pp. 25–56). Mahwah, NJ: Lawrence Erlbaum Associates.

Bonk, C. J., & Cummings, J. A. (1998). A dozen recommendations for placing the student at the centre of web-based learning. *Educational Media International, 35*(2), 82–89.

Bonk, C. J., & Wisher, R. A. (2000) Applying collaborative and e-learning tools to military distance learning: A research framework (Tech. Rep. No. 1107). Alexandria, VA: U.S. Army Research Institute for the Behavioral and Social Sciences.

Brown, A. L. (1988). Motivation to learn and understand: On taking charge of one's own learning. *Cognition and Instruction, 5*, 311–321.

Ciardiello, A. V. (1998). Did you ask a good question today? Alternative cognitive and metacognitive strategies. *Journal of Adolescent & Adult Literacy, 42*, 210–219.

Conway, J. M., & Huffcutt, A. I. (1997). Psychometric properties of multisource performance ratings: A meta-analysis of subordinate, supervisor, peer, and self-ratings. *Human Performance, 10*, 331–360.

Deci, E. L., & Ryan, R. M. (1985). *Intrinsic motivation and self-determination in human behavior.* New York: Plenum.

Dillon, T. J. (1988). *Questioning and teaching: A manual of practice.* New York: Teachers College Press.

Fleishman, E., & Quaintance, M. (1984) *Taxonomies on human performance: The description of human tasks.* New York: Academic.

Garrison, D. R., Anderson, T., & Archer. W. (2000). Critical inquiry in a text-based environment: Computer conferencing in higher education. *Internet and Higher Education, 11*, 1–14.

Glaser, R. (1989). *The fourth R, the ability to reason (Transcript, Science and Public Policy Seminars presentation, June 16, 1989).* Washington, DC: Federation of Behavioral, Psychological and Cognitive Sciences.

Graesser, A. C., & Wisher, R. A. (2001). *Question generation as a learning multiplier in distributed learning environments.* (Tech. Rep. No. 1121). Alexandria, VA: U.S. Army Research Institute for the Behavioral and Social Sciences.

Gunawardena, C. N., Lowe, C. A., & Anderson T. (1997). Analysis of a global online debate and the development of an interaction analysis model for examining social construction of knowledge in computer conferencing. *Journal of Educational Computing Research, 17*, 397–431.

Henri, F. (1992). Computer conferencing and content analysis. In A. R. Kaye (Ed.), *Collaborative learning through computer conferencing: The Najaden Papers* (pp. 117–136). New York: Springer-Verlag.

Jonassen, D. H. (2002). Engaging and supporting problem solving in online learning. *Quarterly Review of Distance Education, 3*(1), 1–13.

Kirkpatrick, D. L. (1984). *Evaluating training programs: The four levels.* San Francisco: Berrett-Koehler.

McCain, M. (2002). *E-learning: Are we in transition or are we stuck?* Washington, DC: National Association of Manufacturers.

National Research Council. (1999). *The changing nature of work.* Washington: National Academy Press.

Oliver, R., & McLoughlin C. (1999). Curriculum and learning-resources issues arising from the use of Web-based course support systems. *International Journal of Educational Telecommunications, 5*, 419–436.

Payne, H. (1999). *A review of the literature: Interactive video teletraining in distance learning courses* (2nd ed.). Atlanta, GA: Spacenet and the U.S. Distance Learning Association.

Phillips, J. J. (1991). *Handbook of training evaluation and measurement methods.* Houston, TX: Gulf.

Phipps, R., & Merisotis, J. (1999). *What's the difference? A review of contemporary research on the effectiveness of distance learning in higher education.* Report prepared at the Institute for Higher Education Policy. Available: www.ihep.com

Rosenshine, B., Meister, C., & Chapman, S. (1996). Teaching students to generate questions: A review of the intervention studies. *Review of Educational Research, 66*, 181–221.

Senge, P. (1994). *The fifth discipline fieldbook: Strategies and tools for building a learning organization.* New York: Doubleday.

Sternberg R. J. (1997). Intelligence: Putting theory into practice. In H. J. Walberg & G. D. Haertel (Eds.), *Psychology and educational practice* (pp. 15–29). Berkely, CA: McCutchan.

Stewart, T. A. (1997). *Intellectual capital: The new wealth of nations.* New York: Doubleday.

Tobias, S. (1994). Prior Knowledge and Learning. *Review of Educational Research, 64*, 37–57.

Viswesvaran, C., Ones, D. S., & Schmidt, F. L. (1996). Comparative analysis of the reliability of job performance ratings. *Journal of Applied Psychology, 81*, 557–574.

Wisher, R. A., & Champagne, M. V. (2000). Distance learning and training: An evaluation perspective. In S. Tobias & J. D. Fletcher (Eds.), *Training and retraining: A handbook for business, industry, government, and military* (pp. 385–409). New York: Macmillan.

Wisher, R. A., & Curnow, C. K. (1999). Perceptions and effects of image transmissions during Internet-based training. *The American Journal of Distance Education, 13*(3), 37–51.

Wisher, R. A., Curnow, C. K., Borman, W. C., & Chase, S. L. (2001, April). *The effects of distance learning on job performance.* Paper presented at the meeting of the American Educational Research Association, Seattle, WA.

Zickar, M. (2002). Modeling data with polytomous item response theory. In F. Drasgow & N. Schmitt (Eds.), *Measuring and analyzing behavior in organizations: Advances in measurement and data analysis* (pp. 123–155). San Francisco: Jossey-Bass.

Open Discussion of Chapter 8

Jenny Franklin: John, I had a thought when you were describing the MBA plus program. Perhaps it would be mutually beneficial if your MBA plus students could be involved in developing the problems for your MBA students. Not only would it contribute to your efforts, but it would also give you an interesting long-range assessment measure to see how the MBA plus students construct those problems. You'll be able to tap into meta-knowledge kinds of considerations.

John Stinson: I think that's a super idea, Jenny. I tie it to Linda or Karen as well, that the faculty that go forward can be individuals who have graduated from the program. If you view the faculty role not as the traditional faculty role but as a multifaceted role, there will be things that those individuals could do.

Jenny Franklin: You could have talent scattered in your MBA plus students as you get them engaged in pedagogy.

John Stinson: Super idea.

Jenny Franklin: Just a crazy thought: Maybe one measure of intellectual capital is how much money these alumni donate back to the university.

Jim Botkin: There is a whole field that some of you know, I'm sure, as intellectual capital, and it's not all financial. It is also relationship capital, there is also customer capital, technological capital, and what they call structural capital. So there are very interesting ways that that might be able to go. The original impetus for developing the concept of capital had to do with a dissatisfaction with the accounting systems that were always looking to the past. There was a wonderful article in the *New York Times* recently that said that maybe we can find a new way to account for the future, or point to the future, as to what companies will be worth or what activities in them are worthwhile, rather than the old accounting systems that get you nowhere. It's an enormous field, and it has great potential.

Jenny Franklin: There was a failed attempt to do that in the early 1970s. It was called human resource asset accounting in Michigan, with Klamholtz and Brummets. It got a big burst of attention for about 3 years, but then I think it ran afoul of the accountants.

Tom Duffy: Returning to John's program, let me ask, Do students pay to be part of community?

John Stinson: The continuing community?

Tom Duffy: Are they going to pay for the problems you give them?

John Stinson: Yes, when they move into the projects there will be some sort of charge there.

Tom Duffy: Do the alumni pay for your community environment?

John Stinson: It's an expensive thing to run, actually, if you are putting articles in and things like that. The president of the university pays for it. It is a focal project for him. So as Linda and I were talking earlier, we really don't have to worry too much—although we have been self-supporting thus far. I didn't mention it here, but we have developed six other graduate programs that will be offered starting in March of this year, and that will be generating some revenues as well.

Jim Botkin: How does it scale, John?

John Stinson: It doesn't scale very well. For example, we build each class as a community of faculty and students. The magic number for us is about 25 students and six faculty. Those people live together all the way through. No faculty member has responsibility for one project and then drops out. We all start together at the beginning of the first week. We all end up together at the end of 2 years. We play different roles as we go through. It is very much a total community from both perspectives. We don't think it would work very well if we tried to do 50 students, 75 students. It can scale only in that you can set up multiple classes.

Jim Botkin: I was using scaling in the terms of your people coming back to each year of the alumni. Pretty soon the alumni becomes everyone who has been attached to Ohio University.

John Stinson: Every program has it's own alumni community. The MBA Without Boundaries community will be the MBA Without Boundaries community. The public administration community will be the public administration community. Now there are some advantages in that there will be objects and resources that will be sitting in our database that can be called out for anyone of those communities. But conceptually, at least at this point in time, we are trying to keep the closeness that existed during a cohort program, and the identification with that program, not with the university as a whole.

Terry Anderson: Could you comment on the workload implication for those—was it six faculty? Is it more or less in the traditional way, do you think?

John Stinson: All of the six faculty are doing it as overloads. It is not on load. This is the beauty—we are sitting out here by ourselves. We pay them for doing it, but they do it as overload. We often will have a diverse faculty. For example, recently we had four of the faculty from the regular business faculty. A fifth is on the faculty of a different university. And the sixth is now in Hawaii and works for a bank in Hawaii.

So the load issue—frankly, the fact that we are online doesn't significantly impact the load. It may actually help the load and the demand. We do the same type of thing and have done the same type of thing in our problem-based learning, face-to-face environment. When you are in the face-to-face environment, you do the project-based action learning using technology mediation but still having face-to-face meetings. But it eats a lot more of your time, so we are much better off with resource application in the distance environment.

Terry Anderson: But are those six involved in each project?

John Stinson: Yes, all the way through.

Tom Duffy: But two had to lead, right?

John Stinson: Typically two or one will. Having them lead means having the administration responsibility. That means they are responsible for introducing the project. That means they are responsible for the original design of the project, which is reviewed by the total team. That means they identified the learning outcomes that come to drive that project. They work with the students in an open forum to establish what the students' learning outcomes will be and how those things meld together. But all of us are engaged and interacting with the students; all of us are tutoring student teams.

Tom Duffy: How much time does the average faculty member, yourself included but the average beyond you, spend dealing with the online discussions? The entire course is online discussions, right, except for the residential thing?

John Stinson: Fifteen to 20 hours per week.

Linda Polin: But on overload?

John Stinson: But well paid on overload. So, for example, we are on a two-course load. So on two face-to-face courses, how much time do you spend there?

Linda Polin: We won't discuss that.

John Stinson: Yeah, I know we won't discuss that.

Tom Duffy: Actually, you told me at one time it was an hour a day you spent dealing with students in the course.

John Stinson: If you average everything out, Tom, that's where I am going with that 15 to 20 hours a week. Because when you are managing administrative...

Tom Duffy: ... the ones that are nonmanagers.

John Stinson: Non managers are probably 10 hours a week. We've got our own standards that we set for ourselves, for example, how frequently are we online is one that I have had problems with here (at Asilomar). But we have to be online—we can't be offline more than 48 hours at any point in time. Normally, I come in the morning and get online, spend maybe an hour unless something is there. Midday I will check it again. Late afternoon I'll check it again—sometimes more, sometimes less.

Raphael Lopez: I have a question about grades. Do you assign grades individually or to a group?

John Stinson: The final grade is an individual grade. The final individual grade is composed of two components. One is for the team projects—a team grade—and one is an individual grade. The team grade is the evaluation of the product produced by the team, and that grade is influenced by peer evaluation. So for every project where you are working together, there is a minimum of one peer evaluation at the end. Early on we will use two or three peer evaluations so that people are getting feedback. That means that somebody can be on a team where the team product was an A but they get a C or a D. We have had that happen. Second the individual grade is roughly half of the course grade. The individual grade is based on the individual's participation in tutoring activities, in discussion of learning issues, learning activities, modules, and things that are more directly content related. Then we put those two together at the end to give a grade on the overall project.

Sally Johnstone: This issue of the time the faculty spent responding to students is obviously a very real issue in an online environment. At the University of Southern Queensland, there is a professor named James C. Taylor who is experimenting with methods to assist faculty with the amounts of time required for online student interactions. They are taking the whole notion of trying to manage the online environment very seriously. They have created a hypothetical professor, who we will call Professor Smith. Smith is really an artificially intelligent system, though he is not horribly sophisticated. Once you have developed a track record of having taught the course three or four times, there are some pretty common questions that students usually ask. Those questions and their answers are fed into a database. When a student sends a question at 3:00 in the morning, the response comes back, "Professor Stinson is not available right now but Professor Smith is. Would you like to have Professor Smith answer your question?" If the student says, "Yes," he or she gets a compilation response that relates to the question the student has asked. The answer is in "real" English and is pretty well set up but drawn from the general database. In comments from students that have been collected after the courses end, Professor Smith is the real hero. Because Professor Smith is online every time the student needs him.

Tom Duffy: That would be interesting. Do get the reference. That would be good to have.

John Stinson: Let me be a contrarian. We don't want our faculty answering students questions. We would much prefer that the students develop the answers to the questions. We would much prefer that they work with one another. They know that if they ask me a question, in all likelihood what they are going to get back is not an answer but another question.

Jamie Kirkley: One of the real issues, I think the toughest issue that has come out of these discussions, is how to assess these things. What kinds of assessments are you concerned about for your audience? What kinds of assessments do you have to deal with in the distance learning program?

John Stinson: Distance really has no factor. When we designed the program, we specified it with a lot of interaction with the business community to generate a set of learning outcomes. These are the things that a student should be able to do when they exit. We built the projects so they are directly related to those learning outcomes. The things we show the external business community, for example, are the products they produce.

The deliverables. About half of the actual deliverables are presented not to faculty but to external business people. About one third of the projects are done for live clients. So they are actually working with a client and presenting that data back. We build all sorts of visuals tools. For that community, that is the important thing.

The accrediting association AACSB sort of loves us. They present us, or we have been presented by them, as an exemplar of how to do holistic education and outcomes-based education. The people who don't like us are the ones, frankly, by far—the ones most trouble selling the program to are the strong discipline-based faculty. They've got this thing called "coveritis." Have you covered this theory? Well, I'm sorry, but I went out into the business world, and nowhere did they say that you had to be able to repeat Maslow's five Levels of Need. They might have said you really need to be able to work with people effectively influencing them and cause them to behave in certain ways and motivate them. But that doesn't mean that it has to be covered in that way. That's a skill or a competency—that's not something that one repeats back.

John Bransford: I was just wondering if your cohorts—as they have formed—do you find that once they have graduated they tend to rely on one another for advice? Because that is a human capital decision.

John Stinson: Yeah, John. Super question. As each cohort graduated, as each class graduated, their intranet stayed. They had continued access to it. Boy, do you know, for the first 2 or 3 months a lot of them were on there very, very frequently. What do you suppose happened after that? They fade. We talked about that when they came together. The thing was that, "Yeah, we still really think about each other and rely on each other and call one another . . . we tend to be close to some members more than others. But we have sort of gotten out of the habit of getting on there every day or every other day. We have gotten out of the habit of that; we really need to interact with one another to accomplish some joint enterprise, which we had." So that's when we said we have to renew the community. We said we've got to find some reason for people to want to come back, some value to add to them that is more than just a place where they can collaborate with one another.

Jim Botkin: I'm not quite sure how to ask this question, but I will try anyway. I noticed in the business community that some unusual topics are coming up that have to do with corporate social responsibility. That have to do with learning through work. It's the sort of thing we would classify under the heading of transformative behavior. This is completely different from what most people think of as the business world or businesspeople's lives. To what degree do you think this program starts to get at that? You started out by asking the question, What will higher education look like in 10, 15 years? Education, after the church, has been known to be one of the things that is most preservative in times of trouble. What would be your thought on this being a move toward a major transformation?

John Stinson: The university or corporation.

Jim Botkin: Either or both?

John Stinson: I took the first part of your question really to mean the focus on transformative experience for the individual and what the individual builds back into their organization. If that is where you are coming from, our focus is much more there than it is with basic business concepts, building, and so forth. We do an awful lot of futures work. We do an awful lot of "Where does the business community fit in within the overall scope of the world as we move forward?" We cause students to be put into situations where they either have to be creative or they don't do very well. Now, in terms of transformative, in the sense of transforming the world or even transforming the university, I don't think that we do very much there.

Tom Duffy: A couple of questions, and then I have to do something for the record. First of all, what is the attrition rate for these classes?

John Stinson: The most that we have lost out of any classes was the first one. We started it with 26 people, 23 graduated. We have lost normally two people on average. And, by the way, the losses occur for both reasons: in some cases the individuals withdraws and there are cases where we ask people to leave.

Tom Duffy: There is a point of clarification that I need to make for the record. Because you started out saying that this is all practical and there is no theory base—let me provide a little context on John. I met John running around AERA 12 years ago or so, sitting in applied learning theory sessions. He brought all the associate deans to Indiana and spent a full day. I think we went to 6.00 in the evening. I was kind of astounded at their stay-with-it-ness. With really exploring issues. He also spent a long time working with Howard Barrows at Southern Illinois University, who started the whole problem-based learning approach. So John is really well embellished in the whole learning theory, applied learning theory framework. (*Group laughs*) Not nearly this kind of "Let's just try to do the practice."

But let me ask a question, John. You moved the residential problem-based learning approach to the undergraduate program. In the program, the students signed up for a set of business courses for a quarter in which, just like the MBA, the notion of courses disappears. They focus on a problem that cuts across the course topics, so they can devote their quarter to the business problem. What is your prediction of the success of moving that undergraduate effort to a distance environment? Could you do it with undergraduates as well?

John Stinson: We are doing it with undergraduates. We have regional campuses. We are doing it with undergraduates in our regional campus. I think it is moderately effective.

Tom Duffy: You mean you are headquartered in Athens, and they are scattered.

John Stinson: I am less comfortable with talking about the 20/20 [undergraduate program]. That's where one quarter of students will take what is called a cluster. That cluster will cover the equivalent of four of the core courses. They can either take it at the beginning level, or they take it at the senior level. The students all have to take one or the other of those. Many of them try to take both. Interesting thing, I'll come back to that. The people who are teaching in the clusters are junior level, non-Ph.D. instructor adjuncts, part-timers. The senior faculty—not all of them—want to make sure they have an auditorium class. They can be the star for 50 students or whatever it might be.

John Bransford: It's hard to give that up.

John Stinson: It's also easier, you know.

Matt Champagne: John brought up the issue of faculty who are early adopters. I wanted to hear more about that. In the FIPSE projects that I have worked on, there is a set number of faculty—6 to 10. They are the early adopters who do all these great things, and then there is everyone else who is sitting and waiting and are very attuned to the notion that it is not easy, and it's not made easy. I'm wondering if there is anything out there that can help manage the information and help remove the burden for these other people to step in. I'm kind of wondering when that point is going to occur when all the other faculty are going to say, "Yeah, I want to do this."

Linda Polin: We are starting to get this in our program. But I think part of it is a misperception on their part: I think they think it's easier. They see that I don't show up much. I tried to give my office away. I think they believe it is somehow easier, but it is not. It will be interesting to see what will happen this year for some of them, because the students are eating them up. It's going to kill the program.

John Stinson: We really focus extensively on faculty education. Duffy was over. Howard Barrows was over. We got a grant from Proctor and Gamble to both conduct faculty development relative to this type of education and to assess particularly that undergraduate component. So there is still an awful lot happening. Our faculty is big—probably about 70. I would say that as many as 30 to 40 or 50% of them have been involved in one way or the other.

Frankly, I know I'm a purist, but it scares me when some of those faculty come in with a little bit of training. Like one of those cluster courses we were talking about—it's supposed to be an integrated course, but what did I find going on? Four faculty—finance, operations, marketing, and strategy—each one of them teaching his or her own class, but they have a common project. The purist in me says, "Dammit, that's not the way you are supposed to do it!" But then I back off and say that's a heck of a lot better than the typical class, where students would get bored. So, hey, we take what we get.

Karen Ruhleder: We also did not have a set group of faculty with our program, and I wanted to clarify that. We actually tried very hard to make sure all faculty taught in the program at least once so that everybody has a common understanding when broader questions came up: "What's the program like?" Some now meet more regularly than others. It's still a policy to move the faculty through so there is a common experience for the program. In fact, I think we've had the opposite problem for the program. We've had so many people involved for a little part of the program that we don't have these strong leaders that seem to happen in other programs. For everyone, it's a class thing. It goes back to the philosophy of having to make it an option rather than a separate program.

Bob Wisher: You mentioned that two faculty withdrew because their values were not consistent with the instructional program. Can you explain?

John Stinson: Beautiful example. At the end of every project, we have a debriefing with the students, and that is not just on content—it's on the project—how did it go, what was good for you, what was good for me? The students started to give one of the faculty some very direct feedback, for example, "Rather than telling us that we did something terrible, you should give us a sample of that accounting problem." And "Gee, you're supposed to be on every 48 hours, but we did not get a response from you for 2 weeks."

He got up and said, "I don't have to take this. I'm the teacher here." And he walked out. And he left the program. The second one was a very similar situation. The faculty member was extremely uncomfortable that he was not in control. The students could actually make determinations and could participate in those determinations—and that did not sit well with him.

John Bransford: Just one other issue about the later adopters and how you can pressure them. I was meeting with a superintendent at a city in New Jersey where they did a big technology thing in middle schools. It is distance learning and things like that. He said it started at middle school, and then when the kids went to high school, the high school teachers didn't want to change. But the middle school kids had a critical mass. You also found out that parents joined the kids. You might want to think about that—seeding the critical mass of freshmen.

John Stinson: That's interesting, John. That is the way the undergraduate units got put into the curriculum, because it was there originally as the experiment. But the students responded and said, "Geez, we'd like to have one of our classes like that." So finally the faculty responded to students.

(End of session)

IV

Innovative Uses of Technology

10

Vanderbilt's AMIGO³ Project: Knowledge of How People Learn Enters Cyberspace

John Bransford, Nancy Vye, Helen Bateman, Sean Brophy, and Bob Roselli

Vanderbilt University

Our goal in this chapter is to discuss Vanderbilt's AMIGO³ project, which is exploring ways to use knowledge about how people learn to design Web-enhanced and Web-based learning environments. The first three letters of AMIGO³ stand for "Anchored Modular Inquiry." This refers to the fact that instruction is inquiry-based and anchored around key challenges that are packaged as modules that can be configured as needed. The remaining letters in AMIGO³ stand for "Generate Ownership, Originality and Organizational Learning." This refers to the fact that the design environment makes it easy to adapt modules to one's individual needs (ownership), to create new resources and challenges (originality), and to learn from one's colleagues by seeing how they have responded to various challenges (organizational learning).

The AMIGO³ project has its roots in earlier research and development projects conducted at Vanderbilt University (e.g., Cognition and Technology Group at Vanderbilt [CTGV], 1990, 1997, 2000; Schwartz, Brophy, Lin, & Bransford, 1999). It emerged in its present form in the context of an engineering research center (ERC) on bioengineering education and technology that was awarded to Vanderbilt University, Northwestern University, the University of Texas, and Harvard University and MIT (VaNTH). The goal of VaNTH is to use new technologies—coupled with state-of-the-art knowledge from the learning sciences—to design new approaches to bioengineering education and to study their effects on student and faculty learning (Harris, Bransford, & Brophy, 2002).

Bioengineering is a rapidly changing field, so the idea of creating modules (as opposed to larger units or entire courses that can be hard to decouple into smaller pieces) was very appealing. The fact that the VaNTH project involves a number of different universities made clear the need for modules that not only traveled intact, but could also be easily adapted to the particular needs of different instructors and institutions—either by adapting existing modules ("ownership") or developing new ones ("originality"). Bioengineering is also a field that requires a great deal of collaboration, both among researchers with specialties in engineering and biology, and between researchers and industry partners. The idea that the AMIGO[3] project promotes "organizational learning" reflects this emphasis on helping faculty and industry partners continually learn from one another, while also helping their students learn (in industry the goal would be to help employees continue to learn).

The AMIGO[3] project has piqued the interest of people from a number of areas, in addition to bioengineering. This interest is allowing us to explore how the AMIGO[3] concept can be adapted to a variety of contexts—including corporate training (Vye, Burgess, Bransford, & Cigarran, 2002), preservice education courses designed to help prospective teachers learn about learning (PT[3] Group at Vanderbilt, 2002) and courses that help principals reorient their practices in ways that help all children succeed (http://ldc.peabody.vanderbilt.edu/). In the discussion that follows, we first explore the theoretical foundations of the AMIGO[3] project and then provide some example applications. More specifically, we discuss

- Issues of educational quality
- The "How People Learn" framework as a guide for designing environments that support high-quality learning
- Basic elements of the AMIGO[3] project and its relationship to knowledge about how people learn
- Needs and opportunities for rigorous research.

ISSUES OF EDUCATIONAL QUALITY

Weigel (2000) argues that most of the current attempts to create online learning environments still fit a "port the classroom" (to the Web) model (e.g., Weigel, 2000). This would be fine if we knew that typical approaches to classroom-based teaching produce high-quality learning. Unfortunately, many argue that typical approaches to K–12 and postsecondary instruction leave a great deal to be desired (e.g., National Research Council, 2000; Weigel, 2000).

Elsewhere, we discuss a tongue-in-cheek analysis of problems with teaching and learning in higher education, plus a proposal for a new kind of university that solves these problems (see Bransford, Vye, & Bateman, 2002). The analysis takes place in the context of a 4-minute comedy routine by Father Guido Sarduci of *Saturday Night Live* (from *Gilda Radnor Live,* 1980). Father Sarduci begins by looking at the knowledge and skills that the average college graduate remembers 5 years after he or she graduates. He accepts these 5-year-later memory performances as his standard and proposes a new kind of university that will have the same outcomes. His innovation is "The Five-Minute University," which will cost only $20. Father Sarduci notes that $20 might seem like a lot for only 5 minutes, but it includes tuition, books, snacks for the 20-second spring break, cap and gown rental, and graduation picture.

Father Sarduci provides examples of the things students remember after 5 years. If they took 2 years of college Spanish, for example, he argues that—5 years postgraduation—the average student will remember only "¿Como esta usted?" and "Muy bien, gracias." So that's all his Five-Minute University teaches. His economics course teaches only supply and demand. His business course teaches "You buy something and sell it for more," and so forth. A video of Father Sarduci's performance demonstrates how strongly the audience resonates to his theme of the heavy emphasis on memorization in college courses, and the subsequent high forgetting rates.

In addition to being humorous, Father Sarduci's performance raises some very important questions. One is whether his claim that educators often overemphasize memorization (e.g., of facts and formulas) has a ring of truth to it. Many argue that the answer is yes (e.g., National Research Council, 2000).

A second question raised by Father Sarduci becomes clear by imagining he launches his Five-Minute University (we'll assume he does it online) and we need to compete with it. What would we do? One approach is to emphasize a suite of "enlightened teaching techniques" that are better than the lecture method that Father Sarduci criticizes. Searching for better teaching techniques is a very common strategy for educational improvement. We have been approached by a number of professors and K–12 teachers who heard that lectures (whether live or online) are a poor way to teach. "Is this true?" they ask. "Is cooperative learning better then lecturing?" "Do [computers, labs, hands-on projects, simulations] help learning?" For Web-based instruction, we are often asked to identify the most important technology features needed for success, including the relative importance of threaded discussions, chat rooms, availability of full-motion video, and so forth. Questions about teaching strategies are important, but they put the cart before the horse.

An alternative strategy, and one we endorse, is discussed in a book by Wiggins and McTighe entitled *Understanding by Design* (1997). They suggest a "working backward" strategy for creating high-quality learning experiences. This involves (1) beginning with a careful analysis of learning goals; (2) exploring how to assess students' progress in achieving these goals; and (3) using the results of 1 and 2 to choose and continually evaluate teaching methods. (Assumptions about Steps 1 and 2 are also continually evaluated). When using a "working backwards" strategy, one's choice of teaching strategies derives from a careful analysis of learning goals.

In Father Sarduci's Five-Minute University, the goal is to teach only what the average college student remembers 5 years after he or she graduates. If that's the goal, 5 minutes of focused instruction might well be sufficient. But consider alternative sets of goals, for example

- Reducing forgetting of a large number of facts (e.g., by using mnemonic techniques)
- Learning with understanding (rather than simply memorizing)
- Problem solving (of well-defined problems) in addition to understanding
- Problem solving of open-ended problems in addition to the preceding
- Learning about oneself as a lifelong learner (e.g., developing metacognitive skills and awareness)
- Learning all of the above, plus learning to use knowledge, strategies, and technology to work smart.

These different sets of goals require different approaches to instruction and different time commitments (see Bransford, Vye, & Bateman, 2002). Additional considerations relevant to choosing effective instructional strategies are discussed next.

The Jenkins Tetrahedral Model

A model developed by James Jenkins (1978) is consistent with Wiggins' and McTighe's (1997) emphasis on "working backwards" (see Fig. 10.1—we have adapted the model slightly to fit the current discussion). It further clarifies the point that different learning goals require different types of teaching strategies and time commitments.

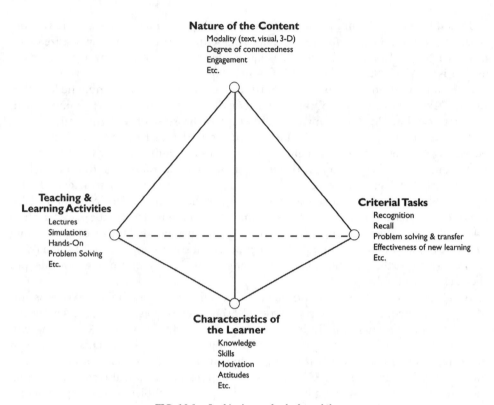

FIG. 10.1.   Jenkins's tetrahedral model.

The model helps instructors see that the appropriateness of using particular types of teaching strategies depends on (1) the nature of the materials to be learned; (2) the nature of the skills, knowledge, and attitudes that learners bring to the situation; and (3) the goals of the learning situation and the assessments used to measure learning relative to these goals. One of the important points of the model is that a teaching strategy that works within one constellation of these variables may work very poorly when that overall constellation is changed.

One way to think about the Jenkins model is to view it as highlighting important parameters for defining various educational ecosystems. A particular teaching strategy may flourish or perish depending on the overall characteristics of the ecosystem in which it is placed. Attempts to teach students about veins and arteries can be used to illustrate the interdependencies shown in the Jenkins framework (Fig. 10.1). Imagine that the materials to be learned include a text, which states that arteries are thicker than veins and more elastic, and carry blood rich in oxygen from the heart. Veins are smaller, less elastic, and carry blood back to the heart. What's the best way to help students learn this information? The Jenkins model reminds us that the answer to this question depends on who the students are, what we mean by "learning" in this context, and how we measure the learning that occurs.

One strategy would be to use mnemonic techniques. For example, students might be taught to think about the sentence "*Art(ery)*" was *thick* around the middle, so he wore pants with an *elastic* waistband." The Jenkins framework reminds us that the ability to use this particular technique presupposes specific types of knowledge and skills on the part of the learners (e.g., that they understand English, understand concepts such as elasticity and why they would be useful in this situation, etc.). Given the availability of this knowledge, mnemonic techniques like the one noted above "work" for remembering factual content. If asked to state important characteristics of arteries (e.g., thick, elastic), the proceeding statement about Art(ery) can be very helpful. If our tests assess only memory, we conclude that our students have learned. But suppose that we change the goal from merely remembering to learning with understanding. The Jenkins framework reminds us that a change in learning goals and assessments often requires a change in teaching and learning strategies as well.

To learn with understanding, students need to understand why veins and arteries have certain characteristics. For example, arteries carry blood from the heart, blood that is pumped in spurts. This helps explain why they would need to be elastic (to handle the spurts). In addition, arterial blood needs to travel uphill (to the brain), as well as downhill, so the elasticity of the arteries provides an additional advantage. If they constrict behind each uphill spurt, they help the blood flow upward.

Learning to understand relationships such as why arteries are elastic should facilitate subsequent transfer. For example, imagine that students are asked to design an artificial artery. Would it have to be elastic? Students who have only memorized that arteries are elastic have no grounded way to approach this problem. Students who have learned with understanding know the functions of elasticity and hence are freer to consider possibilities like a nonelastic artery that has one-way valves (Bransford & Stein, 1993).

Overall, this example illustrates how memorizing versus understanding represent different learning goals in the Jenkins framework, and how changes in these goals require different types of teaching strategies. The details of one's teaching strategies will also need to vary, depending on the knowledge, skills, attitudes, and other characteristics that students bring to the learning task. For example, we noted earlier that some students (e.g., those in the lower grades) may not know enough about pumping, spurts, and elasticity to learn with understanding if they are simply told about the functions of arteries. They may need special scaffolds such as dynamic simulations that display these properties. As a different kind of example, imagine that we want to include mnemonics along with understanding and one of the students in our class is overweight and named Art. Under these conditions, it would seem unwise to use the mnemonic sentence about Art(ery) that was noted above.

Summary of Section 1

Our major goal in this section was to lay the groundwork for a theoretical analysis of the AMIGO³ project. We began this section by noting that most attempts to create online learning environments fit a "port the classroom" (to the Web) model (e.g., Weigel, 2000). This would be fine if we knew that typical approaches to classroom-based teaching produce high-quality learning. Unfortunately, Father Guido Sarduci and many others argue that typical approaches to K–12 and postsecondary instruction leave a great deal to be desired (e.g., NRC, 2000; Weigel, 2000). A major goal of the AMIGO³ project is to create learning opportunities that produce better outcomes than those found in typical face-to-face teaching settings.

We noted that some people approach the goal of improving quality by focusing on teaching methods and asking, "Which ones are best?" An alternative approach— and one we argue is much more productive—is to focus on what we want students to know and be able to do, and to then work backward (Wiggins & McTighe, 1997). We briefly explored the strategy of working backwards in the context of an imaginary set of universities that are set up to compete with Father Sarduci's Five-Minute University. Each tries to differentiate itself from the pack by focusing on different learning outcomes. The choice of outcomes will have a major impact on the choice of teaching strategies—including the length of time that students need to spend in their school (see Bransford, Vye, & Bateman, 2002, for more elaboration).

We next introduced the Jenkins model (see Fig. 10.1). It is compatible with the idea of working backward and reminds us that a change in learning goals is only one of several factors that should impact our choice of teaching methods. Other factors include whom we are teaching and what they already know.

Our goal in the next section is to take the ideas of "working backwards" and the Jenkins tetrahedral model one step further. In particular, we explore the "How People Learn Framework" and show how it influences the AMIGO^3 project.

USING INFORMATION ABOUT HOW PEOPLE LEARN

The How People Learn (HPL) framework has been used in major school reform efforts (e.g. CTGV, 2000) and by several committee reports that were organized by the National Academy of Science and published by the National Academy Press. These publications include *How People Learn: Brain, Mind, Experience and School* (NRC, 1999a) and *How People Learn: Bridging Research and Practice* (NRC, 1999b). These two individual reports have recently been combined to produce an expanded edition of How People Learn (NRC, 2000). We refer to this newest report as HPL. A more recent report, *Knowing What Students Know* (NRC, 2001), builds on HPL and is also relevant to this discussion. Its focus is primarily on assessment.

Figure 10.2 shows the How People Learn framework. The figure depicts a set of four (overlapping) lenses that can be used to analyze any learning situation. In particular, it suggests that we ask about the degree to which learning environments are

- Knowledge centered (in the sense of being based on a careful analysis of what we want people to know and be able to do when they finish with our materials or

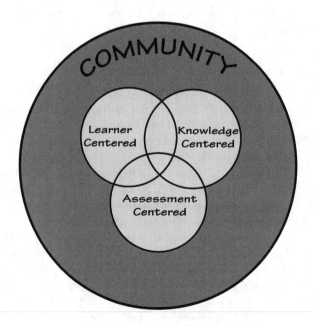

FIG. 10.2. The HPL framework.

course and providing them with the foundational knowledge, skills, and attitudes needed for successful transfer)

- Learner centered (in the sense of connecting to the strengths, interests, and pre-conceptions of learners and helping them learn about themselves as learners)
- Assessment centered (in the sense of providing multiple opportunities to make students' thinking visible so they can receive feedback and be given chances to revise)
- Community centered (in the sense of providing an environment—both within and outside the classroom—where students feel safe to ask questions, learn to use technology to access resources and work collaboratively, and are helped to develop lifelong learning skills)

We discuss each of these next.

Knowledge Centered

Although it seems obvious that learning involves the goal of acquiring new knowledge (we include skills within this category), the HPL framework helps us think more deeply about this issue. An important point that emerges from the expertise literature (see NRC, 2000) is the need to emphasize "connected" knowledge that is organized around foundational ideas of a discipline. Research on expertise shows that it is the organization of knowledge that underlies experts' abilities to understand and solve problems (see, especially, Chap. 2 in NRC, 2000). Bruner (1960) makes the following argument about knowledge organization:

> The curriculum of a subject should be determined by the most fundamental understanding that can be achieved of the underlying principles that give structure to a subject. Teaching specific topics or skills without making clear their context in the broader fundamental structure of a field of knowledge is uneconomical ... An understanding of fundamental principles and ideas appears to be the main road to adequate transfer of training. To understand something as a specific instance of a more general case—which is what understanding a more fundamental structure means—is to have learned not only a specific thing but also a model for understanding other things like it that one may encounter. (pp. 6, 25, and 31)

Courses are often organized in ways that fail to develop the kinds of connected knowledge structures that support activities such as effective reasoning and problem solving. For example, texts often present lists of topics and facts in a manner that has been described as "a mile wide and an inch deep" (e.g., see NRC, 2000). This is very different from focusing on the "enduring ideas of a discipline." In agreement with Bruner (see the previous quotation by Bruner), Wiggins and McTighe (1997) argue that the knowledge to be taught should be prioritized into categories that range from "enduring ideas of the discipline" to "important things to know and be able to do" to "ideas worth mentioning." Thinking through these issues and coming up with a set of "enduring connected ideas" is an extremely important aspect of educational design.

Learner Centered

There are overlaps between being knowledge centered and learner centered, but there are also differences. In Bransford, Vye, and Bateman (2002), we note that one aspect of being learner centered focuses on the need for instructors to examine the gaps between their knowledge as experts and the knowledge their students bring to the learning task.

From the instructor's perspective, an important aspect of being learner centered involves recognition of "expert blind spots." Instructors must become aware that much of what they know is tacit and hence can easily be skipped over in instruction. For example, experts in physics and engineering may not realize that they are failing to communicate all the information necessary to help novices learn to construct their own free-body diagrams (Brophy, 2001). The reason is that many decisions are so intuitive that professors don't even realize that they are part of their repertoire. Studies of expertise (e.g. NRC, 2000) show that experts' knowledge helps them begin problem solving at a higher level than novices, because they almost effortlessly perceive aspects of the problem situation that are invisible to novices (e.g., Chi, Feltovich, & Glaser, 1981; DeGroot, 1965). Shulman (1987) discusses how effective teachers need to develop "pedagogical content knowledge" that goes well beyond the content knowledge of a discipline (see also Hestenes, 1987). It includes an understanding of how novices typically struggle as they attempt to master a domain, and an understanding of strategies for helping them learn.

Being learner centered also involves taking seriously the idea that students are not "blank slates" who are free from preconceptions about subject matter. This point is nicely illustrated in the children's story *Fish Is Fish,* by Leo Lionni (1970). *Fish Is Fish* is the story of a fish who is interested in learning about what happens on land, but it cannot explore land because it can only breathe in water. It befriends a tadpole, who grows into a frog and eventually goes onto the land. The frog returns to the pond a few weeks later and describes the things it has seen, such as birds, cows, and people. As the fish listens to frog's descriptions, he imagines each one to be fishlike. People are imagined to be fish who walk on their tailfins; birds are fish with wings; cows are fish with udders. This story illustrates both the creative opportunities and dangers inherent in the fact that people construct new knowledge based on their current knowledge.

The NRC (2000) summarizes a number of studies that demonstrate the active, preconception-driven learning that is evident from infancy to adulthood (see also Carey & Gelman, 1991; Driver, Squires, Rushworth, & Wood-Robinson, 1994). In many cases, students' preconceptions developed from their everyday experiences and are reasonable in this context yet are at odds with current assumptions that took centuries to formulate (e.g., about physics). If students' preconceptions are not addressed directly, they often memorize content (e.g., formulas in physics), yet still use their experience-based preconceptions (which are often misconceptions from the perspective of mature disciplines) to act on the world.

Being learner centered also involves honoring students' backgrounds and cultural values and finding special strengths (e.g. "funds of knowledge"—see Moll, Tapia, & Whitmore, 1993) that each may have that allow them to connect to information being taught in the classroom. Unless these connections are made explicitly, they often remain inert and hence do not support subsequent learning.

Community Centered

This aspect of the HPL framework is related to being learner centered, but it focuses attention on the norms and modes of operation of any community we are joining. For example, some classrooms represent communities where it is safe to ask questions and say, "I don't know." Others follow the norm of "Don't get caught not knowing something." An number of studies suggest that—to be successful—learning communities should provide their members a feeling that members matter to each other and to the group, and a shared belief that members' needs will be met through their commitment to be together (Alexopoulou & Driver, 1996; Bateman, Bransford, Goldman, & Newbrough, 2000).

The importance of creating and sustaining learning can be traced to Vygotsky's theory in which culture and human interaction plays a central role in developmental processes. Vygotsky (1978) suggested that all learning is culturally mediated, historically developing and arising from cultural activity. An important implication of this perspective is that providing supportive, enriched, and flexible settings where people can learn from one another is essential. Having strong social networks within a classroom, within a school, and between classrooms and outside resources produces a number of advantages. Data relevant to this point are discussed in more detail in Bransford, Vye, and Bateman (2002).

Assessment Centered

In addition to being knowledge, learner, and community centered, effective learning environments are also assessment centered. This aspect of the HPL framework includes two different types of assessments: formative and summative. We discuss each below.

Formative Assessment

Formative assessments are designed to provide feedback to teachers and learners so that they can revise their current thinking and problem-solving approaches and improve their performances. They serve a learning function for teachers who can use the information to improve their overall instruction or to target specific students who are in need of further help. Similarly, students can use feedback from formative assessments to help them improve their actions and their thinking. A number of studies show that providing opportunities for feedback and revision greatly helps students learn (e.g., Barron et al., 1998; Black & William, 1998; CTGV, 1997; Hunt & Minstrell, 1994).

Helping students learn to self-assess (to become more metacognitive) is especially important for learning. (e.g., see NRC, 2000). A major reason is that, ultimately, students need to develop the habits of mind to assess their own progress rather than always rely on outsiders. A number of studies show that achievement improves when students are encouraged to self-assess their own contributions and work (e.g., see NRC, 2000; Lin & Lehman, 1999; White & Frederiksen, 1998). It is also important to help students assess the kinds of strategies they are using to learn and solve problems. For example, in quantitative courses such as physics, many students simply focus on formulas rather than attempt to first think qualitatively about problems and relate them to key ideas in a discipline (e.g., Newton's second law). When they are helped to do the latter, performance on new problems greatly improves (e.g. Leonard, Dufresne & Mestre, 1996).

Summative Assessment

Unlike formative assessments, summative assessments are generally used to index what has been learned at the end of a unit, course, or program of study. These include multiple choice tests, essay exams, and projects that students complete. Most summative assessments do not provide opportunities for students to revise based on the feedback received from their test performances. Their primary function is for quality control and credentialing. Issues of summative assessment are discussed in NRC (2000) and in much more detail in a new National Academy of Science report entitled "Knowing What People Know" (NRC, 2001). The latter report points out both strengths and a weakness of many approaches to summative assessment, such as standardized testing. The report also recommends that course-based formative assessments receive much more attention than they have in the past.

Linking Issues of Assessment to Theories Transfer

Elsewhere (Bransford & Schwartz, 1999), we argue that issues of assessment are fundamentally linked to assumptions about learning and transfer—although this link is often not made explicitly. As an illustration, consider the point that everyone wants summative assessments that provide an indication of students' ability to do something other than "simply take tests." Ideally, our assessments are predictive of students' performance in everyday settings once they leave the classroom. One way to look at this issue is to view tests as attempts to predict students' abilities to transfer from classroom settings to everyday settings. Different ways of thinking about transfer have important implications for thinking about assessment. Central to traditional approaches to transfer is a "direct application" theory and a dominant methodology that Bransford and Schwartz (1999) call "sequestered problem solving" (SPS). Just as juries are often sequestered to protect them from possible exposure to "contaminating" information, subjects in experiments are sequestered during tests of transfer. There are no opportunities for them to demonstrate their abilities to learn to solve new problems by seeking help from other resources, such as texts or colleagues, or by trying things out, receiving feedback, and getting opportunities to revise. Accompanying the SPS paradigm is a theory that characterizes transfer as the ability to directly apply one's previous learning to a new setting or problem (we call this the Direct Application [DA] theory of transfer). Bransford's and Schwartz's thesis is that the SPS methodology and the accompanying DA theory of transfer are responsible for much of the pessimism about evidence for transfer.

This alternative view acknowledges the validity of these perspectives but also broadens the conception of transfer by including an emphasis on peoples' "preparation for future learning" (PFL). Here, the focus shifts to assessments of people's abilities to learn in knowledge-rich environments. When organizations hire new employees, they don't expect them to have learned everything they need for successful adaptation. They want people who can learn, and they expect them to make use of resources (e.g., texts, computer programs, and colleagues) to facilitate this learning. The better prepared they are for future learning, the greater the transfer (in terms of speed and/or quality of new learning). Examples of ways to "prepare students for future learning" are explored in Schwartz and Bransford (1998) and Bransford and Schwartz (1999).

It is important to emphasize that the PFL perspective on transfer does not assume the existence of a set of general learning skills that are content-free. The expertise literature (e.g. NRC, 2000) clearly shows how strategies and knowledge are highly interdependent. Broudy (1977) provides an example: "The concept of bacterial infection as learned in biology can operate even if only a skeletal notion of the theory and the facts supporting it can be recalled. Yet, we are told of cultures in which such a concept would not be part of the interpretive schemata" (p. 12).

The absence of an idea of bacterial infection should have a strong effect on the nature of the hypotheses that people entertain in order to explain various illnesses, and hence would affect their abilities to learn more about causes of illness through further research and study, and the strategies one uses to solve new problems. The acquisition of well-differentiated knowledge is crucial for future learning (e.g., NRC, 2000; Schwartz & Bransford, 1998). The more that this knowledge is acquired with understanding, the higher the probability that appropriate transfer will occur.

The sole use of static assessments may mask the learning gains of many students, plus mask the learning advantages that various kinds of educational experiences provide (Bransford & Schwartz, 1999). Linking work on summative assessment to theories of transfer may help us overcome the limitations of many existing tests.

HPL and Motivation

Many people ask where motivation resides in the HPL framework. We argue that all aspects of the framework are relevant to this issue. If students know they are learning content and skills that will be important in life, that is motivating. If courses connect with their interests and strengths, and provide interesting challenges to their preconceptions, that is motivating (Dweck, 1989). If students receive frequent feedback that lets them see their progress in learning and gives them chances to do even better, that is motivating. If students feel they are a valued part of a vibrant learning community, this is motivating as well.

Summary of Section 2

Our goal in this section was to discuss the How People Learn framework, which highlights a set of four overlapping lenses that are useful for analyzing the quality of various learning environments. The lenses focus on the degree to which these environments are knowledge-, learner-, community-, and assessment-centered, where the latter includes both formative and summative approaches to assessment.

A balance among the four lenses of the HPL framework is particularly important. For example, learning environments can be knowledge centered but not learner centered, and vice versa. Many learning environments fail to promote a sense of community where learning (which includes admissions of "not knowing") is welcomed. In addition, many environments lack frequent opportunities for formative assessment and revision, and their summative assessments often fail to capture the degree to which students are prepared for future learning rather than simply prepared to take a test.

THE AMIGO³ PROJECT

In this section, we discuss Vanderbilt University's AMIGO³ project, which is exploring ways to use knowledge about how people learn to design Web-enhanced and Web-based learning environments. As noted in the introduction to this paper, the first three letters of AMIGO³ stand for "Anchored Modular Inquiry." This refers to the fact that instruction is inquiry-based and anchored around key challenges that are packaged as modules that can be configured as needed. The remaining letters in AMIGO³ stand for "Generate Ownership, Originality and Organizational Learning." This refers to the fact that the design environment makes it easy to adapt modules to one's individual needs (ownership), to create new resources and challenges (originality), and to learn from one's colleagues by seeing how they have responded to various challenges (organizational learning).

Components for Modular Design

• **Overall Course**

• **Mosaics (units)**

• **Modules**

• **Granules (text, video, audio, simulations, etc.)**

FIG. 10.3.   The AMIGO³ architecture.

Overall, the AMIGO³ project is guided by the literature on how people learn (see previous discussion). Please note, however, that the project is far from being the only way to design a learning environment that is HPL compatible. In addition, the AMIGO³ project is a work in progress. One of its benefits is that it is helping us build a technology infrastructure that makes it easier to continue to study the processes by which people learn (e.g., by capturing learners' choices and performances for subsequent analysis).

The AMIGO³ Architecture

Figure 10.3 shows our current architecture for a simple but powerful and flexible modular publishing system. At the base of the system (see Fig. 10.3) is a database of generic

FIG. 10.4.   The design of a module.

resources (granules) such as audio and video clips, simulations, texts, assessment shells, and so forth. The granules become pedagogically useful when put into modules that begin with challenges and then include opportunities for gaining access to other perspectives and for self-assessment (we discuss this in more detail below). Modules can in turn be organized into larger units, called Mosaics. Mosaics can be organized into courses. A database and course management system designed for the bioengineering project (called Courseware Authoring and Packaging Environment (CAPE)) provides the engine for using the modular architecture. For more information about CAPE, see http://www.isis.vanderbilt.edu/projects/VaNTH/index.htm.

The Design for Modules

This design of our AMIGO³ modules is based on previous research at Vanderbilt that explored the learning gains developed through anchored inquiry (e.g., CTGV, 1997, 2000), and that eventually resulted in a software shell for helping people visualize and manage inquiry in a manner that is learner, knowledge, assessment, and community centered. (Schwartz et al., 1999) Called STAR.Legacy (STAR stands for "Software Technology for Action and Reflection"), the software environment provides a framework for inquiry. Chances to solve important problems, assess one's progress, and revise when necessary play a prominent role in the legacy cycle. The environment can also easily be adapted to fit local needs, in part by being able to easily add and delete various resources, and by having teachers and students "leave legacies" for future students and colleagues. Overall, the environment promotes the AMIGO³ goals of generating ownership, originality, and organizational learning. We provide more examples of this later on.

Figure 10.4 shows one of several possible variants of the "homepage" of an inquiry–based module. The software is organized around challenges. After introduction of a challenge, students generate their own ideas. Then they are able to consult resources relevant to the challenges (including the ability to hear ideas from experts). These often result in "Ah-ha" experiences, because the experts raise points that are obviously important but were not initially considered by the students. Students eventually receive opportunities to self-assess and revise before "going public." As noted earlier, the structure of STAR.Legacy is designed to help balance the features of learner, knowledge, assessment, and community centeredness. It's challenge-based design attempts to accommodate a variety of important and successful approaches to learning, such as case-based, problem-based, project-based, and design-based instruction (e.g., see

Barron et al., 1998; CTGV, 1997; Duffy & Cunningham, 1996; NRC, 2000; Kolodner, 1997; Williams, 1992).

Some Advantages of Inquiry-Based Learning

One way to demonstrate the potential value of inquiry-based learning is to contrast it with a teaching situation that is strictly lecture-based. With this goal in mind, imagine a lecture that has very important content (in this case for high school students) but is far from "student friendly" when given in isolation (i.e., as a granule). We created such a lecture and provide a transcript below. When students hear it in isolation, they are far from enthused about its content and delivery. The question we asked ourselves is whether we could make students value the same lecture very highly when it is used as a resource following a challenge rather than as a lecture that simply stands on its own. Here's the lecture:

> The formula for density is $D = M/V$. D stands for density and M stands for the mass of an object. We determine the mass of an object by weighing it.
> V stands for the volume of an object. The volume of a cube is measured by its length times its width times its height. A cube that is 1 centimeter long, tall and wide would have a volume of 1 cubic centimeter.
>   If an object is irregularly shaped, volume can be measured by an immersion technique where the object is placed in a cylinder filled with water. The volume is equal to the amount of water that the object displaces. Volume is measured in units like cubic centimeters.
>   Different types of materials have specific densities. The density of lead is approximately 11.2 grams per cubic centimeter. The density of gold is approximately 19.3 grams per cubic centimeter. The density of a cubic centimeter of sand might be around 3 grams, depending on the coarseness of the sand.

Overall, the concept of density is very important for many aspects of science and engineering. It's a key concept that everyone should know. The STAR.Legacy shell (see Fig. 10.4) suggests a design where the lecture noted above is used as a resource that comes after (a) a relevant challenge and (b) a chance for students to post their initial thoughts about the challenge.

A challenge that is relevant to this lecture has been developed in conjunction with Bob Sherwood, a science educator at Vanderbilt. The challenge is a short 4-minute video entitled *The Golden Statuette*, which was filmed very inexpensively with two high school actors. A high school boy decides to paint a statue gold and try to sell it to the proprietor of a metallurgy shop as being pure gold. "Don't you go cutting into it or anything," he says to the proprietor (obviously worried that this would reveal the true nature of the metal). "It's pure gold and real soft."

The proprietor of the store first weighs the statue and then writes down what she found (908 grams). Next, she immerses it in a cylinder of water and writes down the overflow (80 cm^3). She then divides the mass by the volume. Finally, she looks at a chart of the densities of various metals and a chart of selling prices for these metals. At the end, she gives the boy 10 cents for his statuette. The challenge to the students is to figure out if she was right and, if so, how did she know how much to pay?

We have given this challenge to a number of students—including those who have been in very prestigious high schools. Few knew how to solve the challenge, but most were engaged by the story and wanted to understand how the proprietor knew that the statue was not made of gold. Many realized that they needed to know the answer to questions such as "What are grams a measure of?" and "Why did she put the statute in the flask with water?" They realized that they didn't know what various actions and units meant.

Once students have grappled with the challenge, we find that they are both more motivated and "cognitively ready" (see Schwartz et al., 1999) to learn about the concept of density. One way to test this idea is to use the lecture noted above—the one that students actively dislike when it is presented only in isolation. When presented following the challenge, it is viewed as interesting and informative. The challenge has provided a "time for telling" (Schwartz & Bransford, 1998) that makes the lecture relevant.

A More Complete Example of a Module

The discussion above illustrated how a stand-alone lecture that students undervalue can be transformed into a valuable resource when it is proceeded by a challenge that students want to solve but cannot. The STAR.Legacy cycle invites this kind of design, but it also includes additional components. An example of a more complete module is discussed next.

The Challenge

Consider a module that is designed to help college students learn about principles of How People Learn (in this case about some of the "assessment-centered" principles of HPL). The module begins with a challenge. When used in the Legacy format (see Fig. 10.4), the challenge is displayed on the Web (with high bandwidth media on CD, if that is preferred) in a short (about 45-second) engaging, inexpensive "audio plus picture" format. It introduces an animation of a teacher who gives his students a gift for the holiday season. The narrative reads as follows:

> During the December holiday season, a local newspaper ran a cartoon showing students in a classroom who had each received a wrapped present from their teacher. Upon opening the present, each student discovered the contents—a geometry test. Needless to say, the students were not pleased with their "gift." People who viewed the cartoon could easily understand the students' anguish. Tests are more like punishments than gifts. However, is there any way that a "test" could be perceived as something positive?

As students proceed with this challenge, they go through steps such as those noted below.

Initial Thoughts

Students respond to the challenge by clicking on "Initial Thoughts" (see Fig. 10.4) and publishing them to the Web. As noted earlier, we have presented this challenge to many students and, more often than not, they answer that tests are negative experiences—period. The exception is when they happen to do very well on one—but they don't know this until after the fact.

Students' initial thoughts can be captured as short essays that they can return to later (to compare them to their "later thoughts" once they have completed a module), or they can be multiple choice answers to directed questions, or both. The inquiry shell is designed to be flexible and allow choices among a variety of different response formats at different phases in the cycle.

Perspectives and Resources

After posting their initial thoughts, students proceed to resources. These consist of audio and video clips, texts, simulations, suggestions for hands-on activities, and other tools that give the students a deeper perspective on the challenge. For the preceding challenge, students might hear a 2-minute mini-lecture on differences between formative and summative assessment, plus read a short paper on the topic. They might also see a video interview with a group of middle school children who discuss how valuable it was to get tough feedback (formative assessment) from their friends and teacher prior to an important presentation to outside experts.

Having students write their initial thoughts to a challenge prior to hearing the resources is designed to creates a "time for telling" (Schwartz & Bransford, 1998). Often experts say things that even novices recognize as being familiar to them ("Oh, yeah, I know that"). Nevertheless, the challenge cycle helps students realize that they had not spontaneously generated these ideas during their initial thoughts. This creates an "Ah-ha" experience that results in better memory and a deeper grasp of the significance of new ideas (e.g., see Auble & Franks, 1978; Bransford, 1979).

Self-Assessment

After reviewing resources, students can self-assess their own understanding. This can include multiple-choice tests with automated grading that sends them back to relevant resources when needed. Alternatively, students may write short essays on the Web and receive feedback from teaching assistants or the professor about what needs to be revised. Students also assess the usefulness of each module for their own thinking, hence making it easy to continuously improve the course.

An especially important option for self-assessment is the opportunity for online discussions with others who have taken the same challenge and are trying to articulate their thoughts and opinions about it. As Duffy and Kirkley note (Chap. 6, this volume), online discussions are especially important ways to help students learn.

Go Public

Finally, students "go public." This often involves a written essay, posted to the web, on differences between their initial thoughts (which were captured earlier and can be returned to by the students) and their current thinking about the challenge. Or it may involve class presentations about "big ideas or burning issues." Another option is for students to construct challenges of their own for others to try. The degree to which students truly "go public" is variable. In some cases, their final thoughts go only to the professor the teaching assistants, or both. In other cases, the whole class sees everyone's answers (in our experience, students usually like this option). In still other cases, one group of students may post thoughts to be critiqued by students in another group, course, or university. Once gain, the inquiry cycle can be used in flexible ways.

Students have been particularly appreciative of the opportunity to articulate what they have learned from a module by comparing their later thoughts with their initial thoughts. If initial thoughts are not captured in some format that students can return to, it is easy for them to underappreciate how much their thinking has changed.

Uses of Modules

There are a number of contexts in which students might use the preceding challenge module. Most of our experience has involved "hybrid," or blended, learning environments (combinations of Web-based and face-to-face), rather than totally Web-based environments. As an illustration, students in our courses might receive a challenge in class, write down their initial thoughts, share these in small groups, and then present their thinking to the professor. This provides the professor with the opportunity to learn from students' insights and confusions and to address misconceptions (it also makes teaching much more fun for the professor). The professor can also introduce students to "resources" that are on the Web and that students can explore in class or after class (e.g., as homework).

Another way to use challenges is to have students view the challenges on the Web prior to coming to class, and to publish (on the Web) their initial thoughts on the challenge. This allows the instructor to see students' preconceptions prior to class time—which is extremely helpful. Alternatively, students may finish a number of complete challenge cycles prior to coming to class. This means that they would post (on the Web) not only their initial thoughts, but also their "later thoughts" (after hearing the resources). Class discussion can then focus on discussing the challenges in more detail and on generating analogous challenges or additional resources that are relevant to what is being learned.

Throughout this entire process, it is important to help people feel comfortable interacting online—especially if the course is entirely Web based rather than Web enhanced. In the latter context, a major obstacle is the loss of personal interactions with professors and fellow students (e.g., see Hough, 2000; Palloff & Pratt, 1999). Given a posting to the Web followed by no responses, it is easy to assume that "no one cares" or "my thoughts must have been stupid." In actuality, people may simply have been too busy to respond.

Interacting with people we do not know can exacerbate the difficulties of feeling comfortable in online environments. In *The Social Life of Information*, Brown and Duguid (2000) argue that interactive technologies appear to be more effective in maintaining communication among established communities that in building new communities from scratch. But there are researchers who argue that communities can be built from scratch (e.g., Rose, 2001)

Faculty Learning

We noted earlier that one of the goals of the AMIGO³ project is to facilitate not only student learning, but also faculty learning and learning as an organization. For example, the AMIGO³ project is being designed to allow faculty members to borrow modules (searchable by topic on a database) and tailor them for their own purposes (this includes the AMIGO³ goals of both "ownership" and "organizational learning"). As an illustration, faculty using the "test as a gift challenge" (see previous discussion) may add new examples of formative assessment (as readings, audio, video, and simulations) that better fit their particular areas of emphasis (reading, science, mathematics, etc). They can use comments from other faculty as well. A benefit of the latter approach is that students in a course get to "meet" (via the media) other faculty who are commenting on various challenges. In our experience, students who have seen faculty members in the media frequently approach them in real life and begin to talk (e.g., "I really liked your comments about the Test as a Gift challenge and would love more information about the study you mentioned"). Faculty, too, like to see the perspectives of other faculty who comment on a challenge via the media (e.g. see Schwartz et al., 1999).

The AMIGO^3 project is also designed to support faculty and students' opportunities to create new challenges and resources that can be added to the AMIGO^3 database. This relates to the "originality" goal of the AMIGO^3 project and also its "organizational learning" goal.

From Modules to Mosaics, Courses, and Degree Programs

Our preceding discussion focused on a single module. As illustrated in Fig. 10.3, the AMIGO^3 architecture is designed to connect modules into higher order units such as mosaics and entire courses. We are just beginning to create sets of materials that will cover a whole course and fit the AMIGO^3 architecture. A course in biomechanics (developed primarily by Bob Roselli with consultation from Sean Brophy) is being transformed from a primarily lecture-based course organized around discrete taxonomic domain topics to a more interactive, inquiry-based course organized around challenges that integrate domain topics.

Roselli began by working with VaNTH partners to look at the features of his current course on biomechanics. His traditional approach to teaching was primarily lecture-based, with homework that involved application problems. The course covered important content that students (typically college sophomores) needed for subsequent courses, for meeting the Accrediting Board for Engineering and Tech (ABET) standards for Engineering education, and for success once they graduated. The content for the lectures was organized around specific topics, such as Newton's laws, mechanical advantage, and vector analysis. The lecture approach was an efficient way to cover the content that students needed to learn. Some students did very well in the biomechanics course (although note that what it means to "do well" depends on the nature of the assessments used in the final examinations). As one might expect, others did less well.

Analysis of final exam scores in biomechanics indicated that there was considerable room for improvement in students' learning. Some students did very well on the exams, but many failed to fully grasp key concepts that would be important for their future learning as bioengineering students and bioengineering professionals. For example, many students were unable to generate accurate free-body diagrams for test problems. Once they made this mistake, they were not able to generate the correct result. In addition, carefully documented classroom observations (by Alene Harris) showed that many students were not engaged by the lectures. Students' self-ratings of their level of engagement showed similar results.

Working with Brophy and other VaNTH members, Roselli used the HPL framework, plus the working backward strategy from Wiggins and Mctighe (1997), to redesign his course. This meant that he first had to rethink what he wanted his students to know and be able to do at the end of his course, then define how he would know if they reached his goals.

One of the goals that bioengineering faculty in the VaNTH project adopted was to move students on a path to becoming "adaptive experts" (Hatano & Inagaki, 1986) who were willing and able to struggle with open-ended problems rather than simply learn to solve well-defined problems that essentially required computation without extensive problem analysis (e.g. see also Bransford & Schwartz, 1999; NRC, 2000). Data from a number of studies (e.g., see CTGV, 1997) show large differences between open-ended and well-defined problem solving. Furthermore, these studies indicate that challenge-based approaches to instruction facilitate open-ended problem solving.

Roselli followed suggestions from Wiggins and McTighe (1997) and prioritized his content into "enduring ideas," "things that were important to know and be able to do," and "things that can be covered lightly." The emphasis on enduring ideas shaped the development of challenges, plus resources such as mini-lectures and simulations, that focused on those ideas.

Roselli also created challenges that helped students learn to use multiple concepts to analyze problems. For example, in typical "follow the taxonomy" courses, students might study statics and only later get to dynamics. In Roselli's redesigned course, students get to see how a single challenge problem can integrate statics, dynamics, strength of materials, and other concepts. This allows key concepts to be repeated and deepened throughout the course as students use them to analyze challenges that are posed. During class, Roselli typically follows the challenge-based design of the AMIGO³ modules, although the challenge cycle itself (see Fig. 10.4) is typically not visible to the students (it is often visible as an interface for activities on the Web). Beginning with a challenge allows students to understand the reason for the class inquiry for the day, plus it helps students see what they do and do not understand about the challenge.

Redesigning the course required rethinking the organization of learning activities. Roselli realized that an emphasis on problem analysis and problem solving typically takes more time per unit of content than is true of lectures. Therefore, one of the earliest questions he faced was whether a challenge-based approach would allow coverage of the content and skills that were necessary for subsequent courses in the program, as well as for the ABET standards. It took several iterations, but Roselli is confident that he can now cover the same amount of content that he covered previously while placing much more of an emphasis on helping students develop the knowledge, skills, and attitudes (e.g., tolerance for ambiguity) necessary to become adaptive experts. A major reason for this possibility is that Roselli offloads many resources (additional challenges, mini-lectures, etc.) to the Web. Students sometimes use these prior to coming to class and sometimes after class. In some cases, the students' Web work is graded. In other cases, the Web materials are resources that students can use as the need arises. In all cases, however, students do pre- and postclass work in an anchored inquiry context where they can relate particular drills and activities to a general problem that they are trying to solve.

To make large classes more interactive, Roselli uses an inexpensive wireless "personal response system"(PRS) that allows students to respond to multiple choice questions about challenges and subchallenges he poses, and for each response opportunity, see a graph of the class's responses (see http://www.educue.com). In terms of the HPL framework, this allows his classes to be much more learner-, assessment-, and community-centered than was true in his previous classes. One reason is that everyone in the class (including the instructor) gets to see the (anonymous) distribution of responses to each question. This means that students who are confused realize that they are not alone, because they can see that others choose the (incorrect) answer that they chose. Because of this, students become much more willing to explain their confusions and ask questions during class.

More often than not, Roselli is finding that it takes from two to four iterations through an attempted exploration of a challenge before the PRS data show that a majority of the class begins to sufficiently grasp the point. For those having difficulty even by the end of class, Roselli can point to relevant Web-based resources to study after class. Roselli notes that during his earlier lecture-based approach to teaching, that did not use challenges nor the PRS, he would have had no clear way of knowing how much he needed to back up and reexplain concepts to ensure adequate understanding by his students. Instead,

Roselli would have paused occasionally during his lecture and asked if students understood. Most of the time he would have received nods that prompted him to simply continue with the lecture—unaware of the fact that many students were not understanding important points. In addition, students do not always realize what they know until they are asked to generate a response to a question either for the PRS system or to discuss with a peer in small groups. Each semester, Roselli has discovered innovative ways to pose challenges, organize resources, and query students' current knowledge.

Roselli's use of challenges, coupled with opportunities to make students' thinking visible by using the PRS system, have changed the dynamics of his classrooms. Members of VaNTH have used the same classroom observational systems and student self-assessment systems that we described earlier in the context of observing Roselli's older lecture-based courses (the results showed that most students were often unengaged in class). In his new classrooms, students are much more likely to be on task (as rated by outside observers), and students' self-assessments reflect the same finding. In addition, Roselli currently spends considerably less time lecturing in class and more time in question-and-answer discussions. Students spend more time generating and evaluating what they know during class either individually or working in groups.

Summary of Section 3

The AMIGO^3 architecture is based on the principles of How People Learn and designed to create modules that are inquiry-based and fit the principles of the How People Learn framework. We provided some examples of how resources such as lectures can become much more valuable to students when they follow some kind of challenge. We also showed some examples of modules, plus our attempt to design entire courses that follow the format of anchored inquiry.

Our course-level uses of the AMIGO^3 architecture focused on Bob Roselli's course in biomechanics. Overall, data suggest that students (and Bob himself as the instructor) are more engaged in class, and in thinking through problems, than they were in the earlier lecture-dominated renditions of biomechanics. But the bottom line for success is not simply engagement, it is student and faculty learning. We say more about the challenges and needs of assessing learning in the discussion that follows.

NEEDS AND OPPORTUNITIES FOR RIGOROUS RESEARCH

A major goal of Vanderbilt's AMIGO^3 project is to study changes in learning. The value-added of the technology infrastructure is in part the object of research, and in part makes the research easier because we are increasingly able to capture students' responses and learning paths. The course management component of AMIGO^3 mentioned earlier (CAPE) is currently being developed and will allow us to capture much more detailed data than we can capture currently. (See http://www.isis.vanderbilt.edu/projects/VaNTH/index.htm.) But conducting research also raises a number of procedural and conceptual challenges that are important to understand. We discuss some of these next.

Procedural Challenges

First consider some of the procedural difficulties of attempts to study student learning. These include trying to study a course while also struggling to build it; finding ways to create rigorous experimental designs (e.g., NRC, 2002) in a context where students want the best instruction possible and hence do not relish being in the control group; getting Institutional Review Board (IRB) approval for each set of data to be collected. For example, we obtained IRB approval for all the data collected above, but we need additional approval as we discover the need for additional data. For example, we are currently awaiting IRB approval of college entrance scores so that we can check on the equivalence of certain groups of students.

Conceptual Issues

There are also important conceptual issues that have emerged as we have attempted to study student learning. As an illustration, consider attempts to assess students' learning as a function of "traditional" versus HPL-compatible approaches to teaching biomechanics that were discussed earlier. Our initial plan was to compare students' performances on final exams depending on whether they had taken lecture-based versions of the course (in earlier years) or more challenge-based versions (in later years).

One issue that we quickly encountered involved the types of exam questions that one would expect to be "HPL-sensitive." We know from other research on anchored inquiry that fact-based questions and questions that essentially asked for computation given well-defined problems do not differentiate anchored inquiry from more traditional approaches to instruction (see especially Bransford, & Schwartz, 1999; CTGV, 1997; Michael, Klee, Bransford, & Warren, 1993). We analyzed the exam questions in the early biomechanics courses (as well as other VaNTH courses) and discovered that the vast majority tended to pose well-defined problems that essentially asked students to compute answers. This has made it very difficult to compare the potential value-added of HPL-compatible instruction to older methods of instruction.

Currently, we are creating new sets of exam questions that have the potential to be more sensitive to the kinds of "adaptive expertise" knowledge, skills, and attitudes that represent our ultimate goal. Overall, this exercise has helped everyone involved in the AMIGO³ project (this includes VaNTH members plus many others) to better understand the working backward process. In particular, assessment issues are not something to be considered only at the end of redesign efforts. Once one clearly defines learning goals, the next step is to design assessments (both formative and summative) that are sensitive to progress towards these goals (see Wiggins & McTighe, 1997). In our work in VaNTH, it has become clear that carefully crafted rubrics need to be used to identify where students are successful and where they need increased opportunities to learn.

The importance of finding and developing sensitive measures also relates to issues such as ratings of student satisfaction. Most universities have developed measures that are administered to students at the end of courses, but they typically are not sensitive to the kinds of learning goals that characterize the courses involved in the AMIGO³ project. In addition, it is difficult for students to know if a course is truly engaging and helping them learn with understanding if they have never experienced alternatives to the traditional classroom environments found in most high schools and universities. A "natural experiment" on the importance of experiencing contrasting approaches to instruction occurred in one of the VaNTH courses. The instructor had typically been primarily lecture-based but was engaging and consistently received high student ratings. When participating in VaNTH, she redesigned the first part of her course around the idea of anchored inquiry. She did not have the time to design the second part in this manner, so she reverted to the lecture approach that had been received so well by students in previous years. Her teaching ratings for the course plummeted. Student comments criticized the instructor for abandoning an approach that had made them think and explain during the first part of the course and replace them with the "spoon feeding approach" that occurred during the second half of the semester. Overall, these students had experienced the difference between these approaches to instruction, and this affected the criteria they used to judge what was good versus bad.

A Variety of Research Designs

We are also working on the design of assessments that will allow us to assess progress across smaller units than entire courses. For example, we noted earlier how Roselli currently begins his classes with a challenge and uses the PRS system in order to be more sensitive to the needs of his students. An ideal "mini experiment" would involve comparing students' pre- and postclass performances given a typical lecture on the topic versus the more challenge-based, interactive procedure. At one level it seems obvious that there should be a difference between these two instructional conditions. Therefore, some might think the study superfluous. But the essence of science is "surprise." We would learn a great deal if these findings did not occur. Even if there were differences in learning between the two groups, it would still be beneficial to see if there are still areas that HPL students failed to master effectively. This provides a basis for a continuous improvement model—which is a model that is important for all our AMIGO^3 research.

Some members of VaNTH have been using a "cognitive laboratory" approach to studying anchored inquiry by using students who are in education courses but have enough science background to understand various modules. Initial studies using these cognitive laboratory designs are finding benefits for "anchored inquiry" on open-ended problem-solving tasks (e.g., see Petrosino & Pandy, 2001).

VaNTH members are also making use of the fact that the modular design for the AMIGO^3 project includes the equivalent of a "pretest" (initial thoughts about a challenge) and "posttest" (later thoughts about the challenge after having the benefit of exploring relevant resources). Of course, simply showing that there are pre- to posttest gains is hardly a great discovery. It is easy to view these kinds of findings as trivial unless there is also some sort of control group that received a different intervention between the pre- and postassessment. But there is a value to pre- and postassessments even in the absence of control groups. As noted earlier, the value comes from analyzing what students still do not understand on the posttest. This provides the basis for continually improving the challenges, resources, and opportunities for formative assessment that each module provides.

The Macro Structure of Courses and Programs

Despite the appeal of "mini experiments" and "cognitive laboratories," there is still a need to study the effects of the AMIGO^3 program at the course and program level. For example, we need to study ways to sequence challenges, materials, and activities so that students will develop usable knowledge that prepares them for effective problem solving and future learning once they leave the course. Many courses are essentially a list of topics that tend to remain disconnected in students' minds. For example, when studying learning, students might study the expertise literature, the transfer literature, the development literature, and so forth. Typical exam questions often focus on who did what and what they found. Research on how people learn (HPL) suggests that there are important differences between learning facts about isolated topics and developing connected sets of knowledge and skills that prepare students for continual, future learning by providing a framework or model for guiding thinking and actions once students leave the course (e.g., see Bransford & Schwartz, 1999).

Students also need to discover how different courses taken during their college program fit with one another. The AMIGO³ architecture provides the potential of breaking down some of the silos in our universities and allowing students to see how different faculty bring their expertise to bear on a common set of challenges (this involves "putting the faculty into the modules"). Based on what we know about expert knowledge and how people learn, opportunities to help students make connections both within and across courses, and to work together to form a community designed to continually make new connections, should have a powerful impact on their abilities to excel.

OVERALL SUMMARY AND CONCLUSIONS

We began by noting that many people interested in online learning begin by "porting the classroom to the Web" (Weigel, 2000). This would be fine if classroom-based instruction was always high quality. As Father Guido Sarduci reminds us, classroom-based teaching often leaves a great deal to be desired (see also NRC, 2000).

We discussed strategies that people often use when they set out to improve their current teaching practices (whether classroom based or Web based). They often begin with a focus on teaching (e.g., is cooperative grouping better than lectures?) rather than on student learning. As an alternative approach, we explored the idea of "working backwards" by beginning with a clear articulation of goals for student learning and then deciding how various teaching strategies might help us achieve these goals (Wiggins & McTighe, 1997).

To make this point, we discussed a number of imaginary universities that might compete with one another based on their ultimate goals for their students. Farther Guido Sarduci's Five-Minute University was one competitor. He set as his goal the ability to replicate what most college students remember 5 years after they graduate. Competing universities increasingly raised the bar with respect to what they taught.

We introduced the Jenkins model (Fig. 10.1) as depicting some important characteristics of educational "ecosystems" in which teaching and learning strategies operate. The same teaching strategy may be good or poor depending on the rest of the ecosystem. Especially important are the goals for learning, methods of assessing learning, and the knowledge, skills, and attitudes of the students whom we teach.

In Section 2 we discussed the How People Learn framework (NRC, 2000) and showed how it connects to the idea of working backward (Wiggins & McTighe, 1997) and to the Jenkins model (Fig. 10.1). It is a very general framework that leaves a great deal of room for flexibility (this is both its strength and its weakness). Nevertheless, the framework is useful because it reminds us to analyze situations at a deeper and more complete level than we might do otherwise.

The third section of the chapter focused on special challenges and opportunities provided by new technologies. We discussed Vanderbilt's AMIGO³ project as one way to think about the redesign of online courses (both Web enhanced and entirely Web based), the first three letters in AMIGO³ stand for "anchored modular inquiry," and we showed an inquiry cycle (derived from STAR.Legacy) that can be a shell for modules. The last three letters in AMIGO³ stand for Generate Ownership, Originality and

Organizational learning. Our architecture for modularity is designed to help achieve these goals.

We ended with a discussion of research issues that are currently being explored. The AMIGO[3] architecture is designed to make it easier to capture student choices and learning processes than would typically be true in face-to-face learning situations. Our plan is to use these new capabilities of technology to improve knowledge about how people learn.

ACKNOWLEDGMENTS

Funding for the work described in this paper was provided by EEC-9876363 (the VaNTH Engineering Center), P3421-990348 (a PT[3] Catalyst grant), and Atlantic Philanthropies. We are very grateful for this funding plus feedback from a number of our colleagues in Vanderbilt's Learning Sciences Institute. The opinions expressed in this chapter are those of the authors and should not be attributed to the funding agencies.

REFERENCES

Alexopoulou, E., & Driver, R. (1996). Small group discussion in physics: Peer interaction modes in pairs and fours. *Journal of Research in Science Teaching, 33*, 1099–1114.

Auble, P. M., & Franks, J. J. (1978). The effects of effort toward comprehension on recall. *Memory and Cognition, 6*, 20–25.

Barron, B. J., Schwartz, D. L., Vye, N. J., Moore, A., Petrosino, A., Zech, L., Bransford, J. D., & CTGV. (1998). Doing with understanding: Lessons from research on problem and project-based learning. *Journal of Learning Sciences 3&4*, 271–312.

Bateman, H. V., Bransford, J. D., Goldman, S. R., & Newbrough, J. R. (2000, April). *Sense of community in the classroom: Relationship to students' academic goals.* Paper presented at the annual meeting of the American Educational Research Association, New Orleans, LA.

Black, P., & William, D. (1998). Assessment and classroom learning. *Assessment and Education, 5*(1), 7–75.

Bransford, J. D. (1979). *Human cognition: Learning, understanding and remembering.* Belmont, CA: Wadsworth.

Bransford, J. D., & Schwartz, D. (1999). Rethinking transfer: A simple proposal with multiple implications. In A. Iran-Nejad & P. D. Pearson (Eds.), *Review of research in education* (Vol. 24, pp. 61–100). Washington, DC: American Educational Research Association.

Bransford, J. D., & Stein, B. S. (1993). *The IDEAL problem solver* (2nd ed.). New York: Freeman.

Bransford, J. D., Vye, N. J., & Bateman, H. (2002). Creating high-quality learning environments: Guidelines from research on how people learn. In P. A. Graham & N. G. Stacey (Eds.), *The knowledge economy and postsecondary education: Report of a workshop* (pp. 159–197). Washington, DC: National Academy Press.

Brophy, S. P. (2001). *Exploring the implication of an expert blind spot on learning.* Unpublished manuscript, Vanderbilt University, Nashville, TN.

Broudy, H. S. (1977). Types of knowledge and purposes of education. In R. C. Anderson, R. J. Spiro, & W. E. Montague (Eds.), *Schooling and the acquisition of knowledge* (pp. 1–17). Hillsdale, NJ: Lawrence Erlbaum Associates.

Brown, J. S., & Duguid, P. (2000). *The social life of information.* Boston: Harvard Business School Press.

Bruner, J. (1960). *The process of education.* Cambridge, MA: Harvard University Press.

Carey, S., & Gelman, R. (1991). *The epigenesis of mind: Essays on biology and cognition.* Hillsdale, NJ: Lawrence Erlbaum Associates.

Chi, M. T. H., Feltovich, P. J., & Glaser, R. (1981). Categorization and representation of physics problems by experts and novices. *Cognitive Science, 5*, 121–152.

Cognition and Technology Group at Vanderbilt. (1990). Anchored instruction and its relationship to situated cognition. *Educational Researcher, 19*(6), 2–10.

Cognition and Technology Group at Vanderbilt. (1997). *The Jasper Project: Lessons in curriculum, instruction, assessment, and professional development.* Mahwah, NJ: Lawrence Erlbaum Associates.

Cognition and Technology Group at Vanderbilt. (2000). Adventures in anchored instruction: Lessons from beyond the ivory tower. In R. Glaser (Ed.), *Advances in instructional psychology: Educational design and cognitive science* (pp. 35–99). Mahwah, NJ: Lawrence Erlbaum Associates.

DeGroot, A. D. (1965). *Thought and choice in chess.* The Hague: Mouton.

Driver, R., Squires, A., Rushworth, P., & Wood-Robinson, V. (1994). *Making sense of secondary science: Research into children's ideas.* London: Routledge.

Duffy, T. J., & Cunningham, D. (1996). Constructivism: Implications for the design and delivery of instruction. In D. H. Jonassen (Ed.), *Handbook of research for educational communications and technology* (pp. 170–198). New York: Macmillan.

Dweck, C. S. (1989). Motivation. In A. Lesgold & R. Glaser (Eds.), *Foundations for a psychology of education* (pp. 87–136). Hillsdale, NJ: Lawrence Erlbaum Associates.

Harris, T. R., Bransford, J. D., & Brophy, S. (2002). *Roles for learning sciences and learning technologies in bioengineering education.*

Hatano, G., & Inagaki, K. (1986). Two courses of expertise. In H. Stevenson, H. Azuma, & K. Hakuta (Eds.), *Child development and education in Japan* (pp. 262–272). New York: Freeman.

Hestenes, D. (1987). Toward a modeling theory of physics instruction. *American Journal of Physics, 55,* 440–454.

Hough, B. W. (2000). *Virtual communities of practice in teacher education: Assessing reflection in computer-mediated communication environments.* Unpublished doctoral dissertation, Vanderbilt University, Nashville, TN.

Hunt, E. & Minstrell, J. (1994). A cognitive approach to the teaching of physics. In K. McGilly (Ed.), *Classroom lessons: Integrating cognitive theory and classroom practice* (pp. 51–74). Cambridge, MA: MIT Press.

Jenkins, J. J. (1979). Four points to remember: A tetrahedral model of memory experiments. In L. S. Cermak & F. I. M. Craik (Eds.), *Levels of procession and human memory* (pp. 429–446). Hillsdale, NJ: Lawrence Erlbaum Associates.

Kolodner, J. L. (1997). Educational implications of analogy: A view from case-based reasoning. *American Psychologist, 52*(1), 57–66.

Leonard, W. J., Dufresne, R. J., & Mestre, J. P. (1996). Using qualitative problem-solving strategies to highlight the role of conceptual knowledge in solving problems. *American Journal of Physics, 64,* 1495–1503.

Lin, X. D., & Lehman, J. (1999). Supporting learning of variable control in a computer-based biology environment: Effects of prompting college students to reflect on their own thinking. *Journal of Research in Science Teaching, 36,* 837–858.

Lionni, L. (1970). *Fish is fish.* New York: Scholastic.

Michael, A. L., Klee, T., & Bransford, J. D., & Warren, S. (1993). The transition from theory to therapy: Test of two instructional methods. *Applied Cognitive Psychology, 7,* 139–154.

Moll, L. C., Tapia, J., & Whitmore, K. F. (1993). Living knowledge: The social distribution of cultural sources for thinking. In G. Saloman (Ed.), *Distributed cognitions* (pp. 139–163). Cambridge, UK: Cambridge University Press.

National Research Council, Committee on Developments in the Science of Learning. (1999a). How people learn: Brain, mind, experience, and school [Online]. In J. D. Bransford, A. L. Brown, & R. R. Cocking (Eds.), *Commission on Behavioral and Social Sciences and Education.* Washington, DC: National Academy Press. Also available: http://www.nap.edu/html/howpeople1

National Research Council, Committee on Learning Research and Educational Practice. (1999b). How people learn: Bridging research and practice. In M. S. Donovan, J. D. Bransford, & J. W. Pellegrino (Eds.), *Commission on Behavioral and Social Sciences and Education.* Washington, DC: National Academy Press.

National Research Council, Committee on Developments in the Science of Learning. (2000). *How people learn: Brain, mind, experience, and school* [Expanded ed., Online]. In J. D. Bransford, A. L. Brown, & R. R. Cocking (Eds.), with additional material from the Committee on Learning, Research and Educational Practice. *Commission on Behavioral and Social Sciences and Education.* Washington, DC: National Academy Press. Also available: http://www.nap.edu/html/howpeople1

National Research Council, Committee on the Foundations of Assessment. (2001). Knowing what students know: The science and design of educational assessment. In J. W. Pellegrino, N. Chudowsky, & R. Glaser (Eds.), *Board on Testing and Assessment, Center for Education, Division of Behavioral and Social Sciences and Education.* Washington, DC: National Academy Press.

National Research Council, Committee on Scientific Principles for Education Research. (2002). Scientific research in education. In R. Shavelson & Lisa Towne (Eds.), Washington, DC: National Academy Press.

Palloff, R. M., & Pratt, K. (1999). *Building learning communities in cyberspace: Effective strategies for the online classroom.* San Francisco: Jossey-Bass.

Petrosino, A., & Pandy, M. (April, 2001). *Incorporating learning science research in college biomechanics.* Paper presented at the meeting of the American Educational Research Association, Seattle, WA.

PT³ Group at Vanderbilt. (2002). Three AMIGO³s: Using "anchored modular inquiry" to prepare future teachers. *Educational Technology, Research and Development, 50*(3), 105–123. Gilda Radnor Live 1980. www.amazon.com/exec/obidos/ASIN/6302877628

Rose, A. (2001, October). *The Scope of Virtual Education K–12.* Paper presented at the Vanderbilt PT³ Conference on Teacher Education and Technology, Nashville, TN.

Schwartz, D. L., & Bransford, J. D. (1998). A time for telling. *Cognition & Instruction, 16,* 475–522.

Schwartz, D. L., Brophy, S., Lin, X. D., & Bransford, J. D. (1999). Software for managing complex learning: An example from an educational psychology course. *Educational Technology Research and Development, 47,* 39–59.

Shulman, L. S. (1987). Knowledge and teaching: Foundations of the new reform. *Harvard Educational Review, 57,* 1–22.

Vye, N. J., Burgess, K., Bransford, J. D., & Cigarran, C. (2002). *Using computer-assisted case based instruction in corporate training.* In P. Barker & S. Rebelsky (Eds.), Procedings of Ed Media 2002: World Conference on Educational Multimedia, Hypermedia & Telecommunication (pp. 1997–1999). Norfolk, VA: AACE.

Vygotsky, L. S. (1978, September/October). *Mind in society: The development of higher psychological processes.* Cambridge, MA: Harvard University Press.

Weigel, V. (2000). E-learning and the tradeoff between richness and reach in higher education. *Change,* 10–15.

White, B. C., & Frederiksen, J. (1998). Inquiry, modeling, and metacognition: Making science accessible to all students. *Cognition and Instruction, 16*(1), 39–66.

Wiggins, G., & McTighe, J. (1997). *Understanding by design.* VA: Association for Supervision and Curriculum Development.

Williams, S. M. (1992). Putting case-based instruction into context: Examples from legal and medical education. *The Journal of the Learning Sciences, 2,* 367–427.

11

A Second Look at Learning Sciences, Classrooms, and Technology: Issues of Implementation: Making It Work in the Real World

Terry Anderson
Athabasca University

QUALITY OF ONLINE LEARNING

Online learning, or e-learning, represents the most current onslaught of new education and training programming, delivered by media, that is grounded in a mantra of expanding access. This expansion relates not only to access to greater amounts of education content, but to learning communities, Web-based resources, enhanced student services, and special adaptive services for challenged learners—all of this is accessible "anytime/anyplace." However, access is but one element in a larger set of concerns common to all formats of education. A key issue is the quality of the educational transaction itself.

Recognizing, measuring, and building quality has a timeless attraction to all of us, and my most memorable encounter with its seductive and illusive nature came at my first reading of Robert Pirsig's (1974) *Zen and the Art of Motorcycle Maintenance* some 29 years ago. Pirsig wrote:

> Squareness may be succinctly and yet thoroughly defined as an inability to see *quality* before it's been intellectually defined, that is, before it gets all chopped up into words... We have proved that quality, though undefined, exists. Its existence can be seen empirically in the classroom, and can be demonstrated logically by showing that a world without it cannot exist as we know it. What remains to be seen, the thing to be analyzed, is not quality, but those peculiar habits of thought called 'squareness' that sometimes prevent us from seeing it. (p. 196)

This quotation forces us to remember what *squareness*—a hip term not uniformly understood and rarely used since the 1970s—means. The dictionary defines a *square* as "a person who is regarded as dull, rigidly conventional, and out of touch with current trends." But I think what Pirsig was getting at was the sense of the relative and social basis of our understanding of the world such that quality (in an educational

235

sense) is defined not by analytic measurement of results or outcomes but only sub-jectively within a community of learning—created in often unspoken consensus be-tween and among students, teachers, institutions, and the wider world in which we all operate.

Quality online learning (in Pirsig's words) attenuates the requirement that "a real understanding of Quality captures the system, tames it, and puts it to work for one's own personal use, while leaving one completely free to fulfill his inner destiny" (p. 197). These issues of first creating, then assessing quality has dominated much of the thinking of those interested in fundamental improvements to the way we learn and educate. Bransford, Vye, Bateman, Brophy, and Roselli (Chap. 10, this volume) provide a useful example of quality programming by describing the AMIGO³ project. This exemplar project is:

- Based on meaningful "situated problems" that promote learner engagement and application of knowledge
- Is grounded in theory and models that reflect our understanding of the learning process
- Is conducted visibly through an open Web-based forum
- Is focused on socially validated solutions to the challenges presented
- Contains applications that are capable of being retained and repurposed as edu-cational objects.

Bransford's and his colleagues' chapter on the AMIGO³ project provides an exam-ple that will help both online and classroom teachers and researchers understand the undefinable and to cocreate instances of quality in learning and teaching. In this chapter, I will examine issues of quality in online programming using examples from the work of Bransford, Vye, Bateman, Brophy, and Roselli, as well as my own work.

Most quality education programming is grounded in educational theory and models that reflect understanding of the learning process that educators and researchers have articulated over the years. Bransford and his colleagues begin their chapter with an-other look at Jenkins's 1978 tetrahedral model of appropriate teaching styles. Jenkins's model quite correctly focuses on the unique context of each educational "ecosystem." The model notes the importance of the nature and epistemology of the material to be learned, the prerequisite knowledge, attitudes, skills, and, I would add, the time required of students and the goals or assessment activities that drive measurement of student learning. What is missing from the model is a consideration of the critical im-pact on the educational transaction of the teacher's and the sponsoring educational organization's educational bias, and way of perceiving the world. The role of the teacher in a learner-centered context is discussed later, but the effect of the educational insti-tution also plays a critical role in defining, credentialing, and authenticating student learning. Educational institutions have many roles besides fostering cognitive growth and knowledge acquisition in students. Attainment of educational qualification is used by employers and professional groups as a convenient way of selecting potential staff members based on social capacity to interact with others and meet requirements of external organizations. Governments use these same qualifications to set and maintain standards for both intellectual and social competencies of future citizens. The disci-plines themselves use curriculum standards to maintain quality expectations of new members. Becher's (1989) investigation of the tribal behavior of academics details the epistemological, cultural, personal, and institutional bias that adds significantly to the educational ecosystem in any formal learning context. All of these pressures on formal education caution us to treat learning in a formal context as an ever changing and unique ecosystem. It also helps us to appreciate and assess the degree to which innovation in one component of the educational context has the possibility of disrupting the quality of other components. As important, a deep understanding of the contextual ecosystem of formal education provides guidance for changing and adapting that innovation to generalize its benefit in different contexts. Thus, Jenkins's model and Bransford's and his colleagues' elaboration and instantiation of the model provide motivation to look deeply at the ecosystem within which education functions. But, is this ecosystem readily apparent, or is a great deal of it hidden from all the participants? To answer this question, we turn to a brief discussion of the hidden curriculum of online learning.

QUALITY AND THE HIDDEN CURRICULUM

An underlying determinant of quality in online learning is the capacity for students to understand and deal effectively with the hidden curriculum of formal education. Students, faculty, and supporting infrastructure must share a common understanding of what they are studying and why, to arrive at quality assessment decisions that are congruent with each. The concept of the hidden curriculum has been the focus of much writing by critical educational theorists for the past half century. The term resonates with both theorists and educators, and is perhaps best defined by Sambell and McDowell (1998) when they describe the hidden curriculum as "an apposite metaphor to describe the shadowy, ill-defined and amorphous nature of that which is implicit and embedded in contrast with the formal statements about curricula and the surface features of educational interaction" (p. 391). Many of the salient features of the ecosystem of technologically enhanced learning are both systematically and inadvertently "hidden," and the exposure of these hidden dimensions is a fruitful way to enhance the quality and our understanding of the ecosystem of technically mediated education. The effect and extent of this hidden curriculum in online and other forms of distance education is significantly different from that associated with traditional classroom teaching (Anderson, 2001).

There are many reasons for the existence of the hidden curriculum in education systems (Margolis, 2001). Some are easily revealed through analysis of power structures or the philosophical or religious motivation of the education system's support. Others are deeply ingrained in our social and individual consciousness and not easily revealed without efforts to de- or recontextualize our perspective. This hidden curriculum involves at least four dimensions—learning to learn, learning the profession, learning to be an expert, and learning "the game" (Ahola, 1999).

The "learning to learn" dimension of the hidden curriculum of online education assumes that students have both physical and psychological access to technological tools. Growing evidence of a "digital divide" (National Telecommunications and Information Administration, 1999) documents access inequalities based on family income, formal education level of parents, and other indicators of social economic status. Fortunately, there is early evidence of reductions in differences in participation rates in Internet activities based on age and gender (Angus Reid Group, 2000); however, it is likely that significant differences will remain—especially for those special needs students requiring adaptive technology solutions to overcome individual access problems. Beyond physical access, participants in online education require a sense of technical efficacy that allows them to meet and overcome the too numerous technical problems that often plague online education. Finally, learning to learn in an online context usually requires the acquisition of new skills related to time management, learning outside of a supportive face-to-face classroom, and dealing effectively with vast amounts of unfiltered content. Thus, there exists a formable hidden curriculum that requires institutional and community support for students to acquire the capacity to learn in these environments. Without this capacity, the quality of online education is very markedly reduced.

The "learning the profession" dimension of the hidden curriculum requires students to acquire the often implicit and unstated attitudes and behaviors that define and differentiate professionals from those not holding professional status. These professional skills must be acquired in online contexts without the same type of social intercourse with peers and teachers, and modeling opportunities presented in campus-based education. Quality online programs exploit the opportunities of interactive and distributed education to bring in guest speakers, encourage field study and opportunities for students to interact with professionals in the field, and focus on professional experiences of students themselves in providing ways for students to acquire professional skills. Thus, this hidden curriculum of learning the profession may actually be enhanced in online learning and thus be an indicator of quality that marks online learning.

The "learning to be expert" dimension of the hidden curriculum has been referred to as the university bluff, or learning to act like an expert, even in the absence of any genuine expertise (Bergenhenegouwen, 1987). Online forms of education often force students to be more explicit in their interactions. Forcing students to explicitly state their ideas in text format and otherwise actively and visibly engage with the content and their fellow students, increases accountability and acquisition of true expertise. Quality online forms of education are not hidden behind closed doors but are often accessible and capable of review and criticism, not only by registered students but by all to whom access is granted. This openness threatens some who see education as a private good to be sold in the marketplace, but offers unprecedented opportunity for collaborative development and social contribution for those who see education as a universal tool for human advancement and a means to reduce the inequality of those who have bogus claims of expertise. Thus, the quality of technologically meditated learning and the expertise that is developed through participation may be more transparent, and thus more easily assessed, than classroom-bound forms of education.

Finally, online education, like all of forms education, has a hidden curriculum that requires students to learn to play a new form of the educational game. This game often requires students to go beyond passive reception of lecture-delivered content and to engage in a variety of active learning strategies. Active learning, in online contexts, requires students to have greater understanding of their own capacities to learn, to have the self-confidence and communications skills to interact with others whom they have never physically met, and often requires considerable amount of self-pacing and individually motivated learning. These skills are usually acquired without the close and supportive peer group that marks quality learning in many campus contexts. Thus, quality online education provides opportunities and supports a variety of ways that students can understand themselves and the expectations of the rules of this new form of the educational game.

From this understanding of the education ecosystem (both hidden and explicit) we move to a discussion of Bransford's and his colleagues' major contribution in their paper—that being a summary of their own research on how people learn.

How People Learn

Developing quality educational systems requires that educators have a deep understanding of how individuals and groups of students learn. Bransford provides an impressive, research-backed theory that gives us a "set of four overlapping lenses that can be used to analyze any learning situation." I might prefer to confine the analysis to educational situations, because learning takes place in a myriad of ways, and our applications and those developed by the authors fall squarely in the more formal context of education, rather than the much broader context of learning. The model nicely applies modern constructivist education theories of learning to move beyond, but not deny, the role of objectives and other legacies from early behaviorist models of instruction. In the following sections, I discuss each of these four lenses and relate how they affect online learning context.

QUALITY EDUCATION IS KNOWLEDGE-CENTERED

Appropriately, the knowledge-centered attribute of the learning environment is expanded to include acquisition of skills as well as knowledge, thus furthering its capacity for generalization to training and other more focused learning contexts. The knowledge-centered attribute focuses concentration on the key organizational concepts in the knowledge domain, thus illuminating the deeper structures that grounds expert understanding and decision making. Such an emphasis on a deeper and numerically much smaller number of "key issues" in any disciplines is a necessary antidote to an often self-imposed, yet impossible, task—of attempting to "cover" the full curriculum that plagues undergraduate education today.

Knowledge-centered learning also forces our attention on the way we construct and maintain the structures that are used to express knowledge in our disciplines. The efforts at formally defining these structures through the creation of ontologies (Devedzic, 2002) is a critical issue in the application of intelligent agents to enhance formal education.

QUALITY EDUCATION IS LEARNER-CENTERED

The learner-centered lens resonates well with the current trend to commercial education and consider the student a consumer of an educational service. Again, building from the research literature, the authors neatly relate important concepts of learners' mental models and their active construction of knowledge. This lens could also be expanded to include the students' approach to learning (Entwistle & Tait, 1990) and the literature on learning styles and means by which teachers accommodate both in the design and delivery of programming. However, more affective components of the learners' context are not made explicitly clear, leaving out critical components such as volition (Corno, 1994), motivation (Pintrich & Schunk, 1996), learning styles

(Vermunt, 1996), self-efficacy (Bandura, 1997), and awareness (Langer, 1997). Research by the aforementioned authors shows how these individual and mostly affective components are integral to knowledge construction, and thus their explicit absence from the model is unfortunate.

I was somewhat confused as to whether the learner-centered lens refers to learners (as in their unique attributes, approaches, and motivations) or being learning centered—a more generalized conception of the complete learning process. Learner-centered, in the first usage, acknowledges the important attributes of the learners as individuals and as a group, but seems to negate the other pieces of the learning transaction—namely, those provided by the teacher, the educational institution, and the larger society within which learning takes place. For too long we have built education on models focused on teachers and institutional need. Reversing the priority to an exclusive focus on learners may have equally negative effects. Formal learning is a partnership, negotiated between and among learners and teachers. Focusing on only one side of the partnership obscures necessary input from others. O'Banion (1999) documents the historical evolution of both concepts of learning and learner centeredness, and suggests that it is not enough to make students feel good about themselves, the institution, or their own learning, in the absence of feedback on actual learning accomplishment. O'Banion argues that it is important for a quality learning program to be both learning and learner-centered—a distinction that would enhance our understanding of this important consumer "lens" through which to examine the learning process.

QUALITY EDUCATION IS COMMUNITY-CENTERED

The community-centered attribute allows us to include the critical social component of learning. Thus, we now view the learning context through the lens of social learning and find Vygotsky's popular notions of social cognition, which leads us to Lipman's (1991) community of inquiry and Wenger's (2001) ideas of community of practice. These authors and others note the critical importance to the learning through social and peer interaction that is centered in the learning community. This results in a deepening awareness of the critical function of learning communities in mediating, interpreting, and motivating learners in their acquisition and application of knowledge. The AMIGO[3] project is designed to explicate learning in both virtual and face-to-face contexts and thus does not particularly focus on the special educational attributes of virtual space encountered in online and other forms of distance learning. This is a shortcoming that is not apparent in the content to which the model is applied in this chapter (a networked-enhanced classroom), but one that needs further elaboration if one intends to extend the model to virtual learning communities.

Educators are being challenged in many institutions to redevelop programming so that it can be offered in both distance and campus contexts, thus creating what is referred by some as distributed programming or open and flexible learning. This reformulation from a classroom to a network context raises many questions concerning the way in which communities are defined by face-to-face contact and if they can function effectively in the absence of such contact. Early proponents of online education (Feenberg, 1989; Harasim, 1989) noted that students in discussion-based contexts were quick to engage with each other, exchange information and provide time to develop relationships and exchange personal knowledge with each other. In my own experience of online teaching, I have noted that community can and does form, but that it takes much longer time than in face-to-face context, that it is much easier for the community to be exclusive and to allow nonparticipants to lurk at the edges without active community involvement. Finally, I've discovered that community formation is greatly accelerated when collaborative activities mandate students working together.

In our early work on audio conference–based delivery, we tracked the emergence of the "community of learning" and noted the impact of learning activities, the focus on individual or collaborative pacing, and other features of the instructional design that support or mitigate against the creation of learning communities (Anderson & Garrison, 1995). There is much that educators can learn from the more general work on virtual communities, beginning with Rheingold's (1994) seminal work and later updates (Coate, 1998); however much of this literature and other studies dealing with the emerging sociology, culture, and psychology of cyberspace are focused on informal and voluntary as opposed to formal education context. Although there are many educational enthusiasts who celebrate the capacity to create learning communities at a distance (Harasim, Hiltz, Teles, & Turoff, 1995), there are also those who note problems associated with lack of attention and participation (Mason & Hart, 1997), economic restraints (Annand, 1999), and an in-built resistance among many faculty and institutions to the threatening competition from virtual learning environments (Jaffee, 1998). Ethnographic studies of the Internet (Hine, 2000) illustrate how the lack of "place" and the complications of anonymity attenuate different components of community when located in virtual space. In short, it may be more challenging than we think to create and sustain these communities, and the differences may be more fundamental—linked to lack of place and synchronicity in time and place, and also the mere absence of body language and development of social presence noted.

I have been struck by the wide variation in expectation of learners toward participation in a community of learners. Traditionally, distance education has attracted students who highly value freedom and independence of time and place that independent modes of distance education afford. Contrary to popular belief, the major motivation for enrollment in distance education is not physical access, but temporal freedom to move through a course of studies at a time and pace of the student's choice. Participation in a community of learners almost inevitably places constraints on this independence—even when the pressure of synchronous connection is eliminated by use of asynchronous communications tools. The demands of a learningcentered context may at times force us to modify the proscriptive participation in communities of learning—even though we may have evidence that such participation will further advance knowledge creation and attention. The flexibility of virtual communities allows more universal participation, but a single environment that responds to all students does not exist. Thus, the need for variations that accommodate the diverse needs of learners and teachers at different stages of their life cycles. Finally, one should not underestimate the ethical challenges that uniquely confront the researcher when studying the creation of learning communities and other forms of educational activity in a virtual context (King, 1996). Issues of informed consent, privacy, and confidentiality often must be reinterpreted in a virtual context. (Thomas, 1999). In summary, supportive communities are at the root of most quality education—both that delivered at a distance and online. We are now discovering how best to support and encourage these communities and the unique challenges and opportunities presented to educators by virtual communities.

QUALITY EDUCATION IS ASSESSMENT-CENTERED

Assessment has long been a contentious focus of formal education and one to which educators spend a great deal of attention, but, sadly, I fear our capacity to assess real, long-term learning and transfer is not well established.

The fictional examples provided by Bransford and his colleagues of universities with very different goals for education rather humorously illustrates just how different educational contexts can be once we take seriously the task of defining and building systems to meet particular educational goals. In general, universities and other formal education institutions seem to have little problem in articulating very high-level goals for their graduates—often dressing these goals in the hyperbolic language of "ability to think critically," "appreciate the past and deal effectively with the future," and other rhetorical claims of the highly educated. Where we are less successful is in creating means by which these goals are accurately and meaningfully measured both in the easier, short-term context of the course completion examination or project and the much harder, long-term task of measuring the goal attainment over an extended period of time following graduation. Generally, North American educators are following far behind the quality control and measurement efforts of European or Australian educators (Jackson & Lund, 2000), with resulting lack of ability to expand into new international markets where we must rely on more than stellar reputations to attract sophisticated educational consumers (Marginson, 2002).

Too often, research on educational innovation fails to show significant learning gain (Russell, 2000), not because we fail to test, but because the things easiest to test are often not directly related to the deep, lasting, significant, and transferable learning outcomes. Too often, we adopt strategies that make true the old joke that "the smart students are the ones who forgot the content after the test." Of most significance in Bransford's and his colleagues' model is the ongoing series of formative evaluations that provide feedback for both students and teachers. There are few students or teachers who would not welcome additional formative evaluation of this type; however, we cannot overlook the affect on workload issues imposed by additional evaluation. Strategies that are designed to provide formative feedback with minimal direct impact on teacher workload are most needed. There are a host of potential tools that provide formative evaluation without increased teacher participation: These include

- The use of online computer-marked assessments that extend beyond quizzes to simulation exercises, virtual labs, and other automated assessments of active student learning
- Collaboration learning environments such as Groove (www.groove.net), which allow students to create, document, manage learning projects, and assess their own learning in virtual groups (Woods, 2001)
- Mechanisms that support and scaffold students' evaluation of their own work and that of their peers
- The use of sophisticated software tools such as latent semantic analysis (see http://lsa.colorado.edu/) to machine score even complicated tasks such as students' essays (Kintsch, Steinhart, & Stahl, 2000).

We also need to share these tools. Organizations such as IMS, CANCORE, and SCORM are creating open standards that provide mechanisms for educators to package, acquire, and reuse assessment-orientated learning objects. Each of these techniques and tools are needed to ensure that assessment-centered environments do not contribute to the long list of innovations that work only if large increases in resources or teacher time are required. I next explore how the costs of assessment, as well as other educational innovatives, must struggle to explore new approaches while existing within established institutional and financial constraints.

PRACTICALITY OF INNOVATION

Bransford and his colleagues describe an adaptation of a Web-based development and delivery environment that instantiates the principles of learning in a flexible (suitable for a wide range of disciplines and real world challenges), Web-resource-enhanced (the capacity to make extensive use of the wide range of information and learning content available on the Internet), and relatively easily implemented (lack of sophisticated programming necessary to implement the AMIGO[3] learning environment) learning context. All of these characteristics mark quality online education—but is it affordable?

Looking at the AMIGO[3] project, we see great potential for active learning and construction of knowledge, yet we see little data on development or delivery costing for this approach to education delivery. Our challenge is to understand and appreciate the paradox of developing practical examples of innovative tools that can be utilized in ways that develop the vision for radically improved educational practice, but which at the same time can be sustained within an educational culture and organization bureaucracy that can be brutal in driving decisions based on bottom-line costs. I recently went through an exercise of consulting with a university threatened with complete withdrawal of essential government funding. In this instance, the institution had developed an innovative content development and management system with proven high-quality educational outcomes, yet it could not compete with the cost-efficiencies of much less pedagogically progressive competitors.

Educators currently struggle with the same "productivity paradox" (Fahy, 1998) that marked debate on the use of information technology in business applications in the 1990s. During this period, it was very difficult to justify the expense of information technology purchases within existing productivity measurement rubrics. Similarly in education, it is difficult to measure productivity gains using older models of students assessment based on simple measures of student retention of content. Quality online learning projects require students to gain new knowledge processing and management skills, increased social and negotiation skills, and process skills related to filtering and applying knowledge from diverse sources. To test the efficacy of these techniques, we need to develop new measurement devices. We do not need to fear assessment-based learning, but we must ensure that the learning we assess includes the deeper level skills, attitudes, and competencies that are critical to the emerging information age.

In a related goal, we must ensure that our interventions result in measurable gains in these competencies. Innovation may in the short term not be able to compete economically with existing practice (Christensen, 1997), though it may be essential to allow an organization to adapt to major changes on the near horizon. Decreasing prices of hardware, increasing effectiveness and availability of educational software, plus growing expertise in utilizing powerful educational tools will result in increasing efficiency of online education. Like other organizations, education must be prepared to invest in innovation if it is to remain relevant and effective in changing contexts.

One of the promises of the merging networked context for education is the potential to economically reuse and adapt educational content from multiple sources (Downes, 2000). Thus, I am intrigued by the public nature of knowledge produced and learning documented in the AMIGO^3 project and other educational applications that create Web-based learning resources. The promise of the Web as a self-documenting tool that allows teachers to grow education content from the experience of earlier students is of course large and exiting. However, a number of ethical constraints remain unresolved. Increasing effectiveness of indexing spiders and other automated agent tools allows the discovery and retrieval of student-created information for many years after its creation, with little opportunity for effective ownership control by either students or teachers. This problem has been faced by ethnographic researchers (Hine, 2000) who found that the careful elimination of personal identification indicators from Usenet groups before publication does nothing to prevent more revealing identifiers being revealed through a search of long-term network archiving tools such as DejaNews. A simplistic solution is to suggest that interaction in formal courses reside behind passwords and be protected by firewalls. However, the enduring and easily copied nature of digital transcripts dictates that both students and teachers have a clear understanding of the degree to which such discourse is both a public and a private space. At minimum, both attention to copyright release and means to protect the privacy of those who chose, and attribution for those who demand, recognition of their contribution must be acknowledged. The development of digital rights markup languages and tools (Iannella, 2002) promises to provide sophisticated controls to aide in this protection of copyright, but its development and enforcement over the Web is still some years in the future.

The AMIGO^3 and other student product producing tools may also be useful in creating content that can be searched and harvested by other teachers and students through efforts to develop educational object repositories. In our work on both the MERLOT (www.merlot.org) and the CAREO (www.careo.org) learning object repositories, we have been building databases of educational objects that could be usefully employed as both resources and as a foci for the development of challenges or problem-based application in modularized systems such as the AMIGO^3 project. As educators, we have (to date) failed miserably in effectively distributing and sharing the educational resources that we have created. I recall my training days as an industrial arts teacher, when we all filled up binders of potential shop projects that we could use when we graduated to the field. Sadly, we had no way of ensuring the practicality of these projects, or any system for sharing or managing the knowledge that we gained when the projects were actually implemented. Merlot has established a peer review process designed to assess the quality of content, potential effectiveness as a teaching tool, and ease of use of each object indexed in the repository. This review is designed to ensure quality and also as a means to gain critical scholarly validation critical in systems in which academic review by peers is critical to promotion and tenure. Merlot also allows user reviews, which though simpler and not authenticated, allow teachers, students, and administrators to comment on their impression of the value of the object. Finally, and perhaps of greatest interest to teachers, is a structured assignment section in which teachers can share ways in which they have developed the learning object into classroom projects. It seems that the creation of AMIGO^3 challenges and resources, and their submission to appropriate repositories, would provide a viable means to disseminate and share efforts of individual teachers. To paraphrase the old real estate adage, what practicing teachers require are access, access, and access to quality resources. What we need to create is both the capacity to enter and share (as exemplified by the emergence of these repository models) and the development of incentives and means to reward those who make these contributions.

THE FUTURE OF QUALITY ONLINE EDUCATION

I conclude with a look at the special challenges and opportunities provided by new technologies and that extend the reference to "knowbots" and automated "personal letters" briefly mentioned by Bransford and colleagues. We are seeing the emergence of a new conceptual level of the Web, termed by its founder Berners-Lee (Berners-Lee, Hendler, & Lossila, 2001) as the semantic Web. The original Web was designed to allow seamless navigation and display of content by humans. The semantic Web creates meaningful connections between data stored and displayed on the Web, such that it can be navigated, searched, and filtered by nonhuman, autonomous agents, as well as by humans. The semantic Web does not exist today, although applications linked from sites such as www.semanticweb.org provide interesting glimpses of a context in which agents will act on behalf of students, teachers, and content itself to locate, access, query, process, and exchange data across a distributed heterogeneous network.

In Fig. 11.1, we see a classic look at learning centered in interactions between students, teachers, and content. We focus on interaction because, as Palloff and Pratt explained (2000), the "key to the learning process are the interactions among students themselves, the interactions between faculty and students, and the collaboration in learning that results from these interactions"(p. 5).

This model illustrates the three most common forms of interaction discussed in at least the distance education literature—that between and among students, between teachers and students, and between students and content. However, it goes further to illustrate the collegial effect of teacher-to-teacher interaction on both teaching and research development, the effect of teacher-content development, especially in the

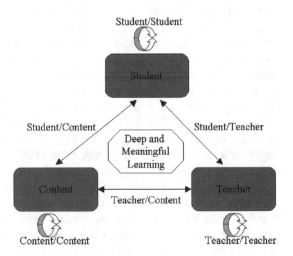

FIG. 11.1. Modes of Interaction in Distance Education (Anderson et al., 1998).

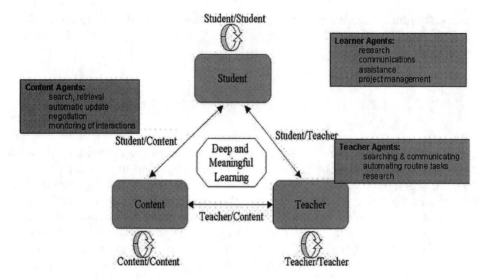

FIG. 11.2.   Agents enhancing interaction on the semantic web.

teacher's role of course developer or adapter, and finally illustrates the newly emerging capacity of content to interact with other forms of content.

Figure 11.2 adds the agents who will act on our behalf on the semantic Web. It is unclear how pervasive and how useful agent technology will be in supporting the educational transaction. However, early projects are demonstrating the capacity of agents to expand access to education "anywhere/anytime"—with resulting time and cost savings for both students and teachers as agents carry out our instructions to the far edges of the Web, on a continuous time schedule (Brusilovsky, 1999).

Teacher agents are being built into tutoring and simulation programs, enhancing earlier forms of intelligent tutoring by providing for facial expressions and other forms of simulated body language if the human form of the teacher agent is deemed useful. (Johnson, Rickel, & Lester, 2000). Agents can be programmed to using "situation-based reasoning that allows for opportunistic learning based on an infinite set of content and student interactions" (Shaw, Johnson, & Ganeshan, 1999). Teacher agents will also be used to manage course process, including alerting students of changes, monitoring participation, marking quizzes, updating content, and other functions associated with high-time requirements of online and classroom teaching.

Student agents will be most useful in coordinating meetings, assisting in coordination and time-line achievement of project groups, and negotiating ways in which students can conveniently and economically provide assistance to each other. For example, colleagues at the University of Saskatchewan have employed a student help system in which student agents (Vassileva et al., 1999) negotiate for help or assistance within specific computer science courses and set appropriate times and payment (in phony money to date) for real-time support for their student owners.

Content agents will function to continually monitor and update learning resources based on changes in external conditions, such as temperature readings, activity levels, or stock exchange activity. In a yet more challenging task, content agents will be designed to adjust the language, language level, complexity, and presentation of their content in response to unique variables of student preference and need.

The educational opportunities provide by the semantic Web are much greater than those provide by the original graphically orientated World Wide Web. Our task as educators seeking to harness the semantic Web will be to act not only as consumers, but also as members of multidiscipline teams that create, test, and adapt this next generation technology to effective educational application.

Challenges for the semantic Web application in formal education extend to defining structured approaches to teaching and learning (such that they can be searched and manipulated by agents) while retaining the flexibility and individuality of teaching design that is so deeply ingrained in education generally and in university instruction in particular. The early work of researchers at the Open University of the Netherlands in developing their education modeling language (Koper, 2001) seems an important step toward developing, producing and delivering semantically enhanced content to diverse and distributed students.

CONCLUSION

In this chapter, I have tried to reflect on the issues of quality in online learning that are inspired by reviewing the work by Bransford and colleagues on defining how people learn and by considering how the application they describe—the AMIGO[3] project—demonstrates these factors of quality. We are just at the beginning of a continuing series of developments known as the semantic Web, which promises to provide very significant new ways to think about and design education experiences. Semantically enhanced education, marked by the extensive use of agents and educational objects, will create new pedagogical, economic, and institutional challenges and create a new form of hidden curricula. Nonetheless, the results when one centers educational experience on learners, assessment, knowledge, and community still defines quality in education—be it campus-based online or enhanced by all of the new tools of the semantic Web.

REFERENCES

Ahola, S. (1999). *Hidden curriculum in higher education.* Available: http://www.utu.fi/RUSE/projektit/piilopro.htm

Anderson, T. (2001). The hidden curriculum of distance education. *Change Magazine, 33*(6), 29–35.

Anderson, T., & Garrison, D. R. (1995). Critical thinking in distance education: Developing critical communities in an audio teleconference context. *Higher Education, 28,* 183–199.

Anderson, T., & Garrison, D. R. (1998). Learning in a networked world: New roles and responsibilities. In C. Gibson (Ed.), *Distance learners in higher education* (pp. 97–112). Madison, WI: Atwood.

Angus Reid Group. (2000). *Second digital gold rush to be led by women.* Available: http://www.angusreid.com/media/content/displaypr.cfm?id_to_view=1006

Annand, D. (1999). The problem of computer conferencing for distance-based universities. *Open Learning, 14*(3), 47–52.

Bandura, A. (1997). *Self-efficacy: The exercise of control.* New York: Freeman.

Becher, T. (1989). *Academic tribes and territories—Intellectual enquiry and the cultures of discipline.* Milton Keynes: Open University Press.

Bergenhenegouwen, G. (1987). Hidden curriculum in the university. *Higher Education, 16,* 535–543.

Berners-Lee, T., Hendler, J., & Lassila, O. (2001, May). The semantic Web. *Scientific American.*

Brusilovsky, P. (1999). Adaptive and intelligent technologies for Web-based education. [Special issue on intelligent systems and teleteaching]. *Künstliche Intelligenz.* 4, (19–25). Also available: http://www2.sis.pitt.edu/~peterb/papers/KI-review.html

Christensen, C. (1997). *The Innovator's dilemma: When new technologies cause great firms to fail.* Boston: Harvard Business School Press.

Coate, J. (1998). *Cyberspace innkeeping: Building online community.* Available: www.cervisa.com/innkeeping.html

Corno, L. (1994). Student volition and education: Outcomes, influences, and practice. In D. H. Schunk & B. Zimmerman (Eds.), *Self-regulation of learning and performance: Issues and educational applications.* Hillsdale, NJ : Lawrence Erlbaum Associates.

Devedzic, V. (2002). What does current Web-based education lack?. In *Proceedings of IASTED International Conference.* Available: http://www.iasted.org/conferences/2002/austria/workshop/351-607.pdf

Downes, S. (2000). *Learning objects.* Available: http://www.downes.ca/files/Learning_Objects_whole.htm

Entwistle, N., & Tait, H. (1990). Approaches to learning, evaluations of teaching, and preferences for contrasting academic environments. *Higher Education, 19,* 169–174.

Fahy, P. (1998). Reflections on the productivity paradox and distance education technology. *Journal of Distance Education, 13*(2), 66–73. Also available: http://www//cade.athabascau.ca/vol13.2/fahy.html

Feenberg, A. (1989). The written world: On the theory and practice of computer conferencing. In R. Mason & A. Kaye (Eds.), *Mindweave: Communication, Computers, and Distance Education* (pp. 22–39). Toronto: Pergamon.

Harasim, L. (1989). On-line education: A new domain. In R. Mason & A. Kaye (Eds.), *Mindweave: Communication, computers, and distance education* (pp. 50–62). Toronto: Pergamon.

Harasim, L., Hiltz, S., Teles, L., & Turoff, M. (1995). *Learning networks: A field guide to teaching and learning online.* London: MIT Press.

Hine, C. (2000). *Virtual ethnography.* London: Sage.

Iannella, R. (2002). *Open digital rights language initiative.* Available: http://odrl.net/

Jackson, N., & Lund, H. (2000). *Benchmarking for higher education.* Milton Keynes: Open University Press.

Jaffee, D. (1998). Institutionalized resistance to asynchronous learning networks. *Journal of Asynchronous Learning Networks, 2*(2). Available: http://www.aln.org/alnweb/journal/vol2_issue2/jaffee.htm

Johnson, L. W., Rickel, L., & Lester, S. (2000). Animated pedagogical agents: Face-to-face interaction in interactive learning environments. *International Journal of Artificial Intelligence in Education, 11* (47–78).

King, S. (1996). Researching Internet communities: Proposed ethical guidelines for the reporting of results. *Information Society, 12*(2), 119–127.

Kintsch, E., Steinhart, D., & Stahl, G. (2000). Developing summarization skills through the use of LSA-based feedback. *Interactive Learning Environments, 8*(2), 87–109. Also available: http://lsa.colorado.edu/papers/ekintschSummaryStreet.pdf

Koper, R. (2001). *Modelling units of study from a pedagogical perspective: The pedagogical meta-model behind EML* Heerlen, The Netherlands: Open University. Available: http://eml.ou.nl/introduction.articles.htm

Langer, E. (1997). *The power of mindful learning.* Reading, MA: Addison-Wesley.

Lipman, M. (1991). *Thinking in education.* Cambridge, UK: Cambridge University Press.

Marginson, S. (2002). The phenomenal rise of international degrees down under: Lucrative lessons for U.S. institutions? *Change, 34*(3), 34–43.

Margolis, E. (2001). *The hidden curriculum of higher education.* London: Routledge.

Mason, J., & Hart, G. (1997). Effective use of asynchronous virtual learning communities. In *Creative collaboration in virtual communities.* University of Sydney. Available: http://www.arc.usyd.edu.au/kcdc/conferences/VC97/papers/mason.html

National Telecommunications and Information Administration. (1999). *Falling through the Net: Defining the digital divide.* Available: http://www.ntia.doc.gov/ntiahome/fttn99/contents.html

O'Banion, T. (1999). The learning college: Both learner and learning centered. *Learning Abstracts, 2*(2). Also available: http://www.league.org/publication/abstracts/learning/lelabs0399.html

Palloff, R. M., & Pratt, K. (2001). *Lessons from the cyberspace classroom: The realities of online teaching.* West Sussex, UK: Wiley.

Pintrich, P., & Schunk, D. (1996). *Motivation in education: Theory, research, and application.* Englewood Cliffs, NJ: Merrill.

Pirsig, R. (1974). *Zen and the art of motorcycle maintenance.* London: Morrow.

Rheingold, H. (1994). *The virtual community.* New York: HarperPerennial.

Russell, T. (2000). *The no significant difference phenomenon.* Available: http://cuda.teleeducation.nb.ca/nosignificantdifference

Sambell, K., & McDowell, L. (1998). The construction of the hidden curriculum: Messages and meanings in the assessment of student learning. *Assessment and Evaluation in Higher Education, 23,* 391–403. Also available: http://www1.appstate.edu/~moormang/wwwboard2/messages/298.html

Shaw, E., Johnson, W. L., & Ganeshan, R. (1999). Pedagogical agents on the Web. In *Proceedings of the Third International Conference on Autonomous Agents.* Seattle, WA: ACM Press. Also available: http://www.isi.edu/ isd/ADE/papers/agents99/agents99.htm

Thomas, J. (1999, Spring). Balancing the ethical antinomies of Net research. *Iowa Journal of Communication, 31,* 8–20. Also available: http://venus.soci.niu.edu/~jthomas/ethics/iowa.html

Vassileva, J., Greer, J., McCalla, G., Deters, R., Zapata, D., Mudgal, C., & Grant, S. (1999). A multi-agent approach to the design of peer-help environments. In *Proceedings of AIED '99.* Artificial Intelligence in Education. Available: http://julita.usask.ca/homepage/Agents.htm

Vermunt, J. D. (1996). Metacognitive, cognitive and affective aspects of learning styles and strategies: A phenomenographic analysis. *Higher Education, 31,* 25–50.

Wenger, E. (2001). *Supporting communities of practice: A survey of community-orientated technologies* [Shareware, 1.3 ed.]. Available: http://www.ewenger.com/tech

Woods, E. (2001). Knowledge management and peer-to-peer computing: Making connections. *KM World, 10*(9). Available: http://www.kmworld.com/publications/magazine/index.cfm?action=readarticle& Article_ID=1104&Publication_ID=56

Open Discussion of Chapter 10

John Bransford: I would like to begin by thanking Terry for his very thoughtful comments. He made a number of points that will be useful to us all. Terry's discussion of agents is one example of his contributions. The "Know-Bot" technology I described, which was developed by my colleague John Bourne, is one kind of agent that has had positive effects. So this area of work seems very fruitful. I might also mention that a group of us at Vanderbilt and Stanford are working on the notion of teachable agents, for example, rather than coaching you, you coach them. In one of our environments, an agent named Betty needs to learn how to assess the quality of the rivers. You can assess her initial knowledge, teach by doing things like drawing graphs and making concept maps, see how she does when trying to use what you have taught her, and continue to help her learn as necessary. We think this is an exciting addition to the general direction of agent-based research.

Tom Duffy: I really appreciate the learning/learner center kind of distinction Terry makes. I think it is an appropriate one. My whole concern with all of this problem-centered stuff is that the faculty get really excited that students talk to each other and talk to them. They forget about anything having to do with the content. They are just happy with discussion, whatever it is.

John Bransford: I, too, like the learning/learner distinction. From the perspective of the How People Learn framework, the entire framework is designed to be learning centered. Being learner-centered is just one part of the overall framework, although it's a very important one. When teachers are happy with having students "just talk," they are not being sensitive to knowledge-, assessment-, or community-centered components of the HPL framework.

Tom Duffy: Another comment and then a question. We tried the automated feedback. I went through a whole variety of evaluations with the executive education courses at Cardean University and tried a variety of strategies of doing things. Satisfaction only occurred with people when they got responses to their test submissions. If they wrote an answer to something and I gave them a model answer, they did not like it. I also tried multiple choice where we asked for correct answers and rationale and then the feedback was which answers were correct or incorrect and why. Even though the students were really positive about the multiple-choice format, they did not like the lack of personalization in getting model answers, or rationales, back. It was only when someone actually went there with an ability to personalize it to them, and respond in some way, did they find it acceptable.

John Bransford: Did you give them a chance to revise after receiving the feedback?

Tom Duffy: No, when we were going through a revision, it was too short of a time frame to do it. We could not do it in that context. Yeah it's a process, that's true.

John Bransford: I think that giving people chances to revise after receiving feedback is an important key to both learning and motivation. If we don't do this, our assessment is essentially summative rather than formative.

Tom Duffy: I agree. Now let me turn to my major question, which has to do with developing your problem or your challenges. I like the strategy. The concern is, what is a workable problem? Near the end of the chapter, you said that if you know it will help you in the future, you will put up with it, and that it will be okay. But, in fact, we do an awful lot of that in education—of saying, this will do you good in the future. There are two things that happen. One, they take it as an act of faith or not. The other is that they can see it is helpful, and they will tolerate it no matter what we do. So I don't know if I buy that as a criteria per se.

John Bransford: Your question is a very important one, and I wish I could say that our team has the answer. But I think I can suggest a few things that may be helpful. The first general point that I hope is helpful is that the HPL framework can be a useful set of lenses for thinking about the design of challenges. The challenges should be knowledge-centered in the sense of getting at important concepts in a discipline. They should be learner-centered in the sense of making some contact with the learner's existing knowledge so that they can generate substantive initial thoughts—rather than simply having to guess or say, "I don't have a clue." Challenges should be assessment centered in the sense of being assessable—that is, there should be "pathways of thinking" that can be defined as more or less fruitful so that students can eventually see the value of the resource and assessment parts of each module for clarifying and refining their thinking. Finally, it's great if challenges can be community centered in the sense of eliciting a range of student responses that lead to lively discussions to help people value the distributed expertise available in the group.

The second general point about the design of challenges is the need to view them in the context of larger sets of activities like mosaics or other kinds of units. Ideally, challenges are viewed as helping prepare people for real activities that they want to learn to perform and that will have consequences beyond the classroom. For example, consider our work in middle school, with one of our Jasper adventures that introduces students to the usefulness of principles of geometry. All our Jaspers are "canned problems." They can be fun and engaging, but solving them does not necessarily have any real consequences for the world. The fifth graders I briefly mentioned in my talk—the ones who wanted tough feedback from us—knew that they had the chance to design a model of a "dream house" that would actually be built by carpenters and placed in child-care settings if the students could to a first-rate job of talking about square footage, front views, side views, and other factors. Solving the Jasper geometry adventure was an important step toward this end. In other cases, middle school students have learned to solve a Jasper problem with the ultimate goal of mentoring college students and adults as they attempt to solve the problem. We refer to instructional units such as these as moving from (canned) problem-based to (actual) project-based learning experiences.

Tom Duffy: Okay. Getting down to the problems you showed. One of them was shooting the bottle rockets up. What you did is kind of create a challenge with the students. You did bring the problem home by asking them, "Is this a good learning environment?"

This is wonderful. So that is how they learn. You have created a cognitive conflict of what is going on.

However, in your presentation you showed another problem dealing with a child whose parents had cancer. It seemed to be very, very separated from the students. There was no conflict produced. It was someone else. It is almost like the beginning of the chapter problem where you can orient your thinking as you go along. But there is not necessarily any reason why I should get involved, like Barrow's notion of bringing it home.

John Bransford: Your point is well taken, and it reminds me that I forget to explain a few things when discussing the cancer challenge. It was created by some undergraduates in my design course who were learning about challenge-based design. The students who developed it were not developing it for a college course. They were actually developing it for a special setting for kids whose parents have cancer.

Tom Duffy: OK. Or so it is for those kids?

John Bransford: Yes, the challenge was highly relevant to the intended audience. I'm sorry I didn't get into this in the chapter.

John Stinson: That is a good point. I've seen the framework used or attempted to be used in an educational setting, where those challenges up-front are so damn trite that the individuals cannot relate to them in any way except to provide context for learning. I think both the paper and, Terry, your comments were extremely good. One thing that you started to do, which I really liked, is that you started to become a little more macro instead of just the micro issues. To me, the macro issues are a hell of a lot more complex and a hell of a lot more challenging to us .... the individual challenges. On your macro studies, you were saying that a challenge in going forward is putting things together so a course becomes more coherent or a curriculum becomes more coherent. Have you ever thought of going the other way, and instead of integrating that which has been artificially sort of differentiating, starting with the overall issue? I ask that because that is my bias. Instead of starting with disciplines in our MBA program, what we do is start out with the overall business.

John Bransford: I totally agree about the importance of macro issues. Also, we try to begin and end with what we call a Grand Challenge that lets students think about the big picture of an entire course and then revisit that challenge, perhaps midway through the course and at the end. This allows students to not only get a better idea of a global context, but also to revisit their earlier thoughts about the Grand Challenge so they can see how much they have learned.

John Stinson: Do you put that master challenge within a single course?

John Bransford: Currently, our largest unit of work is at a course level. Ultimately, we hope that the AMIGO^3 architecture can help break down the silos on individual courses so that an entire program of study can be better connected in the students' minds and related to overall Grand Challenges that might be revisited over the course of the program.

John Stinson: So even if you had a number of different challenges that were all at a holistic level instead of a very focused, discipline-based level, "I challenge you," would probably have something that makes greater integrative sense for the individual.

John Bransford: Yes, for our work on leadership, for example, we have a number of mini challenges that are designed to help students refine their initial thoughts about a Grand Challenge on leadership

Mark Schlager: Let me see if I understand... the approach that you use in totally face-to-face courses and totally online—is it the same pedagogical approach?

John Bransford: We don't have experience with totally online learning at this point, although we are interested in moving in this direction. But we like Pepperdine's approach that also involves face-to-face groups.

Mark Schlager: Well, the interesting thing to me is that we talk a lot about what you can do online that you can't do face-to-face. So you're in the situation now where I think you can shed a lot of light—you already know what you can do face-to-face differently from even what we are all talking about doing face-to-face. The issue moves from "What is the difference between an online course and a face-to-face course?" You are now able to say what can we do online that is different in a really effective face-to-face course and allow our discourse to get away from that false dichotomy of what you can do face-to-face and online. So the question is, as you try to move more online, are there things that you are learning that are constraints or affordances of online, specifically around keeping your pedagogical approach and your content the same? This is a real experimental situation now that we are not comparing apples and oranges anymore.

John Bransford: Yes, down the line this is a direction we'd really like to try. For example, in our How People Learn course, most of these modules are really done as homework. Challenges are posted on the Web, and students post their initial thoughts. So prior to class, I know all their assumptions. I can see what they are thinking. Then they come to class and work in teams to compare their ideas and come up with group thoughts that they share. Then I can act as a resource plus provide them with opportunities for assessment. So I can actually make the time in class much more engaging and productive than I could in the past.

John Stinson: And is there work that you teach that can be done online?

Mark Schlager: That is the question—does it work as well? In the future, yes ...

John Bransford: I agree that this is a very important question and our group is eager for help in how to pursue research in this area. One of the real issues is, of course, community. Helen Bateman, one of the coauthors of our chapter, is studying communities in face-to-face environments and relating it to academic achievement. Issues of trust are huge. We're not sure how we build that trust without letting people meet each other first. I think there are ways to do it. People from the Virtual High School, for example, Ray Rose, claims that it's doable ... He's had a lot of experience, so we're eager to learn more from him.

Mark Schlager: You just type faster. (*Group laughs.*)

Bob Wisher: John, are there any ways when looking at their preconceptions that you could have structured a challenge maybe differently for different groups of people? Have you thoughts about that?

John Bransford: Both challenges and resources could be structured differently, depending on preconceptions. In our newest course architecture, we are building in "ratings bars" that let us see how useful various challenges and resources are to particular users. This helps with the continuous improvement of courses. Simultaneously, our systems engineering group, headed by Larry Howard, is creating an authoring and management system that will let us tailor activities depending on user characteristics, answers to assessments, and other factors. We think this system will be a great research tool.

Jim Botkin: I just want to make an observation rather than ask a question. It's a positive one. The reason I really liked your presentation is that it's one of the few I've seen where you actually "walk the walk." The presentation seems to model as you go through it what you are trying to do—what you are trying to illustrate. Like you start with a challenge—that crazy guy's Five-Minute University. I wonder if that was conscious on your part and whether others agree with me.

Sally Johnstone: He's just internalized the whole thing. (*Group laughs.*)

Tom Duffy: Or it's one big challenge. (*Group laughs.*)

John Bransford: I've definitely been influenced by our group's thinking about challenge-based designs. But given the time constraints, I could only do this partially. If you look at the design of our group workshops and courses, you would see a much more fully implemented challenge-based approach that is much less like the "semilecture" that I gave here.

Jamie Kirkley: A big question and a little question. First, I think AMIGO^3 has an excellent design. It's something that I can see lots of different types of instructors using in other content areas. In the challenge design, you have a circle. Obviously, that is an inquiry model. Can students go back through the circle again?

John Bransford: Yes, especially in Test Your Mettle. But you can always go back.

Jamie Kirkley: Is that explicit in the design?

John Bransford: Yes, it's encouraged.

Jamie Kirkley: And my tougher question is, in the online environment, how do you provide support for this kind of learning? It's really tough knowing how to support and model critical thinking online. For example, I did an analysis on an online problem-based class that I taught and thought everyone was thinking critically and doing a great job. Then I used one of Terry's [Anderson's] scales and was pretty disappointed in the outcome of the critical thinking by students. So it was a real eye-opener. I'd like to know how you got that issue.

John Bransford: Our group feels that students also need formative assessments of their group discussions. This is why we include the assessment or "test your mettle" component in our learning cycle. In some cases, we do this live in class using "personal response systems." In other cases, we can use online multiple choice. In others we can provide models of "moderate to good answers" and have students compare them to one another and their own earlier discussions and thoughts. Ultimately, we hope to incorporate things like latent semantic analysis and immex into our assessments so that they can be less multiple and more generative.

Rafael Lopez: I have a question about the learning objects. How do you define that? It's a very difficult task for you to set a standard to say, "This is this."

John Bransford: I interpret your question to be focused on what we are calling granules. Right now, we're just pretty much catch-as-catch-can. These can include mini-lectures, simulations, assessment routines, and text. We are working on indexing schemes and interoperability standards for all of these—that's part of the work of our systems engineers. Our assumption is that the granules take on their power when they become resources that help students rethink their initial thoughts to initial challenges.

As an example, we have a challenge on attention where you actually get to listen to two tape-recorded messages simultaneously, and we ask to make conjectures about how it works. We then introduce you—through texts and mini-lectures, to the literature on attention. These resources become much more meaningful because you have experienced the phenomena first.

Carson Eoyang: Challenge based, problem centered—at that level, I don't know if you are talking about the same thing or if they are qualitatively different. Yet you kind of wind up with different pedagogical approaches. As I understand it, the way you have designed your curriculum, it's more guided discovery on the part of the students. With Cardean, a lot of the content is engineered much more specifically. The learning with your students is more multipath. With Cardean, it seemed like the paths are predetermined to structure. Yours, Tom, was pretty much asynchronous collaboration, which is hard to bring about. John, your model depends very heavily on collaboration. My question to the two of you is that if you both start out in the same point, basically challenge based, problem centered (I don't know if there's a difference there—I know I can't see one in my mind), do you wind up in different places? Do you see your approaches as variations on the same theme, or are they subsequently different pedagogical approaches?

Tom Duffy: I view the focus as inquiry-based learning—that's really the rubric it all comes under. It's really engaging the student in inquiry and supporting the inquiry process. John's living in a world where he can create the environment he wants. I've got a bunch of business rules. I had that impact on what I had to do versus what I am allowed to do versus what I want to do. That collaboration is difficult is not a pedagogical decision—it is in fact a business rule, an imposed kind of restriction about what we can do. The problems really are more structured, but it really has to do with that asynchronous environment, I think. The goal is to have them open-ended, ill structured—that kind of a label . . . but because we can't get collaborative groups and because the goal was to scale to large numbers, we have to be careful. That is that balancing of structure that I was talking about—the amount of structure versus the amount of inquiry. So my move would be in the direction John is going. But, part of my restrictions are having large numbers of students and the other is a start anytime design—these limit what I can do.

John Bransford: Tom's point about needing to tailor educational designs to the constraints of different environments is very important. It's one of the reasons why we have tried to develop our AMIGO^3 architecture to be flexibly adaptive. I think we could make AMIGO^3 work in an everyday business environment, but some of its functioning would be different. For example, at the end of each mosiac, there might be a "tough love" assessor (live online) who asks questions and provides feedback and asks people to return to resources until they demonstrate an understanding of the major learning goals. Then and only then could the learners proceed—so they could work on their own time. If the assessment is contextualized within a particular mosaic, we could potentially have a set of live people who specialize in each mosaic and don't necessarily need to know everything about what someone is trying to teach. But all this is conjecture, of course.

About the terms *challenge-based, problem based,* and so forth. As we briefly mentioned in the chapter, we adopted the term *challenge based* (actually, I think I like Tom's inquiry-based even better) in an attempt to search for a more generic term for the design of learning environments. There is a rich literature out there of designs that have a family resemblence but also have important differences—this includes problem-based learning, case-based learning in business schools, case-based learning in law schools (which is not quite the same as it is in the business schools), learning by design, and so forth. For us, these differences affect the nature of challenges, resources, and assessments.

Tom Duffy: Right.

John Bransford: For us, the method we use is going to depend on the goals we have for a particular point in the sequence of the course. With engineering, for example, we often start with design challenges. In bioengineering, we began to look at the assessment questions given and noted that they had so much guidance built into them (first compute X and then Y) that they were far closer to computational problems than open-ended problem-solving assessments. So we begin with our learning goals and work backward to see the kinds of challenges, resources, and assessments we need.

John Stinson: If you talk with Barrows, the five steps you have are basically identical to his, but I think the way that they are implemented is somewhat different, but you are basically dealing with the same process.

John Bransford: Yes, we have learned a great deal from Barrows—both from his writings and even more from opportunities to visit him and his program. One difference—and I can't say at this point if it is better or worse or a washout—is that we use more of a blended approach to instruction—we make frequent use of what Dan Schwartz and I have called times for telling, where we think the challenges and discussions have prepared students to learn optimally from a short lecture or demonstration.

Linda Polin: One is that you are really banking on your cognitive transfer . . .

John Bransford: We'll come back to that . . .

Linda Polin: We all have this sense of history of difficulty of accomplishing that, and I was wondering . . .

John Bransford: Can I say something about this?

Linda Polin: You go. (*Laughs.*)

John Bransford: Dan Schwartz and I were asked to review the literature on transfer, and we kind of stumbled onto a set of assumptions that affect most of the transfer literature. The assumption is that transfer is something that occurs only when you can directly apply something learned previously to something new—and apply it under conditions of sequestered problem solving. It's sequestered because you get no extra resources—only the resources that reside "inside your head." Dan and I began to realize that this was a view of transfer that seemed highly constraining. An alternative to sequestered problem-solving assessments were one's that assessed students' preparation for future learning [PFL]. To what extent have we prepared them to use relevant resources—books, the Internet, peers, simulations—to learn to solve important problems. Some of these ideas are briefly discussed in the chapter for this volume. One of the important ramifications of adopting a PFL view of transfer is that educational activities that look poor from sequestered problem solving [SPS] can be seen as very powerful when viewed from a PFL perspective, and vice versa.

Linda Polin: So it's more like bootstrapping—the notion is that you have a set where you are more able to launch from on the next occasion.

John Bransford: Yes. Part of the bootstrapping comes from a deep understanding of powerful ideas in various disciplines, some from general learning strategies and social strategies, and so forth. We actually think that traditional transfer tests often provide mismeasures of the value of various types of learning experiences.

Linda Polin: I think that is a useful discussion. I'm glad you got it in here somehow, given your model. As I listened, I was wonderfully seduced by the engineering. I so badly wanted to get in there and mess around with it. Didn't you all want to do that? I have a recollection about some AI stuff way back when—the attempts to support individualization. I'm wondering ... you have got all these learning objects, and it sounds like you are trying to build little self-contained simulations where one size can fit many people. We can extrapolate what we need to know, and make them all fit and come out the other end. I'm wondering if you have had any problems with tweaking ... when people go through this, does everybody get the same thing out of it?

John Bransford: Actually, our goal is to create an architecture that is flexibly adaptive. I may have a mosaic that you want to use, but chances are pretty great that you will want to change it to fit your goals, students, institutional constraints, and other considerations. So we are trying to make tweaking easier to do.

We're also trying to build a system where granules can be flexibly adapted. For example, in bioengineering we might have a simulation of the bones and muscles of the upper body. You could use that for many different kinds of instruction. One is to use it to explore a challenge of the kinds of muscles that need to be built up for someone to do the iron cross in gymnastics. But the simulation could have many other uses as well. One of the things that happens when simulations are simply provided to people is that they play with them, learn some things by trial and error, but don't necessarily learn what they need to. By introducing simulations in the context of challenges, the learning can be more focused, and it can be easier to assess what students do and do not understand.

Linda Polin: That was my other question, about the authoring tool and what that's like and how hard it is for the students to get their stuff in and create what they need.

John Bransford: Well, the students don't necessarily need an authoring tool.

Linda Polin: Isn't that what they are doing?

John Bransford: Do you mean like publishing their own challenges?

Linda Polin: Yeah, to publish.

John Bransford: This is an activity in some courses, but students still don't have to author the whole course.

Linda Polin: No, no, but like the cancer example where they made that ... did they reuse objects in the database or did they go out and take pictures of the kid and interview people and assemble this?

John Bransford: They took pictures and they used clip art. But they also reused some things that had been developed previously. And they used existing challenges as models for what they wanted to do.

Linda Polin: Ahhh, okay.

Scott Grabinger: Teachers who are intrigued by your challenge, how do you indoctrinate them—how do you help them transform themselves to be able to think about how people learn and why?

John Bransford: The best strategy, in our experience, is to begin by helping them think about what they want to achieve and what's not working. The technology comes well down the line. This is one of the reasons we like the Wiggins and McTighe book, referred to in our chapter. It begins with an analysis of key aspects of skills and knowledge, and then asks how we'll know when students get there and what kinds of benchmarks to look for along the way. Only then do we get into ways to accomplish these goals. This gets us into principles of how people learn and what instructional methods might look like that fits these principles. The AMIGO[3] architecture can accommodate a variety of methods. In fact, we often say that the good news is that AMIGO[3] is flexible. That's the bad news as well, because it's underconstrained.

One of the best examples of a group that has begun to use challenge-based designs quite extensively is our bioengineering project. The bioengineers are a wonderful group to work with. One of the coauthors of this chapter, Bob Roselli, has done an incredible job of transforming his entire course in biomechanics from one that was purely lecture based to one that is challenge based.

Scott Grabinger: And Bob and others are willing to do this?

John Bransford: It helps that we have an National Science Foundation grant that holds our feet to the fire (*Group laughs.*)

Mark Schlager: What we need to do is to get your teacher education curriculum into her (pointing to Linda) program. And she'll turn 'em out. (*Group laughs.*) They'll be fully indoctrinated.

John Bransford: The other end of this is that we don't begin by trying to radically change the teachers. We begin by capturing the knowledge they want their students to learn and why it's important to know. We have a team that is designed to work with instructors to create courses. So that's where we just get you into our studio, and we start capturing the content. Then we create some prototype challenges that set up the content you want to teach. Over time, as you start to use some of these—and understand why they are being used from a "how people learn" perspective—you start to change.

Another method for working with faculty is what we call the Trojan horse method of using really simple technology for beginning change. This involves the use of wireless personal response systems—they are quite inexpensive, but they have big effects. If I'm used to lecturing, I now have to prepare sets of questions to ask my class what they are understanding. I'm restricted to multiple choice, but that's okay. Students press a button. A graph pops up with an anonymous indication of what everybody thinks about a question, and it really changes the dynamics of the classroom. And it sets the stage for lots of discoveries. One is that instructors begin to ask how can they go beyond simply asking factual memory questions. Another is that instructors are often surprised at how many students misunderstand despite the fact that the instructor thought his or her previous mini-lecture was perfectly clear.

Jenny Franklin: John, I want to follow up on Rafael's question. In this world of reusable learning objects and intelligent agents in service of learning and pedagogy, how far have you gone into the extensibility of or extension of meta-data schema to actually encapsulate instructional knowledge about pedagogy? For example, the interactivity of learning objects, those kinds of things. Have you gone into tagging objects in terms of sort of a higher level description of their pedagogical characteristics?

John Bransford: We have just gotten into this, and again, this is work under the leadership of our systems engineering group—especially Larry Howard. We have just gotten a prototype of a really sophisticated system that will allow us to start building things and see what works.

Jenny Franklin: So a teacher could go beyond the typical bibliographic content of metadata schema right now to a highly interactive and high degree of learner control and have response contingent feedback? In other words, are you going there?

Terry Anderson: Actually, John, what I would suggest is that it isn't a systems engineering problem. It's a conceptual and . . .

John Bransford: I agree. Our systems engineers are special breed of cats who know a lot about learning and work very closely with our learning sciences group.

Terry Anderson: . . . you need a librarian or two at least.

John Bransford: Yeah, I agree. I would love information about this.

Jenny Franklin: We're trying to do that for a learning object repository for the purpose of faculty development. I'm sort of hoping that if I can create an environment that fosters inquiry and gets people to ask questions like "Why do I do this for that reason now?" So that they could search a pedagogic repository and use it in that way.

John Bransford: One big issue for me is that what we are calling granules take on very different affordances in different modules. That is the piece that has been missing for me in many attempts to share instructional artifacts.

Tom Duffy: There is one thing we have talked around but have not addressed directly. You are working with community colleges, you're working with a variety of universities building these courses, and the issue you're walking around is faculty involvement—the role of faculty in the whole thing. We've had a lot of discussion about the difficulty of faculty adapting to this inquiry-based approach. But we've got faculty in very different environments—community college, research universities, and a corporate environment. What are the faculty issues in terms of getting them to buy into it—what is their role?

John Bransford: Well, they really differ from community colleges versus the regular colleges and so forth. The biggest one is time, and the second one is payoff. If I use myself as an example, I actually feel like I can teach my How People Learn course better, much better, and with less time teaching it using this approach. For example, using online modules makes it easier to teach from anywhere across the world. Hopefully, we'll get to the point where faculty can see that this ultimately is going to make their life easier. Also, by being able to share modules with my colleagues, my own work is improving because I can collaborate with faculty without having to have a bunch of face-to-face meetings.

Tom Duffy: I understand the long-run sort of thing. I guess it's the issue of getting them involved in the first place. My interpretation right now is that there is faculty involvement, because you can fund it through the grant.

John Bransford: Yes, absolutely.

Tom Duffy: Are they going to start teaching it? What is going to be their role in teaching the course? Are you training them in . . . how do get them so they can actually work with this stuff? I can see you creating an environment for your course . . .

John Bransford: In bioengineering, we have some a seminar every 2 weeks. So we're able to build that capacity. On other grants, we also meet regularly, although usually less frequently than every 2 weeks.

Tom Duffy: So you have ongoing seminars with faculty that are involved in doing this?

John Bransford: Absolutely. You have to . . .

Tom Duffy: Community college level too?

John Bransford: Community college is more sporadic. We try to meet with them at least once a month and provide feedback about modules they create, but by helping them learn how to assess student learning. Not everyone stays the course, but many do, and they do a great job.

Tom Duffy: Thanks a lot, John.
   (End of session)

12

Distance Learning: Beyond the Transmission of Information Toward the Coconstruction of Complex Conceptual Artifacts and Tools

Richard Lesh, Susan K. Byrne, and Pamela A. White
Purdue University

In this chapter, we describe innovative uses of distance education at Purdue University's Center for Twenty-first Century Conceptual Tools (TCCT). At TCCT, the central goal is to investigate the nature of the most important understandings and abilities—in mathematics, science, language and literacy—that are most significant to provide foundations for success beyond school in a technology-based age of information (Lesh, Zawojewski, & Carmona, 2003). In other words, TCCT is investigating ways that the 3 *R*s (Reading, wRiting, and aRithmetic) need to be reconceptualized to meet the demands of the new millennium.

Much of our research is based on the models and modeling perspective (see Lesh & Doerr, 2003). Within this perspective, learning experiences are designed to facilitate students' reasoning and concept development by having them participate in model-eliciting activities where they invent, refine, and extend their own understandings. The models and modeling perspective enables students to reason their way through a problem and a way for teachers to better understand what students do and do not know. This perspective forms the basis of our research in distance learning. Specifically, TCCT research focuses on theory-based and experience-tested prototypes for materials, programs, and procedures that emphasize the following goals:

- To provide early democratic access to powerful conceptual tools (constructs, conceptual systems, plus capability amplifiers) that enable all students to achieve extraordinary results in (simulations of) real-life problem-solving situations that are typical of those where mathematical and scientific thinking is needed (beyond school) in the 21st century.
- To provide experiences in which "students" (who may be either adults or children, inside or outside of school) both develop and document deeper and higher order understandings related to complex achievements that seldom are assessed on brief and easy-to-score standardized tests.

261

- To provide ways to identify a broader range of students whose exceptional abilities and achievements often have not been apparent in settings involving traditional tests, textbooks, and teaching, by recognizing the importance of a broader range of knowledge and abilities that are needed for success in future-oriented fields ranging from agriculture, to business, engineering, medicine, and other fields that are becoming increasingly heavy users of mathematics, science, and technology.

All three projects discussed in this chapter involve technology-mediated learning or problem-solving activities in which not all of the participants and resources reside at the same location. However, they focus on somewhat different types of interactions, and on three different levels or types of participants:

1. Professors and graduate students at remote sites
2. Undergraduate preservice teachers and in-service teachers,[1] or supervising teachers at remote sites
3. College, high school, or middle school students and professionals in fields that are significant users of mathematics, science, and technology, each of which may reside at remote sites.

Before describing these projects, it is useful to identify several general assumptions that apply to most of TCCT's technology-mediated communication, learning, and problem-solving activities.

GENERAL CHARACTERISTICS OF TCCT'S DISTANCE EDUCATION ACTIVITIES

Purdue is similar to other universities we've visited in the use of distance education programs. That is, most can be characterized as using state-of-the-art technologies to simulate traditional (and often notably ineffective) forms of instruction. Therefore, it is significant to emphasize that TCCT projects are investigating ways that traditional conceptions of distance education can be extended to include activities that reach beyond teacher-centered instruction and views of learning that characterize it as a process of transferring information. Instead, we emphasize the use of technology-mediated communication tools so that participants can work together in productive ways that simulate more innovative and effective forms of instruction—such as those that emphasize small group activities and problem-based learning. Consequently, the kind of technology-mediated communication tools emphasized are those that go beyond the transmission of inert information by making it possible for students to be engaged in dynamic, interactive, multimedia exchanges in which simultaneous file sharing capabilities are used to allow small working groups of students to coconstruct complex, sharable, and reuseable artifacts and tools. One way we do this is to gradually morph effective instructional activities into forms that involve increasing numbers of participants ("students" or "teachers") at remote sites. That is, many of TCCT's "distance education" activities involve both face-to-face and remote communication.

Another distinctive characteristic of TCCT's distance education activities is that our goal is seldom simply to create distance education programs for their own sake. Nor is it to provide instruction for new groups of students that we are not already trying to

---

[1] In colleges of education, the term *preservice teachers* refers to undergraduate education majors and others who are engaged in student teaching (or other forms of clinical teaching in K–12 schools) but who are not yet certified and regularly employed teachers. The term *in-service teachers* refers certified and regularly employed teachers who are engaged in professional development activities.

serve. In general, we are trying to better serve the needs of students who are already participating in existing programs, perhaps by providing broader ranges of high-quality resources and experiences, or by eliminating unproductive difficulties (such as those associated with excessive travel times or dealing with inaccessible resources when they are needed).

A third distinctive characteristic of TCCT's distance education activities is that we consider them to be especially productive venues for investigating general principles of teaching, learning, and problem solving. That is, they are productive sites for research. However, when we say this we should emphasize that we are not interested in naive studies, such as those that ask whether synchronous communication is better or worse than asynchronous communication—or whether distance education activities are better or worse than their traditional face-to-face counterparts. In the former case, the question is naive unless we clarify such issues as: better for whom? For what purpose? Under what conditions? In the latter case, the question is naive because, for example, when technology-based communication is used with participants who do not all reside at the same site, our goal usually is to address goals that simply could not be addressed in face-to-face interactions. In fact, TCCT research suggests that, even when instructors begin their distance education experiences by simply trying to do old things in new ways, they usually end up doing significantly new things (Lesh, 2002) and/or significantly reexamining why they are using (or not using) different instructional strategies (Lesh, Crider, & Gummer, 2001). This is why, in TCCT courses and programs, the instructors who use technology-mediated communication often find themselves developing new forms of interaction that aren't simply simulations of activities that were successful in face-to-face encounters. For example, when computers are used to provide the interface with Internet-based communication technologies, the "things" that can be communicated are no longer restricted to written text (e.g., e-mail), or spoken language (e.g., telephone), or visual images (e.g. TV). They also may include complex multimedia artifacts and tools ranging from geometry constructions to PowerPoint presentations, animations, simulations, or the more traditional text documents, spreadsheets, graphs, and graphics. Consequently, rather than simply transmitting inert information from one site to another, complex artifacts may be coconstructed using file sharing interactions that enable participants to work together from remote sites.

ASSUMPTIONS UNDERLYING TCCT'S DISTANCE EDUCATION ACTIVITIES

In TCCT projects, we assume that distance education includes virtually any form of technology-mediated learning or problem-solving activities in which all of the participants and resources do not necessarily reside at the same location. Other relevant assumptions include the following.

No "Single Teacher" Restriction

TCCT projects assume that distance education is not restricted to situations where communication is always mediated through a single teacher (T) who resides at a central hub, as indicated in Fig. 12.1a.

Instead, we assume that students (S) often interact point to point with the teacher and other students, as indicated in Fig. 12.1b, perhaps using Internet-based tools to

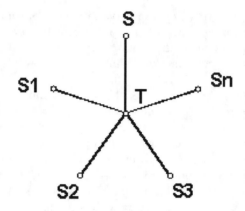

FIG. 12.1a.   Communication occurs only through a hub.

accomplish the communication. Point-to-point communication as described in Fig. 12.1b is consistent with the teacher at the center and students at other points, but because communication now moves from student to student, as well as from the teacher to students, the hub now encompasses everyone involved in the communication instead of only the teacher at the central point.

Redefining the "Teacher"

TCCT projects assume that several levels and types of "teachers" may be available (perhaps at remote sites instead of the local site) and that technology-based communication tools enable them to serve as resources to students (who also may or may not reside at remote sites), as illustrated in Fig. 12.2. Teachers may be mentors, advisors, or consultants; they may also be students—as well as teachers—and as such, they may serve in multiple capacities.

Within Sites and Across Sites

TCCT projects assume that not all of the students are working alone at remote sites. In fact, we assume that many sites may involve several students (S), as well as one or more mentors, as indicated by Fig. 12.3a.

We also assume that face-to-face interactions may occur within sites at the same time that technology-mediated interactions are occurring across sites, as illustrated in Fig. 12.3b.

Consequently, many productive distance education experiences may look less like traditional courses or seminars—and more like project-based learning activities in which cross-site teams of participants (students, teachers, and consultants) work together in small groups that include diverse specialists. A hub no longer exists because of the ability for each participant to communicate independently with any of the others in the network.

Note: At Purdue, WebCT is a well-known hub-oriented courseware development package that enables professors to create Web-based resources for their courses. Groove is Peer-to-Peer (P2P) networking software used for a similar purpose, but emphasizes point-to-point communication and distributed file storage. Currently, we are testing Groove in the classrooms to determine its functionality as it relates to instructional design.

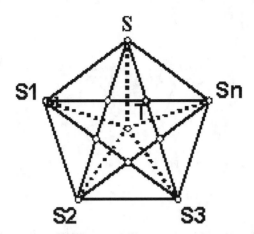

FIG. 12.1b.   Point-to-point communication is possible.

Digital Library

TCCT projects assume that a digital library should be available that includes links to resources distributed across all participating sites. Further, we assume that they include complex artifacts, tools, and resources that support project-based learning; we assume they may be taken out or put in by participants at any site. Consequently, when new resources are submitted, we assume that quality assurance procedures need to be established so they can be assessed, classified, stored, and retrieved in ways that are most useful to participants at all sites. This is not an easy process to manage. As participants share data, a hierarchy needs to be developed for storage and retrieval. A standard must be set to provide each participant with ground rules to follow, with acceptable formats of files, appropriate categories to classify the items, where to place them when they are shared, and information about whether the items may be altered in any way or must be used as they exist. Care must also be taken to protect files against accidental erasure or inadvertent overwriting. A final consideration with a digital library is the issue of ownership. Each participant who adds (or uses) a file needs to know the procedure to provide credit to the contributors. This allows each user to add to or take from the library without danger of copyright issues. More information about a digital library that is currently used in the TCCT projects will be included later in this chapter.

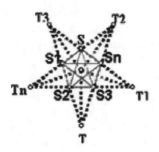

FIG. 12.2.   Several remote teachers (mentors, advisors, or consultants) and several students at the hub.

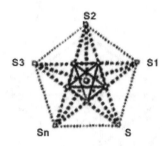

FIG. 12.3a.   Only isolated students reside at remote sites, possibly with a group at the hub, possibly accompanied by a mentor.

Many Kinds of Interactions

TCCT projects assume that productive interactions may involve strategic mixes of face-to-face communication within site and remote communication across site, as well as periodic meetings where all participants meet at a single location. We also assume that it may be productive to encourage participants to interact both inside and outside of formally scheduled class sessions, and that both synchronous and asynchronous forms of communication will be used where appropriate. For this reason, TCCT strives to keep communication costs low, especially for beyond-class communication. We do this by restricting attention to equipment that is sufficiently inexpensive, available, or both, so that participants can use it (perhaps even in their own homes or offices) without depending on special videoconferencing studios or computer laboratories.

Students, Teachers, or Both?

TCCT projects assume that the "participants" may include both students and teachers of several levels and types. In other words, we assume that the "students" may include youngsters or adults who have a variety of educational strengths, experiences, resources, and needs; and, we assume that the "teachers" may function less like lecturers or "worksheet graders" and more like consultants or experienced collaborators. In fact, we assume that, even with a single TCCT project, the "teachers" and the "students" both may be "learners" in the sense that they both may be expected to develop new understandings and abilities as a consequence of interactions that occur. For example, within a single project, using technology-mediated interactions

- Several college professors may serve as in-service instructors for a group of K–12 teachers at remote sites.
- Several K–12 teachers may mentor education majors who are at several different college campuses.
- Several college students may tutor diverse groups of children at several different K–12 schools.
- Several especially interesting K–12 children may serve as interviewed (or observed) "subjects" by a group of college professors who are at remote sites. This will help

Note: One reason that TCCT projects emphasize inexpensive equipment and Internet-based communication is because one of the goals of the Center is to develop models and prototypes for instructional activities that can be modified and used in distance education with children and teachers in K–12 schools where resources for software and hardware are in short supply.

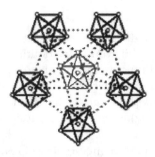

FIG. 12.3b.   Small groups of students reside at most sites.

professors clarify their thinking about the psychology of student learning. There-fore, in such projects, a participant who functions as a "student" at one moment may function as a "teacher" a moment later, or both roles may be played simulta-neously.

Figure 12.4 diagrams the interaction of problem solvers based on the preceding assumptions previously described.

Multitasking

TCCT projects assume that during formally scheduled class periods, synchronous in-teractions may involve multitasking activities in which participants (e.g., students or mentors) may be engaged simultaneously in several layers of communication—both within or across sites. For example, if a distance education seminar involves six sites with three to six participants residing at each site, then sites-as-a-whole may be com-municating using Internet-based videoconferencing at the same time that individ-ual participants also are communicating using networked laptop computers. For in-stance, small groups of participants (who may or may not reside at the same site) may share a "whiteboard" or some other file sharing device to develop shared notes about whole-class discussions, and the shared notes may go well beyond looking like notes from a lecture and include purposeful interpretations based on collaboration from a group.

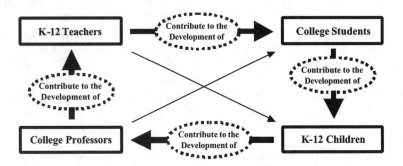

FIG. 12.4.   In projects with interacting learners or problem solvers: Who is learning from whom? Who is remote from whom?

Is It Distance Education?

The assumptions that have been described in this section lead to teaching and learning situations that often look quite different than traditional distance education courses. But, they certainly involve technology-mediated learning or problem solving in which not all of the participants and resources reside at the same location. So, according to our definition of the term *distance education,* they clearly qualify. To see why, consider the following questions. Is it productive to restrict attention to situations where

- None of the sites involve more than a single isolated student?
- Face-to-face interactions are never allowed to occur?
- A single "teacher" is assumed to be the only nonstudent?
- Participants (who are called students) are the only ones who are allowed to reside at remote sites?
- All of the students are considered to be of the same (homogeneous) level and type?
- Students are only able to engage in one interaction at a time in class, when their lives are filled with multimedia/multitasking activities (such as watching a television while doing homework, talking on a cell phone, or both)?

Our answer to all of these questions is: No! In fact, we believe that productive distance education programs of the future will be moving in precisely these directions.

AN OVERVIEW OF SEVERAL TCCT PROJECTS THAT INVOLVE DISTANCE EDUCATION

At any given time, TCCT has many projects (or programs) being conducted by faculty at Purdue. Each may involve significant technology-based interaction among participants at remote sites. Three that are closely interrelated have been chosen for discussion here. They were included because they serve as examples for new directions in distance education and the ability of students to multitask in the classroom.

Purdue University's and Indiana University's Jointly Sponsored Distributed Doctoral Program in Mathematics Education (PU/IU DDPME)

PU/IU DDPME uses technology-mediated communication capabilities associated with Indiana's national hub for Internet II, coupled with well-established intracampus enrollment procedures associated with the Big Ten's Traveling Scholar Program,[2] to enable doctoral students to have access to faculty advisors, research projects, field experiences, and jointly taught courses and seminars that are available at any of the four campuses: Purdue–West Lafayette, IU-Bloomington, IUPUI (Indianapolis), or Purdue-Calumet. For example, in the DDPME, such experiences have included highly specialized courses for mathematics educators on topics that range from research design,

---

[2]The Big Ten's Traveling Scholar Program is available to all Big Ten universities plus the University of Chicago. It is made possible by the Big Ten's Committee on Institutional Collaboration, and it allows students who are enrolled at any participating institution to take courses at any other participating institutions while paying tuition at their home institution. Course credits transfer automatically, just as for courses taken on home campuses.

to software design, to models and modeling in specific content areas, to courses focusing on children's developing knowledge in specific topic areas (algebra, calculus, geometry, or statistics). These courses have included not only virtual seminars that involve participants at several sites throughout the United States (e.g., Rutgers University, Syracuse University, and Arizona State University) or abroad (e.g., Australia, Canada, and Mexico), but they also have included a variety of remote field experiences, multisite coordinated workshops, distributed mini-conferences, or multisite project-based learning activities that involve collaborations among faculty members, students, and other participants at several institutions. Such multicampus collaborations are needed because, in fields such as mathematics education, where only a few universities have more than a handful of doctoral students or faculty members, it's often impossible, using only the resources that reside at a single campus, to offer courses that address many of the highly specialized needs of doctoral students. Yet, most of these topics are not likely to be given adequate attention in generic courses that do not focus on mathematics, science, or other specific content areas.

By drawing on resources at both Purdue and Indiana University's extended campuses, as well as at other collaborating institutions, the goal is not simply to create distance education courses. Other equally important goals include:

1. Providing a launch pad for multiple-campus research projects that are capable of dealing more effectively with realistically complex problems in diverse educational settings throughout the state and nation
2. Developing prototypes for distance education activities that can be used in courses for in-service and preservice teacher education, as well as with students at remote sites in K–12 schools.

With the preceding goals in mind, there tends to be no such thing as a "typical course" in the DDPME. Continuous experimentation is the hallmark of the program. Therefore, significant changes often occur not only from one course to another, or from one instructor to another for a given course, but also within a specific course during the semester in which it is taught. Nonetheless, care is taken to ensure that lessons learned are passed on from one course to another. (A sample of these lessons learned will be described later in this chapter.)

In this section, two courses will be highlighted because they involve significantly different kinds of technology-mediated interactions. Both courses are in the mathematics education content area; the first is about research design, the second software design.

Research Design in Mathematics Education has been taught several times during the past 5 years. Participating institutions usually have included not only the four "core" Indiana campuses but also at least two additional sites in other states, countries, or both. Also, a few individual students sometimes participate from their homes or from their local K–12 schools. Most sites include 3 to 10 doctoral students, plus at least one faculty-level mentor, and a "lead professor" resides at one or more of the "core" Indiana campuses.

Concerning equipment and Internet connections, each site needs to have access to a high-speed Internet connection to our "hub" at Purdue–West Lafayette. Further, for each site that has more than three people, we recommend that the site should have both

1. A dedicated videoconferencing system (such as Polycom) that is intended for communication among sites-as-a-whole
2. At least one computer-based videoconferencing system (such as ViaCom or NetMeeting) for each cluster of two or three students at each site.

In other words, at sites that have more than three participants, more than a single type of videoconferencing system is needed; and, each cluster of three participants should have a computer-based system for communication. Two types of units are needed because dedicated videoconferencing systems usually do not include capabilities for sharing computer-based files, whereas computer-based systems usually do not have sophisticated capabilities for scanning and zooming, and focusing video or audio input.

Concerning course content, the research design course has been organized around readings in the these books: *Handbook of Research Design in Mathematics and Science Education* (Kelly & Lesh, 2001), a *Handbook of Research Design in Mathematics Education* (English, 2002), or *Design Research in Mathematics, Science, and Technology Education* (Kelly & Lesh, (NSF grant in progress). Because it often was the case that some of the relevant readings were not available in print at the time these courses were taught, prepublication versions of chapters were downloadable from a Web site where PowerPoint overviews and other relevant resources also were accessible. Online course materials such as syllabi, outside reading assignments, additional resources, threaded discussions sessions, and so on also were available using a courseware assembly package (WebCT), which is supported by Purdue. Concerning "teachers" for the research design course, arrangements were made, whenever possible, to allow authors of reading assignments to participate in relevant videoconferencing sessions and Web-based threaded discussions during the week(s) when their publications were highlighted. Because they were not participating in the course-as-a-whole, design for both the videoconferencing sessions and the accompanying threaded discussion sessions needed to be structured for relative ease to allow visiting experts and other short-term guests to participate from remote sites.

Weekly seminars for the course generally are held on Thursday evenings from 6:00 to 9:00 (in West Lafayette). Also, in the days between formally scheduled seminars, teams of students often have assignments requiring collaborative work with several students at other sites. Therefore, outside of formally scheduled classes, students need access to inexpensive or readily available facilities for videoconferencing, audioconferencing, file sharing, or synchronously shared whiteboards and chat groups, as well as asynchronous threaded discussions. This means that communication cannot depend on expensive telephone connections, or on expensive equipment that is not readily available.

Software Design in Mathematics Education is a course in which the instructor changes each week. The weekly "instructor" usually is an internationally known software developer who "attends" the session from his or her home site. So, for optimum interactions during formally scheduled classes, most of the students met in small groups of three to five students. Figure 12.5 shows how individual groups worked together in one of several small seminar rooms and were provided with a wirelessly networked

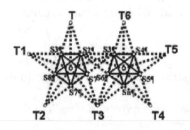

FIG. 12.5.   Two or three groups of students and several teachers at remote sites.

laptop computer-based videoconferencing unit (e.g. Viacom). One unit was available for each pair of students. In this way, within each seminar room, students were able to talk with one another freely, with or without being heard in other seminar rooms. They could also videoconference, audioconference, or file-share with individuals or groups at other sites. Therefore, "teachers of the week" were able to

1. Demonstrate software (using multimedia videoconferencing)
2. Interact with individual students (using file sharing capabilities on the students' individual laptop computers)
3. Participate in follow-up discussions (using file sharing, and Internet-based chat groups and threaded discussions).

Also, outside of class

1. Cross-site "buddy groups" of three to five students used similar capabilities to work together to coconstruct software or other complex artifacts.
2. Individual students were able to engage in videoconferencing and file-sharing activities with individuals (students or teachers) at any participating site.

Concerning teachers for the software design course, each site had a mentor, and mentors had significantly different levels and types of expertise. For example, some were faculty members, whereas others were advanced graduate students. Some were knowledgeable about software development without being experts in mathematics education, whereas others were experienced mathematics educators but were not experts in software development or in using specific software.

Using the kind of multisite, multimedia, and multitasking activities emphasized in the preceding two courses, the DDPME hopes to encourage the development of a research community that is more than just a community of researchers, each "doing their own thing." Indicators of success include the facts that, within the DDPME, students' Ph.D. dissertation committees are beginning to include faculty members from more than a single campus, groups of students are beginning to coordinate their writing and research activities so that more complex problems are being addressed systemically, and faculty members are beginning to develop collaborative multisite research activities so that coordinated projects will build on one another over extended periods of time (Lesh & Doerr, 2003).

Purdue's Program for Preparing Tomorrow's Teachers to Use Technology (P^3T^3)

P^3T^3 interacts with the DDPME. It is designed to provide technology-related professional development activities for professors, graduate teaching assistants in the Purdue's School of Education, and collaborating teachers in specially designated professional development schools associated with School of Education. P^3T^3's goal is to increase participants' proficiencies in using new instructional technologies, including a variety of technology-mediated communication tools used in distance education (as it has been described in this chapter).

P^3T^3 activities that are highlighted in this chapter focuses on two related initiatives— on-the-job professional development activities that use technology-mediated communication tools to promote the continuous development of experienced K–12 teachers who serve as role models and mentors to support field experiences of college students in Purdue's School of Education, and remote field experiences that use technology-mediated communication tools to supplement (not replace) traditional field experiences for college students in Purdue's School of Education.

P^3T^3's on-the-job professional development activities are designed to create something similar to a virtual demonstration school by using technology-mediated communication tools to help develop and maintain close working relationships with a relevant community of mentor-level teachers at sites representing diverse populations of students. The goal is to turn teachers' everyday teaching experiences into learning experiences similar to project-based learning activities for other types of students, so the teachers themselves become the learners—and help is provided when and where it's needed, and on topics that are requested by the teachers themselves. In this way, it is possible to monitor and optimize the quality of field experiences at remote sites.

P^3T^3's remote field experiences use the same distance education equipment that is used for on-the-job professional development activities. They enable college education majors to engage in activities such as

1. Observing excellent teachers teaching a variety of lessons for different levels and types of students in diverse settings
2. Comparing several different teachers teaching similar lessons to different groups of students in different settings
3. Interviewing students or teachers following the preceding teaching and learning episodes
4. Tutoring small groups of students or serving as a consultant on complex projects
5. Analyzing and assessing directions for improvement in student work and returning results in a manner that's sufficiently timely for K–12 teachers and students
6. Teaching specially targeted lessons for students with specifically targeted strengths or needs.

These kinds of virtual field experiences are needed because Purdue University and Indiana University, like many research institutions, are located in relatively small, rural communities where it is impossible to provide large numbers of high-quality field experiences that involve sufficiently diverse populations of students. Therefore, outstanding supervising teachers often must be drawn from remote sites where the following kinds of problems or opportunities arise.

College students in schools of education often must spend large amounts of unproductive time traveling to and from field sites, and, when they arrive, it often is difficult to ensure that relevant activities will be going on in participating K–12 classrooms. Therefore, they often end up watching excellent teachers being engaged in tasks that involve very little significant teaching or learning.

Even if a field experience provides an interesting teaching or learning episode, inexperienced observers often fail to notice more than superficial things that occur. Therefore, if nobody (such as peers or college-based supervisors) shares these experiences, then there may be no effective way to help inexperienced observers develop more sophisticated ways of thinking about what they see.

To get the most out of experiences observing excellent teaching and learning episodes, it often is productive to be able to view several similar activities taking place in a variety of classrooms, in a variety of communities, and with a variety of teachers who have significantly different teaching styles. Also, it often is productive for college students to interview teachers and students in similar classes that they observe, but if the field sites are at different locations, and if only a single college student's needs are being met, it often is not possible to provide opportunities for related live interviews.

Teachers usually are not able to alter their activities to fit the specialized needs of only a single visiting undergraduate student. Therefore, the activities that college students observe often were not chosen to encourage their development. However, if a teacher knows that the classroom is going to be observed (via videoconferencing technologies) by a class of 20 to 30 university students plus their instructor, then he or she often is willing to teach a special lesson that is specially designed to meet the needs of both his or her own students and the college students. Further, the instructor may be especially willing to do so if the college students provide some related service, such as using technology-mediated communication to analyze and provide feedback about geometry proofs, solutions to complex algebra problems, problem-solving situations that involve the construction of graphs, or other complex work that students produce.

Project 3: Purdue's Gender Equity in Engineering Project

The focus of this project is explicitly on project-based learning activities that are designed by and for interacting groups of three to five teachers, professors, or other adults, or students in middle school, high school, or college. An overall goal of the project is to identify a broader range of students whose exceptional abilities and achievements often have not been apparent in settings involving traditional tests, textbooks, and teaching, because the low-level knowledge and abilities that these tests emphasize are not representative of those that are needed for success beyond school in a technology-based age of information. To accomplish this goal, technology-mediated communication is used in a variety of ways:

1. Technology-mediated communication is needed because precollege or college students that we're trying to identify often live at remote sites that can only be reached effectively using some sort of distance education. But the kind of distance education programs that are proving to be most effective often don't resemble traditional courses as much as they resemble project-based learning environments in which small groups of three to five students continually form and reform around projects that usually require between 1 and 10 hours to complete. So, the way groups form to work on projects is similar to the way boy scouts or girl scouts form working groups to complete merit badges. What's needed is a learning environment where students can meet other students with common interests and complementary resources and skills—and where they can share productive experiences and resources—even if collaborators must work together from remote sites.

2. Technology-mediated communication is needed for teachers to make effective use of the activities and tools that the Gender Equity Project provides; special professional development experiences need to be provided for teachers at remote sites.

3. Technology-mediated communication is needed to recognize and reward a broader range of students who have exceptional potential; the Gender Equity Project needs to clarify the nature of a broader range of abilities that are needed for success in future-oriented fields ranging from aeronautical engineering to business management. But, to accomplish this goal, we need to enlist input from

people such as professionals and professors who are in the business of identifying and developing leaders in the preceding kinds of fields. In particular, to develop project-based learning activities that are simulations of "real life" situations in which mathematical thinking is needed, we often need to enlist help from people who are only able to participate at a distance—from remote sites. That is, they are people, teachers, professors, and professionals in business and industry who are in the business of training or hiring tomorrow's leaders in fields that are heavy users of mathematics, science, and technology.

4. Technology-mediated communication is needed, because, in the preceding kinds of case studies for kids, a distinguishing characteristic is that the products that students are asked to produce involve the development of conceptual tools for constructing, describing, or explaining complex systems; and, these conceptual tools need to be sharable (with others), reusable (in other situations), and easily modifiable (for other purposes). They involve much more than just answers to artificially constrained questions. Technology-mediated communication is needed when we talk to professionals and professors who are in the business of identifying and developing leaders in fields where mathematical thinking is needed. In a technology-based age of information, while emphasizing abilities needed for success beyond schools, we are told that in job interviews the kind of capabilities that are given the greatest attention often are those that involve
   - The ability to make sense of complex systems (by quantifying them and in other ways describing them mathematically) so that their behaviors can be predicted, manipulated, or controlled
   - The ability to work well and communicate productively within diverse teams of specialists
   - The ability to adapt to new tools and unfamiliar settings, and the ability to describe situations in forms so that these tools can be used
   - The ability to unpack complex tasks into manageable chunks that can be addressed by different specialists
   - The ability to plan, monitor, and assess progress
   - The ability to describe intermediate and final results in forms that are meaningful and useful to others
   - The ability to produce results that are useful (e.g., timely), sharable (with other people), transportable (to other situations), and reusable (for other purposes).
   TCCT research suggests that in a technology age of information, when the goal is to emphasize what's needed for success beyond school, many of the most important yet neglected mathematical understandings and abilities directly involve the use of technology-mediated communication, as well as multimedia representational fluency. Emphasis shifts beyond just asking what kind of computations and procedures students can do. They also ask: What kind of systems can the students construct, describe, or explain mathematically (Aliprantis & Carmona, 2003; Kardos, 2003; Oakes & Rud, 2003).

5. Technology-mediated communication is needed because TCCT's digital library of case studies for kids includes not only activities and resources that can be downloaded by students collaborating from a variety of remote sites, it also includes

---

Note: We refer to refer to the preceding kinds of simulations of "real life" problems as case studies for kids because they appear to be middle school versions of the kind of "case studies" that often are used for both instruction and assessment in graduate programs in future-oriented fields—such as engineering, medicine, or business management—where mathematical thinking often is needed for success.

systems and procedures for submitting tools that are produced, as well as systems and procedures for giving appropriate credit to contributors. Consequently, if we view TCCT's digital library of case studies for kids as a venue for distance education (for both students and their teachers), then the program looks less like a traditional course and more like a modularized cluster of small-group activities, students can select activities based on their own needs and interests.

SOME LESSONS LEARNED FROM TCCT PROJECTS

For the TCCT activities that have been described in this chapter, many of the most significant general lessons that have been learned can be organized around the following four themes:

1. The need for adequate technical support
2. Increasing productivity through multitasking
3. Increasing meaningfulness using file sharing and multimedia communication
4. The need to make course modifications rapidly and frequently.

Each of these themes will be discussed in the context of the TCCT project where their meaning is most clear, but this does not mean that the theme only applies to the context in which it is described here. In fact, each of the themes could be applied to all of the TCCT activities that have been discussed: DDPME, P^3T^3, and Gender Equity in Engineering.

The Need for Adequate Technical Support

Anytime courseware makes one thing easy to do, it tends to make other alternatives more difficult. For this reason, if a given course or project does not conform to the software designer's vision and instructional philosophy, then difficulties tend to arise:

- Does the project have fixed start and end dates?
- Do the participants remain the same throughout the project?
- Does the project involve small working groups that collaborate inside of class, outside of class, or both? Does membership in these groups always remain the same?
- Is it important for participants to share work spaces with small groups of participants at remote sites? Should all of these work spaces be created, monitored, or controlled by someone (the teacher) at a central hub?
- Are assignments and resources continually evolving and changing—depending on progress that is made?

In DDPME programs, difficulties often arise because courses look less like traditional courses, and look more like projects in which small subgroups of participants work on a series of different projects. They often involve Internet collaborations among several levels and types of participants, and they often go beyond lectures, discussion groups, and individual homework to also involve virtual seminars, virtual working groups, and a variety of remote field experiences: multisite coordinated workshops, distributed mini-conferences, and multisite project-based learning activities. Consequently, many DDPME courses have found it useful to evolve beyond using only monolithic hub-focused courseware (like WebCT) toward also using more distributed peer-to-peer (P2P) communication networks.

P2P software has been touted as the next "killer application" for the Internet (Gartner Consulting, 2001). Groove (available at http://www.groove.net) is an example of a P2P application that has received especially strong reviews. Unlike hub-based software such as WebCT, which was designed to facilitate the creation of Web-based versions of fairly traditional courses, Groove was designed primarily to facilitate collaborations among participants in projects in business settings. Consequently, even though Groove has many of the same features as WebCT—discussion boards, calendars, chat rooms, instant messages, and file sharing—it does not have built-in tools for creating online quiz capabilities or for posting grades, even though it can be grade-posting programmed to provide such capabilities. The main functions that Groove supports were designed to help users to create, reconfigure, and coordinate multisite project-based learning and problem-solving activities.

In DDPME courses, we've found that P2P software does indeed create open-ended environments that make it easy for students to create "shared spaces" where collaboration is possible with a variety of different levels and types of other participants. But, such open-ended environments sometimes create problems, as well as provide opportunities. For example, in DDPME projects, instant messages and electronic copies of weekly readings frequently showed up as missing because there was no single hub to which all materials were sent. Students and instructors simply had not yet developed adequate ways to think about networks in which resources are distributed throughout the system, like DVD music on the Internet. Such problems were compounded by the fact that whenever attempts are made to use new software, relevant technical support staff may be of little help to solve problems.

Of course, when new types of software are adopted, many of the problem that occur can be expected to fade away as students and teachers become familiar with them. Nonetheless, adequate technical support is critical to the success of any form of distance education, and the extent to which it is needed is directly proportional to the degree of innovation that is attempted. So the lesson to be learned here is that if an instructor is going to be innovative, it's often useful to take the additional step of being sufficiently innovative to obtain special support. In the DDPME, we have found that it is much more likely to obtain additional funding and support for projects that are viewed to be innovative.

Increasing Productivity Through Multitasking

DDPME courses have evolved in ways that increasingly enable students to engage (often simultaneously) in both site-to-site videoconferencing and or P2P communication via personal computers. Further, P2P communication usually emphasizes file sharing, as well as other types of synchronous and asynchronous activities that occur both inside and outside of regularly scheduled class periods. Consequently, one of the main lessons that we have learned through DDPME courses is that, when students have access to several different communication media, they often use several at the same time. That is, they often become engaged in multitasking activities even if these activities are not recognized or encouraged by instructors. For example, in DDPME courses, during regularly scheduled class periods, students often interact simultaneously using combinations of: (1) face-to-face discussions that involve sharing materials with other participants at their own site, (2) Internet-based videoconferencing that emphasizes group-to-group interactions among participants at different sites, (3) P2P communication tools that use Internet-based communication to engage in file sharing with one or more individuals (or small groups) who may or may not be at remote sites.

If the preceding kinds of multitasking activities are managed in ways that support rather than subvert the intended goals of the course, then they often make it possible to radically increase the engagement and potential learning payoff to students. For example, during traditional lectures, seminars, and other classroom activities, students often take notes about several relevant themes. Similarly, in DDPME courses, when students are able to engage in P2P communication using wirelessly connected laptop computers, each of these themes may correspond to a computer-based "whiteboard" that is shared with different small groups of students who may or may not reside at remotes sites. In other words, each student may participate simultaneously in several different "discussion groups" using a combination of face-to-face communication, videoconferencing, and file sharing. Further, these working groups often continue outside of formally scheduled class periods. This is why, in DDPME courses, the software and hardware that is emphasized does not require students to come to special classrooms or broadcast studios. A goal is to harness students' energies both inside and outside of formally scheduled class periods.

TCCT courses and projects are only at beginning stages of exploring instructional possibilities related to students' multi-tasking capabilities, but pilot studies are producing promising results. It appears to be only the arrogance of instructors that causes them to imagine that their students' levels of thoughtfulness and engagement should be measured only in terms of devoting all of their attention to the words and actions of the instructor.

Increasing Meaningfulness Using File Sharing and Multimedia Communication

In DDPME courses such as those that focus on software development, P2P communication not only allows students to collaborate on complex projects outside of class, it also enables internationally known experts to make "virtual visits" in which they use file-sharing capabilities to demonstrate their newest state-of-the-art software that is not yet available to the public.

File sharing not only allows "virtually instructors" to demonstrate their software, it also allows them to interact directly with students. Therefore, students are able to have direct experiences with software that neither they nor their schools own, or they are able work together in small groups using software that is owned by only one participant in each group; or they are able to coconstruct their own software-based artifacts, which may range from simulations and animations, to geometric or algebraic constructions, to spreadsheets with graphs, to PowerPoint presentations.

When collaboration environments allow students to use file sharing to coconstruct complex artifacts, communication often involves much more than simply written text (as in chat groups), diagrams and drawings (as on shared whiteboards), and spoken language and video (as on n-way cell phones or Internet-based television transmissions). It also may involve expressing deeper and higher order constructs and conceptual systems in forms that encourage students to not only think with these constructs but to also think about them, by making them explicit objects of reflection and communication.

The Need to Make Course Modifications Rapidly and Frequently

Throughout the evolution of TCCT projects, instructors typically began their courses by imagining that new distance education activities would be similar to their past experiences that involved only face-to-face communication. But, reality typically proved otherwise. For example, even if a course involves nothing more complex than a series of seminars in which videoconferencing and file sharing are used to allow collaboration among six sites with four students at each site, then the interactions that occur during "virtual seminars" should be expected to be very different than those that occur during single-site seminars where 24 participants all sit around a conference in a single room. For example, when people are seen only in computer monitor windows, communication using "body language" tends to be minimized, and the result often leads to significant changes in interactions that occur. Further, because each site includes both real and virtual participants, and because face-to-face communication tends to obey somewhat different rules than technology-mediated communication, new protocols often need to be developed to facilitate communication. Similarly, as soon as students discover how to share whiteboards and other computer-based communication devices, explosions of interaction often begin to occur in which students often participate in several simultaneous conversations.

The preceding situations can result in both difficulties or opportunities, but, in either case, instructors need to be ready to adapt rapidly to feedback of many types. Whenever an interaction depends on technology, the instructor needs to have "Plan B" ready to function based on feedback. In fact, whenever possible, problems and opportunities should be detected without waiting for students to report them, and procedures need to be developed so that participants can help themselves whenever possible. The following examples that occurred during a recent DDPME seminar. They illustrate several ways that multitasking has been used by students to make decisions for their own learning:

- Without disturbing the class, students often would inform a technology support person of problems (such as low batteries or software glitches). The technology-support person also could respond to some problems on an individual basis with minimal interruption to others.
- During an instructor-led face-to-face discussion, a student had questions they preferred not to ask verbally. Using the communication tools, an instant message was sent to another student (or even to the instructor) asking for clarification. In traditional classrooms, this would be considered to be "note passing," but with a variety of technology-mediated communication tools available, it became an opportunity to explore and process information.

When students are given new responsibilities, they often turn them into new opportunities or challenges for the instructor. Therefore, as soon as instructors release tight control over some functions within their courses, participants often used these functions in ways that were unanticipated. In some courses, however, an important instructional goal is for students themselves to learn to govern their own learning and

---

Note: Students sometimes found such abilities to be both an asset and an annoyance, until norms and protocols developed to govern how and when certain types of communication would be appreciated by others. In the early stages of this particular exchange, students remained focused on the coursework, so the instant messages were task oriented. In other instances, however, as students became familiar with tool that were available, some students began to send messages that had nothing to do with the subject matter and reduced the instant message opportunities to the same value as passing notes. However, because this was a graduate-level course, students also recognized their lack of full participation and quickly corrected their behaviors based on nothing more than informal feedback from peers. In general, students used their own problem-solving skills to make judgments about what should and should not be done with the capabilities rather than being managed by the instructor.

problem-solving activities. Further, as participants in a course expand to include many levels of experts and novices, the community itself often exerts powerful norms on individual behavior.

CONCLUDING REMARKS

If we restrict attention to TCCT projects that involve some form of distance education, then a unifying force that distinguishes TCCT's research and development projects from most others results from the underlying theoretical framework and research methodologies that we emphasized. Because our work involves many scientists from fields outside education and psychology, we often draw on theoretical models and research methodologies that are familiar in "design sciences" such as engineering—in addition to being informed by theories and research methods that are more familiar to modern descendants of Piaget, Vygotsky, and Dewey—or more recent leaders in the cognitive sciences.

Foundations of our theoretical perspective have been described recently in a book titled *Beyond Constructivism: Models and Modeling Perspective on Problem Solving, Learning, and Teaching* (Lesh & Doerr, 2003). They also are described in a special issue of the *International Journal for Mathematical Thinking and Learning* (Lesh, 2003). For the purposes of this chapter, the main point to emphasize about models and modeling perspectives is that researchers focus their attention on the models (constructs and conceptual systems) that humans develop to interpret (describe, explain, and predict) their experiences. For example, in elementary mathematics, "thinking mathematically" is considered to be about interpreting situations mathematically at least as much as it is about computing. Similarly, in teacher education, expertise is considered to involve developing a collection of powerful models for making sense of teaching and learning situations; it is not considered to be reducible to the mastery of list of "condition–action" rules.

Models and modeling perspectives recognize that there are at least four distinct types of goals for instruction: affective objectives (AOs), which focus on attitudes, feelings, and values, behavioral objectives (BOs), which focus on facts and skills, cognitive objectives (COs), which focus on the constructs and conceptual systems that are needed to make sense of their experiences, and process objectives (POs), which focus on general learning and problem-solving processes and strategies. Yet, even though all four types of achievements are recognized as being important, models and modeling perspectives emphasize the importance of developing powerful models for describing, explaining, manipulating, and predicting the behaviors of the kind of complex systems that abound in a technology-based age of information. This is why TCCT's instructional programs tend to emphasize instructional activities in which primary goals are for (teams of) students to collaborate to coconstruct powerful constructs or conceptual systems, which often are expressed in the form of conceptual tools that are tested and revised repeatedly.

Another common characteristic of TCCT projects is that students, teachers, and researchers are all considered to be in the model development business. Students develop models (or other conceptual tools) for making sense of a "real life" problem-solving situation. Teachers develop models (or other conceptual tools) for making sense of students' modeling activities. Also, researchers developing models (or other conceptual tools) for making sense of interactions between students and teachers. In each case, the relevant "problem solver" (student, teacher, or researcher) is expressing

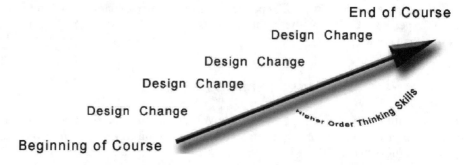

FIG. 12.6.   The process of designing and redesigning throughout a course. The result is always a positive slope with the goal of student's higher order thinking skills.

current ways of thinking in the form of conceptual tools that are tested and revised or refined. Thus, our research methodologies, just like our theoretical perspectives, borrow heavily from traditions that have been refined in "design sciences" such as engineering.

An NSF-supported project on design research (Kelly & Lesh, 2002; Lesh, 2001) currently is enlisting leading researchers—both inside and outside the fields of mathematics, science, and technology education—to codify guidelines for conducting such design experiments in education. Such design experiments are especially useful when the subjects of investigation are complex, dynamic, interacting systems of the type that abound in teaching and learning situations that involve distance education. Such research designs typically integrate both qualitative and quantitative information, and they typically involve a series of iterative refinement cycles (Lesh & Kelly, 2000; Lesh, 2000). Most of all, however, they are designed to generate useful ways of thinking about interactions among teachers and students in new kinds of teaching and learning situations that emphasize the use of technology-mediated communication. The goal is to improve the student's ability to incorporate higher order thinking at the end of the course.

REFERENCES

Aliprantis, C. D., & Carmona, G. (2003). Introduction to an economic problem: A models and modeling perspective. In R. Lesh & H. M. Doerr (Eds.). *Beyond constructivism: Models and modeling perspectives on mathematics problem solving, learning, and teaching* (pp. 255–264). Mahwah, NJ: Lawrence Erlbaum Associates.

English, L. (2002). *Handbook of international research in mathematics.* In L. English (Ed.). Mahwah, NJ: Lawrence Erlbaum Associates.

Kardos, G. (2003). The case of cases. In R. Lesh & H. M. Doerr (Eds.). *Beyond constructivism: Models and modeling perspectives on mathematics problem solving, learning, and teaching* (pp. 241–253). Mahwah, NJ: Lawrence Erlbaum Associates.

Kelly, A., & Lesh, R. (principle investigators, 2001-current). *Design sciences of human.* National Science Foundation. http://gse.gmu.edu/research/de

Kelly, A., & Lesh, R. (2002). Understanding and explicating design experiment methodologies. *Building research capacities.* Cardiff University Press, London.

Lesh, R. (2001). Beyond Constructivism: A new paradigm for identifying mathematical abilities that are most needed for success beyond school in a technology based Age of Information. In Mitchelmore, M. (Ed.). *Technology in Mathematics Learning and Teaching: Cognitive Considerations: A Special Issue of the Mathematics Education Research Journal.* Melbourne: Australia, Australia Mathematics Education Research Group.

Lesh, R. (2002). Research design in mathematics education: Focusing on design experiments. In L. English (Ed.). *Handbook of research design in mathematics education.* Mahwah, NJ: Lawrence Erlbaum Associates.

Lesh, R., & Doerr, H. M. (2003). *Beyond constructivism: Models and modeling perspectives on mathematics problem solving, learning, and teaching.* Mahwah, NJ: Lawrence Erlbaum Associates.

Lesh, R., & Kelly, A. (2000). Multitiered teaching experiments. *Handbook of research design in mathematics and science teaching* (pp. 197–230). Mahwah, NJ: Lawrence Erlbaum Associates.

Lesh, R., Byrne, S. K., & White, P. A. (2003). Center for Twenty-First Century Conceptual Tools (TCCT). West Lafayette, In: Purdue University.

Lesh, R., Byrne, S. K., & White, P. A. (2001). Emerging possibilities for collaborating doctoral programs. In R. E. Reys and J. Kilpatrick (Eds). *One Field, Many Paths: U.S. Doctoral Programs in Mathematical Education* (p. 113). Washington, DC: American Mathematical Society.

Lesh, R., Zawojewski, J., & Carmona, G. (2003). What mathematical abilities are needed for success beyond school in a technology-based age of information? In R. Lesh & H. M. Doerr (Eds.) *Beyond constructivism: Models and modeling perspectives on mathematics problem solving, learning, and teaching* (pp. 205–222). Mahwah, NJ: Lawrence Erlbaum Associates.

Oakes, W., & Rud, A. G. (2002). The EPICS model in engineering education: Perspective on problem solving abilities needed for success beyond schools. In R. Lesh and H. M. Doerr (Eds.). *Beyond constructivism: Models and modeling perspectives on mathematics problem solving, learning and teaching* (pp. 223–239). Mahwah, NJ: Lawrence Erlbaum Associates.

13

Embedded Assessment: An Evaluation Tool for the Web-Based Learning Environment

Matthew V. Champagne
IOTA Solutions, Inc.

The decreasing costs and increasing benefits of information technology have dramatically accelerated the use of Web-based learning. The development of innovative learning platforms, teaching tools, and other educational technologies has similarly accelerated over the past decade. The development of analogous evaluation innovations, however, has been abandoned. The primary evaluation approach within higher education continues to be the "autopsy" (Champagne, 1998). That is, once the learning event is completed, attempts are made to discern what went wrong. The autopsy approach to evaluation fails to deliver timely results to instructors, teaching assistants, and other stakeholders. Even many formative evaluation efforts fail to quickly provide meaningful information to stakeholders so that interim adjustments can be made to improve the learning experience.

Web-based learning provides numerous opportunities to create, test, and implement innovative evaluation methodologies. However, most institutions of higher education have yet to implement even straightforward evaluation techniques such as conducting course evaluations online, despite the overwhelming benefits of doing so (Kronholm, Wisher, Curnow, & Poker, 1999). A survey of 105 of the "most wired" 4-year colleges and universities in the United States (Hmieleski & Champagne, 2000) found that 98% of programs primarily used paper-based evaluation forms; two schools reported using an institute-wide Web-based evaluation system, and four schools used Web-based evaluation for distance education courses. All reported administering evaluation forms solely at the end of the term (the autopsy approach). More disturbing is the finding that faculty at only 25% of these schools received the results of their course evaluations within 2 weeks; 10% of faculty did not receive results for more than two months, if at all. No school reported having a mechanism in place whereby faculty received feedback from their course evaluations while classes were still in session.

FORMATIVE EVALUATION

Mosston and Ashworth (1990) argued that teaching and all classroom behaviors of instruction are governed by decision making. Decisions can occur before (e.g., choice of instruction materials), during (e.g., pace of discussion), or after (e.g., decision to repeat a particular topic) the class interaction. A good instructor, therefore, is one who makes good decisions. It follows that good decision makers need to be provided with knowledge based on reliable and valid information.

Traditional formative evaluation approaches, however, typically fail to provide timely and meaningful information required to make these decisions. Statistical results generated by an evaluation are often unwieldy and the narrative results too general to facilitate improvement. Evaluative measures generally focus on the "average" student, rather than on the results and needs of each individual student. Learning styles, motivation, experience, and other individual differences among students are often ignored in data gathering, or are analyzed well after the course has ended.

What is needed in higher education are formative evaluation methodologies that are as innovative as the current educational technologies. These methodologies should include reliable and valid evaluative measures, frequently administered to learners, with meaningful results and interpretation made immediately and conveniently available to the appropriate stakeholders. This form of evaluation would help instructors improve the delivery of learning in "midstream" with a minimal time investment. Students would receive feedback to their feedback ("closing the loop"), thus removing obstacles to learning and demonstrating that students are an important part of the learning process. Administrators would receive more useful information for course and faculty evaluations. This methodology would inform the summative evaluation by allowing evaluators to systematically collect, analyze, store, and compare a wealth of data from multiple courses and programs to make meaningful comparisons within and across programs to advance the field. Finally, innovative uses of evaluation might also spark pedagogical changes, such as shifting the definition of high-quality instruction from "students are satisfied" to "instructor uses student feedback to facilitate change."

EVALUATION INNOVATIONS IN PRACTICE

The Center for Twenty-first Century Conceptual Tools (TCCT), as described by Lesh, Byrne, and White (2003), houses an impressive array of learning technology and can support a wide range of courses and pedagogies. However, the TCCT does not support any similarly impressive evaluation mechanisms. In this chapter, I will describe a particular evaluation process called "embedded assessment" (Champagne, 1998), which would take advantage of the strengths of the TCCT and other technology-based classrooms. Embedded assessment has been successfully used in evaluating Learning Anytime Anywhere Partnerships (LAAP) projects for the Fund for the Improvement of Postsecondary Education (FIPSE) to assist faculty, organize and manage student feedback and information, and improve the Web-based learning experience.

In a small traditional classroom, there are few obstacles to interactions among students and instructors. A good instructor can read the body language of each student to determine when a point should be restated or when an illustrative example should be given. A good instructor can adapt the style and pace of the classroom engagement based on the direction or passion of the discussions. There are a limited number of sources competing for students' attention (i.e., instructor, instructional materials, other students), permitting students more time for thoughtful reflection, a key characteristic for differentiating a constructivist learning environment (Jonassen, 1994).

The TCCT is a highly interactive and technically oriented environment, less conducive to reflection. Students are asked to manage information presented by instructors, teammates, students at remote locations, Web sites, remote information centers, and other sources. It is difficult to attend to all these various sources of information, yet the concept of attention is a key component of most theories of learning (e.g., Bandura, 1986). How can attention be maintained and reflection occur in this highly interactive environment? Can all students differentiate between facts, informed opinion, and speculation among these information sources?

The TCCT is also more challenging for instructors. The ability to read body language and gather feedback from students, particularly those off-site, is difficult. How can teachers obtain meaningful feedback from students to make good pedagogical decisions?

It is unlikely that all students, regardless of background, experience, maturity, and other individual characteristics, learn equally well in the TCCT environment. It is also unlikely that all students possess high levels of motivation, willingness to share and collaborate, desire to build on the collective knowledge, and other characteristics typically ascribed to successful Web-based learning. At what point are students ready to learn in this fashion? Is the TCCT appropriate for all types of courses?

Each of these questions point to the need for evaluative tools that can provide frequent feedback and an evaluation system that can efficiently collect, store, analyze, and interpret information. There is considerable demand for the benefits of feedback tools. In the most comprehensive survey of online teaching, Bonk (2001) found that faculty with Web-based teaching experience perceived a high need and placed a high value on online tools that provided interactive feedback.

EMBEDDED ASSESSMENT

Embedded assessment is an online tool that contains a wide range of evaluative measures that instructors and evaluators can use to facilitate teaching and accelerate learning. Embedded assessment systems serve as knowledge centers, housing various attitudinal, behavioral, and learning measures, distributing those measures to students when needed and immediately delivering organized and meaningful results to instructors, teaching assistants, evaluators, and other stakeholders in a Web-based learning program. Although embedded assessment systems could also house quizzes, examinations, and other performance measures, the objective of the system is faculty assistance, program improvement, and addressing student needs, rather than as an online testing system.

In the TCCT-based courses, there are multiple stakeholders, including faculty leaders, faculty mentors, technicians, teaching assistants, administrators, and students. The embedded assessment system would provide different levels of access and content for different stakeholders. Each stakeholder would receive the type of knowledge they need, when they need it, in the form that they need it, and in the amount that they need it. For example, teaching assistants might continually and independently monitor the Web-based results and address each student concern or problem as it occurs; technicians might periodically check e-mail containing a summary of problems with the course Web site reported by students; faculty leaders might download student comments or individual student learning measures at the end of each class engagement; and administrators might print an anonymous summary of results of all quantitative measures at the end of each course. This system would improve communication among stakeholders and close the feedback loop by providing timely responses to all stakeholder questions and concerns.

The embedded assessment system would be accessible by Web browser via passwords given to all stakeholders of a TCCT-based course. The system would be highly scalable, housing any number of evaluative measures and an almost unlimited amount of data. The common database would permit timely and appropriate comparisons within and between courses. For example, faculty leaders would compare learning outcomes across multiple courses, faculty mentors would compare class results across time, and the TCCT evaluator would compare multiple administrations of a single measure.

The results of a traditional formative evaluation are not available until the data is analyzed and the results are generated. The embedded assessment system would deliver immediate textual and graphical results in both online and hard-copy formats. This richer and timelier knowledge would reduce the number of written interim reports to stakeholders. The automation of distribution and analysis of evaluative measures would free the TCCT evaluator to focus on more integrative evaluation questions.

In the remainder of this chapter, I will focus on the application of embedded assessment to the Distributed Doctoral Program in Mathematics Education (DDPME), which is conducted via the TCCT. It should be noted that this discussion also applies to most distance learning and technology-based learning programs. The steps to integrating an embedded assessment follow a "who-what-when-how-where" framework.

WHO: THE STAKEHOLDERS

Stakeholders are the individuals who will use the results of the evaluation to make decisions. The stakeholders in the DDPME exist across a variety of positions within and

TABLE 13.1

DDPME example of the Who, What, and When of Embedded Assessment

	Measure Administered Through Embedded Assessment		
Stakeholders	Utility of Web Site	Faculty Attitudes	Learning-Styles Battery
Primary stakeholder (course instructor)	Printed full report upon completion	Printed full report upon completion	Printed partial report upon completion
Other faculty leaders		Printed partial report at end of course	Printed partial report upon completion
Faculty mentors		Printed partial report at end of course	Printed partial report upon completion
Teaching assistants			Online raw data immediately
TCCT technical staff	Online raw data immediately		
Chairs at partner institutions	Printed report at end of course	Printed full report upon completion	Printed full report at end of course
Students	Online summary upon completion		

across institutions, including students, faculty leaders, and mentors (residing at primary and secondary sites), administrators at each institution, teaching assistants, and TCCT technical support personnel. However, the needs and interests of the primary stakeholder must be the focus of the evaluation (Champagne & Wisher, 2000; Cummings, 1998). Because the purpose of embedded assessment is to provide knowledge to faculty so that good decisions can be made, the faculty leader would be considered the primary stakeholder.

Secondary stakeholders, those who would benefit from the knowledge gained from the evaluation, would also be identified. The first column in Table 13.1 lists the stakeholders in the DDPME. In a traditional evaluation, addressing the individual needs of multiple stakeholders would be time-consuming. Distributing a general report to all stakeholders would save time, but would be of limited value if the results were intended for the specific needs of the primary stakeholder. An embedded assessment, however, permits multiple levels of access to results. Each stakeholder receives customized reports targeted to their individual needs, providing meaningful knowledge.

WHAT: THE OBJECTIVES, MEASURES, AND RESULTS

Evaluation objectives of the primary stakeholder must be specific, measurable, and obtainable. Evaluation objectives of other stakeholders must not conflict with those of the primary stakeholder. Appropriate measures of attitudes, learning, behavior, and other performance indicators related to these objectives must be reliable, accurate, and practical, and can be constructed or obtained from published or nonpublished sources.

An embedded assessment system can store an enormous amount of data and share a vast number of evaluative measures. Evaluators can: (1) choose among measures already created; (2) edit existing measures to fit the primary stakeholder's objectives; or (3) create new measures from scratch. Types of measures would include surveys (e.g., faculty attitudes), self-reports (e.g., student perceptions), objective tests (e.g., learning outcomes), questionnaires (e.g., learning styles), behavioral measures (e.g., retention), and cost/efficiency measures (e.g., utility of a Web site).

Qualitative responses are especially important and are well suited to an embedded assessment. Comments and explanations can be easily tied to quantitative responses, permitting insight into an individual response or the pattern of responses. A survey of graduate management courses found that students typed an average of four times as many comments (62 words per student) as students completing a paper-based version of the same evaluation form at the end of class (Champagne & Wisher, 2001). In addition, comments delivered through the embedded assessment were automatically sorted by categories and could be searched by key words, generating individual results and patterns of recommendations. Comments written on the paper-based form needed to be retyped to hide recognizable handwriting and provided no means of organizing the information for the stakeholders' benefit.

Stakeholders would receive various levels of reports. Some stakeholders will simply want an overall report of findings; others will want detailed analysis of each measure; and others may want the raw data to conduct additional analysis. The breadth and depth of results and the type of analysis can be easily customized in the embedded assessment. The format of the results (e.g., online graphics, printed copy, and detailed statistics) can be tailored to each stakeholder.

Table 13.1 illustrates three possible measures to implement in the DDPME: utility of Web site, faculty attitudes, and learning styles battery. The utility of Web site measure would survey students' opinions regarding ease of navigation, availability of information, and usefulness of the DDPME home page and related Web sites. The faculty attitudes survey would consist of self-report items regarding the collaborative DDPME effort, availability of resources, suggested improvements, and related questions to be answered by the faculty leaders and mentors. The learning styles battery would consist of several nonoverlapping measures of students' preferred way of using their intellectual abilities (Sternberg & Grigorenko, 1997).

Research suggests that students whose learning styles are compatible with the instructional technology and teaching style available in the classroom may perform higher than students whose learning styles are not compatible (Furnham, 1992; Ingham, 1991). Because there currently exists over 80 published and validated learning style measures, the choice of measure is an important task. Based on the validation information and dimensions of the measures, and the structure of the DDPME environment, measures such as the Grasha-Reichmann Student Learning Style Scale (GRSLSS: Reichmann & Grasha, 1974) and the Learning Orientation Grade Orientation scale (LOGO II: Eison, 1981) would be appropriate.

An example of the amount and type of reported results for each stakeholder can be found at the intersection of each row and column in Table 13.1. Not all stakeholders would need to view the results of each measure. For example, TCCT technical staff would receive the raw data containing each student's comments and responses regarding the usefulness and concerns with the course Web site, but the teaching assistants, who do not have the ability to act on this information, would not receive these results. The primary stakeholder would receive a final printed report to compare student concerns with future courses once the technicians had addressed these concerns. Because the purpose of student comments is for faculty development, these comments would be available to faculty leaders and mentors, but not shared with administrators.

WHEN: FREQUENCY OF MEASURES AND REPORTS

All measures must be converted to a Web-based format such as HTML or ASP to be used in an embedded assessment. The primary stakeholder must decide the timing and schedule for delivering the measures (e.g., before or during class, twice per course). Each stakeholder must decide when they wish to view the reports or data (e.g., immediately, on completion, at end of course).

An example of the timing of reported results for each stakeholder in the DDPME is found at the intersection of each row and column in Table 13.1. For example, in terms of the faculty attitudes survey, the faculty leaders and mentors would share all comments to make adjustments based on the results provided by their colleagues. The chairs at the partner institutions would receive an executive summary of the quantitative results with the individual comments suppressed. Teaching assistants would not receive any information regarding this measure because they would not be able to act on the information.

HOW: ANNOUNCING AND COMPLETING THE MEASURES

The manner in which data is gathered from students, faculty, partners, and other populations is consistent (i.e., measures are accessed via a Web browser), but the process for announcing the measures can vary. No single method is universally more effective than another and is a choice the evaluator and primary stakeholder must make.

Choices include: (1) sending an e-mail containing an embedded URL associated with the measure; (2) linking the measure to the course home page; or (3) having the instructor verbally announce the URL to students. The pros and cons of each approach in terms of ease of use, technical complexity, and motivation of users must be addressed. The evaluator of the DDPME, in conjunction with the faculty leader would also have to make decisions regarding the use and type of incentives to complete the measures, the method and frequency of reminders for those individuals who have not responded, the wording of instructions, and designation of the individual(s) responsible for addressing questions or problems that arise with the delivery or content of the measures.

WHERE: THE EMBEDDED ASSESSMENT

The embedded assessment serves as a common source for delivering measures that will address the objectives of the evaluation. Once the questions of who, what, when, and how are answered, the system automatically administers measures to selected individuals at different times and with different levels of urgency. The system is also a place for accessing, communicating, and distributing knowledge to all stakeholders. The decision of where is made by determining the level and degree of access by each stakeholder. User IDs and passwords not only protect the data and prevent unwarranted access, but also reduce the amount of irrelevant data distributed to each stakeholder. By receiving only the knowledge they need in an organized and meaningful format, better decisions can be made by each stakeholder. The faculty leader of the DDPME course would hold the highest level of access with the ability to view all results and reports. Teaching assistants need to conduct deeper analysis at an individual student level and would have access only to the learning style battery results. Students would be allowed to see how their feedback compares to other students and would be given access only to a summary of results for the utility of Web-site measure.

DISCUSSION

Although the need for rigorous evaluation in distance learning programs has been widely established, it is usually poorly performed or conducted post hoc. Embedded assessment, a system centered on the concept of feedback, is best used in conjunction with a thoughtful evaluation plan. By rapidly organizing feedback into knowledge, it can successfully assist faculty, address individual student needs, and improve course content and delivery.

Innovative ideas, tools, and technology for Web-based learning have multiplied over the past decade. In the same time period, innovations in evaluative measures and methodology have consisted solely of the idea to convert existing paper-and-pencil measures to an online format. Even the timing of evaluative measures has failed to improve, as colleges continue to deliver autopsy measures, frustrating both instructors and students, providing neither with the feedback required to make necessary changes while classes are in session.

Successful technology-based classrooms will continue to require a stronger and more comprehensive evaluation component. Embedded assessment serves students, instructors, and administrators alike by removing obstacles to learning, providing a means to rapidly improve delivery, and reducing the costs of evaluation. Incorporating innovative evaluation tools into existing learning tools will likely spark pedagogical changes and assist schools in objectively judging the effectiveness of technology-based classrooms.

REFERENCES

Bandura, A. (1986). *Social foundations of thought and action: A social cognitive theory.* Englewood Cliffs, NJ: Prentice Hall.

Bonk, C. J. (2001). *Online teaching in an online world.* [Online]. Bloomington, IN: CourseShare.com. Available: http://courseshare.com/Reports.php

Champagne, M. V. (1998). Dynamic evaluation of distance education courses. In *Proceedings of the 14th annual conference on distance teaching and learning,* (pp. 89–96), Madison, WI.

Champagne, M. V., & Wisher, R. A. (2000). Design considerations for distance learning evaluations. In K. Mantyla (Ed.), *The 2000–2001 ASTD distance learning yearbook: The newest trends and technologies* (pp. 261–286). New York: McGraw-Hill.

Champagne, M. V., & Wisher, R. A. (2001). Online evaluation of distance learning: Benefits, practices and solutions. In K. Mantyla & J. Woods (Eds.), *The 2001 ASTD distance learning yearbook* (pp. 360–376). New York: McGraw-Hill.

Cummings, O. W. (1998). What stakeholders want to know. In S. Brown & C. Seidner (Eds.), *Evaluation corporate training: Models and issues* (pp. 41–62). Boston: Kluwer.

Eison, J. A. (1981). A new instrument for assessing students' orientations towards grades and learning. *Psychological Reports, 48,* 919–924.

Furnham, A. (1992). Personality and learning style: A study of three instruments. *Personality and Individual Differences, 13,* 429–438.

Hmieleski, K. M., & Champagne, M. V. (2000). Plugging in to course evaluation [Online]. *The Technology Source.* Available: http://ts.mivu.org:8000/default.asp?show=article&id=795

Ingham, J. M. (1991). Matching instruction with employee perceptual preference significantly increases training effectiveness. *Human Resource Quarterly, 2,* 53–64.

Jonassen, D. (1994). Thinking technology. *Educational Technology, 34,* 34–37.

Klein, H. (1989). An integrated control theory model of work motivation. *Academy of Management, 14,* 150–172.

Kronholm, E. A., Wisher, R. A., Curnow, C. K., & Poker, F. (1999). *The transformation of a distance learning training enterprise to an Internet base: From advertising to evaluation.* Paper presented at the Northern Arizona University NAU/web99 Conference, Flagstaff, AZ.

Mosston, M., & Ashworth, S. (1990). *The spectrum of teaching styles from command to discovery.* White Plains, NY: Longman.

Riechmann, S. W., & Grasha, A. F. (1974). A rational approach to developing and assessing the construct validity of a student learning style scales instrument. *The Journal of Psychology, 87,* 213–223.

Sternberg, R. J., & Grigorenko E. L. (1997). Are cognitive styles still in style? *American Psychologist, 52,* 700–712.

Wisher, R. A., & Champagne, M. V. (2000). Distance learning and training: An evaluation perspective. In D. Fletcher & S. Tobias (Eds.), *A handbook for business, industry, government, and the military* (pp. 385–409). New York, NY: Macmillan.

Open Discussion of Chapter 12

Dick Lesh: Let me begin the discussion by commenting on a couple of topics Matt raised. First, the role of theory. We call what we produce *models* and we take a *modeling* perspective. It comes out of Dewey and the pragmatists at least as much as out of Vygotsky and Piaget and others. The premiere thing that the pragmatists were talking about—they did not use the word *model,* but they could have—is that they had a pretty strong belief that grand theories rarely should or can inform real decision-making as most real decisions need to draw on a variety of perspectives and theories. For example, a teacher starts out making a psychological decision about doing something, but that turns into a classroom management problem, which turns into a parent problem, which turns into an administrative problem, which turns into something that changes the psychology of the situation. Engineers regularly tell us that interesting problems don't fall into a single discipline. They have to take into account costs, as well as quality, as well as something else, and often those are in conflict. They need to find some way to reach a balance and to draw on two things that are completely different and put them together.

A modeling perspective doesn't say that you don't need powerful theories to draw on, but it does say don't expect one. So a modeling perspective tries to come up with kind of a blue-collar theory. If it is a theory at all, it is a theory that focuses on the decision making that we really make as program designers and teachers make. I haven't figured out nice ways to talk about all this yet, because I am definitely not saying theory is not important. Theory building is very important. If we are going to get anywhere, we have to build theory, because that is knowledge. On the other hand, our job is to build programs, to build other kinds of things, and don't expect that to happen using just one theoretical perspective. It simply won't do.

My second point is to emphasize the importance of thinking about systems. You need to think of a classroom as a bunch of conceptual systems—you guys are not only a bunch of people, you are a bunch of conceptual systems. If I want those systems to evolve, I have to have diversity, but I also have to have selection. I also have to have spread of those that survive, and I've got to have some way of preserving it. So it's true that in some respects we are pushing our instructors to put together interaction situations that look a bit chaotic, because you see an explosion of ideas. On the other hand, there is a rapid selection, and the instructor doesn't have to be the one filtering all of this. We try to off-load as much as we can.

To give you one simple example, we have had Internet-based interactions where everybody is sitting in the same room. So we could put all of you on a computer in groups, and we could all be watching the teacher teach live up in Calumet. Each group would have a whiteboard writing comments, so that at the end we would compare comments and flash your whiteboard up. We would see an explosion of interesting ideas if we did that, but there would also be a bunch of ways to test your thinking. It doesn't have to be the teacher testing everything. So getting the teacher out of that role is one of the things we need to do.

Now that isn't a distance thing. But what we're trying to do here—what I was trying to emphasize here—is interaction types. Once we figure out how to do those, then we try to port them out and use them at a distance and maybe to assemble whole programs. But my assumption up-front is going to be is that most of our programs—at least the ones that I am looking at—are not going to be entirely Internet based. They are not going to be entirely face-to-face. They are going to blend the best of both of those. The question then is how, when, and why. Those are the biggies, I think.

John Bransford: At a meta-theoretical level, I think that you are a constructivist. You are just not a naive constructivist. (*Group laughs.*)

Dick Lesh: Well, in the last chapter of my book, I spent 30 pages denying it. (*Group laughs.*)

John Bransford: That is naive constructivism. I just wanted to reinforce your idea of creating artifacts that have generalities. I think it is one of the things we learned in our Jasper series, where we might have a video on rescuing an eagle and you have to do all this computation in math. It only solves one problem, rescuing the eagle. But that is just computing for a situation. We want students to develop tools for solving problems like these, so we restructured all the problems. Now . . . she has a company, and she is in the rescue and delivery service, and you have to work smart and invent tools that can off-load all the problem solving. You create graphs, charts, spreadsheets and that generality. That has had a huge effect on the kinds of information that kids get out of it.

Let me also comment on your view of classrooms built with or without a theory. Another way to think about it is that they are always built with a theory. Usually the theory is tacit, probably inconsistent. If you can make it explicit, then you can figure out how to make it better. Designing for flexibility is kind of a theory in a way, or at least a model of what you want to do.

Dick Lesh: We found the language of models and modeling to be sufficiently focused that people from many different points of view can fit into it and actually behave differently because they are doing it. It puts enough constraints on but it doesn't put too many. That is really the trick.

John Bransford: Fair enough.

Linda Polin: There were a couple of things that intrigued me. One was the digital library case study by students, for students and all those good things. I thought of it is an intriguing junior level peer review and social construction of knowledge. I want to steal it, actually. (*Laughs.*) I was wondering if you could say a little more about what it looked like when kids make those decisions and how they sort of get there.

Dick Lesh: One of my research projects used this multitiered approach where teachers were developing case studies that they thought would help prove their claim that their students were learning higher order things that the tests weren't showing. They claimed that there were some kids that were real good that the tests weren't identifying. So

I told them, if these problems aren't doing it, design problems that will. I did that probably with seven different groups, each working half a year. They developed not only problems, but principles for writing them. One of the principles that they felt would make or break a problem was that you not only have to have students produce a complex artifact, but there also needed to be a client and a purpose—a realistic situation.

Almost no math or science problems have that. You know how they say: Here is the volleyball stuff—find the average. For whom? For what reason? You don't know, and if you don't know for whom and for what reason, how can you possibly know if they want my 5-minute answer, or my 5-hour answer, or my 5-year answer? One of the keys in all the modeling activities—whether they were for kids, teachers, or anyone else who participates in our stuff—is to have a client and a purpose. Once you got that, then kids can put themselves in the role of the client for the purpose and make judgments of how it works. That is the single thing that makes it fly. Unfortunately, you are not going to find a rack of problems that are going to have that characteristic. It takes one person a month to write an activity.

Peter Shea: I was interested in the issue of scaleability especially in the context of your PT^3, where you have video in somebody's classroom and a student teacher goes to that classroom. How do you scale that kind of thing?

Dick Lesh: We were actually already faced with scale meltdown because we couldn't provide all the clinical experience we were supposed to. So one thing we had to do is to say we're going to cut those back by about half—just an arbitrary number, I don't know what it was exactly—so instead of sending, say, 30 people out to see 30 different classrooms, we are going to send one teacher where one part of the clinical experience is 30 people watching that one classroom. Then you have some other experiences where you will go out and see individuals. So we're already at scale meltdown. I think we can handle this with Purdue's program, where we might turn half of the clinical experiences into things that use Internet kinds of technology. We can have our students do file sharing and interviews or be a tutor to kids up in a school site. We just plain couldn't do that before.

Peter Shea: Do you imagine those videos could be used not in real time?

Dick Lesh: One of the things we keep experimenting with is whether there is any reason that it needs to be real time. We want some portion to be real time, because one of the things that we found is for the 30 people to be making observations it is important to then be able to talk to the teacher immediately and say, "I saw this. Why did you do that?" to get that feedback fast is critical for some things. Do we need it everytime? I doubt it. If we can pull it off, then we do.

Linda Polin: The thing that intrigued me in your modeling cycles was the notion of roles. Certainly, that is an issue in the education world—in teacher ed. I mean, one of the things that we always ask students when they are studying community of practice and it's curriculum is, what is the practice of schooling? There is a huge debate. A lot of it has to do with roles. What is the role of the student? What is the role of the teacher? Who is what to whom? What is the relationship between the roles? I like your strategy. The problems should be a junior version of legitimate issues. Then I was thinking, Well, that is interesting in teacher ed. and teaching and K–12 and all that. But a lot of us aren't just dealing with that—we are all dealing with people who are professionals or practicing something or engaged in something. We need to be exploring the role relations of those students. I was thinking in terms of my own program. There is finally a better reason for having our exhibitions than the reason we use, which is that we needed to have something that is public to be sure people realize, "Yeah, they are just not giving out degrees." (*Group laughs.*) You put them in a role where they actually have to talk to other people about education. Stand up and give different information. Do a different role than teachers or educators typically have. They were in the practice of mini AERA poster sessions, in a sense. That was really interesting if we were trying to impact identity and inform people. The more we can move them out of roles they are already in and get them to see things with new eyes, the better this is for them.

Dick Lesh: As far as transferring to new audiences in concerned, I think it helps enormously that we are actually adopting these problems. We are starting with the aeronautics department and the business schools at Purdue. We go around Indiana, where I grew up, and say, "If you want to prepare for Purdue, why don't you do what Purdue does right now? They like that.

John Bransford: One question. When I deal with mathematicians often, they kill me as soon as I put application into mathematics. Do you run into that problem?

Dick Lesh: Sure. But these modeling listening activities are not what they are thinking of as applications. Because when they think applications, they teach something, and then you apply it. I think for good reason that good mathematicians don't like the traditional application problems. I'm afraid they are right in some respects. It's not that you couldn't teach mathematics so it would be useful—that would be nice. They don't very often. But this is very different than that.

John Bransford: So they would like modeling?

Dick Lesh: No. Nobody likes it. This is why we talk about the evolving expert. We tell them, "you think you have strong opinion? You think you are right, then fine, you have to play with us for a semester and help us devise things." They have never had to look at student responses before. So we try to get them to express their thinking in a form that is testable, whereas most mathematicians do not want to do that. They like to express their opinions in a form that nobody can test. It's the nature with us math guys.

(End of session)

V

Scaling Up

14

Collaborative Learning at Monterrey Tech–Virtual University

José Rafael López Islas
Monterrey Tech–Virtual University

The Instituto Tecnológico de Monterrey (known in English as Monterrey Tech, or MT) is a Mexican private university system with campuses in 29 cities in Mexico and more than 100 satellite receiving sites in as many cities in Mexico and nine other Latin American countries. Throughout its Virtual University (VU), MT offers a variety of educational services to more than 80,000 students per year, with more than 5,000 of them working on graduate degrees in business, engineering, computer science, and education. The courses in these graduate programs are the focus of this paper.

At its inception in 1989, the original VU model was based on satellite-delivered lectures with some degree of student–instructor interaction through a proprietary e-mail system known as Remote Interaction System (SIR, in Spanish). By 1996, most courses had their own web pages, and in some of them, faculty included access to threaded discussions, for both academic purposes and informal discussions (cyber café and the like).

In 1998, the VU revised its learning model and identified four critical components: (1) lectures, which take place either as a video session delivered through satellite or through a combination of Internet and CD-ROM, (2) autonomous learning activities carefully designed from an instructional design standpoint, (3) collaborative learning activities, conducted mostly in an asynchronous mode using a variety of Internet tools, and (4) tutoring, which allows participants to interact with an expert and receive feedback and support in a timely fashion. According to an institutional policy, all courses had to include the four components as best as it was appropriate for the nature of each course. Faculty were trained and assisted in the redesign process by a team of instructional designers.

Of all four components, collaborative learning represented the main challenge due to the difficulty of designing collaborative activities for a distributed learning system and the lack of familiarity of faculty with this online pedagogy. Collaborative learning required a revision of the instructional design model to take advantage of the asynchronous communication tools that complemented the synchronous satellite sessions.

This chapter is the story of the VU journey in elaborating and implementing this pedagogical model. We begin with a discussion of the theoretical foundations of the model. Here, we take as a given that meaningful student collaboration is an essential component of online learning in academic courses; that is, the collaborative construction of knowledge is essential.

Next, we examine the initial implementation of the "requirement" for discussion, examining the variability in the amount and nature of the discussion in courses. Through these early analyses, we identified best practices that helped to define a more appropriate instructional design model for collaborative learning.

As a result of this work, Monterrey Tech adopted problem-based learning (PBL). The second section of this chapter analyzes the initial results of VU's experience with PBL, as a recommended active learning technique that should be used to promote more relevant learning.

THEORETICAL FOUNDATIONS

A concept proposed by Collis and Moonen (2001) seems to engulf the kind of transformation that Monterrey Tech has experienced since the inception of its Virtual University. This concept is flexible learning, "a movement away from a situation in which key decisions about learning dimensions are made in advance by the instructor or institution, towards a situation where the learner has a range of options from which to choose with respect to these key dimensions" (p. 10). Although "not everything can be flexible and still be scalable beyond a small number of students" (p. 10), the development of a flexible learning model has implications at all levels, from pedagogical issues to administrative, university-wide strategic decision making. Network technologies are at the core of the implementation of a flexible learning model, not determining it but as an enabler.

This paper concentrates on the pedagogical dimension. Therefore, the review of the literature covers four topics: (1) a notion of how people learn online at the higher education level, (2) the foundations of collaborative learning as a process of social construction of knowledge, (3) the role of an active learning strategy such as PBL as the pedagogical design that guides collaborative learning, and (4) the notion of communities of inquiry in the context of social interactions with a learning purpose that occur through asynchronous, computer-based communication.

Learning As Acquisition and Participation

Sfard (1998) identifies two types of educational models: the acquisition model and the participation model. In the knowledge acquisition model, a student learns predetermined concepts delivered through some sort of medium (including a face-to-face situation). This individualized perspective on learning emphasizes the instructional design of educational materials with the purpose of facilitating the acquisition of predefined concepts. On the other hand, the participation model recognizes that learning involves becoming a member of a community of practice. Rather that focusing on acquiring predetermined concepts, this social perspective of learning emphasizes the process by which an individual learns from the community of practice while contributing to the development of new knowledge that could not be predetermined.

Besides identifying these models, Sfard (1998) argues that higher education should be based on both. Although the participation model contributes to meaningful learning, the members should acquire the foundational concepts on which the community of practice is based before engaging in interaction processes. Otherwise, interaction may not be meaningful.

As the learning acquisition model has been prevalent for many years, there is an abundant experience (as well as literature) regarding the instructional design of educational materials (Dick & Carey, 1990), particularly those based on multimedia (Schwier & Misanchuk, 1993). However, there is much less experience designing processes of social construction of knowledge, particularly when interactions are supposed to occur through a computer network. The most common decision at colleges is to simply add the Internet as a medium for interaction among students and teachers that complements regular activities.

Computer-mediated communication (CMC) has been extensively researched (Rafaeli, Sudweeks & McLaughlin, 1995; Rice & Love, 1987; Sproull & Kiesler, 1991; Sudweeks, Collins & December, 1995; Walther, 1992). Most research has concentrated on understanding the emergence of interaction patterns when people participate in CMC, including issues such as how the participants manage emotions, how leadership emerges, and how participants discuss, collaborate, and deal with agreement and disagreement. However, CMC researchers have traditionally assumed that a "characteristic of CMC groups is the democratic nature of the mode in which people interact" (Sudweeks & Rafaeli, 1996, p. 118). Therefore, more remains to be learned about CMC when groups interact with a specific purpose and under the formal direction of someone with authority, such as in a collaborative learning activity led by a teacher.

A common complaint by students and faculty about electronic bulletin boards and other online interaction spaces is that frequently, interaction does not evolve into meaningful discussions, and participation becomes scarce. Sometimes, a look at the discussion boards shows isolated messages that do not relate to one another and, therefore, it is hard to argue that such a discussion has yielded relevant learning to the participants. Clearly, the sole availability of technological resources, such as newsgroups or other group interaction software, does not guarantee academic success, in the same way that just putting together a group of students inside a classroom without the guidance of faculty or at least a clear purpose does not automatically result in a productive experience.

In traditional, democratic CMC, research shows that a group of strangers can work together online, but it also recognizes that "an extensive coordinating overhead is necessary to resolve conflict and foster cooperation" (Sudweeks & Rafaeli, 1996, p. 132). This is particularly important in a learning situation, where the general purpose of the CMC activity is defined by the teacher, who also facilitates the process by providing coordination and resolving conflict. Group learning activities, particularly those that occur through the Internet, should be designed with a pedagogical model in mind. The pedagogical foundations for designing online collaborative learning activities can be found in the literature regarding the process of social construction of knowledge.

THE PROCESS OF SOCIAL CONSTRUCTION OF KNOWLEDGE

According to the literature (Gunawardena, Lowe, & Anderson, 1997; Pinheiro, 1998; Slavin, 1995), collaborative activities enrich the learning experience when they promote the social construction of knowledge. Pinheiro (1998) defines collaborative learning as "the process of students working in teams to pursue knowledge and learning" (p. 118). This definition is wide enough to include organized, purposeful discussion, as well as solving problems and cases in teams. Learning is no longer viewed as a mere transmission of knowledge from a teacher to a student, but a process of knowledge construction in which each participant contributes and benefits from the ideas shared by the group. Collaborative learning is a form of what Sfard (1998) calls the "participation model of learning."

At the core of the notion of learning as a social process resides a concept proposed by Vygotsky (1978), known as "the zone of proximal development." This concept is defined by its author as "the distance between the actual developmental level as determined by independent problem solving and the level of potential development as determined by problem solving under adult guidance or in collaboration with more capable peers."

This notion is important for several reasons. First, it recognizes the dual nature of learning, which is both individual and social, although the social component is the one that helps learners to reach their true potential for learning. Second, it explains why a pedagogical model requires a combination of autonomous (or individual) learning, teaching (both as lecture and tutoring), and collaborative learning. It is interesting that with the advent of interactive communication technologies, distance education is now capable of constructing a pedagogical model with all these components, as opposed to the limited nature of the old forms of distance learning, such as correspondence studies, with their dependence on autonomous learning. Third, it advances the idea of active learning as a result of solving meaningful problems, rather than the traditional transmission model of education.

The premise of the Monterrey Tech distance learning system is that all components of its pedagogical model—including collaborative learning as a process of social construction of knowledge—can take place at a distance at least as well as in a face-to-face situation. Gunawardena, Lowe, and Anderson (1997) developed an interaction analysis model for examining social construction of knowledge in computer conferencing. This model has five phases, each with several types of messages:

- Sharing and comparing information: observation or opinion, definition, description, or identification of a problem
- Discovery and exploration of dissonance: cognitive dissonance, defined as inconsistency between a new observation and the learner's existing framework of knowledge and thinking skills
- Negotiation of meaning/coconstruction of knowledge: negotiation to clarify the meaning of terms, identification of agreement and disagreement areas, and coconstruction of knowledge
- Testing and modification of proposed synthesis: testing the coconstructed knowledge and comparison of formal data, existing cognitive schema, personal experiences, and contradictory testimony in the literature
- Agreement statements of newly constructed meaning: summarization of agreements, application of new knowledge, and metacognitive statements by the participants illustrating their understanding.

This model is not only useful to analyze online processes of social construction of knowledge, but it may also function as a cognitive strategy that a group could apply to guide its collaborative process. The process could be applied to both solving problems and discussing ideas with the objective of reaching an agreement that integrates the contributions of the members of the group.

Collaborative learning makes sense only when the nature of the task falls into the "zone of proximal development" (Vygotsky, 1978). Otherwise, students could learn more by themselves in an autonomous mode. Designing collaborative learning activities represents an important challenge, and the use of an active learning technique, such as problem-based learning (PBL), may be helpful to construct more meaningful scenarios for collaborative learning.

Problem-Based Learning as a Pedagogical Strategy

Problem-based learning is an active learning, student-centered approach that anchors learning in concrete problems (Savery and Duffy, 1995). Students work on ill defined problems through free inquiry and a social process of knowledge construction (Antonietti, 2001, p. 344). This approach to learning is also related to cognitive constructivism (Duffy & Jonassen, 1992), a view that stresses the importance of prior knowledge and social interaction in the active and reflective process of learning. An important form of social interaction for learning is the cooperative (or collaborative) learning approach (Slavin, 1995).

Another critical form of interaction is between faculty and students. For groups participating in a PBL situation, Barrows and Tamblyn (1980) propose the notion of tutors as facilitators rather than as instructors. According to them, if the problems that trigger the process are well designed, what a good tutor needs, instead of being an expert on the subject matter, is to know how to facilitate a group process—an assertion that has been disputed. For example, Neville (1999) after reviewing the research on the role of tutoring in PBL, concluded that the "degree of tutor content knowledge required for effective learning facilitation in PBL is not an absolute quantity but needs to be tailored to the particular student groups' level of prior knowledge and familiarity with PBL" (p. 11). Therefore, it is necessary to have a strategy to organize and administer the tutoring function in a PBL context.

In summary, the literature suggests that two critical aspects of PBL in a distributed learning model are related to the teaching function: the design of problematic situations or scenarios and the role of tutors as facilitators of group processes.

Communities of Inquiry

According to Garrison, Anderson and Archer (2000), "a worthwhile educational experience is embedded within a Community of Inquiry that is composed of teachers and students" (p. 3). Learning occurs in this community as a result of the interaction of "three essential elements: cognitive presence, social presence, and teaching presence" (p. 3). This notion is important, as it recognizes that collaborative learning is more than a cognitive process. The social–emotional dimension of group process, and the presence of someone—usually a teacher—who assumes the role of designing and facilitating the process, as well as providing direct instruction, complement the cognitive dimension, as previously discussed, based on the Gunawardena, Lowe, and Anderson (1997) model for the analysis of the social construction of knowledge process.

The notion of community is also important. Rheingold (1993) coined the notion of a "virtual community," and several authors have adapted this notion to the educational environment (Harasim, 1990; Hiltz, 1998; Palloff & Pratt, 1999; Turoff, 1995). From the perspective of a learning community or a community of inquiry, online education transcends earlier conceptions of computer-based learning as individualized, behaviorist transmission of knowledge and becomes a learning experience potentially as rich (or richer) as residential, face-to-face education. Moreover, the community perspective provides a larger context for collaborative learning. Instead of designing isolated learning activities, faculty and instructional designers may attempt to create communities of inquiry where students and faculty can collaborate to socially construct significant knowledge.

In summary, collaborative learning as a participatory learning mode is a process of social construction of knowledge that takes place in the context of communities of inquiry. Besides a cognitive component—the social construction of knowledge process—there are two additional elements that play a significant role in the functioning of a community of inquiry: the social presence and the teaching presence. The teaching presence involves the design of the process—which could be improved by the adoption of an active learning didactic technique such as problem-based learning (PBL)—and the facilitation of the group process, as well as the provision of direct instruction.

The remainder of the chapter analyzes Monterrey Tech–Virtual University's experience with collaborative learning at two moments: during the first attempts to incorporate collaborative learning and during the current stage, when PBL has become a didactic technique used to design the collaborative learning activities for several Virtual University courses.

THE FIRST STAGE OF COLLABORATIVE LEARNING: EXPLORING ASYNCHRONOUS COLLABORATION

By 1999, practically all Virtual University (VU) faculty had responded to the Monterrey Tech mandate and included some sort of collaborative learning in their graduate and undergraduate courses. However, in most cases, it was just a novelty that took the form of optional threaded discussions that were frequently unrelated to the academic content of the courses. Moreover, as one might expect with "add on" discussions, in some courses student participation was very limited. However, in some cases, participation was not only heavy but substantive in terms of its relationship to course content. For example, in some cases, there were group activities, such as solving a problem or writing a group paper, that were truly collaborative. In other instances, students had to reflect on their own learning and discuss their thoughts to generate a group metacognitive statement. The initial experience with collaborative learning was analyzed both in quantitative and qualitative terms. First, it was necessary to understand student participation patterns to make decisions aimed at optimizing technical resources such as servers. Yet the most important research had to do with documenting the results of the initial attempt to design and execute collaborative learning activities in a distributed learning environment. This section discusses the results of both quantitative and qualitative analyses of the initial stage of collaborative learning at VU.

A Quantitative Analysis of Student Participation

Graduate student participation in collaborative learning activities was analyzed for the entire year of 1999. The analysis included all graduate programs in engineering, computer science, and business. During 1999, around 100 graduate courses were offered to

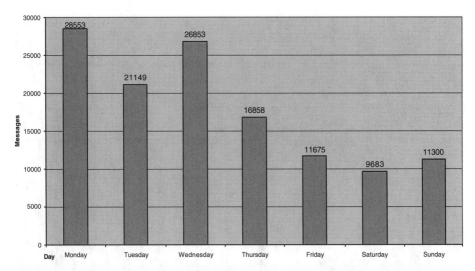

FIG. 14.1. Message distribution by day of the week. A total of 171,585 messages were registered, but information about the specific day when they were sent was available only for 126,574 of them ($n = $ 126,574 messages).

a student population of approximately 10,000 students (students typically take from two to four courses per year). A total of 171,500 messages related to collaborative learning activities were produced and exchanged by these students.

First, considering the logistics and demographics of online collaboration, we found that student participation is heavier during the first part of the week (Monday through Wednesday), declining notoriously toward the weekend (see Fig. 14.1). These data were helpful for the network engineers to make decisions about server resource allocation.

The data also show two peaks for student participation during the day: one around 8 and 9 p.m., mostly from Monday to Wednesday, and another around noon, especially during the weekends (Fig. 14.2).

These results suggest that most students work on their collaborative learning activities from the workplace right after work hours, or from home during the weekends. As expected, the distribution of messages by month varies according to the academic calendar, with peaks in February–March, May–June, and September–October (Fig. 14.3).

The primary focus of our analysis of these contributions is to understand the contexts that promote high participation. In that regard, the analysis of messages by course revealed that although student participation in some courses was heavy (up to 73 messages per student during the entire semester), in other courses participation was null (Table 14.1). Out of the 113 courses, five were labeled as "high participation," with over 70 messages per student; 25 courses as "medium participation," with over 35 messages per student; 40 courses as "low participation," with five messages per student; and 43 courses as "null participation," with less than one message per student. Evidently, although some faculty members complied with the policy of incorporating collaborative learning by creating newsgroups and online bulletin boards, they did not promote it and kept it as an optional, peripheral component of their courses.

The syllabi of the courses were reviewed, and some characteristics were found in the instructional design of the courses with high student participation. These highly participative courses included

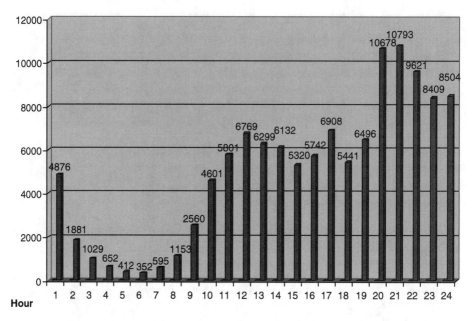

FIG. 14.2.   Message distribution by time of the day. A total of 171,585 messages were registered, but information about the time when they were sent was available only for 126,574 of them ($n = 126,574$ messages).

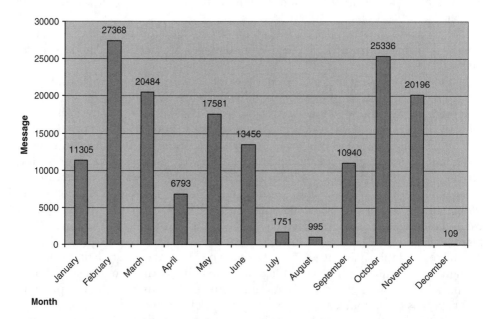

FIG. 14.3.   Message distribution by month. A total of 171,585 messages were registered, but information about the month when they were sent was available only for 156,314 of them ($n = 156,314$ messages).

TABLE 14.1
Course Classification According to Level of Student Participation

Type of Student Participation	Number of Courses	Number of Students	Total Messages	Messages per Student (Average)
High	5	1,180	51,169	76.76
Medium	25	3,238	68,365	37.16
Low	40	7,124	36,126	5.20
Null	43	3,637	881	0.16

Note. A total of 113 courses were classified according to the level of student participation. The total student population was 15,179, and the total amount of messages exchanged by these students was 156,541.

- *Specific directions about how to participate, as well as to what was expected from the students.* In most courses, directions for the collaborative learning activities were simple and general (for example, "Go to the bulletin board and discuss with your classmates a topic of interest for you"). The high-participation courses provided specific instructions about what the nature of the collaborative activity was, how students were expected to collaborate, and in some instances, students could find concrete suggestions about how to organize their collaborative process, step by step.
- *Participation that represented a considerable percentage of the final grade.* Although in the low or null participation courses, collaborative activities were optional or accounted for less than 5% of the grade, in the high-participation courses, collaborative activities represented from 20% to 70% of the final grade. This 70% was not because a single activity accounted for it by itself, but because it was a requirement to participate in other learning and evaluative activities that, together, accounted for 70% of the grade.
- *Students being able to obtain technical support for the use of the different technologies for interaction.* The high-participation courses offered specific directions and tutorials for the use of the technologies, so that lack of knowledge about the technology would not hinder student participation. Low- and null-participation courses did not offer technical support for the students.
- *Faculty members being actively involved in collaborative processes, both moderating group processes and modeling collaboration behavior.* An overview of the messages showed that in the high-participation courses, faculty (including tutors) actively participated in the process. Their participation usually took the form of modeling the kind of behaviors and messages that were expected from the students, and moderating the process when the group could not find a way to move ahead or solve a conflict. In the low and null participation courses, faculty participation was practically nonexistent.

A qualitative analysis was conducted to answer the obvious question of whether students participating in high-participation courses were actually engaged in a process of social construction of knowledge. The results of this analysis are presented in the next section.

Analyzing the Process of Social Construction of Knowledge

To explore to what extent participation in collaborative learning experiences was a process of social construction of knowledge, a qualitative analysis was conducted of the collaboration in one class. We used Gunawardena's, Lowe's, and Anderson's (1998) interaction analysis model to evaluate the degree to which the interaction reflected the social construction of knowledge. This model has five phases, each with several types of messages:

- Sharing and comparing information
- Discovery and exploration of dissonance
- Negotiation of meaning/coconstruction of knowledge
- Testing and modification of proposed synthesis
- Agreement statements of newly constructed meaning.

A total of 1,078 messages were analyzed using the model. This was the total number of messages exchanged by 24 groups (five participants per group), during the process of participating in collaborative learning activities. Each group had to complete three collaborative activities: (1) constructing a conceptual map based on a reading, (2) discussing a case, and (3) writing a brief article based on Internet and library research. Typically, what a team had to do with each activity was to read some materials, post an initial reaction or comment on the reading or situation, discuss each one's ideas, reach an agreement, and post a joint statement or document.

The activities took place between February 2 and February 24, 2000, and were selected for analysis because they were part of the course with the highest participation. This course was an information systems management seminar, taught by an adjunct faculty member who also was the chief information officer (CIO) at a large Mexican corporation. This seminar was traditionally well regarded by students, because of the day-to-day, top-level strategy experience of the teacher, who was also one of the most innovative faculty members at the Virtual University.

Because the purpose of the study was exploratory, aimed at identifying best practices in the design and execution of collaborative learning activities in a distributed environment, rather than being randomly selected, the sample had to be constructed because of its potential theoretical contribution. The level of participation in this course was much higher than in the other courses, and therefore its analysis could identify practices that promoted student participation in collaborative processes.

The unit of analysis was a statement that expressed an idea related to one of the model's categories. Most of the 1,078 messages analyzed included only one statement, but given that in some cases there were two or more statements in a single message, the total number of units analyzed was 1,340. For the sake of simplicity, in the following paragraphs these units are called messages.

The coding was performed by three research assistants who were trained for this purpose. Prior to the full coding procedure, intercoder reliability was measured by asking the three assistants to independently code the same set of messages ($n = 125$). Coders agreed in their coding decisions 94% of the time.

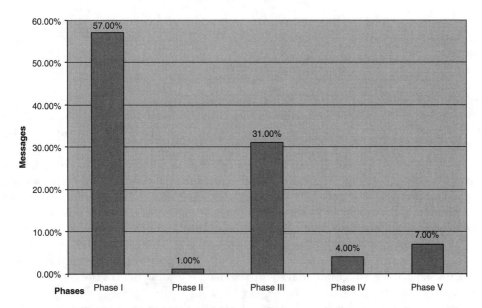

FIG. 14.4. Message distribution by Gunawardena's, Lowe's, and Anderson's model phases. This figure includes only 935 messages, because 405 messages could not be assigned to any of the model's categories.

Each student group worked independently, which made it possible to compare group processes aimed at achieving the same goal. The number of messages needed by each group to reach its goal varied from 25 to 163, with a mean of 56 messages. The length of the messages varied from two to three sentences to one page. Generally speaking, only those messages that presented group conclusions were longer than one or two paragraphs. Despite the large difference in the number of messages per group, all the groups reached the final goal—exploring an issue and coming to consensus. However, only 5 of the 24 groups passed through all the phases of the Gunawardena, Lowe, and Anderson (1998) model.

As Fig. 14.4 shows, in general, the second phase (discovering dissonance) was the one with the least amount of messages, followed by the fourth phase (testing and modification of proposed synthesis). This finding could be attributed to cultural reasons: Latin culture has not traditionally favored the open expression of disagreements. Therefore, with few disagreements openly expressed (second phase), there is no need to extensively test and modify group proposals (fourth phase).

A total of 405 messages (29% of the total number of coded messages) could no be assigned to any of the model's categories. Rather than discarding those messages, two additional categories were proposed to complement Gunawardena's, Lowe's, and Anderson's model: housekeeping and organizational messages; and feedback/moderating messages from the faculty. Although these messages were not part of the model per se, they contributed to the group process by providing organization among the students and direction from the tutor. These two new categories coincide with the social and teaching presences proposed by Garrison, Anderson, and Archer (2000). Implicitly, the analysis supported the notion of communities of inquiry, with its three presences—cognitive, social and teaching—although the researchers where not aware by then of the existence of this concept.

When the results of this study were published in an internal Virtual University newsletter, some faculty members and instructional designers decided to adopt Gunawardena's model as a cognitive resource to organize their collaborative learning activities for the next academic term. Their purpose was to use the model not for analysis, as it was originally designed, but as a tool to scaffold student participation in collaborative activities. When these activities were designed, it was made explicit to the students that they were expected to go through the five phases of the model, and examples of adequate messages from each phase were included in the syllabi.

From the initial Virtual University's experience with collaborative learning, it was clear that students engage in productive processes of social construction of knowledge if collaborative learning activities are adequately designed and the students perceive them as relevant. The easy way to encourage the perception of relevance was increasing the degree to which the activity contributes to the final grade. However, the most important challenge was to improve the design of the activities. This could be achieved by adopting an integrative didactic technique, such as problem-based learning. Similarly, the experience suggested that the role of faculty as designers of the activities, and as tutors facilitating the group process, was critical.

The next section discusses the current stage of collaborative learning at the Vitual University. Two main themes emerge in this new stage: how the use of PBL may contribute to improve the design of collaborative learning activities and what the role of faculty should be in the process of social construction of knowledge. For analytical purposes, in this new stage, the concept of "communities of inquiry" (Garrison, Anderson, & Archer, 2000) was adopted.

THE CURRENT STAGE OF COLLABORATIVE LEARNING: INCORPORATING PROBLEM-BASED LEARNING

Monterrey Tech adopted in 1997 a student-centered learning model. By 1999, more than half of all undergraduate and graduate courses were redesigned, or were in the process of being redesigned, to comply with the new model. The Virtual University, as a component of the Monterrey Tech System, was also involved in the redesign of its courses. The redesign implied the adoption of collaborative learning, as well as the use of a computer platform for asynchronous interaction among students and instructors. The main goal was to transform faculty from instructors to facilitators of learning processes.

Although there were some positive results with specific components of the model (as it was discussed in the previous section regarding collaborative learning), by 2000 it was clear that in most cases, the resulting learning model was a mixture of several components without a unifying strategy. Frequently, collaborative learning activities were not necessarily related to the content of lectures or to contents that should be researched by students in an autonomous way. Therefore, Monterrey Tech—and the Virtual University—decided to adopt integrative learning techniques such as problem-based learning (PBL), project-oriented learning (POL) and case study.

Faculty members from all campuses of the system and the Virtual University were trained in PBL by experts from the University of Maastricht, which is one of the most experienced universities in the use of PBL. The "train the trainers" strategy had two steps: first, a group of 70 faculty members spent the summer of 2000 at Maastricht, the

Netherlands, being trained in PBL. Besides participating in lectures and workshops, faculty worked on the redesign of their own courses into PBL and collaboratively designed a training program that they would offer to their colleagues. Second, over 200 faculty members from the entire Monterrey Tech System participated, during the fall semester of 2000, in the training program designed and taught by the initial team with the support of experts from Maastricht. By mid 2001, over 150 residential undergraduate courses were completely redesigned using PBL. To achieve this, Maastricht's seven-step PBL model (Van Til & van der Heijden, 1998) was adopted with minor changes to the MT residential environment.

However, for the Virtual University, adopting PBL was a serious challenge, mainly because Maastricht's experience with PBL is based on a residential model. Six of the seven steps of the Maastricht model are supposed to occur in face-to-face group meetings. Therefore, in a distributed learning system such as the VU's, the PBL model could not be adopted without revising it. The most difficult challenge was to preserve the richness of student teams working face-to-face, when they have to interact instead completely through an asynchronous, computer-based discussion system.

Another important issue was the fact that in the VU, online courses are designed by senior faculty members who are not supposed to nor are they expected to do the tutoring of large numbers of students. Therefore, the VU's revised PBL strategy had to address the issue of defining the role of the faculty and tutors, and the way in which students should be organized to function as small, productive teams.

Despite the difficulties, PBL was considered an appropriate integrating approach that would foster socially constructed and pertinent knowledge, and it was also adopted—with important adaptations—for the redesign of VU's courses. During the fall semester of 2001, 19 graduate courses were offered online under the revised PBL model. The next section discusses the Virtual University adaptation of the Maastricht, face-to-face based PBL model.

Adapting PBL to the Virtual University's Model

The adoption of PBL by the Virtual University implied solving several issues: how to deal with the lack of face-to-face teamwork; the definition of new roles for senior faculty, tutors and students (who participate in large numbers in a single course); how to employ asynchronous interactive technology as a platform for collaborative learning; and how to scaffold students' online collaboration. This section discusses the decisions made regarding these issues.

Maastricht's approach to PBL is based on seven steps: clarifying concepts; defining the problem; analyzing the problem/brainstorming; problem analysis/systematic classification; formulating learning objectives; self-study; and reporting results (Van Til & van der Heijden, 1998). Maastricht University implements this model through small teams, with a high level of face-to-face interaction among the team members and their mentor(s). With the exception of independent research, each step is supposed to occur in intensive team meetings. Because of the face-to-face nature of these meetings, it is possible to finish one or more steps in a single session. However, in a distributed learning model, where students interact mostly asynchronously, each step could take days before the team reaches an agreement.

The VU decided to condense the process into four steps (Tobias, 2001). Although clarifying terms, brainstorming, and classifying ideas were eliminated as steps on their own, the actual results expected from these steps were incorporated in the remaining four steps. The VU's PBL version is as follows:

- Defining the problem: Students (working in teams of four or five) read the problematic scenario and discuss their ideas about what the problem is. Students usually identify more than one problem in a single scenario.
- Establishing learning objectives: Students identify their prior knowledge and discuss what kind of new knowledge they need to obtain if they want to solve the problem defined in Step 1. The team expresses the new knowledge as learning objectives for the exercise.
- Independent research: Students conduct research individually, consulting academic and nonacademic sources to accomplish their learning objectives. Each student should post her or his results, and the team thoroughly discusses what they learned, as well as how the new knowledge permits them to solve the problem.
- Solving the problem: Students discuss until they agree on a solution to the problem, write a report, a presentation, or both, and reflect about their knowledge, in a metacognitive analysis of their own learning process.

Besides the students' effort, the success of this process depends on three critical components: the design of the problematic scenarios (and the entire learning activity), the guidance provided by mentors and tutors, and the appropriateness of the technological platform for the asynchronous group process. In this regard, the VU has also made decisions to accommodate PBL into its distributed learning model, where students in a single course generally surpass 150, reaching on occasions 250.

The large number of students taking a single course through the VU demands a redefinition of the role of faculty. On the one hand, the design of problematic situations for the courses, and the entire curricular structure, should be in the hands of senior faculty members with substantial content expertise. On the other hand, hundreds of students working in teams of five or six require an army of tutors who must hold at least a master's degree and some experience in the content area, and who need to be highly qualified as facilitators of group learning processes. There is one tutor for each 50 students enrolled in a course. Tutors obtain supervision and coordination, as well as support from senior faculty members. Although most of the interaction occurs between students and tutors, senior faculty members also get involved occasionally in discussions. For students, it is important to have access to well-known experts besides the continuous interaction with tutors.

Another critical issue to deal with is the computer platform used to run the distributed learning model. For some time, the VU has used several commercial platforms with varying degrees of success. Evidently, there is no commercial platform available that fits the specific needs of a multimodal higher education institution such as Monterrey Tech. Moreover, for the distributed learning operation of the Virtual University, now based on PBL, it is impossible to find a platform able to support its operation without major adaptations. Therefore, MT has undertaken to develop its own platform to support the PBL approach.

During the last few years, several units of Monterrey Tech have developed computer modules aimed at solving the peculiar institutional needs derived from its learning model. Currently, there is a prototype of a distributed learning platform that integrates those modules, as well as new ones. The platform is currently used on a limited basis, because stability and performance are still issues that need to be solved. However, the importance of this platform resides in the fact that it was put together with the objective of supporting the redesigned learning model developed by MT, including the Virtual University's approach to PBL.

This support includes the use of templates for the design of courses so that faculty members are taken step-by-step through the process of designing their courses directly into the platform. Other components, particularly relevant for the Virtual University, are the collaborative learning module and the tutoring system. The collaborative learning module allows students to work in collaborative activities with directions embedded in the system. For example, students are reminded about what step they are working in and what they are supposed to produce at the end of the step. In a sense, the module scaffolds student participation by providing orientation for the collaboration process.

This feature is further supported by the fact that tutors are trained to moderate collaborative learning following the Gunawardena, Lowe, and Anderson (1998) model of social construction of knowledge. The tutoring system is helpful both for tutors and administrators. Tutors can follow each student progress through the system, and they can communicate with their students in a closed environment that does not use external e-mail accounts. Administrators (or senior faculty members in charge of supervising a group of tutors) use the system to monitor the performance of each tutor, both in terms of their students' progress and the quality of their communication with them.

The first VU graduate courses running completely under a PBL model were taught during the fall of 2001. However, due to technical difficulties, these courses could not use the Monterrey Tech computer platform and had to operate through a commercial platform. An analysis of the experience is presented in the next section.

Results of the First VU's Online PBL Model Experience

During the fall of 2001, a total of 22 online graduate courses were offered by the Virtual University, 19 of them designed under the PBL model. Four PBL courses and two non-PBL courses were analyzed to compare the collaboration that occurred, and in particular the degree to which we can infer the social construction of knowledge in that collaboration. This comparison was intrinsically difficult, because the analysis was based on different courses in different areas of content, taught by different faculty members and tutors. However, applying a consistent analytical approach might offer at least some evidence about how the use of PBL was related to the resulting processes of social construction of knowledge. Because the reason for adopting PBL in first place was to enrich collaborative learning activities, it was expected that the processes of social construction of knowledge in the PBL courses would more closely follow the Gunawardena, Lowe and Anderson (1997) model (previously discussed) than those from the non-PBL courses.

The selection of courses was as follows: Three courses were selected at random from the list of PBL courses; two more were selected randomly from the list of non-PBL courses; and one more was selected on purpose, because the faculty member in charge of that course adopted a modified, eight-step PBL model. Five courses were in the area of business, and one was a literary analysis course. The following paragraphs present information about each of these courses.

The first course was in business strategy and had 26 students. The course included one PBL activity that accounted for 20% of the final grade. The problematic scenario was, in summary: What should Singer (a company specialized in domestic appliances) do to succeed with the introduction of a new product, after two consecutive failures with the Facilita models? A detailed rubric was included showing the criteria for evaluation for each step of the PBL process.

The second course was in literary analysis and had 21 students. The problematic scenario accounted for 35% of the final grade. A short text that the faculty member considered that contained all the elements of literary discourse was published on the course web page. Students had to research the elements and techniques of literary analysis and come up with a collaborative analysis of the text. A detailed explanation about the PBL process was included in the syllabus.

The third PBL course was on business models for the Internet and had 19 students. The PBL activity accounted for 20% of the final grade. The problematic scenario was, in summary: A couple decided to buy an electronic airplane ticket. During the trip, the couple had a series of problems related to the fact that few employees knew how to proceed with an electronic ticket. On their return, the couple wrote a letter to the airline, complaining about the poor service. The public relations manager responded to the letter with an offer of two complimentary tickets to compensate for the inconveniences,

TABLE 14.2
Message Distribution by Phase and PBL Step—Course 1

| Presence | Phase/Type | PBL Model | | | | Total | % Abs | % Rel |
		Step 1	Step 2	Step 3	Step 4			
	Phase 1	111	62	82	31	286	43.60	66.82
	Phase 2	12	6	3	2	23	3.51	5.37
Cognitive	Phase 3	0	31	22	20	73	11.13	17.06
	Phase 4	0	1	0	6	7	1.07	1.64
	Phase 5	10	6	11	12	39	5.95	9.11
	Total	133	106	118	71	428	65.24	100.00
	Organization	10	7	8	1	26	3.96	22.03
Teaching	Facilitation	17	14	16	4	51	7.77	43.22
	Direct instruction	10	12	16	3	41	6.25	34.75
	Total	37	33	40	8	118	17.99	100.00
	Student organization	6	15	27	13	61	9.30	55.45
Social	Student facilitation	9	9	26	5	49	7.47	44.55
	Total	15	24	53	18	110	16.77	100.00
Total		185	163	211	97	656	100.00	

Note. % Abs indicates the absolute percentage of the category with respect to the total number of messages. % Rel indicates the relative percentage of the category with respect to its corresponding presence (cognitive, teaching, or social).

and an explanation of how electronic tickets work. Evidently, the airline company does not want to have more problems with electronic tickets. A detailed rubric with the criteria for evaluation was included.

The fourth course was a special case, because the faculty member decided to modify the PBL model. Instead of four steps, the modified version included eight steps. In reality, some of the eight steps were subdivisions of the four steps, but the faculty wanted to be more specific. The course—on economics and management—had 57 students who had to work on three scenarios. Overall, the PBL activities accounted for 30% of the final grade. Summarized, the scenarios were: (1) The company you are working for is considering investing in highway construction, under a privatized model. What economic analyses could you present to the board to avoid the failure of previous experiences with privatized highways? (2) You are hired as a consultant by a company that needs a production plan and a compensations program to reduce inefficiencies. (3) Again, you are hired as a consultant by a company that decided on a hostile takeover of a new competitor, but the government is blocking the operation, arguing that a more competitive environment is needed. What should the company do?

The fifth course—in finance—did not include PBL and had 86 students. The course included a newsgroup activity where students were expected to discuss, in small teams,

TABLE 14.3
Message Distribution by Phase and PBL Step—Course 2

| | PBL Model | | | | | | |
Phase/Type	Step 1	Step 2	Step 3	Step 4	Total	% Abs	% Rel
Phase 1	21	17	7	4	49	20.08	34.51
Phase 2	6	0	3	0	9	3.69	6.34
Phase 3	7	6	30	16	59	24.18	41.55
Phase 4	0	0	3	5	8	3.28	5.63
Phase 5	1	1	3	12	17	6.97	11.97
Total	35	24	46	37	142	58.20	100.00
Organization	5	5	4	4	18	7.38	30.51
Facilitation	9	5	9	5	28	11.48	47.46
Direct instruction	3	3	4	3	13	5.33	22.03
Total	17	13	17	12	59	24.18	100.00
Student organization	7	6	3	1	17	6.97	39.53
Student facilitation	6	3	12	5	26	10.66	60.47
Total	13	9	15	6	43	17.62	100.00
Grand total	65	46	78	55	244	100.00	

Note. % *Abs* indicates the absolute percentage of the category with respect to the total number of messages. % *Rel* indicates the relative percentage of the category with respect to its corresponding presence (cognitive, teaching, or social).

the concepts studied through the trimester. Participation in this activity accounted for 5% of the final grade.

The final course was also a non-PBL course on knowledge management and had 19 students. During the entire trimester, students were expected to participate in online discussions about specific questions related to the content of the course. This activity accounted for 10% of the final grade.

The qualitative analysis of these courses was also based on the Gunawardena, Lowe, and Anderson (1997) model for the analysis of the social construction of knowledge. However, in this case, those messages that could not be analyzed according to the model were analyzed under the Garrison, Anderson and Archer (2000) notion of communities of inquiry. Therefore, the Gunawardena Lowe and Anderson model was considered the "cognitive presence"; the faculty or tutor generated messages were the "teaching presence"; and the noncognitive student-generated messages were the "social presence." The categories of analysis for teaching presence were based on Garrison, Anderson and Archer (2000): design and organization, process facilitation, and direct instruction. The categories for social presence were organizational messages and process facilitation messages.

TABLE 14.4
Message Distribution by Phase and PBL Step—Course 3

Phase/Type	PBL Model				Total	% Abs	% Rel
	Step 1	Step 2	Step 3	Step 4			
Phase 1	11	4	1	2	18	17.31	32.14
Phase 2	1	0	0	0	1	0.96	1.79
Phase 3	2	10	8	4	24	23.08	42.86
Phase 4	0	0	1	1	2	1.92	3.57
Phase 5	1	2	5	3	11	10.58	19.64
Total	15	16	15	10	56	53.85	100.00
Organization	2	0	1	0	3	2.88	11.54
Facilitation	1	9	4	5	19	18.27	73.08
Direct instruction	0	0	2	2	4	3.85	15.38
Total	3	9	7	7	26	25.00	100.00
Student organization	1	3	7	0	11	10.58	50.00
Student facilitation	1	4	4	2	11	10.58	50.00
Total	2	7	11	2	22	21.15	100.00
Grand total	20	32	33	19	104	100.00	

Note. % *Abs* indicates the absolute percentage of the category with respect to the total number of messages. % *Rel* indicates the relative percentage of the category with respect to its corresponding presence (cognitive, teaching, or social).

The units of analysis were statements that corresponded to one of the categories, either for the cognitive, teaching, or social presence. Most of the 1,335 messages analyzed included only one statement, but given that in some cases there were two or more statements in a single message, the total number of units analyzed was 1,525. For the sake of simplicity, in the following paragraphs these units are called messages.

Two research assistants coded the messages. One of the coders participated in the analysis reported in the previous section. Intercoder reliability was measured by assigning the same set of messages ($n = 115$) to both coders to analyze them independently. The coders agreed in 92% of their coding decisions.

Tables 14.2, 14.3, and 14.4 show the distribution of messages by the presence (cognitive, teaching, and social) categories and by the step of the PBL process for each of the PBL-based courses. As expected, messages corresponding to the more advanced phases of the cognitive model occur in the later steps of the PBL process, when the groups approach the solution of the problematic scenario. The data show some differences (not statistically validated) among the courses. In Course 1, for example, students exchanged a higher percentage of Phase 1 messages, compared to the other two courses. Similarly, in Course 1 there were more Phase 2 messages, and less Phase 3 messages with respect to the other courses. However, generally speaking,

TABLE 14.5
Message Distribution by Phase in the PBL Modified Version—Course 4

Presence	Phase/Type	PBL Model			Total	% Abs	% Rel
		Scenario 1	Scenario 2	Scenario 3			
Cognitive	Phase 1	48	28	32	108	33.64	62.43
	Phase 2	0	0	1	1	0.31	0.58
	Phase 3	11	21	26	58	18.07	33.53
	Phase 4	1	0	4	5	1.56	2.89
	Phase 5	0	0	1	1	0.31	0.58
	Total	60	49	64	173	53.89	100.00
Teaching	Organization	1	0	0	1	0.31	50.00
	Facilitation	0	0	0	0	0.00	0.00
	Direct instruction	0	0	1	1	0.31	50.00
	Total	1	0	1	2	0.62	100.00
Social	Student organization	15	36	22	73	22.74	50.00
	Student facilitation	19	41	13	73	22.74	50.00
	Total	34	77	35	146	45.48	100.00
Grand total		95	126	100	321	100.00	

Note. % Abs indicates the absolute percentage of the category with respect to the total number of messages. % Rel indicates the relative percentage of the category with respect to its corresponding presence (cognitive, teaching, or social).

the three courses showed a similar pattern than the student discussions analyzed 2 years before (reported in the previous section) prior to the adoption of PBL, with fewer messages in Phases 2 and 4. The apparent advantage of PBL is that students create more Phase 5 (concluding) messages, and that some of these messages are more complex in the sense that the conclusions or problem solutions synthesize the group work and reflect the construction of new knowledge. In average, about 22% of the total messages corresponded to teaching presence and 17 to social presence. The data show support for the communities of inquiry notion, as it is clear that what happens in online collaborative learning is more than a cognitive process.

Table 14.5 shows the results for the modified, eight-step PBL course. Although this course provided students with more specific steps for collaboration, no time frame-work was presented to the students for the completion of each step, nor were specific directions provided. The table includes the results for each of the three problematic scenarios. The data show that students practically did not go beyond Phase 3 in each of the scenarios and that participation in Phase 2 was null. Similarly, whereas 45% of the total messages correspond to social presence, less that 1% of the messages were classified as teaching presence.

Although generalizing from this single case would be inappropriate, these results, at first sight, seem to indicate that the four-step PBL model is more productive than the

TABLE 14.6
Message Distribution by Phase (No PBL)—Course 5

Presence	Phase/Type	PBL Model			Total	% Abs	% Rel
		Team 1	Team 2	Team 3			
Cognitive	Phase 1	46	30	42	118	83.69	88.72
	Phase 2	3	1	5	9	6.38	6.77
	Phase 3	3	0	3	6	4.26	4.51
	Phase 4	0	0	0	0	0.00	0.00
	Phase 5	0	0	0	0	0.00	0.00
	Total	52	31	50	133	94.33	100.00
Teaching	Organization	0	0	0	0	0.00	0.00
	Facilitation	0	0	0	0	0.00	0.00
	Direct instruction	0	0	0	0	0.00	0.00
	Total	0	0	0	0	0.00	0.00
Social	Student organization	0	0	8	8	5.67	100.00
	Student facilitation	0	0	0	0	0.00	0.00
	Total	0	0	8	8	5.67	100.00
Grand total		52	31	58	141	100.00	

Note. % Abs indicates the absolute percentage of the category with respect to the total number of messages. *% Rel* indicates the relative percentage of the category with respect to its corresponding presence (cognitive, teaching, or social). The discussion processes of three teams were analyzed.

modified version. However, a closer analysis of the data offers another possible conclusion: that the tutor plays a fundamental role in the success of the student collaborative learning process. While in the three 4-step PBL courses, the tutors contributed to one fifth of the total messages; in the modified version the tutor participation was practically null. It is interesting that in the modified version course, students devoted 45% of the total messages to housekeeping and organizing purposes, probably because of the lack of structure and tutor participation.

Tables 14.6 and 14.7 show the results of the analysis of two courses where PBL was not used. The table includes the analysis of the discussion processes of three teams (Table 14.6) and two teams (Table 14.7).

The courses show two different scenarios. In Course 6 (Table 7), students reached Phases 4 and 5 (though with a lower percentage of messages than in the four-step PBL model courses), with a tutor participation of 29%. In Course 5 (Table 6), students did not go beyond Phase 3, and the tutors did not participate. These findings reinforce the conclusion that tutors play a fundamental role in the process of social construction of knowledge.

Moreover, the results of the entire analysis seem to imply that although the use of PBL contributes to enrich the cognitive component of the social construction of knowledge process, an adequate participation of faculty and tutors (teaching presence)

TABLE 14.7

Message Distribution by Phase (No PBL)—Course 6

Presence	Phase/Type	PBL Model		Total	% Abs	% Rel
		Team 1	Team 2			
Cognitive	Phase 1	3	3	6	10.17	26.09
	Phase 2	0	0	0	0.00	0.00
	Phase 3	6	7	13	22.03	56.52
	Phase 4	0	2	2	3.39	8.70
	Phase 5	0	2	2	3.39	8.70
	Total	9	14	23	38.98	100.00
Teaching	Organization	3	0	3	5.08	13.04
	Facilitation	10	0	10	16.95	43.48
	Direct instruction	9	1	10	16.95	43.48
	Total	22	1	23	38.98	100.00
Social	Student organization	0	6	6	10.17	46.15
	Student facilitation	0	7	7	11.86	53.85
	Total	0	13	13	22.03	100.00
Grand total		31	28	59	100.00	

Note. % *Abs* indicates the absolute percentage of the category with respect to the total number of messages. % *Rel* indicates the relative percentage of the category with respect to its corresponding presence (cognitive, teaching, or social). The discussion processes of two teams were analyzed.

is critical for the process. Similarly, the data show that social presence is also important, particularly when there is limited or null teaching presence. In summary, this analysis of the Virtual University experience suggests that online collaborative learning works better when balanced communities of inquiry (with their three presences) are created.

CONCLUSIONS AND NEXT STEPS

Monterrey Tech's Virtual University experience with collaborative learning has been extensive, intense, and varied. From irregular and dispersed threaded discussions, to integrated collaborative activities in the context of communities of inquiry, the evolution of collaborative learning at the VU suggests that pedagogical considerations are critical for the success of collaborative learning. Simply stated, collaborative learning activities should be adequately designed; otherwise, students get lost in the process. In this respect, the use of a course design technique such as problem-based learning contributes to integrate collaborative learning with other forms of learning—such as autonomous learning—to create a richer learning experience. Moreover, MT's experience also shows that the role of the faculty and tutors (teaching presence) is critical, as they facilitate student social processes and provide direct instruction. Similarly, social presence is necessary to round the development of productive communities of inquiry.

The results of the current experience with PBL promise a more homogeneous pattern of collaboration among students, compared to previous experiences, where the design of the activities was not integrated by a single strategy. However, research should go beyond analyzing whether collaborative activities actually become a process of social construction of knowledge, and emphasis should be put on measuring the quality of learning. Similarly, research should focus on analyzing the effectiveness of scaffolding techniques, either as a component of tutoring or as embedded features of the computer platform.

Further analysis of the Monterrey Tech experience should adopt a wider scope, paying more attention not only to the cognitive aspects of online collaborative learning, but also to the social and teaching components. The notion of communities of inquiry, as proposed by Garrison, Anderson, and Archer (2000), could provide an adequate theoretical framework for deepening the analysis of the Monterrey Tech experience. A comprehensive point of view could contribute to develop a better understanding of the nature of online collaborative learning.

ACKNOWLEDGMENTS

This chapter was based on research conducted by José Rafael López Islas, Noemí Ramírez Angel, Raúl Julián Rojo Aguirre, Rosa María Megchún Alpizar, Aída Cerda Cristerna, Dora Luz Candanosa Salazar, and Gerardo Tobías Acosta. Special thanks to Noemí Ramírez for her valuable support.

REFERENCES

Antonietti, A. (2001). Problem-based learning: A research perspective on learning interactions. *The British Journal of Educational Psychology, 71,* 344.

Barrows, H. S., & Tamblyn, R. (1980). *Problem-based learning: An approach to medical education.* New York: Springer.

Collis, B., & Moonen, J. (2001). *Flexible learning in a digital world: Experiences and expectations.* London: Kogan Page.

Dick, W., & Carey, L. (1990). *The systematic design of instruction* (3rd ed.). New York: HarperCollins.

Duffy, T. M., & Jonassen, D. H. (1992). Constructivism: New implications for instructional technology. In T. M. Duffy & D. H. Jonassen (Eds.), *Constructivism and the technology of instruction: A conversation* (pp. 1–16). Hillsdale, NJ: Lawrence Erlbaum Associates.

Garrison, D. R., Anderson, T., & Archer, W. (2000). Critical inquiry in a text-based environment: Computer conferencing in higher education. *The Internet and Higher Education, 2,* 1–19.

Gunawardena, C., Lowe, C., & Anderson, T. (1997). Analysis of global online debate and the development an interaction analysis model for examining social construction of knowledge in computer conferencing. *Journal of Educational Computing Research, 17,* 395–429.

Harasim, L. M. (Ed.). (1990). *Online education: Perspective on a new environment.* New York: Praeger.

Hiltz, S. R. (1998). Collaborative learning in asynchronous learning networks: Building learning communities. In *Proceedings of WebNet '98 World Conference on WWW, Internet and Intranet* (pp. 1–7). Norfolk, VA.

Neville, A. J. (1999). The problem-based learning tutor: Teacher? Facilitator? Evaluator? *Medical Teacher, 21,* 393–401.

Palloff, R., & Pratt, K. (1999). *Building learning communities in cyberspace: Effective strategies for the online classroom.* San Francisco: Jossey-Bass.

Pinheiro, E. (1998). Collaborative learning. In D. G. Oblinger & S. C. Rush (Eds.), *The future compatible campus* (pp. 118–130). Bolton, MA: Anker.

Rafaeli, S., Sudweeks, F., & McLaughlin, M. (Eds.). (1995). *Network and netplay: Virtual groups on the Internet.* Menlo Park: AAAI/MIT Press.

Rheingold, H. (1993). *The virtual community: Homesteading on the electronic frontier.* New York: HarperCollins.

Rice, R. E., & Love, G. (1987). Electronic emotion: Socioemotional content in a computer-mediated communication network. *Communication Research 14,* 85–108.

Savery, J., & Duffy, T. (1995). Problem-based learning: An instructional model and its constructivist framework. *Educational Technology 35,* 31–38.

Sfard, A. (1998). On two metaphors for learning and the dangers of choosing just one. *Educational Researcher, 27,* 4–13.

Slavin, R. (1995). *Cooperative learning.* Needham Heights, MA: Allyn & Bacon.

Sudweeks, F., Collins, M., & December, J. (1995). Internetwork resources. In Z. Berge & M. Collins (Eds.), *Computer mediated communication and the online classroom: Vol. I. Overview and perspectives* (pp. 193–212). Cresskilp, NJ: Hampton.

Schwier, R. A., & Misanchuk, E. R. (1993). *Interactive multimedia.* Englewood Cliffs, NJ: Educational Technology.

Sproull, L., & Kiesler, S. (1991). *Connections: New ways of working in the networked organization.* Cambridge, MA: MIT Press.

Sudweeks, F., & Rafaeli, S. (1996). How do you get a hundred strangers to agree? Computer-mediated communication and collaboration. In T. M. Harrison & T. Stephen (Eds.), *Computer networking and scholarly communication in the twenty-first-century university* (pp. 115–136). Albany: State University of New York Press.

Turoff, M. (1995). *Designing a virtual classroom.* Available: http://www.njit.edu/Department/CCCC/VC/Papers/Design.html

Van Til, C., & van der Heijden, F. (1998). *PBL study skills: An overview.* Maastricht, the Netherlands: Vakgroep O&O.

Vygotsky, L. (1978). *Language and thought.* Cambridge, MA: MIT Press.

Walther, J. B. (1992). Interpersonal effects in computer-mediated interaction: A relational perspective. *Communication Research, 19,* 52–90.

15

Using Theory-Based Approaches to Architect Online Collaborative Problem-based Learning: Lessons Learned from Monterrey Tech–Virtual University

Jamie Kirkley

Indiana University, and Information in Place, Inc.

In recent years, there has been a growing emphasis on implementing learner-centered practices within various educational environments. These practices focus on supporting learners in constructing their own understandings through complex learning experiences that emphasize interpersonal reasoning and social interaction (see American Psychological Association, 1997, for a complete discussion of learner-centered principles). Reflective of and consistent with a constructivist perspective of learning as a process of sense making (Duffy & Cunningham, 1996), the learner-centered approach often places learners in the role of collaborators and problem solvers. Thus, one goal for using collaborative and problem-based approaches is to support learners in the process of communicating with and challenging each other for the purpose of improving knowledge construction and understanding (Zech, Gause-Vega, Bray, & Goldman, 2000).

Learner-centered practices are particularly relevant to distance learning as we design (and redesign) online instruction so that learners are engaged in the knowledge construction and negotiation process (Wagner & McCombs, 1995). The need for a more student-centered approach to online learning is reflected in the variety of guidelines for designing online instruction. In 1998, Bonk and Cummings documented over a dozen guidelines for using the Web in teaching that were linked to learner-centered principles. In 2001, the Institute for Higher Education Policy's *Quality on the Line* report recommended that Web-based courses be designed to "require students to work in groups utilizing problem-solving activities in order to develop topic understanding" and to use materials that "promote collaboration among students." Yet designing online courses solely for the purpose of having collaborative or problem-solving activities should not be a primary goal of any instructional designer. Those designing and providing online education must first determine the vision and goals for the learning experience, as well as how theoretical commitments to teaching and learning can guide their design.

This is the value of Rafael López-Islas's chapter (Chap. 14, this volume) as he shares with us the design, wide-scale implementation, and evaluation of collaborative problem-based learning (PBL) at the Instituto Tecnológico de Monterrey (or Monterrey Tech–Virtual University, MT–VU). This is an important story of how a large virtual university consisting of 29 campuses made a system-wide commitment to pedagogical innovation. From his story, the distance education community can better understand one university's road map from satellite lectures to a theory-based pedagogical model that includes online collaboration via problem-based learning. However, it is important to note that the map is not a straightforward one. It involves wide scale change in faculty, student, and teaching assistant roles as well as pedagogical training, course structures, and technological tools. From the story of MT–VU, we learn how they:

- Moved from approaching collaboration as an ill-defined add-on component of online courses to a well-defined strategy used within a theory-based framework of PBL
- Adopted and adapted their own pedagogical model designed for the online learning environment
- Implemented theory-based design with up-front consideration of social structures and roles, as well as technological tools used
- Evaluated the implementation of the model in a variety of courses to determine patterns of shared knowledge construction among students
- Used the evaluation results to inform the best practices for implementing online problem-based courses in their context.

Clearly, Monterrey Tech is to be lauded for taking on this type of massive organizational change. It is not often that we see theory-based pedagogical change on this scale in higher education—one that impacts over 80,000 students. Although change often occurs at the course or department level, it becomes many times more complex when it involves many locations, departments, courses, stakeholders, and degree programs. From López-Islas's story, we can learn valuable lessons about how to use theory to design, develop, implement, and evaluate a large-scale pedagogical innovation. Inversely, our efforts with design can feed back into the development of theory. Specifically, MT–VU began with the participation model of learning (Sfard, 1998), and later adopted PBL as their learning methodology. They did not begin with theory, but instead with a goal to improve online teaching and learning. It was through the adoption and adaptation of a theory-based approach, specifically problem-based learning, that MT–VU was able to create a consistent blueprint for designing, implementing, and evaluating a pedagogical change from satellite lectures to distributed PBL.

In this chapter, I will focus on reviewing the design and implementation of MU–VT's collaborative problem-based methodology as a theory-based innovation as well as how theory can provide an architectural blueprint for the design and implementation of online environments. Second, I will review López-Islas's research on students' shared knowledge construction process and the implications of his research on the design of learning environments. Lastly, I will provide an outline of a framework for architecting theory-based design.

THE IMPORTANCE AND CHALLENGES OF THEORY-BASED DESIGN

Before addressing MT–VU's sweeping pedagogical change addressed in López-Islas's chapter, I will first address the challenges and importance of using learning theory to guide design. Although learning theory is more often seen as a hot topic of debate among academics and seemingly distant from practice, it actually can serve as a powerful design tool. The true value of theory-based design is that it can provide a blueprint for designing, developing, researching, and evaluating the design of learning environments. Theory provides the structure and guidance for applying a certain design methodology (at the macro level) or a teaching strategy (at the micro level). It gives context and meaning to how methodology and strategy should be applied based on the beliefs of how learning occurs (Reigeluth, 1999). Learning theory also helps researchers identify significant variables related to learning, unify a variety of findings, assimilate them into a cohesive and interrelated body, and identify areas for further research (Krathwohl, 1998).

Learning theory plays an interesting role for instructional designers. First, we each possess our own beliefs about how learning occurs. Given that we usually have 12 to 18 years of experience with our own schooling, we have beliefs about what makes learning successful. Yet, depending on if and how we have explored these beliefs, they may not be explicit in our own minds. Second, our beliefs may not be aligned with current educational theories, or they may not be consistent with one theory. Regardless of whether we purport to use theory or not, our beliefs show up in our designs. They are indicated by our choices in how we design learning activities, support the learning process, and develop learner assessments. In this chapter, I advocate that we make these beliefs explicit, align them consistently with theory, and use theory as a purposeful tool to inform methodology and design choices. I also advocate that we examine the implementations of our designs and participate in a process of sharing findings with other designers, researchers, and theorists. This not only provides information about what works with regard to aspects of methods and designs, it serves to inform and advance theory and build closer links among theory and practice.

Although I advocate using theory as a design tool, there are challenges with doing so. First, understanding the nuances of theory and how to apply it in real world contexts can be challenging, even for those with expertise. There are usually debates even among experts on how to translate theoretical values into practice. If little guidance exists in the form of methodologies or frameworks, it can be challenging for those with limited knowledge of theory to use theory as a design tool. Without a theoretical foundation, designers often abstract and interpret these methods through their own existing frameworks, which may or may not match the theory (Bednar, Cunningham, Duffy, & Perry, 1992). This can result in designers engaging in trial-and-error that can result in problematic designs, as well as significant investments needed for redesign work. It also results in misunderstandings about how theory can and should be applied.

Second, there are limited methodologies that provide guidance on how to use particular theories to design learning environments. This has been due to the result of the gap between researchers and practitioners. According to Robinson (1998), this gap occurs when the theories of researchers do not address the theories and problem-solving processes of practitioners. "This gap persists because we do not know the methodological resources that are required to forge such an articulation" (p. 25). As a result, many instructional designers choose to ignore theory altogether. Yet by ignoring the role of theory, we are limiting the advancement of our own understanding of learning. Schwen (personal communication, October 2002) has argued that one problem with the field of instructional design is that our basis in theory is weak, and we have created correspondingly weak design approaches. To address this need, Hannafin, Hannafin, Land, & Oliver (1997) have proposed using a grounded-systems learning design approach, which involves establishing links between the practice of learning systems design and related theory and research. By using a grounded design approach, they propose that we develop models and examples of high quality theory-into-practice frameworks for other designers to use, critique, revise, and adapt. By sharing the outcomes of usage and adaptation, such as López-Islas has done in his chapter, we advance the field of instructional design through examining the relationships among theory and design practice.

Third, there is a long history of instructional designers relying on the pragmatic approach. With this approach, instructional problems are viewed from a variety of theoretical perspectives, and results are then compared (Wilson, 1999). This eclectic or toolbox approach advocates drawing on methods abstracted from different learning theories and applying them as tools in a toolbox. Yet Bednar, Cunningham, Duffy, & Perry (1992) argue that abstracting a method or strategy from its theory strips it of its meaning and context. This creates a situation where methods may not applied in a way that is consistent with the goals and beliefs about learning. For example, problem-solving is one example of an instructional method that may be viewed from a variety of theoretical perspectives. Well-structured problem-solving (e.g., solving an equation) is based on an information-processing theory of learning, while ill-structured problem-solving (e.g., determining whether to purchase a new car) is based on a constructivist approach. These differ in that well-structured problems are constrained by a limited number of rules and principles and have convergent solutions, while ill-structured problems have multiple paths for solving the problem and have multiple solutions (Jonassen, 1997). Applying problem-solving with these two different approaches will result in different learning activities, processes, and outcomes in the learning environment. By not understanding the implications of these differences, problems may occur due to inconsistencies in design.

Acknowledging that theory-based design is challenging, the aforementioned issues provide reasons for why we should use theory-based approaches. In fact, using theory to inform design, and vice versa, has become an important movement in educational research. Design experiments (Brown, 1992; Collins, 1992) and design research (Cobb, Confrey, diSessa, Lehrer, & Schauble, 2003) have emerged as an effort to connect theory, research, and practice. Design research has been characterized by iterative design and formative research in complex, real world settings (Edelson, 2002). Traditionally, theory and research are used to inform design. However, with design experiments, the role of design is to implement a theory so that the theory can be evaluated and refined (Edelson, 2002). Ideally, design experiments result in a helping us better understand a complex, interacting system of elements for the purpose of long term, generative learning (Cobb, Confrey, diSessa, Lehrer, R, & Schauble, 2003). Although MT–VU did not formally engage in a design experiment as described above, they did engage in systematically designing, implementing, and evaluating a pedagogical change. This is a valuable endeavor that enables us to explore the intertwined nature of theory, research and design and how this impacts implementation.

In the following section, I will address specific issues with regard to using theory-based design as a tool for architecting pedagogical innovation. In discussing this approach, I will use specific examples from the MT–VU case with regard to how theory informed the design and evaluation of their online problem-based learning model.

MT–VU: A CASE OF THEORY-BASED PEDAGOGICAL INNOVATION

It is important to note that Monterrey-Tech did not begin with theory-based design in their initial implementation of collaborative learning. In revising their learning model, MT–VU worked their way back to theory through their adoption and adaptation of problem-based learning. In fact, this is why their story is valuable as it helps illustrate lessons learned in their process. Throughout his chapter, López-Islas nicely establishes linkages among theory and practice as he discusses the evolution of MT–VU's movement from a flexible learning model to the development and implementation of a distributed PBL model. As his story illustrates, the movement was not always a straight path. Lessons were learned along the way that enabled MT–VU to enhance the design, implementation, and evaluation of their model as well as clarify their beliefs about learning. Like any real world application, design was informed and influenced by the context and circumstances under which it was implemented. By understanding these relationships, we can learn more about how context affects implementation.

With regard to the use of theory to inform design, López-Islas stated that the first implementation of collaboration was more of "a novelty that took form of optional threaded discussions, frequently unrelated to the academic content . . . a supplemental activity to enhance learning." With no explicit theory or methodology to guide the use of collaborative activities and threaded discussion, both ended up serving as supplements rather than as ways to facilitate specific learning goals. MT–VU then realized the need for a more unified instructional approach and chose PBL as a methodology. With the development of an online model of PBL, collaborative learning became a method for supporting students in constructing shared knowledge for the purpose of solving content-related problems. However, it is not clear from López-Islas's chapter when theory came into play or how it was related to the purposeful choice of the problem-based learning framework. Although we see the outcomes of using socioconstructivism as a theoretical guide for evaluating student learning in an online learning environment, it is not clear what role that particular theory played in the actual design of the online learning model. This could possibly be a case of equating method with theory. That is, it would seem that the method of problem-based learning is seen by López-Islas as, by definition, a theoretical representation. However, theory must guide the application, and the way in which the theory is guiding the implementation of PBL in this context is not made explicit.

Interestingly, MT–VU obtained training in PBL from the University of Maastricht, where PBL is applied primarily using a cognitive-based framework. In this application of PBL, there is an emphasis on using students' prior knowledge and elaboration to ground the learning process (Schmidt 1993). The problem, in addition to being motivational, provides a real world reference that the learner may recall later, when similar real world cases are encountered. From a constructivist perspective (Savery and Duffy, 1996), the goal of PBL is to develop problem-solving skills in the content area. The critical issue within the PBL environment, from this perspective, is the learner's authentic engagement in an issue that is a legitimate and central issue in the discipline. The problem prompts authentic engagement with the issue. Further, the ability to generate hypotheses, gather information to evaluate those hypotheses, and be able to discuss and defend a perspective are all central to the learning outcomes. Clearly, how PBL is implemented–the focus in the learning environment—depends on which theoretical perspective one holds. In fact, both of these perspectives are expressed within the Maastricht model (Gijselaers, 1996). Thus, how MT–VU implemented PBL in their first efforts, may well depend on which Maastricht perspective guided their training. Regardless of when theory formally came into play, MT–VU was committed early on to participatory learning through interaction and collaboration, which is matched with the social constructivist learning theory.

Considering how things happen in the real world, it is important to note that sometimes a methodology may take root before the full theoretical implications of using that methodology can be fully explored and understood. Or perhaps the application of a methodology may be adapted to fit the context or values of a specific learning environment, and thus, theoretical commitments may be emerge or even shift over time. In fact, it was MT–VU's valuing of student interaction that promoted the adoption of collaboration as a key part of their flexible learning model, and the later adoption/adaptation of a problem-based approach. What is important is that the application of the methodology be grounded in theory so as to help ensure consistency of methodology and design.

The context and situation of the learning environment are a critical part of the design process and must be considered in any adoption or adaptation of any methodology. By not addressing contextual factors such as organizational or technological factors, a design may simply fail. Wilson (1995) argues that design and implementation are ultimately inseparable, and many good designs have failed to be adopted due to not considering situational issues. Therefore, it is important in choosing a methodology to consider the adaptations needed in order to apply that methodology to your own context. For example, MT–VU chose to begin with the Maastricht model of PBL, but they adapted it in several ways to fit their own context. MT–VU had to design it to work with students who were distributed and communicating via asynchronous threaded discussion. This meant that they had to consider how both the distribution of students and the design of the communication technology would impact their model of PBL as well as the implementation. To address these issues, MT–VU adapted the seven-step Maastricht model of PBL to a four-step model due to the complexity of the online learning environment. Specifically, asynchronous communication can add time to the decision making process because learners post messages and then have to wait for responses, so using the more complex learning model could have caused confusion and time delays. Hence, the four-step model was a good solution for streamlining the PBL process. Also, I found it interesting that some instructors began using the five stages of the Gunawardena, Lowe, & Anderson's (1997) content analysis framework as a cognitive scaffold for students. This is an excellent idea and an interesting example of how research can directly impact design. If we are truly going to understand the success of an innovation, it is important to provide scaffolds to the instructors and students as they participate in that innovation.

Theory impacts not only the methodology, but it also impacts methods used to research and evaluate the implementation of the methodology. In MT–VU's examination of student knowledge construction, social constructivism is used as a lens to better understand the process of how students develop online shared knowledge. MT–VU chose Gunawardena, Lowe, & Anderson's (1997) content analysis framework as a way to research patterns of interaction in their distributed problem-based learning courses. To develop this framework, Gunawardena and her colleagues used the social constructivist theory of learning as a basis. The values of the framework are that learning is:

- An active, changing, and constructive process and not a static entity
- Occurring among a group and not just at the individual level
- A process that is distributed among multiple contributions
- A process that is ever evolving and not frozen at one point

Using this framework was a choice that was consistent with the design of their learning environment as well as MT–VU's values about learning. Had they used a cognitivist-based PBL implementation, the framework for evaluating the learning process would have needed to reflect that orientation. Such a framework may instead focus on how prior knowledge and elaboration supported problem-solving. Yet by using an evaluation framework that was consistent with their design and values, they were able to gain important understandings about the social interaction and shared knowledge building. Choosing a research framework that is aligned with theory is critical because it enables one to focus on examining themes that are congruent with the design. The issue of consistency among theory, methodology, design, research, and even implementation is critical for any learning environment. The values set forth through the theory guide each part. Without alignment, there are likely to be problems that impact the design, learning process, research, and evaluation outcomes.

Contextual and situational factors, such as technological and organizational factors, are a critical part of implementing theory-based design. López-Islas discussed some of the limitations of the threaded discussion for supporting the PBL process, specifically time delay and logistics. To support learning environments that focus on knowledge construction, online learning tools need to graphically represent, support, and signify multiple stages of the learning process through a variety of representations. Specifically with regard to PBL, this may include tools that provide an overall visualization of the PBL process (e.g., where the student or group is in relation to the end goal), different learning tools to support different stages of the process (e.g., identification of problem, brainstorming, and reflection), functions of the process (e.g., negotiating and decision-making), and interface supports for each type, such as discussion labels (see Duffy, Dueber, and Hawley, 1998). In fact, MT–VU is currently embarking on designing a tool to support their model of PBL. As constructivist online learning environments continue to expand, it is critical that we develop learning tools need to reflect the cognitive and social activities and processes of students. In particular, these tools should enhance the cognitive powers of human beings during thinking, problem-solving, and learning (Jonassen and Reeves, 1995). With regard to designing tools to specifically support PBL, Koschmann (1996) examined the phases of PBL and looked for ways that technology could support each of the processes, such as problem presentation and reflection. In my own experience with teaching a distributed PBL course, I found there was a need to provide tools that support instructors with facilitating, mentoring, and tracking process and participation of groups as well as individual students. As designers continue to develop innovative online learning environments, they must consider how tools and technology can support the learning process as well as instructional goals.

Another important aspect of context is how organizational structures and logistics will impact the implementation of a methodology. There are often changes in structures, roles, and processes of learning and teaching. Without considering and accounting for these changes in the design, the new design implementation is likely to experience problems. In implementing their distributed PBL model, MT–VU had to address issues such as who would design and teach the courses as well as how the roles would change for everyone involved. We learn that MT–VU restructured many aspects of design and teaching in order to meet their goal of implementing the distributed PBL format. Because senior faculty members were content experts, they served as designers of the courses. This required a considerable investment in training for a primary set of faculty members because they went to Maastricht to receive this training. In fact, MT–VU had the primary faculty redesign not only one course using PBL but also had them develop a workshop to train other faculty on PBL methods. Once implemented, MT–VU restructured how students and tutors worked together to facilitate the learning process. With hundreds of students working in four to five member teams, a large number of tutors must supervise and coordinate the student teams. Even though López-Islas did not focus on organizational planning and implementation of the model in his chapter, it is clear that this endeavor required a major commitment to change as well as much logistical coordination. Due to planning and foresight in the management of implementation issues, MT–VU was able to successfully implement their new pedagogical model and then have the opportunity to evaluate that implementation.

As addressed above, the case of MT–VU provides many interesting issues to consider in using theory-based design. First, the boundaries among theory, research, and practice are not always clear. As demonstrated by MT–VU, one impacts the others in many ways both explicit and inexplicit. Second, real world implementation of a methodology often requires adjustments and adaptations to fit the learning context. As with MT–VU, these should be considered ahead of time in order to facilitate a more successful implementation. Third, by examining the implementation, designers can gain an understanding of important issues with regard to the issues with application of theory. By sharing our stories, such as MT–VU, we all benefit from the experience of knowing what worked and did not work well. From examining cases such as this one, best practices and guidelines can begin to emerge. Perhaps then design can become both more effective and efficient, with less time spent reinventing the wheel for every new innovation. Researching and evaluating the implementation of the MT–VU PBL methodology is another contribution of López-Islas's chapter. In the following section, I will review López-Islas research on this and address issues related to researching online collaborative learning environments.

EXAMINING MT–VU'S IMPLEMENTATION OF DISTRIBUTED PBL

By sharing the design and implementation of their problem-based learning methodology, MT–VU enables us to gain a better understanding of their model and how it was adapted from a traditional PBL model to fit their unique context. However, it is their research and evaluation of the implementation of that methodology that enables us to learn about resulting best practices and the online process of student knowledge construction. It is this sharing of best practices and research outcomes that informs our critical understandings of online learning processes, student interactions, facilitation, and technological tool use and design.

In the MT–VU study, López-Islas examined best practices during the initial stage of collaborative learning. The purpose of this research was to identify those practices that contributed to further refining our understanding of issues related to the instructional methodology for asynchronous collaboration. In this study, he examined graduate student participation in collaborative learning activities in 100 graduate courses for the year of 1999. The analysis included all graduate programs in engineering, computer science and business. From the 100 courses, López-Islas identified those courses with high student participation and examined their syllabi. The following characteristics were found:

- Directions and expectations were made clear through specific instructions
- Participation made up a considerable portion of the final grade
- Faculty members were actively involved in the collaborative process through moderation and modeling
- Students were able to obtain technical support as needed.

While these best practices are typical to good instruction, they are especially important for the area of online learning. In an online environment, various factors may inhibit understanding or participation, e.g., limited technology capabilities, unclear directions. Therefore, López-Islas's findings remind us of basic learner expectations. As a minor point, I would have liked further information about his analysis, such as how many courses were deemed "high participation courses" and what criteria were used to classify a course as high participation. Also, more information on whether the courses were spread across all subject areas or located in just one or two areas would have been helpful. Having data from student interviews would increase the validity of López-Islas's analysis and provide specific examples of the issues with regard to distributed PBL environment. Specifically, the best practices defined by López-Islas translate back into design considerations for future PBL courses. They also inform the understanding of online learning processes and interactions with regard to distributed PBL and contribute to research on methodology as well as the understanding of theory.

In his chapter, López-Islas described content analysis research conducted on the MT–VU distributed PBL learning process in order to better understand research data on shared knowledge construction within teams across several different types of courses using the MT–VU PBL model. The goal was to determine whether students in high participation courses were actually engaged in a process of social construction of knowledge. Three courses were randomly selected from the list of PBL courses, and two were selected from the list of non-PBL courses. Additionally, one other PBL course was purposefully selected because the faculty member in charge of the course used an eight-step PBL model instead of the MT–VU four-step model. To examine cognitive presence, he used Gunawardena, Lowe, & Anderson's (1997) content analysis framework for examining shared knowledge construction. Using this framework, the five stages of shared knowledge construction are:

1. Sharing and knowledge information
2. Discovery and exploration of dissonance
3. Negotiation of meaning and co-construction of knowledge
4. Testing and modification of proposed synthesis
5. Agreement statements of newly constructed meaning

As noted earlier in this chapter, the choice of the Gunawardena, Lowe, & Anderson (1997) framework was an appropriate choice given that it is consistent with the social constructivist goals of the PBL learning methodology. It has also been used to investigate other online environments (Gunawardena & Lowe, 1999). In the analysis of messages across PBL courses, López-Islas reports the following findings:

1. Messages corresponding to the more advanced stages of the process occurred later in the PBL process, which makes sense given the process itself.
2. Across the courses, there was a pattern of more Phase 2 and Phase 4 messages as compared with an earlier analysis before the PBL model was implemented.
3. There was evidence of Phase 5 messages reflecting synthesis and construction of new knowledge.
4. Analysis of a single course reflected the need for structure and facilitator interaction as it had a high number of housekeeping-type messages. (There was little interaction by the facilitator and little instruction for how to interact using a seven-instead of four-step PBL model).

These findings offer some important insights into the implementation of distributed collaboration model within the MT–VU context. Specifically, they are useful for providing evidence of knowledge construction through the latter stages of the PBL model as well as the co-construction of new knowledge. Because the outcome of PBL is to support students in construction of new knowledge, this framework was helpful for understanding this issue. Having structure and a method for supporting process (e.g., logistics) is also important as seen in the last finding. In fact, this is an important point because some designers have naïve misconceptions that constructivist methodologies do not provide structured learning environments.

With regard to this specific research, there are several issues to consider. First, obtaining such a high level of interrater reliability, 92% agreement, is extremely difficult. As Cronbach (1970) states, "the process by which constructs are translated and induced from observable behaviors are largely private, informal, and undocumented." This is one of the major challenges of content analysis. I do not challenge López-Islas's rating agreement, but I would like further explanations and examples of how the messages were coded as well as more information on the process of how interrater agreement was obtained. For example, is not clear whether this rating is before or after negotiation of the coding decisions or if a negotiation process was needed or used. Second, student and faculty perspectives gathered through some interviews would have validated findings and provided further insights into issues specific to implementing this methodology. Content analysis alone is a very useful research tool; however, interviews or other multiple data sources enable data triangulation (Denzin, 1989). Third, I wanted to see some examples of the student knowledge building process from MT–VU classes, e.g., student messages reflecting each of the stages. This would have provided more insight into their processes, as well as helped readers understand the context in which the research method was applied. These are some suggestions for enhancing the research as well as the reader's understanding of the findings and methodologies used.

By using the Gunawardena, Lowe, & Anderson (1997) framework, MT–VU was able to examine shared knowledge construction. This is at the same time powerful and limiting. This framework does enable the examination of whether collaborative activities led to group knowledge construction. However, as López-Islas points out, we need to also get at measuring the quality of learning. Specifically, this means that we need to consider process as well as product. Although it is important to understand the process of shared knowledge construction within a collaborative environment, the purpose of an educational experience is usually to support students in meeting certain goals or outcomes. Hence, the research method should support examining learning process as well as product or outcome (e.g., team developed projects). One issue of concern is how we define collaboration and understand how those definitions impact research outcomes. For example, López-Islas cites Pinheiro's (1998) definition of collaborative learning as "the process of students working in teams to pursue knowledge and learning." This seems to be more closely aligned with cooperation where there is not necessarily a shared labor. Roschelle and Teasley (1995) define collaboration as the mutual engagement of participants in a coordinated effort to solve a problem together. These definitions can result in quite different learning processes; hence they are important to clarify as part of the research and design process. Another issue of concern is that the quality of each student's contribution to the shared knowledge construction or the final product is unknown. This is a limitation of most content analysis frameworks as they focus on supporting analysis of individual students (e.g., through messages) rather than supporting analysis of both individual and group process and product. Although there are a number of frameworks for examining learner interactions within collaborative groups (Curtis and Lawson, 1999; Hathorn and Ingram, 2002; Koschmann, Hall, & Miyake, 2002; Newman, 1996), they usually focus on very specific aspects of collaborative behaviors rather than a holistic group portrait. In fact, we need portraits of student interaction and the challenging ways that students work out problems together (Barron, 2000). To address this issue, I am currently developing a holistic framework to evaluate portraits of group collaboration that includes evaluating group process and product as well as individual contributions to group (Kirkley, forthcoming).

The role of theory is to inform our thinking about collaborative learning environments as well as the research methods used to examine them. Yet the role of theory is also a confusing one as there is tension between the individual and the group in collaborative learning that is of critical importance to consider. This also reflects the division in the theoretical field between cognitive constructivism (Piaget, 1932) and socioconstructivism (Vygotsky, 1978). Because group interdependency is a key element of collaboration, learning and knowledge can be shared at the individual level and at the group level. If knowledge and learning is distributed in a way that the sum equals more than the parts (Salomon & Perkins, 1998), can we even begin to isolate cognition in a distributed sense, or even point to the evidence of the contribution of individuals in this case? Simply assessing individual student contributions is not adequate to understand the quality of the collaboration, and assessing the quality of the collaboration will not necessarily indicate what individual students have learned. Some may argue that individual learning is no longer important, but I do not subscribe to that view. Also, there needs to be an assessment of the outcome of the collaboration—what was produced and how did the outcome relate to the quality and patterns of collaboration. This is tall order for computer supported collaborative learning (CSCL) research as we seek to examine the expanses and boundaries of theories focusing on the individual (e.g. radical constructivism) and the group (e.g., socioconstructivism).

With research in CSCL growing in both education (e.g., see Koschmann, 2002) and computer supported collaborative work growing in the workplace (e.g., see Ackerman, 1996), we need a range of high quality and flexible research methods that help us get at the heart of evaluating collaboration. López-Islas's chapter provides insight into how we might apply research methods in order to better understand the impact of a pedagogical innovation on the student learning process, course design, faculty support, and student interactions. From the MT–VU story, we are able to gain insights into real world adaptation, implementation, and evaluation of a pedagogical innovation. We also learn that application of theory, methodology, design and research are intimately intertwined, and if we approach each of these consistently, we can gain important understandings with regard to the holistic design process.

In evaluating new pedagogical innovations, the heart of the issue is determining how and how well they support the learning process and product. Designers, researchers, and theorists need to know more about the trade-offs or gains made with various types of collaborative elements and supports (e.g., scaffolding approaches). As we continue to develop new research methods, it is critical that these be informed by theory so that we can examine instructional methods, learning processes, and technological tools in a grounded approach. We also need to critique these innovations and not simply fall in love with them. As there is a continued push to implement learner-centered environments both online and face-to-face, it is critical that researchers have the necessary tools to examine student interactions and address issues related to real world applications as well as theory development.

In the final section of this chapter, I will propose a framework for architecting theory-based design. In presenting this, I hope to assist other designers and educators who are grappling with the challenging issues related to using theory-based design.

FRAMEWORK FOR ARCHITECTING THEORY-BASED DESIGN

As educators endeavor to create and implement new learning environments both online and face-to-face, we have three responsibilities. First, we need to consider how to best use, adapt, and advance theory-based methodologies. It is only through application that the nuances of theory and methodology can be better understood. Second, we need to actively research and evaluate the implementation of these methodologies in real world settings. This will facilitate an informed understanding of the issues with regard to application of methodologies. Lastly, we need to discuss and publish findings so that the linkages among theory, research, and practice can be better established. For it is through discussion that we create shared understanding of innovative learning processes, well-designed technology tools, and best practices for design. These best practices can, in turn, be used to inform theory and enhance our understanding of the complex process of learning. In this framework, I am presenting a process for conducting theory-based design.

The purpose of this framework (see Figure 1) is to provide a process for educators who wish to develop theory-based designs for real world settings. It has been developed and informed by my seven years of work with Tom Duffy and others at Indiana University who have practiced theory-based design, specifically how to implement PBL in a variety of constructivist learning environments (Duffy and Kirkley, this volume; Malopinsky, Kirkley, & Duffy, 2002). Although my colleagues' work has informed this framework, they hold no responsibility for its imperfections.

In the following paragraphs, I will explain issues to consider at each stage and include examples. Before reviewing the framework, it is important to note several assumptions. First, although this framework has seven stages, one may not go through the stages in a linear manner. In real world application, there is often much overlap among stages as indicated in my discussion of these specific overlaps. Second, the process is iterative, so stages should be revisited and reordered as necessary. In fact, it is through iteration that inconsistencies as well as design issues can be addressed. Third, This is an outline of a framework, and there are many issues that go beyond the length of this chapter. But

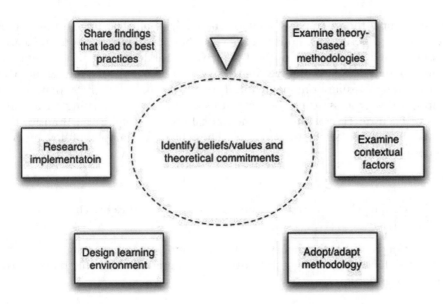

FIG. 15.1.   Framework for theory based design.

this serves as a starting place. Lastly, this was developed for the designer or instructor who is a novice with theory-based design and will hopefully provide insights for those with more expertise.

Briefly, the seven stages are listed below. A discussion of each stage with particular issues and examples follows.

Stage 1: Identify beliefs and values about learning.
Stage 2: Examine theory-based methodologies and related research
    and design issues.
Stage 3: Examine contextual factors of targeted learning environment.
Stage 4: Adopt/adapt a methodology.
Stage 5: Design (or redesign) learning environment.
Stage 6: Implement and research the implementation.
Stage 7: Share findings and contribute to best practices.

Stage 1: Identify Beliefs and Values about Learning

As stated earlier, not all instructional designers have explicitly stated their beliefs and values with regard to learning. Understanding those personal beliefs and how they impact the understanding of the learning and design process is of critical importance. As a first step, it is recommended that you take inventory of those beliefs and values. In doing this, you should read and discuss issues on learning theory and determine which one aligns with your beliefs. This is not an easy endeavor if you are just beginning, and it helps to work with designers or researchers who have expertise in these issues. Articles that link theory and methodology are helpful as a way to examine beliefs as well as principles (e.g., Savery & Duffy, 1996).

Second, consider and document how your beliefs have influenced past design choices either through assumptions made about the learning environment on the design of particular learning processes and activities. This is important for helping understand how theory impacts assumptions made about learning through design. Note that I view design as a holistic endeavor where assumptions about the learning environment may be apparent not just in instructional design but also through interface and content design. By linking your design decisions to theory, you can help tease out covert design assumptions that may not consistent with your beliefs about learning. To support this process, it may be helpful to examine other learning environments that have been developed based on theoretical commitments (e.g., Bransford, Vye, Bateman, Brophy, & Roselli, this volume). These provide examples of how theory impacts design.

Stage 2: Examine Theory-based Methodologies and Related Research and Design Issues

The next step is to identify theory-based methodologies that are congruent with the theory with which you are aligned. In examining a methodology, the following issues should be considered:

1. Is it really a methodology? There are sometimes teaching frameworks and strategies that pose as methodologies. In fact, a teaching technique, strategy, or method is not methodology. A methodology is a cohesive, principle-based process of instruction (e.g., problem-based learning, case based reasoning) that often employs certain types of strategies and techniques in order to bring about a desired goal.

2. Is the methodology grounded in theory and well documented in research? First, research articles that ground the methodology by discussing its linkages to theory should be available. These are helpful for understanding not only theory but also the implications of putting theory into practice. Second, there should be research published on a variety of issues related to research and use of a methodology, and research reviews are particularly helpful for understanding the larger perspective. If there is little research on a methodology, it may be due to the fact that it new, or that it has not been widely adopted for a variety of reasons. Research on real world implementations of the methodology in various settings will not only confirm its utility but its transferability to various settings. Also, guidelines and examples of the methodology being applied are helpful with understanding the teaching and learning process in a tangible manner.

3. From research outcomes as well as interviews with those using the methodology, document factors (past and present) that may impact:
    a. learning process
    b. curriculum design
    c. student and faculty roles
    d. use of technology
    e. logistical issues
    f. other factors that may be relevant (e.g., state requirements, funding available to support innovation)

Knowing and understanding these issues before you approach your own design will support a more successful design and implementation. It is also helpful to conduct site visits to places with experience in using the methodology in order to better understand design as well as implementation and logistical issues.

Stage 3: Examine Contextual Factors of Targeted Learning Environment

In education, we have much experience with good designs failing due to contextual factors not being addressed ahead of time. This is a critical stage of the process. Knowledge gained about contextual factors can provide structure for a successful design and implementation of a methodology and design. Contextual factors include a wide range of issues, including: characteristics of students, faculty, and administration; the type of school or training center; the characteristics of the professional environment; and past experiences with certain types of methodologies.

Without fully analyzing contextual factors, a design, no matter how well done, may experience problems with fully realizing success (see Duffy & Kirkley, this volume). As with the MT–VU case, much planning went into considering how faculty, student, and tutor roles would change, the technology needed to support the distributed PBL, and even how the PBL model needed to be adapted to support distributed learners using an asynchronous discussion. Documenting frame factors that may limit implementation through interviews with people at the targeted learning environment will not only inform decisions about design, it will also provide for a smoother implementation process. Regardless of how well planned an implementation is, there are always lessons to be learned. By documenting lessons learned from the implementation, others can learn how to improve their own designs and implementations, and theorists and researchers can use these to further examine or advance knowledge of the learning process.

Stage 4: Adopt/Adapt a Methodology

Once there is an understanding of the methodological research issues as well as the contextual factors involved, you may be ready to adopt and adapt a methodology. This can be a contentious stage, as a variety of factors need to be addressed. First, in making an adoption, are you choosing a methodology that matches your targeted learning environment? For example, are there constraints such as organizational structures or cost that would inhibit this adoption? Note that adoption of a methodology may not be wide-scale as with MT–VU. In fact, many methodology adoptions are often at the department or even course level.

Once you are clear on the methodology, consider what adaptations need to be made for designing and implementing the methodology. For example, MT–VU simplified the PBL process from seven to four steps due to the distributed nature of their learning environment. Adaptations may be related to a variety of factors such as student outcomes, technology and support systems available, and instructor expertise. It is important to consider these but not to entirely limit the design based on these factors. If limitations completely defined design, there would rarely be new innovations. The goal is to apply creative and realistic solutions to address these factors and document why specific approaches worked or did not work. Keeping a design diary is one method helpful for documenting decisions and the impact on design.

In making adaptations, it is important to ensure that changes made are aligned with theory and methodology. If certain things are changed, it can be argued that the design is no longer grounded in either the purported theory or methodology. Hence, theory-based design is no longer being practiced, and you may be representing your design as something that it is not.

Stage 5: Design (or Redesign) Learning Environment

In creating a design based in a specific methodology, it is important to view examples of other designs using this specific methodology. Compare and contrast those designs and define and consider the following:

a) How do specific learning goals, assessments, processes, and activities reflect the methodological principles?
b) How does the overall design of the learning environment instantiate values and beliefs about theory?
c) How might technological factors support or inhibit the design?
d) How might organizational factors support or inhibit the design?

After reflecting on other designs, prototype your own design with these factors in mind. As you do this, consider and address factors related to learning environment goals and context. Because designs are rarely perfect the first time, obtaining feedback from experts or clients is a must. With rapid prototyping techniques (Tripp, & Bichelmeyer, 1990) and usability testing (Nielsen, 1994), aspects of the instruction, learning process, interface, and technology can evaluated and improved until a final version is reached. Implementing the design in a small scale test environment will reveal problematic issues not found in prototyping or usability testing, e.g., technology failures, logistical problems.

If you are conducting redesign work, it is important to document needed changes or improvements to the design from a standpoint of research and evaluation. These results can greatly inform what changes need to be addressed not only to your design but will serve others as well. For redesign work, it may also be review previous stages listed in this framework as a way to generate additional ideas for improvement or a realignment of theory and methodology.

Stage 6: Implement and Research the Implementation

Long before implementation, the research and evaluation process should be planned and organized. Research and evaluation processes and methods should be chosen based on current knowledge as well as be congruency with theoretical commitments and learning goals. For MT–VU, using the Gunawardena, Lowe, & Anderson (1997) framework was consistent with their beliefs about learning.

There are a wide variety of research and evaluation techniques available, and the choices made should reflect the purpose of the evaluation as well as how the information will be used (e.g., to support redesign work, to document methodological best practices/lessons learned, to inform theory). Both summative and formative evaluation are important, and there are a wide variety of research and evaluation methods available to support both (see Hannafin & Peck, 1988). Action research (Calhoun, 1993) is also a useful framework that supports practitioners in examining their problems in order to evaluate decisions and actions. Regardless of the evaluation method and process chosen, it should do the following: provide specific outcomes with regard to purpose of evaluation; be aligned with theoretical values and methodological principles; and be able to support translation of the evaluation outcomes to research, theory, and practice (although not all are likely to be met equally).

Stage 7: Share Findings and Contribute to Best Practices

Evaluation findings can be shared in a wide variety of formats from white paper discussions and best practices guidelines to more formal conference presentations and journal articles. By sharing lessons learned and developing best practices from theory-based design instantiations, the field of instructional design and education in general can be greatly enhanced by developing designs from tested models.

Once you complete the stages, it is assumed that you will continue to cycle back through various stages as necessary. By using theory to develop informed and consistent design and sharing those developments and evaluations on a wide scale, we can develop a greater understanding of interlinked issues related to theory, research, methodology, and practice. By grounding our work in theory and methodology, we can create stronger design approaches that can be used and adapted by others. This framework, as outlined here, is one attempt to provide a process for architecting theory-based design.

CONCLUSION

In this chapter, the goal has been to address, through the case of MT–VU, the issues related to and importance of using theory-based design. We have much work to do in education with gaining better understandings of the complexities of theory and practice in technology-based learning environments. In examining the case of MT–VU's adoption, adaptation, and implementation of collaborative PBL, López-Islas has provided us with some ideas on how to proceed.

By understanding that theory, methodology, design are not only intimately intertwined but function as a result of each other, instructional designers can capitalize on developing high quality learning environments that are based on sound principles of theory and practice. This calls for changing our practices. The traditional one-way street between theory and practice needs to become a six lane highway where theorists, designers, researchers, instructors, administrators, and students (as clients) all contribute to the development, implementation, and evaluation of innovative learning environments. By using theory-based design to inform our designs and implementations, we can create stronger design approaches that enhance not only theory and methodology but the field of instructional design as well.

REFERENCES

Ackerman, M. (Ed.), (1996). CSCW '96: Proceedings of the conference on computer supported cooperative work. New York: ACM.

Barron, B. (2000). Achieving coordination in collaborative problem-solving groups. *Journal of the Learning Sciences, 9*(4), 403–436.

Bednar, A. K., Cunningham, D., Duffy, T. M., & Perry, J. D. (1992). Theory into practice: How do we link? In T. M. Duffy, & D. H. Jonassen (Eds.), *Constructivism and the technology of instruction: A conversation* (pp. 17–34). Hillsdale, NJ: Lawrence Erlbaum.

Bonk, C. J., & Cummings, J. A. (1998). A dozen recommendations for placing the student at the center of Web-based instruction. *Educational Media International, 35*(2), 82–89.

Brown, A. L. (1992). Design experiments: Theoretical and methodological challenges in creating complex interventions in classroom settings. *The Journal of the Learning Sciences, 2*(2), 141–178.

Calhoun, E. (1993). Action research: Three approaches. *Educational Leadership, 51*(2), 62–65.

Collins, A. (1992). Toward a design science of education. In E. Scanlon, & T. O'Shea (Eds.), *New directions in educational technology* (pp. 15–22). Berlin: Springer-Verlag.

Cobb, P., Confrey, J., diSessa, A., Lehrer, R., & Schauble, L. (2003). Design experiments in educational research. *Educational Researcher, 32*(1), 9–13.

Cronbach, L. J. (1970). Essentials of psychological testing, 3rd Ed. New York: Harper, & Row.

Curtis, D., & Lawson, M. (1999). Exploring collaborative online learning. *Journal of Asynchronous Learning Networks, 5*(1), 21–34.

Denzin, N. K. (1989). Interpretive biography, Qualitative research methods Series, 17. Newbury Park: Sage.

Duffy, T. M., Dueber, W., & Hawley, C. L. (1998). "Critical thinking in a distributed environment: A pedagogical base for the design of conferencing systems." In C. J. Bonk and K. S. King (Eds.), *Electronic Collaborators: Learner-Centered Technologies for Literacy, Apprenticeship, and Discourse* (pp. 51–78). Mahwah, NJ: Lawrence Erlbaum Associates.

Duffy, T. M., & Cunningham, D. J. (1996). Constructivism: Implications for the design and delivery of instruction. In D. Jonassen (Ed.), *Handbook of research for educational communications and technology* (pp. 170–198). New York: Macmillan.

Edelson, D. C. (2002). Design research: What we learn when we engage in design. *The Journal of the Learning Sciences, 11*(1), 105–121.

Garrison, D. R. (1991). Critical thinking and self-directed learning in adult education: an analysis of responsibility and control issues. *Adult Education Quarterly, 42*(3), 136–148.

Gijselaers, W. H. (1996). "Connecting problem-based practices with educational theory." In L. Wilkerson, & W. Gijselaers (Eds.), *Bringing Problem-Based Learning to Higher Education: Theory and Practice*. San Francisco: Jossey-Bass.

Gunawardena, C. N., & Lowe, C. A. (1998). Transcript analysis of computer-mediated conferences as a tool for testing constructivist and social-constructivist learning theories. *Proceedings of the Fourteenth Annual Conference on Distance Teaching and Learning* (pp. 139–145). Madison, WI: University of Wisconsin-Madison.

Gunawardena, C. N., Lowe, C. A., & Anderson, T. (1997). Analysis of a global online debate and the development of an interaction analysis model for examining social construction of knowledge in computer conferencing. *Journal of Educational Computing Research, 17*(4), 397–431.

Hannafin, M. J., & Peck, K. L. (1988). *The design, development, and evaluation of instructional software.* New York: Macmillan.

Hannafin, M. J., Hannafin, K. M., Land, S., & Oliver, K. (1997). Grounded practice in the design of learning systems. *Educational Research and Development, 45*(3), 101–117.

Hathorn, L. G., & Ingram, A. L. (2002). Cooperation and collaboration using computer-mediated communication. *Journal of Educational Computing Research, 26*(3), 325–347.

Institute for Higher Education Policy (2000). Quality on the line: Benchmarks for success in internet-based distance education. Washington, DC: The Institute for Higher Education Policy. Available: http://www.ihep.com/Publications.php?parm=Pubs/Abstract?30

Jonassen, D. H. (1998). Designing constructivist, case-based learning environments. In C. Reigeluth (Ed.), *Instructional design theories and models: A new paradigm of instructional theory* (Vol. 2). Mahwah, NJ: Lawrence Erlbaum Associates.

Jonassen, D. H., & Reeves, T. C. (1995). Learning with technology: Using computers as cognitive tools. In D. H. Jonassen (Ed.), *Handbook of research for educational communication and technology* (pp. 693–724). New York: Simon, & Schuster/Macmillan.

Kirkley, J. (Forthcoming). Developing a content analysis framework to holistically evaluate collaboration in asynchronous learning environments.

Koschmann, T., Hall, R., & Miyake, N. (Eds.) (2002). CSCL 2: Carrying forward the conversation. Mahwah, NJ: Lawrence Erlbaum Associates.

Koschmann, T. (1996). Computer-Supported problem-based learning: A principled approach to the use of computers in collaborative learning. In T. Koschmann (Ed.), *CSCL: Theory and Practice* (pp. 83–124). Mahwah, NJ: Lawrence Erlbaum Associates.

Krathwohl, D. R. (1998). Methods of educational and social science research: An integrated approach, (2nd ed.). New York: Longman.

Malopinsky, L., Kirkley, J. R., Duffy, T. (2002). Building performance support systems to assist preK-12 teachers in designing online, inquiry-based professional development instruction. Paper presented at the Annual Meeting of American Educational Research Association, New Orleans, LA.

Nielsen, J. (1994). Usability engineering. San Francisco: Morgan Kaufmann.

Newman, D. R. (1996). How can WWW-based groupware better support critical thinking in CSCL? In proceedings of the ERCIM workshop on CSCW and the Web, Sankt Augustin, Germany.

Newman, D. R., Johnson, C., Webb, B., & Cochrane, C. (1996). Evaluating the quality of learning in computer supported cooperative learning, *Journal of the American Society for Information Science, 48,* 484–495.

Piaget, J. (1932). The moral judgment of the child. London: Routledge and Kegan Paul.

Pinheiro, E. (1998). Collaborative learning. In D. G. Oblinger, & S. C. Rush (Eds.), *The future compatible campus* (pp. 118–130). Bolton: Anker Publishing.

Presidential task force on psychology in education, (1993). Learner-centered psychological principles: Guidelines for school redesign and reform. Washington, DC: American Psychological Association/Mid-continent Regional Educational Laboratory.

Reigeluth, C., Ed. (1999). Instructional design theories and models: A new paradigm of instructional theory (Vol. 2). Mahwah, New Jersey: Lawrence Erlbaum Associates.

Robinson, V. (1998). Methodology and the research-practice gap. *Educational Researcher, 27*(1), 17–26.

Roschelle, J., & Teasley, S. D. (1995). Construction of shared knowledge in collaborative problem-solving. In C. O'Malley (Ed.), *Computer-supported collaborative learning* (pp. 69–97). New York: Springer-Verlag.

Salomon, G., & Perkins, D. (1998). Individual and social aspects of learning. In P. Pearson & A. Iran-Nejad (Eds.), *Review of research in education, 23,* 1–24.

Savery, J., & Duffy, T. (1996). Problem-based learning: An instructional model and its constructivist framework. In B. Wilson (Ed.), *Constructivist learning environments: Case studies in instructional design* (pp. 135–148). Englewood Cliffs, NJ: Educational Technology Publications.

Schmidt H. G. (1993) Foundations of problem-based learning: Some explanatory notes. *Medical Education, 27,* 422–432.

Sfard, A. (1998). On two metaphors for learning and the dangers of choosing just one. *Educational Researcher, 27*(2), 4–13.

Tripp, S., & Bichelmeyer, B. (1990). Rapid prototyping: An alternative instructional design strategy. *Educational Technology Research, & Development, 38*(1), 31–44.

Vygotsky, L. S. (1978). Mind in society. Cambridge, MA: Harvard University Press.

Wagner, E. D., & McCombs, B. L. (1995). Learner-centered psychological principles in practice: Designs for distance education. *Educational Technology, 35*(2), 32–35.

Wilson, B. G. (1999). The dangers of theory-based design: A paper for discussion on IT Forum. Available: http://itech1.coe.uga.edu/itforum/paper31/paper31.html

Wilson, B. G. (1995). Situated instructional design: Blurring the distinctions between theory and practice, design and implementation, curriculum and instruction. In M. Simonson (Ed.), *Proceedings of selected research and development presentations.* Washington, DC: Association for Educational Communications and Technology.

Zech, L., Gause-Vega, C., Bray, M., & Goldman, S. (2000). Content-based collaborative inquiry: A professional development model for sustaining educational reform. *Educational Psychologist, 35*(3), 207–217.

Open Discussion of Chapter 14

Rafael Lopez: Just a brief comment on the data set and the analysis issues. We have also got these personal profiles of students. The only problem we have is that just from these programs, we have 8,000 students. So how we put this together is very hard. My database is incredibly rich, and as a consequence, the analysis is very complicated. So, for example, what kind of program these students are from—they are from humanities, and also engineering, also business, and education. So it's very hard for me to analyze it. But, of course, over time we will be conducting much richer and more detailed analyses. It just takes time.

Terry Anderson: Three quick comments. You talked about the lack of dissonance in the student discussion. I don't think it is peculiar to the Latin culture, but rather, it is common in educational settings. We call it pathological politeness. It's funny, because in the literature on noneducational use of asynchronous text messaging, you get this flame war thing—it's huge stuff. But you don't get this happening in educational settings. I wouldn't worry about it being a particularly Latin thing.

My second comment has to do with the reliability of your measures. I think it's critical that you publish it. You indicated that the unit of analysis is not the message but the thematic unit. It is real tricky to describe how you pulled those thematic units out. It would be very valuable and important for you to document that.

My final quick comment: You talked about the development of the learning objects that model the learning processes. The most interesting work that I have found in this area is the educational modeling language developed at the Open University in the Netherlands. IMS, the instructional design group, is probably going to adopt this. It goes a small way toward developing an ecology for looking at learning transactions, as well as objects. We are a long ways from it, but that is the best lead I know.

Scott Grabinger: I am interested in tools, theory, and practice, especially for the PBL process you are doing. You mentioned at the end that technology is a constraint and not an enabler. What tools do you need to make the PBL process richer? For example, thinking through the problems is a critical part of the PBL process. Do you have in mind the tool that you might be able to use to enable the students to work together and think through this process?

Rafael Lopez: I can think of two things here. One is that I believe that the technology can help to scaffold the process. It provides a way to organize. I think we can embed in technology some of the structure I think we should provide. I don't want to constrain interaction, but I want to provide some structure. I believe the technology can do this. That is what we are trying to develop with this system we are dealing with.

The other one is for the interactive capabilities of the system. We did not decide to go asynchronous, because we did not want synchronicity. Rather, it is very hard to provide the space for 8,000 students to come and chat and keep things organized. So we are designing a system, with the technology that allows students to interact synchronously and asynchronously as they want to.

All these issues we raise about agents and that kind of stuff is very helpful to me. We are also working on the learning object things, but we are really not very far along. However, we are also working with a repository that can be used by different courses.

Scott Grabinger: So if you have a group of six students now and they get a problem, what kind of process do they go through in terms of generating hypotheses or ideas?

Rafael Lopez: They have to discuss this according to the instructions. The instructions are in the scenario. They have to read it. They have to come up with first the impressions about what the problem is. They have to come up with the definition of the learning. This is how they move through all the phases. There is a tutor that calls the students.

Scott Grabinger: Okay, so they are working individually?

Rafael Lopez: No, they are collaborating.

Scott Grabinger: They do it groups.

Rafael Lopez: There is one component where they are doing independent research. They go back to the library. They review some resources that we provide. They come back with an answer. They discuss the answer. They have to agree on the answer.

Scott Grabinger: Does the tutor then participate in an ongoing assessment of the different parts?

Rafael Lopez: Yes, there is an ongoing assessment. The teacher is part of the process—she is very important to us.

(End of session)

16

Faculty Development, Student Satisfaction, and Reported Learning in the SUNY Learning Network

Peter J. Shea, Eric E. Fredericksen, Alexandra M. Pickett, and William E. Pelz
State University of New York

Online teaching and learning environments have evolved only recently to the point where not only courses, but entire degree programs, may be completed via the Internet. How best to structure such environments has been a challenge, one that many institutions are only beginning to address. Added complexity arises when the system implementing an online teaching and learning environment is a very large one, as in the case of the State University of New York (SUNY), by some measures the largest unified system of public higher education in the United States. This chapter will examine issues of pedagogy, faculty development, student satisfaction, and reported learning in the State University of New York Learning Network, the forum for online learning leading to complete degree programs for 53 SUNY colleges.

BACKGROUND

The SUNY Learning Network (SLN) is the online instructional program created for the 64 colleges and nearly 400,000 students of the State University of New York. The primary goals of the SUNY Learning Network are to bring SUNY's diverse, high-quality instructional programs within the reach of learners everywhere and to be the best provider of asynchronous instruction for learners in New York state and beyond. Strategic objectives for this initiative are threefold:

1. To provide increased, flexible access to higher education within and beyond New York state
2. To provide a mechanism for maintaining consistently, high-quality online teaching, and learning across the SUNY system
3. Leverage the resources of the State University of New York system to contain the costs associated with the development, design, and delivery of online education.

This chapter focuses primarily on the second goal—that of providing a mechanism for maintaining consistently high-quality online teaching and learning.

The SUNY Learning Network started as a regional project in the Mid-Hudson Valley involving eight SUNY campuses. Initially, the development and delivery of asynchronous courses was a new activity for SUNY campuses and faculty. With generous support from the Alfred P. Sloan Foundation, combined with enthusiasm and resources from SUNY System Administration and participating campuses, the SLN successfully met the challenges of an early developmental phase that focused on "proof of concept" and "expansion—scalability."

Successful experiences led to an expanded vision and goals for the SLN, and the scope and objectives of the project have grown substantially. The annual growth in courses, from eight in 1995–1996 to more than 2,500 in 2001–2002, and annual growth in enrollment, from 119 in 1995–1996 to more than 40,000 in 2001–2002, with courses offered at all undergraduate and graduate levels from 53 of our institutions, illustrates that the project has met, and in many ways exceeded, original projections. The program has recently been recognized by EDUCAUSE as the 2001 award winner for Systemic Improvement in Teaching and Learning and by the Sloan Consortium for its 2001 Excellence in ALN Faculty Development Award.

CONCEPTUAL FRAMEWORK

The SUNY Learning Network represents a formal online teaching and learning environment. To understand how best to structure such an environment to ensure effective pedagogy, it is useful to begin by looking at what works well in traditional learning environments and to attempt to attend to models of best practices identified for effective education. Of course, such an examination must be done in light of our understanding that differences exist between online and classroom-based teaching and learning. But starting with best practices in structuring traditional learning environments is a good foundation for further investigation.

The National Research Council's Commission on Behavioral and Social Sciences and Education provides guidance in this area, especially in the publication *How People Learn* (Bransford, Brown, Cocking, Donavan, & Pellegrino, 2000). The authors offer a model for effective learning environments in which a system of four interconnected components combine and mutually support each other. These interconnecting components are foci that provide a foundation for learning environments, the best of which appear to be learner centered, knowledge centered, assessment centered, and community centered. The model may be seen as a set of overlapping circles, as illustrated in Fig. 16.1.

The authors detail each of these foci—briefly summarized here. Good learning environments are knowledge centered in that they are designed in consideration of desired outcomes. Guiding questions for creating a knowledge-centered learning environment include: What do we want students to know and be able to do when they have completed our materials or course? How do we provide learners with the "foundational knowledge, skills, and attitudes needed for successful transfer" (Bransford et al., 2000)?

Good learning environments are also learner centered, that is, they function in a manner that connects to the strengths, interests, and preconceptions of learners (Bransford et al., 2000) and help students to gain insight into themselves as learners. In such environments, teachers work to bridge new content with students' current

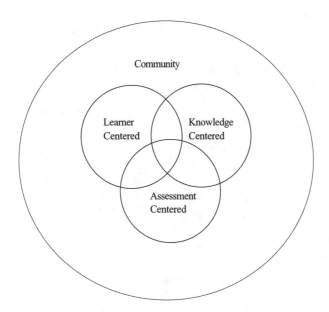

FIG. 16.1.   Perspectives on learning environments. (Source: Bransford et al., 2000).

understandings and to facilitate growth, while attending to the learners' interests, passions, and motivations.

Another characteristic of good learning environments is that they are community centered; that is, they promote and benefit from shared norms that value learning and high standards. Ideally, good learning environments connect to relevant external communities and provide a milieu within the classroom where students feel safe to ask questions, work collaboratively, and in which they are taught to develop lifelong learning skills.

Finally, the authors emphasize that good learning environments are assessment centered, meaning that they provide learners with many opportunities to make their thinking visible (Bransford et al., 2000) and to get feedback to create new meaning and new understanding.

The guidelines in *How People Learn* provide an excellent framework from which to consider the design of online learning environments, in that they summarize much of what is known about good learning environments generally. However, in addition, we must also consider the specific needs of higher education learners and focus on lessons learned from research in college-level teaching and learning, as these are most relevant to the SLN. Are there guidelines that help to determine how to implement a learning-, assessment-, knowledge-, and community-centered environment—one that is designed to engage higher education students specifically?

Certain institutional practices are known to lead to high levels of student engagement. Perhaps the best-known set of engagement indicators is the "Seven Principles of Good Practice in Undergraduate Education." (Kuh, 2001)

The seven principles of good practice in undergraduate education identified by Chickering and Gamson (1987) reflect much of what is identified by Bransford and colleagues (2001) in the design of good learning environments. These principles distill decades of research on the undergraduate experience, providing some guidance on

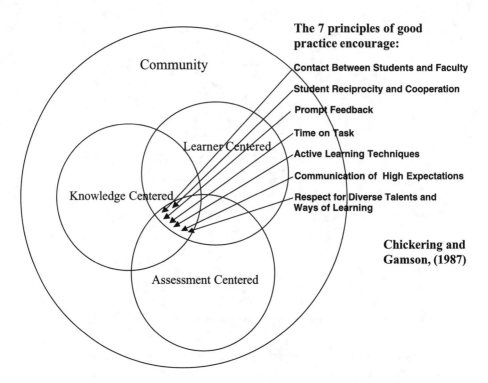

FIG. 16.2. Principles of good practice and perspectives on learning environments. (Source: Chickering & Gamson, 1987).

how best to structure learning in higher education. Chickering and Gamson (1987) encourage the following general conditions and behaviors for successful learning: (1) frequent contact between students and faculty, (2) reciprocity and cooperation among students, (3) active learning techniques; (4) prompt feedback, (5) time on task, (6) the communication of high expectations, and (7) respect for diverse talent and ways of learning.

We feel that the principles of good practice outlined by Chickering and Gamson (1987) are at the heart of the model presented by Bransford and colleagues (2000) and provide a focus specific to higher education learning environments. Figure 16.2 details this relationship.

Although these principles provide guidance in developing higher education learning environments, they are written at a relatively high level of abstraction without a specific focus on the needs of higher education students learning at a distance, as in the case of the SLN. Further, the SLN was specifically designed as an asynchronous environment, and for many courses in the program, it depends largely on text-based interaction to carry out teaching and learning. A specific set of indicators that *does* focus on higher education at a distance in primarily text-based, asynchronous environments may be found in the model proposed by Garrison, Anderson, and Archer (2000). This framework also reflects the principles of good practice and, we propose, the model presented by Bransford and colleagues (2000). It is to the Garrison, Anderson, and Archer (2000) framework we will now turn, with the goal of providing a more comprehensive conceptual background and to provide a more developed and detailed set of categories through which to examine issues of pedagogy, faculty development, student satisfaction, and reported learning in the SLN.

In the model of critical thinking and practical inquiry proposed by Garrison, Anderson, and Archer (2000), three overlapping lenses—cognitive presence, social presence, and teaching presence—provide mutual support to create a framework in which interaction in an asynchronous online educational experience may be assessed. The model seeks to explain how to best analyze and ultimately promote higher order learning in computer mediated, largely text-based environments such as the SLN. Later, we will look at social, teaching, and cognitive presence in greater depth.

In this model, social presence is viewed as the "ability of students to project themselves socially and affectively into a community of inquiry" and is deemed critical in the absence of physical presence and attendant teacher immediacy necessary to sustain learning in the classroom. Teaching presence is referred to as "the design facilitation and direction of cognitive and social processes for the realization of personally meaningful and educationally worthwhile learning outcomes." (Anderson, Rourke, Garrison, Archer, 2001). Teaching presence has three components—instructional design and organization, facilitating discourse, and direct instruction.

The authors define cognitive presence as "the extent to which students are able to construct and confirm meaning through sustained discourse in a community of inquiry," and it is achieved in concert with effective teaching presence and satisfactory social presence. The authors provide a visual representation of the model, reproduced in Fig. 16.3.

How does this model relate to the principles of good practice in undergraduate education espoused by Chickering and Gamson (1987)? Again, one might revise the model to locate the seven principles of good practice, as shown in Fig. 16.4.

We feel that the principles of good practice are also essential elements of the teaching and learning transaction, and crucial in creating and sustaining student engagement

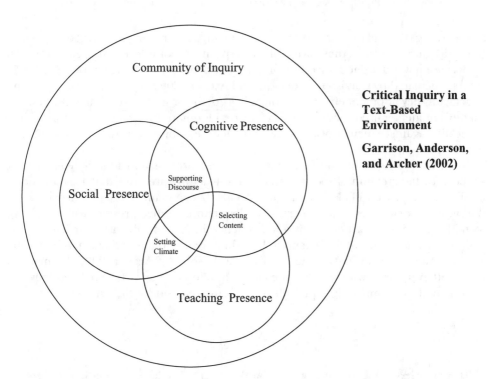

FIG. 16.3.   Elements of an educational experience. (Source: Garrison, Anderson, & Archer, 2000).

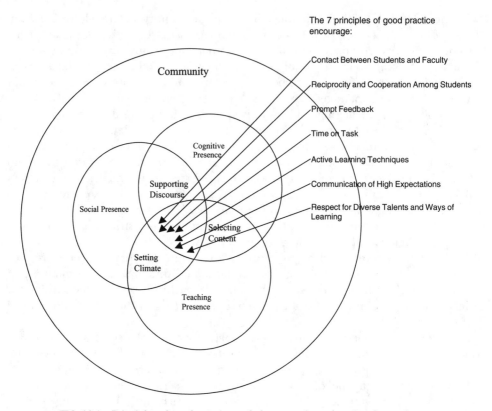

The 7 principles of good practice encourage:

Contact Between Students and Faculty

Reciprocity and Cooperation Among Students

Prompt Feedback

Time on Task

Active Learning Techniques

Communication of High Expectations

Respect for Diverse Talents and Ways of Learning

FIG. 16.4.   Principles of good practice and elements of an educational experience.

and learning. We feel that the Garrison, Anderson, and Archer (2000) model specifies how to identify and enact these principles in a specifically online learning environment.

Because it was designed for online learning environments, the framework and indicators articulated by Garrison, Anderson, and Archer (2000) is useful in analyzing the SLN faculty development efforts. Although it is not the original intention of the authors that this model be used for assessing faculty development programs, it does provide a "checklist" against which efforts to create an effective online learning environment can be analyzed.

Next, we will describe the faculty development process and identify elements of support for the creation of social presence and teaching presence that are embedded in SLN training. We will also explain how faculty become aware of and enact these in the online courses they teach to create and sustain cognitive presence. By attending to both the general principles of good practice in higher education articulated by Chickering and Gamson (1987) and to how they are identified and enacted in online, asynchronous environments in the Garrison, Anderson, and Archer (2000) framework, we will attempt to discover whether the faculty development efforts were likely to result in good pedagogy and a high-quality learning environment for SLN students.

FACULTY TRAINING

They are peers in the execution of "real work." What holds them together is a common sense of purpose and a real need to know what each other knows. (John Seely Brown on communities of practice)

All faculty teaching through the SLN participate in a program of training. The goals of this faculty development initiative are to help new instructors understand the nature of online learning and how to transform what they do in the classroom to best exploit the affordances and mitigate the constraints of Internet-based teaching and learning. Below, we describe this training and highlight the components of the experience that we feel reflect principles of good pedagogical practice that support the creation of social and teaching presence.

Faculty Development: A Community Approach

All faculty who participate in the SUNY Learning Network agree to participate in a 5-month preparatory training, and engage in an ongoing dialogue and receive ongoing support during the entire time they develop and teach their courses. The dialogue and supportive interaction takes place within the SLN community of trainers, multimedia instructional design partners, experienced faculty, SLN program staff, and the faculty help desk.

Faculty report a number of motivators for deciding to develop and teach an online course. In our most recent survey of faculty, with 255 respondents, we found that most faculty chose to participate because of an interest in online teaching (Table 16.1).

Training begins with participation in an online, all-faculty conference that mirrors the environment in which faculty will eventually instruct. Through participation in this online conference, new faculty come together with experienced faculty and conference facilitators to experience what they and their students will do in this new learning environment. The online conference helps faculty to understand, firsthand, the affordances and constraints of an online environment, allowing them to have the perspective of the online student. This conference also allows new faculty to connect to experienced faculty, and models an effective online course design, effective learning activities, and productive course management practices. This initial online experience for new faculty is designed to provide encouragement, support, and responsiveness, and facilitates entry into the community of SLN online course developers and educators.

In this phase of the faculty development and course design process, new faculty also have the opportunity to observe "live" ongoing courses, examining and discussing the course designs and instructional styles of experienced SLN instructors in a variety of disciplines. Again, through these activities, embedded in the real work of developing a

TABLE 16.1

Why Did You Choose to Develop and Teach an Online Course?

	Frequency	Percent
Course only offered online	4	1.6
Fear of being left behind	5	1.9
Want/need to telecommute	11	4.3
Marketability of skills	14	5.5
Curiosity	17	6.7
Interest in technology/Internet	22	8.6
Interest in online teaching	152	59.6
Other	30	11.8
Total	255	100.0

course, new faculty are encouraged to become members of the larger SLN community, to learn its norms, practices, and vocabulary. Entry into this community is symbolized in part through the distribution of T-shirts with the SLN logo and the phrase "replicate–work–replicate," a practice required in the software that faculty use to create their courses.

In addition to the online faculty conference, new instructors also engage in 20 hours of face-to-face training. During three full-day trainings, implemented over an ongoing 5-month synchronous and asynchronous training cycle, faculty receive a comprehensive course development guide, and meet their instructional design partner, training facilitators, help desk staff, the SLN program staff, and other new instructors. Through participation in this emerging community, faculty explore the idea that online instruction does not simply entail mimicking what happens in the classroom, but rather requires a considerable transformation and rethinking of course components.

Common issues that arise include understanding new roles and new technology. For example, writing and posting online course materials in cooperation with an instructional design partner represents a break with familiar, frequently individual, higher education practices. New faculty frequently struggle with the idea that their instructional design partner will view and provide feedback on their materials. Building trust and understanding through frequent communication is essential in this new relationship. Facilitating the understanding that this practice has assisted hundreds of previous instructors is also helpful in building trust.

Other challenges include learning how to manage a database-driven online course site. Throughout face-to-face training, faculty are introduced to various features of the software and provided best practices on how to integrate good pedagogy while learning the new features. For example, in learning how to edit documents in this environment, faculty write a profile that helps students see them as "real people" with interests, concerns, and lives outside the course.

In concert with their instructional design partner, the help desk, experienced instructors, and trainers, the new faculty work on how to best create a teaching and learning environment in which students get to know the instructor, each other, and have ample opportunities for quality interaction and feedback. To fully exploit the unique opportunities of online instruction faculty are initially encouraged to reflect on course learning outcomes and then to investigate, with the ongoing support of the SLN community, how best to translate and achieve these outcomes online. The faculty help desk provides continuous support to answer technical questions and make the technology as invisible as possible, reducing confusion about technology and helping faculty focus on their key role—facilitating learning. Figure 16.5 provides an overview of the faculty development process.

After 7 years of faculty development efforts, more than 1,400 instructors have engaged in training offered through the SUNY Learning Network. This training and the accompanying support reflects what Buckley (2002) referred to as "lavish care" necessary (though not always sufficient) to ensure a transforming experience. During this initial faculty development cycle, new instructors receive what Buckley calls "boutique-level" service that, we believe, has helped establish the reputation of the SUNY Learning Network and resulted in interest and enthusiasm of later adopters.

The SLN Course Management System (CMS)

The SLN CMS was developed by higher education professionals specifically for the purpose of higher education teaching and learning. The design team focused on

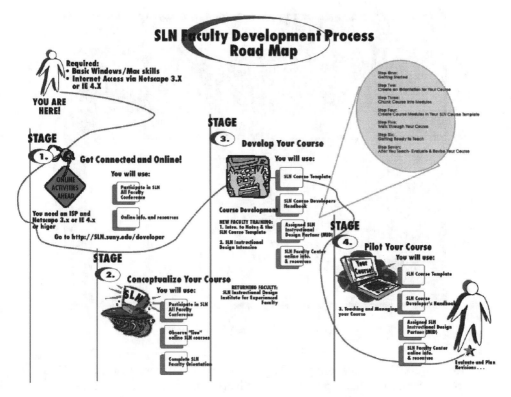

FIG. 16.5.   SLN faculty development and course design process.

providing sound pedagogical tools that provided maximum design flexibility while maintaining an attractive and informative graphical interface that students could easily learn to use. Courses created in the SLN CMS may include text, images, sound, and multimedia appropriate to meet course-learning objectives. Figure 16.6 shows the SLN CMS interface, as seen from a student's perspective on the Web.

We believe this common interface reduces the burden that might arise from a nonstandard course environment and helps students focus on learning content, rather than navigation of the course.

HELPING FACULTY CREATE AND SUSTAIN QUALITY ONLINE TEACHING AND LEARNING

How does the faculty development process outlined above help faculty to engage in behaviors that are likely to result in productive learning environments? Clearly, to achieve this goal, there is a need to focus on the elements put forth by Bransford and colleagues (2000); that is, the trainings need to emphasize the importance of learning-centered, knowledge-centered, assessment-centered, and community-centered environments. In addition, because the SLN is a higher education learning environment, we emphasize the importance of the specific principles of good practice in undergraduate education outlined by Chickering and Gamson (1987). Finally, because the goals of the trainings are to help faculty understand the nature of online, asynchronous learning, we emphasize many of the indicators of social presence outlined by Rourke, Garrison, Anderson,

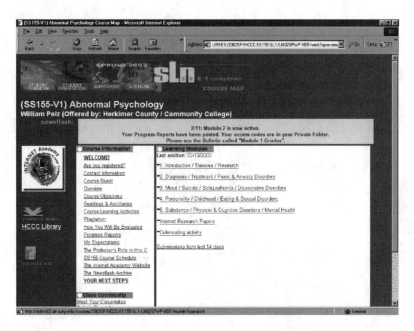

FIG. 16.6.   SLN course Web interface.

and Archer (2001) and teaching presence outlined by Anderson, Rourke, Garrison, and Archer (2001) that lead to better online learning. Later, we will discuss faculty development in greater detail, especially as it relates to social and teaching presence, and examine how faculty learn about ideas and practices related to these concepts through SLN trainings.

Rourke, Garrison, Anderson, and Archer (2001) identified social presence as the "ability of learners to project themselves socially and emotionally into a community of inquiry." Social presence is important in that it supports learning by making interaction, "appealing, engaging, and thus intrinsically rewarding" (Rourke et al., 2001). The model also presents a more specific set of online indicators for facilitating engagement than those represented by the general principles of good practice in undergraduate education. Attention to social presence is also necessary, though not necessarily sufficient, to attain the learner-centered environment emphasized by Bransford and colleagues (2000). Rourke and colleagues proposed three categories for analyzing computer conferencing transcripts for evidence of social presence—affective, interactive, and cohesive.

Affective indicators can be described as expression of emotion, feeling, and mood, which may be evidenced by the use of emoticons, humor, and self-disclosure. The authors define interactive indicators as messages of a "socially appreciative nature" that are found within the threaded interchanges of online discussion. (These may be found in other parts of an online course, though Rourke and colleagues (2001) focused primarily on threaded discussions.) In the absence of the physical cues of verbal and nonverbal communication, interactive indicators provide evidence that "somebody is out there 'listening.'" This evidence that your professor or fellow students are attending to your communications may be seen through the continuation of a "thread," or interchange; by directly quoting or by referring directly to another's message; by asking questions to elicit clarity; by complimenting or expressing appreciation; and by expressing agreement.

The authors also identify "cohesive indicators," which are evidenced by the use of "vocatives," for example, addressing participants by name, the use of inclusive pronouns (*we, our, group*), as well as "phatics and salutations," or verbal exchanges that serve a purely social function such as greetings and closures (Rourke et al., 2001). These indicators equate with the Chickering and Gamson (1987) principle encouraging contact between students and faculty, while providing appropriate concern for making such contact authentic in an online learning environment.

Support for Building Social Presence in SLN Training

Affective Dimensions

SLN training facilitators emphasize the affective nature of online learning in a number of ways. For example, the use of humor and appropriate methods for self-disclosure are discussed in both online forums, the face-to-face trainings they precede, and with their instructional design partner. In these forums, faculty learn that humor, although useful and potentially socially binding, can also backfire and cause misunderstanding and even anger in the absence of physical presence and verbal and nonverbal signals that often facilitate humor. The training forums provide opportunities to discuss humor and, again where appropriate, to model it, along with suggestions about the affordances and constraints of an online environment.

Faculty are encouraged to model appropriate levels of self-disclosure in their introductory course documents. Trainers provide faculty with examples of introductory documents that give students background information on instructor interests, research specialization, and even personal Web sites. These examples are meant to help instructors understand how to begin to create a sense of togetherness, shared mission, and to begin to put students at ease about studying online. Trainers emphasize that modeling appropriate levels of self-disclosure will help lower the barriers that a lack of physical immediacy may create online.

Interactive Dimensions

The importance of interaction is strongly emphasized in faculty development efforts. Certain interactive indicators identified by Rourke and colleagues (2001) are integrated into the technology used by the faculty; others are specifically highlighted through the various training forums. Faculty explore different forums for interacting with students within their course management system. Interaction may be done publicly—in topical open class discussions and course related bulletin boards—or in private, as appropriate, through "virtual office hours," private folders, and individualized feedback to specific assignments. Faculty discuss the pros and cons of small group forums and learning activities designed and implemented to encourage student–student interaction.

Faculty are encouraged to require certain levels of interaction, that is, to begin to help students get into the habit of interacting online (which may be relatively foreign to both the students and the instructor), faculty examine guidelines and rubrics on what constitutes significant or meaningful interaction. Rules, such as requiring a minimum number of postings, help get the class into the habit of reading and thoughtfully responding to each other's messages. In time, these rules fade into the background as students become authentically engaged in discussions. Requiring students to post messages to "get credit" in online threaded discussions ensures a minimum level of interaction, and the other indexes identified by the authors—continuing a thread, quoting from other's message, and referring to other's messages, occur more naturally as they are needed for effective communication. That being said, faculty are also specifically encouraged to refer to student comments to engage and elicit student interest and participation.

Early on, faculty explore the nature of "substantive comments" in online discussions. Trainers encourage faculty to articulate what constitutes high-quality comments with the goal of encouraging students to thoughtfully respond rather than to merely post "I agree" messages in online discussion. Trainers also offer faculty rubrics that provide a more systematic means of assessing significant student interaction. Rubrics can allow for more precise feedback on course participation. They also facilitate the attainment of higher levels of discourse in support of cognitive presence and critical thinking by "setting the bar" at a level that is higher than might evolve without them.

Cohesive Dimensions

The importance of addressing students by name is highlighted and modeled in online and face-to-face trainings. Although the authors emphasize the importance of inclusive pronouns in online communication, such as *we* and *our*, it may be just as important to emphasize the avoidance of other modes of address, such as *the student* and other third-person vocatives. The use of both inclusive pronouns (*we, our, us*) and the second person (the appropriate use of *you* when referring directly to students) is specifically recommended and modeled in trainings forums.

Greetings and salutation that serve a purely social function are implemented in at least two ways. Students are automatically greeted by name when they enter the SLN system, with a randomly generated greeting such as "Aloha Jim" or "Welcome Jim." The course template has areas that are designed to provide initial greetings early in the course, such as the Newsflash area, which by default offers students a "Welcome to the course" message. Welcome messages are also contained in standard course documents.

Beyond these low-level, automated, cohesive messages, faculty discuss the importance of warmly welcoming student and of responding to social posting with greater frequency and in a rapid fashion, especially early on in the course, when the cohesiveness of the class is still fragile and emerging. Trainers routinely encourage faculty to use student names in responses to help create a sense of cohesion.

Helping Faculty Create and Sustain Teaching Presence

The component of the Garrison, Andersen, and Archer (2000) framework that details "teaching presence" is also quite useful in helping to explain and to analyze the faculty development process implemented within the SUNY Learning Network. We will provide a brief description of this part of the framework and then return to it when discussing the SLN faculty development and course design process in greater depth.

Anderson and colleagues (2001) defined teaching presence as "the design, facilitation, and direction of cognitive and social processes for the realization of personally meaningful and educationally worthwhile learning outcomes." Although the authors were principally concerned with analyzing course discussion transcripts for evidence of these categories, it is our belief that teaching presence is also evident in other areas of online courses. Anderson and colleagues (2001) acknowledge this and encourage others to investigate teaching presence beyond course discussions. We will use the categories devised by Anderson and colleagues (2001) and provide additional examples of teaching presence (beyond what may be found in discussion transcripts), and describe how faculty are supported to understand and create teaching presence in SLN online courses.

Teaching presence in this model has three components—instructional design and organization, facilitating discourse, and direct instruction. Under the category "Instructional Design and Organization," the authors include: setting curriculum, designing methods, establishing time parameters, utilizing the medium effectively, and establishing netiquette. This aspect of the model equates with Chickering's and Gamson's (1987) concern for active learning techniques, time on task, communication of high expectations, and prompt feedback, again, providing more consideration of the affordances and constraints of online environments.

Support for Instructional Design and Organization

Support for instructional design and organization is provided in many ways. For example, all faculty are provided a shell structure from which to build their courses. The SLN CMS embeds a common instructional design format and organization into each course. It is however, flexible, and faculty can alter the format to suit their needs and the specific learning outcomes for their courses. This CMS provides several advantages for achieving the goals of building an asynchronous learning network on the scale of SLN. Each course has a common look and feel, so students do not need to learn a new interface every time they enroll in a new course. Placeholder documents also serve to remind faculty to include information that students will need to feel well oriented in any course. The CMS helps faculty to establish teaching presence in accordance with several of the categories identified by Anderson and colleagues (2001). These are—setting the curriculum, establishing time parameters, utilizing the medium effectively, and establishing netiquette.

Setting the Curriculum

Common course information placeholder documents provide a reminder to faculty of the importance of this element of teaching presence, and that they need to inform the students about the course, how it will proceed, and how students can succeed. Common issues confronted include the sequence, quantity, and pacing of learning activities in each section of the course.

Each course contains documents into which course-specific information may be inserted. Trainers, using the hard copy and online-faculty development guide provided to all faculty, give examples of appropriate content that can be tailored for a standard set of course information documents. Documents that touch on setting the curriculum include: a welcome document, a course overview, course learning objectives, "how you will be evaluated" and "my expectations" documents, as well as readings and course materials. Such signposting begins to fulfill the role of creating a "narrative path through the mediated instruction and activity set such that students are aware of the explicit and implicit learning goals and activities in which they participate" (Anderson et al., 2001). In addition to creating the narrative path, we feel it is also important to provide a "table of contents" to the narrative, so faculty can also create course-level, section-level overview documents with the goal of reminding students where they are and what they will be working on throughout each section of the course.

Establishing Time Parameters

This element of teaching presence is critical; keeping students moving along at a similar pace is foundational to supporting meaningful interaction in asynchronous learning environments such as the SLN. For students to engage in coconstruction of knowledge, they need to work together, and well-articulated time parameters facilitate effective interaction.

Faculty in SLN learn about the importance of establishing time parameters in several ways. Again, the SLN CMS provides standard documents and instructional cues that help establish time parameters. For example, it contains a preformatted course schedule, into which learning activities, topics, assignments and due dates may be recorded. Each course segment (module) contains a standard "What's Due?" document for that section of the course. At the document level, "discussion starter" documents contain start and end date reminders so that faculty remember to provide these time parameters to students. Assignment starter documents contain similar due date reminders to help faculty to keep students on track. In addition, the SLN CMS permits faculty to activate and deactivate learning modules to control course pace.

Utilizing the Medium Effectively

Under this category, Anderson and colleagues (2001) included helping students understand how to use the technology appropriately, for example, the proper use of the reply and quote functions in online discussion. Again, the SLN CMS contains standard course documents that help faculty to help students understand these functions, and they are placed immediately before the task to which they refer or in which they will be used. Such shared documentation on effective use of the medium reduces the burden on individual faculty to "reinvent the wheel" in each course.

Occasionally, students will need extra help with the technology, so in addition to documentation within each course, a central student help desk exists to assist students to make effective use of the medium. But rather than take a merely reactive role, the help desk facilitates an interactive, online orientation to SLN. This course, modeled on all other SLN courses, is offered each semester and helps students understand the medium and its effective uses, as well as practice the skills necessary for success before they enter a specific, credit-bearing course.

To help faculty understand and address instances when students are not using the medium well, one of the roles of the SLN instructional design partner is to monitor each course, especially in its very early stages, and to make sure that the faculty member is aware of communication breakdowns, such as misplaced postings and unanswered questions, so that they may be repaired.

Designing Methods

Under this category, the authors include the provision of instructional strategies that help structure learning activities. One of the greatest challenges in online learning is the clear articulation of how learning activities will be structured and paced, and new online faculty frequently struggle with providing clear instructions on how to accomplish a particular activity. Cooperative learning methods in particular require clear directions and close monitoring. The ability to draw on hundreds of courses that have been developed, designed, and delivered through the SLN provide some assistance in overcoming these challenges. Faculty are able to review examples of learning activities that were either successful or unsuccessful to understand how their design and method may impact their effectiveness. Examples include student-designed surveys, journals, observations, individual and collaborative projects, and jointly constructed annotated bibliographies. Through the SLN Faculty Developers Center and the all-faculty conference, instructors can view entire archived courses, "sit in" on live courses, and access excerpted examples of well-designed, or previously successful, learning activities. These faculty-support resources are detailed next.

Faculty Center

Through this online resource, faculty can access their SLN e-mail, explore a common set of library resources, search a repository of discipline specific learning objects (MERLOT), access the online version of the SLN handbook, participate in an online faculty orientation, and access instructional design tips and online teaching tools, beyond those included in the SLN CMS. The Faculty Center is one resource for promoting understanding of this element of "teaching presence."

Archived Courses

Faculty are encouraged to browse from a broad selection of previously delivered and now archived courses across disciplines and to examine them for ideas regarding how they will design their own course. These courses provide a "static" view of previous designs that have proven effective in the eyes of the instructional designer, faculty members, and students.

Live Courses

New faculty may enter a selection of live, ongoing SLN courses to get an understanding of how experienced instructors conduct and facilitate a course. This guided discovery process occurs during the all faculty online conference and allows faculty to see and discuss the dynamic process by which a course unfolds and through which teaching, social, and cognitive presence may evolve.

Excerpted Activities

Instructional designers have developed a database of innovative online teaching and learning activities from previous courses that new instructors can access. This resource is smaller than a complete course but represents a greater concentration of examples from across many courses.

Establishing Netiquette

Rourke and colleagues (2001) referred to "netiquette," that is, behaviors that are deemed appropriate in online communication. Newcomers to online communication are often unaware that certain acts may violate established norms. One example is typing in uppercase, which is viewed as "shouting" in online communication and thus inappropriate for most messages. Dominating conversations with long postings is another potentially problematic violation of netiquette. Trainers review these concepts, and the hard copy and online versions of the SLN handbook provide examples of simple policies for acceptable interaction in online college courses.

Support for Facilitating Discourse

Another element of teaching presence in the Anderson and colleagues (2001) framework is facilitating discourse. The task of facilitating discourse is necessary to sustain learner engagement and refers to "focused and sustained deliberation that marks learning in a community of inquiry" (Anderson et al., 2001). The authors provide indicators of the act of facilitating discourse, which include identifying areas of agreement and disagreement; seeking to reach consensus and understanding; encouraging, acknowledging, or reinforcing student contributions; setting climate for learning; drawing in participants and prompting discussion; and assessing the efficacy of the process. This aspect of the model equates with Chickering's and Gamson's (1987) encouragement of contact between students and faculty and reciprocity and cooperation among students—further delineating these for online learners. This activity is also essential for sustaining the knowledge-centered and community-centered learning environment emphasized by Bransford and colleagues (2000). We will look at the components of facilitating discourse and identify how faculty in SLN learn about this skill.

Trainers and instructional design partners encourage faculty to consider the early stages of their courses as an opportunity to begin to create a nonthreatening environment in which students can begin to engage in discourse. A standard practice designed to help meet this goal is the use of an "ice-breaking" module. In this initial course section, students engage in ungraded activities where they can practice the skills needed to participate in the course. These might include open class and small group discussions, submitting a profile, or taking a learning style quiz. These activities are designed to encourage class discourse in a safe, supportive, and unassessed (at least in terms of course grade) environment.

Two indicators of discourse facilitation, identifying areas of agreement and disagreement and seeking to reach consensus and understanding, depend on the ability to frame a thought-provoking topic of discussion. Students need to be encouraged to engage in dialogue to express thoughts that others may then acknowledge or refute. Before consensus can exist, ideas must be expressed and examined. Faculty learn how to start and extend such discussion in several ways. Through face-to-face and online forums, faculty explore resources that document effective, engaging online discussion practices. For example, in face-to-face trainings, faculty examine and discuss a list of 14 ways to enhance online discussion that correspond to the categories identified by Anderson and colleagues (2001). Faculty "experience" these tips by participating in facilitated discourse in the online all faulty conference. Examples of discourse facilitation tips to faculty are

1. *Include a grade for participation.*   Be clear about how students can succeed in discussion with reference to quality and quantity guidelines, as well as requirements for timeliness. Entering an asynchronous discussion after it is nearly over can be unproductive (though there are ways around this problem, such as asking a late student to summarize the discussion that has already occurred).
2. *Provide an overview of what is due for each week.*   This weekly agenda will help keep students working as a cohort and ensure a "critical mass" for getting discussions off the ground.
3. *Make the discussion interesting or provocative.*   Asking students to respond to "known answer" questions is unlikely to generate sustained involvement. Discussion questions should be open-ended, focused on learning objectives, and likely to spur some controversy or interaction.

4. *Participate wisely.*   The instructor should not dominate the discussion. Nor should he or she be absent. It is the instructor's job to keep the discussion on track by guiding without pontificating. Frequently, an instructor will provide a comment that students perceive as the "official answer," and discussion can come to a halt.
5. *Require a product that is based on or the result of discussion.*   A "hand-in" assignment that is based on class discussion can help students to synthesize, integrate and apply what has been discussed.

With the ongoing assistance of an instructional design partner for implementation, tips such as these help faculty to understand how to facilitate productive discourse in the service of creating teaching presence and ultimately cognitive presence.

Direct Instruction

Anderson and colleagues (2001) also included indicators of direct instruction in their framework for the analysis of teaching presence. These indicators include presenting content and questions, focusing the discussion on specific issues, summarizing discussion, confirming understanding, diagnosing misperceptions, injecting knowledge from diverse sources, and responding to technical concern. This aspect of the model equates with Chickering's and Gamson's (1987) concerns for prompt, assistive feedback, again with emphasis on the needs of online learners. Attention to direct instruction is also essential for sustaining the knowledge-centered learning environment emphasized by Bransford and colleagues (2000).

Regarding the final indicator of direct instruction, responding to technical concerns, it should be noted that faculty in the SLN are specifically instructed not to respond to student technical difficulties, as this diverts instructor resources away from their primary role, facilitating learning. It is the role of the SLN Help Desk to address all technical issues, and faculty are advised to refer all such questions to the help desk to avoid students becoming dependent on instructors for technical support.

New online faculty struggle with how to engage in direct instruction. Novice instructors frequently raise questions about how they will "teach" in the absence of visual and aural clues reflective of students misunderstanding. So, how do new SLN faculty learn about effective practices for direct instruction in this lean medium of online courses? Again, there are a variety of forums in which this topic is explored. For example, new faculty interact and learn from experienced faculty in the "Managing and Teaching your Course" workshop, the last in a series of three face-to-face workshops for new instructors. In this meeting, experienced instructors present lessons they have learned from designing and facilitating their own courses, including how they present content, focus and summarize discussions and issues, and identify and remedy misunderstanding.

New faculty learn that direct instruction takes place most commonly through dialogue with the instructor (as well as more able peers). Some examples of suggestions for effective dialogue discussed in training forums include

- Resist the temptation to respond to every student's response. Otherwise, the discussion may become a series of dialogues between you and each student, rather than among the students.
- Assign individual students the task of summarizing the discussion, and check for accuracy and comprehensiveness.

- Employ student-led discussion where assigned students devise critical thinking questions and are evaluated on the quality of their questions and how they facilitate the discussion.
- Create a discussion response that calls on specific students that have not yet participated in the discussion.
- Create a discussion response that asks a specific student to clarify a point, or that asks a student to reassess a response in light of another student's response.
- Create a discussion response that asks a follow-up question of the group or of an individual student. (*SLN Faculty Developer's Guide*)

Through suggestions and tips such as these, as well as participation in online forums such as the all-faculty conference, new faculty gradually learn from experienced faculty and trainers how to engage in effective dialogue and to implement direct instruction online.

STUDENT SATISFACTION AND REPORTED LEARNING

As part of the revision cycle of the course design and faculty development Processes, we have engaged in systematic efforts to evaluate and analyze online teaching and learning in SLN. Each semester, we conduct surveys of participating faculty and students through an integrated, Web-based data collection infrastructure.

Questions driving this assessment include: How do students who have taken online courses through SLN feel about the experience? (For example: Is there sufficient interaction with instructors and students to sustain satisfactory levels of social presence and engage students in learning?) Do students feel there are any disadvantages to the online format relative to the classroom? (For example: Does the online format and pedagogy foster or inhibit thoughtful discussion of course topics, effective written communication, or the likelihood that students will ask for help when they don't understand something?) Are there other downsides? (For example: Do these online students find that they waste time because of the distractions of the Internet and thus spend less time engaged in learning, or does the online environment make them feel isolated?) Finally, how do students feel that the environment compares to the classroom overall?

To assess whether this online learning environment has been successful from a student perspective, it is necessary to remind ourselves what our "student" goals were. To determine whether and to what extent we were achieving this goal, we administered an online student satisfaction survey, which consisted of 35, Likert-type and open-ended questions. To define high-quality teaching and learning in devising the survey, we framed questions around the principles of good practices in higher education (Chickering & Ehrmann, 1995; Chickering & Gamson, 1987). We believe that these practices reflect good pedagogy in classroom and online learning environments. Approximately one third of the questions we asked were based on the *Flashlight Evaluation Handbook and Current Student Inventory*, developed by the Flashlight Program of the Teaching, Learning, and Technology Group (Ehrmann & Zuniga, 1997).

In the most recent survey (summer of 2001), we received surveys from 935 students, about 26% of student enrollments for that period. This response rate, while low, is quite typical of e-mail and Web-based survey returns, which have been declining in recent years (Sheehan, 2001). It may be necessary to admit that the entire field of survey research suffers from this trend (Bradburn 1992; Hox & De Leeuw, 1994). For example, a recent study of academic and non-for-profit research organizations (O'Rourke &

Johnson, 1998) revealed that, even when using well-designed, random sampling survey techniques, the 36 organizations polled averaged only a 46.8% return rate. The authors admitted that although they had asked for typical return rates, it was possible that the organizations gave figures for the most successful efforts, making the actual, typical rates even lower than 46.8%.

An examination of the demographics of the students who responded to the SLN student survey reveals that they appear to be a fairly representative sample of the entire population of students taking courses for the semester in which the survey was conducted. Students' ages, employment status, distance from campus, reasons for taking an online course, matriculation status, computer types, full- or part-time status, and other variables are a close approximation of these demographics for the entire population of SLN students for that semester (see Appendix, Tables A1–A8). This being said, caution must be taken when interpreting these results due to the low response rate. The results must be viewed as suggestive rather than conclusive.

Students are asked, via e-mail, to complete the Web-based survey by both SLN administration and their instructor. Follow-up reminders are sent to nonrespondents 2 weeks and 4 weeks after the initial request. Although the survey is completely voluntary, the format of the instrument requires that all questions be answered before the survey may be submitted successfully, so for these surveys, students respond to all items. Students are instructed that the results of the survey will not be revealed to their instructor and that it is a voluntary activity that will have no bearing on their grade.

RESULTS

High-Quality Online Teaching and Learning

To discuss the strategic goal relevant to this chapter—providing a mechanism for maintaining consistent, high-quality online teaching and learning across the SUNY system—requires that we define what we mean by "quality." Again, we used the best practices identified by Chickering and Gamson (1987) in the design and evaluation of faculty development efforts. We feel that these principles of good practice, based on decades of research on the undergraduate experience, are at the heart of recent understandings of the structure of high-quality, higher education, online learning environments (Bransford et al., 2000; Garrison, Anderson, & Archer, 2000). These principles are presented here, followed by survey comments and results related to each:

A. Good Practice Encourages Contact Between Students and Faculty
   Being a shy person, I am able to think questions and answers through before I respond. In a regular classroom setting, I often don't get my question out before we are on to another topic. I really like the online classes. I wish I could complete my degree online ... (Survey comment)

This online course is exciting to me because you can always ask a question and expect an answer. In the class, questions are somewhat limited because of time. (Survey comment)

I have taken seven online courses, and this was the best one by far, due largely to the amount of input and continual feedback from the professor. You never had to wait for a reply; you had the feeling he was right there with you all the time. He's a great one, and a great asset to online teaching. I also want to praise the SLN Help Desk. I never saw such fast responding. Regardless of what I asked, they were helpful, supportive, and prompt!!! Anytime, any day. Applause, applause!! (Survey comment)

The communication is lacking with the instructor, and so I don't even know what I sent that she didn't get. This is changing my mind about taking any future online courses. An e-mail from the instructor just letting me know that she didn't receive something would have alerted me that something was wrong; but now I still don't know what she is missing because she is now on vacation!!! Not a phone call or e-mail, just an incomplete grade. This would have never happened in a classroom. (Survey comment)

The comments above testify to the importance of dialogue between faculty and students. When present, students report enthusiasm for their experience; without it, students report frustration, even anger. It has been suggested that information technologies "can increase opportunities for students and faculty to converse" (Chickering & Ehrmann, 1995) and that such conversation is critical to learning and satisfaction. So, we asked students whether they had high levels of interaction with their instructors and other students and about the quality of the interaction. Overall, more that 75% of respondents reported high levels of interaction with their instructors, and approximately 73% felt they had high levels of interaction with their online classmates. In addition, approximately 78% of respondents felt that the quality of the interaction with their instructors was very high, and approximately 70% felt the quality of interaction with fellow students was very high. When asked to compare the level of interaction to similar classroom-based courses, a majority felt there was as much or more interaction with their instructor and fellow students as in similar classroom-based courses.

Emphasizing the importance of social discourse and contact with and between students and faculty, principles of good practice would predict that the amount and quality of interaction will relate to satisfaction and learning, and our results suggest that they do. Table 16.2 shows the correlations between students' reports of the quantity and quality of interaction with faculty and with other students and their reports of satisfaction and learning in SLN courses.

If interaction is crucial to student reports of satisfaction and learning, then reported isolation, or lack of interaction, is just as important. We asked students about feelings of

TABLE 16.2
Correlations Between Interaction, Satisfaction, and Learning (N = 935)

		Quantity of Interaction with Instructor	Quality of Instructor Interaction	Quantity of Interaction with Fellow Students	Quality of Interaction with Fellow Students
Satisfaction	Spearman's rho	.605**	.636**	.376**	.408**
Reported learning	Spearman's rho	.585**	.607**	.378**	.392**

**Correlation is significant at the 0.01 level (two-tailed).

isolation due to the format of the course. We found that approximately 30% of students did report some feelings of increased isolation, but about 70% did not. We also found that students who had more experience in online learning (those who had taken three or more online courses) were somewhat less likely to report feelings of isolation than those taking their first online course. Results seem to indicate that feelings of isolation may diminish with greater experience in negotiating the new learning environment. This is a finding that may warrant further study:

B. Good Practice Uses Active Learning Techniques

   This was a good experience for me. This course made me do a lot of deep thinking and allowed me to further my education. I cherish the fact that I can learn at this stage of my life. Thanks very much for offering this course. (Survey comment)

I have to tell you that I read the chapters more carefully as it was my responsibility to learn the subject matter. This course has helped me with my concentration skills. I was surprised how much I enjoyed the course. It was a real challenge to me and I love a challenge. (Survey comment)

We read and then had assignments, few of which related to the textbook. My grade was above average, but I do not feel that I received much out of this course. (Survey comment)

As the comments above suggest, meaningful learning requires active student engagement. When students are active participants, they tend to report excitement; when they are passive, they tend to report disappointment.

How well do traditional classroom practices actively engage students? Frequently, not very well. Barnes (1980) found that, even among faculty who actively solicited student participation, students only responded 50% of the time when called on. Karp and Yoels (1987) reported that in classes of less than 40, 4 to 5 students accounted for 75% of all interactions, and that in classes of more than 40, 2 to 3 students accounted for more than half of all interactions. Stones (1970), in a survey of more than 1,000 students, found that 60% stated that a large number of classmates listening would deter them from asking questions, even when encouraged to do so by the instructor.

In contrast, in the most recent SLN survey, 93.4% of respondents reported active participation in their online class. To get a sense of how active and in what sense the students engaged in active learning, we asked them to compare their levels of participation in online discussions about course material with comparable classroom discussions (Table 16.3). We found that students were about twice as likely to report more active participation in online discussions than in classroom-based discussions.

Think about a similar classroom-based course you have taken. Compared to that course, because of the way this course uses online communication and interaction, how likely were you to actively participate in scheduled discussions about the course material?

Active learning implies a certain level of ownership of the learning process. Taking responsibility to ask for clarification when misunderstandings arise can be seen as an element of active learning and productive discourse. Students reported that they were about twice as likely to ask for clarification when they did not understand something online as compared to in similar courses they had taken in the classroom (Table 16.4).

Think about a similar classroom based course you have taken. Compared to that course, because of the way this course uses online communication and interaction, how likely were you to ask for clarification when you did not understand something?

TABLE 16.3
Active Participation

		Frequency	Percent	Cumulative Percent
Valid	Much more than in the classroom	186	19.9	19.9
	More than in the classroom	260	27.8	47.7
	The same as in the classroom	308	32.9	80.6
	Less than in the classroom	139	14.9	95.5
	Much less than in the classroom	42	4.5	100.0
	Total	935	100.0	

TABLE 16.4
Requests for Clarification

		Frequency	Percent	Cumulative Percent
Valid	Much more than in the classroom	151	16.1	16.1
	More than in the classroom	216	23.1	39.3
	The same as in the classroom	396	42.4	81.6
	Less than in the classroom	124	13.3	94.9
	Much less than in the classroom	48	5.1	100.0
	Total	935	100.0	

One side benefit, because all of this communication occurred through written means, was that about 83% felt that the online format helped them improve their ability to communicate effectively in writing.

It has been suggested that information technologies allow students and faculty to converse "more thoughtfully and safely than when confronting each other in a class-room or faculty office" (Chickering & Ehrmann, 1995) and that this increased comfort and level of thought contributes to learning and satisfaction. We asked students to com-pare the amount of thought they put into their online discussion comments with those they made in the classroom. We found that about 86% of respondents reported that they put more thought into online discussion comments than into comparable classroom discussion, providing support for this hypothesis. As would be predicted, a significant

TABLE 16.5

Correlation Between Thought in Discussion Comments, Satisfaction, and Learning
(N = 935)

		Satisfaction	Reported Learning
Discussion thought	Spearman's rho	.252	.268
	Sig. (two-tailed)	.000	.000

correlation exists between amount of thought invested in discussion responses, and learning and satisfaction (Table 16.5).

To confirm whether online conversations did occur "more safely," that is , with more opportunity to explore topics that might be difficult to explore face-to-face, we asked students how likely they were to ask an awkward question online as compared to the classroom, and whether they were more likely to ask for clarification online than in the classroom. Approximately 69% of respondents reported they were more likely to feel comfortable asking an awkward question online. Approximately 40% reported that were more likely to ask for clarification online, which was about twice the rate of those reporting that they were more likely to ask for clarification in the classroom (18%).

Authentic interaction implies that student participants feel empowered to disagree, not only with each other, but also with the instructor. When asked whether they felt more comfortable disagreeing with the instructor online, a large number of respondents (42%) reported that they did feel more comfortable dissenting in this environment.

C. Good Practice Gives Prompt Feedback and Communicates High Expectations

I absolutely love this class. (The professor) expects a lot, but it's all so clear and interesting that it actually is fun. I've learned so much! I wish more classes were online. (Survey comment)

I enjoyed this class because the teacher was helpful; she was prompt with answering questions and grading assignments. The teacher was very clear with what she wanted the class to do. (Survey comment)

What I've appreciated most about this course has been the instant feedback and evaluations, critiques, etc. from my professor. It's helped to keep me motivated and striving for better each week of the class. This has been a fantastic experience! (Survey comment)

There was very prompt response to discussion threads and test and assignment evaluations. Responses to comments were made within a day in most cases. This encouraged students to discuss with the instructor and other students on a regular basis. It felt like the course was alive, and help was there when you needed it. (Survey comment)

... my only problem with the class was that I like to get an answer to my questions immediately, but I did get used to it, and my instructor did get back to me as soon as possible. (Survey comment)

TABLE 16.6
Correlations Between Satisfaction, Learning, Expectations, and
Feedback ($N = 935$)

		Prompt Feedback	Quality Feedback	Clear Expectations
Satisfaction	Spearman's rho	.562**	.590**	.581**
Learning	Spearman's rho	.485**	.556**	.543**

**Correlation is significant at the 0.01 level (two-tailed).

I don't think it was actually the instructor's outline for the course that wasn't specific, but what was expected for a "discussion" or what the quiz would be like. I felt as though I were going into those areas "blind." I personally would have liked maybe an online example of what the quiz would look like, even saying it is a multiple choice, books are ok to use, etc. (Survey comment)

The comments above demonstrate the importance of clear expectations and timely feedback. When they are present, students are satisfied, when absent, less so. We asked students about the speed and quality of the feedback they received in their online courses. Approximately 85% of respondents reported that they received very prompt feedback, and about 87% felt that they had received high-quality, constructive feedback. In addition, more than 90% reported that the instructor provided clear expectations of how students could succeed in the course. As demonstrated in Table 16.6, each of these variables correlates significantly with reports of satisfaction and learning.

D. Good Practice Emphasizes Time on Task

I have learned more from this course than any other graduate course I have taken. There was a lot of work involved, but it only enhanced my understanding of lessons taught and has improved my teaching abilities in the classroom. I have, and will continue to recommend, this system to fellow teachers who are trying to obtain a graduate degree. Thank You!!! (Survey comment)

I love the learning experiences gained from the online courses. I find that I actually work harder, because generally it does take more time and effort to complete the online courses. With this in mind, the time used is very valuable and adds more meaning and depth to the overall learning experience. (Survey comment)

This was my final course for my degree. I will never try to take another math course (online or not) in a 5-week session—it is just not enough time for me. (Survey comment)

As the comments above suggest, time on task is an important contributor to learning. When students understand and recognize the opportunities afforded by additional time, they report higher levels of satisfaction and increased learning. Without sufficient time, learning is impaired. We asked students to think about the format of their courses and the fact that there was "anytime–anywhere" access. Did they feel that this increased level of access resulted in more time studying? Approximately 71% of students reported

TABLE 16.7
Correlation Between Amount of Time Spent Studying, Learning, and
Satisfaction ($N = 935$)

		Satisfaction	Learning
Time	Spearman's rho	.247**	.288**
	Sig. (two-tailed)	.000	.000

**Correlation is significant at the 0.01 level (two-tailed).

that they did spend more time studying as a result of the increased access afforded by the online format (Table 16.7).

However, the possibility for wasting time in online courses, due to the distractions of the Internet, is also possible. Approximately 13% of respondents did report that the online format resulted in more wasted time browsing, and about 87% did not.

Wasting time can take other forms. For example, technical difficulties can consume time that would otherwise be devoted to more productive purposes. So we asked students about technical difficulties and their effect on the students' learning and satisfaction. Approximately 88% of respondents felt that taking a course through SLN was no more technically difficult than taking a classroom based course. We also found that students who were less likely to report technical difficulties were more likely to report higher levels of satisfaction and learning.

E. Retention

Currently, we do not have a process for tracking completion rates for each of the campuses that participate in the SUNY Learning Network. This is related to the different roles played by participants in the program. As with traditional courses, campuses track enrollment, maintain students grades, and record completion rates at the local level, and there is no centralized mechanism for storing and reporting all such data. We do, however, have some evidence from particular campuses that suggests that course completion rates may be similar between face-to face and online courses. For example, at the university at Albany, the completion rates for certain online courses have been statistically similar to face-to-face offerings. If anything, they have been slightly higher than classroom based versions (see Figs. 16.7 & 16.8).

Similar results were reported at Herkimer County Community College. Tracking 21 different courses in the spring 2001 semester, offered by the same professors both online and in the classroom, the college reported no significant differences in completion rates between the online and the face-to-face versions of these courses.

Clearly, these results are inconclusive and require additional study. Inasmuch as we do not have more complete information on this issue, these results are merely suggestive of a comparison of completion rates that are not, necessarily, lower online.

Overall, approximately 87% of respondents reported being satisfied or very satisfied with their courses; about 90% report learning a great deal; about 94% reported being satisfied or very satisfied with SLN services; and 97% reported satisfaction with the SLN Help Desk. When asked whether they would take another SLN course, only 1.7% responded that they would definitely not want to do this. Finally, overall, these

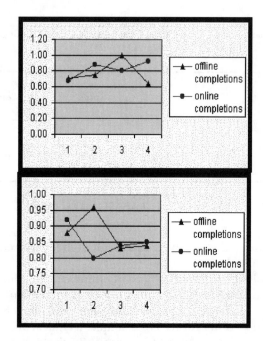

FIG. 16.7.   Comparison of Completion Rates for ETAP 426 and 526 (Computing in Education) for four semesters—traditional and online versions.

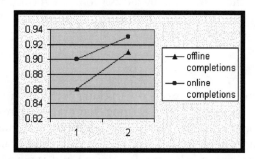

FIG. 16.8.   Comparison of course completions in face-to-face and online versions of ETAP 523 (Media in Teaching and Learning) for two semesters.

935 students were 1.7 times as likely to report learning more in their online courses (35.9%) than in comparable classroom-based courses (20.8%), though the majority felt they were equivalent (43.3%).

Faculty Survey Results

In addition to collecting data on student satisfaction and learning, we also collect data on faculty attitudes about teaching in this online environment. For the most recent semester, we heard back from 255 faculty from more than two-dozen institutions, ranging from community college through four-year and university centers. To understand student responses to online learning, it is useful to explore the faculty experience as well. The following section provides information on faculty reactions and work that gives insight into student-reported satisfaction and learning. Three instructional variables that

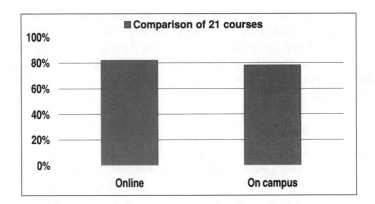

FIG. 16.9.   Comparison of 21 online and classroom-based course attrition rates.

seem most relevant are interaction, opportunities to implement alternative means of assessment, and opportunities to implement more systematic instructional design.

In the spring 2001 semester, faculty responded to a 31-item online survey about their experience of developing and teaching an online course through the SUNY Learning Network. As with the student survey, all items had to be completed to submit the survey, so all items were answered in all of the returned surveys. Two hundred and fifty-five surveys were returned, which represents approximately 52% of the faculty who were teaching in that semester. Again, because of this relatively low response rate, these results are more suggestive than conclusive.

Interaction

We feel that the importance of interaction in teaching and learning cannot be understated. Through interaction with the instructor, peers, and course content, students have the opportunity to negotiate meaning and connect new concepts to previous knowledge. One measure of this important variable is faculty perceptions of interaction. To the item "Compared to classroom based teaching, rate your level of interaction with your online students," respondents were, again, more than twice as likely to rate their interaction with online students as higher than their classroom students. Approximately 49.4% felt that their level of interaction with students was higher online than in the classroom, approximately 23.9% saw no difference, and about 22.7% thought the level of interaction was lower online than in the classroom. The remainder did not teach the course in the classroom.

We asked a similar question regarding interaction between students and found the following results: Respondents were about 1.7 times as likely to rate interaction between their online students as higher than their classroom students. About 43.2% rated interaction between online students higher than their classroom students; about 27.5% saw no difference, and 25.5% rated interaction between their classroom students as higher than their online students. The remainder did not teach the course in the classroom.

Alternative Means of Instruction and Assessment

For instruction to become more learner centered, faculty must have an opportunity to consider alternatives to traditional methods and to be able to engage in more systematic design of instruction that incorporates those alternatives. Considering all the time and effort that faculty reported expending in the creation of courses (more than

150 hours), we wondered whether the experience of developing and teaching an online course afforded such opportunities. Apparently it does. Approximately 97% of survey respondents reported that developing and teaching their online course offered them a new opportunity to consider alternative means of instruction, and approximately 93% reported that the experience offered them a new opportunity to consider alternative means of assessment.

Systematic Design of Instruction

Regarding instructional design, we asked the following question: "Think about similar courses you have developed for the classroom. Relative to those courses, how likely were you to systematically design instruction before teaching the course?" Respondents were more than nine times as likely to report more systematic design of instruction for their online courses than for their classroom courses. Approximately 58% of respondents reported higher levels of systematic instructional design online, about 37% reported no difference, and about 6% reported less systematic design of instruction online.

Student Performance

We also wanted to understand how faculty perceived student performance in online courses as compared to similar classroom courses. To the question, "If you have ever taught this course in the classroom, how would you rate your online students' performance to your classroom students' performance?" respondents were twice as likely to report better performance from their online students then their classroom students. Approximately 32.5% reported better performance from online students; about 41.2% reported no difference in performance; and approximately 14.1% reported better performance from classroom students. The remainder did not teach the course in the classroom.

Inasmuch as faculty and students rated their online teaching and learning experiences superior to similar classroom experiences, does this mean that we are suggesting that online learning should replace the classroom? Absolutely not. Obviously, there is a great deal more to residential higher education than this study reports on. But would the experience of designing and teaching an online course improve classroom teaching and learning? We asked SLN faculty this question, and 85% agreed that it would.

Relevance to Other Institutions

Are these findings relevant to other institutions? We believe they may be useful in a number of ways. Online learning environments are not easy to implement successfully. Effort, coordination, planning, and expense are required. If an institution is considering systematic implementation of online education, it is useful to know that success, as measured by traditional notions of best practice in higher education, is possible.

In general, although we acknowledge that these results are for the most part suggestive, to find that nearly 1,000 students from dozens of institutions from associate level through graduate level programs reported high levels of learning and satisfaction in online courses offered through a single, unified system should be helpful to the decision making of other institutions. Positive student response to this learning environment suggests that it is possible to overcome the complexity and challenges involved in system-wide online learning initiatives, to provide increased flexible access, and to maintain high standards across courses.

For those who are concerned that online learning is, by its very nature, cold, sterile, and isolating, finding that the vast majority of these respondents reported high levels and high-quality interaction with their instructors and other students, and that the majority were unlikely to report feeling isolated, is potentially helpful. Knowing that most respondents reported fast and high-quality feedback, as well as clear expectations for success, is also encouraging. It is important to understand that such results are not likely without considerable planning. We believe a focus on developing systems (such as the student help desk and overall faculty development process) that emphasize the importance of student support and interaction is critical to success in this area. Fostering existing communities that can grow to take on expanded roles in these areas may also prove helpful. The learning community embodied in SLN evolved gradually. Wenger (1998) summarizes the importance of this process succinctly, "To develop the capacity to create and retain knowledge, organizations must understand the processes by which these learning communities evolve and interact. We need to build organizational and technological infrastructures that do not dismiss or impede these processes, but rather recognize, support, and leverage them" (p. 6).

Our research suggests that a number of variables correlate significantly with high levels of satisfaction and learning. Before embarking on the implementation of new online learning environments, it would be wise to consider the following: high levels of interaction with the instructor and the quality of that interaction, interaction with fellow students and its quality, prompt and high-quality feedback on assignments, clear expectations on how to succeed in the course, and low levels of technical difficulties. These are all variables that correlate highly with both satisfaction and learning and, therefore, need to be given a high priority in planning and developing an online environment. Perhaps not surprisingly, these are also variables that correlate highly with satisfaction and learning in the classroom.

IS ONLINE LEARNING "AS GOOD AS" THE CLASSROOM?

This is a question that continues to appear in the popular media and is a cause for concern among online learning critics. From these results, the answer appears to be "No, it may be much better." We see reason for optimism in the knowledge that, in the most recent term for which data was collected, nearly the majority of nearly 1,000 online students from dozens of institutions not only reported high levels of satisfaction and learning, but, when asked to compare their online course to similar classroom courses, these students were: twice as likely to report active participation in such important activities as discussion of course materials; twice as likely to report asking instructors for clarification; twice as likely to report putting more thought into discussion; and twice as likely to report spending more time studying. We also found that faculty were twice as likely to report higher levels of interaction with and between their online students; that they were able to explore and implement alternative means of assessment and instruction, and that they were nine times as likely to report engaging in more systematic design of instruction in their online class compared to similar classes they had developed and taught in the classroom.

It may be that the instructional improvements and more active student behaviors account for the fact that students were nearly twice as likely to report learning more online than in the classroom, and that faculty were twice as likely to report better performance from their online students than from students in the same course taught in the classroom. Does this mean that online learning should replace the classroom? Of course

TABLE 16.8
Student Satisfaction for the Past Six Terms in SLN*

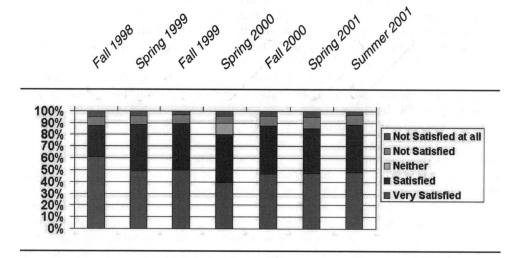

*Responses to: "Overall I was very satisfied with this online course."

TABLE 16.9
Reported Learning for the Past Six Terms in SLN*

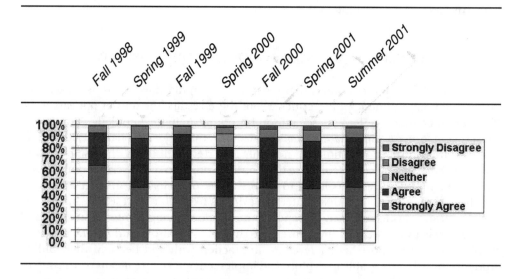

*Responses to: "Overall, I learned a great deal in this online course."

not. Do faculty feel that the experience of developing and teaching an online course can improve what they do in the classroom? In our most recent survey the answer was yes.

These high levels of satisfaction and learning replicate findings from six previous surveys in the period 1998 to 2001 (Tables 16.8 & 16.9).

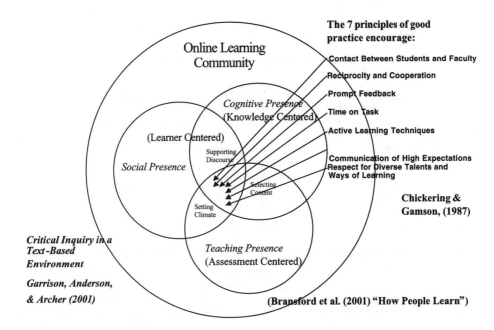

FIG. 16.10.   A conceptual framework for high-quality, higher education, online learning environments.

In summary, we feel that an emphasis on multiple perspectives may be a step forward in the development of online learning environments. Attention to the principles espoused by Bransford and colleagues (2001), Chickering and Gamson (1987), as well as Garrison, Anderson, and Archer (2000) may be the best approach to ensuring high quality in the development of future online learning forums. We will endeavor to facilitate understanding of this emerging model (Fig. 16.10) to the SLN community as we seek to improve the experience of students and faculty in the SUNY Learning Network.

APPENDIX: COMPARISON OF SUMMER 2001 SURVEY SAMPLE AND ENTIRE SLN POPULATION FOR SUMMER 2001 ON DEMOGRAPHIC VARIABLES

TABLE A1
Employment Status

Employment Status	SLN Population (n = 3596)	Survey Sample (n = 935)
Full-time	54%	59%
Not employed	17%	16%
Part-time	29%	25%
Total	100%	100%

TABLE A2
Age

Age	SLN Population (n = 3596)	Survey Sample (n = 935)
15–24	47%	36%
25–34	24%	26%
35–44	19%	24%
45–54	9%	13%
55–64	.5%	1%
65+	.5%	0%
Total	100%	100%

TABLE A3
Distance From Campus

Distance from Campus	SLN Population (n = 3596)	Survey Sample (n = 935)
On campus	1%	1%
< 30 minutes	44%	42%
30 minutes–1 hour	24%	23%
1–2 hours	11%	12%
> 2 hours	20%	22%
Total	100%	100%

TABLE A4
Primary Reason for Taking an Online Course

Primary Reason	SLN Population (n = 3596)	Survey Sample (n = 935)
Conflict with personal schedule	31%	39%
Not offered on campus/schedule conflict	15%	13%
Distance/lack of transportation	20%	14%
Family responsibility	16%	20%
Interest in technology/ Internet	7%	5%
Other	12%	9%
Total	100%	100%

TABLE A5
Gender

Gender	SLN Population (n = 3596)	Survey Sample (n = 935)
Female	67%	77%
Male	33%	23%
Total	100%	100%

TABLE A6
Matriculation Status

Matriculation Status	SLN Population (n = 3596)	Survey Sample (n = 935)
Matriculated	74%	75%
Nonmatriculated	26%	25%
Total	100%	100%

TABLE A7
Computer Type Use for Online Course

Computer Types Used	SLN Population (n = 3596)	Survey Sample (n = 935)
486 PC	2%	1%
Macintosh	2%	3%
Other/don't know	39%	38%
Pentium PC	13%	13%
Pentium II PC	19%	17%
Pentium III PC	24%	27%
Pentium IV PC	1%	1%
Total	100%	100%

TABLE A8
Full- or Part-Time Academic Status

Full-Time or Part-Time	SLN Population (n = 3596)	Survey Sample (n = 935)
Full-time	39%	33%
Part-time	61%	67%
Total	100%	100%

REFERENCES

Anderson, T., Rourke, L., Garrison, D. R., & Archer W. (2001, September). Assessing teaching presence in a computer conferencing context. *Journal of Asynchronous Learning Networks, 5*(2).

Barnes, M. (1980, April). *Questioning: The untapped resource.* (ERIC Document Reproduction Service No. 1888555). Paper presented at the annual meeting of the American Educational Research Association, Boston.

Bradburn, N. M. (1992). A response to the non-response problem. *Public Opinion Quarterly, 56,* 391–397.

Bransford, J., Brown, A., Cocking, R., Donovan, M., & Pellegrino, J. W. (2000). *How people learn.* Washington DC: National Academy Press.

Brown, J. S. & Gray, E. S. (1995). The people are the company. Fast Company, P. 78 Available: http://www.fastcompany.com/online/01/people.htm)

Buckley, D. (2002). In pursuit of the learning paradigm: Coupling faculty transformation and institutional change. *Educause Review, 37*(1), 28–38.

Chickering, A. W., & Ehrmann, S. C. (1995). Implementing the seven principles: Technology as lever. *American Association for Higher Education.* Available: http://www.aahe.org/Bulletin/Implementing%20the%20Seven%20Principles.htm

Chickering, A. W., & Gamson, A. F. (1987). *Seven principles for good practice in undergraduate education.* Racine, WI: Johnson Foundation/Wingspread.

Fulford, C., & Zhang, S. (1993). Perceptions of interaction: The critical predictor in distance education. *American Journal of Distance Education, 7*(3), 8–21.

Garrison, D. R., Anderson, T., & Archer, W. (2000). Critical inquiry in a text based environment: Computer conferencing in higher education. *The Internet and Higher Education, 2*(23), 1–19.

Hox, J. J., & De Leeuw, E. D. (1994). A comparison of non-response in mail, telephone and face-to-face surveys—Applying multilevel modeling to meta-analysis. *Quality and Quantity, 28,* 329–344.

Karp, D., & Yoels, W. (1987). The college classroom: Some observations on the meanings of student participation. *Sociology and Social Research, 60,* 421–439.

Kuh, G. (2001). *The national survey of student engagement: Conceptual framework and overview of psychometric properties.* Available: http://www.indiana.edu/~nsse/acrobat/framework-2001.pdf

Lave, J. (1988). *Cognition in practice: mind, mathematics, and culture in everyday life.* Cambridge, England: Cambridge University Press.

O'Rourke, D., & Johnson, T. (1998). An inquiry into declining RDD response rates: Part III a multivariate review. *Survey Research, 30*(2), 1–3.

Pickett, A. M. (1996). SUNY Learning Network Course Developers Handbook, Version 9, March 2003, published in house State University of New York, Albany, New York.

Rourke, L., Anderson, T., Garrison, D. R., & Archer, W. (2001) Assessing social presence in asynchronous text-based computer conferencing. *Journal of Distance Education.* Available: http://cade.athabascau.ca/vol14.2/rourke_et_al.html

Sheehan, K. (2001). Email survey response rates: *A Review Journal of Computer Mediated Communication 6*(2). http://www.ASCUSC.org/jcmc/vol6/issue2/sheehan.html

Stones, E. (1970). Students' attitudes to the size of teaching groups. *Educational Review, 21*(2), 98–108.

Teaching, Learning and Technology Group, the American Association for Higher Education, & the Corporation for Public Broadcasting, Washington DC. Ehrmann, S. C., and Zuniga, R. E. (1997). *Flashlight evaluation handbook and current student inventory.*

Wenger, E. (1998, June). Communities of practice—Learning as a social system. *The Systems Thinker.* Available: http://www.co-i-l.com/coil/knowledge-garden/cop/lss.html

17

Promises and Challenges of Web-Based Education

Carson Eoyang
Naval Postgraduate School

As widely recognized by the authors of these chapters, as well as throughout academia (e.g., Duderstadt, 2000), higher education is at the cusp of major and dramatic change. Not only is the impact of rapidly evolving information technology shaping how we conduct our business, but also more fundamentally what our business is. Our primary student base is growing well beyond young adults who can study full-time to the entire adult population, most of whom are also employed in full-time jobs. As many of these working professionals receive financial support and sometimes released time for their education, their employers frequently influence the type, quality, length, and even the location of the education that is subsidized. Thus, the choices of what and where students study are no longer simply the province of students and their parents, but increasingly the domain of employees and employers. Such customers will inevitably be more demanding, skeptical, and impatient with the quality, quantity, and price of education than inexperienced and partially informed young adults.

In this new education environment, the costs of taking courses is no longer simply the price of tuition and books, but now reflects the total costs to the employee and employer of making the learners available for learning, that is, the opportunity costs of not being on the job or with the family, the time and costs of commuting, and even the costs of attrition or dropping out. As our students make more sophisticated and informed choices about which education constitutes the best value for their money and time, we educators must be more attentive to the economics of demand pull rather than the traditional supply push we became accustomed to in the 20th century. Only premier universities will be able to afford the luxury of intense brand recognition and largely offer what their distinguished faculty deem appropriate, whereas most other universities become even more more attentive and responsive to what the learning market is willing to pay for.

We have been sadly disappointed by the early promises of information technology over the last 4 decades, expecting that the costs of developing, producing and delivering education would decline significantly. On the contrary, there is no university that hasn't experienced a veritable explosion in the level of resources and staff that have been allocated to information technology, communications, and computers. This is undoubtedly a major factor in the growth of tuition that substantially exceeds the national rates of inflation. Moreover, because tuition alone does not cover all the costs in any university, the growth of higher education costs have burgeoned over the last 5 decades. Fortunately, these technological advances are also contributing to the rising quality and growing content of our curricula, as well as allowing us to accommodate a larger number of students, both on campus and off. There is growing consensus among universities engaged in online education that the true costs to the education provider of development and delivery of e-learning are likely to be greater than the development and delivery of traditional classroom learning. However, the economic benefits to the students in terms of reduced time and effort to access and acquire quality education will presumably induce them to pay the higher costs of online learning.

In the midst of these economic changes, there appears to be a controversial trend of growing commercial interests of our faculty, who may be seduced by the potential profits of retaining their intellectual property rights to their individual curricula, which heretofore were largely controlled by their academic employers. Traditionally, the process of education was largely limited to the geographic constraints of the classroom and campus, and intellectual property rights led to royalties, patents, and speaking fees. With the Internet making some education accessible virtually anywhere, some faculty envision themselves as intellectual entrepreneurs with global revenue potential that should accrue to them rather than to their host universities. The confounding of educational motivations with commercial ones will most likely be more pervasive throughout academia, with a variety of consequences, not all of which will be benign for the ultimate customer—the student.

Another shift in education is the weakening of the regional oligopolies that residential and commuter campuses have enjoyed. As online education grows and the constraints of distance and geography become less binding, many institutions will aggressively expand their market reach beyond their local boundaries to reach students anywhere in the world. Obstacles such as state accreditations and legal degree-granting authority will not permanently deter education providers from transcending state, regional, or even national borders. As universities face increasing competition not only from crosstown rivals, but from potentially anywhere in the world, the quality, relevance, and value of their curricula will come under constant competitive pressure to keep up with national expectations, if not with global benchmarks. Moreover, this competition will not only come from other universities, but also from profit-seeking corporations, government agencies, employers, and corporate universities, and even entire nations that seek to compete in the global information economy.

In the face of all these massive trends, our universities face several handicaps in coping with such turbulence. First, our individual and even collective experience in Web-based education is relatively new and short; there are only a handful of schools that have as much as 10 years experience in online learning of any kind. Second, there are few established standards, procedures, and specifications that govern the design, development, and delivery of online learning. Although a few government–industry partnerships have been working for more than 5 years to evolve some industry standards, their influence on the current state of e-learning has been modest at best. Finally, the pace of change in e-learning is increasing at breathtaking speeds, whether it's in technology, customer preferences, economic markets, or information infrastructure. It is an almost overwhelming challenge for any single university to keep up with all the relevant developments that will directly affect their core business of education.

Thus, there is a compelling need for the educational community as a whole, as well as for individual institutions, to engage in rapid learning, imitation, innovation, and experimentation. We cannot afford our environment to "settle down"; there will be no market equilibrium when it comes to learning. The time scales of decades (some may say centuries) that have traditionally governed institutional change in universities are not only irrelevant but are likely to be fatal, except for those few who enjoy the luxury of enormous financial and intellectual endowments, and even they may not be immune from rapid transformation. As a consequence, those institutions that have long, rich, and proven e-learning programs constitute an important national resource that will help other universities guide their own destinies on the Internet. The accumulated experience of the early e-learning pioneers will help the rest of us manage our own growth and development by minimizing the delays and expense of avoidable errors and blind alleys, by improving our efficacy and economy in providing e-learning, and by illuminating the direction and focus of significant research and development that will ensure the vitality of e-learning into the 21st century.

The helpful descriptions of current progress and program evolution of e-learning in universities and university systems such as the State University of New York (SUNY) are therefore timely, instructive and important guides as other institutions navigate their way across the turbulent, uncharted seas of e-learning. The chapter presented by Shea, Fredericksen, Pickett, and Pelz (Chap. 16, this volume) is of interest at two levels. First as a role model as a large, nationally recognized, well-established e-learning program, SUNY's early pioneering efforts have much to teach us. Second, as a study of the fundamentally different learning dynamics on the Web, this chapter is an object lesson in the conceptual and methodological difficulties of conducting such research. Both foci have instructive lessons and implications.

As one of the oldest and largest e-learning programs in higher education today, the SUNY Learning Network the (SLN) commands both attention and respect. The size alone of the SLN is impressive, encompassing 47 campuses, 1,500 online courses reaching 38,000 online students. With a 7-year history, the SLN is fully a whole generation (measured in Internet or dog years) ahead of institutions starting today. The SLN infrastructure is also very impressive in its scope and depth. SLN provides intensive faculty development in Web-based education, multimedia instructional designers, faculty help desks, mentors, system-wide learning and course management systems, and even workbooks, templates, and course structure. These are resources that most faculty at a single campus could only dream of; a statewide system of this scale boggles the mind of any faculty or administrator who scavenges for enough copying paper or for the odd teaching assistant simply to meet their day-to-day requirements. Especially for those of us who labor in public institutions, our curiosity, envy, and awe can be captured in the simple question, "How on earth did you do that?" or to put it in Disney cinematic terms, "How did SUNY build this online El Dorado?" Although the specific features of this shining virtual city are dazzling, those of us living in the impoverished countryside, unable to relocate, are hungry to learn how to create even the modicum of such an infrastructure in our own neighborhoods. Let me elaborate this curiosity through a dozen topics on the economic, programmatic, and institutional aspects of online education:

1. How much does e-learning cost SUNY annually? If the start-up and operating costs of the SLN are prohibitive except for the largest or richest universities, then most institutions of higher learning may well be left behind in the

e-learning market or alternatively seek smaller, more scalable niches in the online domain.

2. Where did the funding come from to build the SLN? Was there a single budget appropriated centrally to establish the SLN, or did the various SUNY campuses contribute appropriate shares to support the enterprise? To what degree did tuition or other revenues offset the development and operating costs of the SLN?

3. What are the economics of the program, especially in light of the recent news that NYU-Online has failed after only 3 years of operation and that the Open University of Great Britain has withdrawn for the U.S. market? Has the SLN reached financial break-even yet? If not, when is it projected to become profitable?

4. What was the inside story of the political infighting to create, launch, and protect SLN? Was it a top-down initiative driven by the senior leadership of SUNY, or was it a bottoms-up grass roots revolution inspired by entrepreneurial faculty? With most academic faculty committed, professionally, culturally, and psychologically to traditional classroom instruction, how did SUNY overcome the inevitable resistance to such radical change that potentially threatens the very identity of the professoriate?

5. Who are and were the champions of the SLN, and why were they successful? What change strategies and tactics proved to be most effective and which least? Assuming that coalitions were formed to carry out this state-wide program, who were the key stakeholders, and how was their support enlisted? Did faculty unions/and associations play any major role in the approval or endorsement of the SLN?

6. What incentives and inducements were most successful in attracting faculty to the SLN? Beyond the financial incentives, were there other inducements, such as positive consideration of online instruction in pay, promotion, and tenure decisions? If so, how was the natural controversy over such an emotionally charged issue managed? Do SUNY faculty enjoy any intellectual property rights to their online curricula?

7. How did SUNY get traditionally fractious faculty at different campuses to conform to common practices, standards, and formats? If inducements are not adequate to ensure compliance, what sanctions or discipline are appropriate and effective?

8. What are the secrets for getting multiple campuses to participate in a state-wide online program? Because getting academic departments and schools on only one campus to cooperate is already a daunting challenge, how did SUNY get even more independent and powerful chancellors agree to commit to a common program that potentially promoted greater competition among themselves for online students?

9. What are the challenges and obstacles to scaling up the SLN at such a rapid rate? Obtaining funding, recruiting faculty, building infrastructure, stimulating demand, and developing policies and procedures are all familiar problems for start-up corporations. For universities to solve such problems in the space of only a few years are rare and exceptional cases. Indeed, SUNY may in fact be the singular multicampus university system to be so successful in such a short period of time.

10. What are the current threats and dangers to the SLN—economic, political, technological, and cultural? Can SUNY sustain continued growth and proliferation of the SLN throughout the state? Are there competitive pressures from other universities both within and outside New York state? Are the New York State Legislature and the U.S. Department of Education advocates or skeptics of e-learning and the SLN? What are the problems of getting online courses and degree programs accredited? How do traditional residential and commuting students respond to the availability of online

courses? Are they migrating from the classroom to the Web? Is cheating or plagiarism more problematic for online students than for traditional students?

11.   How are system-wide changes and refinements to the SLN decided, implemented, and evaluated? In short, what is the current governance structure and process for the SLN? As the SLN continues to evolve to keep pace with market demand, information technology, and educational competition, how are changes institutionalized across the state while respecting the necessary discretion and flexibility of specific campuses and individual faculty? There are constant tensions between innovation and stability, between academic freedom and interdependence, and between creativity and economy. Although there are never easy or universal answers to the right balance, SUNY's experiences may instruct the rest of us in how to find our own.

12.   What are the most important lessons to be learned from the evolution of the SLN? Besides what we as individual institutions of higher learning may learn from SUNY's experiences, the scope and scale of the SLN may be harbingers of what the entire industry of online learning may expect in the decades to come. The demonstrable success of the SLN on a variety of levels strongly suggests that e-learning will not suffer the same fate of more recent and well-publicized failures in the dot.com economy. Although the irrational exuberance of the earliest prognosticators of Web-based education may not be realized in the near future, there would be few academic Luddites that would claim that universities will not be permanently affected by online learning. As an early e-learning pioneer, SUNY not only serves as an institutional exemplar for those who follow but also shapes the future evolution of our profession.

To raise these questions is not intended as a criticism of the SLN chapter, which clearly has a focus different from the one embedded in the questions above. On the contrary, these curiosities are a testament to the impressive sophistication and scale of the SUNY program. The SLN is a vibrant case study that deserves to be widely examined and discussed, and I sincerely hope that the authors continue to publicize more information and explanations of what they have accomplished and, perhaps of even more interest, what their plans are for the future of the SLN. Obviously, these are the programmatic curiosities of university administrators, program managers, and educational entrepreneurs who wrestle with the mundane realities of administration. More respected members of academe, such as cognitive scientists, educational psychologists, instructional designers, and curriculum specialists, would likely have stronger interests on the psychological, pedagogical, and technical dimensions of the SLN, that is, the dynamics of online learning, which is the second focus of the chapter.

One of the explicit purposes of the Shea, Fredericksen, Pickett, and Pelz chapter is to study the variables correlated with satisfaction and perceived learning. The data were derived from a recent survey in which 935 students responded. Unfortunately, the generalizability of the reported results is undermined by a variety of imperfections, some mundane, such as flawed statistical treatment, but others are more serious, such as potentially fatal sample bias. In the interests of brevity, I address only three, the first being the problem of sample bias. The 935 students responding is only 26% of the defined population, and this sample was derived from only those who completed all items on the survey. Since no description was given on how the sample was constructed, we can only infer that this was a collection of students who volunteered to respond and were conscientious enough to fill out all the items. Even if we accept the assertion that some of the demographic characteristics of the respondents compared closely to the entire population, there are inescapable differences between the respondents and nonrespondents, namely, in volition and diligence. Without evidence, we cannot reject the possibility that the population of nonrespondents was less satisfied, less diligent, less motivated, less involved and perhaps lower achieving than the respondents. Therefore, we can neither generalize to the population at large nor have confidence that even the underlying factor structure is reliable. In his chapter, Shea notes that they did not have funding to track down all of the nonrespondents. A point worth making is how one might check on the nonrespondents. The strategy is simply to go after a sample of them, making personal contact or paying them, to get responses, and then comparing that sample to a demographically similar group.

Second, the data reported are so incomplete as to cast doubt on the objectivity of the analysis. Two examples should suffice. First, all of the statements quoted are with exceptions favorable to distance learning. It is simply not credible that so few of the 935 respondents had negative or unfavorable comments. If in fact there were none, this is convincing confirmation that the sample is unrepresentative of the larger population. Without disputing the authors' conclusion that the predominant reactions of the respondents were indeed favorable, research obligations of accuracy and objectivity require at least some presentation of the full range of comments. The second omission is no description of the dropout or attrition rate, nor recognition if the sample included those who failed to complete the course. Since 74% if the population is unaccounted for, it is very likely that nonrespondents included all the course dropouts. Any study of satisfaction that systematically excludes those students most likely to be dissatisfied has serious problems, not the least of which is restriction of range.

Finally, the study suffers from problematic construct validity. One central conclusion of the study is that the interactions lead to satisfaction and perceived learning because of the significant positive correlations between the purported independent and dependent variables. Without seeing a copy of the survey instrument used to collect the data, the influence of response bias cannot be discounted. If the items on satisfaction and reported learning came at the end of the survey, and all the surveys had identical item order, then significant response bias cannot be rejected as an explanatory hypothesis. Put another way, correlations between alternate ways of expressing satisfaction may be statistically significant but theoretically unremarkable. For example, in a restaurant customer survey, would we expect anything other than a positive correlation between items asking satisfaction with the food, wine, service, and ambience, and a final item asking whether customers enjoyed the meal?

These criticisms notwithstanding, it is important to study the nature and efficacy of student interactions online. However, rather than scratching the surface by verifying the accepted wisdom that interactions between students and faculty is essential, it would be more insightful to dig a bit deeper and address some of the following questions: What kinds of learning interaction are most efficacious, not only in terms of satisfaction and perceptions, but also in actual performance? Because not all human learning is social (e.g., self-discovery), what does independent learning look like online? How can independent and social learning best be integrated? Finally, should we always try to replicate traditional face-to-face learning in an online environment, or are there some pedagogies unique to e-learning that have no traditional analog?

In summary, all works in progress are flawed to some degree, and the present case is no exception. Nevertheless, often the value of field research is less in what it proves than what it illuminates. In this respect, the Shea, Fredericksen, Pickett, and Pelz chapter is stimulating because of the number and richness of issues raised, both programmatic and theoretic. Without recapitulating these again, it is clear that the SUNY Learning Network has much to teach us. The lessons from its vast experience can be invaluable for any institution so bold as to venture where few have gone so far. I sincerely hope that SUNY continues to share its extensive insights in a variety of forums, and I pay homage to its pathbreaking enterprise.

Open Discussion of Chapter 16

Carson Eoyang: Let me begin the discussion by following up with some questions, or, more accurately, some concerns about the design and interpretation of the data. The value of field research is less what it proves than what it illuminates. In this respect, I was stimulated by the number and richness of issues raised both statistically and implicitly. However, there seem to be some limitations in what conclusions we can draw because of sampling issues.

Primarily, I think there is a problem of sample bias: The 935 students responding is only 26% of the defined population. This sample is taken from only those students who completed all items. Because no description was given on how this sample was constructed, we can only infer that it was a collection of students who completed the course, volunteered to respond, and who were conscientious enough to fill out all the items. Without evidence, we cannot reject the possibility that the population of nonresponders and noncompleters were less satisfied, less diligent, less motivated, less involved, and lower achieving than the responders. I also worry that there seems to be nothing negative in the data—no problems.

Peter Shea: When you start looking at sample sizes, I don't know of any research that shows that dissatisfied people do not respond to opportunities to vent their frustrations, anger, dissatisfaction, and so on. So when you look at eight different surveys across 5 or 6 years and you get the same results from survey to survey, it couldn't be a phenomenon where only satisfied people answered.

Carson Eoyang: The fact that the instrument is the same, the sample procedure is the same, the fact that it is consistent all the time suggests that there could be consistent problems with the methodology.

Tom Duffy: When is it administered?

Peter Shea: It is administered at the end of the semester.

Tom Duffy: So dropouts don't fill it out?

Linda Polin: That is the main problem with the survey.

Jenny Franklin: There is actually some student ratings literature indicating that students who fill out the open-ended comments are the students most satisfied. Without some extraordinary effort to sample, that encourages the participation by all students; you will not hear from 80% of the students in the middle. You have to ask, "So what do the comments mean when so many subjects are lost?"

Peter Shea: Are you talking about students who fill in comments, or are you talking about students who fill in surveys?

Jenny Franklin: I see the comment area as very analogous to student ratings. But let me sneak in a different question: You adapted Chickering and Gamson as a conceptual base, but there is a huge volume of empirically based research about this measure and how it correlates to actual learning, as well as with student variables. The course disciplinary area, for example, is a strong correlate of student satisfaction.

Peter Shea: We did not find any differences in satisfaction across disciplines.

Jenny Franklin: I am really surprised! One of the strongest relationships between satisfaction and student and context variables is course discipline and course level. You can broadly characterize courses by their relationship to predicted ratings. Courses that are high in quantitative content, like math, statistics, and logic, get lower ratings.

Peter Shea: Well, this is asking thousands of students—just the most recent survey had 2,600 students—and we do not find the relationship.

Jenny Franklin: It would be very interesting to understand why, because this is well replicated.

Tom Duffy: That is the issue, and it relates to what Carson was saying about potential methodological concerns.

John Bransford: Well, it just occurred to me that you have such a wonderful test bed, and the sample bias issue is really huge. One way to do this is to do it the way they do advertising—telephone survey, stratified random sampling.

Peter Shea: We have thought about doing a follow-up survey for nonrespondents, randomly sampling them.

John Bransford: I think it is really important. We have actually hired a couple firms to do this for us. The other reason for doing it is for continuous improvement; the most valuable data for improvement is from the group that has dissatisfaction. For selling to your board, you want the good sample, but for learning purposes, you want the bad group.

Tom Duffy: Do you find differences by campuses and by types of campuses?

Peter Shea: I have to look at that.

Tom Duffy: Community colleges versus universities?

Peter Shea: I would have to look that up. I would think we have a higher level of satisfaction at the community college.

Linda Polin: I am thinking of triangulation. It seems to me that surveys may be self-fulfilling. You just paid for something you've gone through. And are you going to say that it is bad—kind of like buying a car—are you going to say you did not like it? I think how many people are repeat customers would be a good indicator.

Peter Shea: If you saw higher satisfaction or lower satisfaction by repeat customers, what would that tell you?

Linda Polin: If I saw lower satisfaction by a repeat customer, I would wonder about that.

Tom Duffy: No, the important triangulation bit of data is simply what proportion of students who take other courses. It is another index of satisfaction. But I am not sure how to evaluate an isolated number—it would have to be looking at the satisfaction and repeat relationship across subgroups or over time.

Sally Johnstone: That is the value of the data, not the distance learning. It is a diagnostic tool to see what you need to do to increase the satisfaction in the performance of the students. There are no absolutes.

Matt Champagne: This conversation walks right across one of my pet peeves. This is a larger issue in terms of course evaluations. Universities... online universities... universally tend to use the autopsy approach—to wait until the class is over to figure out what went wrong, which is totally inappropriate. A graduate student of mine did a survey of the top 200 most wired schools in the country in 1999 and found that 98% of even the most wired schools who obviously have the technology to find out from the students on an ongoing basis used the autopsy approach.

The learning anywhere, anytime program, FIPSE, has taken the lead on this, and is doing an adaptive continual monitoring of the students and helps create tools. They have been able to survey student satisfaction and find out what is going wrong and get that information in quickly, and change while the course is still in session. The dead giveaway is the table in which Peter shows that the level of *strongly disagree* and *disagrees* remains relatively stable, at about 7% to 10% across 7 years. Well, what you find is that when you do this adaptive monitoring, asking the questions a month or two into the courses, over time those disappear, the *strongly disagree* and *disagree*. You want to continually improve so that is zero.

Peter Shea: In terms of reducing the number of dissatisfied, or students reporting low levels of learning, you want those to be shrinking. But considering the other side, how this program has grown. We continually feel that the numbers of dissatisfied students stays relatively small. Another issue that dropout rates carry with them is the assumption that students are dropping out of courses because something is going wrong with the course. Do you feel that that is the primary reason students are dropping out of online courses? You don't feel there are other variables that may be more likely to cause students to drop out of online courses?

Matt Champagne: I am just worried about the obstacles to learning. I guess that is what I looked at, 7%–10% or so continue to be dissatisfied about something. They provide the opportunity to learn how to improve your program even more.

Peter Shea: We started with 56 students online, and last year it was 25,000 and the level of dissatisfaction has stayed relatively low. I would be more concerned if the level of dissatisfaction started growing instead of staying stable. I would say that student satisfaction this high, together with growth at this level, is not only acceptable but should also be applauded.

John Bransford: Again, I think you have such a neat project. Two things you might look at: If you could look at the same course taught once and then twice and then three times and the level of satisfaction goes up, that tells you something about continuous improvement. The other things that you have is a faculty development model. So if you could find some professors who taught, let's say, statistics very badly prior to coming into this, but then over time you follow the changes in satisfaction ...

Rather than taking a sample survey across everything, I'd say let's keep the focus on this particular courses or this particular instructor or something like that. I think you have lots of potential.

Peter Shea: I don't want it to come out that this is the only way that we are looking at what is happening in this program. Karen Swan at the University of Albany is looking at social presence issues; others are looking at how to drill down into what is going on and getting into the whole program. There are other people that are looking at what's happening in classes. It is a huge program.

Karen Ruhleder: Let me change the subject a bit and ask about student access to resources. One of the things that we have struggled with is equal access to all kinds of resources. We have had all kinds of intrastructural problems, such as the university trying to assess our students for a sports facility fee when they are probably not going to use it if they live in Japan. We have a real problem in that we want them to be independent learners as well as good learners, and part of that is we want them to be able to access the library facilities that our on campus students have access to. We only have one campus for one specific body of students, but you have a vast network. So I am wondering how you make sure that the resources are equal or somehow equalized.

Peter Shea: For the library, there is a program called SUNY Connect that provides access to library resources and databases on every campus. It allows you to access different databases.

Linda Polin: We have invested a lot of money each semester putting things online by ourselves.

Mark Schlager: So I have 1 minute. (*Group laughs.*) Do you have any data on actually how much synchronous and asynchronous activity is going on, even though it is not required?

Peter Shea: I would say that the vast majority of interaction is asynchronous and not synchronous.

Mark Schlager: To me, this gets to the heart of the theory-of-practice question. As I understand it, being able to get together and engage in real-time dialogue is a good thing. In fact, Peter's program has senior instructors come together for face-to-face training. How come they are so privileged and their students are not?

Peter Shea: I guess it has to do with the goals of the program ...

Sally Johnstone: . . . and of the individuals. We are coming together face-to-face because Tom can't even get us to read e-mails when he sends them out to us, because we are just so busy.

Mark Schlager: Forget all the practical reasons. Let's talk about how people learn. We are not talking about the impossibility of scheduling synchronous interaction [among instructors and students in online programs]. We have heard from programs [at Pepperdine University and LEEP] that have no problems with synchronous interactions. In fact, there are data to show that synchronous interaction can be extremely valuable in learning, especially in social learning activities, and that asynchronous interaction, which is claimed to be so highly reflective, can be completely vacuous. The point is why some programs insist on the a priori exclusion of synchronous modes of interaction.

Sally Johnstone: That's a real easy one. Sloan funded them, and their focus is on asynchronous.

Mark Schlager: The Sloan Foundation has somehow convinced a generation of developers of online courses that you don't need synchronous interaction, even if you can [overcome scheduling issues], even if it is a good thing, even if your content material would benefit from it. Sloan has set a stake in the ground and said this is the way that online activity should go, and everybody just believes.

Carson Eoyang: It is a real serious issue. In the Navy, we have one of our senior officials who is trying to drive the asynchronous distance learning as the dominant pedagogy for any training education throughout the entire Navy. At the graduate school, we believe that a blended approach, depending on the objective and the content, is more sensible. It is a real political and economical problem for us to fight that.

Peter Shea: Let me back up and say there is no mandatory ban on synchronous.

Mark Schlager: But if your instruction to instructors does not include why and when it is valuable, how to do it—faciliate synchronouse interaction—well, and it is not something they [instructors] practice, who is going to do it, much less do it well?

Peter Shea: But what is the value added? What is the unique advantage to synchronous interaction versus asynchronous?

Tom Duffy: Let me answer with an example from Unext. Mark Schlager and Carlos Olgin worked with me on the study. We ran two classes of 20 students each. They were paid participants, but the only requirement was that they completed the tasks. They did not have to do anything else. They did not have to interact asynchronously (using Domino) or synchronously (using WebEx). They had access to the asynchronous as I described in my paper. For one of the classes, when they were first accepted for the study, we sent out an e-mail saying we're going to have a synchronous discussion where we will get to know each other, get to know the faculty. We will give you the 10 best strategies for being successful in the course; you don't have to be there for it, but we will run it three different times taking care of time zones and work habits.

They almost all showed for at least one session. There were 10 in one session, and we used a survey tool in WebX, and we said, "So do you want to do this again ever, and if you want to do it again, do you want to do this again after 3 weeks, or do you want to do it every week?" Eight out of the 10 said they want to do it every week. They tended to participate in those sessions. I don't know the numbers, but they tended to participate. At the end, the difference between those two classes (only asynchronous or both synch and asynch) was dramatic. They had different instructors, but other than that, there wasn't anything different about them.

The group that had the synchronous, they came together much more to talk online. At one point, they e-mailed me and asked if they could get together because they were all from the Chicago area. I did not want that to happen during the study so I said no, "we will do that at the end. You cannot do it during the course." We ran a focus group two different nights, one for each group, and brought in five or six students from each class. When the students from the synchronous group came together, it was "You're Jamie! Hi, Jamie." It was a whole sense of familiarity. For those that were in the asynchronous class, there was no sense of that familiarity. It was just sort of a formal tone. So that sort of social thing that everybody is talking about does make a difference.

Peter Shea: The Virtual High School project uses Lotus Domino as well. They started using it because they believed in asynchronous learning—and it would not have a chat room.

Sally Johnstone: Which project was that?

Mark Schlager: The Concord Consortium of virtual high schools. What they found was they had sort of an e-mail passing thing. The students, not so much the faculty, but the students, would get online at night and fire off e-mails to one another to converse because they needed the conversation to understand the concepts they felt. The only way they could do it was to quickly fire off e-mails sort of like instant messages. In fact, early on, the designers of the system said, "We'll see, that is the affordance of our system." That's not the affordance of the system, that's a bug in the system because of their failure to support synchronous.

Tom Duffy: I just want to do a shift to the faculty development to get some focus on that. Why do faculty participate? You talk about the mandatory training. How much time does that take? Are they compensated in any way?

Peter Shea: We looked at the relation of faculty satisfaction to the amount of work they reported with any course with the expressed concern that the faculty were putting so much time into the development and delivery of these courses that they were going to be reporting very, very dissatisfactory, unsatisfactory experiences. We found just the opposite. The faculty that report the highest number of hours report the highest level of satisfaction, which is sort of counterintuitive but really points to the fact that these are faculty that really care about what they are doing.

Tom Duffy: That is interesting. Clearly, people happy with their job put in more time. But let me pursue the mandatory training. How many hours are there? How did it get started in the first place? You are talking about satisfaction about having done it. But hell, I have my research program to do. I have my other classes to teach. I know that it is going to take more time. How am I going to get into that?

Peter Shea: We have questions on the faculty survey on why are you teaching this course. Why are you teaching this course online? Most of the responses have to do with interest in online teaching and learning, interest in learning how to do this stuff. They are intrinsically motivated.

Tom Duffy: The length of time on the mandatory? How long is the mandatory?

Peter Shea: Face-to-face, there are three all-day trainings that happen over a course of a 5-month period. Overall, most commonly, they spend more than 150 hours per course. Compensation varies by institution. Initially, we were funding courses . . .

John Bransford: So is this an add-on course by unit, or do I substitute?

Peter Shea: Typically, the online course becomes part of the regular teaching load, not an add-on.

Sally Johnstone: In a number of states that have strong unionized faculty, there has been some interesting approaches as to how the unions have chosen to respond to distance education. In some states, the unions have chosen to take it off the table for a while. What has happened within the SUNY system?

Peter Shea: There was a report that came out recently in which SUNY was listed as an exemplary institution in its management of faculty participation in online courses. It's voluntary.

Sally Johnstone: So it has not been a negotiation issue yet?

Peter Shea: Because we at the SUNY system level are not hiring faculty to teach courses, these issues become moot . . .

Tom Duffy: I think we need to wind up at this point. Thank you all.
    (End of session)

VI

Alternate Views

18

A Policy Perspective on Learning Theory and Practice in Distance Education

Sally M. Johnstone
WCET at WICHE

The technologically enabled practices described in the previous chapters are allowing the ideal of individualized learning to be realized. Most put the learner in the center of all the decisions about the structure of the learning activities, the time allowed to complete the learning goals, the tools used in the learning environment, and the curriculum. This is wonderful for the learner; however, it poses some serious challenges for the way that colleges and universities operate. It affects the semester system, classes and credits as units of analysis to measure progress, the range of technologies used to capture academic content, and the practice of individual departments independently defining the curriculum. These are no small challenges. In the following pages, I would like to elaborate on these and other areas where new practices are challenging higher education traditions. I do not propose many solutions, but sometimes understanding the problem can be a good first step. The best uses of technology for teaching and learning will continue to push a lot of changes in the ways things are done at colleges and universities.

In this chapter, I will address the following issues related to policy in distance education: classroom practices, institutional policies, academic sharing, institutional costs, state policies, regional policies, federal policies, and international policies. This chapter is not meant to be comprehensive in scope, but instead raises issues specifically from the chapters in this volume, as well as the chapter discussions. It also includes work in which my colleagues and I are currently engaged.

NEW CLASSROOM PRACTICES

One of my favorite new "classroom" practices is described by John Stinson (Chap. 8, this volume). It is a simple artifact that comes out of online, as opposed to face-to-face, student discussions. Stinson describes the assessment rubric he uses to assess online students' engagement to the discussion. The result is a new metric for student engagement in the learning process—if we can use the quality of the comments in a discussion as a reflection of engagement, that is. Stinson uses threaded discussion in his online classes. He requires students to participate in these discussions and evaluates their participation. Faculty grading class participation in a classroom usually use a checklist system or a general impression of how often a student asks questions, makes comments, maintains eye contact, does not fall asleep, and other indexes. Rarely does the instructor have an objective measure of the quality of the student's participation.

On the other hand, Stinson has a written record of all his students' comments. He evaluates them on four levels. First he looks for the student's immediate personal reaction. Then he also checks for reports of some type of research (including informal discussions with experts). He says he always expects his students to comment at these first levels, but he also pushes them for even more engagement. John checks for evidence of synthesis and generalization of the material within the comments. His last level is my favorite. It is both practical to administer and seems valid. At the end of the term, John looks at the responses from other students that each student's comments generate. If the original comment was not very thought provoking, other students are not likely to react to it. He can actually count the number of responses. That is pretty hard to do in a classroom discussion unless the instructor uses outside observers.

With capabilities like these available, it makes our traditional ways of evaluating certain aspects of a student's performance seem obsolete. It seems to call for a systematic analysis of the new evaluation methods now available to teaching faculty that could be used to guide new student assessment practices.

INSTITUTIONAL POLICIES

One institutional practice that is challenged by distance learning focuses on who should be doing the "teaching." Are full-time faculty members really the best ones to assist students online? Several of the seminar participants mentioned that their programs, enabled by technology, require special teaching behaviors. They require new ways of working with students that fully utilize the capabilities of the technologies. These new ways require training, and Linda Polin from Pepperdine University (Chap. 2, this volume) and Karen Ruhleder from the University of Illinois (Chap. 4, this volume) both raised the issue of whether or not their full-time faculty members were ready to adapt so completely. If part-time faculty members, or adjunct faculty, are to be the core workforce for online instruction, then institutions that use a lot of online teaching may need to develop a new category of professional employees. The requirements for promotions of these new professionals should look quite different from those of the traditional faculty. Research and improvement in online teaching would be a more germane requirement for a teacher's promotion than simple professional development within his or her field of study.

Another institutional shift that becomes critical for effective distance learning is providing full support for students who do not come to a campus. If a program is fully online, then students who enroll in that program need academic advising, tutoring, and career counseling, just like students who enroll in on-campus programs. Few institutions are ready to offer all the student support services to noncampus students, and yet they charge as much or more as their on-campus counterparts to be part of the academic institution.

Another practice that needs examination has to do with the ownership of the materials used in a class. In a traditional face-to-face class, the faculty member teaching the class usually develops all the lecture and supporting materials. When good distance learning courses are developed, there are frequently teams involved. These teams are likely to include faculty members, instructional designers, technologists, and others (e.g., see Duffy & Kirkley, Chap. 6, this volume). This challenges our traditional approaches to intellectual property rights for a course. Whose intellectual property is the final product? Who holds the copyright? Who decides what uses of the course materials are possible? If students' work is incorporated into future versions of the course material, what are the ownership implications? There are multiple models being used at the campus level to solve this dilemma, and some will fit an individual institution better than others, but every institution should have a formal policy to which all members of the community must agree. This all becomes more complex when the development teams are not all from a single institution. We are seeing incentive funding for the development of distance learning courses that requires multi-institutional collaboration. There are few models in operation to handle this circumstance, but as they evolve, the WCET will make them available on our Web site (http://www.wcet.info).

ACADEMIC SHARING

The chapter by Bransford, Vye, Bateman, Brophy, and Roselli (Chap. 10, this volume), discusses a way of capturing knowledge as part of the online teaching and learning experience. For example, the distance learning tools now in use allow us to create and capture demonstrations of certain statistical principles. A faculty member in a social science department can create a simulation for his or her students of what happens to the various measures of central tendency when the level of variation in the sample change. Once that is done in one department, it is neither necessary nor efficient to replicate it by the business faculty or the many other departments and colleges across a university campus. The replication is currently the case when each has it's own unique statistics course. What is possible, and what is likely to happen as financial constraints come into play? I believe we will see things like the electronic statistics demonstration being captured and reused by other faculty members.

This is part of what Bransford and his colleagues called knowledge capturing. Even as there is not a need to have this replicated within a campus, there is also no need to replicate these time-consuming but valuable learning tools across campuses. However, that means we need to figure out how to share them. Institutions need to sort that out. We don't have models for this other than the textbook model, wherein institutions are readily willing to adopt the same textbook as other institutions. MERLOT, an emerging project that began a few years ago, is one attempt to set up a vehicle for this cross-campus sharing of learning objects, or captured knowledge. However, the biggest challenge is overcoming the inertial and cultural practices that do not include faculty sharing-learning tools with one another.

In 2002 some additional projects developed that will be of value in helping faculty share teaching materials. One of those, the Connexions Project, is housed at Rice University. Connexion (cnx.rice.edu) offers faculty members both the software and the repository to strre course-related materials that others can use. The Creative Commons (www.creativecommons.org) is housed at Stanford University's law school. It is an online licensing system for web-based materials. It offers authors control options over the material they create for the web. Authors can choose among options, such as "no commercial use," "no derivative works." This enables authors of web materials to have more choices than just "open-to-all" or "open to no one." Finally, the MIT OpenCourseWare project is setting an example for colleges and universities all over the world. By posting the materials used in hundreds of their courses on the web and allowing any educator to use them and modify them, MIT has opened a new way of thinking about the value of sharing academic materials. There are universities in many countries already using their resources and beginning to create their own. In the summer of 2002, the United Nations Educational, Scientific and Cultural Organization (UNESCO) recognized this activity and dubbed it Open Educational Resources. I believe we will see this movement grow.

The implications of sharing captured knowledge, course objects, or electronic courses themselves are enormous for shifting current campus practices. The changes are likely to emerge gradually as faculty members begin to see changes in the focus of their activities. They are likely to spend less time developing new materials for teaching their subject and more time assessing the needs of their students, as well as directly mentoring (teaching) their students. The students' local institutions will likely devote more resources to managing and providing student and administrative support services, as well as managing the brokering of materials for instruction. This is the model that the large distance learning programs use to enable them to make their services affordable to students.

To assist institutions in this transition, the WCET has worked on the issue of providing good support for online learners. We have created some resources that are freely available. With support from the U.S. Department of Education's Fund for the Improvement of Post Secondary Education (FIPSE), we created a "Guide to Developing Online Student Services". This resource is on our Web site (http://www.wcet.info), and it allows the user to virtually tour a wide range of solutions for effective support for online students. The William and Flora Hewlett Foundation is supporting a Web-based decision tool that allows institutional decision makers to compare different solutions to the student support challenge. An additional set of resources evolved from our previous work with support from the U.S. Department of Education's Learning Anyplace Anytime Project (LAAP). We are working with a community college, a private university, and a research university to develop models for the integration of these support services into the core activities of the institution. The process of placing the Web-based support of students at the core of an institution's mission results in changes at many levels of the campus. This is discussed in more detail in a chapter in another book (Johnstone & Shea, 2003).

INSTITUTIONAL COSTS FOR DISTANCE LEARNING

Very few departments or campuses really know what distance learning is costing them. As distance learning goes from being a peripheral activity as described in several of the cases in previous chapters to being an integral part of campus activity, administrators do need to know the costs. In partnership with Dennis Jones from the National Center for Higher Education Management Systems (NCHEMS) and with support from the FIPSE and the Andrew Mellon Foundation, the WCET created the Technology Costing Methodology project. The analytic framework has been pilot tested in more than 20 higher education settings and a virtual high school. The materials include a handbook, a casebook, and a tabulator that lets the user plug in numbers to play out different costing scenarios. It has been valuable to campuses looking at costs across departments, as well as states looking across institutions.

When institutions know what their current practices in distance learning cost, it begins to drive decisions. The most telling finding from these cost analyses is that the types of people that are used for different tasks and activities for online teaching and for supporting students is the single most influential variable for costs. The specific technologies used for a distance learning program are important for costs only in so far as they affect how and which people are used. The actual cost of the technology has very little effect on the overall costs of a program. There are more details on this issue in a recent article in *Change* magazine (Johnstone & Poulin, 2002).

An additional institutional policy related to distance learning costs is the way in which revenue is shared among departments or colleges. In many institutions, the distance learning programs are run as stand-alone operations through a separate unit within the institution. These programs usually develop as self-supporting programs, and if full-time faculty members are involved, they are paid according to one of a few different schemes, such as overload or incentive pay. As this type of activity becomes more popular, many institutions are pulling the programs into the academic departments that have attracted the most distance learning students. If this trend continues, the formulae for distributing tuition revenue, technology-support fees, and even state full-time equivalency (FTE) funding will have to be adjusted to reflect the costs of the distance learning courses.

An additional institutional policy issue that seems to be under examination, in part, as a result of increased distance learning activity is the acceptance of transferred credits. As it becomes easier for a student to sit in his or her dormitory room on a campus and take a class from another institutions, transferring credits becomes a real issue. Students usually do this for convenience, but sometimes they may be seeking a better quality course than the one offered locally. Regardless of the reason, they expect the online course to transfer into their home institution. The faculty at the home institution may have some valid concerns about accepting credits toward a degree program when they do not know if the material in the course to be transferred in actually fits into the curriculum they have designed. One solution to this problem is to move away from credits and academic currency and look more toward assessments of student learning. This is not a short-term solution, but it would help to eliminate another institutional barrier for students choosing to learn online. This issue is examined more thoroughly in a monograph published by the American Council of Education (Johnstone, Ewell, & Paulson, 2002; Johnstone & Shea, 2003).

STATE POLICIES

As more and more institutions are offering distance learning programs, costs become more visible. Some new strategies are developing at the state level to reflect the cost realities. In some states, policy makers are beginning to recognize that public universities and colleges cannot be allowed to compete among themselves in the "E-learning marketplace." State leaders are starting to create noncompetitive strategies for state funding for distance learning. Different states are doing this in different ways. In South Dakota and Montana, there are incentive grants for projects that include interinstitutional collaboration in the development of distance learning projects. The University of Texas has eight campuses working together to offer students a master's degree with some courses from each campus. There are also statewide consortia developing within both the university and community college arenas. They are designed to allow the sharing of some of the expenses of administering distance learning programs. These do not require that institutions give up their autonomy with regard to offering degrees. They are not in charge of the academic function, but act as a vehicle for sharing some aspects of the whole administrative framework. Kentucky, Michigan, Arizona, Georgia, Ohio, Washington, Colorado, South Dakota, and Oregon all have aspects of these.

New funding models are also beginning to emerge that recognize the costs to both sending and receiving institutions. Most funding sources focus on the creation of distance learning academic material, that is, the courses. When you start looking at the real costs of supporting students in a teaching/mentoring environment using captured knowledge/courseware that is brought in from elsewhere, one has to recognize that the receiving institution also has expenses. There are few models for sharing these costs, but one state, Oklahoma, is implementing such a system. It is being watched very closely by several other states. The Oklahoma system allows institutions to receive state funding for students within their areas of responsibility. The responsible institution may serve those students with courseware that originates elsewhere, but the local staff is providing direct support to the students and that is being recognized and reimbursed by the state.

State higher education officials are also seeking new accountability measures for institutions. As individualization of learning is enabled by distance learning technologies, the completion rates (that old dyed-in-the-wool standard) may not be very informative. Completion rates have been used widely by states and by the accrediting community as a measure of institutional performance. This is getting very tricky, because a student is now able to define his or her own learning goals, which may or may not match what an institution defines as a degree. We do not have methods to deal with this.

In addition, funding institutions based on full-time equivalency (or FTE) gets to be very complex as institutions are serving students that may or may not be in the same state as the institution. The students may not be behaving in the way that their peers did 30 years ago, when these systems were devised. The rules are changing very fast, and the staffs of the state coordinating and governing boards do not have any experiences or models to help them interpret what this all means. No one really does.

As students begin using distance learning resources from multiple institutions, the question of in-state and out-of-state tuition charges for public institutions for distance learning comes up. There is very little policy consistency among states regarding this issue. A few states have no policies at all, and how much tuition is charged is decided by the institutions. In many states, distance learning students are expected to pay full out-of-state tuition. In one state, there have been discussions in the legislature about this issue that reflect a broader perspective and view of the future. These legislators recognize that by making their state universities and colleges charge out-of-state tuition for all distance learning students, they are making their institutions noncompetitive in other states and around the world. They recognize that their previous investments in their institutions might be better served by allowing them to be competitive. There has not been formal action on this yet, but at least there is talk about it.

REGIONAL POLICY ISSUES

Just as institutions are using distance learning to reach students beyond their local areas, they are also reaching students across the country and around the world. For the last century, U.S. higher education has been organized into geographical regions for purposes of accreditation. Institutions that serve students in multiple regions are challenging the regional accrediting community's historical autonomy. The regional accrediting associations have recently begun to work together. They formed an organization called the Council of Regional Accreditation Commissions (C-RAC). The C-RAC is made up of the CEOs and the chairs of the individual boards of each association. They meet regularly to address issues that affect all of them. One of their early projects was to contract with the WCET to help them develop a common set of principles for quality distance learning programs. All the boards have adopted these "Principles of Good Practice" (Johnstone & Poulin, 2002), [1] though they are used differently in each region. A part of this work on the Principles of Good Practice includes a set of protocols for each section. These are questions that can be asked to get at the information needed to assess the broad quality of the distance learning program. All the regional associations and the discipline accrediting groups recognize the need for more qualified assessors for distance learning programs. They are working on developing pools of evaluators.

FEDERAL POLICIES

As several of the previous authors noted in our discussions, it has become common practice for the number and length of face-to-face class meetings to be defined by federal financial aid policies, rather any pedagogical theory or active assessment of the efficacy of the meetings. Because student financial support is still based on full-time study as defined by class credit indices and is based on seat time, it cannot reflect what happens when learning is individualized in a learning anytime, anyplace setting. As technology allows a student to work toward mastery of a set of materials at his or her own pace, federal financial support for the student becomes a problem. The U.S. Department of Education does have a demonstration project under way to address this difficulty. This project is carefully examining how institutions with different types of learning environments can administer financial aid (http://www.ed.gov/offices/OPE/PPI/DistEd/).

Another development in federal practice is worth noting. The National Science Foundation, the U.S. Department of Education, and even the Department of Commerce through its National Technology Infrastructure Assistance program, all fund distance learning–related projects that have embraced totally asynchronous programs. Several of the authors of the previous chapters in this book have questioned when and under what circumstances totally asynchronous learning environments are most effective. The governmental agencies previously mentioned are all legislatively motivated to address access issues. They are trying to enable as many people as possible to have access to higher education resources, and have interpreted this to mean "anytime, anyplace," and, consequently, asynchronous approaches. Perhaps there should be a broader approach that is supported by theory and practice and matched to the needs of the student. The E-Army University project and the new navy distance learning project demand totally asynchronous programs of classes for purposes of logistics. In the coming years, these projects may well provide evidence to let us really test the scope and understand the parameters of asynchronous learning situations.

---

[1] The C-RAC Principle's of Good Practice can be found on all the regional association's Web site and also at www.wcet.info.

SOME INTERNATIONAL ISSUES

The World Trade Organization currently has higher education on the table for negotiations. It will be a few years before the negotiations are complete, but we can speculate about some of the consequences. It could mean that a university in Spain will find it easier to offer distance learning programs to students throughout Illinois than the University of Illinois would find it. The state of Illinois will not be able to mandate what the Spanish University does under the fair trade agreement, even though it can restrict its own institutions from enrolling students in another institution's service area. This could well be a critical influence on how states regulate of their own institutions.

Another important international issue for U.S. university and college educators relates to how we share what we have and what we do with others in the world. We have as resources in this country besides just fast food and action movies to export, and those include higher education. Not all of what we choose to export in higher education needs to or should be profitable. The basis of our intellectual growth for faculties in universities and colleges rests on sharing information with peers. Our definition of *peers* needs to expand as far as technological communication allows. One of the vehicles emerging for this is the open courseware movement. The Massachusetts Institute of Technology (MIT) announced in 2001 its goal to put almost all of their intellectual capital on the Web for use anywhere. This is not distance learning in the traditional sense. MIT will not be awarding degrees based on their open courseware, but they are confronting some of the same issues that arise in a distance learning setting. They are exploding our simplistic notions of intellectual property related to a course. It is hoped that the MIT project can become a model for ways to increase the quality of course materials. Because the materials are all online, they are open to the public and instructors can get feedback on them.

With the support of the Hewlett Foundation, MIT is working with the WCET to begin exploring some of the intercultural issues inherent in sharing course materials. The report of the first international meeting on open courseware is available on WCET's website (www.wcet.info). The representatives from universities in developing countries who attended this meeting hosted by the United Nations Educational, Scientific and Cultural Organization (UNESCO) embraced the concept but adopted the name "open educational resources." We hope it is a movement in which many faculty from the developed world will engage. It is already the case that individual faculty members at community colleges and in the health sciences are voluntarily putting their course materials on the Web for everyone in the world to see. In the cases of which I am aware, these faculty members are getting feedback from a wide range of colleagues and opening up opportunities for collaboration.

SUMMARY

Academic practice and research are both ahead of policies applied to distributed and distance learning. This is true of policies at the campus, college and university systems, states, and even the federal government levels. This results in teaching and learning activities that are not shaped by research and demonstrated good practices, but rather by policies that reflect the state of practice that was in place when those who made the policies were in school. The advent of easy Internet and high-speed computing access has radically altered the range of useful learning activities. Yet, federal financial aid policies are dictating classroom practices, and in some states, the reimbursement policies are dictating the types of technologies colleges can use to serve students.

There are not easy solutions to this dilemma. In this chapter, I have pointed out several instances of where policy and good practice are in conflict. Sometimes knowing the problem is the first step toward a solution. At this point in time, our federal government is examining new authorization legislation for higher education. At this writing, the congressional hearings are not yet complete, but the testimony thus far seems to be pushing for the removal of policies that inhibit distance learning.

Open Discussion of Chapter 18

Tom Duffy: Sally, I would like to start the discussion. During this time together, we have had interesting discussions, but we have played around in our own little sandbox talking about our designs. How do we influence change? You presented a whole lot of policy issues, and all of those have a huge impact. What is the mechanism for building a linkage?

Sally Johnstone: If there were a simple mechanism, it would have been built. There isn't a simple mechanism. Part of the reason there isn't a simple mechanism is that we have 50 higher education systems in this country. We've got a few things that our federal government does and can influence, but it's at a state-by-state level. Then there are the meta-players—I mean the regional accreditors, as well as the specialized accreditors. They have an impact as they can push certain kinds of activities. So the Western Association of Schools and Colleges [WASC], for instance, is trying very hard to base accreditation on outcomes. The transition is not a simple one. But it is through vehicles like that we can see change occurring. To shift anything on a large scale, there are issues with the legislatures in the states and in the state higher education executive offices. In this country, we don't have one place to go to change everything. That is part of the problem we face. I am not saying that this is a bad thing—that's just the way it is.

Tom Duffy: As far as influence, is it important to go to American Association of Higher Education (AAHE) or somewhere like that, or is it more important to talk to the regional accrediting agencies?

Sally Johnstone: It depends on what you are trying to accomplish. That is why I have been whining about how much I have to fly around, but I have to talk to all of them. I deal with the accreditors. I deal with the legislators. I deal with American Association of Higher Education (AAHE), ACE, ASCU—whoever is looking at the issues around e-learning. I think the key to all of this, just as we were talking about how you approach a learner by knowing where the learner is, you need to do the same thing in the policy world. You've got to know what the hot issue is that is pushing the button of the legislature or the committee in the legislature or the faculty committee that is part of AAHE, or the hottest topic that is beating an accreditor over the head that is your wedge to get in. It would be nice if it were simpler for those of us trying to deal with policy change, but part of the beauty of the higher education system in the U.S. is its diversity and, hence, complexity.

Brian Lekander: At the national level, there are issues that need to be resolved before there is likely to be federal funding for distance education. For example, there are concerns among many associations that distance education is impacting the academic environment in ways that may not be positive. For example, there is a reasonable amount of data as to the workload increase in distance education and the possible impact on disaggregation of faculty roles.

Sally Johnstone: My sense though, Brian, is that there is a softening on these issues.

Brian Lekander: Yes and no.

Sally Johnstone: But I think that ACE, for instance, has really changed the voice that they've had on a lot of these issues over the last 5 years.

John Bransford: Is this mainly at the college level—just a clarification—or is this also at the K–12 level that you've got the resistance?

Sally Johnstone: You know, I don't know, because I pay attention to higher education. My involvement with K–12 is only where there are links to higher education. We are just starting to host a new K–12 organization focusing on virtual schools. In a couple of years, I will probably be able to answer that question.

John Bransford: The National Education Association (NEA) is actually ready to totally transform the union back into helping schools. They want to do it all by distance learning.

Sally Johnstone: Well . . .

John Bransford: This is the group to help them do it.

Sally Johnstone: Yes, absolutely. I was at the American Federation of Teachers (AFT) meeting last year—the higher education part of it, not the K–12 part. After my presentation, I really could not address all the defensive issues they had with the concept of using technology in teaching and learning. All I could really do was say, "OK guys, fine, but here is the reality—here is what the data tells us is going on out there. Do you want to do it, or do you as leaders in your union want to fight it and have your union focus on dying issues?" I think the shear scope of the activity is what will bring them around.

Terry Anderson: First, I really wanted to thank you, Sally, for that. I didn't realize that we had brought up so many topics.

Sally Johnstone: Yes, yes! (*Group laughs.*)

Terry Anderson: I think it is a significant addition that you have added just with that piece. Common link question—I think one other piece that should be added just on institutional issues is the whole ethics thing of when you have knowledge objects there, the sense of privacy protecting students and professors and giving them both copyright credit and giving them protection to make it anonymous is a real hard issue on both the research side and the teaching side. It is especially tough when knowledge gets commodified and reused for subsequent groups of students. This goes on and on forever. But my question is, given the churn of issues that need to be dealt with, plus the very quick evolution of the tools and the people's social conceptions of cyberspace and e-learning, I can understand a real reluctance for legislators to do too much too fast. Are we really at a "Let all flowers bloom for another few years," or is it time to start hunkering down into solid policy?

Sally Johnstone: You know what is going to change it, Terry? It's the cost realities—not just our Technology Costing Methodology project, but the whole effort to uncover the real costs. As the costing tools develop and costing data comes out, I believe it will drive a more unified policy on distance education. Legislators are screaming for costing management tools, as are college presidents. They are running into problems, because they do not know how the money is being spent. Legislators have fiscal responsibilities, and it drives a lot of their thinking on many issues. That is true whether they are in U.S. or Mexico or Canada.

Terry Anderson: But we don't have activity-based costing running profitably in hardly any of our campuses on face-to-face courses, so how is distance learning going to make that much difference?

Sally Johnstone: The difference it will make is that it will allow you to break it down, just like everything else. All of you have encountered this in using distance learning technological tools as a lever or a change agent, to begin to have things be done differently. That's the same thing that is going to go on with costing. That is the most profound thing in which I have ever been involved. It is scary in some ways.

Carson Eoyang: I also wanted to say thank you, because I have been both simultaneously exhilarated and terrified . . .

Sally Johnstone: . . . and with good reason.

Carson Eoyang: I mean, it's an absolutely great addition, especially coming in having this view of 30,000 feet looking down across not only the whole nation but the whole world on these sets of issues. The exhilaration part is to see how much is going on in so many different places, and there are at least a few of you trying to make sense and order of all this stuff. The terror comes from the perception that there is so much stuff going on. If you look at the pace of change, and now that you have confirmed that the scope of change nationally and internationally, it is like an avalanche. I think now my despair is just riding the avalanche, because it seems to be totally out of control.

Sally Johnstone: It is completely out of control. I was serious in my introductory comments. This has been my day job for over 13 years now. I really do characterize it as trying to help create or enable the most graceful transition possible. Some of the projects we do are because people need the information, and nobody else is going to do it, so we do it. However, another part of it is that it is that some of the projects are an important aspect of some ephemeral quality that those of us who work on these kinds of things believe is important to preserve. Whether we can or not, I don't know.

Carson Eoyang: One observation: I think because the movement is so large and so incredibly fast, the traditional governance model that we have used in our country to manage it is just totally inadequate. Therefore, the only other choice we have really is basically market dynamics. The question is how do we make that market efficient and quick in terms of dissemination of information and coordination of coalitions, because

I think if we have to rely solely on the Congress and accrediting bodies to bring order to this, they won't be able to do it on time, and they won't bring about the right order.

Sally Johnstone: No, they are not going to bring order to it. What they may do is enhance certain aspects of it versus others. I don't think we're going to see order in our lifetimes. I mean, think about how old what we now think of the World Wide Web is and how pervasive it is. The last statistic I heard was I think in January of this year, that more than 75% of all kids between the ages of 12 and 18 used the Web. They don't just have it—they were online during the month of January—all kids between 12 and 18. That is profound.

Terry Anderson: That is in the United States?

Sally Johnstone: Yes. It falls off a little bit in Canada, but if you guys go through with your national Internet connectivity funding, it is going to shoot way up, although I understand that it has stalled. Maybe you can brief me on that. In northern Europe, it is 40%, and in the southern hemisphere it drops radically. But the reality is that we've got a tool, a brand new tool that is 7 to 8 years old that we can think about. Are we going to try and control it? I mean we can't, there won't be control. I think about this a lot, and I think we will see certain aspects of what we think of as higher education moving in the direction of the market portion. I hope, in addition to that, we are to see other aspects of higher ed moving more in the framework of public service. There is a public good in the higher levels of education for the citizenry. That is the message I use with legislators. They have a public mandate to do something in this area, and they can't just go out and make contracts with the University of Phoenix and bring them in to teach all the business courses—it just doesn't work that way. What about literacy training? What about special types of education that are relevant to specific states, like environment issues? There is no profitable market in a lot of these areas. What we are likely to see is going to be the octopus that comes out in different ways. There are days when I think I can see three or four of the arms and there are other days when I just want to put a cover on my head. I don't think there is just going to be one approach. I don't think we are going to see order to it anytime soon.

Bob Wisher: To what extent do you see e-learning industry—those who build or enhance the systems' content hardware vendors—trying to influence any of the policy? Do they have a voice?

Sally Johnstone: Sure, they have some money and some interest in policy, but my sense is that it is mostly in policy affecting the use of networks and pricing of systems. There is a lobbying group of commercial universities, as I am sure that you are aware. It is trying to push for things like a federal or national accrediting system. They are pushing very hard for opening up full financial aid to distance learning students. They are also paying attention to a lot of other federal policies that they would like to see changed to make their products and services more available. Now, how successful they are going to be, I don't know. But yes, there is a voice.

Brian Lekander: This is an observation more than a question, but one of the reactions that I've had is that the programs that are described, while all terrific, are to a certain extent comparatively of a lot of these policy problems or constraints. It is no accident that most are master's programs, for example, which completely eliminates all those student financial aid issues. Having a fixed cohort going through an entire program enabled certain kinds of freedoms or creativity, permitting the designers to even imagine the possibility that the program could be constructed as a series of projects or activities as opposed to courses. Regardless, I guess I just want to raise a question: To what extent have we featured things that are either a characteristic or at the very least happening in pockets of innovation that are isolated from the whole? The question would be, if that is the case, how do we translate the possibilities, the sense of creativity that is happening in those programs, to those other places?

Terry Anderson: The SUNY program doesn't fit that, though.

Sally Johnstone: It is undergraduate and institutionally based, so they sidestep a lot of the issues. They are going to get hit with a lot of the things we have discussed. I do not think we will see competitive programs developing in multiple institutions in the same state system in the next few years.

Tom Duffy: The difficulty in figuring out the innovation at the undergraduate level is the level of coordination that is required because of the course requirements. You have to figure out where you can contain it.

Sally Johnstone: ... and there is no precedent. It will be interesting.
   (End of session)

19

Pulling It All Together: A Business Perspective on Web-Based Learning

Jim Botkin
Executive Coaching

Prasad Kaipa
SelfCorporation

Corporate education has become a second system of learning, which has grown silently over the past 2 decades to the point where it is now larger than the formal traditional higher education system in America. For example, "If the education arms of GE, AT&T, or IBM were spun off as public universities, their revenues would exceed the budgets of Big Ten powerhouses like Ohio State, Michigan, and Purdue" (Davis & Botkin, 1994, p. 97).

OBJECTIVES

Business and academia have much to learn from one another. Our objective in this chapter is to provide a business perspective on learner-centered theory and practice in Web-based learning. More specifically, our thesis is that(1) business is looking to education for theoretical foundations that are learner-centered, (2) business has much to offer to academia in the domain of measuring learning results, and (3) both business and education would benefit by focusing on transformational learning. These ideas are presented, respectively, in Parts 1, 3, and 4; Part 5 contains our conclusions.

Many of our ideas are based on the presentations from the conference Distance Education: Theory and Practice, held in December 2001, which has resulted in this book. Our intention is to contribute toward pulling together many of these both so they can be better understood by business readers, and also to expand and build on the ideas expressed by educators in many of the other chapters in this book.

Some Context

Since the conference took place, the business world and society at large have been buffeted by scandals in poor, possibly illegal accounting practices in companies such as Enron and too many others. Companies are now engaged in a painful review of their values, and how these can be made more explicit and accountable to CEOs, employees, investors, and society in general. The gap between academia and business—a gap already wide, and one we hope to bridge in this chapter—has grown even wider. In this climate, it may seem foolhardy to suggest that educators should learn from business, and vice versa. However, in the world of learning, both sectors have a track record of accomplishments, perspectives, and future needs that can benefit by cross-sharing; indeed, learning may be one of the best vehicles for transforming companies to become more responsive to people in the form of leadership development, innovation, and creativity—all of which form part of this chapter in the following sections.

Resource Comparisons

According to best estimates, more than $60 billion (Davis & Botkin, 1994) is spent on corporate education, which exceeds the budgets of all the traditional 4-year institutions of higher education combined. (The Masie Reports [2000] put the figure at $62 billion for business and $40 billion for government spending on learning, education, and training). The corporate university "nonsystem" has grown to be extensive, big, and global. It comes from large enterprises (like IBM and AT&T), as well as smaller ones (like the Print & Copy Factory in San Francisco or Accurate Threaded Fasteners in the Midwest). Companies like Hewlett-Packard talk about enterprise workforce development and see learning as one of its key strategic assets.

The figures for corporate spending on education are estimates only. A reason why it is difficult to make such a calculation depends on costing strategies, for example, on whether a manager's salary during training time is included or excluded, or how we put a dollar figure on recent efforts to promote "learning through work," a strategy that is beginning to replace time spent in the corporate classroom (InterClass Report, 2001).

Not only do businesses have the resources for learning, they have the ability to do a lot of experimentation. They can try nontraditional methods, because they do not have to contend with legacies that have grown up over the 300 years or more of higher education history. Tenure would be but one example. Businesses seldom have a permanent faculty. Further, courses do not have to have a fixed length or starting time. This flexibility allows them to react to, or occasionally foresee, problems ahead so they can be more agile and changeable than can most traditional formal postsecondary institutions.

Language and Perspective Comparisons

Executives and academics often use different language to designate ideas that are similar or substantially the same. For instance, academics use the term *distance education*, whereas businesspeople speak of *e-learning*. Both use *Web-based learning*. Although each of these terms may have different connotations, in this chapter we tend to use them interchangeably. The two worlds of business and academia also have differing perspectives on learning and knowledge. Many business executives use the model that goes from data to information to knowledge, where data is a single transaction, information is data made meaningful, and knowledge is information put to productive use. Conventional learning is a process of acquiring new knowledge that leads to improving the capacity and competence to act (Davis & Botkin, 1994). Formal education, executives maintain, seldom builds that capacity and competence. Apprenticeship, they say, builds competence, whereas coaching and mentoring build dialogue, reflection, and experiences essential to lifelong learning.

In an academic setting, education creates a context for knowledge that focuses not just on first-order learning processes (acquiring new knowledge and skills), but also on a second-order learning process (learning to learn). Although academics maintain that students thus develop broader awareness in education settings, executives think that too much focus on second-order learning tends to be too broadly focused without linkages to application. Thus, for business, the traditional education focuses on inert knowledge, which can only be applied in other classroom work.

Businesspeople consider school-based education to be some years behind the corporate world. They complain that it does not take into account the changing landscape of information and the use of cutting-edge technologies. Academics, however, make a distinction between education and business training. Academics eschew training as too narrowly focused on first-order learning, and generally ignore the business complaint about lack of linkages to application.

Corporate training, still the dominant approach in business, is focused on certain clearly defined bodies of knowledge and the need to drill down to the needed detail. For example, managers and workers may get information on how to use a software package, how to operate a machine, or how to apply principles of aerodynamics to building aircraft. Hence the educators' argument that there is little ability to generalize is often valid. That is, intentional corporate focus on learning how to do something may build skills in workers, but those skills are not easily transferable, because the change of technology or tools require additional training. Academics, for the most part, do not want to be identified with anything that smacks of Microsoft or Cisco Systems certifications, whereas corporations cannot do without them. Certifications allow their employees to develop required skills quickly, and when employees meaningfully apply those skills in their job context, they develop to the required level of competence.

In the larger context, "learning to learn"—the process of acquiring new knowledge and the ability to apply old knowledge to new problems, are not often enough acknowledged by businesspeople, and thus are not yet the dominant part of corporate education. Inquiry-based learning, as described in this book, seems to hit a proper middle ground and could be useful to both educators and corporate trainers.

Far-seeing academics, as well as enlightened corporate trainers, are recognizing that today's learners need both approaches. All learners need to be engaged in more ways than one to achieve lifelong learning. Business, as well as academia, prizes a type of learning that is transformational—variously called "generative" (Senge, 1990); "innovative" (Botkin, 1980) or "discontinuous" (Kaipa, 2003). We will say more about such transformational learning later in this article.

Drivers

What is basically driving all this corporate emphasis on learning is the shift from an industrial economy to a knowledge economy, where good ideas become the currency (Webber, 1999).

It is as if "knowledge is bursting out everywhere." It is not just in the economy or business. The same trend is evident in health care, medicine, astronomy, and space exploration, in both the military and civilian spheres. In each of these fields, We can say "we know 10 times more about that field than we did five years ago," and this knowledge is growing exponentially.

With the total knowledge in the world doubling every 7 years or sooner, it becomes essential that learning does not stop with academic institutions, but somehow becomes part of the workplace and beyond. Hence, lifelong learning has become more of a necessity than a cliché. Recognizing that their competitiveness, innovation, and long-term sustainability is dependent on employees continually engaging in the learning processes, corporations have been actively creating corporate universities, from McDonald's University to Cisco University. The corporate world is well ahead of most of academia in looking at ways of supporting continuous learning—through communities of practice (Botkin, 1999) and just-in-time learning resources. Although traditional universities dislike corporate training centers being called universities, educators are beginning to recognize that there is an unmet need that is being addressed by these corporate universities. Some traditional universities and management schools even are aggressively creating executive and corporate education centers through their university extension programs and distance learning approaches. Harvard, Stanford, INSEAD, and the University of Michigan are some examples of business schools that have created successful executive education programs.

In addition to business–education partnerships that are considered a win–win proposition to both partners, universities are beginning to identify the importance of distance learning and situated learning programs as ways to bridge the gap between their traditional education programs and business-oriented training programs. What academic institutions call distance education programs have attracted the attention of business leaders, when a subset of distance education programs became popular under the name, e-learning. E-learning is very well suited for the performance-focused executives, because employees can take those distant learning courses just-in-time. They can also be taken anywhere, anytime. Further, the focus is to provide enough basic concepts, skills, or both to complete the job that is in front of you.

E-learning courses span a wide variety of applications and audiences. They can be short or long—20 minutes or several years, as in the case of complex multimodule courses that result in certification and accreditation. Academic faculty, in general, are having a hard time to switch from a "talking heads" approach, as executives call stand-up lectures in academia, to media rich, customizable learner centric and Net-dependent courses that are growing in the business world. This book contains several chapters that bridge the gap between the two approaches and have the potential to impact a traditional teacher's mind-set in a significant way. This chapter also addresses different approaches and methodologies that increase the effectiveness of distance learning in general and e-learning in particular. We will include discussion about measuring the effectiveness of e-learning and its applicability in business and academic settings.

WHAT EDUCATION OFFERS: THEORIES THAT ARE LEARNER-CENTERED

Academia has traditionally been the institution that builds and tests theory. This is no less true in the domain of learning as it is in general. The experience of the past decade, however, is one where practice has outrun theory. Thus, business has proceeded to develop its learning systems without the benefit of very much sound theory, but which worked in practice. Business is looking over its shoulder to find in academia one or more theories that can advance their work, especially in the direction of having the learner at the center of the learning process. Training, while still the bulk of corporate education, is being superceded by e-learning and learning through work, both of which rely on autonomous learners.

Next, we discuss a number of issues that arise in business learning, which chief learning officers, for example, hope could result in superior, future-oriented learning.

Learning Theory

Although this book has focused on case studies, it has put appropriate and necessary focus on learning theory. Even though the open discussion did not lead to agreement on the pedagogical theory underlying e-learning/distance education, none of the business books that we have seen in this area have covered any meaningful theory at all. Corporations too often ignore the fact that without appropriate theory, practices do not spread. The key to bridging business and academics is to raise good questions on theory. Once the questions are raised, those might be meaningfully answered by either corporate educators or academic scholars. Meaningful answers are likely to come first from the education sector to inform and improve the business sector—that is, the domain of deep theory is a natural one, where business can learn from and possibly collaborate with education.

Lifelong learning means that people are in a continuous learning mode—that learning is in fact situated. This is not only job based—it is equally relevant to our role as citizens, in the world, our country, and our community. The complexity and number of issues that are relevant to our performance as citizens, even in our community, is phenomenal. If we had to take a course every time we needed to engage in learning, we would be in courses continuously, but only 10% or so would be relevant to our needs, and hence that amount, at most, would be retained.

Peter Henschel, former executive director of the Institute for Research on Learning, makes a strong case for continuous learning in the workplace. According to Henschel (quoted in Botkin, 1999), "the manager's core work in this new economy is to create and support a work environment that nurtures continuous learning. Doing this well moves us closer to having an advantage in the never-ending search for talent" (Henschel, 1999).

The corporate world is well advanced in looking at ways of supporting continuous learning—through communities of practice (Botkin, 1999) and through just-in-time learning. They may not have it right, but they are addressing the issues. The chapters in this volume are excellent examples of inquiry-based courses, either capitalizing on the learners interests and needs or creating that interest through the presentation of problems. But what role are these courses going to play in meeting the growing need for continuous learning? John Stinson, in his move to create an alumni environment, is on to one of the potential strategies for supporting continuous learning. Of course, this is a pilot study, and the ROI in terms of revenue streams is still unclear.

There are many issues still unresolved in the area of e-learning and its replacement potential in businesses and academia. As long as we know the knowledge that we want students to learn, we can create courses. How do we evolve new knowledge that is beyond the immediate focus of the learner or the business? We have to pay attention to problem-finding and inquiry-based approaches, because we cannot construct courses on something that is still unclear. Asking the right questions and exploring the right areas, and predicting where the discontinuities exist in the models, theories, and frameworks, is part of discontinuous learning that is not yet being addressed either in schools or in businesses. In addition, there are a few more issues that we would like readers to explore further and come up with their own answers.

Ways to Evolve "Communities of Practice" Online

The basic unit of analysis is moving from individual learning to the group, especially community, learning. For the business world, the emphasis is on groups of any sort rather than on individuals. This does not mean that quick-to-learn individuals are forgotten or put by the wayside, it simply means that group learning is seen as equally or more important than individual learning (see Nonaka & Takeuchi, 1995), but the ability to collaborate with other teams or community members, as well as to nurture and grow communities of practice, is more highly valued than ever. What would it take to create online communities of practice? How do we learn and dialogue in a focused way? The second aspect that stood out in the book was the emphasis on communities of practice. Here we are seeing a fundamental shift both in education and the business world (Henschel, 1999).

The reason for collaboration has a simple explanation: The complexities that business and all sectors of society face are so great that not even the best and the brightest can get their arms around the issues. So any theories that we cite or develop need to account for this group or community aspect. Thus, we encourage digging deeper into what is meant by community and what opportunities or obstacles it presents for our thinking.

Just-in-Time Learning

We referred to the concept of just-in-time learning in the earlier part of this chapter. E-learning allows employees to know that what they need to learn can be made available any-time, anywhere. By dividing the subject matter into byte-sized chunks, choice is left for the learner and her or his manager to decide how much and what needs to be learned at the time of contact. Were we to take a trip to Dell Computer in Texas and its Dell University, we would be astounded by the instant just-in-time learning broken down into less than 10-minute learning modules. Here one can legitimately challenge whether this can reasonably called learning or whether this should be called following instructions. Yet the Dell case illustrates that there are people who go all the way from the 5-minute learning modules to 5 hours learning. The key here is receptivity to problem solving and knowledge doled out one nugget at a time. By calling them courses, businesses are moving into the domain of schools and will have similar issues regarding missing the big picture and nonapplicability of the content to other situations. Nonetheless, many companies are looking for ways to get out of or beyond this in-built structural issue. Although what this indicates is a continuous learning approach, just-in-time learning is differentiated, because it is learner driven and need based. Beyond the courses, though, we need to explore where the boundaries of our current knowledge limits our future, and that cannot be done through offering more courses. We have to get the students and workers to ask good questions and identify opportunities for discontinuous learning (Kaipa, 2003).

Learning as Working—Performance-Centered Learning

Let us take an example of how large companies are integrating e-learning in their workplaces. Companies like HP are beginning to use a blended learning model in which Web-based learning (practice and learn) is supplemented through performance support systems (knowledge on demand), and face-to-face learning. Face-to-face learning is not a trainer–learner model but a peer-to-peer one, a learn together approach. When combined with virtual classrooms to learn the content and a face-to-face approach to collaborate together, the results are noteworthy.

The business case for e-learning is made based on four goals: (1) improved economics, (2) better quality, (3) improved performance, and (4) increased personalization. Hewlett-Packard's (HP's) Change Management Challenge, according to one HP manager, is to move the philosophy of requesting training classes as routine to learning business requirements first and then determining how much of training is appropriate. In other words, classroom learning is being phased out and a continuous "learning through work" approach is being phased in. The learning and performance processes are understood to be two sides of a coin and are considered interconnected. They are managed through gathering business and performance requirements that link content with appropriate delivery mechanisms like e-services that focus on learning. HP is using electronic packages like learning management systems and content management systems to "e-enable" learning management processes to be effective and efficient. With these systems, the delivery of learning is channeled through a variety of online courses, just-in-time learning modules, and videos.

HP's approach is innovative and effective. Even so, typical corporate e-learning today achieves only about 10% effectiveness. The only way we can improve the effectiveness of learning in the workplace is to move it away from the e-training and courses approach and toward performance improvement based on a continuous learning model, and inquiry-based learning as being pioneered by companies like Cisco.

Learner Accountability for Results

When the learner is absorbed in the learning process and can quickly demonstrate his or her own competency, the learner begins to get deeply engaged with the process. If that is coupled with productivity, low costs and capturing the imagination of the employee. Then the learner creates the content and becomes both effective and productive. Because there is a close connection between what the learner is interested in and what the business is recommending, it leads to the learner taking accountability for results. This is when the learner becomes either an intrapreneur an or entrepreneur. They are no longer looking outside for motivation, clarity, or content. They are dynamically engaged in solving the business problem. Thus results become an automatic outcome.

Cisco has taken e-learning very seriously and started integrating e-learning with day-to-day working in Cisco. This is Cisco's way of introducing its learning to its own employees. On its Web site is the following:

Cisco E-Learning is a world class, learner focused, just in time, easy-to-use, highly integrated, Learning Solution, that exemplifies the Internet Economy in action.

Single model & framework with company-wide Integration

—Learner Focused (just in time)
—Integrated content and applications
—Adapts to Learner's needs
—Closed Loop
—Global

Learning-Style Differences

Each of us learn differently. One may learn auditorily through listening to somebody. Another learns by doing, practicing, and improving on the previous performance. Yet another learns by visual images and making sense of those images and reading rather than listening to the teacher. Each of us have our own learning styles and preferences when the e-learning module, course, or methods take into account the reader's communication and learning styles. The learner engagement and absorption become high, and time to competency becomes quick. We found that the learning styles are not paid sufficient attention in applications that we were exposed to till now.

WHAT BUSINESS OFFERS—PRACTICE AND MEASUREMENT

The best way to understand some of the many different practices and experiences of business in e-learning is to view them as consisting of five stages of evolution.

Five Stages of the Evolution of E-learning in Business

Cisco has done pioneering work in the area of corporate e-learning, which it defines as "learning enabled or enhanced by the Internet." Such Internet-based learning reduces travel and classroom costs, increases relevance of and accessibility to content and online collaboration, and enables accountability for the learner, developer, and content owner. It also expands the scope of e-learning beyond the classroom. Even though all the five stages described below are simultaneously available, the later stages provide a higher return on investment for businesses and produces more effective learner engagement.

Stage 1: Content Focus: Having Information Does Not Mean I Know How to Use It Well

When e-learning first started, its developers focused on creating content and information to be more available to users. As knowledge multiplied at a faster and faster rate, the difficulty was to locate the right information. This used to take a long time because of lack of appropriate search mechanisms. Learning outcomes were not the focus, because the information was seen as a valuable resource. The resources were useful, just as a well-written book might be, and clearly, learning outcomes are not incorporated in books. CD-ROM-based cases and content-based sites were rich in data and information but poor in knowledge. They were also poor by not including learner's differences, questions, and the learning process itself. These initial attempts seldom impacted business outcomes, because the translation of knowledge to learning and performance did not occur well. In addition, users began to realize that they were lacking ways to approach this information to learn better, for example, through posing good questions or hearing memorable stories. This led to a second generation of e-learning approaches.

Stage 2: Portal Focus: It's the Eyeballs, Stupid!

The second-generation of e-learning focused on creating portals. The portal approach took off quickly, and everybody created portals for their constituents. There were portals for salespeople, marketing groups, HR professionals, and accountants. It made them efficient within their own circles but ineffective in learning how to serve their customers, colleagues, and partners. There was very little integration from the perspective of the customer, and this approach did nothing to reduce silos that already were a problem in some business organizations. While the learner got a bit more value from these portals (decrease in time to competency and higher absorption), it did not necessarily translate any better into business outcomes (such as productivity, cost, or employee retention). Portals also did not require anything from the learner, and they "pushed" the content to the learner, assuming that he or she knew what to do with it. Hence, learners were passive and not informed about how to integrate their work with their learning. Similar to the first stage of e-learning, the focus was still on content, though more tailored to the needs of individual users. The effectiveness of these portals was measured based on how many people ("eyeballs") access them and which pages they visit. This measurement is similar to what some schools measure—the number of students registered in a class or in their school. Neither tells much about what they learned.

The portal approach could take off if cross-functional team portals are created for partner support. Similarly, portals are good for online training delivery, receiving feedback from the learners and creating competency maps and road maps. Aetna, Dow Chemical Co. and Lucent Technologies have used portal approaches in creating competency road maps effectively.

Stage 3: Module Focus: Modularize and Conquer

The next stage was the creation of learning modules that were built based on linking together various modules from various sources. Using standardized tools and templates, e-learning developers started chunking content into various modules based on learning objectives. Using dynamic processes for identifying proficiency and competency levels, various modules were integrated together to present one standard learning module with an integrated user interface. Many just-in-time learning modules that are discussed later in the chapter are based on this modular approach. It was used to create 5-minute courses to multihour courses. This modular approach was more effective in terms of absorption, time to competency for the person, and increased return on investment (ROI) business. This is the first stage that increased ROI for businesses while continuing to engage the individual.

The modular approach is effective for creating standard e-learning platforms. Many e-learning companies use modules to create subscription-based courses based on proficiency or competency levels. Over time, the module approach is being found useful in standardizing tools and templates for content creation.

Stage 4: Performance Focus: Doing Is More Critical Than Knowing

The next stage of evolution in e-learning adopts a performance-centered approach. There are many good examples, from teaching Java programming classes to teaching professional certification courses. Business simulations also have performance focus, and it is also possible to do real-time coaching and mentoring using these systems. Because learning is now being translated into performance improvement, the return on investment is considered high when business outcomes are measured. This is where ROI becomes high enough that businesses get interested in e-learning applications and begin to explore e-learning as an alternative to face-to-face classes. It also means that the learner can take the course just when they need to learn it. In addition, the just-in-time learning approach is valuable because it reduces travel costs, instructor errors, and other fees, and it becomes possible to continually improve an e-learning course because there is no ego to offend. Users stay motivated because the courses address another important issue mentioned above: just-in-time learning. When someone wants to develop slides, they can learn how to use PowerPoint, or go to courses offered by SmartForce or Saba, or some other e-learning company and come back satisfied with skills to apply their learning right away. It is more dynamic than the previous approaches. By being based on what the learner brings to the class, it engages the learner for the first time, thus beginning to tap into the intrinsic motivation of the learner.

Performance-focused approaches allow learner assessment, remediation, collaboration, and simulations to be chosen by the learner without having to use just the training mode. When learner experiences are captured through feedback, it is possible to create newly tailored content in these e-learning programs. The expertise is no longer limited to stored content; subject matter experts could offer real-time coaching and development.

The effectiveness of these courses depends on the instructional design rather than information design, unlike the first two stages. The learning outcomes are more closely tied to both individual effectiveness and business results. Adobe and Dell have begun to use these approaches to let employees collaborate and share applications. Business simulations are being used in many companies more effectively than before. Microsoft has been integrating the e-learning platform with individual performance and competency management by dynamically generating career road maps for each employee on demand.

Learner accountability is still not very high in this stage, because design is instruction centered rather than learner-centered. The dependence is still on the packaging of existing content rather than allowing for new knowledge to be created.

Stage 5: Learner Focus: The Learner Shall Inherit the Earth

Finally, the most valuable design for e-learning is going to be a totally learner-centered approach. Here, the learner defines the problem and actively engages in designing the learning experience. The majority of the time, it is focused on solving a problem that the learner brings with her or him. So far, in technical and professional skill development, e-learning is slowly gaining the edge and is becoming more efficient compared to regular teaching approaches in universities. To assist learners, communities of practice (highlighted in other parts of this book) and electronic mentoring (this book) are beginning to approach the much required mediation for the learner. How do we effectively coach, mentor, and assist the learner to solve real problems? How do we help him or her formulate a bounded problem or ask real questions that would help identify tacit issues? Finally, the issue of knowledge creation is still to be satisfactorily resolved for the e-learning to compete with the training and education of the future.

This is not panacea, either. Because the context is continuous learning, whatever the user is learning is focused and too particularized. The questions of purpose and bigger vision are not appropriately addressed, and without appropriate use of communities of practice, mentoring and other checks and balances, knowledge creation that takes place is of limited long-term consequence.

Still, learner-centered design creates high value and is business critical. Ford uses a system that dynamically prescribes learning content based on individual profiles and performance histories. It is with this method that we can help the learner to become accountable for results. Because it is possible to create a global and standard document sharing and collaboration environment, virtual laboratories and communities can be created and connected. Knowledge creation becomes the effective means of learning. Continuous knowledge mining by automatically scanning knowledge repositories, e-mail archives, and Internet sites to create new learning content is an approach that is emerging in consulting and knowledge management firms.

Although the initial stages improve operational performance of the company, Stages 4 and 5 emphasize new value creation and innovation. All the five stages are appropriate for different purposes, and in this book, many of them are addressed in individual chapters. These five stages incorporate many issues where education could learn from business. But chief among those is measurement and learning assessments, which are described next from a business perspective.

Measurement and Learning Assessment: ROI, and More, in Business;
Tests in Education

We especially empathized with one of the authors who in the conference discussion asked whether we actually achieve better learning by examining things like new venues, teacher training, and synchronous or asynchronous systems. Indeed, sometimes we get so enthralled with new technologies, new methods, and new avenues to be explored, than we sometimes forget the ultimate reason why we are engaged in this endeavor—does it lead to better learning? Corporations are not looking at e-learning just as performance improvement alone.

The corporate world tends to measure the effectiveness of e-learning in two ways, One is the learner outcomes, such as productivity, performance, effectiveness, and innovation. Another is business outcomes like return on investment (ROI), competitiveness, cycle time reduction for innovation, and new product development. In contrast, in academic settings the learner is evaluated based on what he or she can reproduce in tests, assignments, and quiz-based measurements.

In the business world, this question of measurement and assessment is asked over and over again. Sometimes the measurement issue is no more than an attempt to justify budgets and funding, perhaps for your corporate university or training program. If you are a chief learning officer in corporate America or the European Community, you know the first thing your CEO is going to ask is, How will you measure learning? Will we do better than our competition? How much better? If we are behind, how far behind and how long will it take our company to catch up with others and surpass them? What will be the return on our investment in learning? Do we really get better learning by introducing Web-based tools, deeper understanding, and genuine contributions to knowledge—and if so, how much?"

Jay Cross, the chief executive officer of e-learning forums, (www.elearning forum.com), gives the following examples on payback on his web site, http://www.internettime.com:

> A Fortune 50 company used eLearning, knowledge management, and collaboration to bring new-hire sales people up to speed in six months instead of fifteen—a time savings of nine months. Nine months multiplied by 1400 new hires per year times a $5 million sales quota for each employee yields $5 billion of incremental revenue. To be sure, better products, sales campaigns, and a host of factors contributed to the gain but even a small faction of $5 billion still yields a significant ROI.

(The specifics here refer to new-hire training at a well-known Silicon Valley based electronics firm, but equivalent cases could be cited from any number of large companies.)

Another example: 10,000 consultants at a Fortune 100 technical services company earned professional certifications via e-learning. The result? Less attrition, better esprit de corps, and $100 million increased revenue per year attributable to higher billing rates.

A software firm launches a new system into a $250 million global market with e-learning and virtual meetings. This accelerates time-to-market by 2 months, gives the firm first-mover advantage over a major competitor, builds a more confident and enthusiastic sales force, and gets a new sales channel up to speed. Result? Increased revenue, from $80 to $100 million.

A very large retailer of personal computers realizes that customers are frustrated with their products, because they don't understand the software that accompanies them. The company offers customers free admission to an online learning community created by SmartForce. More than 100,000 customers sign up to learn Windows, Word, and Office applications online. Value of increased customer loyalty? Conservatively, $20 million in repeat business over 3 years.

As it is clear from the examples above, e-learning, or distance education, makes a significant difference in corporations. Unlike the analogous usages of technology for learning in the education sector, companies can measure the value of their e-learning more easily than schools can. How might schools think about measurement beyond their usual focus on tests and quizzes? One way would be to combine the testing with observable practices. KaosPilots University, a Danish management school, uses such a method. The school gives team assignments that are evaluated as the work takes place. The outcomes are a measurements that go beyond what a student has achieved in the past.

Types of Learning

Aurelio Peccei, the late president of the Club of Rome (see Botkin, Elmandjra, & Malitza, 1979) was fond of saying that the question is not learning, which will largely determine the fate of humanity, it is: What kind of learning? This issue is one that escapes most authors' chapters, and during the conference, there was very little differentiations of the types of learning. Mostly, we deal with "problem-based learning," or problem-solving abilities. Although important, problem-solving learning is relatively low on the list of priorities of some employers, especially those interested in transformation of their organizations.

TRANSFORMATIONAL LEARNING

Both business and education could benefit by a greater focus on what we call transformational learning. It starts with soft skills, such as leadership or creativity, but it's basic goal is to transform the learner and the organization in which he or she works. The chapters in this volume generally do not address learning for creativity, or what some call generative learning or innovative learning.[1] These terms refer generally to creativity, or the generation of something completely new. Nor did the authors address "problem avoidance learning"—problem avoidance so one does not need to spend effort on solving yesterday's problems rather than focus on a system that may spawn future problems. We can think of learning in many different ways depending on the context, and we may have more work to do to stimulate "generative learning" in distance education.

Soft Skills, Such as Leadership and Creativity

How does distance learning address topics like leadership development? Is leadership a skill? Knowledge that we can read? A practice that we engage with? A capacity to be developed? How do we develop leadership using e-learning approaches? How would we

---

[1]In the Club of Rome book *No Limits to Learning*, we used the term *innovative learning*, Some years later, in the *Fifth Discipline*, Senge refers to "generative learning." Similar concepts, different names.

develop capacities like learning to learn, unlearn, thinking to think (critical thinking), strategic thinking? The classical economist Joseph Schumpeter introduced the term *creative destruction*. How do we make good decisions that enhance creativity and allows us to let go of what does not work (even though it worked great before)?

Relating and sharing—collaborating and networking—these are practices of increasing importance in leading companies. But where does one go for information on these processes? How reliable will that information be? What quality will it have? In consulting companies, a majority of such firms focus on "professional services." To be successful, people have to learn how to relate, share, collaborate, and network—all of which require learning and communicating with others. Most distance education, as reflected in this volume, seems to move in this general direction, but much more could be done. Too much e-learning seems to concentrate on analyzing and differentiating. Although these are important, equally essential is to learn how to integrate information. For example, can you take the information that your colleagues have learned and put it together for a presentation as part of a team? The Internet makes copying and sharing information so easy that the boundaries between sharing and plagiarizing become blurred. The business world could use some guidance in this domain, because intellectual property rights are becoming more and more important, and educators might be in a position to provide that guidance.

Alan Mullaly, president of Boeing Commercial Aircraft, once said, "building a great airplane means not coming up with great doors, great engines, or great parts that may be poorly integrated. It is about building a system optimized at a system level and not at the parts level. That is what makes our planes great!" (personal communication, 2001).

Assessment, competencies, storytelling—how do you integrate them to design an e-learning system that is effective? How do we weave these into systems what we are building? Companies like Skillsoft and Saba are addressing these issues. Their initial offerings of skill-based modules are being replaced by sophisticated business simulations. Still, we would like to see this area addressed much more than it has been.

Learning for Creativity

What we lacked was to go all the way back to the beginning of a learning cycle. So, for example, what about "problem identification"? Before one can solve a problem, one has to determine a problem exists. As any consultant can tell us, the number one job is identifying the problem in the first place and ask right questions that will provide a frame for seeking right answers.

Transformational Learning

One more point needs to be covered. We have an opportunity for an other book on what could be called transformational learning. Recent events of the last months have illustrated the need for such activity. We need to find ways of doing things entirely differently. Both business and education need to put learning in a context with content that can fundamentally transform the ways we go about learning. What this means is that the very structures of business and education need to be reconceived so that everyone becomes a learner, and the organization values and encourages learning of individuals and of "learning communities." If we do not do something fundamentally differently in the next 5 to 10 years, we are at risk of having one of our greatest national assets—higher education—become less and less relevant at a time when a shadow system—business education—grows larger and larger. This is not a role that business wants to take on.

Nonetheless, it is real and is happening. There are not enough cross relationships between education and business to satisfy the needs of the business workforce or, for that matter, the needs of an American society that is increasingly interdependent both domestically and globally.

Business guru Tom Peters asks important and interesting questions about women in the workplace. He asks: What do they do, and how are they doing in their new roles? forty eight percent of working wives earn more than 50% of family income. Women control 48% of the purse strings and write 80% of the checks. They pay 61% of the bills, own 53% of the stock, and have contributed to the boom in mutual funds in a significant way. They make 95% of a household's financial decisions, and 29% do so single-handedly, according to Tom Peters.

Collaboration

Women use collaborative approaches to learning more than men do. To the extent this is true, most of the approaches we have explored so far tend to be more oriented to males than to females. How do we design distance education in ways that encourage diversity—male, female, rich and poor, black and white? In other words, is there a way that we could focus on meta-learning and "learning to learn" skills while we are working on learner-centered approaches? These are useful questions to explore together.

Creativity and Change

We have to pay as much attention to building capacity in creativity as we do in competence development and skills transfer. For example, Intel introduces new products on a regular basis. Pentium 4 was introduced last year, Pentium 3 the year before that, Pentium II two years ago, and so on. In the course of a year, Intel makes price adjustments once or twice, and the primary reason is increasing sales and keeping competitors at a disadvantage. As cycle times become shorter and shorter, the need for creativity, innovation, and leadership becomes more and more evident. How do we address this kind of focus on knowledge creation, innovation, and leadership using distance learning methods?

Storytelling

Another issue to be more fully developed is one that was only addressed by Bransford, Vye, Bateman, Brophy, and Roselli (Chap 10, this volume) and this has to do with the value of storytelling. We need more context, we need more "fish is fish" stories that Bransford identified. Business schools are taking this subject more seriously. Rather than relying on numbers to make its point, the business world is seeking stories that are more meaningful and memorable than numbers are. What businesses want are short crisp stories that illustrate what you've learned, often with a moral or a point that managers need to get across to lots of people. (Large numbers of students at the State University of New York comes quickly to mind, but other authors also tell of vast numbers of students being served). Business schools need to deal with large numbers of students, as do government agencies (for example, The U.S. postal system, which has over half a million employees, or the Veterans Administration, which has over a quarter of a million). So the business world also needs ways to summarize and make known what large numbers of employees need to learn and hear.

Particularly in the brainstorming, innovation, or creative areas, business is in the business of making everybody quite different, but companies need a set of guiding principles to be create "autonomous" learners, who don't need to wait for directions to proceed with their learning, and those guiding principles are best communicated through storytelling. How do we capture those stories and how do we evaluate them in some way that relates them to the effectiveness of learning?

Often, such stories are meant to illustrate a company culture or a best practice. An example would be 3M, and Art Frye, the person who invented Post-It notes. It wasn't until the 40th try to launch the effort that he actually got the funding for it. That story is known throughout the company as an example of persistence in overcoming adversity.

CONCLUSIONS

To review our main points in this chapter: We suggest that both business and education have much to learn from one another—business from the theoretical side and educa-tion from the measurement side. Yet both institutions have another step to pursue: how to create and enhance more generative learning whose outcome nurtures transforma-tion and brings new knowledge into being. From the perspective of business, we would value a way to bridge the gap between business and academia in ways that are "out of the box" thinking. We need to get educators and businesspeople alike on the track of generative learning, enhancing the very structures through which learning is delivered. Distance education and e-learning constitute an excellent domain for collaboration, and possibly the tools for doing so.

REFERENCES

Botkin, J. (1999). How knowledge communities can revolutionize your organization. In J. Botkin (Ed.), *Smart business: How knowledge communities can revolutionize your organization*. New York: Free Press.

Botkin, J., Elmandjra, M., & Malitza, M. (1979). *No limits to learning: A report to the Club of Rome*, Oxford, UK: Pergamon.

Cisco Systems. (2000). Available: http://www.cisco.com/warp/public/752/2000

Cross, J. (2002). *Examples of payback.* Available: http://www.internettime.com

Conference on Distance Education (2001, December). Theory and Practice.

Davis, S., & Botkin, J. (1994). *The monster under the bed.* New York: Simon & Schuster.

E-learning Forum. Available: http://www.elearningforum.com

Henschel, P. (1999). The manager's core work in the new economy. In J. Botkin (Ed.), *Smart business: How knowledge communities can revolutionize your organization* (pp. 244–249). New York: Free Press.

Kaipa, P. (2003). *Discontinuous learning.* Palo Alto, CA: Vinakaya Media.

MASIE Reports The (2000). Available: http://www.ma.umist.ac.uk/jm/MASIE/news.html

Nonaka, I., & Takeuchi, H. (1995). *The knowledge-creating company.* New York: Oxford University Press.

Peccei, A. (1978). In Botkin, J., Elmandjra, M., Malitza, M. *No Limits to Learning: A Report to the Club of Rome*, Oxford, UK: Pergamon.

Peters, T. (2000, November 14). Seminar 2000 *Distinet or Extnet* TechLearn 2000 & The World E-Learning Congress, Orlando, FL.

RuHenbur, B. W., Spickler, G., & Lurie, S. (2000, July). *e-learning: The engine of the knowledge economy.* Memphis, TN: Morgan Keegan.

Senge, P. (1990). *Fifth discipline: The art and practice of the learning organization.* New York: Doubleday Currency.

Thornsberry, J., & Yozzo, A. (2001). *Learning through work.* (Internal Rep.). Cambridge, MA: Interclass.

Webber, A. (1999), Foreword. In J. Botkin (Ed.), smart business: *How knowledge communities can revolutionize your organization.* New York: Free Press.

Open Discussion of Chapter 19

John Stinson: I am so happy we are bringing the corporate perspective in. I sat here the past 2½ days with primarily a group of academics. We have been talking about distance learning on the Web, and we have been talking about e-learning, or whatever it means. Most of our conversations have been around courses or around programs that are based to produce some type of an outcome. I was in New York City in September, sitting in a conference of the corporate university exchange. The topic of that conference was e-learning. I heard entirely different types of things being discussed. The topics being discussed there were primarily coming from corporate universities. The topics were around just-in-time learning, they were about learning objects, they were about knowledge management, they were around learning content management systems. Now, I am not saying it is my judgment that one might be right or that one might be wrong, but it seems to me that it would be beneficial to us if we sort of integrated the two. What I heard at the university corporate exchange was a deep need to be able to do these things, but in many ways a lack of capability or ability to actually do them. What I heard here was a lot of learning talent that is really looking for better applications than what is already provided. I would love to put this group together with that group and instead of writing papers focus on talking to one another—I'd love to put you heterogeneously into some projects that says redesign education for this particular organization in terms of what is needed in that organization and have both the corporate environment and the learning experts talking to one another. I think we would get some marvelous things that would be very beneficial for both.

Tom Duffy: I agree with you whole heartedly, but let me push in another way. One of the things I found really fascinating in the industry are the two issues that you mention and that Prasad and Jim mentioned. One is a real focus on community. How do you build community? I had a video conference with CRC Research Group, and one of the people from CRC was talking about 354 communities of practice within CRC. Okay, that is general in virtually any company that you go to. Now my immediate response is, and I expect yours is to, is, "Oh yeah, what do they really mean by that? It is probably listservs in many cases, and it's not going to be very sophisticated and not be very well done." But I am impressed by their recognition of the need and their attempt to do something. We are outliers in trying to do those things. It is certainly not recognized in the academic administration, even though those communities exist. You can say we are all face-to-face, but that is nonsense. We have a lot to learn from the corporations in terms of assessing need—and they a lot from us, I suspect, in terms of design and implementation.

The other issue I wanted to comment on is the notion of learning objects. A Fortune 100 company I worked with was talking about every learning object being no more than

30 minutes long. When you look at the Ninth House, which does executive education training with Ted Blanchard and Tom Peters and all that, they now started adding 2-minute learning objects. There is a little video that pops up and talks about some issue—not very helpful, quite frankly—because it is so short. I worry about learning objects for exactly the reasons you talked about—they are chunks of information, so why are we calling them "learning" objects?

But my sense about what is going to happen across corporations is that learning objects and communities will be adopted because they are cost efficient—they use internal resources, and they provide just-in-time training and education. If you put the two together, you now have a potentially really meaningful environment. You have a community environment with objects people can use and talk about. But now those isolated little pieces of information get situated in the particular work contexts through the community discussion. In my sense, that is what I suspect we will see in industry that I think will be very exciting.

John Stinson: If those learning objects are not very good now, we could have John Bransford and others, rather than doing those 30 minutes, they could be just a hell of a lot better by putting them into a challenge or problem context and really engaging people in the challenge. But most of the people out there producing the learning objects don't really have the type of learning expertise that sits in this room.

Tom Duffy: You see, I would almost argue that the learning objects will increasingly be internal, community-developed products rather than externally designed items. More in line with the Xerox project originally called Eureka.

John Stinson: They have to learn how to do it.

Terry Anderson: I would just like to respond to something that Jim said about the thing he liked was the emphasis on theory. Frankly, I didn't see it that much. I felt like I have been reading so many years about distance ed research, which is little more than "Here is what we did at my shop," with some exceptions and lots of references to Vygotsky in here... (*Group laughs.*) I guess maybe it is a challenge for ourselves I'm just as guilty as anyone else, I'm sure, but is to maybe read Glaser and Strauss about grounded theory work. The experiment ends with some hypotheses that are at least testable or with trying to make some generalizations. We tend not to do either. Some of us, or maybe all of us, collectively are some of the best minds in the world in this distance ed stuff. Why are we afraid to make the big statements to sort of really go out on the limb and try to push this field in major ways? I am not sure that I feel comfortable even with calling this book "learning theory and practice." I don't know. Maybe I am just being too critical.

Jim Botkin: Well, I at least appreciated that many of you gave thought to the fact that we should be thinking about theory, even if not that much of it appeared in your conversations. The business community would barely raise the issue of what's the theory about. Their theory is fairly implicit—it is what works.

John Bransford: They don't reference Vygotsky? (*Group laughs.*)

Jim Botkin: No, I have never seen a reference to Vygotsky.

Carson Eoyang: I would like to pick up on a point of storytelling and use that more in the design of learning. What occurs to me is that storytelling in corporations is not so much motivated by the desire to teach and to educate but to socialize. Good stories, corporate stories, the 3M story, the Hewlett-Packard story, all those stories, the point is that they are really trying to make a statement about the values that the company stands for and how they will conduct themselves. Which leads to the issue of whether we are missing something about learning when we don't look at the socialization dimension. That is, besides the content, besides the skills, besides the cognitive tools, doesn't learning especially in higher education have a very important socialization function? Let me give you a couple of examples. In the Marine Corps, boot camp is one of the most powerful socialization, learning experiences we have I think in an educational institution. It is enormously effective. If you finish boot camp and you finish your first time enlisted as a Marine, you are a Marine for life. Other Marines treat you as a Marine for life. The training and education that goes on in boot camp—how to clean a rifle, how to navigate over terrain, how to clean the uniform, all that stuff—is the surface learning. The deep learning is the socialization that is very intentional.

The second example of very intensive education training, which has an unintended socialization consequence, again from the military, is the way we train our nuclear power submariners. It's incredibly technical. It's incredibly analytic. It's extremely rigorous. It is very hard. It is nuclear science literally. Because of this, the submarine community overvalued that so much that there evolved a technocratic social mentality that puts machinery and technical expertise above people, above leadership, and above communication. We are still living with that today. The French have a proverb that says something on the order of "Years after graduation the information is forgotten but the education remains." What is it about the education that is enduring for people? How do we capture that online? If we don't pay attention to those deeper educational responsibilities as we design online systems, then we are only training and are not truly educating.

Scott Grabinger: I forgot who said this—I think it was Terry, about the lack of theory. I guess the lack of theory kind of disturbed me too, because it wasn't as theoretical as I expected. On the other hand, I think what disturbs me more when it comes to linking theory and practice is our lack of "stick-to-it-ness". A little story . . . when I started teaching in Colorado, I went into a school that was in its 5th year of not having walls and having modular scheduling—A, B, C, D, E, F, K. The place was just chaos. It was so bad that at the end of the semester, they dropped F day because they realized that nobody had any classes. (*Group laughs.*)

In the summer, they gave up and built walls all over the place. I was sorry to see that, because I believed in the theory behind the open classroom. I thought it could have worked. I thought it was making people more active, more involved. The thing is the teachers were never trained to use the approach, to teach in that way. They took the same teachers, put them in the building, and expected everything to change. It didn't. After 5 years, it was so chaotic and so controversial, they had to change it. That is kind of what I am concerned about. There seems to be a lack of intellectual commitment or a lack of intellectual consistency. If we buy into a theory such as social cultural or constructivism or behaviorism, don't we have a certain obligation to make that work?

Jamie Kirkley: Scott, I wanted to follow up on your comment because I strongly agree. I believe we also have a responsibility to our practitioners. For my teaching methods course, I like to organize things, so we discuss the theory, the frameworks, and the strategies, and practices that they imply. I think we have done a good job with that here. I think that is something that our book will contribute: breaking down the theory in our distance ed practices through our frameworks, our strategies, our practices. That is something I'm really excited about.

Linda Polin: I am less disturbed by our approach to theory. To me, theory is not liturgy; it is the tool to think with. Jumping to your example, Jamie, I had an interesting experience when I used to teach in the teacher ed lab. At the time, we were doing a curriculum class, and the students had to bring in something they created to show what they could do with constructivism in the classroom. One student brought in a spelling lesson that was a constructivist spelling lesson. She tried to present it, and I asked, "Do you think constructivist do spelling lessons?" It was sort of a difference between seeing theory as clothing, like I am going to put on constructivism now and take this and make it constructivist or take this thing and make it sociocultural and an approach in which you take a stand on education and learning. The notion is wrapping yourself and building or writing from the perspective of theory; that, to me, is one of the reasons that I feel comfortable. If that is indeed where you are, your theoretical connections can be very tacit. They are not as overt, because you are not visibly brushing stuff up. It is a little harder to point to and see, here, I am referencing this idea, or here, I am referencing that idea. To me, part of the value of having multiple opinions is that we have a lot more disagreement in this room than we were willing to make obvious. I think the value of that is that it makes us be clear.

Brian Lekander: What I would like to do is add another issue that I think has been ignored. I am thinking of the increasing interdependence between faculty and curriculum designers, and the world of business as represented by the makers of commercial software products. The adoption of those products limits or defines the way the course or program is constructed, and the choice of those products is not necessarily even in the hands of the faculty or the curriculum designer because of the procurement or acquisition policies. I guess, in the worse case scenario, a course will be strictly defined by the capability of the product chosen. We saw some of this in Karen's discussion of the LEEP program.

With respect to theory, I would have liked to have heard a little bit more discussion along the lines of what Tom was talking about in his chapter on the conflicts between theory and practical constraints. The Cardean University approach was so heavily shaped by the conflicting interest of the business plan. I thought that was an interesting point and something to think about in a different setting.

Tom Duffy: The technology constraint—that same sort of thing in the business world. A large amount of constraints—I agree.

Mark Schlager: I'd like to respond to Carson's issues around the culture and values and things like that. I think this culture and value approach is the kind of thing Tom talked about if he could do the Cardean University part of Unext rather than the course part. It is also the thing that John Stinson talks about that he is trying to do at a university level. I think this is actually an area we can look at with optimism: sharing online and disseminating values online is a very natural kind of thing. The online environment becomes a different kind of place. You can have elders and leaders that model those values to the newcomers, and they are taken up like that. The best example that I know is Pepperdine. I keep telling Linda that she is the Lucy of Tapped In (aka, Lucy, the first human being).

Linda Polin: Ooooohh. That's interesting. (*Group laughs.*)

Mark Schlager: If I were to do a social network analysis of Tapped In, everybody can be traced back to Linda Polin. She is like the dirty secret of the way Tapped In has grown, because I have seen that the values that she has instilled in her students have spread like wildfire through the environment. Her students have graduated and continue to use our system wherever they go. They infect people around them, and then they come into Tapped In. They feel at home already in Tapped In, because the values that are being spread by the Pepperdine students are already there, and they are already in Tapped in as well. So it becomes an extremely powerful cultural and inculturation kind of thing. This is an area where we really can help become change agents in online environments. It's not the course, necessarily. It's the overriding—the Cardean University level—where we have those values that we can disseminate.

John Bransford: The next level is to have a virtual university football team. That is what brings people back.

Sally Johnstone: This is already here among virtual universities. They came together and formed a football league. The students play, they put together fantasy teams. This is an organized league within virtual universities. I think it was Magellan University that won the championship last year, and Kentucky came in second.

Bob Wisher: Something I foresee coming out of the military as we adopt e-learning more and more is what is going on now. This might be true in business and maybe the entire education system, but since the draft ended in 1973, one of the main reasons people join the military is for the education and training opportunities. When people leave the military, they fill out an exit survey about what they liked and didn't like. They don't like all the deployments overseas. They don't like the housing, they don't like the food, but training and education always come out very high.

In a recent survey the Army did (a random last two digits of social security numbers, about 10,000 respondents, from privates to colonels), the results show a lot of skepticism on the part of the troops about what they seem to be learning. Only about 10% reported having taken any online learning courses, and about one fourth were unsure about whether they would—they were ambivalent. About one third said they don't want to take e-learning. They want to stay with the classroom because that is what they trust. My concern is that there is a perception that the quality is going down even though we have evaluations that show otherwise.

Jim Botkin: The point you are making on the business side is known as the war for talent. The number one issue is in the decision of whether you want to retain talent or you want to attract new talent as the opportunity to learn and grow. Money only comes in two or three or four further down the list.

Tom Duffy: I want to shift just a little and echo Linda's view of not being disturbed by the theory–practice kind of linkage. If people are disturbed, I think it is important to understand what the concern is. In essence, what do you expect to see in terms of the theory representation? I do think theory is imbedded. I think it is the practice we are engaging—the way we are talking about things is very different, as Jim pointed out, from business.

John Bransford: The other thing on that—we talked about it earlier—rather than theory to practice, it really is the theory–practice linkage. A lot of what these chapters have is actually a theory guiding what you notice about practice that then comes back and improves. I think it is that cycle that everyone of us is looking at.

Terry Anderson: I don't have a problem with the implicit theory that is guiding all the projects that we have seen. I guess what I was looking more for is the theory generation, for the new theory coming out of the practice being emphasized. Not that we don't have different ones.

Tom Duffy: I am not feeling a need for new theory. I mean, seriously, if you look at the certain stuff that is being written about distance learning environments—it's incredible—it's "here is the technology we're using, here is when I hold my lectures." There is no kind of rationale for what they are doing and why they are doing it. It's incredible what's going on.

Linda Polin: But Terry wants the next step, which is "Okay, we have theory. You came in, you built the thing, you had an experience, you thought about it, now what do you think?" None of us wrote, "Now, what do we think?"

Mark Schlager: What would you do differently?

Linda Polin: Yeah, yeah—what I would do differently now that I have heard everybody's stuff.

John Bransford: Rafael, the example you talked about in Monterey—you said you tried it one way and the conversation was not good, so you went to problem-based learning. What the theory does is affect what you notice. The problem is that when you have no theory, you are never surprised. The essence of science is to make a prediction so that you will be surprised by something so that you can improve. But we all need to say that a little more like you did.

Tom Duffy: We have to wind this up now.
    (End of session)

Author Index

Subject Index